TJ
211
.M86

Multisensor
integration
and fusion fc
intelligent
machines and

Multisensor Integration and Fusion for Intelligent Machines and Systems

Contents

10	Dynamic Multisensor Data Fusion System for Intelligent Robots *Ren C. Luo, Min Hsiung Lin and Ralph S. Scherp*	217
11	Geometrical Fusion Method for Multisensor Robotic Systems *Yoshihiko Nakamura and Yingti Xu*	241
12	Optimal Combination and Constraints for Geometrical Sensor Data *John Porrill*	261
13	Feature Space Mapping for Sensor Fusion *Gerald M. Flachs, Jay B. Jordan, C. L. Beer, D. R. Scott and Jeffrey J. Carlson*	283
14	An Inference Technique for Integrating Knowledge from Disparate Sources *Thomas D. Garvey, John D. Lowrance and Martin A. Fischler*	309
15	Measuring Consensus Effectiveness by a Generalized Entropy Criterion *Harry E. Stephanou and Shin-Yee Lu*	327

Part III Object Recognition

16	Introduction to Part III *Ren C. Luo and Michael G. Kay*	357
17	Integrated Analysis of Thermal and Visual Images for Scene Interpretation *N. Nandhakumar and J. K. Aggarwal*	375
18	Integrating Vision and Touch for Object Recognition Tasks *Peter K. Allen*	407

Part IV Multisensor-Based Mobile Robots

19	Introduction to Part IV *Ren C. Luo and Michael G. Kay*	443
20	Multisensor Fusion and Navigation of Mobile Robots *Su-shing Chen*	467
21	Building, Registrating, and Fusing Noisy Visual Maps *Nicholas Ayache and Olivier D. Faugeras*	495

Multisensor Integration and Fusion for Intelligent Machines and Systems

edited by

Ren C. Luo and Michael G. Kay

North Carolina State University

Ablex Publishing Corporation
Norwood, NJ

Copyright © **1995** by Ablex Publishing Corporation

All rights reserved. No part of this publication may be reproduced, stored in a retrieval system, or transmitted, in any form or by any means, electronic, mechanical, photocopying, microfilming, recording or otherwise, without permission of the publisher.

Printed in the United States of America

Library of Congress Cataloging-in-Publication Data

Multisensor integration and fusion for intelligent machines and
  systems / edited by Ren C. Luo and Michael G. Kay
    p. cm. — (Computer engineering and computer science)
  Includes bibliographical references and indexes.
  ISBN 0-89391-863-6 (cl)
    1. Robotics. 2. Artificial intelligence. 3. Multisensor data
  fusion. I. Luo, Ren C. II. Kay, Michael G. III. Series.
  TJ211.M86   1994
  629.8'92—dc20   93-45356
                                                                CIP

Ablex Publishing Corporation
355 Chestnut Street
Norwood, New Jersey 07648

Contents

List of Contributors
Preface
Acknowledgements

1 Introduction
   Ren C. Luo and Michael G. Kay

Part I Multisensor Integration

2 Introduction to Part I
   Ren C. Luo and Michael G. Kay
3 A Survey of AI Approaches to the Integration of Information
   Thomas D. Garvey
4 Logical Sensor Systems
   Thomas C. Henderson and Esther Shilcrat
5 Neural Network Approach to Sensory Fusion
   *John C. Pearson, Jack J. Gelfand, W. E. Sull
   Richard M. Peterson and Clay D. Spence*
6 Knowledge Representation Approaches in S
   L. Pau
7 MKS: A Multisensor Kernel System
   Thomas C. Henderson and Wu S. Fai

Part II Multisensor Fusion

8 Introduction to Part II
   Ren C. Luo and Michael G. Kay
9 Fusion of Multisensor Data
   John M. Richardson and Kenneth

Part V Applications

22	Introduction to Part V *Ren C. Luo and Michael G. Kay*	541
23	Data Fusion and Decision Support for Command and Control *Edward L. Waltz and Dennis M. Buede*	563
24	Theoretical Approaches to Data Association and Fusion *Samuel S. Blackman*	597
25	Joint Probabilistic Data Association in Distributed Sensors Networks *Kuo-Chu Chang, Chee-Yee Chong and Yaakov Bar-Shalom*	611
26	Optimal Distributed Decision Fusion *Stelios C. A. Thomopoulos, Ramanarayanan Viswanathan and Dimitrios K. Bougoulias*	637
27	Optimal Serial Distributed Decision Fusion *Stelios C. A. Thomopoulos, Ramanarayanan Viswanathan and Ramakrishna J. Tumuluri*	647

Author Index 673
Subject Index 683

List of Contributors

J. K. Aggarwal
Computer and Vision Research Center
College of Engineering
University of Texas
Austin, TX 78712

Peter K. Allen
Department of Computer Science
450 Computer Science Building
Columbia University
New York, NY 10027

Nicholas Ayache
INRIA–Rocquencourt
Domaine de Voluceau
B.P. 105–78153 Le Chesnay Cedex
France

Yaakov Bar-Shalom
Dept. of Electrical Engr. and Computer
  Science
University of Connecticut
Storrs, CT 06268

C. L. Beer
Dept. of Electrical and Computer
  Engineering
New Mexico University
Las Cruces, NM 88003

Samuel S. Blackman
Hughes Aircraft Company
El Segundo, CA 90245

Dimitrios K. Bougoulias
Department of Electrical Engineering
Southern Illinois University
Carbondale, IL 62901

Dennis M. Buede
Decision Logistics, Inc.
2139 Golf Course Dr.
Reston, VA 22091

Jeffrey J. Carlson
Sandia National Laboratories
Albuquerque, NM 87185

Kuo-Chu Chang
Advanced Decision Systems
1500 Plymouth St.
Mountain View, CA 94040–1230

Su-Shing Chen
Artificial Intelligence Laboratory
University of North Carolina at
  Charlotte
Charlotte, NC 28223

Chee-Yee Chong
Advanced Decision Systems
1500 Plymouth St.
Mountain View, CA 94040–1230

Wu S. Fai
Department of Computer Science
3190 Merrill Engineering Building
University of Utah
Salt Lake City, UT 84112

Olivier D. Faugeras
INRIA–Rocquencourt
Domaine de Voluceau
B.P. 105–78153 Le Chesnay Cedex
France

Martin A. Fischler
Artificial Intelligence Center
SRI International
333 Ravenswood Ave.
Menlo Park, CA 94025

Gerald M. Flachs
Dept. of Electrical and Computer
  Engineering
Frenger and Sweet, Suite 106
New Mexico University
Las Cruces, NM 88003

List of Contributors

Thomas D. Garvey
Artificial Intelligence Center
SRI International
333 Ravenswood Ave.
Menlo Park, CA 94025

Jack J. Gelfand
David Sarnoff Research Center
Subsidiary of SRI International
Princeton, NJ 08543-5300

Thomas C. Henderson
Department of Computer Science
3190 Merrill Engineering Building
University of Utah
Salt Lake City, UT 84112

Jay B. Jordan
Dept. of Electrical and Computer
  Engineering
New Mexico University
Las Cruces, NM 88003

Michael G. Kay
Dept. of Industrial Engineering
North Carolina State University
Raleigh, NC 27695-7906

Min H. Lin
Dept. of Electrical and Computer
  Engineering
North Carolina State University
Raleigh, NC 27695-7911

John D. Lowrance
Artificial Intelligence Center
SRI International
333 Ravenswood Ave.
Menlo Park, CA 94025

Shin-Yee Lu
Long Range Research Division
Exxon Production Research Co.
Houston, TX 77001

Ren C. Luo
Dept. of Electrical and Computer
  Engineering
North Carolina State University
Raleigh, NC 27695-7911

Kenneth A. Marsh
Communications and Signal Processing
Rockwell International Science Center
1049 Camino Dos Rios
P.O. Box 1085
Thousand Oaks, CA 91360

Yoshihiko Nakamura
Center for Robotic Systems in
  Microelectronics
University of California
Santa Barbara, CA 93106

N. Nandhakumar
Department of Electrical Engineering
Thornton Hall
University of Virginia
Charlottesville, VA 22901

L. Pau
Electromagnetics Institute
Building 348
Technical University of Denmark
Lyngby, DK-2800
Denmark

John C. Pearson
David Sarnoff Research Center
Subsidiary of SRI International
Princeton, NJ 08543-5300

Richard M. Peterson
David Sarnoff Research Center
Subsidiary of SRI International
Princeton, NJ 08543-5300

John Porrill
Artificial Intelligence Vision Research
  Unit
University of Sheffield
Sheffield S10 2TN
United Kingdom

John M. Richardson
Communications and Signal Processing
Rockwell International Science Center
1049 Camino Dos Rios
P.O. Box 1085
Thousand Oaks, CA 91360

Ralph S. Scherp
Dept. of Electrical and Computer
  Engineering
North Carolina State University
Raleigh, NC 27695-7911

D. R. Scott
Dept. of Electrical and Computer
  Engineering
New Mexico University
Las Cruces, NM 88003

Esther Shilcrat
Department of Computer Science
3190 Merrill Engineering Building
University of Utah
Salt Lake City, UT 84112

Clay D. Spence
David Sarnoff Research Center
Subsidiary of SRI International
Princeton, NJ 08543-5300

Harry E. Stephanou
Center for Advanced Technology in
 Automation and Robotics
Rensselaer Polytechnic Institute
Troy, NY 12180-3590

W. E. Sullivan
Department of Biology
Princeton University
Princeton, NJ 08544

Stelios C. A. Thomopoulos
Department of Electrical Engineering
Pennsylvania State University
University Park, PA 16802

Ramakrishna J. Tumuluri
Department of Electrical Engineering
Purdue University
West Lafayette, IN

Ramanarayanan Viswanathan
Department of Electrical Engineering
Southern Illinois University
Carbondale, IL 62901

Edward L. Waltz
Bendix Communications Division
Allied-Signal Aerospace Company
1300 East Joppa Road
Baltimore, MD 21204

Yingti Xu
Center for Robotic Systems in
 Microelectronics
University of California
Santa Barbara, CA 93106

Preface

There has been a growing interest over the past few years in the use of multiple sensors to increase the capabilities of intelligent machines and systems. This book is a compendium of some of the most important and influential work that has appeared in this area. In addition, it contains comprehensive introductory material and an extensive survey and review of related research.

This book grew out of a paper* we wrote that surveyed the entire subject of multisensor integration and fusion. We realized, however, that it was impossible to provide enough details in one paper to make it the single source of information a person would need to consult. Due to the interdisciplinary nature of the subject, many of the most important research papers have appeared in a wide range of technical journals and conference proceedings of limited access. This book makes available a number of these papers in a single volume. We hope it will be useful to anyone interested in the development of more intelligent machines and systems through the synergistic use of multiple sensors.

The first chapter of the book provides a general introduction to multisensor integration and fusion. The distinction between multisensor integration and fusion is defined, and typical integration functions are described to both introduce the subject and to provide a common framework for discussing various methods of integration presented in the book. The remainder of the book is organized into five parts: multisensor integration, multisensor fusion, object recognition, multisensor-based mobile robots, and applications. Each part includes

---

* *IEEE Transactions on Systems, Man and Cybernetics*, vol. SMC-19, no. 5, pp. 901–931.

an introductory chapter that provides an extensive survey and review of the topic.

Ren C. Luo
Michael G. Kay
North Carolina State University

Acknowledgements

We wish to acknowledge the following sources for the respective chapters that appear in this book. We are grateful to the authors, and their publishers, for permission to include their work in our book.

Chapter:
3. Reprinted, with permission, from *Proceedings of the SPIE,* vol. 782, *Infrared Sensors and Sensor Fusion* (pp. 68–82), R. G. Buser and F. B. Warren (Eds.), Orlando, FL, 1987. © SPIE.
4. Reprinted, with permission, from *Journal of Robot. Systems,* vol. 1, no. 2, 1984, pp. 169–193. © John Wiley & Sons.
5. Reprinted, with permission, from *Proceedings of the SPIE,* vol. 931, *Sensor Fusion* (pp. 103–108), C. W. Weaver (Ed.), Orlando, FL, 1988. © SPIE.
6. Reprinted, with permission, from *Automatica,* vol. 25, no. 2, 1989, pp. 207–214. © Pergamon Press.
7. Reprinted, with permission, from *IEEE Transactions on Systems, Man, and Cybernetics,* vol. SMC-14, no. 5, 1984, pp. 784–791. © IEEE.
9. Reprinted, with permission, from *International Journal of Robotics Research,* vol. 7, no. 6, 1988, pp. 78–96. © The MIT Press.
10. Reprinted, with permission, from *IEEE Journal of Robotics and Automation,* vol. RA-4, no. 4, 1988, pp. 386–396. © IEEE.
11. Reprinted, with permission, from *Proceedings of the IEEE International Conference Robotics and Automation* (pp. 668–673). Scottsdale, AZ. © IEEE.
12. Reprinted, with permission, from *International Journal of Robotics Research,* vol. 7, no. 6, 1988, pp. 66–77. © The MIT Press.
13. Reprinted, with permission, from *Journal of Robotic Systems,* vol. 7, no. 3, 1990, pp. 373–393. © John Wiley & Sons.

14. Reprinted, with permission, from *Proceedings of the 7th International Joint Conference Artificial Intelligence* (pp. 319–325), Vancouver, BC, Canada, 1981. © International Joint Conference on Artificial Intelligence, Inc., copies of this and other IJCAI proceedings are available from Morgan Kaufmann Publishers, Inc., 2929 Campus Drive, San Mateo, CA 94403.
15. Reprinted, with permission, from *IEEE Transactions on Pattern Analysis and Machine Intelligence,* vol. PAMI-10, no. 4, 1988, pp. 544–554. © IEEE.
17. Reprinted, with permission, from *IEEE Transactions on Pattern Analysis and Machine Intelligence,* vol. PAMI-10, no. 4, 1988, pp. 469–481. © IEEE.
18. Reprinted, with permission, from *International Journal of Robotics Research,* vol. 7, no. 6, 1988, pp. 15–33. © The MIT Press.
20. Reprinted, with permission, from *International Journal of Intelligent Systems,* vol. 2, no. 2, 1987, pp. 227–251. © John Wiley & Sons.
21. Reprinted, with permission, from *International Journal of Robotics Research,* vol. 7, no. 6, 1988, pp. 45–65. © The MIT Press.
23. Reprinted, with permission, from *IEEE Transactions on Systems, Man, and Cybernetics,* vol. SMC-16, no. 6, 1986, pp. 865–879. © IEEE.
24. Reprinted, with permission, from *Proceedings of the SPIE,* vol. 931, *Sensor Fusion* (pp. 50–55), C. W. Weaver (Ed.), Orlando, FL, 1988. © SPIE.
25. Reprinted, with permission, from *IEEE Transactions on Automatic Control,* vol. AC-31, no. 10, 1986, pp. 889–897. © IEEE.
26. Reprinted, with permission, from *IEEE Transactions on Aerospace and Electronic Systems,* vol. AES-25, no. 5, 1989, pp. 761–765. © IEEE.
27. Reprinted, with permission, from *IEEE Transactions on Aerospace and Electronic Systems,* vol. AES-23, no. 5, 1988, pp. 644–653. © IEEE.

1
Introduction

Ren C. Luo and
Michael G. Kay

The synergistic use of multiple sensors by machines and systems is a major factor in enabling some measure of intelligence to be incorporated into their overall operation so that they can interact with and operate in an unstructured environment without the complete control of a human operator. The use of sensors in an intelligent system is an acknowledgement of the fact that it may not be possible or feasible for a system to know a priori the state of the outside world to a degree sufficient for its autonomous operation. The reasons a system may lack sufficient knowledge concerning the state of the outside world may be due either to the fact that the system is operating in a totally unknown environment, or, while partial knowledge is available and is stored in some form of a world model, it may not be feasible to store large amounts of this knowledge; it may not even be possible in principle to know the state of the world a priori if it is dynamically changing, and unforeseen events can occur. Sensors allow a system to learn the state of the world as needed and to continuously update its own model of the world. The motivation for using multiple sensors in a system can be considered as the response to the simple question: If a single sensor can increase the capability of a system, would the use of more sensors increase it even further? Over the past decade a number of researchers have been exploring this question from both a theoretical perspective and by actually building multisensor machines and systems for use in a variety of areas of application. Typical of the applications that can benefit from the use of multiple sensors are automatic target recognition, mobile robot navigation, target tracking, aircraft navigation, industrial tasks such as assembly, and military command and control for battlefield management. This book provides a thorough survey of much of this work and includes a number of papers that describe some of the most important theoretical as well as applied research in this area.

There are a number of different means of integrating the information provided by multiple sensors into the operation of a system. The most straightforward approach to multisensor integration is to let the information from each sensor serve as a separate input to the system controller. This approach may be the most appropriate if each sensor is providing information concerning completely different aspects of the environment. The major benefit gained through this approach is the increase in the extent of the environment that is able to be sensed. The only interaction between the sensors is indirect and based on the individual effect each sensor has on the controller. If there is some degree of overlap between the sensors concerning some aspect of the environment that they are able to sense, it may be possible for a sensor to directly influence the operation of another sensor so that the value of the combined information that the sensors provide is greater than the sum of the value of the information provided by each sensor separately. This synergistic effect from the multisensor integration can be achieved either by using the information from one sensor to provide cues or guide the operation of other sensors, or by actually combining or fusing the information from multiple sensors. The information from the sensors can be fused at a variety of levels of representation, depending upon the needs of the system and the degree of similarity between the sensors. The major benefit gained through multisensor fusion is that the system can be provided with information of higher quality concerning, possibly, certain aspects of the environment that cannot be directly sensed by any individual sensor operating independently.

This chapter first describes the role of multisensor integration and fusion in intelligent systems in terms of the typical functions performed during integration, the different levels at which fusion can take place, and the potential advantages and possible problems involved in integrating multiple sensors. Examples are then given of the synergistic integration of multisensor information in both humans and snakes. Speculations are then given concerning possible future research directions and a short description is given of previous survey and review papers in the area of multisensor integration and fusion. The chapter concludes with an overview of the subsequent parts of the book.

1. THE ROLE OF MULTISENSOR INTEGRATION AND FUSION IN INTELLIGENT SYSTEMS

This section describes the role of multisensor integration and fusion in the operation of intelligent machines and systems. The role of multisensor integration and fusion can best be understood with reference to the type of information that the integrated multiple sensors can uniquely provide the system. The potential advantages gained through the synergistic use of this multisensory information can be decomposed into a combination of four fundamental aspects: the redundancy, complementarity, timeliness, and cost of the information. Multisensor integration and the related notion of multisensor fusion are defined and distinguished. The different functional aspects of multisensor integration and fusion in the overall operation of a system are presented, and they serve to highlight the distinction between the different types of integration and the different types of fusion. The potential advantages in integrating multiple sensors are discussed in terms of four fundamental aspects of the information provided by the sensors, and then the possible problems associated with creating a general methodology for multisensor integration and fusion are discussed in terms of the methods used for handling the different sources of errors or uncertainty.

Multisensor integration, as defined in this book, refers to the synergistic use of the information provided by multiple sensory devices to assist in the accomplishment of a task by a system. An additional distinction is made between multisensor integration and the more restricted notion of multisensor fusion. *Multisensor fusion,* as defined in this book, refers to any stage in the integration process where there is an actual combination (or fusion) of different sources of sensory information into one representational format. The information to be fused may come from multiple sensory devices during a single period of time or from a single sensory device over an extended time period. Although the distinction of fusion from integration is not standard in the literature, it serves to separate the general system-level issues involved in the integration of multiple sensory devices at the architecture and control level from the more specific mathematical and statistical issues involved in the actual fusion of sensory information.

1.1. Multisensor Integration

The means by which multiple sensors are integrated into the operation of an intelligent machine or system are usually a major factor in the overall design of the system. The specific capabilities of the individual sensors and the particular form of the information they provide will have a major influence on the design of the overall architecture of the system. These factors, together with the requirements of the particular tasks the system is meant to perform, make it difficult to define any specific general-purpose methods and techniques that encompass all of the different aspects of multisensor integration. Instead, what has emerged from the work of many researchers is a number of different paradigms, frameworks, and control structures for integration that have proved to be particularly useful in the design of multisensor systems.

Many of the paradigms, frameworks, and control structures used for multisensor integration have been adapted with little or no modification from similar high-level constructs used in systems analysis, computer science, control theory, and artificial intelligence (AI). In fact, much of multisensor integration research can be viewed as the particular application of a wide range of fundamental systems design principles. Common themes among these constructs that have particular importance for multisensor integration are the notions of modularity, hierarchical structures, and adaptability. In a manner similar to structured programming, modularity in the design of the functions needed for integration can reduce the complexity of the overall integration process and can increase its flexibility by allowing many of the integration functions to be designed to be independent of the particular sensors being used. Modularity in the operation of the integration functions enables much of the processing to be distributed across the system. The object-oriented programming paradigm and the distributed blackboard control structure are two constructs that are especially useful in promoting modularity for multisensor integration. Hierarchical structures are useful in allowing for the efficient representation of the different forms, levels, and resolutions of the information used for sensory processing and control, for example, the NBS Sensory and Control Hierarchy (see Section 2.2 of Chapter 2) and logical sensor networks (see Chapter 4). Adaptability in the integration process can be an efficient means of handling the error and uncertainty inherent in the integration of multiple sensors. The use of the artificial neural network formalism (see Section 1.3 of Chapter 2) allows adaptability to be directly incorporated into the integration process.

Although the process of multisensor integration can take many different forms depending on the particular needs and design of the overall system, certain basic functions are common to most implementations. The diagram shown in Figure 1.1 represents multisensor inte-

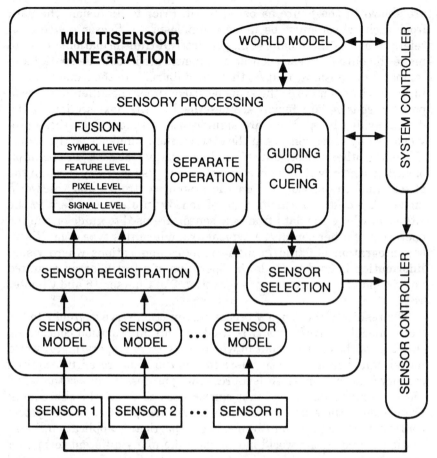

Figure 1.1. Functional diagram of multisensor integration and fusion in the operation of a system.

gration as being a composite of these basic functions. A group of n sensors provide input to the integration process. In order for the data from each sensor to be used for integration it must first be effectively modeled. A *sensor model* represents the uncertainty and error in the data from each sensor and provides a measure of its quality that can be used by the subsequent integration functions. A common assumption is that the uncertainty in the sensory data can be adequately modeled as a Gaussian distribution. After the data from each sensor have been modeled, they can be integrated into the operation of the system in accord with three different types of *sensory processing:* fusion, separate operation, and guiding or cueing. The data from Sensors 1 and 2 are shown in the figure as being fused. Prior to its fusion, the data from each sensor must be made commensurate. *Sensor registration* refers to any of the means (e.g., geometrical transformations) used to make the data from each sensor commensurate in both its spatial and temporal dimensions, that is, that the data refer to the same location in the environment over the same period of time. The different types of possible sensor data fusion are described in the next section. If the data provided by a sensor are significantly different from those provided by any other sensors in the system, their influence on the operation of the other sensors may be indirect; that is, the *separate operation* of such a sensor will influence the other sensors indirectly through the effects that the sensor has on the system controller and the world model. A *guiding* or *cueing* type of sensory processing refers to the situation where the data from one sensor are used to guide or cue the operation of other sensors. A typical example of this type of multisensor integration is found in many robotics applications where visual information is used to guide the operation of a tactile array mounted on the end of a manipulator (see Section 2 of Chapter 16 and Chapter 18).

The results of the sensory processing function serve as inputs to the world model. A *world model* is used to store information concerning the state of the environment in which the system is operating. A world model can include both a priori information and recently acquired sensory information. High-level reasoning processes can use the world model to make inferences that can be used to direct the subsequent processing of the sensory information and the operation of the system controller. Depending on the needs of a particular application, information stored in the world model can take many different forms; for example, in object recognition tasks (see Part III) the world model might contain just the representations of the objects the system is able to recognize, whereas in mobile robot navigation tasks (see Part IV) the world model might contain the complete representation of the robot's local environment (e.g., the objects in the environment as well as local terrain features). The majority of the research related to the development of multisensor world models has been within the context of the development of suitable high-level representations for multisensor mobile robot navigation and control. Chapter 19 describes a number of examples of different world models used in mobile robots. The last multisensor integration function, *sensor selection*, refers to any means used to select or allocate the particular group of sensors to be used by the system. The selection process may take place during the initial design of the system or during its actual operation. When selection takes place during operation it can be used to determine the most appropriate sensor or group of sensors to use to guide the operation of other sensors in response to changing environmental or system conditions such as sensor failure.

1.2. Multisensor Fusion

The fusion of the data or information from multiple sensors or a single sensor over time can take place at different levels of representation (sensory information can be considered data from a sensor that has been given a semantic content through processing and/or the particular context in which it was acquired). As shown in Figure 1.1, a useful categorization is to consider multisensor fusion as taking place at the signal, pixel, feature, and symbol levels of representation. Most of the sensors typically used in practice provide data that can be fused at one or more of these levels. Although the multisensor integration functions of sensor registration and sensor modeling are shown in Figure 1.1 as being separate from multisensor fusion, most of the methods and techniques used for fusion make very strong assumptions, either explicitly or implied, concerning how the data from the different sensor is modeled and to what degree the data is in registration. A fusion method that may be sound in theory may be difficult to apply in practice if the assumed sensor model does not adequately describe the data from a real sensor; for example, the presence of outliers due to sensor failure in an assumed normal distribution of the sensory data may render the fused data useless, or the degree of assumed sensor registration may be impossible to achieve, for example, due to the limited resolution or accuracy of the motors used to control the sensors.

The different levels of multisensor fusion can be used to provide information to a system that can be used for a variety of purposes: Signal-level fusion can be used in real-time applications and can be considered as just an additional step in the overall processing of the signals; pixel-level fusion can be used to improve the performance of many image processing tasks such as segmentation; and feature- and symbol-level fusion can be used to provide a system performing an object recognition task with additional features that can be used to increase its recognition capabilities. The different levels can be distinguished by the type of information they provide the system, how the sensory information is modeled, the degree of sensor registration required for fusion, the methods used for fusion, and the means by which the fusion process improves the "quality" of the information provided the system. A comparison of the different levels of fusion is given below and summarized in Table 1.1.

Table 1.1. Comparison of fusion levels

Characteristics	Signal Level	Pixel Level	Feature Level	Symbol Level
Type of sensory information	single- or multi-dimensional signals	multiple images	features extracted from signals and images	symbol representing decision
Representation level of information	low	low to medium	medium	high
Model sensory information	random variable corrupted by uncorrelated noise	stochastic process on image or pixels with multidimensional attributes	non-invariant geometrical form, orientation, position, and temporal extent of features	symbol with associated uncertainty measure
Degree of registration:				
spatial	high	high	medium	low
temporal	high	medium	medium	low
Means of registration:				
spatial	sensor coalignment	sensor coalignment or shared optics	geometrical transformations	spatial attributes of symbol if necessary
temporal	synchronization or estimation	synchronization	synchronization	temporal attributes of symbol if necessary
Fusion method	signal estimation	image estimation or pixel attribute combination	geometrical and temporal correspondence, and feature attribute combination	logical and statistical inference
Improvement due to fusion	reduction in expected variance	increase in performance of image processing tasks	reduced processing, increased feature measurement accuracy, and value of additional features	increase in truth or probability values

Signal-level fusion refers to the combination of the signals of a group of sensors in order to provide a signal that is usually of the same form as the original signals but of greater quality. The signals from the sensors can be modeled as random variables corrupted by uncorrelated noise, with the fusion process considered as an estimation procedure. As compared to the other types of fusion, signal-level fusion requires the greatest degree of registration between the sensory information. If multiple sensors are to be used for signal-level fusion, their signals must be in temporal as well as spatial registration. If the signals from the sensors are not synchronized, they can be put into temporal registration by estimating their values at common points of time. The signals can be registered spatially by having the sensors coaligned on the same platform. Signal-level fusion is usually not feasible if the sensors are distributed on different platforms due to registration difficulties and bandwidth limitations involved in communicating the signals between the platforms. The most common means of measuring the improvement in quality is the reduction in the expected variance of the fused signal. One means of implementing signal level fusion is by taking a weighted average of the composite signals, where the weights are based on the estimated variances of the signals.

Pixel-level fusion can be used to increase the information content associated with each pixel in an image formed through a combination of multiple images; for example, the fusion of a range image with a two-dimensional intensity image adds depth information to each pixel in the intensity image which can be useful in the subsequent processing of the image. The different images to be fused can come from a single imaging sensor (e.g., a multispectral camera) or a group of sensors (e.g., stereo cameras). The fused image can be created either through pixel-by-pixel fusion or through the fusion of associated local neighborhoods of pixels in each of the component images. The images to be fused can be modeled as a realization of a stochastic process defined across the image (e.g., a Markov random field), with the fusion process considered as an estimation procedure, or the information associated with each pixel in a component image can be considered as an additional dimension of the information associated with its corresponding pixel in the fused image (e.g., the two dimensions of depth and intensity associated with each pixel in a fused range–intensity image). Sensor registration is not a problem if either a single sensor is used or multiple sensors are used that provide images of the same resolution and share the same optics and mechanics (e.g., a laser radar operating at the same frequency as an infrared sensor and sharing the same optics and scanning mechanism). If the images to be fused are of different resolution, then a mapping needs to be specified between corresponding regions in the images. The sensors used for pixel-level fusion need to be accurately coaligned so that their images will be in spatial registration. This is usually achieved through locating the sensors on the same platform. The disparity between the locations of the sensors on the platform can be used as an important source of information in the fusion process, for example, to determine a depth value for each pixel in binocular fusion. The improvement in quality associated with pixel-level fusion can most easily be assessed through the improvements noted in the performance of image processing tasks (e.g., segmentation, feature extraction, and restoration) when the fused image is being used as compared to their performance when only the individual component images are used.

Feature-level fusion can be used both to increase the likelihood that a feature extracted from the information provided by a sensor actually corresponds to an important aspect of the environment and as a means of creating additional composite features for use by the system. Features provide for data abstraction. A primary feature is created through the attachment of some type of semantic meaning to the results of the processing of some spatial and/or temporal segment of sensory data, whereas a composite feature is created through a combination of existing features. Typical features extracted from an image and used for fusion include edges and regions of similar intensity or depth. When multiple sensors report similar features at the same location in the environment, the likelihood that the features are actually present can be increased and the accuracy with which they are measured can be improved; features that do not receive such support can be regarded as spurious artifacts and eliminated. A feature created as a result of the fusion process may be either a composite of the component features (e.g., an edge that is composed of segments of edges detected by different sensors) or an entirely new type of feature which is composed of the attributes of its component features (e.g., a three-dimensional edge formed through the fusion of corresponding edges in the images provided by stereo cameras). The geometrical form, orientation, and position of a feature, together with its temporal extent, are the most important aspects of the feature that need to be represented so that it can be registered and fused with other features. In some cases, a feature can be made invariant to certain geometrical transformations (e.g., translation and rotation in an image plane), so that all of these aspects do not have to be explicitly represented. The sensor registration requirements for feature-level fusion are less stringent than those for signal- and pixel-level fusion, with the result that the sensors can be distributed across different platforms. The geometric transformation of a feature can be used to bring it into registration with other features or with a world model. The improvement in quality associated with feature-level fusion can be measured through the reduction in processing requirements resulting from the elimination of spurious features, the increased accuracy in the measurement of a feature (used, e.g., to determine the pose of an object), and the increase in performance associated with the use of additional features created through fusion (e.g., increased object recognition capabilities).

Symbol-level fusion allows the information from multiple sensors to be effectively used together at the highest level of abstraction. Symbol-level fusion may be the only means by which sensory information can be fused if the sensors are very dissimilar or refer to different regions of the environment. The symbols used for fusion can originate either from the processing of the information provided by the sensors in the system, or through symbolic reasoning processes that may make use of a priori information from a world model or sources external to the system (e.g., intelligence reports indicating the likely presence of certain targets in the environment). A symbol derived from sensory information represents a decision that has been made concerning some aspect of the environment. (Symbol-level fusion is sometimes termed "decision-level fusion".) The decision is usually made by matching features derived from the sensory information to a model. The symbols used for fusion typically have associated with them a measure of the degree to which the sensory information matches the model. A single uncertainty measure is used to represent both the degree of mismatch and any of the inherent uncertainty in the sensory information provided by the sensors. The measure can be used to indicate the relative weight that a particular symbol should be given in the fusion process. Sensor registration is usually not explicitly considered in symbol-level fusion because the spatial and temporal extent of the sensory information upon which a symbol is based has already been explicitly considered in the generation of the symbol; for example, the underlying features upon which a group of symbols are based are already in registration. If the symbols to be fused are not in registration, spatial and temporal attributes can be associated with the symbols and used for their registration. Different forms of logical and statistical inference can be used for symbol-level fusion. In logical inference the individual symbols to be fused represent terms in logical expressions, and the uncertainty measures represent the truth values of the terms. In statistical inference the individual symbols to be fused are represented as conditional probability expressions, and their uncertainty measures correspond to the probability measures associated with the expressions. The improvement in quality associated with symbol-level fusion is represented by the increase in the truth or probability values of the symbols created as a result of the inference process.

Figure 1.2 provides an example of how the different levels of multisensor fusion can be used in the task of automatic target recognition. Additional information concerning the multisensor integration and fusion aspects of automatic target recognition can be found in Section 3 of Chapter 16. In the figure, five sensors are being used by the system to recognize a tank: two millimeter-wave radars (which could be operating at different frequencies), an infrared sensor, a camera providing visual information, and a radio signal detector that can identify characteristic emissions originating from the tank. The complementary characteristics of the information provided by this suite of sensors can enable the system to detect and recognize targets under a variety of different operating conditions; for example, the radars provide range information and their signals are less affected by atmospheric attenuation as compared to the infrared image, whereas the infrared sensor provides information of greater resolution than the radars and, unlike the camera, it is able to operate at night.

The two radars are assumed to be synchronized and coaligned on a platform so that their data are in registration and can be fused at the signal level. The fused signal is shown in the figure as being sent both to the system, where it can be immediately used for the improved detection of targets, and as input to generate a range image of the target. The range image from the radars can then be fused at the pixel level with the intensity image provided by the infrared sensor located on the same platform. In most cases, an element from the range image can only be registered with a neighborhood of pixels from the infrared image because of the differences in resolution between the millimeter-wave radars and the infrared sensor. The fused image is sent both to the system, where it can be immediately used to improve target segmentation, and as input to a feature extraction process. The features extracted from the pixel-level fused image can then be fused at the feature level with similar features extracted from visual image provided by the camera. The camera may be located on a different platform because the sensor registration requirements for feature-level fusion are less stringent than those for signal- and pixel-level fusion. The fused features are then sent both to the system, where they can be used to improve the accuracy in the measurement of the orientation or pose of the target, and as input features to an object recognition process. The output of the recognition process is a symbol, with an associated measure of its quality (0.7), indicating the presence of the tank. The symbol can then be fused at the symbol level with a similar sym-

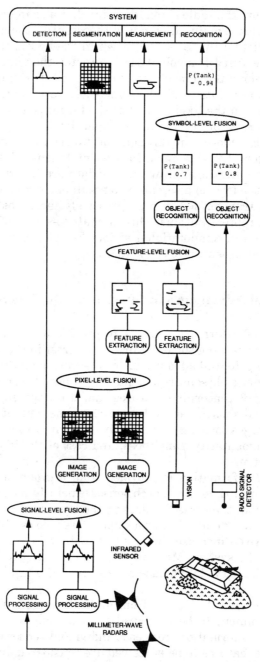

Figure 1.2. Possible uses of signal-, pixel-, feature-, and symbol-level fusion in the automatic recognition of a tank.

bol derived from the radio signal detector that also indicates the presence of the tank. The fused signal is then sent to the system for the final recognition of the tank. As shown in the figure, the measure of quality of the fused symbol (0.94) is greater than the measures of quality of either of the component symbols and represents the increase in the quality associated with the symbol as a result of the fusion, that is, the increase in the likelihood that the target is a tank.

The transformation from lower to higher levels of representation as the information moves up through the target recognition structure shown in Figure 1.2 is common in most multisensor integration processes. At the lowest level, raw sensory data are transformed into information in the form of a signal. As a result of a series of fusion steps, the signal is transformed into progressively more abstract numeric and symbolic representations. This "signals-to-symbols" phenomenon is also common in computational vision (Fischler & Firschein, 1987) and AI (Chandrasekaran & Goel, 1988).

1.3. Potential Advantages in Integrating Multiple Sensors

The purpose of external sensors is to provide a system with useful information concerning some features of interest in the system's environment. The potential advantages in integrating and/or fusing information from multiple sensors are that the information can be obtained more accurately, concerning features that are impossible to perceive with individual sensors, as well as in less time, and at a lesser cost. These advantages correspond, respectively, to the notions of the redundancy, complementarity, timeliness, and cost of the information provided the system.

Redundant information is provided from a group of sensors (or a single sensor over time) when each sensor is perceiving, possibly with a different fidelity, the same features in the environment. The integration or fusion of redundant information can reduce overall uncertainty and thus serve to increase the accuracy with which the features are perceived by the system. Multiple sensors providing redundant information can also serve to increase reliability in the case of sensor error or failure.

Complementary information from multiple sensors allows features in the environment to be perceived that are impossible to perceive using just the information from each individual sensor operating separately. If the features to be perceived are considered dimensions in a space of features, then complementary information is provided when each sensor is only able to provide information concerning a subset of features that form a subspace in the feature space; that is, each sensor can be said to perceive features that are independent of the features perceived by the other sensors. Conversely, the dependent features perceived by sensors providing redundant information would form a basis in the feature space.

More timely information, as compared to the speed at which it could be provided by a single sensor, may be provided by multiple sensors due either to the actual speed of operation of each sensor, or to the processing parallelism that may possibly be achieved as part of the integration process.

Less costly information, in the context of a system with multiple sensors, is information obtained at a lesser cost as compared to the equivalent information that could be obtained from a single sensor. Unless the information provided by the single sensor is being used for additional functions in the system, the total cost of the single sensor should be compared to the total cost of the integrated multisensor system.

The role of multisensor integration and fusion in the overall operation of a system can be defined as the degree to which each of these four aspects is present in the information provided by the sensors to the system. Redundant information can usually be fused at a lower level of representation compared to complementary information because it can more easily be made commensurate. Complementary information is usually either fused at a symbolic level of representation, or provided directly to different parts of the system without being fused. Whereas in most cases the advantages gained through the use of redundant, complementary, or more timely information in a system are related to technological benefits, in multisensor target tracking (see Section 4 of Chapter 22), fused information is sometimes used in a distributed network of target tracking sensors just to reduce the bandwidth (and cost) required for communication between groups of sensors in the network.

Figure 1.3 illustrates the distinction between complementary and redundant information in the task of object recognition. Four objects are shown in Figure 1.3(a). They are distinguished by two independent features, shape and temperature. Sensors 1 and 2 provide redundant information concerning the shape of an object, and Sensor 3 provides information concerning its temperature. Figure 1.3(b) and (c) show hypothetical frequency distributions for both "square" and "round" objects, representing each sensor's historical (i.e., tested) responses to such objects. The bottom axes of both figures represent the range of possible sensor readings. The output values $\mathbf{x}_1$ and $\mathbf{x}_2$ correspond to some numerical "degree of squareness or roundness" of the object as

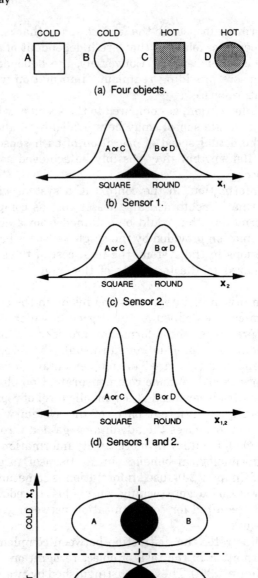

(a) Four objects.

(b) Sensor 1.

(c) Sensor 2.

(d) Sensors 1 and 2.

(e) Sensors 1, 2, and 3.

determined by each sensor, respectively. Because Sensors 1 and 2 are not able to detect the temperature of an object, objects A and C (as well as B and D) can not be distinguished. The dark portion of the axis in each figure corresponds to the range of output values where there is uncertainty as to the shape of the object being detected. The dashed line in each figure corresponds to the point at which, depending on the output value, objects can be distinguished in terms of a feature. Figure 1.3(d) shows the frequency distribution resulting from the fusion of $\mathbf{x}_1$ and $\mathbf{x}_2$. Without specifying a particular method of fusion, it is usually true that the distribution corresponding to the fusion of redundant information would have less dispersion than its component distributions. Under very general assumptions, a plausible argument can be made that the relative probability of the fusion process not reducing the uncertainty is zero (Chapter 10). The uncertainty in Figure 1.3(d) is shown as approximately half that of Figure 1.3(b) and (c). In Figure 1.3(e), complementary information from Sensor 3 concerning the independent feature temperature is fused with the shape information from Sensors 1 and 2 shown in Figure 1.3(d). As a result of the fusion of this additional feature, it is now possible to discriminate between all four objects. This increase in discrimination ability is one of the advantages resulting from the fusion of complementary information. As mentioned above, the information resulting from this second fusion could be at a higher representational level; for example, the result of the first fusion, $\mathbf{x}_{1,2}$, may still be a numerical value, whereas the result of the second, $\mathbf{x}_{1,2,3}$, could be a symbol representing one of the four possible objects.

1.4. Possible Problems

Many of the possible problems associated with creating a general methodology for multisensor integration and fusion, as well as developing the actual systems that use multiple sensors, center around the methods used for modeling the error or uncertainty in 1) the integra-

←

Figure 1.3. The discrimination of four different objects using redundant and complementary information from three sensors. (a) Four objects (A, B, C, and D) distinguished by the features "shape" (square vs. round) and "temperature" (hot vs. cold). (b) 2-D distributions from Sensor 1 (shape). (c) Sensor 2 (shape). (d) 2-D distributions resulting from fusion of redundant shape information from Sensors 1 and 2. (e) 3-D distributions resulting from fusion of complementary information from Sensors 1 and 2 (shape), and Sensor 3 (temperature).

tion and fusion process, 2) the sensory information, and 3) the operation of the overall system including the sensors. For the potential advantages in integrating multiple sensors to be realized, solutions to these problems have to be found that are both practical and theoretically sound.

Error in the integration and fusion process: The major problem in integrating and fusing redundant information from multiple sensors is that of "registration"—the determination that the information from each sensor is referring to the same features in the environment. The registration problem is termed the *correspondence* and *data association* problem in stereo vision and multitarget tracking research, respectively. Barniv and Casasent (1981) have used the correlation coefficient between pixels in the grey level of images as a measure of the degree of registration of objects in the images from multiple sensors. Hsiao (1988) has detailed the different geometric transformations needed for registration. Lee and Van Vleet (1988) and Holm (1987) have studied the registration errors between radar and infrared sensors. Lee and Van Vleet have presented an approach that is able to both estimate and minimize the registration error, and Holm has developed a method that is able to autonomously compensate for registration errors in both the total scene as perceived by each sensor ("macroregistration"), and the individual objects in the scene ("microregistration").

Error in sensory information: The error in sensory information is usually assumed to be caused by a random noise process that can be adequately modeled as a probability distribution. The noise is usually assumed to be uncorrelated in space or time (i.e., white), Gaussian, and independent. The major reason that these assumptions are made is that they enable a variety of fusion techniques to be used that have tractable mathematics and yield useful results in many applications. If the noise is correlated in time (e.g., gyroscope error (see Section 5 of Chapter 22)) it is still sometimes possible to retain the whiteness assumption through the use of a shaping filter (Maybeck, 1979). The Gaussian assumption can only be justified if the noise is caused by a number of small independent sources. In many fusion techniques the consistency of the sensor measurements is increased by first eliminating spurious sensor measurements so that they are not included in the fusion process. Many of the techniques of robust statistics (Huber, 1981) can be used to eliminate spurious measurements. The independence assumption is usually reasonable so long as the noise sources do not originate from within the system.

Error in system operation: When an error occurs during operation due to possible coupling effects between components of a system, it may still be possible to make the assumption that the sensor measurements are independent if the error, after calibration, is incorporated into the system model through the addition of an extra state variable (Maybeck, 1979). In well-known environments the calibration of multiple sensors will usually not be a difficult problem, but when multisensor systems are used in unknown environments it may not be possible to calibrate the sensors. Possible solutions to this problem may require the creation of detailed knowledge bases for each type of sensor so that a system can autonomously calibrate itself. One other important feature required of any intelligent multisensor system is the ability to recognize and recover from sensor failure (cf. Bullock, Sangsuk-iam, Pietsch, & Boudreau, 1988; Jakubowicz, 1988).

2. BIOLOGICAL EXAMPLES OF THE SYNERGISTIC INTEGRATION OF MULTISENSOR INFORMATION

Two of the major abilities that a human operator brings to the task of controlling a system are the use of a flexible body of knowledge and the ability to synergistically integrate information of different modalities obtained through his or her senses. The increasing use of knowledge-based expert systems is an attempt to capture some aspects of this first ability; current research in multisensor integration is an attempt to capture, and possibly extend to additional modalities, aspects of this second ability. Thus, a human's, or other animal's, ability to integrate multisensory information can provide an indication of what is ultimately achievable for intelligent systems (i.e., an existence proof) and insight into possible future research directions. Multisensor integration in the higher vertebrates appears in at least three different forms (Brooks, 1990): duplicate sensing, (e.g., the use of two eyes); sensor fusion (e.g., seeing and touching the same object); and distributed sensing (e.g., networks of sensors in the skin).

2.1. Ventriloquism

A well-known example of human multisensory integration is ventriloquism, in which the voice of the ventriloquist seems to an observer to come from the ventriloquist's dummy. The ability of visual information (the movement of the dummy's lips) to dominate the auditory information coming from the ventriloquist demonstrates the existence of some process of integration whereby information from one modality (audition) is interpreted solely in terms of information from another modality (vision). Howard (1982, Chapter 11) has reported research that found the discordance between visual and auditory information becomes noticeable only after the source of each has been separated beyond 30° relative to the observer (see Figure 1.4). Notwithstanding

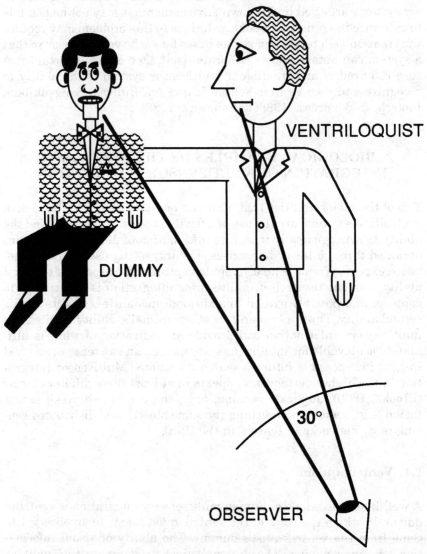

Figure 1.4. Ventriloquism demonstrates the existence of some process of human multisensory integration through the ability of visual information (movement of the dummy's lips) to dominate auditory information (from the ventriloquist) for up to a 30° separation of these information sources relative to the observer.

ventriloquism, the use of information from these two modalities can increase the probability of detecting an event in the environment when compared to the use of either modality alone.

2.2 Pit Vipers and Rattlesnakes

Although in humans the processes of multisensory integration have not yet been found, research on the less complex nervous systems of the pit viper and the rattlesnake has identified neurons in these snakes' optic tectums (a midbrain structure found in vertebrates) that are responsive to both visual and infrared information (Newman and Hartline, 1982). As shown in Figure 1.5, both the left eye and pit organ of a rattlesnake are receiving information from Region 1 in the environment. Infrared information from the pit organ, together with visual information from the eye, are represented on the surface of the optic tectum in a similar spatial orientation so that each region of the optic tectum receives information from the same region of the environment. This allows certain "multimodal" neurons to respond to different combinations of visual and infrared information. Certain "or" neurons respond to information from either modality and could be used by the snake to detect the presence of prey in dim lighting conditions, while certain "and" neurons, which only respond to information from both modalities, could be used to recognize the difference between a warm-blooded mouse and a cool-skinned frog. The "and" neurons have been whimsically described as mouse detectors. In evolutionary terms, it seems likely that similar integration processes take place in the tectums of most other vertebrates.

3. FUTURE RESEARCH DIRECTIONS

In addition to multisensor integration and fusion research directed at finding solutions to the problems already mentioned, research in the near future will likely be aimed at developing integration and fusion techniques that will allow multisensory systems to operate in unknown and dynamic environments. As currently envisioned, multisensor integration and fusion techniques will play an important part in the Strategic Defense Initiative in enabling enemy warheads to be distinguished from decoys (Adam, 1989). Many integration and fusion techniques will be implemented on recently developed highly parallel computer architectures (e.g., Kjell and Wang's (1988) use of the Connection Machine (Hillis, 1985) for data fusion using hierarchical simulated annealing) to take full advantage of the parallelism inherent in

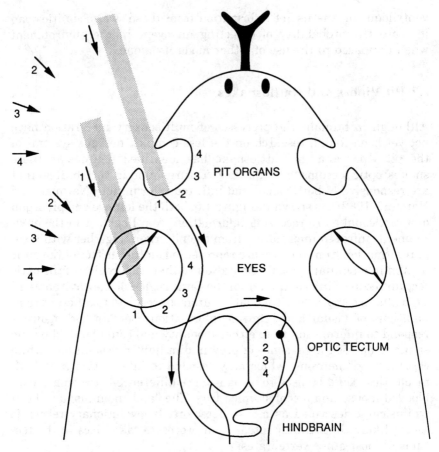

Figure 1.5. The left eye and pit organ of the rattlesnake are receiving information from Region 1 in the environment. Information from both sources is represented on the surface of the optic tectum in a similar spatial orientation. (Adapted from Newman and Hartline (1982), p. 121.)

the techniques. The development of sensor modeling and interface standards would accelerate the design of practical multisensor systems (Henderson et al., 1987). Lyons and Arbib (1989) have initiated the construction of a formal model of computation for sensory-based robotics that they term "robot schemas." Future extensions to their model will make it possible to reason about sensory interactions in a consistent and well-defined manner, and should facilitate the creation of the complex control programs required for multisensor robots. Continued research in the areas of artificial intelligence and neural networks will continue to provide both theoretical and practical insights. AI-based research may prove especially useful in areas such as sensor selection, automatic task error detection and recovery, and the development of high-level representations; research based on neural networks may have a large impact in areas such as object recognition through the development of distributed representations suitable for the associative recall of multisensory information, and in the development of robust multisensor systems that are able to self-organize and adapt to changing conditions (e.g., sensor failure).

The development of integrated solid-state chips containing multiple sensors has been the focus of much recent research (Rojder & Lauber, 1990; Stauffer, 1987; Wise, 1986). As current progress in VLSI technology continues, it is likely that so-called "smart sensors" (Middelhoek & Hoogerwerf, 1985) will be developed which contain many of their low-level signal and fusion processing algorithms in circuits on the same chip as the sensor. In addition to a lower cost, a smart sensor might provide a better signal-to-noise ratio and the ability to perform self-testing and calibration. Currently, it is common to supply a multisensor system with just enough sensors for it to complete its assigned tasks; the availability of cheap integrated multisensors may enable some recent ideas concerning "highly redundant sensing" (Tou & Balchen, 1990) to be incorporated into the design of intelligent multisensor systems—in some cases, high redundancy may imply the use of up to ten times the number of minimally necessary sensors to provide the system with a greater flexibility and insensitivity to sensor failure. In the more distant future, the development of micro or "gnat" (Flynn & Brooks, 1988) robots will necessarily entail the advancement of the state of the art in multisensor integration and fusion.

4. PREVIOUS SURVEYS AND REVIEWS

A number of recent papers have surveyed and reviewed different aspects of multisensor integration and fusion. An article on multisensor integration in the *Encyclopedia of Artificial Intelligence* has focused on the issues involved in object recognition (Bajcsy & Allen, 1986). Mitiche and Aggarwal (1986) discuss some of the advantages and problems involved with the integration of different image processing sensors and review recent work in that area. Mann (1987) provides a concise literature review as part of his paper concerning methods for integration and fusion which are based on the maintenance of consistent labels across different sensor domains. Luo and Kay (1988, 1989) have surveyed some of the issues of and different approaches to multisensor integration and fusion, and Hackett and Shah (1990) have surveyed a number of multisensor fusion papers and have classified them into the following six categories: scene segmentation, representation, three-dimensional shape, sensor modeling, autonomous robots, and object recognition. Recent research workshops have focused on the multisensor integration and fusion issues involved in manufacturing automation (Henderson, Allen, Mitiche, Durrant-Whyte, & Snyder, 1987) and spatial reasoning (Kak & Chen, 1987). Techniques for multisensor integration and fusion have been included in recent textbooks on AI (Dougherty & Giardina, 1988, pp. 273–277) and pattern recognition (Therrien, 1989, pp. 232–242).

5. OVERVIEW OF THE BOOK

The remainder of the book is divided into five parts, each covering a particular aspect or application of multisensor integration and fusion. The first chapter of each part provides a general introduction to the subject of the part and a comprehensive survey of existing research.

Part I covers multisensor integration exclusive of fusion. The chapters included in this part serve both to supplement the material presented in this chapter and to present approaches to different aspects of multisensor integration that are quite general in terms of their range of applicability. Part II includes chapters that describe a variety of methods of multisensor fusion. Each method is quite general in scope and can provide a viable means of fusion for a number of different applications. Part III describes a variety of approaches to object recognition using the integration of information from different combinations of sensors. Chapters are included that describe the integration of visual and thermal images, and the use of vision and touch by a robot to recognize objects. Part IV details the role played by multisensor integration and fusion in enabling mobile robots to operate in uncertain or unknown environments. Chapters are included that describe high-level representations suitable for the creation of world models for multisensor-based mobile robots. Part V describes the use of multisensor integration and fusion in a variety of areas of application. Chapters are included that detail the use of multiple sensors for the tasks of target tracking and battlefield command and control. Chapters 26 and 27 in Part V discuss parallel and distributed decision fusion.

REFERENCES

Adam, J.A. (1989). Star Wars in transition. *IEEE Spectrum, 26*(3), 32–38.
Bajcsy, R., & Allen, P. (1986). Multisensor integration. *Encyclopedia of artificial intelligence* (pp. 632–638). New York: Wiley.

Barniv, Y., & Casasent, D. (1981). Multisensor image registration: Experimental verification. W.H. Carter (Ed.), *Proceedings of the SPIE, vol. 292, Processing Images and Data from Optical Sensors* (pp. 160–171). San Diego, CA.

Brooks, M. (1990). Highly redundant sensing in robotics—Analogies from biology: Distributed sensing and learning. In J.T. Tou & J.G. Balchen (Eds.), *Highly redundant sensing in robotic systems* (pp. 35–42). Berlin: Springer-Verlag.

Bullock, T.E., Sangsuk-iam, S., Pietsch, R., & Boudreau, E.J. (1988). Sensor fusion applied to system performance under sensor failures. In C.W. Weaver (Ed.), *Proceedings of the SPIE, vol. 931, Sensor Fusion* (pp. 131–138). Orlando, FL.

Chandrasekaran, B., & Goel, A. (1988). From numbers to symbols to knowledge structures: Artificial intelligence perspectives on the classification task. *IEEE Transactions on Systems, Man and Cybernetics*, SMC-18(3), 415–424.

Dougherty, E.R., & Giardina, C.R. (1988). *Mathematical methods for artificial intelligence and autonomous systems.* Englewood Cliffs, NJ: Prentice-Hall.

Fischler, M.A., & Firschein, O. (1987). *Intelligence: the eye, the brain and the computer* (pp. 241–242). Reading, MA: Addison-Wesley.

Flynn, A.M., & Brooks, R.A. (1988). MIT mobile robots—What's next? *Proceedings of the IEEE International Conference on Robotics and Automation* (pp. 611–617). Philadelphia, PA.

Hackett, J.K., & Shah, M. (1990). Multi-sensor fusion: A perspective. *Proceedings of the IEEE International Conference on Robotics and Automation* (pp. 1324–1330). Cincinnati, OH.

Henderson, T.C., Allen, P.K., Mitiche, A., Durrant-Whyte, H., & Snyder, W. (Eds.). (1987). *Workshop on multisensor integration in manufacturing automation* (Tech. Rep. UUCS-87-006). University of Utah, Snowbird: Department of Computer Science.

Hillis, W.D. (1985). *The Connection Machine.* Cambridge, MA: MIT Press.

Holm, W.A. (1987). Air-to-ground dual-mode MMW/IR sensor scene registration. In R.G. Buser & F.B. Warren (Eds.), *Proceedings of the SPIE, vol. 782, Infrared Sensors and Sensor Fusion* (pp. 20–27). Orlando, FL.

Howard, I.P. (1982). *Human visual orientation.* Chichester, UK: Wiley.

Huber, P.J. (1981). *Robust statistics.* New York: Wiley.

Hsiao, M. (1988). Geometric registration method for sensor fusion. In P.S. Schenker (Ed.), *Proceedings of the SPIE, vol. 1003, Sensor Fusion: Spatial Reasoning and Scene Interpretation* (pp. 214–221). Cambridge, MA.

Jakubowicz, O.G. (1988). Autonomous reconfiguration of sensor systems using neural nets. In C.W. Weaver (Eds.), *Proceedings of the SPIE, vol. 931, Sensor Fusion* (pp. 197–203). Orlando, FL.

Kak, A., & Chen, S. (Eds.). (1987). *Spatial reasoning and multi-sensor fusion: proceedings of the 1987 workshop.* Los Altos, CA: Morgan Kaufmann.

Kjell, B.P., & Wang, P.Y. (1988). Data fusion and image segmentation using hierarchical simulated annealing on the Connection Machine. In D.P.

Casasent (Ed.), *Proceedings of the SPIE, vol. 1002, Intelligent Robots Comp. Vision: Seventh in a Series* (pp. 330–337). Cambridge, MA.

Lee, R.H., & Van Vleet, W.B. (1988). Registration error analysis between dissimilar sensors. In C.W. Weaver (Ed.), *Proceedings of the SPIE, vol. 931, Sensor Fusion* (pp. 109–114). Orlando, FL.

Luo, R.C., & Kay, M.G. (1989). Multisensor integration and fusion in intelligent systems. *IEEE Transactions on Systems, Man and Cybernetics,* SMC-*19*(5), 901–931.

Luo, R.C., & Kay, M.G. (1988). Multisensor integration and fusion: Issues and approaches. In C.W. Weaver, Ed., *Proceedings of the SPIE, vol. 931, Sensor Fusion* (pp. 42–49). Orlando, FL.

Lyons, D.M., & Arbib, M.A. (1989). A formal model of computation for sensory-based robotics. *IEEE Transactions on Robotics and Automation,* RA-5(3), 280–293.

Mann, R.C. (1987). Multi-sensor integration using concurrent computing. In R.G. Buser & F.B. Warren (Eds.), *Proceedings of the SPIE, vol. 782, Infrared Sensors and Sensor Fusion* (pp. 83–90). Orlando, FL.

Maybeck, P.S. (1979). *Stochastic models, estimation, and control* (Vol. 1). New York: Academic.

Middelhoek, S., & Hoogerwerf, A.C. (1985). Smart sensors: When and where? *Sensors and Actuators, 8,* 39–48.

Mitiche, A., & Aggarwal, J.K. (1986). Multiple sensor integration/fusion through image processing: A review. *Optical Engineering, 25*(3), 380–386.

Newman, E.A., & Hartline, P.H. (1982). The infrared "vision" of snakes. *Scientific American, 246*(3), 116–127.

Rojder, P., & Lauber, A. (1990). Using VLSI circuits for optimal signal handling in multisensorial robotic systems. In J.T. Tou & J.G. Balchen (Eds.), *Highly redundant sensing in robotic systems* (pp. 149–156). Berlin: Springer-Verlag.

Stauffer, R.N. (1987). Integrated sensors extend robotic system intelligence. *Robotics Today,* Aug.

Therrien, C.W. (1989). *Decision, estimation, and classification: An introduction to pattern recognition and related topics.* New York: Wiley.

Tou, J.T., & Balchen, J.G. (Eds.). (1990). *Highly redundant sensing in robotic systems.* Berlin: Springer-Verlag.

Wise, K.D. (1986). Intelligent sensors for semiconductor process automation. *Proceedings of the International Conference on Industrial Electronics, Control and Instrumentation* (pp. 213–217). Milwaukee, WI.

PART I
Multisensor Integration

2
Introduction to Part I

Ren C. Luo and
Michael G. Kay

Part I presents approaches to different aspects of the multisensor integration problem discussed in Chapter 1. Although some of the approaches were originally presented in terms of a specific application or combination of sensors, they are distinguished by their applicability to a broad range of systems in a number of possible areas of application. Additional, more application-specific approaches to multisensor integration are described in Parts III through V of the book.

This chapter first describes a number of different paradigms and frameworks that have been proposed for multisensor integration, and then various control structures that have been used for integration are reviewed. Many of the different frameworks and control structures described can be distinguished by the degree to which they enable the notions of modularity, hierarchical structures, and adaptability (as discussed in Chapter 1) to be effectively incorporated into the integration process. A number of different sensor selection strategies (one of the basic integration functions described in Chapter 1) are then described. Various approaches to the other basic integration functions are not specifically reviewed in this chapter, but are instead included in the other chapters of the book; for example, different representations suitable for creating world models are described in Chapters 6 and 7 and in Section 2 of Chapter 19; multisensor fusion is the subject of Part II of this book, and an example of the guiding type of sensory integration is given in Chapter 18. This chapter concludes with an overview of the remaining chapters of Part I.

1. PARADIGMS AND FRAMEWORKS FOR INTEGRATION

This section describes a number of different paradigms and frameworks that have been proposed for multisensor integration. A paradigm for multisensor integration is more abstract than a framework, and can be thought of as the inspiration behind the development of more concrete frameworks for integration. A framework, in contrast to a paradigm, typically includes specifications as to the particular form of processing to be used for integration. A single paradigm, such as sensory processing using artificial neural networks, may give rise to a variety of different frameworks, such as multilayer Perceptrons and associative memories. A number of AI inspired frameworks for integration are described in Chapter 3, and a particularly influential framework for multisensor integration—logical sensor systems—is described in Chapter 4.

1.1. Hierarchical Phase-Template Paradigm

Luo, Lin, and Sherp (see Chapter 10 in Part II) have proposed a general paradigm for multisensor integration in robotic systems based upon four distinct temporal phases in the sensory information acquisition process (see Figure 2.1). The four phases, "far away," "near to," "touching," and "manipulation," are distinguished at each phase by the range over which sensing will take place, the subset of sensors typically required, and, most importantly, the type of information desired. During the first phase, "far away," only global information concerning the environment is obtained. Typical information at this stage would be the detection, location, or identity of objects in a scene. The most likely types of sensors to be used during this phase would be noncontact sensors like vision cameras and range finding devices. If the scene is found to be of sufficient interest during the first phase, the manipulator can zoom in to obtain more detailed information. This leads to the second phase, "near to." Usually at this close range it is not possible to see the entire object, so noncontact sensors such as proximity sensors or "eye-in-hand" vision systems, mounted on the gripper of the manipulator, are used. If it is desired to confirm or integrate the information from the previous two phases, one can proceed to the third phase, "touching." Contact sensors such as tactile sensors might be used at this phase. Finally, if it is necessary to manipulate the object, one can proceed to the fourth phase, "manipulating." Sensors providing information concerning force/torque, slippage, and weight would typically be used during manipulation.

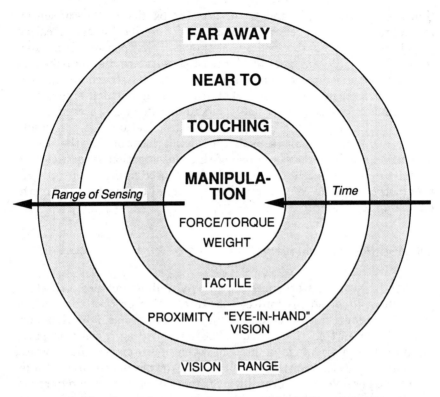

Figure 2.1. The four phases of the Hierarchical Phase-Template paradigm.

The information acquired at each phase is represented in the form of a distinct framelike template. Each template represents information that is both common to all phases (e.g., position and orientation of an object) and specific to the particular phase. During each phase of operation, the information acquired by each sensor is stored as an instance of that phase's template. The information from each sensor can then be fused into a single instance of the template (Chapter 10 in Part II provides a description of the fusion method used).

1.2. The Sensor Effect Cube

The number and variety of possible sensors available for use in an intelligent system (e.g., an autonomous multisensor mobile robot) leads one to try to classify these sensors so that it may be possible to develop methods of integrating the operation of each different sensor that are to some degree independent of the particular type of sensor. Middelhoek and Hoogerwerf (1986) have described a classification paradigm for solid-sate sensors that they call the "sensor effect cube" in which the different possible types of sensors are distinguished on the basis of the energy or mass carrier (i.e., radiant, mechanical, thermal, electrical, magnetic, and chemical) through which signals are first input to the sensor, possibly modulated during processing, and then output from the sensor. Using this classification it is possible to represent each possible sensor type as a location in the three-dimensional cube. A possible use of this classification scheme is as a means to measure the generality of the proposed multisensor integration method in terms of the range sensor signal types which the method is able to integrate.

1.3. Artificial Neural Networks

Artificial neural networks provide a fairly well-established formalism with which to model the multisensor integration process. Current research in neural networks (e.g., Hinton & Anderson, 1989; Kohonen, 1989; Rumelhart & McClelland, 1986) is providing a common paradigm for the interchange of ideas between neuroscience and robotics; Pellionisz (1987) has even introduced the term "neurobotics" to describe the possible use of brainlike control and representation in robotic systems. Kung and Hwang (1989) have examined several neural network architectures for robotic applications and have proposed a ring VLSI systolic architecture for their implementation. An example of sensory fusion using a biological neural network is given in Chapter 5.

Maren, Pap, and Harston (1989) have developed a hierarchical data structure for multisensor fusion between dissimilar sensors. The hierarchical data structure is created by the unsupervised clustering of maximally-related nodes in a multilayer cooperative/competitive neural network (Maren, Minsky & Ali, 1988). The hierarchical network architecture allows a system to identify the most "perceptually salient" regions in an image or temporal data stream for possible fusion.

Multilayer Perceptrons: In contrast to most methods of statistical pattern recognition, the use of multilayer Perceptrons (Minsky & Papert, 1988; Rumelhart & McClelland, 1986) requires no assumptions be made concerning the form of the distribution associated with sensory data; for example, the data may have multiple modes and a non-Gaussian form of distribution. Given enough training samples and a long enough time for training, a multilayer Perceptron can learn to classify arbitrary patterns of sensory data into different categories. As opposed to a single-layer Perceptron, a multilayer Perceptron can use hidden layers of nodes together with a learning procedure such as "back-propagation" (Rumelhart, Hinton & Williams, 1986) for classification using data that is not linearly separable.

Associative memories: Neurons can be trained to represent sensory information, and, through associative recall, complex combinations of the neurons can be activated in response to different sensory stimuli presented to an associative memory (Hopfield, 1982; Kohonen, 1989). The optical implementation of associative memories (Farhat, Psaltis, Prata & Paek, 1985) can significantly increase their storage capacity and will allow their use in more complex multisensory systems. "Simulated annealing" (see Section 2 of Chapter 8) is one of the many different techniques that can be used to find a global optimal state in the memory based upon the local state of activation of each neuron. An associative memory can be used in two modes: in a "heteroassociative" mode where the output of the memory is different than the input (e.g., the sensory data is the input and an object label is the output of the memory) and in an "autoassociative" mode where the output is the complete version of a partial or noise corrupted input data. A heteroassociative memory can be said to perform a recognition function while an autoassociative memory performs a feature extraction function. It is possible to combine a heteroassociative memory in series with an autoassociative memory to take full advantage of each. The use of an autoassociative memory allows for the possibility of using global features (e.g., moments, Fourier descriptors (Wechsler & Zimmerman, 1988)) even in the case where the object may be partially occluded.

Self-organizing maps: Layers of topologically correct self-organizing feature or sensorimotor maps are used in the nervous system for the processing of multisensor and motor information (Knudsen, du Lac & Esterly, 1987). Feature maps can be used to reduce the dimensionality of sensor signals while preserving their topological relationships so that sensory information from different sources can be efficiently fused. Kohonen (1989) developed one of the first algorithms for the creation of general abstract self-organizing feature maps, that is, maps not tied to a specific biological sensor modality. Graf and LaLonde (1988, 1989) have used self-organizing sensorimotor maps to represent the actuator signals controlling two independent cameras and a manipulator to learn the "hand/eye" correspondence for various locations in the environment; the learned sensorimotor maps were then used to plan collision-free manipulator movements.

The self-organizing and autonomous reconfiguration capabilities of neural networks have been used by a number of researchers as part of their development of methods of mobile robot control. Priebe and Marchette (1988) have proposed a self-organizing neural network architecture for multisensor integration on an autonomous sentry robot. The outputs for various sensors are correlated and fused based on their temporal co-occurance. Jakubowicz (1988, 1989) has presented a neural network-based multisensor system that is able to adaptively reconfigure itself in response to sensor failure. Dress (1987) and Barhen, Dress, and Jorgensen (1988) have developed a frequency-based neural network model that is able to self-organize and learn in a simulated environment using multiple sensors. The use of frequency for coding sensory information allows for an improved noise response as well as a common framework for integrating different types of sensors.

1.4. Object-Oriented Programming

In a similar manner to the logical sensors mentioned above, object-oriented programming is a methodology that can be used to develop a uniform framework for implementing multisensor tasks; Henderson and Weitz (1987) have, in fact, discussed the development of logical sensor specifications (see Chapter 4) within an object-oriented programming context. In most object-oriented multisensor applications, each sensor is represented as an object. Objects communicate by passing messages that invoke specialized sensor processing procedures ("methods") based on the sensor's attributes and behavior. Each method is transparent to other objects, allowing different physical sensors to be used interchangeably. Rodger and Browse (1987) have used object-oriented programming for multisensor object recognition, and Allen (1987) has developed an object-oriented framework for multisensor robotic tasks.

1.5. Logical Behaviors

Henderson and Grupen (1990) describe a framework for multisensor integration that is based on what they term "logical behaviors." Logical behaviors are an extension to Henderson's previous work on logical sensors (see Chapter 4) and, like logical sensors, serve as a uniform framework for multisensor integration. Elemental robot tasks which span a particular problem domain are described in terms of logical behaviors which are themselves composed of both logical sensors and logical actuators. The distinction between execution and planning tasks relates, respectively, to whether the logical sensors and actuators comprising the task terminate at an actual physical device, or only represent hypothetical state transitions that comprise cognitive planning tasks. The use of logical behaviors can increase the portability of a robot's control system because the details of actual physical sensors and actuators are separated from their functional use in the system.

1.6. Generalized Evidence Processing

Thomopoulos (1990) has developed a generic architecture and analytical framework that addresses the sensor fusion problem in a single coherent fashion, and has offered three design criteria required of any fusion method. In his fusion architecture, processing takes place at three different levels: the signal level, the level of evidence, and the level of dynamics, where it is assumed that a mathematical model exists of the dynamical process providing the sensory information. At the level of evidence a new "generalized evidence processing" theory is presented that unifies Bayesian and Dempster-Shafer evidence processing (see Sections 3.1 and 3.2 of Chapter 8) in a general framework.

2. CONTROL STRUCTURES

This section presents different structures that have been used to control the overall integration and fusion process. Although some of the control structures described in this section are mentioned in relation to a specific application, each can potentially be used in a wide range of applications. A number of structures that have been used to control the integration process on multisensor mobile robots are described in Chapter 19.

2.1. Bayesian Networks and Rule-Based Systems

Networks and rule-based systems are the most common forms of control structures used for multisensor integration. They can be used either individually or combined together as part of an overall control structure. They are especially useful when the sensors in a system are very dissimilar and the data they provide needs to be fused at multiple levels of representation, that is, from signal- through symbol-level fusion. Due to the particular advantages of each type of structure, rule-based structures are most effective when used for top-level control, and network structures (e.g., Bayesian and neural networks) are most effective when used for lower-level control functions. Mitiche, Henderson, and Laganiere (1988) have advocated the use of "decision networks" for multisensor integration. In a decision network, Bayesian and neural networks can be used as evaluating mechanisms at the nodes of a tree-structured production rule-based control network.

The use of networks enables hierarchical structures to be efficiently represented (e.g., the networks of logical sensors described in Chapter 4) and allows the same formalism to be used to encode their representational as well as control structure; for example, a hierarchical network can be used to both model an object and to control the decision process in multiple-hypothesis object recognition. The use of rule-based systems enables the implementation of many AI-based control schemes (see Chapter 3) that offer extreme flexibility for integrating multiple sensors in complex systems because knowledge, in the form of production rules, can be added to the control structure in a modular and incremental fashion. The production rules used in many systems can themselves be used for symbol-level fusion (see Section 3 of Chapter 8).

The major problem with rule-based systems that limits their application to all levels of the control structure needed for multisensor integration is that, unless each rule in the system represents an inference that is independent of all the other rules in the system (i.e., the rule base forms a tree structure), improper conclusions can be drawn during the reasoning process; for example, bidirectional inferences are not correctly handled, conclusions can not be easily retracted, and correlated sources of evidence are improperly treated (Pearl, 1988, pp. 6–9). A means of overcoming these difficulties in portions of the control structure where individual rules can not be isolated from the effects of other related nodes is through the use of the Bayesian formalism in which conditional probability expressions are used to represent factual or empirical information. A problem with the straightforward use of conditional probability expressions is that in order to assert a fact one must know its conditional dependencies with all of the other known facts. Bayesian networks (Pearl, 1988, pp. 116–131) can be used to encode these dependencies as directed arcs between neighboring nodes in an acyclic graph so that they can be quickly identified. The network offers a complete inference mechanism that can identify, in polynomial time, every conditional dependence relationship.

Miltonberger, Morgan, and Orr (1988) and Morgan, Miltonberger, and Orr (1989) have used Bayesian networks for multisensor object recognition. Continuously-valued estimates of an object's state (e.g., position and orientation) arising from the outputs of the multiple sensors are represented at the nodes of the network in the form of hierarchical Kalman filters. Geometry reasoning is used for both forward and backward propagation through the networks in the course of determining a joint estimate of the object's state.

2.2. The NBS Sensory and Control Hierarchy

The Center for Manufacturing Engineering at the National Bureau of Standards (NBS or, as it has recently been renamed, the National Institute of Standards and Technology) is implementing an experimental factory called the Automated Manufacturing Research Facility (AMRF). As part of the AMRF, a multisensor interactive hierarchical robot control system (Albus, 1981; Barbera, Fitzgerald, Albus & Haynes, 1984; Kent & Albus, 1984; McCain, 1985; Shneier et al., 1983; Swyt, 1989) is being developed. As shown in Figure 2.2, the structure of the control system in AMRF consists of an ascending "sensory processing" hierarchy coupled to a descending "task-decomposition" control hierarchy via "world models" at each level. Input to the world model at each level comes from both the task unit at that level and other unspecified locations in the system. The use of multiple levels is motivated by the observation that the complexity of a control program grows exponentially as the number of sensors and their associated processing increases. By isolating related portions of the required processing at one level, this complexity can be reduced. The large number of low-level processing tasks, which usually have to be done in real time, can be separated from the fewer, more complex, higher-level processing tasks so that the required processing time at each level can become nearly equal. Assuming the required communication between processing levels will be much less than the communication within levels, complexity is reduced by requiring only a limited number of communication channels between levels. If the processing at each level can be done in parallel, the addition of more levels will not result in an exponential increase in complexity. The amount of processing at each level is further reduced by the use of a priori knowledge from the world model. The world models provide predictions to the sensory system concerning the incoming sensory information so that the amount of processing required can be reduced. Use of a world model promotes modularity because the specific information requirements of the sensory and control hierarchies are decoupled.

Figure 2.2 provides an example of the control of a multisensor robot using the NBS hierarchy. Raw sensory data from the environment

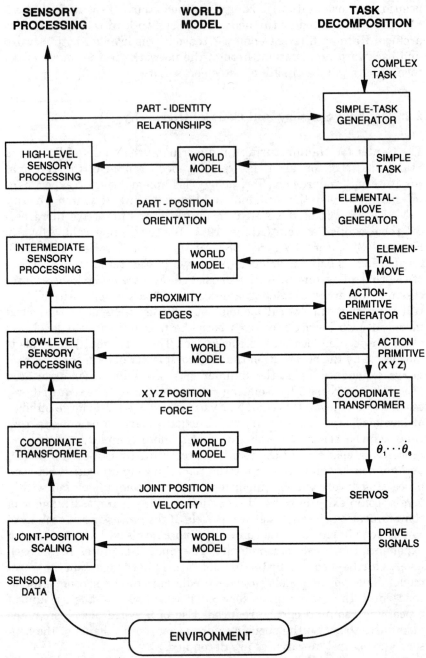

Figure 2.2. The NBS sensory and control hierarchy used to control a multisensor robot. (Adapted from Figs. 5.24 and 9.6 in Albus (1981).)

enter the system at the bottom. At this lowest level, most of the required sensory processing will be continuous monitoring of the robot's joint positions. Any deviation between the actual and expected data is sent as feedback information to the servos, and as summary information to the next level in the sensory processing hierarchy. More complex data, such as that from vision sensors, are sent through to higher levels unmodified. At the very highest level in the system, the complex task and the top-level world model filter down to lower levels in the hierarchy both expected and desired information values. It is at the intermediate levels where both of these information flows meet and interact. Based upon current sensory information, the world models are updated. The updated world models can then serve to modify the desired task control actions until, at the lowest level, the necessary drive signals are sent to the robot to initiate actions in the environment.

Shneier, Kent, and Mansbach (1984), Kent, Shneier, and Hong (1986), and Shneier, Lumia, and Kent (1986) have described the kinds of processes involved in the higher levels of the sensory system of the NBS hierarchy. World models at each level in the hierarchy are used to created initial expectations about the form of the sensory information available at that level and then to generate predictions for the task control units in the hierarchy so that they do not have to wait for sensory processing to finish. Errors between the sensed information and the world model are used initially to register the model and later to maintain the consistence of the model during operation of the system.

2.3. Distributed Blackboards

A blackboard architecture allows economical communication between distributed sensory subsystems in an integrated multisensor system. Each subsystem can send time-stamped summary output to a blackboard where it becomes available to any fusion process as well as to the various integration functions. The time stamp on the output in the blackboard allows for sensor information to be made commensurate before being fused. The blackboard can contain any system information needed by the integration functions. Any number of different fusion methods can be implemented using the output from the blackboard. Capocaccia, Damasio, Regazzoni, and Vernazza (1988) have developed a method of multisensor fusion that can be used for mobile robot obstacle detection and identification. An object-oriented blackboard organization is used for both inference (fusion) and control. Harmon, Bianchini, and Pinz (1986) have used a blackboard architecture to compare different methods of multisensor fusion, and Johnson, Shaw, Reynolds, and Himayat (1989) discuss the advantages of a blackboard style software architecture as a means of implementing the concept of object-oriented, data-flow programming that is useful in multisensor fusion. Sikka and Varshney (1989) have used a blackboard for distributed fusion and object identification, and Harmon (1990) has used a tree-structured blackboard architecture to support multisensor fusion on autonomous robots.

2.4. Adaptive Learning

Adaptive learning is a method of control in which a system discovers the appropriate signals for control based on the output of its sensors. The system is taught a representative sample of correlated control signals and associated sensory outputs over the range of signals and sensory outputs encountered by the system. Based on the associations developed during this teaching phase, it is possible to have the system respond to any combination of sensory outputs with an appropriate control signal. The system requires no a priori knowledge of the relationship between the structural kinematics of the robot, or the desired control signals and their associated sensory outputs. It is the feature of the adaptive learning approach that makes it attractive when there are possibly multiple sensors interacting to produce complex outputs.

Some of the earliest biologically inspired approaches to the control of a robot manipulator through adaptive learning were based on the mathematical formalism called the Cerebellar Model Articulation Controller (CMAC) (Albus, 1975a, 1975b, 1981). Handleman, Lane, and Gelfand (1989a, 1989b, 1990) have used CMAC modules for adaptive learning as part of an integrated neural network and knowledge-based system for robotic control.

3. SENSOR SELECTION STRATEGIES

Sensor selection is an integration function that can enable a multisensor system to select the most appropriate configuration of sensors (or sensing strategy) from among the sensors available to the system. In order for selection to take place, some type of sensor performance criteria need to be established. In many cases the criteria require that the operation of the sensors be modeled adequately enough so that a cost value can be assigned to measure the sensor's performance. Two different approaches to the selection of the type, number, and configuration of sensors to be used in a system can be distinguished: *preselection* during design or initialization, and *real-time selection* in response to changing environmental or system conditions.

3.1. Preselection

Hager (1990) has defined a descriptive framework for sensor selection that uses geometric, sensor, and task models to determine what to observe, the group of sensors needed to observe it, and how much effort to spend on the sensing task. Tou (1990) has used Markov renewal analysis to develop reliability measures for redundant sensors that can be used in the selection process, and Balchen and Dessen (1990) have investigated the performance versus cost trade-offs in using a large number of less accurate and lower cost sensors as opposed to a few highly accurate but more expensive sensors.

As an initial step towards a general methodology for optimal sensor selection and design, Beni, Hackwood, Hornak, and Jackel (1983) have derived a general relationship between the number and operating speed of available sensing elements as a function of their response and processing times. This relationship can be used to determine the optimal arrangement of the sensing elements in a multisensor system. In addition to the actual geometric arrangement of the sensing elements, consideration of the choice between adding sensing elements (static sensing) and moving the elements (dynamic sensing) is used in determining the optimal arrangement.

Hovanessian (1988, pp. 279–298) has used an "expert matrix" method to obtain a quantitative ranking of the performance of a group or suite of sensors in different operational scenarios (e.g., automatic target recognition under different battlefield conditions). Expert knowledge is used to determine a "sensor-condition matrix" which estimates the relative performance of each sensor in relation to a variety of operating conditions. Relative sensor effectiveness values for each scenario are then obtained by multiplying the sensor-condition matrix by a "condition-scenario matrix," which estimates the relative importance of each operating condition in the different scenarios. An overall ranking of the sensors can then be obtained through relative weighting methods.

Ikeuchi and Kanade (1988, 1989) have proposed a means of automatically generating multisensor object recognition programs based on the types of object features that can be detected by different sensors under what operating conditions and with how much accuracy. These sensor characteristics are represented in a feature configuration space and are used to determine detection constraints in order to predict the appearance of an object viewed from different aspects.

3.2. Real-Time Selection

Hutchinson, Cromwell, and Kak (1986) and Hutchinson and Kak (1989) have presented an approach to planning sensing strategies for object recognition in a multisensor robotic workcell. One sensor in the workcell is used to form an initial set of object hypotheses and then subsequent sensors are chosen so as to maximally disambiguate the remaining object hypotheses. Grimson (1988) has also considered the problem of recognizing objects in the workspace of a robot using minimal sets of sensory information, and Taylor and Taylor (1988) have used "dynamic error probability vectors" to select the appropriate sensors necessary for the recovery from errors during an automatic assembly process.

Blackman (1986, pp. 387–391, and in Chapter 24 of Part V) has outlined a utility theory approach to sensor selection for target tracking. Individual sensors are allocated to target tracks so as to maximize the overall utility of the system. The expected gain in marginal utility associated with the allocation of a particular sensor to a target track is expressed as the improvement in the estimate of a kinematic quantity (e.g., the target's range) given a measurement from the sensor. The utility of a kinematic quantity is estimated using the prediction covariance matrix of a Kalman filter.

Zheng (1989) has proposed a systematic approach to evaluating the real-time performance of multisensor integration in robotic systems. The integration process is modeled using logical sensors (see Chapter 4) and its performance is measured by determining the number of levels of control into which the logical sensors are integrated. The cost of integration is measured using the sensors' response time and the uncertainty associated with their data.

4. OVERVIEW

This section presents an overview of the remaining chapters in Part I.
  Chapter 3: Garvey discusses multisensor integration and symbol-level fusion in relation to current research in AI. Symbol-level fusion is implemented in most AI systems through the inference process. A generic system architecture is used to illustrate

the different means by which the inference process can be controlled in AI systems in order to limit their overall processing workload. A thorough discussion is provided of a variety of different control structures for high-level multisensor integration which serves to supplement the material presented in Section 2 of this chapter.

Chapter 4: A number of researchers have used Henderson and Shilcrat's definition of logical sensor systems as a common framework with which to model the integration process in multisensor systems. A logical sensor is a specification for the abstract definition of a sensor that can be used to provide a uniform framework for multisensor integration. Through the use of an abstract definition of a sensor, the unnecessary details of the actual physical sensor are separated from their functional use in a system. In a manner similar to the way an abstract data type separates the user from unnecessary algorithmic detail, the use of logical sensors can provide any multisensor system with both portability and the ability to adapt to technological changes in a manner transparent to the system. Each logical sensor can serve as an element in a network of logical sensors, which itself can be viewed as a logical sensor. Recent research that has extended the basic idea of logical sensors includes: Henderson, Hansen, and Bhanu (1985a, 1985b, 1985c), Luo and Henderson (1986), Henderson and Weitz (1987), Henderson, Weitz, Hansen, and Mitiche (1988), and Henderson and Hansen (1988).

Chapter 5: Pearson, Gelfand, Sullivan, Peterson, and Spence have presented a neural network model for multisensor fusion based on the barn owl's use of visual and acoustic information for target localization. Separate visual and acoustic maps are fused into a single map (corresponding to the owl's optic tectum) which is then used for head orientation. A recent extension of their model can be found in Spence, Pearson, Gelfand, and Peterson (1989).

Chapter 6: Pau presents a formal knowledge representation architecture for feature- and symbol-level multisensor fusion. The architecture is hierarchical in nature with feature vectors at the lowest level, feature graphs at the next level, and rules invoked by the nodes in feature graphs at the highest level. Fusion takes place through transformation, matching, and projection operations defined for each level in the hierarchy. Examples are given that illustrate the application of the representation for the tasks of integrated circuit inspection and object recognition using multiple Doppler processed interferometric measurements.

Chapter 7: The multisensor kernel system presented by Henderson and Fai is a means of providing a representation for sensor information that is compatible with the specification of logical sensors (see Chapter 4). Object features are extracted from low-level sensory data and organized into a three-dimensional "spatial proximity graph" that makes explicit the neighborhood relations between features. Each feature is defined in terms of a logical sensor and is available to the system as the output of the logical sensor's characteristic vector. Subsequent sensory data can then either be matched in terms of the spatial proximity graph, or a "k-d tree" (a binary tree with k-dimensional keys that allows the nearest neighbors of one of k features to be found) is constructed, using the proximity graph, for faster processing.

REFERENCES

Albus, J.S. (1975a). Data storage in the Cerebellar Model Articulation Controller (CMAC). *Journal of Dynamic Systems, Measurement and Control, 97*(3), 228–233.

Albus, J.S. (1975b). A new approach to manipulator control: The Cerebellar Model Articulation Controller (CMAC). *Journal of Dynamic Systems, Measurement and Control 97*(3), 220–227.

Albus, J.S. (1981). *Brains, behavior, & robotics.* Peterborough, NH: Byte Books.

Allen, P.K. (1987). A framework for implementing multi-sensor robotic tasks. In R. Raghavan & T.J. Cokonis (Eds.), *Proceedings of the ASME International Computers in Engineering Conference and Exhibition* (pp. 303–309). New York, NY.

Balchen, J.G., & Dessen, F. (1990). Structural solution of highly redundant sensing in robotic systems. In J.T. Tou & J.G. Balchen (Eds.), *Highly redundant sensing in robotic systems* (pp. 264–275). Berlin: Springer-Verlag.

Barbera, A.J., Fitzgerald, M.L., Albus, J.S., & Haynes, L.S. (1984). RCS: The NBS real-time control system. *Robots 8 Conference Proceedings* (pp. 19.1–19.33). Detroit, MI.

Barhen, J., Dress, W.B., & Jorgensen, C.C. (1988). Applications of concurrent neuromorphic algorithms for autonomous robots. In R. Eckmiller & C. v.d. Malsburg (Eds.), *Neural computers* (pp. 321–333). Berlin: Springer-Verlag.

Beni, G., Hackwood, S., Hornak, L.A., & Jackel, J.L. (1983). Dynamic sensing for robots: An analysis and implementation. *International Journal of Robotics Research 2*(2), 51–61.

Blackman, S.S. (1986). *Multiple target tracking with radar applications.* Dedham, MA: Artech House.

Capocaccia, G., Damasio, A., Regazzoni, C.S., & Vernazza, G. (1988). Data fusion approach to obstacle detection and identification. In P.S. Schenker (Ed.), *Proceedings of the SPIE, vol. 1003, Sensor Fusion: Spatial Reasoning and Scene Interpretation* (pp. 409–419). Cambridge, MA.

Dress, W.B. (1987). Frequency-coded artificial neural networks: an approach to self-organizing systems. *Proceedings of the IEEE 1st International Conference on Neural Networks* (pp. II-47–II-54). San Diego, CA.

Farhat, N.H., Psaltis, D., Prata, A., & Paek, E. (1985). Optical implementation of the Hopfield model. *Applied Optics, 24*(10), 1469–1475.

Graf, D.H., & LaLonde, W.R. (1988). A neural controller for collision-free movement of general robot manipulators. *Proceedings of the IEEE International Conference on Neural Networks* (pp. I-77–I-84). San Diego, CA.

Graf, D.H., & LaLonde, W.R. (1989). Neuroplanners for hand/eye coordination. *Proceedings of the International Joint Conference on Neural Networks* (pp. II-543–II-548). Washington, DC.

Grimson, W.E.L. (1988). Disambiguating sensory interpretations using minimal sets of sensory data. *Proceedings of the IEEE International Conference on Robotics and Automation* (pp. 286–292). Philadelphia, PA.

Hager, G.D. (1990). *Task-directed sensor fusion and planning: A computational approach.* Norwell, MA: Kluwer.

Handelman, D.A., Lane, S.H., & Gelfand, J.J. (1989a). Integrating neural networks and knowledge-based systems for robotic control. *Proceedings of the IEEE International Conference on Robotics and Automation* (pp. 1454–1460). Scottsdale, AZ.

Handelman, D.A., Lane, S.H., & Gelfand, J.J. (1989b). Integration of knowledge-based system and neural techniques for autonomous learning machines. *Proceedings of the International Joint Conference on Neural Networks* (pp. I-683–I-688). Washington, DC.

Handelman, D.A., Lane, S.H., & Gelfand, J.J. (1990). Integrating neural networks and knowledge-based systems for intelligent robotic control. *IEEE Control Systems Magazine, 10*(3), 77–87.

Harmon, S.Y. (1990). Tools for multisensor data fusion in autonomous robots. In J.T. Tou & J.G. Balchen (Eds.), *Highly redundant sensing in robotic systems* (pp. 103–125). Berlin: Springer-Verlag.

Harmon, S.Y., Bianchini, G.L., & Pinz, B.E. (1986). Sensor data fusion through a distributed blackboard. *Proceedings of the IEEE International Conference Robotics and Automation* (pp. 1449–1454). San Francisco, CA.

Henderson, T.C., & Grupen, R. (1990). Logical behaviors. *Journal of Robotic Systems, 7*(3), 309–336.

Henderson, T.C., & Hansen, C. (1988). Multisensor knowledge systems. In A.K. Jain (Ed.), *Real-time object measurement and classification* (pp. 375–390). Berlin: Springer-Verlag.

Henderson, T.C., & Weitz, E. (1987). Multisensor integration in a multiprocessor environment. In R. Raghavan & T.J. Cokonis (Eds.), *Proceedings of the ASME International Computers in Engineering Conference and Exhibition* (pp. 311–316). New York, NY.

Henderson, T.C., Hansen, C., & Bhanu, B. (1985a). A framework for distributed sensing and control. *Proceedings of the 9th International Joint Conference on Artificial Intelligence* (pp. 1106–1109). Los Angeles, CA.

Henderson, T.C., Hansen, C., & Bhanu, B. (1985b). The specification of distributed sensing and control. *Journal of Robotic Systems, 2*(4), 387–396.

Henderson, T.C., Hansen, C., & Bhanu, B. (1985c). The synthesis of logical sensor specifications. *Proceedings of the SPIE, vol. 579, Intelligent Robots and Computer Vision* (pp. 442–445). Cambridge, MA.

Henderson, T.C., Weitz, E., Hansen, C., & Mitiche, A. (1988). Multisensor knowledge systems: Interpreting 3D structure. *International Journal of Robotics Research, 7*(6), 114–137.

Hinton, G.E., & Anderson, J.A. (Eds.). (1989). *Parallel models of associative memory* (updated ed.). Hillsdale, NJ: Erlbaum.

Hopfield, J.J. (1982). Neural networks and physical systems with emergent collective computational abilities. *Proceedings of the National Academy of Science of the USA, 79*, 2554–2558.

Hovanessian, S.A. (1988). *Introduction to sensor systems.* Norwood, MA: Artech House.

Hutchinson, S.A., & Kak, A.C. (1989). Planning sensing strategies in a robot work cell with multi-sensor capabilities. *IEEE Transactions on Robotics Automation, RA-5*(6), 765–783.

Hutchinson, S.A., Cromwell, R.L., & Kak, A.C. (1986). Planning sensing strategies in a robot work cell with multi-sensor capabilities. *Proceedings of the IEEE International Conference on Robotics and Automation* (pp. 1068–1075). San Francisco, CA.

Ikeuchi, K., & Kanade, T. (1988). Automatic generation of object recognition programs. *Proceedings of the IEEE, 76*(8), 1016–1035.

Ikeuchi, K., & Kanade, T. (1989). Modeling sensors: Toward automatic generation of object recognition program. *Computer Vision, Graphics, and Image Processing, 48*, 50–79.

Jakubowicz, O.G. (1988). Autonomous reconfiguration of sensor systems using neural nets. In C.W. Weaver (Ed.), *Proceedings of the SPIE, vol. 931, Sensor Fusion* (pp. 197–203). Orlando, FL.

Jakubowicz, O.G. (1989). Multi-layer multi-feature map architecture for situational analysis. *Proceedings of the International Joint Conference on Neural Networks,* (pp. II-23–II-30). Washington, DC.

Johnson, D., Shaw, S., Reynolds, S., & Himayat, N. (1989). Real-time blackboards for sensor fusion. In C.B. Weaver (Ed.), *Proceedings of the SPIE, vol. 1100, Sensor Fusion II* (pp. 61–73), Orlando, FL.

Kent, E.W., & Albus, J.S. (1984). Servoed world models as interfaces between robot control systems and sensory data. *Robotica, 2*, 17–25.

Kent, E.W., Shneier, M.O., & Hong, T.H. (1986). Building representations from fusions of multiple views. *Proceedings of the IEEE International Conference on Robotics and Automation* (pp. 1634–1639). San Francisco, CA.

Knudsen, E.I., du Lac, S., & Esterly, S.D. (1987). Computational maps in the brain. *Annual Review of Neuroscience, 10*, 41–65.

Kohonen, T. (1989). *Self-organization and associative memory* (3rd ed.). Berlin: Springer-Verlag.

Kung, S.Y., & Hwang, J.N. (1989). Neural network architectures for robotic applications. *IEEE Transactions on Robotics and Automation,* RA-5(5), 641–657.

Luo, R.C., & Henderson, T. (1986). A servo-controlled robot gripper with multiple sensors and its logical specification. *Journal of Robotic Systems, 3*(4), 409–420.

Maren, A.J., Minsky, V., & Ali, M. (1988). A multilayer cooperative/competitive method for creating hierarchical structures by clustering maximally-related nodes. *Proceedings of the IEEE International Conference on Neural Networks* (pp. II-95–II-105). San Diego, CA.

Maren, A.J., Pap, R.M., & Harston, C.T. (1989). A hierarchical data structure representation for fusion multisensor information. In C.B. Weaver (Ed.), *Proceedings of the SPIE, vol. 1100, Sensor Fusion II* (pp. 162–178). Orlando, FL.

McCain, H.G. (1985). A hierarchically controlled, sensory interactive robot in the automated manufacturing research facility. *Proceedings of the IEEE International Conference on Robotics and Automation* (pp. 931–939). St. Louis, MO.

Middelhoek, S., & Hoogerwerf, A.C. (1986). Classifying solid-state sensors: The "sensor effect cube." *Sensors and Actuators, 10,* 1–8.

Miltonberger, T., Morgan, D., & Orr, G. (1988). Multisensor object recognition from 3D models. In P.S. Schenker (Ed.), *Proceedings of the SPIE, vol. 1003, Sensor Fusion: Spatial Reasoning and Scene Interpretation* (pp. 161–169). Cambridge, MA.

Minsky, M.L., & Papert, S.A. (1988). *Perceptrons* (expanded ed.). Cambridge, MA: MIT Press.

Mitiche, A., Henderson, T.C., & Laganiere, R. (1988). Decision networks for multisensor integration in computer vision. In P.S. Schenker (Ed.), *Proceedings of the SPIE, vol. 1003, Sensor Fusion: Spatial Reasoning and Scene Interpretation* (pp. 291–299). Cambridge, MA.

Morgan, D., Miltonberger, T., & Orr, G. (1989). A sensor algorithm expert system. In Y. Lin & R. Srinivasan (Eds.), *Proceedings of the SPIE, vol. 1075, Digital Image Processing Applications* (pp. 357–372).

Pearl, J. (1988). *Probabilistic reasoning in intelligent systems: Networks of plausible inference.* San Mateo, CA: Morgan Kaufmann.

Pellionisz, A.J. (1987). Sensorimotor operation: A ground for the co-evolution of brain-theory with neurobotics and neurocomputers. *Proceedings of the IEEE 1st International Conference on Neural Networks* (pp. IV-593–IV-600). San Diego, CA.

Priebe, C.E., & Marchette, D.J. (1988). Temporal pattern recognition: A network architecture for multi-sensor fusion. In D.P. Casasent (Ed.), *Proceedings of the SPIE, vol. 1002, Intelligent Robots and Computer Vision: Seventh in a Series* (pp. 679–685). Cambridge, MA.

Rodger, J.C., & Browse, R.A. (1987). An object-based representation for multisensory robotic perception. *Proceedings of the Workshop on Spatial Reasoning and Multi-Sensor Fusion* (pp. 13–20). St. Charles, IL.

Rumelhart, D.E., & McClelland, J.L. (Eds.). (1986). *Parallel distributed pro-*

cessing: Explorations into the microstructure of cognition. Cambridge, MA: MIT Press.

Rumelhart, D.E., Hinton, G.E., & Williams, R.J. (1986). Learning internal representations by error propagation. In D.E. Rumelhart & J.L. McClelland (Eds.), *Parallel distributed processing: Explorations into the microstructure of cognition* (pp. 318–362). Cambridge, MA: MIT Press.

Shneier, M.O., Kent, E.W., & Mansbach, P. (1984). Representing workspace and model knowledge for a robot with mobile sensors. *Proceedings of the 7th International Conference on Pattern Recognition* (pp. 199–202). Montreal, Canada.

Shneier, M.O., Kent, E.W., Albus, J., Mansbach, P., Nashman, M., Palombo, L., Rurkowski, W., & Wheatley, T. (1983). Robot sensing for a hierarchical control system. *Proceedings of the 13th International Symposium on Industrial Robots and Robots 7* (pp. 14.50–14.64). Chicago, IL.

Shneier, M.O., Lumia, R., & Kent, E.W. (1986). Model-based strategies for high-level robot vision. *Computer Vision, Graphics and Image Processing, 33*, 293–306.

Sikka, D.I., & Varshney, P.K. (1989). A distributed artificial intelligence approach to object identification and classification. In C.B. Weaver (Ed.), *Proceedings of the SPIE, vol. 1100, Sensor Fusion II* (pp. 73–84). Orlando, FL.

Spence, C.D., Pearson, J.C., Gelfand, J.J., & Peterson, R.M. (1989). Neuronal maps for sensory-motor control in the barn owl. In Touretzky (Ed.), *Advances in Neural Information Processing Systems I* (pp. 366–374). San Mateo, CA: Morgan Kaufmann.

Swyt, D.A. (1989). AI in manufacturing: The NBS AMRF as an intelligent machine. *Robotics and Autonomous Systems, 4*, 327–332.

Taylor, G.E., & Taylor, P.M. (1988). Dynamic error probability vectors: A framework for sensory decision making. *Proceedings of the IEEE International Conference on Robotics and Automation* (pp. 1096–1100). Philadelphia, PA.

Thomopoulos, S.C.A. (1990). Sensor integration and data fusion. *Journal of Robotic Systems, 7*(3), 337–372.

Tou, J.T. (1990). A knowledge-based system for redundant and multi-sensing in intelligent robots. In J.T. Tou & J.G. Balchen (Eds.), *Highly redundant sensing in robotic systems* (pp. 3–20). Berlin: Springer-Verlag.

Wechsler, H., & Zimmerman, G.L. (1988). 2-D invariant object recognition using distributed associative memory. *IEEE Transactions on Pattern Analysis and Machine Intelligence*, PAMI-*10*(6), 811–821.

Zheng, Y.F. (1989). Integration of multiple sensors into a robotic system and its performance evaluation. *IEEE Transactions on Robotics and Automation*, RA-*5*(5), 658–669.

3
A Survey of AI Approaches to the Integration of Information

Thomas D. Garvey

The integration of information is a central issue for artificial intelligence (AI) research and development. The *inference process* in AI is the fundamental mechanism for combining information, and a significant aspect of most AI systems is the means by which they manage their overall workload by focusing processing attention and by controlling which inferences are drawn and when it is appropriate to draw them. Several perspectives on the control of inferential processes and their access to information have evolved. One view of the problem treats the control task as a goal-driven perceptual process, where specific information is explicitly sought from the world through selected sensor modalities, translated into a common "vocabulary," fused with other relevant information, and finally translated back into an understanding of critical aspects of the environment. Another view relies on a flexible structure, known as the blackboard architecture, for enforcing control and communication activities. In this chapter, we first review briefly a variety of AI inference techniques, focusing primarily on logical inference and uncertain reasoning methods. We conclude with a survey of approaches currently used to control inference processes, to mediate their access to real-world information, and to schedule their activities.

1. INTRODUCTION AND OVERVIEW

A motorist stops a pedestrian in a suburban area and asks for directions to a particular address. The pedestrian tells the motorist, "Continue down the street for several blocks until you pass a shopping center on the left. Take the first right, then a left, and your destination will be across from the train station." After repeating the directions to ensure he has them, the motorist continues on his way.

A cat hears a faint rustling in the tall grass a few feet away. Crouching down, she continues to scan the area. When she sees the flash of motion out of the corner of her eye, she springs.

The radar seeker head in a missile scans a wedge-shaped area in front of it. When a significant return from the radar's signal is detected, the radar processor analyzes the signal and, based on its amplitude and spatial extent, determines that it is a target. It narrows its field of view to include just the area containing the target and begins a turn toward the target area.

Each of these activities requires that information from one or more sources be integrated in order to provide a picture of the environment that can be effectively used to accomplish the goals and objectives of the "system" acquiring the information. The motorist must integrate the pedestrian's words into a model in order to interpret the utterances; this process may be aided by gestures on the part of the pedestrian. The motorist's interpretation of the utterances yields an abstract, specialized map of the area which must, in turn, be integrated into the spatial model of the environment that he or she already possesses. The cat integrates sounds of movement with a visual indication of motion. The sound provides *cueing* information which allows a more precise process, with a narrower field of view, to be used effectively. The radar seeker must integrate electromagnetic energy until it determines that a possible target is present. This information is then integrated with a file of target descriptions to determine whether the signal represents a target of interest.

An effective understanding of the environment based on the integration of information is central to any sort of purposeful behavior. Humans excel in their ability to integrate information from a wide variety of sources, simple and complex, and draw accurate and far-ranging conclusions from it. This performance is primarily due to humans' ability to effectively integrate data from distinct sources into an all-encompassing framework. Artificial intelligence (AI) researchers use human activities as models for numerous types of intelligent behavior, including sensing and perceiving, interpretation and reasoning, planning and problem-solving, and language understanding and speech. Each of these general areas involves the integration of information as a central theme. AI approaches to problems in these areas typically use one or more *inference* methods as the basic mechanism for integrating information.

Inference, a fundamental AI operation, is the process of drawing a new conclusion from two or more pieces of information. The most fundamental logical inference technique, *modus ponens,* uses a statement of fact and a related implication statement to generate a new statement of fact. For example, the integration of the statement SUNNY-DAY and the rule (SUNNY-DAY *implies* GO-TO-THE-BEACH) asserts GO-TO-THE-BEACH.

Complications arise when it is important to control which conclusions are drawn, or more importantly, to ensure that certain conclusions are drawn when necessary. One of the most important tasks in any AI system is to control the exploration of a potentially huge space of possible inferences, by focusing toward "useful" ones.

In this chapter we shall discuss some of the methods that AI practitioners use for drawing inferences, both Boolean, where all conclusions will be either true or false, or weighted by their likelihood of being true. We will then discuss general methods for controlling an inference process, and conclude with a brief discussion of system issues.

1.1. The Role of Artificial Intelligence

An AI approach[1] offers a number of benefits for the solution of problems involving the integration of various types of information, both in the development of a system and as a component in the subsequent operation of the system. These benefits include:

- **Flexibility**—By making inferences and decisions explicit, an AI system is (typically) easier to change and update than a conventional system accomplishing an equivalent task. Furthermore, if the target environment is highly dynamic or complex (or poorly understood), an AI system can offer the flexibility necessary to adapt to the particular conditions that hold when it is employed.
- **Ability to handle complex problems**—Recognition and assessment of real-world activities can result in highly complex interactions among pieces of data, with multiple interpretations possible

---

[1] In this paper, we shall use the term "*AI* approach" to indicate a solution method based primarily on the use of explicit AI formalisms, which typically include inference and search. The terms "*algorithmic* approach" and "*conventional* approach" will be used interchangeably to mean non-AI methods.

in general. AI offers effective representations and computational methods for managing this complexity.
- **Understandability**—By making decisions and chains of inference explicit, an AI system is often able to provide explanations for its findings and actions that are not feasible with algorithmic approaches.

The utility of AI techniques for use in a fielded system depends roughly on the complexity of the sources of information that must be accessed and the environmental states that may need to be recognized. These levels of complexity may be characterized as follows:

1. The sources of information and their organization are well understood with respect to the information provided and the types of errors expected. For example, an engine control system that monitored temperature and pressure in order to regulate fuel flow would fall into this category.
2. The number and types of sources are bounded, but the specific data provided and the possible types of errors in the data are not predictable in detail. A military battlefield information system would be an example of this level.
3. The sources of information and their errors are essentially unbounded. A system for interpreting natural language utterances about widely varying topics would fit into this category.

In the first case described above, techniques for integrating information may generally be prespecified, along with methods necessary for eliminating noise and refining estimates. Activities that are based upon this type of information may be thought of as *instinctive*, and the role of AI is relatively small in these applications. In the third case, the amount of background knowledge and the uses to which it might be put are essentially unpredictable. These problems, while certainly requiring intelligent behavior, are significantly beyond the current operational state of the art in AI. In the second case, however, there is enough prior knowledge about the environment and available information sources to constrain the activities of the system, while requiring a flexible, intelligent capability for combining, manipulating, and interpreting information. Problems in this class seem most appropriate for the application of AI techniques, and will form the focus of this chapter.

A number of other factors will influence the detailed choice of methods used to acquire and integrate information. These include, for example, the use to which the information will be put; the number, types and quality of information sources; the degree to which the sources are understood in advance; the complexity of the environment being monitored; the dynamics of the environment; and the degree and quality of environmental knowledge available to the integration system.

1.2. Knowledge, Information and Representation

The types of knowledge and information that may be available or useful to an information-integration process are likely to be quite varied. Raw data in an image might represent intensity, color, range, texture, surface shape, surface type, elevation, optical density, X-ray absorbance, or geometric relationships. Different types of data will suggest different representations. For example, intensities are simply represented as numeric values of continuous quantities; texture might be best represented as a certain statistical distribution of intensity; color might be represented either as a vector of intensity values for the primary colors, red, green, and blue, or in terms of hue, saturation, and brightness; simple surface shapes might be represented as superquadrics; complex surfaces may be represented by collections of small patches or by articulated combinations of simple surfaces; and surface type might be represented by a set of symbolic names. The knowledge used for understanding the information in the image might be derived from a variety of experiences and prior knowledge and might include declarative statements such as, "The color RED signifies danger"; imperative knowledge such as "To find intensity edges, convolve the image with the Laplacian operator"; procedural knowledge such as that embodied (at a low level) in an image-operator description or (at a high level) in a *script* for an analysis process; and causal knowledge such as "The intensity at a point is a combination of the incident intensity, the local surface orientation, and the reflectance function of the surface."

In addition, the information available may have a variety of other qualities. In particular, information is often uncertain, incomplete, inaccurate, and ephemeral (i.e., it ages). It may be acquired out of sequence with other information. It may often vary in "granularity" or level of abstraction. The sources of information may be dependent or independent, inconsistent with other sources, of varying reliability, and few or numerous. The amount of information that must be handled may be appropriate for the available processing resources and problem requirements, potentially overwhelming (necessitating some means for throttling the data to a manageable level), or insufficient for the task (requiring some means for inferentially filling information gaps or an effective method for acquisition of additional information).

A wide variety of applications have information integration components where the information sources and the necessary interpretations are bounded and amenable to AI approaches. Examples include autonomous vehicle navigation; personnel identification systems and access-control and monitoring systems; business management systems; battle management systems and intelligence analysis; photointerpretation, cartography, and map-making; medical diagnosis; and military threat-detection and warning systems.

2. GENERIC SYSTEM ARCHITECTURE AND DEFINITIONS

In general, we shall treat the architecture shown in Figure 3.1 as an informal, generic perception/action model that links sensing and effecting through an inferential information-integration module (IM). This model joins a collection of information *producers* with a set of information *consumers* (users). Each producer will be associated with a single source of environmental information, but will have one or more distinct output channels. (A multichannel producer will be said to be *multimodal*.) These channels will be treated as distinct (although of-

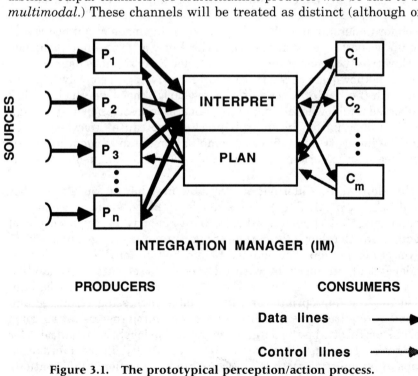

Figure 3.1. The prototypical perception/action process.

ten highly correlated) information input to the IM. Inputs to the producers from the IM will include control information, commands, and parameters. In a *multilevel* or *hierarchical* system, each producer may itself be composed of a complete perception/action process as described here.

Integrated output from the IM is provided to the consumers, who will determine their behavior based on the information they receive. Consumers may make information requests of the IM. These requests are further processed by the IM, and appropriate instructions are then issued to the producers. A consumer may also be a producer. Feedback occurs through adaptive information requests from the consumers.

The IM may be functionally partitioned into two components, an integration and interpretation part and a planning and control part. The integration and interpretation component processes and combines information received from the producers before it updates appropriate databases and makes the processed information available to the consumers. The planning and control unit interprets consumer information requests in light of overall system goals and requirements, plans and schedules producers' activities, and closes the loop by feeding necessary control and processing information back to the producers

This simple architecture captures the essence of a wide variety of systems. Three principal subarchitectures of the generic architecture cover most current and contemplated systems: the single-source, single-model (channel) system; the single-source, multimode system; and the multi-source system.

A radar tracker for a missile is an example of the single-source, single-mode system. It integrates reflections from a target into a model of the target's motion dynamics. It continuously maintains its model by predicting a new position, comparing acquired information with its predictions, and updating its model. Even this simple system must control its access to information,[2] integrate the information into a model, and adjust its model to accept new information.

A radar system that computes both range and velocity information is an example of a single-source, multimode system. In this case, signal-processed information is integrated into two separate dynamic models, which in turn yield two distinct (correlated) channels of information. These channels may then be used by completely separate consumer processes. The human optic system is another single-source, multimode system which produces several distinct channels of information providing spatial, topological, and temporal information.

---

[2] A common radar technique is to use a *range gate* to set the elapsed time before it looks for returned pulses.

The multisource, multimode system is exemplified by many human organizations.[3] Intelligence gathering and interpretation, by both government and commercial organizations, is a key instance of this type of system. A simpler example would be a combined threat-warning system consisting of a radar intercept receiver, a laser warning receiver, and an infrared (IR) detector. The integrated results of processing could include information for warning a crew member of a possible threat, as well as detailed information for use by an automatic countermeasures system.

In Figure 3.2, we illustrate a prototypical view of an information-integration process. Two distinct information-manipulation processes are shown: *fusion* (*integration* or *combination*) processes and *translation* (*interpretion*)[4] processes. This simple network can be thought of as an *inference module*. Input comes from producers; output goes to consumers. These modules may be combined by identifying the consumers for one module as the producers for the next. A common view of the information-integration process as moving from "signal to symbol" emphasizes the concept of the data moving through ever more complex (and abstract) interpretations.

2.1. The Information-Integration Process

Information acquired from external sources must normally be combined with a model and *interpreted* in order to draw conclusions about the world. For example, a radar system makes a direct measurement of the intensity of the electromagnetic field at its antenna; an interpretation of the electromagnetic radiation may yield the conclusion that a real radar pulse was received. A further interpretation of the pulse information could lead to the determination that an aircraft was the source of the energy. This interpreted information is the output typically provided to a user: Raw information (particularly that which is received directly from sensors) rarely describes the world in ways that are of direct interest to a user. In one sense, the information is almost always in the wrong "language," and a *translation* operation is required to convert the information to statements that are meaningful, that is, to a form that can be integrated with the current model of the situation. This leads to an important observation: Information is not combined directly with other information, but is integrated into an evolving *model* of some aspect of the situation. The current characteristics of the model are a function of information received earlier.

---

[3] As well as by cats!
[4] Translation can also be thought of as a process of *synchronizing* information.

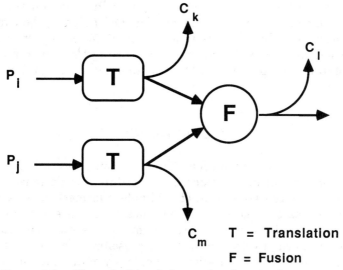

Figure 3.2. The primitive information-integration process.

The process of integrating information, then, can be envisioned as one of first translating the information to an appropriate framework, and then combining it with other information in the same framework. This process is appropriate regardless of the number and types of the sources. A key ingredient in the process of integrating information is the inferential framework that defines the interactions between different types and sources of data.

The process of acquisition and assimilation of information may require significant effort, and, therefore, must be effectively managed to ensure that a system has adequate information for achieving goals. Acquisition and integration of new information into a model is a goal-driven, purposeful process, with attendant requirements for planning and reasoning capabilities that must be met before it can be carried out effectively.

The information-integration process described above raises issues that must be addressed in system design and implementation. First, based upon the nature of the information available to the process and the uses to which the derived information is to be put, the system designer must select an appropriate representation of that information (for example, information expressed as a series of precise statements will be represented differently from information expressing weighted judgments). Second, based on the information sources, the process goals, and the characteristics of the environment, the designer must determine appropriate means for controlling the process. Third, the designer must implement means for manipulating the available information and drawing inferences from it for interpretation and translation, as well as the means for converting from one representation to another as appropriate. The remainder of this chapter discusses these issues.

3. INFERENCE

A fundamental AI computation is that of combining information in order to *infer* a conclusion. Inference procedures are designed to work on a particular representation of available information. A variety of representations and methods of inference have proven useful for AI problems. The selection of a particular method is ordinarily based on the type of information available to the reasoning process, the types of output required, the computational complexity of the available mechanisms, and the degree to which assumptions are necessary and possible in order to carry out the computation.

The basic inferential modes addressed by AI researchers are logical inference and uncertain inference. Formal logical inference methods center on propositional and predicate logics. They are particularly useful for reasoning about situations where available information is *Boolean,* that is, statements are either true or false. Logical methods are typically based on formal properties that make it possible to characterize the results of their operations. For example, in a predicate calculus system, it is guaranteed that any statement which can be deduced from axioms (statements that are true by assumption or definition) using valid rules of inference is a theorem, and therefore true. Formal logical systems are *consistent;* if a statement is a theorem, its negation cannot be. They are also *complete;* any statement that can be proved from a consistent set of axioms is a theorem in the system. At the same time, predicate calculus is not *decidable;* there are statements which can be neither proven or disproven. Logical systems traditionally have traded ease of expressiveness and computational simplicity for formality.

Uncertain inference methods are based on various models of probability theory. Such methods typically have an underlying propositional structure that allows statements to be made. In addition, they provide a means for representing uncertainty about whether the statement is strictly true and sometimes provide ways of representing imprecision or ignorance.

3.1. Logical Inference

The style of logical reasoning most commonly used is *deductive,* and can be best exemplified by *theorem proving.* A proof of a theorem is derived by creating a chain of inferences from axioms to the theorem of interest. In this regard, theorem proving involves a search process, where candidate statements are combined in an attempt to get "closer" to the target theorem. The key characteristic of deductive reasoning is that the results, by the nature of the computations, are known to be valid and consistent.

Propositional logic: Propositional calculus (Mendelson, 1964) deals with constant statements (or *propositions*), which are known to be either true or false. Propositions may be either atomic propositions, consisting of a single statement, or more complicated statements, composed of other propositions joined by valid connectives. The legal connectives in propositional calculus are conjunction (represented as AND or "$\wedge$"), disjunction (OR or "$\vee$"), negation (NOT or "$\neg$"), and implication (IF or "$\Rightarrow$").

The fundamental rule of inference in propositional logic is *modus ponens,* which states that $\mathcal{B}$ is a direct consequence of $\mathcal{A}$ and $\mathcal{A} \Rightarrow \mathcal{B}$. Thus, an indication from a visual sensor, LIGHT-IS-RED, may be combined with an implication (LIGHT-IS-RED $\Rightarrow$ DANGER) to infer DANGER.

Predicate calculus: By virtue of its restriction to constant statements, propositional logic is limited in its ability to express complex concepts (Charniak & McDermott, 1985; Fischler & Firschein, 1987). While retaining the connectives from propositional calculus, the first-order predicate calculus provides additional expressive power by permitting the use of terms, variables, functions, predicates, and quantifiers.

Predicates denote properties and relations among objects, and can take on a value of true or false when their arguments are specified. An *atomic formula* is a predicate with the terms that constitute its arguments. A *literal* is a single (negated or unnegated) predicate and its terms. A *term* is either a constant, a variable, or a function application. A *variable* is a symbol that stands for an unspecified object. *Functions* represent arbitrary, fixed expressions whose arguments are terms.

For example, the expression *BLUE* (x) is a literal which states that x, an unspecified variable, is blue. The expression, *BLUE(SKY)* is true (in general) for California skies, while *BLUE(TREE)* is false (in general). Quantifiers come in two forms, universal and existential. Universal quantifiers (written "∀" and pronounced "for all") permit the statement that something is true for all possible values of a variable. Existential quantifiers (written "∃" and pronounced "there exists") allow the assertion that a statement is true for at least one possible value of a variable. Existential and universal quantifiers may be combined in the same expression.

Thus, we may represent the statement, "Where there's smoke, there's fire," by the predicate calculus statement

$$\forall x(SMOKE(x) \Rightarrow \exists y(FIRE(y) \land SAME\text{-}LOC(x, y))),$$

where $SMOKE(x)$ means that there is smoke at location x, $FIRE(x)$ means that there is fire at location y, and $SAME\text{-}LOC(x, y)$ means that x and y are the same location.

Predicate calculus uses the *Rule of Universal Instantiation* in addition to *modus ponens* as its fundamental rules of inference. Modus ponens is exactly the same for propositional and predicate logic. Universal instantiation merely states that universally quantified variables may be replaced by constants in a theorem, in which case a new theorem will result. Universal instantiation of x with MARY in the formula $\forall x(HUMAN(x) \Rightarrow \exists y(MOTHER\text{-}OF(x, y)))$ yields $(HUMAN(MARY) \Rightarrow \exists y(MOTHER\text{-}OF(MARY,y)))$.

Systems for automated theorem proving typically use a rule of inference called *resolution* (Nilsson, 1980). The resolution principle allows the deduction of the statement $\mathcal{U} \lor \mathcal{V}$ (the *resolvent*) from the two statements $\neg \mathcal{A} \lor \mathcal{U}$ and $\mathcal{A} \lor \mathcal{V}$, where $\mathcal{A}$, $\mathcal{U}$, and $\mathcal{V}$ are arbitrary, valid formulas. $\mathcal{A}$ and $\neg \mathcal{A}$ are the literals resolved upon.

In order to apply resolution to logical statements, one statement must contain the literal to be resolved upon and the other the negation of the literal. The two literals must contain the same predicate (otherwise, there is no possibility of resolving them); however, there is no guarantee that the terms of the predicates will be identical. In order to determine whether there is a substitution that, when applied to each of the literals, will make them identical (except for the negation), a process called *unification* is performed. Unification attempts to match the two literals by finding the most general substitution that will render them identical. Once this substitution is applied (using the rule of Universal Instantiation) to each of the statements involved (that is, to all literals in the statements, not just the ones resolved upon), resolution may proceed, and the new resolvent may be computed.

Unification and resolution are another example of the basic information-integration principle mentioned in the beginning of this chapter. That is, the process consists first of a translation step, where the two "sources" are transformed so that they are both concerned with the same thing. Second, an inference step is performed that completes the integration. Planning (Wilkins, 1984, 1988) and robot control systems (Hart, Fikes, & Nilsson, 1972) have been developed using formal theorem-proving techniques as the information-integration mechanism.

The concept of programming a computer by specifying goals as theorems to be proven, situational facts as axioms, and rules as implications has been attractive to AI researchers ever since effective theorem-proving procedures were developed. **Prolog,** (Clocksin & Mellish, 1981) one of the most popular *logic-programming* languages currently available, makes this possible. **Prolog** uses a *clause* form of logical representation, containing only constant terms and universally quantified variables. While **Prolog** uses a simple syntactic, top-down (discussed below) scheme to determine the order of processing facts and rules as a default, the system provides built-in procedures for altering the flow of processing under programmer control.

> *Other logical representations:* The basic logical representations as discussed above consist of formulas and statements in propositional or predicate logic. Other representations of great value to AI developers include production rules, frames, semantic nets, and state transition networks.

A *production rule* is the most common representation of information used in expert systems development (Buchanan & Feigenbaum, 1984). It is roughly equivalent to an implication in the propositional or predicate logic. It consists of *evidence* (also called the left-hand-side or LHS) and a *hypothesis* (also called the right-hand-side or RHS). Establishing the existence (i.e., the truth) of evidence enables a production rule system to infer the hypothesis. Furthermore, a system that needs to establish the truth of the hypothesis can seek to establish the truth of the evidence—this is termed backward-chaining, and will be discussed below. Production rules with appropriate updating formulas can be used for uncertain reasoning; this will also be discussed below.

Frames group knowledge about particular objects and situations. Properties of an object and interrelationships among objects are represented as *slots* in the frame; values for the properties are stored in the slots. Frames provide useful mechanisms for focusing attention, as they collect relevant information into a single element. Default values are often provided for slots.

Semantic nets are quite similar to frames in concept. A semantic net uses arcs to represent properties and relations (which are slots in frames) and nodes to represent entities and values (the contents of slots).

State-transition networks are graphical representations of sequential machines. States are represented by nodes; conditions for state change are represented as predicates (expressions that evaluate true or false) on the arcs connecting the nodes. State-transition networks provide useful computational mechanisms for handling temporal changes. The evolution of a system may be expressed through changes in a state-transition network.

Other logics: First-order predicate calculus does not allow relationships among predicates, beliefs, temporal relations, or statements of possibilities. In addition, there is no means for deleting assertions from the database. For this reason, a variety of alternative logics and inference methods have been explored. AI workers are actively researching problem-solving and inference methods based on these logics, which we will briefly describe here. (For more details, see Turner, 1985.)

Modal logics are concerned with necessity and possibility. They are primarily used to represent statements of belief. A modal logic of particular interest is *epistemic logic,* a formalism suitable for representing states of knowledge (Moore, 1985).

Temporal logics deal with the representation of time and statements whose truth-value is tied to the temporal interval over which it is evaluated. Temporal logic is important for planning and interpreting situations where time is a critical factor.

Higher-order predicate logics can express properties of predicates. Certain problems, particularly those involving concepts of equality, can be worked more easily in a higher-order predicate logic.

Nonmonotonic logics address the problem of nonmonotonic changes in the database. In a standard logical system, it is assumed that the axiom base is consistent (that is, that it contains no contradictions), and therefore that all theorems derived from the axiom set are true. In practical situations, it is common to treat the axiom base as the current data base of facts about the world. All consistent new facts that are added, then, cause *monotonic* changes to the knowledge base (i.e., the "amount" of knowledge is always increasing). When a fact is inserted that contradicts an earlier axiom, a *nonmonotonic* change has occurred, and all theorems derived from the invalidated axiom must be updated. Nonmonotonic logics assist in this updating process.

3.2. Uncertain Reasoning

Most real-world activities involve varying degrees of uncertainty about the true situation. This type of information is not well or easily described in formal logical terms. As a result, several schemes for representing and reasoning about uncertain information have evolved. Most of these approaches begin with classical, Bayesian probability theory as a base, and then extend it either formally or heuristically to handle situations that are difficult or impractical to address using the pure theory.

Most systems that deal with uncertainty use a propositional framework to represent interrelated statements about situations of interest. The chosen uncertainty representation is then overlaid on the propositions in this framework. Most developers of uncertain-reasoning systems will follow some or all of the following steps: framing the problem, creating a background knowledge structure representing key problem elements and their interrelations, creating a structure for analysis of situational data, and, finally, using the system to interpret and analyze data acquired about the situation. Differences in approach arise primarily from particular assumptions about the nature of the underlying information being interpreted. These assumptions motivate the choice of an *updating mechanism* for uncertain information which, in turn, dictates the requisite infrastructure to support the choice.

In this section, we focus on several types of uncertain reasoning formalisms. We shall highlight *evidential reasoning* as a particular form of uncertain reasoning developed specifically to address problems in interpreting real-world information.

Statistical reasoning: The simplest form of uncertain reasoning is statistical inference. A primary motivation for the use of statistics is the need to summarize and describe populations of events and situations based on relatively small subsets of those events. An important statistical method is the process for estimating population parameters with prespecified confidence levels and intervals (Moore, 1979). Such estimators are useful for determining whether acquired data indicate a possibly significant event. For example, a radar detector must accumulate and average several samples of possible radar pulses before determining (with acceptable confidence) that there is a target in its field of view. The integration process carried out by the radar (and by most statistical operations) combines information into the current *model* of the target. This model will, for example, include information about the current position and vector velocity of the target. The model is *predictive* in nature, as it enables a new estimate of position to be derived. This information can be used to control acquisition of information (by using a "range gate," for example), as well as to verify the current model (see Swerling,

1970, for a detailed discussion). Kalman filters integrate position data into a model of an objects state parameters in order to estimate future positions. This information is (typically) used to track the object.

A familiar form of statistical inference is pattern recognition or pattern classification (Duda & Hart, 1973). A typical approach to classifying input features as belonging to particular objects begins by creating a partitioned feature space. An ideal feature space would consist of well-spaced, compact clusters; interpreted features would map to single clusters, and the recognition problem would be trivial. In real life, however, feature measurements associated with one object typically overlap the feature measurements for other objects. To add to the difficulty, the measurements themselves may be corrupted, leading to further imprecision. This situation requires the developer to select a partition of the feature space that will minimize the likelihood and the costs of wrong decisions. This transforms the problem into a statistical decision-theory task.

Probabilistic inference: The primary means for estimating the probability of a hypothesis based upon the measured probability of supporting evidence is the familiar *Bayes's Rule of Conditioning*. While formally defined using strictly a priori probabilities and conditionals, Bayes's rule is often used to *update* belief in a hypothesis based on new evidence. Bayes's rule is expressed mathematically as

$$p(A|B) = \frac{p(B|A)p(A)}{p(B)}.$$

This shows how estimating the value of $p(B)$ changes the prior value $p(A)$ to the a posteriori likelihood, $p(A \mid B)$.

An interesting situation occurs when more than one piece of evidence has been acquired, and a new a posteriori likelihood based on the combination is desired. In this case, input descriptions typically consist of the individual conditional probabilities and the individual prior probabilities. For example, starting information might consist of the following a priori specifications:

$$p(B), p(C), p(B|A), \text{ and } p(C|A).$$

New probabilities are measured for events B and C, and $p(A \mid B \wedge C)$, the a posteriori likelihood, is desired. Bayes's rule provides

$$p(A|B \wedge C) = \frac{p(B \wedge C|A)p(A)}{p(B \wedge C)}.$$

Note that in order to compute this expression, values for $p(B \wedge C \mid A)p(A)$ and $p(B \wedge C)$ must be available or computable. Since determining all of the required conditional and prior probabilities needed to solve such updating problems exactly is onerous if not impossible in complex situations, various assumptions are typically made to facilitate the computation. Frequent assumptions are *conditional independence* and the *principle of insufficient reason*. Conditional independence states that $p(B \wedge C \mid A) = p(B \mid A)p(C \mid A)$. That is, given conditioning statement A, events B and C are independent, and their probabilities may be multiplied to compute the joint conditional probability. If B and C are strictly independent, then by definition, $p(B \wedge C) = p(B)p(C)$.[5] These independence assumptions allow us to rewrite the above expression

$$p(A \mid B \wedge C) = \frac{p(B \mid A)p(C \mid A)p(A)}{p(B)p(C)},$$

which is now composed of known quantities.

Often, necessary probability values are unavailable when computations are to be performed. In such cases, it is common to use the principle of insufficient reason to assign missing probability values. Simply put, if the probability of a disjunction of events is known, but the probabilities of the individual components are not, and there is no particular reason to expect that one event is more likely than any other, then the principle of insufficient reason dictates that equal probabilities, totaling to the original probability, be assigned to the individual components. A more sophisticated version of this approach is the *maximum entropy principle* (Jaynes, 1957). In this approach, probability values are selected that maximize the entropy (or the "disorderedness") of the assignment. The use of a maximum-entropy computation corresponds to making a *minimal commitment* in estimating unknown probabilities.

It is important to note that for many real-world problems, most uncertainty methods based on classical Bayesian probability will require information that is not available, and must be estimated. Often these estimate will turn out to be close to the "correct" probabilities, particularly when the space of possibilities is well understood and the estimation procedure is matched to the situation. However, they are *only* estimates; they may well be incorrect, and must be accounted for in the final results.

---

[5] In most practical systems, *ratios* of quantities such as *odds* are used for the probability computations. This scheme avoids the need to handle *joint,* prior probabilities explicitly.

Evidential reasoning: Information acquired about real-world situations provides *evidence* about the possible states of the world that might have given rise to it (Garvey, Lowrance, & Fischler, Chapter 14, this volume). This evidential information is typically uncertain and usually incomplete (that is, it contains residual *ignorance*), and it may contain errors. Based on a formal theory, the *Dempster-Shafer Theory of Evidence* (Shafer, 1976) *evidential reasoning*[6] makes a formal departure from classical probability to address these issues. In particular, evidential reasoning allows belief[7] to be associated directly with combinations (disjunctions) of possible events. That is, rather than forcing probabilities to be distributed across the set of possibilities, evidential reasoning maintains the direct association between the measure of belief and the disjunction itself.

For example, we may know that a particular radar signal may be generated by any one of several distinct radar systems. Upon intercepting such a signal, we can only identify the source as belonging to this set. Therefore, we may assign our belief that the signal is present to the *set* of possibilities. In a Bayesian framework, we would be forced to distribute this belief to the individual elements of the set (thereby introducing new "information" into the process); in evidential reasoning we are not forced to make this distribution. This approach avoids the need for assumptions for values of missing data. When beliefs of components are later needed, they are underconstrained as a result of the disjunction, and an interval representation is needed to capture the true constraints. This interval enables the explicit modeling of both what is known (although with uncertainty) and what is unknown.

The fundamental entity in evidential reasoning is the *frame of discernment* (commonly called the frame and indicated by "Θ"). Θ consists of a set of mutually exclusive, exhaustive statements which represent concepts of interest to the developer. Propositions are made up of elements of the power set (i.e., the set of all subsets) of Θ, indicated by 2^Θ. Belief can be assigned to any proposition, including to Θ itself; any belief assigned to Θ expresses total ignorance to that extent. An *evidential mass function* (or just mass function) represents the distribution of a unit of belief across selected (focal) elements of 2^Θ. A *body of evidence* is the frame of discernment and a particular mass function.

---

[6] Evidential reasoning is a term coined by SRI International (Lowrance & Garvey, 1982) to denote the body of techniques specifically designed for manipulating and reasoning from evidential information.

[7] Although *beliefs* are not strictly probabilities, we will use the terms interchangeably in this informal chapter.

For manipulating bodies of evidence, evidential reasoning provides explicit formalisms for both combination and translation, the two aspects of the information-integration problem discussed in the beginning of this paper. *Dempster's rule of combination* is used to combine two distinct bodies of evidence over a common frame of discernment to yield a new body of evidence. *Compatibility relations* are used to translate statements from one frame to another. Because Dempster's rule is both commutative and associative, multiple (independent) bodies of evidence can be combined in any order without affecting the result. If the initial bodies of evidence are independent, then the derivative bodies of evidence are independent as long as they share no common ancestors.

Evidential reasoning supports a number of primitive operations for reasoning from evidence. All of these operations have a formal basis in the Dempster-Shafer mathematical theory of evidence and have intuitive appeal as well. Thus, both flexibility and understandability are retained without sacrificing validity.

- **Fusion**—This operation pools multiple bodies of evidence into a single body of evidence that emphasizes points of agreement and deemphasizes points of disagreement.
- **Discounting**—This operation adjusts a body of evidence to reflect its source's credibility. If a source is completely reliable, discounting has no effect; if it is completely unreliable, discounting strips away all apparent information content; otherwise, discounting reduces the apparent information content in proportion to the source's unreliability.
- **Translation**—This operation moves a body of evidence away from its original context to a related one, to assess its impact on dependent hypotheses. For example, a body of evidence pertaining to the activities of an object can be translated to estimate observables that ought to be associated with it.
- **Projection**—This operation moves a body of evidence away from its original temporal context to a related one. For example, evidence about an object's state parameters can be projected to estimate future locations.
- **Summarization**—This operation eliminates extraneous details from a body of information. The resulting body of evidence is slightly less informative, but remains consistent with the original.
- **Interpretation**—This operation calculates the "truthfulness" of a given statement based upon a given body of evidence. It produces an estimate of both the positive and negative effects of the evidence on the truthfulness of the statement.

- **Gisting**—This operation produces a single statement that captures the general sense of a body of evidence, without reporting degrees of uncertainty.

Evidential reasoning techniques have been automated in a system called **Gister**[8] (Lowrance, Garvey, & Strat, 1986). **Gister** provides graphical facilities for constructing a background knowledge base, creating frames of discernment, defining compatibility relations among them, and interactively creating and evaluating analyses of situational information. The steps in using **Gister** to develop an evidential reasoning solution to a problem are exactly those listed in the beginning of this section. First, background knowledge is structured. The various "vocabularies" are selected and represented as frames of discernment. Compatibility relations linking these frames are specified next. To provide a structure for analyzing situation data, an *analysis graph* is developed. The analysis graph describes exactly the evidential operations that are to be performed on the input bodies of evidence. Information from a body of evidence flows through the network of operations specified in the analysis graph in a *dataflow* fashion, until all operations are complete. Information computed for selected output frames may then be examined in order to determine the results of the analysis.

Gister provides a graphical, interactive aid for *argument construction* (Lowrance, 1986) the creation of explanations for evidence received about the environment. An *argument* can be thought of as a way of explaining evidence. Particularly in highly complex domains such as intelligence analysis, it is often the case that it is not obvious how to interpret information until that information is in hand. Essentially, no single style of explanation can account for all possible input. Traditional expert systems, on the other hand, typically use models that can be thought of as the generic argument for explaining all input to the system. Argument construction may be viewed as the analogue to a logical proof in the field of uncertain reasoning. **Gister** gives the developer flexibility in operating on evidence, in creating arguments, and in evaluating alternative explanations until a suitable one is found.

Evidential reasoning relaxes some of the extensive information requirements of classical Bayesian probability theory while maintaining its formal appeal, and is therefore more natural for a wide range of problems. In addition, a wide variety of primitive evidential operations with a rigorous theoretical basis have been defined to facilitate manipulation of evidence.

---

[8] **Gister** is implemented in Lisp on the Symbolics 3600-series Lisp Machines.

3.3. Heuristic Methods

Early work in expert systems addressed the problem of reasoning from uncertain data using the production rule formalism. The very nature of expert systems, which attempt to suppress insignificant information and focus on the data deemed useful by an expert, makes it effectively impossible to use formal probabilistic methods to update hypotheses based on new evidence. The work on MYCIN (Shortliffe, 1976) an expert system to diagnose and recommend treatment for certain blood diseases, resulted in an informal approach which used *certainty factors* between −1 and 1 to represent degrees of belief. A goal of the early research that led to the Prospector mineral exploration consultant (Duda, Hart, & Reboh, 1977) was to formalize the updating process, using classical probability.

Prospector was forced to assume conditional independence in order to update hypotheses. Although it led to an inconsistent (that is, noninvertible) procedure, this was an acceptable compromise because of the nature of the probability values that were typically associated with the presence of ore bodies. These probabilities tend to be very small, and errors due to the updating rule were minimal (Duda, private communication).

4. CONTROL OF THE INTEGRATION PROCESS

Inference procedures are typically quite simple and straightforward to perform. In general, each inference generates a new piece of information to add back into the database. Since it is simple to fill a database with irrelevant data from uncontrolled inference, a key problem in AI is to control these processes effectively in order to reach correct, useful, and desirable conclusions. This means that the processing framework that controls the acquisition of information and the selection and application of inference procedures is of critical importance. In this section, we discuss certain basic AI control paradigms, along with architectures that have evolved specifically to address problems of real-world, real-time information-system control.

In order for a system to behave *purposefully,* it must know what its (or its developer's) goals are. These goals, which may be well understood by the developer, must be made explicit and meaningful to the system itself. In addition, the system must have some means for recognizing when it is making progress toward its goals. Typical informational goals include detecting the presence of certain activities, identifying the activity and the actors, measuring interesting features of an activity (such as its location, status, and state variables), discriminating among possible identifications, and predicting future activities. In addition, however, *meta-goals* may be operative. These might include requirements for real-time operation, a need for explanation of results, a requirement for effective man-machine interaction, a need for "quiet" (i.e., passive) operation, and a desire for the system to learn and adapt to new situations. These meta-goals will likely have as great an impact on the selection of an approach as do the nominal informational goals.

4.1. Top-Down/Bottom-Up Methods

Two basic control paradigms used in AI are *top-down* and *bottom-up* methods. Top-down methods are also termed *goal-driven, model-driven,* or *backward-chaining* techniques. Bottom-up methods are also called *data-driven* or *forward-chaining* techniques.

Top-down methods begin with a statement of the problem or goal and attempt to solve it by finding subproblems that can be solved. For example, an expert system may contain a rule that states, "If a fruit is red and round, then it is an apple." Inverting the rule provides a means for finding apples: try to find fruits that are both red and round. This is the source of the word "back-chaining"; the system chains backward through its rules until it finds a subgoal it can solve. *Hierarchical* methods are top-down (typically) methods that break a problem into ever finer parts, solving problems at one level before filling-in details at the next.

Because certain subgoals may be impossible to achieve, failure of the solution procedures must be expected from time to time. In this case, the system (usually) has no recourse except to *backtrack* to an earlier choice point (normally the most recent) and try another alternative. Should the system exhaust all of its options, then the procedure fails, and the top-level goal also fails. Each time the system chooses a new alternative to consider, it typically must switch its evaluation context to that of the new alternative. Context switching, a direct result of backtracking, can be an extremely costly operation, and a typical design goal is to minimize the number of times it occurs. Effective procedures try to use knowledge to make good choices in the first place, and to learn enough from those failures that do occur to eliminate alternatives that might have otherwise been considered.

Clearly, top-down processing can involve *searching* a potentially huge database of possibilities. Much of early AI research was concerned specifically with controlling search. A number of formal and heuristic search techniques such as *alpha-beta search* were developed and are still part of the AI developer's tool kit (Nilsson, 1980).

Bottom-up processing draws conclusions by reasoning forward from data to conclusions. Using the same rule about apples mentioned above, a stem could infer that it had an apple after it had determined that it had a fruit that was also red and round. Data-driven methods are useful for determining the implications of new information; however, by their nature they are difficult to focus.

A typical approach to interpreting real-world information is to use a combination of top-down and bottom-up techniques. This, for example, was the procedure used in Prospector, an expert system for geological exploration. The user would enter data that had been collected in the field. Implications derived from these data in a forward-chaining manner provided an initial context of hypotheses for evaluating the likelihood of ore bodies of interest. This initial context helped Prospector, in a top-down fashion, to frame queries to the user in order to refine its initial hypotheses. At any time, the user could enter new data to be interpreted in a data-driven fashion. This *hybrid* method facilitated an interactive paradigm known as *mixed initiative,* where the system has the initiative part of the time and can ask questions; at other times, the user could take the initiative and volunteer information.

Generally speaking, top-down, model-driven approaches are useful when the models are restrictive and the data are noisy. Noisy data cause problems to a data-driven system. If there are no safeguards for data quality (and in a data-driven mode there is rarely enough information to ensure quality in a noise environment), it is quite likely that corrupted data will generate errors which may be costly to rectify. Noisy data require effective data acquisition and data management techniques based on an understanding of the system's goals and its environment.

4.2. Perceptual Reasoning

As mentioned previously, the acquisition and interpretation of information may be considered a *perceptual* task and, therefore, is a purposeful activity, undertaken to support definite system goals. In that regard, a perceptual system must be capable of interpreting overall system objectives and using them to focus the system's resources to optimize the collection and interpretation of information. By updating the underlying model of the situation from new information and altering its detailed information goals, a system can adapt to new situations.

A straightforward architecture designed to control a perpetual process in a top-down mode is the *perceptual reasoning loop* (Garvey & Fischler, 1980; Lowrance & Garvey, 1987) shown in Figure 3.3. This architecture consists of three functional modules, ANTICIPATE, PLAN, and INTERPRET. This architecture was first elaborated for use in a simulation of an electronic warfare (EW) multisensor situation-assessment system (Garvey & Fischler, 1979; Garvey & Lowrance, 1983) but it serves as a general, functional architecture for perception.

The ANTICIPATE module attempts to predict aspects of the situation that might be expected, but for which there is no direct evidence. These include events that will take place by virtue of the passage of time or because of interactions among actors. Other anticipated events include activities associated with previously identified events. The goals of the EW system were to detect, identify, and locate possible threats to the aircraft. Examples of the types of events anticipated included undetected components of identified systems and system mode changes due

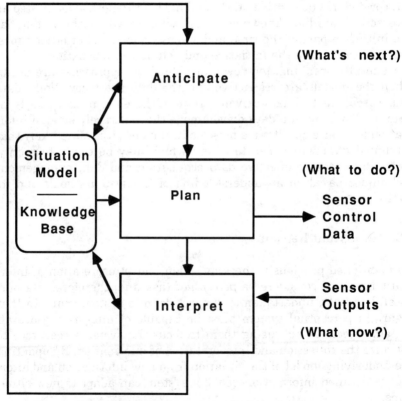

Figure 3.3. The perceptual reasoning loop.

to actions of the platform. For instance, the fact that certain types of surface-to-air missile systems were defended by anti-aircraft guns enabled the system to consider looking for the guns before they became a threat. Similarly, knowledge of the standard operating procedures of the missile systems allowed the system to predict probable mode changes (for example, from an acquisition mode to a target-tracking mode—definitely an interesting development) based on the computed range to the missile. A state-transition network was used to represent a process model; anticipation of mode changes was made on the basis of state changes in the network, which were in turn predicated on the satisfaction of conditions placed on the arcs. Based on the predicted events likely to be of interest, the ANTICIPATE module would assemble a set of information requests for the PLAN function.

The PLAN module was given the task of determining an optimal plan for satisfying as many information requests as possible. There was always competition for sensor resources, so it was, in general, impossible to satisfy all the requests made. The first step in the PLAN function was to order the information requests by their priority. This priority was computed based on two key parameters: a determination of the overall effect that acquiring the information would have on the system's goal, and the degree of importance of the information (which was typically based on the lethality of the threat being considered). For each available sensor a probability model of its performance (modified for the current environment) was used to determine the utility of using that particular resource to acquire the desired information. The utility values were used by a heuristic, dynamic-programming allocation routine to make the ultimate assignment of sensor resources to information requests. In the course of computing utility values, a determination was made of the optimal control parameters for the sensors. These control data were communicated to the (simulated) sensors, and they were operated in the simulated environment to acquire their data.

The INTERPRET module analyzed the acquired sensor data in terms of the expected information. Information that matched expectations typically resulted in increased likelihoods, whereas information that was expected, but not acquired, typically resulted in decreased likelihood. Evidential reasoning was used to integrate new information into the situation model. In addition, data that were received that were unanticipated were interpreted in a data-directed mode to determine possible unexpected threats. The updated situation model was the primary, *short-term* database, used in turn by the ANTICIPATE module.

This system was highly adaptive and could adjust to varying environmental conditions by altering its selection of sensors. It exhibited various interesting behaviors, but one of the most useful was a *cueing*

74 Garvey

capability that used information received from one sensor to point to another sensor.

4.3. The Blackboard Architecture

The *blackboard architecture* provides a very flexible control structure for interpretation and problem solving. The name "blackboard" attempts to capture the notion of a collection of asynchronous processes writing messages on a blackboard, which are in turn read by anyone looking at the blackboard and acted upon by those able to do so. A less anthropomorphic view would characterize the architecture as a mediated, limited-broadcast communication structure.

As shown in Figure 3.4, the three basic components of a blackboard system (as implemented in AGE (Nii & Aiello, 1979) consist of the

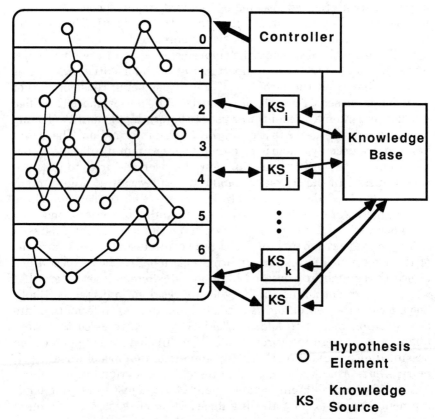

Figure 3.4. The blackboard architecture.

blackboard itself, a controller, and the knowledge base. The blackboard is a hierarchical data structure organized to represent the problem domain as a hierarchy of analysis level. Facts about objects are stored in the knowledge base; production rules represent the knowledge for using these facts and information on the blackboard. Related rules are grouped together into *knowledge sources.*

The controller's selects knowledge sources for activation, based on the contents of the blackboard. By specifying different control structures, the developer can explore different problem-solving strategies. The default control mechanism has two distinct functions, *inference generation* and *focus of attention.*

The primary contents of the blackboard are organized into one or more *hierarchical hypothesis structures.* These structures are oriented toward particular parts of the problem. Each level in a hypothesis structure is integrated with levels above and below by links joining hypothesis elements in the various levels. Links that represent support from above are called *expectation links;* those representing support from below are called *reduction links.* Hypothesis elements can be thought of as *abstractions* or *summarizations* of lower-level elements, and *components* of higher-level ones.

A solution is built incrementally by rules that add or modify the hypothesis elements or relationships among them. Hypothesis formation is a process where the rules do one of the following: interpret data at a lower level, instantiate a more-general model at a higher level, or generate expectations that must be verified by data.

Blackboard systems have been developed for a variety of applications including speech and natural-language processing (London, Erman, & Fickas, 1981; Lowerre, 1976) multi-sensor signal analysis (Nii & Feigenbaum, 1978) and image understanding (Hansen & Riseman, 1978).

4.4. Planning Methods

Early AI work addressing the integration of information from multiple sources focused on the task of locating objects in unregistered range and color images (Garvey, 1976). This research resulted in a system that developed plans for locating specific objects based on their expected appearance in each sensor modality (the information used was hue, saturation, intensity, surface orientation and extent, and reflectance at the wavelength of the laser used in the range sensor) and its expected relation to other objects.

More recent work (Wesley, 1986, 1987; Wesley, Lowrance, & Garvey,

1984) has taken the view that planning itself is an evidential process. That is, a system does not know for sure what the outcome of using a particular procedure in a plan will be, and can only estimate the likely outcome based on evidence about the operation. This is particularly true of processes that acquire information from the environment. The work uses evidential reasoning to draw conclusions about which process to invoke next in a scene interpretation task.

4.5. Local/Global Methods

Information in an image is both *local* and *global*. Local information includes point properties such as intensity and range and properties of small patches such as texture and surface orientation. The facts that several pixels appear to be in single line or that surface slope is constant over a wide area may be included in global information. It is clear to vision researchers that being able to recognize such global concepts and bring them to bear on the local computations would make the overall interpretation more robust. Unfortunately, detecting global similarities is quite expensive and, furthermore, requires that certain local determinations be made first.

Relaxation (Hummel & Zucker, 1983) methods provide a control architecture that introduces global information into a local interpretation in an iterative manner. They do this by computing local properties from a combination of current interpretations for a pixel and its immediate neighbors. These local computations may be Boolean or probabilistic. A single iteration involves performing local computations and updating at each pixel in the image. A number of iterations are performed until the system "relaxes," and further changes will be minimal. Relaxation has been shown to be equivalent to constrained optimization, and offers particular utility for *enhancing* certain image features.

Another method that attempts to bring global information to bear on local interpretations is *simulated annealing* (Gelatt, Kirkpatrick, & Vecchi, 1983). In this approach, an *energy function* is defined that is (typically) based on local interpretations and an overall, global interpretation. In effect, the initial system of data is brought to a very high "temperature," generating disorder in the possible local interpretations. Very slowly, the system is "cooled" and the energy of the system is reduced. This occurs by randomly selecting pixels and making local changes in interpretation that reduce the overall "energy." Changes that will result in a slight increase in overall energy are made on a probabilistic basis, where the probability is a function of the system temperature—when the system is at a high temperature, there is a greater likelihood that energy-increasing changes will be permitted. What this means is that an interpretation of a pixel that leads to a local energy minimum may yet be changed, allowing it to "pop" out of the local minimum and continue seeking the true minimum. Over time, the system converges toward interpretations that result in a minimal, ground-energy state. Simulated annealing is being explored as a technique for computing stereo disparity in two images (Barnard, 1987) and for many other applications.

5. SUMMARY AND CONCLUSIONS

In common to all purposeful activities is a continuing need for up-to-date environmental information. Directly perceived information is used to detect new events, to monitor dynamic events, and to measure parameters of the environment. By exploiting redundancy, a situation "mosaic" may be created from a diverse collection of information sources, each with a partial view of the situation. In addition, the combination of information from multiple sources will provide a means for overcoming the imprecision, inaccuracy, and occasional errors inherent in most sensing processes. As situations in which such activities occur become more complex, great quantities and greater diversity of information sources are typically needed. The integration of information by inference is a fundamental process in intelligent systems—both natural and artificial. In this brief survey, we have discussed a number of AI representations, inference methods, and control strategies for inference procedures.

REFERENCES

Barnard, S.T. (1987). Stereo matching by hierarchical, microcanonical annealing. *Proceedings of the International Joint Conference on Artificial Intelligence* (pp. 128–134). Milan, Italy.

Buchanan, B.G., & Feigenbaum, E.A. (1984). *Rule-based expert systems*. Reading, MA: Addison-Wesley.

Charniak, E., & McDermott, D. (1985). *Introduction to artificial intelligence*. Reading, MA: Addison-Wesley.

Clocksin, W.F., & Mellish, C.S. (1981). *Programming in Prolog*. New York: Springer-Verlag.

Duda, R.O. Private communication.

Duda, R.O., & Hart, P.E. (1973). *Pattern classification and scene analysis*. New York: John Wiley.

Duda, R.O., Hart, P.E., & Reboh, R. (1977). A rule-based consultation program for mineral exploration. *Proceedings of the Lawrence Symposium on Systems and Decision Sciences* (pp. 306–309). Berkeley, CA.

Fischler, M.A., & Firschein, O. (1987). *Intelligence—the eye, the brain, and the computer.* Reading, MA: Addison-Wesley.

Garvey, T.D. (1976). Perceptual strategies for purposive vision. Unpublished doctoral dissertation, Stanford University.

Garvey, T.D., & Fischler, M.A. (1979, October). Machine intelligence based multi-sensor esm system. (Final Report SRI Contract 6804). Menlo Park, CA: Artificial Intelligence Center, SRI International. (Distribution limited to US Government Agencies.)

Garvey, T.D., & Fischler, M.A. (1980). Perceptual reasoning in a hostile environment. *Proceedings of the First Annual National Conference on Artificial Intelligence* (pp. 253–255). Stanford, CA.

Garvey, T.D., & Lowrance, J.D. (1983, November). Machine intelligence for electronic warfare applications. (Final Report SRI Contract 1655). Menlo Park, CA: Artificial Intelligence Center, SRI International. (Distribution limited to US Government Agencies.)

Gelatt, C.D., Kirkpatrick, S., & Vecchi, M.P. (1983). Optimization by simulated annealing. *Science, 220,* 671–680.

Hansen, A.R., & Riseman, E.M. (1978). Computer vision systems. In James C. Bezdek (Ed.), *Computer vision systems.* New York: Academic Press.

Hart, P.E., Fikes, R.E., & Nilsson, N.J. (1972). Learning and executing generalized robot plans. *Artificial Intelligence, 3,* 251–288.

Hummel, R.A., & Zucker, S.W. (1983). On the foundation of relaxation labeling processes. *IEEE Transactions on Pattern Analysis and Machine Intelligence,* PAMI-5(3), 267–287.

Jaynes, E.T. (1957). Information theory and statistical mechanics. *The Physical Review, 106,* 620–630.

London, P.E., Erman, L.D., & Fickas, S.F. (1981). The design and an example use of hearsay-iii. *Proceedings of the International Joint Conference on Artificial Intelligence* (pp. 409–415), Vancouver, BC, Canada.

Lowerre, B.T. (1976). The HARPY speech recognition system. Unpublished doctoral thesis, Carnegie-Mellon University, Pittsburgh, PA.

Lowrance, J.D. (1987, March). Automating argument construction. *Proceedings of the Workshop on Assessing Uncertainty (November 13–14, 1986).* Stanford, CA: Stanford University, Department of Statistics, Stanford University and the Navy Center for International Science and Technology.

Lowrance, J.D., & Garvey, T.D. (1982). Evidential reasoning: A developing concept. *Proceeding of the International Conference on Cybernetics and Society* (pp. 6–9).

Lowrance, J.D., & Garvey, T.D. (1983, December). Evidential reasoning: An implementation for multisensor integration. (Tech. Rep. 307). Menlo Park, CA: Artificial Intelligence Center, SRI International.

Lowrance, J.D., Garvey, T.D., & Strat, T.M. (1986). A framework for evidential-reasoning systems. *Proceeding of the Fifth National Conference on Artificial Intelligence* (pp. 896–903). Philadelphia, PA.

Mendelson, E. (1964). *Introduction to mathematical logic.* New York: Van Nostrand Reinhold.

Moore, D.S. (1979). *Statistics—concepts and controversies.* San Francisco: W.H. Freeman.

Moore, R.C. (1985). *A formal theory of knowledge and action.* Norwood, NJ: Ablex Publishing.

Nii, H.P., & Aiello, N. (1979). Age (attempt to generalize): A knowledge-based program for building knowledge-based programs. *Proceedings of the International Joint Conference on Artificial Intelligence* (pp. 645–655). Tokyo, Japan.

Nii, H.P., & Feigenbaum, E.A. (1978). Rule-based understanding of signals. In D.A. Waterman & F. Hayes-Roth (eds), *Pattern-directed inference systems* (pp. 483–501). New York: Academic Press.

Nilsson, N.J. (1980). *Principles of artificial intelligence.* Palo Alto, CA: Tioga Publishing.

Shafer, G. (1976). *A mathematical theory of evidence.* Princeton, NJ: Princeton University Press.

Shortliffe, E.E. (1976). *Computer-based medical consultations: MYCIN.* New York: Elsevier.

Swerling, P. (1970). *Radar measurement accuracy* (see especially Chapter 4). New York: McGraw-Hill.

Turner, R. (1985). *Logics for artificial intelligence.* Halsted/Wiley.

Wesley, L.P. (1986, March). Evidential knowledge-based vision. *Optical Engineering, 25*(3), 363–379.

Wesley, L.P. (1987). Evidential-based control in knowledge-based systems. Unpublished doctoral dissertation, University of Massachusetts, Amherst, Department of Computer and Information Science.

Wesley, L.P., Lowrance, J.D., & Garvey, T.D. (1984, July). Reasoning about control: An evidential approach. (Tech. Rep. 324). Menlo Park, CA: Artificial Intelligence Center, SRI International.

Wilkins, D. (1984). Domain-independent planning: Representation and plan generation. *Artificial Intelligence, 22*(3), 269–301.

Wilkins, D.E. (1988). *Practical planning: Extending the classical AI planning paradigm.* Los Altos, CA: Morgan Kaufmann.

4
Logical Sensor Systems*

Thomas C. Henderson and
Esther Shilcrat

Multisensor systems require a coherent and efficient treatment of the information provided by the various sensors. In this chapter, we propose a framework, the Logical Sensor Specification System, in which the sensors can be defined abstractly in terms of computational processes operating on the output from other sensors. Various properties of such an organization are investigated, and a particular implementation is described.

1. INTRODUCTION

We describe and motivate a particular sensor system methodology, that of Logical Sensors, and its linguistic implementation, the Logical Sensor Specification Language. The overall goal of Logical Sensors and the Logical Sensor Specification Language is to aid in the coherent synthesis of efficient and reliable sensor systems (Hansen, Henderson, Shilcrat, & Fai, 1983; Henderson, Shilcrat, & Hansen, 1983; Shilcrat, Panangaden, & Henderson, 1984).

Both the availability and need for sensor systems is growing, as is the complexity in terms of the number and kind of sensors within a system. For example, most robotic sensor-based systems to date have been designed around a single sensor or a small number of sensors,

---

* This work was supported in part by the System Development Foundation and NSF Grants ECS-8307483 and MCS-82-21750.

and *ad hoc* techniques have been used to integrate them into the complete system and for operating on their data. In the future, however, such systems must operate in a reconfigurable multisensor environment; for example, there may be several cameras (perhaps of different types), active range-finding systems, tactile pads, and so on. In addition, a wide variety of sensing devices, including mechanical, electronic, and chemical, are available for use in sensor systems, and a single-sensor system may include several kinds of sensing devices. Thus, at least two issues regarding the configuration of sensor systems arise:

1. how to develop a coherent and efficient treatment of the information provided by many sensors, particularly when the sensors are of various kinds;
2. how to allow for sensor system reconfiguration, both as a means toward greater tolerance for sensing device failure, and to facilitate future incorporation of additional sensing devices.

The Multisensor Kernel System (MKS) (see Chapter 8) has been proposed as an efficient and uniform mechanism for dealing with data taken from several diverse sensors (Henderson & Fai, 1983a, 1983b; Fai, 1983). MKS has three major components: low-level data organization, high-level modeling, and logical sensor specification. The first two components of MKS concern the choice of a low-level representation of real-world phenomena and the integration of that representation into a meaningful interpretation of the real world, and have been discussed in detail elsewhere (Fai, 1983). The logical sensor specification component aids the user in the configuration and integration of data such that, regardless of the number and kinds of sensing devices, the data are represented consistently with regard to the low-level organization and high-level modeling techniques that are contained in MKS. As such, the logical sensor specification component is designed in keeping with the overall goal of MKS, which is to provide an efficient and uniform mechanism for dealing with data taken from several diverse sensors, as well as facilitating sensor system reconfiguration. However, the logical sensor specification component of MKS can be used independently of the other two MKS components, for example, in conjunction with any desired low-level organization and high-level modeling technique. Thus, a use for logical sensors is evident in any sensor system which is composed of several sensors, and/or where sensor reconfiguration is desired.

The emergence of significant multisensor systems provides a major motivation for the development of logical sensors. Monitoring highly automated factories or complex chemical processes requires the integration and analysis of diverse types of sensor measurements; for example, it may be necessary to monitor temperature, pressure, reaction rates, etc. In many cases, fault tolerance is of vital concern, for example, in a nuclear power plant (Nelson, 1982). Our work has been done in the context of a robotic work station where the kinds of sensors involved include:

- cameras: an intensity array of the scene is produced.
- tactile pads: local forces are sensed.
- proximity sensors: the proximity of objects to a robot hand is sensed.
- laser range finders: the distance to surface points of objects in the scene are produced, and
- smart sensors: special algorithms implemented in hardware for detecting features such as edges.

Oftentimes, if the special hardware is not available, then some of these sensors may be implemented as a software/hardware combination which should be viewed as a distinct sensor and which ultimately may be replaced by special hardware. Other examples of sophisticated sensor systems include automatic target recognition (ATR) systems (Bhanu, 1983) and the Utah/MIT Dextrous Hand (Jacobsen, Wood, Knutti, & Biggers, 1983). ATR systems integrate data from three (or more) sensors: microwave, FLIR, and LADAR (see also Section 3 of Chapter 16). The Utah/MIT Hand includes a tactile sensing system which is composed of tactile element sensors gathered into tactile pads and placed on the Hand.

Other principal motivations for logical sensor specification are:

Benefits of data abstraction: the specification of a sensor is separated from its implementation. The multisensor system is then much more portable in that the specifications remain the same over a wide range of implementations. Moreover, alternative mechanisms can be specified to produce the same sensor information but perhaps with different precision or at different rates. Thus, several dimensions of sensor granularity can be defined. Further, the stress on modularity not only contributes to intellectual manageability (Wirth, 1979) but is also an essential component of the system's reconfigurable nature. The inherent hierarchical structuring of logical sensors further aids system development.

Availability of smart sensors: the lowering cost of hardware combined with developing methodologies for the transformation from high-level algorithmic languages to silicon have made possible a system view in which hardware/software divisions are transparent. It is now possible to incorporate fairly complex algorithms directly into hardware. Thus, the substitution of hardware for software (and vice versa) should be transparent above the implementation level.

2. RELATED WORK

The work most related, in a high-level way, to logical sensor specification has been done in computer graphics. The need for some device-independent interactive system has been so widely recognized in the area of graphics that the Graphical Kernel System (GKS) is now a Draft International Standard, and is under consideration as an American National Standard. The main idea behind GKS is to provide "a means whereby interactive graphics applications could be insulated from the peculiarities of the input devices of particular terminals, and thereby become portable" (Rosenthal, Michener, Pfaff, Kessenere, & Sabin, 1982). This was accomplished by allowing only a restricted view of an input device; the only aspect of an input device which could be viewed was the *type* of its output. Input devices so restricted are called *virtual input devices*.

Criticisms of GKS have focused on the need for virtual devices to have visible aspects other than type alone. This led to the adoption of the *logical* device concept, which is a virtual device with an enlarged view whereby other details of importance are visible.

Logical sensors are also proposed as a means by which to insulate the user from the peculiarities of input devices, which in this case are (generally) physical sensors. Thus, for example, a sensor system could be designed around camera input, without regard to the kind of camera being used. However, in addition to providing insulation from the vagaries of physical devices, logical sensor specification is also a means to create and package "virtual" physical sensors. For example, the kind of data produced by a physical laser range-finder sensor could also be produced by two cameras and a stereo program. This similarity of output result is more important to the user than the fact that one way of getting it is by using one physical device, and the other way is by using two physical devices and a program. Logical sensor specification allows the user to ignore such differences of how output is produced, and treat different means of obtaining equivalent data as logically the same.

Another related graphics interface system is SYNGRAPH (Olsen & Dempsey, 1983). This system automatically generates graphical user interfaces. The user expresses the desired interface in a modified BNF wherein a primitive input device must be declared so that a set of special features as well as output type are visible. A grammar-driven approach is favored because the syntactic description makes automated analysis of the interface possible.

The need for higher-level robotics languages has also been articulated by Donner (1983) in his work on the OWL language. OWL is not a sensor specification language, but rather a simple programming language for describing concurrent processes to control a walking machine.

3. LOGICAL SENSORS

We have touched briefly on the role of logical sensors above. We now formally define logical sensors.

A *logical sensor* is defined in terms of four parts:

1. A *logical sensor name.* This is used to uniquely identify the logical sensor.
2. A *characteristic output vector.* This is basically a vector of types which serves as a description of the output vectors that will be produced by the logical sensor. Thus, the output of a logical sensor is a set (or stream) of vectors, each of which is of the type declared by that logical sensor's characteristic output vector. The type may be any standard type (e.g., real, integer), a user-generated type, or a well-defined subrange of either. When an output vector is of the type declared by a characteristic output vector (i.e., the cross product of the vector element types), we say that the output vector is an "instantiation" of that characteristic output vector.
3. A *selector* whose inputs are alternate subnets and an acceptance test name. The role of the selector is to detect failure of an alternate and switch to a different alternate. If switching cannot be done, the selector reports failure of the logical sensor.
4. *Alternate subnets.* This is a list of one or more alternate ways in which to obtain data with the same characteristic output vector. Hence, each alternate subnet is equivalent, with regard to type, to all other alternate subnets in the list, and can serve as backups in case of failure. Each alternate subnet in the list is itself composed of (a) a set of *input sources.* Each element of the set must either be itself a logical sensor, or the empty set (null). Allowing null input permits *physical* sensors, which have only an associated program (the device driver), to be described as a logical sensor, thereby permitting uniformity of sensor treatment. (b) A *computation unit*

over the input sources. Currently such computation units are software programs, but in the future, hardware units may also be used. In some cases, a special "do-nothing" computation unit may be used. We refer to this unit as PASS.

A logical sensor can be viewed as a network composed of subnetworks which are themselves logical sensors. Communication within a network is controlled via the flow of data from one subnetwork to another. Hence, such networks are *data flow* networks.

Alternatively, we present the following inductive definition of a logical sensor:

A logical sensor is an acceptance test which checks (sequentially and on demand) the output of either (base case 1):

1. A list of computation units, with specified type (the characteristic output vector), which require no input sources.
2. A list of computation units, with specified output type, whose input sources are logical sensors.

Figure 4.1 gives a pictorial presentation of this notion. The characteristic output vector declared for this logical sensor is (x–loc:real, y–loc:real, z–loc:real, curvature:integer). We present two examples to clarify the definition of logical sensors, and in particular to show how the inputs to a logical sensor are defined in terms of other logical sensors and how the program accepts input from the source logical sensors, performs some computation on them, and returns as output a set (stream) of vectors of the type defined by the characteristic output vector. Figure 4.2 shows the logical sensor specification for a "camera"

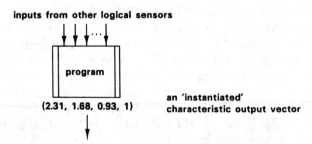

Figure 4.1. Graphical view of a logical sensor.

Figure 4.2. The logical sensor specification of a "camera."

which happens to have no other logical sensor inputs. The specification for a stereo camera range finder called "Range_Finder" is given in Figure 4.3. The program "stereo" takes the output of the two cameras and computes vector of the form (x, y, z) for every point on the surface of an object in the field of view. The idea is that a logical sensor can specify either a device driver program which needs no other logical sensor input, but rather gets its input directly from the physical device and then formats it for output in a characteristic form, or a logical sensor can specify that the output of other logical sensors be routed to a certain program and the result packaged as indicated. This allows the user to create "packages" of methods which produce equivalent data, while ignoring the internal configurations of those "packages."

3.1. Formal Aspects

Having described how logical sensors are developed and operate, we now define a logical sensor to be a *network* composed of one or more subnetworks, where each subnetwork is a logical sensor. The computation units of the logical sensors are the nodes of the network. Currently, the network forms a rooted directed acyclic graph. The graph is rooted because, taken in its entirety, it forms a complete description of a single logical sensor (versus, for example, being a description of two logical sensors which share subnetworks). We also say that it is rooted because there exists a path between each subnetwork and a computation unit of the final logical sensor. Logical sensors may not be defined in terms of themselves (that is, no recursion is allowed) and hence the graph is acyclic.

All communication within a network is accomplished via the flow of

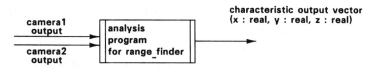

Figure 4.3. The logical sensor specification of "Range_Finder."

data from one subnetwork to another. No explicit control mechanism, such as the use of shared variables, alerts, interrupts, etc., is allowed. The use of such control mechanisms would decrease the degree of modularity and independent operation of subnetworks. Hence, the networks described by the logical sensor specification language are data flow networks, and have the following properties (Keller, 1978).

- A network is composed of independently, and possibly concurrently, operating subnetworks.
- A network, or some of its subnetworks, may communicate with its environment via possibly infinite input or output streams.
- Subnetworks are modular.

Since the actual output produced by a subnetwork may depend on things like hardware failures (and because the output produced by the different subnets of a logical sensor are only required to have the same type), the subnetworks (and hence the network) are also indeterminate.

3.2. Logical Sensor Specification Language

We have shown that a logical sensor has the following properties:

- A logical sensor is a network composed of subnetworks which are themselves logical sensors.
- A logical sensor may be defined only in terms of other, previously defined, logical sensors.
- A computation unit is an integral part of the definition of a logical sensor.
- A logical sensor produces output of the type declared by its characteristic output vector, and the declaration of the characteristic output vector is also an integral part of the definition of a logical sensor.

It should be noted that there may be alternate input paths to a particular sensor, and these correspond to the alternate subnets. But even though there may be more than one path through which a logical sensor produces data, the output will be of the type declared by the logical sensor's characteristic output vector.

With these points in mind, a language for describing the logical sensor system can be formed. We give the syntax below.

Syntax:

⟨logical-sensor⟩	→	⟨logical-sensor-name⟩
		⟨characteristic-output-vector⟩
		⟨selector⟩
		⟨alternate-subnet-list⟩
⟨logical-sensor-name⟩	→	⟨identifier⟩
⟨characteristic-output-vector⟩	→	⟨name-type-list⟩
⟨name-type-list⟩	→	⟨identifier⟩:⟨type⟩
		{; ⟨name-type-list⟩}
⟨selector⟩	→	⟨acceptance-test-name⟩
⟨alternate-subnet-list⟩	→	⟨computation-unit-name⟩ ⟨input-list⟩
		{⟨alternate-subnet-list⟩}*
⟨acceptance-test-name⟩	→	⟨identifier⟩
⟨input-list⟩	→	⟨logical-sensor-list⟩ | null
⟨logical-sensor-list⟩	→	⟨logical-sensor⟩
		{⟨logical-sensor-list⟩}*
⟨computation-unit-name⟩	→	⟨identifier⟩

Semantics: Below we present a high-level description of the *operational* semantics (i.e., the execution effect) for each rule of the grammar:

1. A *logical sensor* declaration provides an associated name for the logical sensor used for identification purposes, a characteristic output vector to declare the type of output for that logical sensor. A selector performs the test and switch after the acceptance test and the alternate subnet list establishes the alternative ways of providing the characteristic output vector.
2. A *logical sensor name* declaration associates a (unique) identifier for the logical sensor.
3. A *characteristic output vector* declaration establishes the type of output for the logical sensor.
4. A *name-type list* declaration establishes the precise nature of the output type as declared by the characteristic output vector. It consists of a cross product of types, with an associated name.
5. A *selector* declaration specifies the order in which the alternates in the alternate subnet list will be tested by the acceptance test.
6. An *alternate subnet list* declaration establishes a series of input sources and computation unit name tuples, thus making known which logical sensors and computation units are part of the definition of the logical sensor being declared.
7. An *input list* declaration establishes which legal input sources

(either none or a series of logical sensors) are to be used as input to the computation unit.
8. A *logical sensor list* declaration establishes the set of logical sensors to be used as input.
9. A *computation unit name* declaration establishes the name of the actual program which will execute on the declared input sources.
10. A *acceptance test name* declaration establishes the name of the actual program which will be used to test the alternate subnets.

We are also currently working on providing more formal semantics for the logical sensor specification language. Many works provide *denotational* semantics (i.e., semantic schemes which associate with each construct in the language an abstract mathematical object) for general data flow networks (Keller, 19778; Kahn, 1974; Kahn & McQueen, 1977). When such semantics have been given for the networks represented by logical sensors, we will be able formally to prove desired network properties, such as that a network can execute forever (Kahn, 1974). We will also be able to prove that the output of a specified logical sensor has particular properties of interest (e.g., that its type matches that of the characteristic output vector).

3.3. Implementation

We currently have two implementations of the logical sensor specification language running: a C version (called C-LSS) running under UNIX, and a functional language version (called FUN-LSS). The C version has been described elsewhere (Henderson et al., 1983) and produces a shell script from the specification. We give details here of the functional language version.

FUN-LSS provides a logical sensor specification interface for the user and maintains a database of s-expressions which represents the logical sensor definitions (see Figure 4.4). The operations allowed on logical sensors include:

Create: a new logical sensor can be specified by giving all the necessary information and it is inserted in the database.
Update: an existing logical sensor may have certain fields changed; in particular, alternative subnets can be added or deleted, and program names and the corresponding sensor lists can be changed.
Delete: a logical sensor can be deleted so long as no other logical sensor depends on it.

Logical Sensor Systems 91

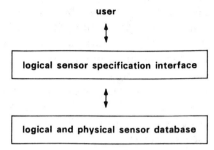

Figure 4.4. The logical sensor system interface.

Display: show all parts of a logical sensor or list all logical sensor names.
Dependencies: show all logical sensor dependencies.

The Appendix gives a sample session with the logical sensor specification interface.

Once the logical sensors are specified, they are stored as s-expressions in the database. In order to actually execute that logical sensor specification, it is necessary to translate the database expressions into some executable form, for example, to produce a source for some target language, and then either interpret or compile and run that source. Our approach is displayed in Figure 4.5.

We have written a translator which converts the s-expressions in the database into abstract syntax trees for a Function Equation Language (FEL) (Shilcrat, Panangaden, & Henderson, 1984). These are then passed to the FEL complier which produces a function graph which can then be evaluated, using a combination of graph reduction and data

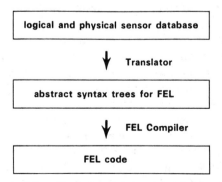

Figure 4.5. Steps to obtain executable code.

flow strategies. More on these topics can be found elsewhere (Shilcrat, Panangaden, & Henderson, 1984). In that paper we discuss a methodology for configuring systems of sensors using a functional language. The use of abstraction and of functional language features leads to a natural and simple approach to this problem. The features of a particular functional programming environment, Function Equation Language (FEL) running on the REDIFLOW simulator, are exploited to develop a scheme that avoids complicated issues of state restoration and switching protocols. Moreover, the use of reduction allows us to store that part of the alternate subnet list which is currently backup in a skeletal form. Thus, a large savings in runtime space requirements may be achieved.

4. FAULT TOLERANCE

The Logical Sensor Specification Language has been designed in accordance with the view that languages should facilitate error determination and recovery. As we have explained, a logical sensor has a selector which takes possibly many alternate subnets as input. The selector determines errors and attempts recovery via switching to another alternate subnet. Each alternate subnet is an input source–computation unit pair. Selectors can detect failures which arise from either an input source or the computation unit. Thus, the selector together with the alternate subnets constitute a failure and substitution device, that is, a fault-tolerance mechanism, and *both* hardware and software fault tolerance can be achieved. This is particularly desirable in light of the fact that "fault tolerance does not necessarily require diagnosing the cause of the fault or *even deciding whether it arises from the hardware or software* [emphasis added]" (Randell, 1977). In a multisensor system, particularly where continuous operation is expected, trying to determine and correct the exact source of a failure may be prohibitively time-consuming.

Substitution choices may be based on either *replication* or *replacement*. *Replication* means that exact duplicates of the failed component have been specified as alternate subnets. In *replacement* a different unit is substituted. Replacement of software modules has long been recognized as necessary for software fault tolerance, with the hope, as Randell states, that using a software module of independent design will facilitate coping "with the circumstances that caused the main component to fail" (Randell, 1977). We feel that replacement of physical sensors should be exploited both with Randell's point in view and because extraneous considerations, such as cost, and spatial limitations as to placement ability are very likely to limit the number of purely back-up physical sensors which can be involved in a sensor system.

4.1. Recovery Blocks

The recovery block is a means of implementing software fault tolerance (Randell, 1977). A recovery block contains a series of alternates which are to be executed in the order listed. Thus, the first in the series of alternates is the *primary* alternate. An acceptance test is used to ensure that the output produced by an alternate is correct or acceptable. First the primary alternate is executed and its output scrutinized via the acceptance test. If it passes, that block is exited; otherwise the next alternate is tried, and so on. If no alternate passes, control switches to a new recover block if one (on the same or higher level) is available; otherwise, an error results.

Similarly, a selector tries, in turn, each alternate subnet in the list and tests each one's output via an acceptance test. However, while Randall's scheme requires the use of complicated error recovery mechanisms (restoring the state, and so on), the use of a data flow model makes error recovery relatively easy. Furthermore, our user interface computes the dependency relation between logical sensors (Shilcrat, Panangaden, & Henderson, 1984). This permits the system to know which other sensors are possibly affected by the failure of a given sensor.

The general difficulties relating to software acceptance tests, such as how to devise them, how to make them simpler than the software module being tested, and so on, remain. It is our view that some acceptance tests will have to be designed by the user, and that our goal is simply to accommodate the use of the test. Unlike Randall, we envision the recovery block as a means for both hardware and software fault tolerance, and hence we also allow the user to specify general hardware acceptance tests. Such tests may be based, for example, on data link control information, two-way handshaking, and other protocols. It is important to note that a selector must be specified even if there is only one subnet in a logical sensor's list of alternate subnets. Without at least the minimal acceptance test of a "time-out," a logical sensor could be placed on hold forever even when alternate ways to obtain the necessary data could have been executed. Given the minimal acceptance test, the selector will at least be able to signal failure to a higher-level selector which may then institute a recovery. However, we also wish to devise special schemes for acceptance tests when the basis for substitution is replacement. While users will often know which logical sensors are functionally equivalent, it is also likely that not all possible substitutions of logical sensors will be considered. Thus, we are interested in helping the user expand what is considered functionally equivalent. Such a tool could also be used to automatically generate logical sensors.

We give an example logical sensor network in Figure 4.6. This example shows how to obtain surface point data from possible alternate methods. The characteristic output vector of Range_Finder is (x:real, y:real, z:real) and is produced by selecting one of the two alternate subnets and "projecting" the first three elements of their characteristic output vectors. The preferred subnet is composed of the logical sensor

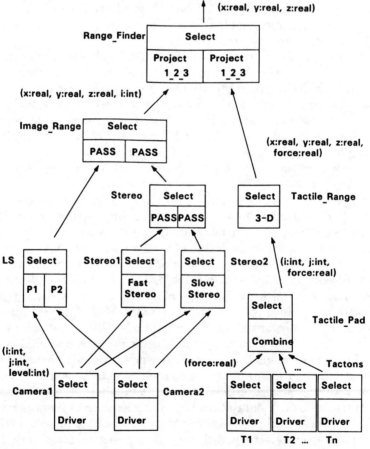

Figure 4.6. Logical sensor network for Range_Finder.

Image_Range. This logical sensor has two alternate subnets which both have the dummy computational unit PASS. PASS does not effect the type of the logical sensor. These alternatives will be selected in turn to produce the characteristic output vector (x:real, y:real, z:real, i:integer). If both alternates fail (whether due to hardware or software), the Image_Range sensor has failed. The Range_Finder then selects the second subnet to obtain the (x:real, y:real, z:real) information from the Tactile_Range's characteristic output vector. If the Tactile_Range subsequently fails, then the Range_Finder fails. Each subnet uses this mechanism to provide fault tolerance.

4.2. Ramifications of Fault Tolerance Based on a Replacement Scheme

Many difficult issues arise when fault tolerance is based on a replacement scheme. Because the replacement scheme is implemented through the use of alternate subnets, the user can be sure that the *type* of output will remain constant, regardless of the particular source subnet. Ideally, however, we consider that a replacement-based scheme is truly fault tolerant only if the effect of the replacement is within allowable limits, where the allowable limits are determined by the user. As a simple example, consider a sensor system of one camera, A, and a back-up camera of another type, B. Suppose camera A has accuracy of $\pm 0.01\%$, and camera B has accuracy of $\pm 0.04\%$. If the user has determined that the allowable limit on accuracy is $\pm 0.03\%$, then replacement of camera A by camera B will not yield what we call a truly fault-tolerant system; if the allowable limit is $\pm 0.05\%$, the replacement does yield a truly fault-tolerant system, as it will if the user has determined that the system should run regardless of the degree of accuracy.

As mentioned above, determining functional equivalence may necessitate seeing more of a logical sensor than merely its type. This example illustrates this point in that we have isolated a need to know more about leaf logical sensors (physical sensors). However, we also mentioned that the above example was simplified. Let us now assume, in addition, that the user can use a variety of algorithms to obtain the desired final output. Suppose one of those algorithms incorporates interpolation techniques which could increase the degree of accuracy over camera B's input. In this case, the user may be able to use camera B and this algorithm as an alternate subnet and have a truly fault-tolerant system, even if camera B's output is not itself within the allowable accuracy limit. Thus, when we consider a slightly more complex example, we see a general need for having features (beside type of output) of logical sensors visible, and a need to propagate such information through the system.

Feature propagation, together with allowable limit information, is needed for replacement-based fault-tolerance schemes and constitutes an acceptance test mechanism. In addition, such feature propagation has a good potential for use in automatic logical sensor system specification/optimization. For example, consider a workstation with several sensors. Once various logical sensors have been defined and stored, feature propagation can be used to configure new logical sensors with properties in specified ranges, or to determine the best (within the specified, perhaps weighted, parameters) logical sensor system. Thus, feature propagation is necessary for both fault tolerance and automatic generation of logical sensor systems, and it is our view that the basic scheme will be the same in either case.

5. FEATURES AND THEIR PROPAGATION

Our view is that propagation of features will occur from the leaf nodes to the root of the network. In sensor systems, the leaf nodes will generally be physical sensors (with associated drivers). Thus, we first discuss the important features of physical sensors.

5.1. Features of Physical Sensors

Our goal here is to determine whether a set of generally applicable physical sensor features exists, and then to provide a database to support the propagation mechanism. In addition, it is possible for the user to extend the set of features. Currently, the system provides a small set of generally applicable features (see below).

All physical sensors convert physical properties or measurements to some alternative form, and hence are transducers. Some standard terms for use in considering transducer performance must be defined (Wright, 1983). We have selected a set of features defined by Wright which we feel are generally applicable to physical sensors.

- *Error*—the difference between the value of a variable indicated by the instrument and the true value at the input.
- *Accuracy*—the relationship of the output to the true input within certain probability limits. Accuracy is a function of nonlinearities, hysteresis, temperature variation, and drift.

- *Repeatability*—the closeness of agreement within a group of measurements at the same input conditions.
- *Drift*—the change in output that may occur despite constant input conditions.
- *Resolution*—the smallest change in input that will result in a significant change in transducer output.
- *Hysteresis*—a measure of the effect of history on the transducer.
- *Threshold*—the minimum change in input required to change the output from a zero indication. For digital systems this is the input required for 1-bit change in output.
- *Range*—the maximum range of input variable over which the transducer can operate.

Based on this set of physical sensor characteristics, the next step in arriving at a characterization of logical sensors is to "compose" physical sensor feature information with computation unit feature information.

5.2. Algorithm Features

There are several difficult issues involved in choosing a scheme whereby features of algorithms can be "composed" with features of physical sensors such that the overall logical sensor may be classified. As Bhanu (1983) has pointed out: "The design of the system should be such that each of its components makes maximum use of the input data characteristics and its goals are in conformity with the end result."

One issue to be resolved is how to represent features and feature composition. One approach is to record feature information and composition functions separately. Thus, it would be necessary to classify an algorithm as having a certain degree of accuracy, and, in addition, provide an accuracy function which, given the accuracy of the physical sensor, produces the overall accuracy for the logical sensor which results from the composition of the physical sensor and the algorithm. A major difficulty in resolving such issues is presented by the great variety of sensor systems, both actual and potential, and the varying level of awareness of such issues within different sensor user communities. For example, experienced users of certain types of sensors may have a fairly tight knowledge of when and why certain algorithms work well, whereas other user communities may be aware in only a vague way which algorithms work well under which circumstances. Indeed, even within a sensor user community, algorithm evaluation techniques may not be standardized, hence yielding a plethora of ways in which properties of algorithms may be described. This problem is manifest in Bhanu's survey of the evaluation of automatic target recognition (ATR) algorithms (1983).

The state of the art in algorithm evaluation techniques effects the choices made regarding the use of classifying physical sensors whether we wish to simply catalog information or maximize criteria. For example, if the user cannot provide information about the degree of resolution for the algorithms being used, then an overall logical sensor resolution figure cannot be determined, even if the resolution of all physical sensors is known. Also, if such is the case, then the system cannot be used to help the user maximize the degree of resolution of the final output.

On the other hand, there are some encouraging results reported in the literature; a systematic study of robotic sensor design for dynamic sensing has recently been undertaken by Beni et al. (1983), and more of that kind of work is required if we are to achieve comprehensive sensor systems.

6. FUTURE RESEARCH: AUTOMATIC LOGICAL SENSOR GENERATION

We are investigating ways in which to generate logical sensor systems automatically. We recognize that, considering the number of unanswered questions we listed above, we will not be able to establish a fully automatic logical sensor system, and therefore our proposal is to confine ourselves to an automatic logical sensor system of limited generality.

6.1 Tupling/Merging Data

We now describe some techniques to allow for dynamic specification and allocation of logical sensors. Though the kinds of logical sensors which we consider represent only simple extensions to the existing logical sensor system, this type of work is a first step toward generally extensible logical sensor systems. The goal here is to show how, given information about logical sensors which can be configured in the system, new logical sensors can be defined automatically. There are two techniques under investigation, tupling and merging data.

Tupling Data: Tupling data is a technique which can be used to generate automatically new logical sensors in a feature-based sensor system. In such systems, the logical sensors would be returning information about certain features found in the scene, such as number of edges, number of holes, temperature, metallic composition, and so on. The user may then request that a new logical sensor be established by specifying the name for the new logical sensor, and giving the names of the input logical sensor(s). The output of the new logical sensor will be, simply, a set of tuples (one for each object in the scene), where the tuple is composed of the Cartesian product of the features which were input from the source logical sensors. Thus, we are basically packaging together features of interest so that they will be in one output stream. For example, suppose that the features "number of edges" and "number of holes" are sufficient to determine the presence of bolts. Then a logical sensor *bolt-detector* could be created by tupling the output of the logical sensors *edge-detector* and *hole-detector*. It should be noted that we assume that the latter two logical sensors produce output of the form (object No., feature 1, feature 2, . . . , feature N). For the sake of simplicity, in this example we assume that logical sensor *edge-detector* produces output of the form (object No., number or edges) and logical sensor *hole-detector* produces output of the form (object No., number of holes). Logical sensor *bolt-detector* will match an object number, and produce tuples of the form (object No., number of edges, number of holes).

Merging Data: Another facility we are investigating dynamically incorporates, in response to a system demand, a newly defined logical sensor which outputs the merge of three-dimensional logical sensor inputs. The idea is to accommodate an interactive request to allow the output of two physical sensors to be treated as one, for example, to create a multiple-view laser range-finder logical sensor from what had been two different laser range-finder logical sensors. In this example, a logical sensor *multiview-laser* is created with input logical sensors of both laser range finders, and the inputs are merged to produce output. Thus, the user can decide, interactively, to get more views without having to reconfigure the entire system. Also, such a facility obviates the need for having multiple program units where the only difference is in the number of expected inputs.

6.2. Choosing Algorithms Based on Appropriateness/Reliability

Our view is that a feature propagation mechanism is useful for both fault-tolerance checking and logical sensor optimization. Some difficulties are involved in using the feature propagation mechanism in a logical sensor optimization system. From the optimization viewpoint, the task which we wish the logical sensor system to perform is not merely to produce output, but to produce output which is optimal. One difficulty is that what makes the output optimal may change from application to application, or from use to use. Hence, the logical sensor system should produce output of the specified type which is optimized according to the *user-specified optimization criteria*.

In light of the above-discussed difficulties in developing a feature propagation mechanism, we are considering optimization facilities which could also be used in the absence of a general feature propagation mechanism. Our goal is to help the user choose algorithms which maximize desired capabilities of a logical sensor system. Therefore, in addition to providing what may only constitute a catalog of physical sensor characteristics, we wish to establish a database of algorithms which can be searched to determine how to configure the optimal logical sensor system for the task at hand. Since, once again, we are forced to consider the level of information detail which the user can provide in setting up the database, we recognize that this database may or may not be part of a general feature propagation mechanism. In other words, if the user tells us only that a certain algorithm works well, for example, then this database will basically serve merely as an automatic cataloging device. On the other hand, if we can be provided with numerical estimates of certain parameters for each algorithm and with composing functions, the database can be used as part of a feature propagation mechanism. In the latter case, not only can we provide a much closer realization of the user's goal, but we may also be able to indicate which performance attributes cannot be met by any known configuration of physical sensors and algorithms; in such cases, the system may actually specify a new configuration of the parameters on an algorithm which would make the demanded performance possible.

6.3. Automatic Generation of Algorithm Feature Information

Several approaches to the incorporation of algorithm feature information into a logical sensor specification system have been discussed. As an extension to this idea, we intend to investigate ways in which to use a logical sensor specification system to *generate* algorithm feature information. We are looking into the use of models for algorithm evaluation, together with a database of training data, that is, sample data to be used as a standard against which algorithms are evaluated. For the ATR (Automatic Target Recognition) systems, Bhanu (1983) states that the models for algorithm evaluation should be chosen such that each part of the system should be evaluated with respect to its own figures of merit but also against its effect on the overall classification (i.e., the overall goal of the system). In this view, statistical measures of an algorithm's performance such as edge point measures and structural measures, the ability of an algorithm to make maximal use of the specific characteristics of FLIR images, and the three general parameters which are used to determine the overall performance of an ATR system (probability of target detection, probability of classification, and false alarm per frame) must all be taken into account when evaluating an algorithm. In addition, these statistical, heuristic, and parametric models are to be used in establishing the requirements of the database in terms of data collection and organization, with the end goal of generating databases of FLIR images which are increasingly representative of the real world. Thus, Bhanu envisions a training database–algorithm database interaction such that the original figures of merit for algorithms are refined, on the basis of sample data, to reflect ability to make maximal use of specific characteristics of particular physical sensor data toward the end of promoting the overall system performance (1983). We agree with the philosophy that sensor systems should be viewed as the best source of information on how to improve themselves, and intend to investigate the use of training databases, and possible training database–algorithm database interaction schemes.

7. CONCLUSION

We have defined a Logical Sensor Specification Language as a framework facilitating efficient and coherent treatment of information provided in multisensor systems. In addition to the issues raised when considering the language implementation itself, various extensions have been suggested. In particular, we have implemented:

1. a Logical Sensor Specification Language compiler,
2. general fault-tolerance features such as
    (a) a mechanism for detecting two types of sensor failure,
    (b) a technique by which switching to an alternate subnet is accomplished,
    (c) a method for determining when a sensor failure dictates top-level sensor failure.
3. a database of physical sensors.
4. automatic generation of tupling/merging logical sensors.

In addition, we intend to investigate formal semantics for the Logical Sensor Specification Language; features and feature propagation, in particular, how to arrive at a classification scheme for algorithm features and composing functions; the establishment of an algorithm database for at least optimization purposes; inference schemes by which to determine a need for new physical sensors; and training databases, and training database-algorithm database interaction schemes.

APPENDIX

The following session demonstrates the logical sensor specification system. Comments have been added in bold.

[PHOTO: Recording initiated Thu 8-Mar-84 1:19PM]

@psl
Extended 20-PSL 3.1, 15-Jun-83
1 lisp> (dskin "start.sl")

    Welcome to LSS!

Allowed options:

1. Create Logical Sensor
2. Update Logical Sensor
3. Delete Logical Sensor
4. Show Logical Sensor
5. Show Dependency Graph
6. Exit LSS

First, display all the existing logical sensors. They are either physical sensors or previously defined logical sensors.

    Enter option number: 4   **Show Logical Sensor**

    Enter name of logical sensor to be shown, or L for list: l

    Defined logical sensors: CAMERA1 CAMERA2

Enter name of logical sensor to be shown, or L for list: camera1
    Logical sensor CAMERA1:

Acceptor: TIMEOUT
COV: (I:INT J:INT LEVEL:INT)
Alternate Subnets: ((DRIVERCAM1 NIL))

The two logical sensors CAMERA1 and CAMERA2 are already known to the system. They are both physical sensors since they are leaf nodes.

Enter option number: 4   **Show Logical Sensor**

Enter name of logical sensor to be shown, or L for list: camera2

Logical sensor CAMERA2:
Acceptor: TIMEOUT
COV: (I:INT J:INT LEVEL:INT)
Alternate Subnets: ((DRIVERCAM2 NIL))

Next, create the logical sensor laser-range-finder as shown in Figure 4.6 in the text

Enter option number: 1   **Create Logical Sensor**

Enter name of logical sensor to be created: laser-range-finder

Enter name of acceptance test: timeout

Enter characteristic output vector: (x:real y:real z:real intensity:int)

Enter program name: P1

Enter the list of input logical sensors: (camera1)

Do you want to define another subnet? (yes or no): y

Enter program name: P2

Enter the list of input logical sensors: (camera2)

Do you want to define another subnet? (yes or no): n

Enter option number: 4

Enter name of logical sensor to be shown, or L for list: laser-range-finder
   Logical sensor LASER-RANGE-Finder:
   Acceptor: TIMEOUT
   COV: (X:REAL Y:REAL Z:REAL INTENSITY:INT)
   Alternate Subnets: ((P1 (CAMERA1)) (P2 (CAMERA2)))

Next, create the logical sensor stereo of Figure 4.6.

Enter option number: 1   **Create Logical Sensor**

Enter name of logical sensor to be created: stereo

Enter name of acceptance test: timeout

Enter characteristic output vector: (x:real y:real z:real intensity:int)

Enter program name: ^V   **Hit wrong key. Fix later.**

Enter the list of input logical sensors: (Camera1)

Do you want to define another subnet? (yes or no): y

Enter program name: slow-stereo

Enter the list of input logical sensors: (Camera1 Camera2)

Do you want to define another subnet? (yes or no): n

Display the logical sensors defined to this point.

Enter option number: 4   **Show Logical Sensor**

Enter name of logical sensor to be shown, or L for list: l

   Defined logical sensors: CAMERA1   CAMERA2   LASER-RANGE-FINDER STEREO

Enter name of logical sensor to be shown, or L for list: stereo

   Logical sensor STEREO:
   Acceptor: TIMEOUT
   COV: (X:REAL Y:REAL Z:REAL INTENSITY:INT)

Alternate Subnets: ((^V (CAMERA1)) (SLOW-STEREO (CAMERA1 CAMERA2)))

Note the ^V for program name.

Correct the typo made when creating the logical sensor stereo. Also, correct the input list for the first alternative.

Enter option number: 2   **Update Logical Sensor**

Enter name of logical sensor to be updated, or L for list: stereo

Add, delete or modify an alternate? (a, d or m): m

Alternates defined for logical sensor STEREO are:
Number Alternate
1   (^V(CAMERA1))
2   (SLOW-STEREO (CAMERA1 CAMERA2))

Enter the NUMBER of the alternate you wish to modify: 1

Enter p to modify program name, i to modify input list: p

Here is the alternate you wish to change: (^V (CAMERA1))
Enter the new program name.

Enter program name: fast-stereo   **Correct the program name.**

More changes to this sensor? (y or n): y

Add, delete or modify an alternate? (a, d or m): m

Alternates defined for logical sensor STEREO are:
Number Alternate
1   (FAST-STEREO (CAMERA1))   **Stereo requires 2 cameras.**
2   (SLOW-STEREO (CAMERA1 CAMERA2))

Enter the NUMBER of the alternate you wish to modify: 1

Enter p to modify program name, i to modify input list: i

Here is the alternate you wish to change: (FAST-STEREO (CAMERA1))
Enter the new input list.

Enter the list of input logical sensors: (camera1 camera2)

More changes to this sensor? (y or n): n

Display the updated logical sensor.

Enter option number: 4   **Show Logical Sensor**

Enter name of logical sensor to be shown, or L for list: stereo

> Logical sensor STEREO:
> Acceptor: TIMEOUT
> COV: (X:REAL Y:REAL Z:REAL INTENSITY:INT)
> Alternate Subnets: ((FAST-STEREO (CAMERA1 CAMERA2)) (SLOW-STEREO (CAMERA1   CAMERA2)))

Create the logical sensor image-range of Figure 4.4.

Enter option number: 1   **Create Logical Sensor**

Enter name of logical sensor to be created: image-range

Enter name of acceptance test: timeout

Enter characteristic output vector: (x:real y:real z:real intensity:int)

Enter program name: pass

Enter the list of input logical sensors: (stereo)

Do you want to define another subnet? (yes or no): n

Display the logical sensor image-range.

Enter option number: 4   **Show Logical Sensor**

Enter name of logical sensor to be shown, or L for list: image-range

> Logical sensor IMAGE-RANGE:
> Acceptor: TIMEOUT
> COV: (X:REAL Y:REAL Z:REAL INTENSITY:INT)
> Alternate Subnets: ((PASS (STEREO)))

Next, we add an alternative subnet to an existing sensor.

Enter option number: 2   **Update Logical Sensor**

Enter name of logical sensor to be updated, or L for list: image-range

Add, delete or modify an alternate? (a, d or m): a

    Alternates defined for logical sensor IMAGE-RANGE are:
    Number Alternate
    1 (PASS (STEREO))

Enter the NUMBER you wish for the new alternate: 1 **The switching order can be rearranged.**

Enter program name: pass

Enter the list of input logical sensors: laser-range-finder

    Inputs must be a list. What you gave LASER-RANGE-FINDER is not

Enter the list of input logical sensors: (laser-range-finder)

    More changes to this sensor? (y or n)n

Display the new version of the logical sensor.

Enter option number: 4   **Display Logical Sensor**

Enter name of logical sensor to be shown, or L for list: l

    Defined logical sensors: CAMERA1 CAMERA2 LASER-RANGE-FINDER STEREO IMAGE-RANGE

Enter name of logical sensor to be shown, or L for list: image-range

    Logical sensor IMAGE-RANGE:
    Acceptor: TIMEOUT
    COV: (X:REAL Y:REAL Z:REAL INTENSITY:INT)
    Alternate Subnets: ((PASS(LASER-RANGE-FINDER)) (PASS(STEREO)))

Enter option number: 5

Dependency Table:

CAMERA1	0	0	1	1	1
CAMERA2	0	0	1	1	1
LASER-RANGE-FINDER	0	0	0	0	1
STEREO	0	0	0	0	1
IMAGE-RANGE	0	0	0	0	0

Exit the system. The sensor database is automatically updated.

Enter option number:6   **Exit LSS**

Your requests have been handled!

NIL
NIL
2 lisp> (quite)
@pop

[PHOTO: Recording terminated Thu 8-Mar-84 1:29PM]

REFERENCES

Beni, G., Hackwood, S., Hornak, L.A., & Jackel, J.L. (1983). Dynamics sensing for robots: An analysis and implementation. *International Journal of Robotics Research, 2*(2), 51–61.

Bhanu, B. (1983). Evaluation of automatic target recognition algorithms. *Proceedings of the SPIE, vol. 435* (pp. 18–27).

Donner, M.D. (1983). The design of OWL: A language for walking. *ACM SIGPLAN Notice, 18*(6), 158–165.

Fai, W.S. (1983, June). A multi-sensor integration and data acquisition system. Unpublished masters thesis, University of Utah, Department of Computer Science.

Hansen, C., Henderson, T.C., Shilcrat, E., & Fai, W.S. (1983). Logical sensor specification. *Proceedings of the SPIE Conference on Intelligence Robots* (pp. 578–583).

Henderson, T.C., & Fai, W.S. (1983a). A multi-sensor integration and data acquisition system. *Proceedings of the IEEE Conference on Computer Vision and Pattern Recognition* (p. 274). New York, NY.

Henderson, T.C., & Fai, W.S. (1983b, July). *Pattern recognition in a multi-sensor environment* (Tech. Rep. UUCS 83-001). University of Utah: Department of Computer Science.

Henderson, T.C., Shilcrat, E., & Hansen, C. (1983, November). *A fault tolerant sensor scheme* (Tech. Rep. UUCS 83-003). University of Utah: Department of Computer Science.

Jacobsen, S., Wood, J.E., Knutti, D.F., & Biggers, K. (1983). The Utah/MIT dextrous hand. *Proceedings of the MIT/SDF IRR Symposium.*
Kahn, G. (1974). The semantics of a simple language for parallel programming. *Proceedings of the IFIP* (pp. 471–475).
Kahn, G., & MacQueen, D. (1977). Coroutines and networks of parallel processes. *Proceedings of the IFIP* (pp. 993–998).
Keller, R.M. (1978). Denotational models for parallel programs with indeterminate operators. In E.J. Neuhold (Ed.), *Formal descriptions of programming concepts* (pp. 337–366). Amsterdam: North-Holland.
Nelson, W.R. (1982). REACTOR: An expert system for diagnosis and treatment of nuclear accidents. *Proceedings of the Second National Conference on Artificial Intelligence* (pp. 296–301). Pittsburgh, PA.
Olsen, D.R., & Dempsey, E.P. (1983). SYNGRAPH: A graphical user interface generator. *SIGGRAPH '83 Conference Proceedings* (pp. 43–50).
Randell, B. (1977). *System structure for software fault tolerance.* Englewood Cliffs, NJ: Prentice-Hall, pp. 195–219.
Rosenthal, D.S., Michener, J.C., Pfaff, G., Kessenere, R., & Sabin, M. (1982). The detailed semantics of graphics input devices. *Computer Graphics, 16*(3), 33–38.
Shilcrat, E., Panangaden, P., & Henderson, T.C. (1984, February). *Implementing multi-sensor systems in a functional language* (Tech. Rep. UUCS 84-001). University of Utah, Department of Computer Science.
Wirth, N. (1979). On the comparison of well-structured programs. In E.N. Yourdan (Ed.), *Classics in software engineering* (pp. 153–172). London: Yourdan Press.
Wright, J.D. (1983). *Measurement, transmission, and signal processing* (pp. 80–112). New York: Van Nostrand Reinhold.

5
Neural Network Approach to Sensory Fusion*

John C. Pearson,
Jack J. Gelfand,
W.E. Sullivan,
Richard M. Peterson, and
Clay D. Spence

We present a neural network model for sensory fusion based on the design of the visual/acoustic target localization system of the barn owl. This system adaptively fuses its separate visual and acoustic representations of object position into a single joint representation used for head orientation. The building block in this system, as in much of the brain, is the neuronal map. Neuronal maps are large arrays of locally interconnected neurons that represent information in a map-like form; that is, parameter values are systematically encoded by the position of neural activation in the array. The computational load is distributed to a hierarchy of maps, and the computation is performed in stages by transforming the representation from map to map via the geometry of the projections between the maps and the local interactions within the maps. For example, azimuthal position is computed from the frequency and binaural phase information encoded in the signals of the acoustic sensors, while elevation is computed in a separate stream using binaural intensity information. These separate streams are merged in their joint projection onto the external nucleus of the inferior col-

---

* This work was supported by internal funds of the David Sarnoff Research Center.

liculus, a two-dimensional array of cells which contains a map of acoustic space. This acoustic map and the visual map of the retina jointly project onto the optic tectum, creating a fused visual/acoustic representation of position in space that is used for object localization. In this chapter we describe our mathematical model of the stage of visual/acoustic fusion in the optic tectum. The model assumes that the acoustic projection from the external nucleus onto the tectum is roughly topographic and one-to-many, while the visual projection from the retina onto the tectum is topographic and one-to-one. A simple process of self-organization alters the strengths of the acoustic connections, effectively forming a focused beam of strong acoustic connections whose inputs are coincident with the visual inputs. Computer simulations demonstrate how this mechanism can account for the existing experimental data on adaptive fusion and makes sharp predictions for experimental test.

1. INTRODUCTION

Neural network research is largely oriented towards solving "high-level" problems such as pattern recognition, categorization, and associative memory. Recent developments in this field have produced powerful new architectures and algorithms for solving such problems (see review by Cowan and Sharp, 1988). Due to our relative ignorance of how such problems are solved by animals, these "high-level" neural networks are only loosely based upon known principles of brain organization and function, and do not directly correspond to any known brain structures. However, there are other equally important problems for which the corresponding brain structures are well characterized. Object localization and identification is one such problem, and sensor fusion plays an important role in the brain's solution to this problem. In this chapter, a neural network approach to sensor fusion is presented that is based upon the map-like brain structures that solve the acoustic object localization problem in the barn owl.

Neuronal maps are key building blocks of nervous system function, ranging from perceptual classification to motor control. These structures consist of locally interconnected arrays of neurons whose response properties vary systematically with position in the array, thus forming a map-like representation of information. Computation is achieved through transforming the representation from one map to the next. The fidelity of these transformations is maintained through dynamic processes of self-organization, endowing them with self-optimizing and fault tolerant properties. These structures are linked together in modular, hierarchical processing systems, which employ some of the same problem solving approaches used in technical applications, such as sensor fusion.

In this chapter we first briefly describe the stages in the chain of neuronal processing that generate a map of space from acoustic timing cues, and adaptively fuse it with the map of space derived from the retina. We then describe our proposed neuronal mechanism for the stage of visual/acoustic fusion and present results of computer simulations. This mechanism exploits the coincident signals produced by an object in the visual and acoustic representations, using adaptive, nonlinear, neuron-like processing elements.

2. BARN OWL VISUAL/ACOUSTIC FUSION SYSTEM

Behavioral and physiological studies have revealed that owls use interaural intensity cues to specify the elevation of sounds, and interaural timing cues to localize the azimuthal direction (Knudsen & Konishi, 1979; Moiseff & Konishi, 1981). The neuronal processing leading to azimuthal sound localization and visual fusion is accomplished by a series of four so-called "computational maps", as shown in Figure 5.1, and reviewed by Knudsen, du Lac, and Esterly (1987). The processing for elevation follows a similar design and is omitted from the present discussion for clarity and brevity.

The nucleus laminaris (N. lam.) generates a map of interaural phase delay vs. frequency given phase-locked input signals from the cochlear nucleus. The central nucleus of the inferior colliculus (ICc) transforms the N. lam. map into a map of frequency vs. interaural delay. The external nucleus of the inferior colliculus (ICx) transforms the ICc map into a map of space, forming an "acoustic retina." The acoustic space map (ICx) and the visual space map (retina) are fused in their joint projection onto the optic tectum. This fused map of object location is then used in orienting the head to center the object in the visual field for closer scrutiny.

The neuronal processes of visual/acoustic fusion are known to be adaptive during the growth period of the owl (Knudsen, 1983). This is essential for the young owl, for during this time the distance between the ears increases severalfold, and this distance is a critical parameter in computing azimuthal position. Laboratory experiments have shown that perturbations to either the visual or auditory transducers (e.g., goggles or ear plugs) initially cause registration errors between the auditory and visual space maps. As a consequence, head orientation driven by acoustic cues fails to center the object in the visual center of

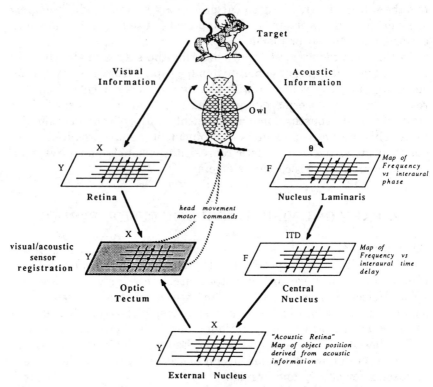

Figure 5.1. Illustration of the series of transformations in neuronal representation that produce adaptive visual/acoustic fusion in the object localization system of the barn owl. Only the azimuthal acoustic system is shown for clarity. A similar parallel series of transformations between neuronal arrays computes elevation.

view. However, with time, fusion is reestablished, and proper localization behavior is restored in a continuous manner.

The fused sensory map of space in the optic tectum is also a motor map that orients the head to center objects in the visual field, as illustrated in Figure 5.2. The static topographic projection of the retina onto the tectum, and the fact that the eyes do not move relative to the head, establishes head centered retinotopic coordinates on the tectum. Because the acoustic map (ICx) is fused with the visual map, the same region of the tectum will be activated by either visual or acoustic signals from a particular location in space. A vector from this point to the point representing the center of the retina represents the magnitude and direction of the head movement necessary to bring this source to the center of the visual field. Possible neuronal mechanisms for this

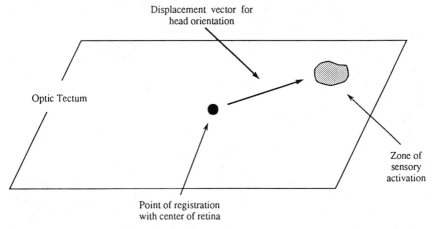

Figure 5.2. Representation of motor command for head orientation by position of activation on neuronal map in head-centered retinotopic coordinates.

have been presented by Grossberg and Kuperstein (1986) for the similar case of saccadic eye movements. Multiple objects presumably create multiple regions of activation on the tectum, and the system must select a single target for the head orientation response. Didday (1976) and Arbib (1984) have presented neuronal models of this function for the case of the frog.

3. NEURONAL MECHANISM FOR SENSORY FUSION

Recent work by Pearson, Finkel and Edelman (1987) demonstrated a solution to a problem related to the neuronal map fusion problem. They modeled the cortical map of touch sensation of the hand, which contains a topographic representation of both front and back hand surfaces. The representation of these two surfaces is not fused. Each cell in the map responds to stimulation of only one surface, and cells with the same preference are clustered into regions that are separated from regions with the opposite preference by sharp borders. Experiments have shown (see references within Pearson et al., 1987) that the borders between these regions dynamically shift so that more highly stimulated regions of the hand have larger regions of representation in the map and greater resolution. In the model, each cell received equal numbers of connections from corresponding regions of both surfaces. A rule for changing the strengths of the connections strengthens inputs that are spatially and temporally correlated, and weakens those that aren't. Since the two surfaces are rarely stimulated at the same time, cells weaken their connections with one surface while strengthening their connections to a small, compact region of the other.

Our model for fusion in the tectum is a simplified version of this model of the map of the hand. The front and back surfaces of the hand correspond to the visual and acoustic space maps. Fusion is produced instead of segregation, because stimulation of corresponding regions of the two input maps is correlated rather than uncorrelated. Figure 5.3 is a pictorial representation of the flow of signals from an object in the environment through the visual and acoustic space maps to a cell (marked with a filled dot) in the optic tectum. The light lines from the marked ICx cell to the tectum delimit its divergent region of projection, whereas the heavy line from the ICx cell to the tectum represents the functional projection created by strengthening that subregion of the total projection and weakening all others. This divergent projection is an assumption of the model. The dashed prism indicates schematically what would happen if there is a distortion added to the visual field. Immediately after the perturbation, the visual and acoustic maps in the tectum are out of register. The new point of activation in the retina (marked with an unfilled dot) immediately leads to the activation of a different cell in the tectum (marked with an unfilled dot), whereas the acoustic input fires the same cell in the tectum as before (filled dot). As a result, a single object will activate two cells in

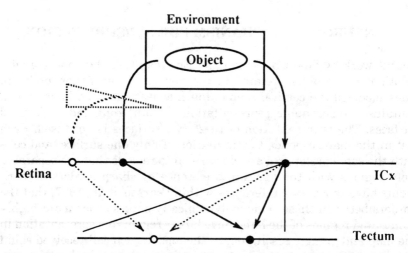

Figure 5.3. Proposed neuronal architecture for adaptive registration of visual (retina) and acoustic (ICx) neuronal maps of object position in the tectum of the barn owl following perturbation to the visual input (prism).

the tectum instead of one, and the input to a tectal cell will be half of what it was before the perturbation. However, with sufficient correlated stimulation of the visual and acoustic input maps, the connection strengths are altered so as to strengthen those acoustic connections that are coincidently activated with the visual input, and to weaken the original acoustic connections that are no longer activated at the same time as the visual connections. To test these ideas a simplified computer model was constructed.

4. COMPUTER MODEL OF SENSORY FUSION

Figure 5.4 shows preliminary results of a simulation of adaptive fusion following the type of perturbation to the visual input described in Figure 5.3. These drawings are plots of the input connection strengths from the acoustic space map (ICx) onto the cell at the center of the fused map (tectum). The series of six drawings shows these connections as initially assigned (0), after 1000 time steps of unperturbed input (1000), and at four successive times after the perturbation that moved the center of coincident input to the upper right as indicated by the arrow.

In this simulation a visual/acoustic stimulus 3 × 3 grid points in size was applied in a random sequence over the entire input grid, coincidently activating topographically corresponding points in the space maps of the retina (R) and ICx (X). The tectal cell received a visual input from one fixed location (R_0) that was activated when the stimulus covered it. The stimulus-generated input was summed to yield the cell's potential, v, shown in Equation 1.

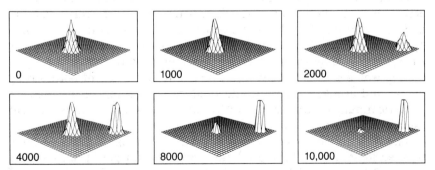

Figure 5.4. Simulation of reestablishment of visual/acoustic fusion following visual perturbation. Arrow indicates site of acoustic input coincident with visual input after the perturbation.

$$v = \sum_j c_j X_j + c_0 R_0 \qquad (1)$$

where:

c_j = variable acoustic connection strength, $(0 < c_j < 1)$
c_0 = fixed visual connection strength, $(c_0 = 10)$
X_j = acoustic input, $(X_j \in \{0,1\}, 1 = \text{ON}, 0 = \text{OFF})$
R_0 = visual input, $(R_0 \in \{0,1\}, 1 = \text{ON}, 0 = \text{OFF})$

The acoustic connection strengths were then modified according to a simplified version of the synaptic rule proposed in Pearson et al. (1987) shown in Equation 2.

$$\Delta c_j = \kappa \cdot \sigma(v, \theta_1, \epsilon_1) \cdot X_j - \delta \cdot \sigma(v, \theta_2, \epsilon_2) \cdot |1 - X_j| \qquad (2)$$

where:

κ = growth constant, $(\kappa = 0.05)$
δ = decay constant, $(\delta = 0.05)$
σ = sigmoidal function, $\sigma(v, \theta, \epsilon) = [\exp(\theta - v)/\epsilon + 1]^{-1}$
θ = threshold parameter, $(\theta_1 = 9.5, \theta_2 = 16)$
ϵ = sharpness parameter, $(\epsilon_1 = 0.01, \epsilon_2 = 0.01)$

Parameters θ_1 and θ_2 set the thresholds for significant strengthening and weakening, respectively. Significant strengthening of an acoustic connection requires that its input be active $(X_j = 1)$ and that enough other strong connections (whether visual or acoustic) be active so that $v > \theta_1$. Weakening an acoustic connection requires that its input be inactive $(X_j = 0)$ and that enough other strong connections be active so that $v > \theta_2$. Given the fixed value of c_0 (arbitrarily chosen) and the stimulus size (chosen based on simple considerations of scale), θ_1 was set so that weak acoustic connection strengths would grow very slowly unless they were activated coincidently with the visual input, and θ_2 was set so that only the coincident activation of both strong visual and acoustic inputs would produce weakening in the inactive acoustic inputs. Parameters κ and δ simply determine the time scale, or "smoothness," of the simulation.

The reestablishment of fusion is robust to changes in the parameters, as long as the above guidelines are met. Larger stimuli simply enlarge the region of the strong acoustic connections. Larger values of ϵ soften the nonlinearity in σ, making it easier to strengthen and weaken connections, but do not significantly affect the results. Regular stimulation, in which the stimulus moves over the input grid one point at a time, works as well as random stimulation. Changes in the threshold parameters affect the rate at which the original peak decays and the new peak grows, but not the final outcome, because the region of the new peak has the advantage of a fixed visual input. Of course, θ_1 must be less than the voltage due to the visual input, R_0, or the new peak cannot grow, and θ_2 must be less than the maximal potential.

The model makes several biological predictions that could be tested. The model assumes a topographic, divergent projection from the ICx to the tectum (see Figure 5.3). This could be tested with various anatomical tracing methods. The width of the divergence sets the maximum range over which registration errors can be corrected. During the adaptation to the perturbation, the auditory responsiveness of cells in the tectum should change in a characteristic way. A new region of auditory responsiveness should appear along with the original region, and as the new region gains in strength the original region should weaken, eventually vanishing. At first, this appears to be in contrast with the behavioral result, which is that the localization error vector slowly decreases in magnitude. However, it is consistent with recent findings that the motor output is determined by the vector average of activity on the tectum (du Lac & Knudsen, 1987).

5. CONCLUSIONS

Study of the visual/acoustic localization system in the barn owl has disclosed a potential neuronal mechanism for adaptive multisensor registration. Computer simulations of a neural network model of this system have successfully tested the proposed mechanism and produced predictions for experimental testing. Future work must determine the suitability of this method for technical applications.

REFERENCES

Arbib, M.A. (1984). Visuomotor coordination: From neural nets to schema. In Sulfridge, et al. (Eds.), *Adaptive control of ill-defined systems* (pp. 207–225). New York: Plenum Press.

Cowen, J.D., & Sharp, D.H. (1988, Winter). Neural nets. *Daedulus*.

Didday, R.L. (1976). A model of visuomotor mechanisms in the frog optic tectum. *Mathematical Biosciences, 30,* 169–180.

du Lac, S., & Knudsen, E.I. (1987). The optic tectum encodes saccade magnitude in a push-pull fashion in the barn owl. *Society for Neuroscience Abstracts,* 393.

Grossberg, S., & Kuperstein, M. (1986). *Neural dynamics of adaptive sensory-motor control.* Amsterdam: North-Holland.

Knudsen, E.I. (1983). Early auditory experience aligns the auditory map of space in the optic tectum of the Barn Owl. *Science, 222,* 939–942.

Knudsen, E.I., & Konishi, M.J. (1979). Mechanisms of sound localization by the barn owl (Tyto alba). *Journal of Comparative Physiology, 133,* 13–21.

Knudsen, E.I., du Lac, S., & Esterly, S.D. (1987). Computational maps in the brain. *Annual Review of Neuroscience, 10,* 41–65.

Moiseff, A., & Konishi, M.J. (1981). Neuronal and behavioral sensitivity to interaural time differences in the owl. *Journal of Neuroscience, 1*(1), 40–48.

Pearson, J.C., Finkel, L.H., & Edelman, G.M. (1987). Plasticity in the organization of adult cerebral cortical maps: A computer simulation based on neuronal group selection. *Journal of Neuroscience, 7*(12), 4209–4223.

6
Knowledge Representation Approaches in Sensor Fusion*

L. Pau

This chapter first discusses the motivation for, and basic approaches to, sensor fusion: The primary goal is to extract better features and to achieve sensor diversity. Thereafter a formal knowledge representation architecture is described which makes sensor fusion possible. Some example implementations are finally mentioned using this knowledge representation.

1. INTRODUCTION

SENSOR FUSION is the scene understanding approach which uses data or information of more than one type (Mitiche & Aggarwal, 1986; Kak & Chen, 1987). The information types may differ through the following:

- physical sensing principle,
- sensor location,
- sensor design or setting,

---

*The original version of this paper was presented at the 10th IFAC World Congress, which was held in Munich, F.R.G. during July, 1987. The Published Proceedings of this IFAC meeting may be ordered from: Pergamon Press plc, Headington Hill Hall, Oxford OX3 0BW, England.

- sensor environment,
- bandwidth,
- gain,
- wavelength or spectral detectivity profile of the sensor,
- data rate,
- preprocessing software,
- lighting mode.

The physical sensing principles themselves belong to three categories:

1. signals (analog, digital, logic),
2. 2- or N-D arrays such as images or radiation field,
3. procedural information, such as text, speech, software, or behavioral rules.

In any event, sensor diversity and parallelism are intrinsic to sensor fusion (Figure 6.1). Each sensor/information type is used in parallel for feature extraction from specific sensor information. Different features are thus extracted in parallel. The knowledge-based understanding process then takes place afterwards by accessing features of the different sources through a hierarchical retrieval and inference/recognition process.

Table 6.1 gives some known examples of sensor combinations, and the additional effects expected from such combinations. Most experiments have so far been in the areas of defense and nondestructive testing (Drazovich, 1983; Henderson & Wu So Fai, Chapter 7; La Jeunesse, 1986; Workshop, 1987). More and more application-specific systems, however, are developed for industrial vision applications using similar approaches.

Little basic work has been published which highlights unified approaches and tools in sensor fusion.

Previously, the usual approach has been to build a semantic context net or a blackboard architecture (Nii, 1986; Lyons & Arib, 1985; Rao &

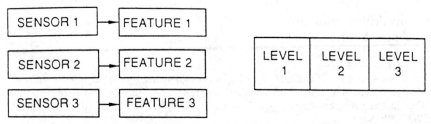

Figure 6.1. Parallelism in sensor fusion (see Figure 6.2).

Table 6.1. Examples of sensor fusion combinations and effects for two sensors

Sensor 1	Sensor 2	Effect
TV	IR	Penetration day/night
MMW	IR	Penetration/discrimination
TV	SAR	Mapping
TV	Lidar	Control, shape, motion
IR	Lidar	Control, shape, motion, penetration
TV	Laser (highpower)	Induced vibration signatures
IR	UV	Background discrimination
Multispectral	Panchro	Discrimination features and context
All	Digital terrain maps, considered as a sensor	Discrimination and location
Laser (pulsed)	TV/IR	Thermal signature

Jain, 1988) to fuse the diverse sensor data. In practice, however, such blackboards may lead to several classes of problems:

- control structure among knowledge sources, requiring task related scheduling and planning when the agendas change,
- widely differing response times,
- large memory occupation overheads in case of high sensor data rates,
- reliable deletion of blackboard items in a continuously operating system,
- difficulties in debugging errors in large shared data areas,
- difficulty of storing context information between activations of a knowledge source.

A testimony hereof is found in Alvey (1984). Although blackboards may be useful sensor fusion design methods, efficiency requirements within the context of state-of-the-art hardware and software development require multilevel sensor fusion knowledge representation schemes of the type described below and in Pau (1981, 1987) and Pau, Xiao, and Westphal (1989); some attempts have been made towards hierarchical blackboards (e.g., CODGER at Carnegie Mellon University) or distributed blackboards (Harmon, Bianchini, & Pinz, 1986).

2. IMPLEMENTATION ISSUES

In specific implementations, the issues are the following:

1. The main goal is to require better discriminating features, e.g., features giving the highest correct recognition rates with lowest false alarms and rejections.
2. The next goal is to avoid having to use high performance and high cost (single) sensors and computers.
3. The third goal is to achieve sensor diversity, and thus integrity, in order to cope with sensor failures or data link failures and destruction.
4. The fourth goal is to achieve higher recognition, segmentation, or understanding speeds through parallel sensor data preprocessing (see Figure 6.1).
5. Sensor diversity offers segmentation, characterization, and feature extraction clues when retrieving and processing features from other sensors. This is the cross-fertilization effect at the query and understanding level.
6. Sensor fusion allows one to avoid stereo sensors and processing if one sensor, or several sensors of different types in combination, provide range data.

There is also a relation between parallel or distributed processing and sensor fusion (Chiu, Morley & Martin, 1986; Lyons and Arib, 1985). If preprocessing is performed in connection with each sensor output and provides sensor-specific icons (see Table 6.2), then the fusion processor correlates, matches, and aggregates these icons and the fusion processor is then relieved from much of the preprocessing. This requires that a suitable knowledge representation framework is available to make it possible to combine such icons, even if they originate in different information sources. At the same time, this means that the selection and structuring of the knowledge representation is highly critical for the performance of any sensor fusion system.

3. KNOWLEDGE REPRESENTATION

This chapter will now formalize a general knowledge representation scheme applicable to sensor fusion problems. This scheme is hierarchical, and can be simplified whenever possible owing to specific cases. It has been tested out in a number of very concrete cases; Section 5 discusses two examples by relating the levels of sensor fusion to physi-

Table 6.2. Higher level icons provided by different sensor data types

SENSOR	ICONS RESULTING FROM PRE-PROCESSING AT SENSOR LEVEL
Imaging array (d=2)	. Segments . Features (time, space) . Graphs
Imaging array d=3 or more	. Shape-from-methods . Relational structures
Maps and spatial data structures (d=2 or 3)	. Primal sketches . Features, e.g. morphology . Relational structures
Signal series (T = [o,T])	. Features (time, frequency, space) . Causal models . Other models
Point measurements (d=0)	. Coding . Features
Text	. Grammar/ATN . Semantic/relational structures
Software	. Functional parsing . Relational structure
Planning	. Scenarios/scripts . Segmentation . Causal models

cal objects, and by explaining the operations involved in moving between levels.

3.1. Knowledge Representation Structure (K)

Notation

- d: dimension of a vector space E_i,
- i: sensor/information channel index, $i \in S$,
- E: vector space, with its norm,
- X_i: feature vector in $E_d(i)$; dim $(X_i) = d$,
- G: structural graph, with nodes which are features f_i; the arc labels are a_{jk},
- $L_i(X)$: *list of feature nodes in the feature vector X_i, with the corresponding labels a,*

M: semantic graph, or grammatical description hereof with rules expressed in predicate form,
$N_i(X)$: list of rules from $M(i)$ invoked by features in $L_i(X)$, with the corresponding labels b_1,
r: rule number in the predicate form representation of M.

Moreover, the term fused is used to express the fact that sensor fusion is applied.

The output of the sensor fusion representation is $X_s = (X_i, L_i(X), N_i(X); i \in S)$, covering all sensors in S. Three representation levels are considered (see Figure 6.2 and 6.3).

Level 1. **The lowest level of the representation is a vector space $E_d(i)$ of dimension d, for each sensor i. This space is supplied with a specific metric.**

The coordinates in $E_d(i)$ are furthermore separated into two classes:

- measurements x in X_i obtained passively,
- measurements x in X_i observed actively, that is, by controlling the illumination or another context/environmental parameter.

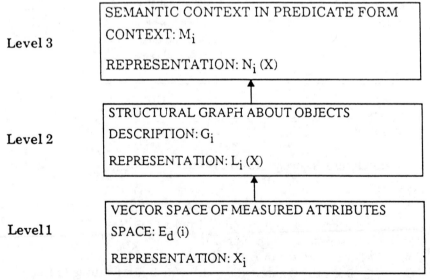

Figure 6.2. Knowledge representation levels and knowledge bases (see also Figure 6.3).

SENSOR $\eta \in S(.)$

LEVEL 1	○ VECTOR X IN SPACE E(i)
	⟶ PASSIVE MEASUREMENTS
	⟶ ACTIVE MEASUREMENTS
	○ METRIC IN E(i)

LEVEL 2		LIST $L_i(X) = (L_i^1, L_i^2)$
	L_i^1	○ LIST OF FEATURE NODES IN FEATURE GRAPH G(i)
	L_i^2	○ LIST OF LABELS OF ARCS IN SECOND SUBLIST

LEVEL 3	RULES $N_i(X)$ REPRESENTING THE CONTEXT IN M_i
	○ PREDICATE RULES FROM M WITH FEATURES IN $L_i(X)$
	○ LABELS OF THESE RULES

K	$(X_i, L_i(X), N_i(X))$

Figure 6.3. Sensor fusion knowledge representation (K).

Example 1. In a typical $d = 3$ dimensional scene, observed through a laser sensor associated with a 2-D CCD array, the attribute vector X_i is given as follows:

x_1: first coordinate of point (passive),
x_2: second coordinate of point (passive),
x_3: third coordinate (range) (active),
x_4: amplitude of signal (grey level) (passive),
x_5: frequency of laser source (active),
x_6: wavelength of measurement x_4 (passive)
x_7: time (passive)
x_8: estimated reflectivity (active),
x_9: irradiation field (active).

Level 2. If X_i is the feature vector in $E_d(i)$ provided by Level 1, the Level 2 representation is the list $L_i(X)$ defined as follows:

- let $G(i)$ be the feature graph, which specifies all feature types which can be encountered in $E_d(i)$, and establishes the relations between them which are feasible/allowable,
- the first sublist of $L_i(X)$ is the list of features present in X_i,
- the second sublist contains all the labels attached to the features in X_i, that is, labels attached to the arcs of nodes, one of which, at least, is in the first sublist.

Example 2. If a picture is considered as all of the elements of which are composed of primitive shapes, then $G(i)$ is the graph representation of the corresponding picture description language for objects allowed/expected in the scene (Fu, 1974).

The primitive shapes are straight segments, curved segments, and regions of specific shape. The labels of graph G_i are the length of these primitives, as observed in the scene and registered through coordinates in X_i, as well as other feature attributes (e.g., curvature, area, orientation, etc.). The values of these labels are a_{jk}.

Level 3. The third level is a set of rules representing the context of the scene. If M is the predicate form representation (Giannesini et al., 1987) of the context grammar, then the result $N_i(X)$ of the Level 3 knowledge representation will be the list of predicate rules containing features encountered in $L_i(X)$, with the corresponding attribute labels of the rules.

More specifically, if the global scene context is represented through the semantic grammar M_i, M_i is supposed to be represented by a set of logical predicates which correspond to rewriting rules in M_i:

Rule r_l: ($w \to v$, with label b_l, is true),

where w, v are concatenated lists of terminal and nonterminal symbols which the language M_i generates. The terminal symbols of this language include all the features of $G(i)$, supplemented by other symbols related to the context.

The list $N_i(X)$ will be defined by:

- a first sublist of rules r_l, such that at least one feature in $L_i(X)$ is encountered in v; this means that L_i will be unified with the predicate representing r_l,
- a second sublist, made of the labels b_l of such rules which are unified with $L_i(X)$.

Example 3. If M_i is a language describing the context and features about a specific problem, then $N_i(X)$ will contain in the first sublist the predicate rules which use at least one key word about the scene found in $L_i(X)$. The attributes hereof would say when such a rule may be encountered.

Knowledge bases. In the above scheme, the knowledge bases are as follows:

- Level 1: $E_d(i)$.
- Level 2: G_i.
- Level 3: M_i.

4. SENSOR ATTRIBUTE FUSION OPERATIONS (SEE TABLE 6.3)

The knowledge representation $(X_i, L_i(X), N_i(X))$ is derived for:

- each sensor/information channel i, for which the sensor and knowledge bases are available,
- each observation of the scene or event.

Therefore, to be able to interpret, recognize, or understand the joint set of observations about the scene obtained from all sensors, one must be able to combine the above knowledge provided from each channel. The basic combinations serve different purposes. The main combinations are:

1. fusion operations, used in knowledge query and inference;
2. matching operations, used in recognition and understanding goals;
3. projection operations, used to jointly display the outcomes of the different sensors.

4.1. Fusion Operations

Level 1. **Fusion operations on vector spaces E_d can only be carried out for spaces of same dimension d (typically the largest dimension, in that lower dimensional spaces are extended with dummy dimensions). These fusion operations are derived from linear algebra in euclidean spaces:**

- translate, rotate,
- superimpose by merger, after translation and rotations,
- define combination metrics, which includes scaling to the same scales on each axis,
- warp, which includes rescaling on each axis by an isomorphism in order to fix the maximum range of the coordinates.

Level 2. **To merge the structural graphs $G(i)$, the operations are:**

- merge the lists $L_i(X)$ of feature nodes, and merge the corresponding graphs $G(i)$,
- reduce graph in case of redundant arcs in the merged $G(i)$.

Level 3. **To merge the semantic grammars M_i or predicates, the operations are:**

- merge the terminal vocabularies $G(i)$, link the predicate/rule sets M_i, and choose the same initial symbol for all M_is;
- apply unification rules, insertions rules, deletion rules, and truncation rules to the sentences w, v.

4.2. Matching Operations

Level 1. **In the fused vector space, the matching operations involve assigning the measurements x from X_is into the same labelled classes; they are:**

- all matching procedures from pattern recognition, based on neighborhood relations (Fukunaga, 1972);

- clustering procedures;
- entropy minimization procedures (Fukunaga, 1972);
- orthographic projections from projective geometry:
  — match points in $d = 3$ (3 translations and 3 rotations)
  — match sets of two points (2 translations, 1 rotation, 1 scaling, 2 length warpings, 2 length parametrizations)
  — match line segments in $d = 2$ (2 translations, 1 rotation, 1 warping)

Level 2. **In the fused graph G, all matching operations are subgraph matches (Wong and Goldfarb, 1982); they require a combinatorial search for the symmetric difference between subgraphs of the same degree. One special case is the matching of anchor or reference nodes.**

Level 3. **In the fused semantic grammar M, the matching operations are related to symbolic parsing techniques:**

- structural matching of strings,
- structural matching of strings with unknown elements
- context dependency,
- ranking of matches by numbers of joint occurrence.

4.3. Projection Operations

Level 1. **They are of two sorts, originating in the fused vector space, or in a subspace of the latter.**

1. Linear projections are possible from the joint space, using the joint norm and unitary transforms from linear algebra.
2. Nonlinear projections or operations are possible among subspaces of the fused vector space; they involve functional relations in space, or derivation manifolds.

   - Change of scale by the $g(x) = 1/f(x)$ transform: spatial domain to spatial frequency time domain; time–time frequency domain; and phase domain to phase frequency domain.
   - Derivation by the $g(x) = \partial f(x)/\partial x$ transform:
     —time to speed,
     —color–color differences,
     —signal level to differential level,
     —spectral value to spectral derivative.

- Nonlinear projections through a structuring element onto which x is projected:
  —closed area to skeleton mapping (Serra, 1982),
  —region to boundary mapping (Serra, 1982).
- Quaternion operations for time-dependent entities.
- Chromaticity triangle (quotient operations), by the $x = \alpha c_1 + \beta c_3$ transform (Ohta, 1985).

Level 2. **In the fused graph G, projections are identical to the selection of graph cut sets, or cycles, onto which other nodes are mapped.**

Level 3. **In the semantic rule set M after fusion, a projection corresponds to a filter enabled by propagating the same set of constraint rules through all of the rules in M, thus resulting in a constrained unification.**

Remark. **The most obvious form for Level 1 projection operations by linear mappings are the overlay operations:**

- visible/IR overlay,
- visible/radar overlay,
- multispectral/map overlay,
- IR/UV overlay, etc.

These types of projections are carried out by using display units with several video input channels, to which the same synchronization signal is applied.

5. EXAMPLES

It is difficult to present here a complete overview of sensor fusion applications, and also to present in great detail an example of the above knowledge representation. But we will discuss a few cases, of entirely different nature, to relate the above concepts and mathematical formulations to applications.

Example 4. Integrated circuit (IC) inspection: Pau (1983, 1985) describes a novel approach to integrated testing of ICs which combines imaging inspection with electrical testing. This patented process can be briefly described as follows. The IC is subject to two sets of active stimuli:

- a narrow beam of radiation, typically a laser or ion beam of known wavelength, modulation, amplitude, and phase.
- electrical voltage stimuli coming from a tester.

It is also the object of three sets of sensed information.

- Sensor 1: imaging the IC at another wavelength in order to give a signal at each position related to the emittance at the detection wavelength; the attribute vector X_1 is given in Example 1, Section 3.1 for any point in the image.
- Sensor 2: current sensor applied to the output signal, which is the sum of the test stimuli and of the location dependent beam induced current; the attribute vector X_2 gives the currents measured at a finite number of probing points, as just defined.
- Sensor 3: CAD layout and position dependent properties of the circuit; the attribute vector X_3 is given by (x_1, x_2, x_4, x_7) in Example 1, Section 3.1 for each cell in the layout.

The knowledge representation of Section 3 then provides the following total circuit description, after fusion by the procedures of Section 4 (see Figure 6.4).

- Level 1: position-dependent emissivity, induced current, phase shift, wavelength shift.
- Level 2: active layered patterns, signal shapes; labels are: sizes, tolerances, alignment, and signal values.
- Level 3: defect propagation rules, rules with open circuits, and isolation structure rules; the attribute values are: voltage, capacity, intensity, and distributed resistance along the paths.

The matching operations performed are (see Table 6.3):

- subgraph matching in the current visible images (Pau, 1983)
- matching strings of correct conductor pads with the CAD layout,
- fuzzy matching, where the class membership value is dictated by the process tolerance and imaging resolution (Pau, 1983).

The query/inference operations performed are (see Table 6.3):

- merge lists of nodes at Level 2 for Level 1 features located at same physical position,

```
Level 1        o   Vector X in spaces   E(i)
                   —> Passive E(1) : wavelength shift, position depen-
                                     dent emissivity
                   —> Active  E(2) : induced current
                   —> Passive E(3) : IC layout
               o   Euclidean metrics in E(1)  E(2)  E(3)
```

```
Level 2        List L_i (X) = L_i^1 , L_i^2 , L_i^3

               L_1^1 : observed patterns    L_2^1 : sizes, tolerances,
                                                    alignment
               L_1^2 : signal shapes        L_2^2 : signal values
               L_1^3 : CAD patterns         L_2^3 = L_2^1
```

```
Level 3        Rules N_i(x) representing the context in M_i
               o   Rules:  (M_1,M_2) : defect propagation rules
                           (M_1,M_2) : rules with open circuits
                           (M_1,M_3) : isolation structure rules
               o   Labels: M_2 : voltage, capacity, intensity,
                                 distributed resistance
```

Figure 6.4. Sensor fusion knowledge representation (K): IC inspection case.

- merge the Level 3 vocabularies for syntactic descriptions of the image, current values, and CAD layout.
- unify rules to find missing pads, out of order connections, etc., by pure backtracking.

The projection operations are (see Table 6.3):

- image of the current density at any point of the circuit for any given logical test state.
- overlay of the above with the circuit image at another wavelength,

Table 6.3. Sensor attribute fusion (C)

JSE	FUSION (B) QUERY INFERENCE	MATCHING RECOGNITION UNDERSTANDING	PROJECTION DISPLAY OVERLAY
LEVEL 1: x_i	Translate Rotate Combination metrics Warping	Neighborhood operations Clustering Entropy minimization Orthographic projections	Linear projections Change of scale Derivation Structuring elements Chromaticity
LEVEL 2: $L_i(x)$	Merge lists of nodes Graph reduction	Subgraph matching (symmetric difference) Combinatorial search of graph elements	Cut sets Cycles
LEVEL 3: $N_i(x)$	Merge vocabularies Unify rules Insert rules Delete rules Truncate rules	-Match strings -Context dependency -Ranking of occurences by co occurence matrix -Fuzzy match	Constraint propagation

- photoluminescence image of the circuit to reveal substrate defects when no voltage is applied by the tester.

Once the knowledge has been acquired according to the fused knowledge representation, this representation $(X_i, L_i(X), N_i(X))$ for $i = 1, 2, 3$ can be evaluated through a set of diagnostic and defect detection rules supplemented by test stimuli generation. Later, knowledge-based processing can be used for acceptance/rejection testing of the circuits and to provide feedback to the manufacturing process.

Example 4. Object imaging for identification and classification. The sensor data in this example are Doppler processed interferometric measurements, derived from a set of different identical sensors at two instants (for detecting the shift). The received signals from the scatterer comprising the object are processed at Level 1 to obtain estimates of the net Doppler shift producing velocities resulting from the respective motions of the radar/interferometric platforms and the object.

Three spaces E_i are used for fused projection operations:

E_1—range/azimuth angle projection,
E_2—azimuth angle/elevation profile projection,
E_3—range/elevation profile projection.

These three spaces are scaled jointly.

Matching rules in the fused space are used for object classification:

- clustering of targets in the product space (range × azimuth × elevation × time-interval),
- derivation of binary skeleton image in all three spaces E_i, and matching of these skeletons by subgraph matching.

The query/inference operations performed are:

- combination metrics to sort targets by type and location jointly.
- rule-based unification to find targets with similar properties in either spaces E_i.

6. CONCLUSIONS

Original and efficient solutions to a number of tasks may be found by sensor fusion. This approach is especially useful when no sensor alone gives good features, or only does so at the expense of heavy processing and the use of context information. Knowledge representation techniques and knowledge processing are indispensible for these sensor fusion tasks, and it is suggested that a hierarchical decomposition (fusing, matching, and projecting) is useful. The formal validation or proof of this approach cannot yet be given due to the lack of general evaluation criteria which can be aggregated amongst nonindependent information sources.

REFERENCES

Alvey Directorate. (1984). IKBS applied to sensor data processing, Minutes Alvey IKBS interest group meeting 17, October 1984. London: Alvey Directorate.

Chiu, S.L., Morley, D.J., & Martin, J.F. (1986). Sensor data fusion on a parallel processor. *Proceedings of the IEEE Conference on Robotics and Automation* (pp. 1629–1633). San Francisco, CA.

Drazovich, R.J. (1983). Sensor fusion in tactical warfare. AIAA Paper No. 83-2398, American Institute of Aeronautics and Space.

Fu, K.S. (1974). *Syntactic methods in pattern recognition.* New York: Academic Press.

Giannesini, F., Kanoui, H., & Pasero, R. (1987). *Prolog.* Reading, MA: Addison Wesley.

Harmon, S.Y., Bianchini, G.L., & Pinz, B.E. (1986). Sensor fusion through a distributed blackboard. *Proceedings of the IEEE Conference on Robotics and Automation* (pp. 1449–1454). San Francisco, CA.

Henderson, T.C., Allen, P.K., Mitiche, A., Durrant-Whyte, H., & Snyder, W. (Eds.). (1987, February). *Workshop on multisensor integration in manufacturing automation* (Technical Report UUCS-87-006). Snowbird, UT: University of Utah, Snowbird, Department of Computer Sciences.

Kak, A., & Chen, S.S. (Eds.). (1987). *Spatial reasoning and multi-sensor fusion.* Los Altos, CA: Morgan Kaufman.

La Jeunesse, T.J. (1986, September). Sensor fusion. *Defense Science and Engineering*, pp. 21–31.

Lyons, D., & Arbib, M. (1985). *A task level model of distributed computation for sensory based control* (COINS-TR-85-30). Amherst, MA: University of Massachusetts.

Nii, P.H. (1986). Blackboard systems. *AI Magazine, 7*(2/3), 38–53/82–106.

Ohta, Y. (1985). *Knowledge based interpretation of outdoor natural colour scenes.* Boston: Pitman.

Pau, L. (1981). Fusion of multisensor data in pattern recognition. In J. Kittler, K.S. Fu, & L. Pau (Eds.), *Pattern recognition theory and applications, NATO ASI series.* Dordrecht, The Netherlands: D. Reidel.

Pau, L. (1983). Integrated testing and algorithms for visual inspection of integrated circuits. *IEEE Transactions on Pattern Analysis and Machine Intelligence, PAMI-5,* 602–608.

Pau, L. (1985). Image understanding of defects in GaAs integrated circuits: Experiments with laser beam induced currents. In J. Bonnafé (Ed.), *Defect recognition and image processing in III-V compounds.* Amsterdam: Elsevier.

Pau, L. (1987). Knowledge representation approaches in sensor fusion. *Proceedings of the IFAC World Congress—1987.* Munich, Federal Republic of Germany.

Pau, L., Xiao, S., & Westphal, C. (1989). A knowledge based sensor fusion editor. In J. Aggarwal (Ed.), *Multisensor fusion, ASI series.* Heidelberg, FRG: Springer-Verlag.

Rao, A.R., & Jain, R. (1988). Knowledge representation and control in computer vision systems. *IEEE Expert, 3,* 64–79.

Serra, J. (1982). *Image analysis and mathematical morphology.* New York: Academic.

Wong, A.K.C., & Goldfarb, L. (1982). Pattern recognition of relational structures. In J. Kittler, K.S. Fu, & L.F. Pau (Eds.), *Pattern recognition theory and applications* (pp. 157–176). Boston: D. Reidel.

7
MKS: A Multisensor Kernel System*

Thomas C. Henderson and
Wu S. Fai

The Multisensor Kernel System (MKS) is proposed as a means for multisensor integration and data acquisition. This system is being developed in the context of a robot workstation equipped with various types of sensors, including tactile sensors mounted on a dexterous hand and cameras. Specific goals are to:

1. Develop a suitable low-level representation of raw data and/or features extracted from the raw data of the various sensors,
2. Provide a method for efficient reconfiguration of the sensor system in terms of "logical sensors" (see Chapter 4) which map onto physical sensors and computation, and
3. Provide a basis for 3-D object modeling techniques which allow the derivation of constraints useful in controlling and directing the acquisition of data for object recognition.

---

* This work was supported in part by the System Development Foundation. The original range data for the object shown in Figure 7.14 were obtained with a laser range finder developed by Francois Germain at INRIA (l'Institut National de Recherche en Informatique et en Automatique) located in Roquencourt, France.

1. INTRODUCTION

The long-term goal is the development of a flexible and programmable robot workstation involving several sensors and several robot arms and hands. The object of such a robot workstation is the automatic inspection or assembly of parts. Clearly such a system requires a capacity for planning actions, modeling objects, and integrating vast amounts of sensor data to those ends. Therefore, a prerequisite to intelligent action is a method for representing and integrating data from several different types of sensors.

Various 2-D low-level representations have been proposed by workers in the image analysis community; however, we propose the *spatial proximity graph* as a means of describing 3-D spatial relations between features, and a sensory data protocol which allows for efficient integration of nonvisual information and features. The significance of such a representation is that it allows uniform handling of data from diverse types of sensor systems, and that given an efficient representational scheme, it allows more rapid exploitation of the sensor data for object identification and manipulation.

Such a system should be easily reconfigurable (perhaps even automatically). Thus, a mechanism will be provided for defining logical sensors which may involve several physical sensors and some amount of computation; for example, a "range finder" can be defined in terms of two cameras and a program which computes stereo disparity (see Section 4.1 of Chapter 4). Then the sensor system can be compiled or used interpretively once all the logical and physical sensors have been defined.

Many methods exist for modeling 3-D objects, and the Multisensor Kernel system supports a wide range of 3-D object modeling techniques. Such high-level models allow the automatic derivation of constraints which can then be used to control the acquisition of data. This provides a mechanism to limit the amount of sensor data acquired, and thus reduces the amount of computation necessary to identify objects. Although the methods proposed here are developed in the context of a robot workstation, the results will be applicable to any multisensor system, including distributed sensing systems, situation assessment systems, etc.

Multiprocessor and multisensor systems are being proposed to solve a wide range of problems. In particular, distributed sensing systems and general robot workstations require real-time processing of information from visual, auditory, tactile and other types of sensors. Three major issues must be addressed:

1. Low-level representation of the sensory data,
2. High-level specification and organization of the sensor systems, and
3. High-level control of processors and sensors.

We propose the *spatial proximity graph* as a low-level representation of sensory data from diverse sources and use this as the basis for high-level organization and control over the acquisition of data. The notion of a logical (or abstract) sensor allows for a flexible hardware/software mix in terms of a multisensor system and permits a simple method of reconfiguration whenever logical or physical sensors are added to or removed from the system.

The first major goal is to provide a mechanism for the integration of data available from different sensors into a coherent low-level representation of the 3-D world. Such a representation is crucial to the successful application of multisensor systems, and in particular, robot technology. Shneier, Nagalia, Albus, and Haar (1982) argue that "the use of easily acquired information from a number of sources can lead more easily to understanding a scene than can exhaustive analysis of an image from a single source." Although their work dealt only with visual information, we heartily concur in principle and propose the spatial proximity graph (see Section 2.1) as a structuring mechanism for the integration of data from different sensors.

The second major goal is to provide a simple, yet complete, method for (re)configuring a multisensor system. We propose the logical sensor (see Chapter 4) as a key notion toward this end. A logical sensor either maps directly onto a physical sensor, or provides a description of how data from one or more physical sensors is combined to produce the desired data. (See Foley & Van Dam, 1982; Pfaff, Kuhlmann, & Hanusa, 1982; Rosenthal, Michener, Pfaff, Kessener, & Sabin, 1982 for a similar approach to computer graphics systems.) Ultimately, such logical sensors could be implemented in special hardware (a "sensor engine").

The third major goal is to provide a context in which constraints, both physical and logical, can be brought to bear to reduce the amount of computation required to solve problems. A prominent example of a multisensor system is the *distributed sensing system* for situation assessment (Wesson, Hayes-Roth, Burge, Stasz, & Sunshine, 1981). Distributed sensing systems consist of several independent stations interacting to produce an assessment of the activity being monitored collectively by the stations. Most research in this area is directed toward organizing the information flow between stations so as to achieve an efficient and successful interpretation of the sensed data (see also Smith, 1981). Usually the stations transmit reports or evaluations of their own data rather than the raw data themselves. Thus, there is a need for a high-level model to provide an interpretation of the various patterns of information provided by the sensors, and a mechanism for controlling the acquisition of data. Several high-level modeling methods will be investigated, including standard feature models and structural models. Although the system organization and modeling capabilities proposed here are generally applicable to multisensor systems, the focus of this proposal is the design of a multisensor robot workstation. In particular, the system is presented in terms of the integration of visual and tactile data toward the goal of forming a model of the 3-D objects within the range of a robot arm.

2. ACQUISITION AND ORGANIZATION OF 3-D DATA

The Multisensor Kernel System (MKS) must coordinate the active control of several sensors—for example, turn a sensor off or on, aim a camera, etc., and integrate the data from the various sensors into a coherent and useful description of the world. Figure 7.1 shows the flow of data and control in such a system, where C_1 to C_n are the controllers or actuators for the sensor systems S_1 to S_n, respectively. In this section, we describe the organization of incoming data into the low-level representation.

Each sensor system, S_i, in Figure 7.1 has an associated controller, C_i; for example, a camera may be aimed, focused, or have the shutter speed changed. A sensor system may have several components:

- a camera system: a camera and a light source,
- a laser ranger finder: a laser, mirror system, diode arrays, and optics.

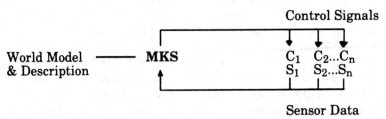

Figure 7.1. MKS: Multisensor Kernel System.

That is, a sensor system consists of all the sensor components and the associated controller.

The prototype system consists of two sensors: a camera and a dexterous hand; these provide visual and tactile data, respectively. Visual information arrives as digital images which must be processed, whereas the tactile information is provided by a multifingered dexterous hand currently under development by the University of Utah Center for Biomedical Design in conjunction with the MIT AI laboratory. This is a four-finger dexterous hand which includes touch sensors on palm and finger surfaces. The contact sensors are based on the use of birefringent materials in conjunction with optical fibers (Jacobsen, personal communication). However, other contact sensors such as that described by Hillis (1982) or Raibert and Tanner (1982) may also be used as they become available.

In general, any set of sensors can be used, and the system is organized such that each sensor contributes information independently of the other sensors. However, as will be described later, a high-level model is used to control the acquisition of data so that as time goes on, fewer data are demanded from the sensors. Constraints from the already processed data control the sensors' acquisition of new data.

2.1. Spatial Proximity Graphs

In the context of digital image analysis, various schemes have been proposed for organizing properties or features recovered from 2-D images, for example, Marr's primal sketch (1975) the intrinsic images of Barrow and Tennenbaum (1978) and in a more limited context, the region adjacency graph of Pavlidis (1977). However, all of these representations were developed with 2-D images in mind, and we propose a more general 3-D organization called the *spatial proximity graph*.

The spatial proximity graph provides a means for organizing information about the 3-D world. In particular, the approach is to:

1. obtain raw sensory data,
2. extract features from the data and the 3-D locations of these features, and
3. dtermine the spatial relationships between the features.

The nodes of the spatial proximity graph correspond to the positions in 3-space of the features extracted from the raw sensory data. Nodes are linked by an edge if they are within some prespecified distance. This then provides a means for organizing information from different sources. Moreover, high-level analysis can be performed on this graph (Henderson, 1982).

Thus, given a set of sensors, we assume that each sensor provides raw data in the form of two pieces of information. Namely, each datum from a sensor consists of a feature and a location (in 3-space) of that feature. In this manner, data from various sensors can be treated uniformly. This data protocol places an additional burden on some types of sensors (e.g., cameras) but for most sensors, techniques are available to determine the required information, and for many sensors (e.g., laser range finders, tactile sensors, etc.) the information is directly available.

The spatial proximity graph has been studied in the context of 3-D range data (Henderson & Bhanu, 1982). For example, consider the surface points of the synthetic cube shown in Figure 7.2. The spatial proximity graph (SPG) for those points is given in Figure 7.3. Figures 7.4 and 7.5 show the same process for a set of points obtained with a laser range finder used to scan an industrial object. There are about 2000 point samples. Various views of the object points and the spatial proximity graph are shown in Figures 7.6 through 7.13. The original object is shown in Figure 7.14.

The spatial proximity graph is a graph G, having a distinct node for each distinct feature location. An edge exists between two nodes if either of the two nodes has the other as one of its m-nearest neighbors, for some small m. If the features are not used in forming the key, then the spatial proximity graph imposes a direct Euclidean nearest neighbors on the features; for example, such a graph can be used to recover planar faces approximating the data when the features are simply surface points (Henderson, 1982).

On the other hand, if the features are encoded as part of the key, then an appropriate choice of the feature values in the feature space dimension can lead to tremendous gains in object recognition efficien-

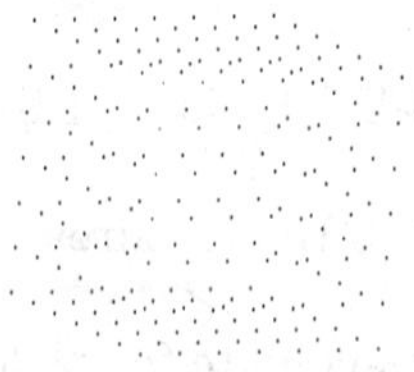

Figure 7.2. Surface Points of Cube.

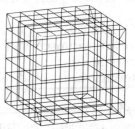

Figure 7.3. SPG for Cube.

MKS: A Multisensor Kernel System   145

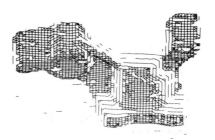

Figure 7.4. 0 Degree View of Surface Points.

Figure 7.5. 0 Degree View of SPG.

Figure 7.6. 85 Degree View of Surface Points.

Figure 7.7. 85 Degree View of SPG.

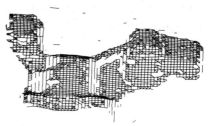

Figure 7.8. 180 Degree View of Surface Points.

Figure 7.9. 180 Degree View of SPG.

Figure 7.10. Bottom View of Surface Points.

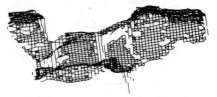
Figure 7.11. Bottom View of SPG.

cy. For example, if linear edges and flat surfaces are features assigned a large positive value in the first key dimension, whereas curved edges and surfaces are assigned a large negative value, then the spatial proximity graph of a scene containing a sphere and a cube, for example, will be disconnected. Obviously, one would like to take advantage of this whenever possible.

This method of representation seems well suited to organizing multisensor data. Intuitively, the spatial proximity graph makes explicit the neighborhood relations of selected features extracted from the data.

2.2. Feature Selection

Feature extraction plays a prominent role in image analysis, and there is every indication that it will do so for tactile sensors, also. Features range from the intrinsic characteristics found in images (edges, reflectance, depth, etc.) to physical characteristics of a surface (temperature, smoothness, compressability).

Features are often used to characterize objects, and as time efficiency is of utmost importance, features are usually chosen so as to provide an adequate description which can be obtained cheaply and reliably. Discovering useful features will no doubt be an outcome of this project, but such features as edges, surface texture, and surface shape will be

Figure 7.12. Top View of Surface Points.

Figure 7.13. Top View of SPG.

Figure 7.14. Original Object.

used initially. We view feature extraction as a distinct step performed on the raw sensor data, but obviously a "smart" sensor might provide such features directly.

2.3. Feature Organization

The cost is prohibitive to try to form the spatial proximity graph directly from the sensor data. Therefore, as a first step, the feature–location pairs are organized into a special tree structure (called the *kd-tree*) which can be built in Order($n$log$n$) time for n keys, and which allows the m-nearest neighbors of any given key to be found in Order(log$n$) time complexity. See Freidman, Bentley, and Finkel (1977) for a detailed explanation of *kd*-trees. Basically, a *kd*-tree is a binary tree of k-dimensional keys which is organized such that at each subdivision step, the data are split at the median along the axis having greatest spread in vector element values along that axis. In our application the feature–location pairs are used as the keys of the tree, and the spatial proximity graph is built by finding for each node the m-nearest neighbors. This approach has already been studied in the context of feature encoding for satellite imagery (Henderson & Triendl, 1981a, 1986b).

3. CONFIGURING THE MULTISENSOR KERNEL SYSTEM

The Multisensor Kernel System (MKS) permits the specification of:

1. both physical and logical sensors,
2. the meaning of the low-level representation in terms of any particular high-level representation, and
3. high-level models.

We will consider the requirements of each of these capabilities. Figure 7.15 shows how physical and logical sensors are specified. Physical sensors are defined by parameters associated with the individual sensor of some known class (e.g., CCD array, TV camera, tactile sensor, etc.). Moreover, some indication of operationality of the sensor should be provided. Logical (or abstract) sensors are defined in terms of physical devices and algorithms on their data, for example, an "edge image" sensor or "surface normal" sensor. It may be possible that logical sen-

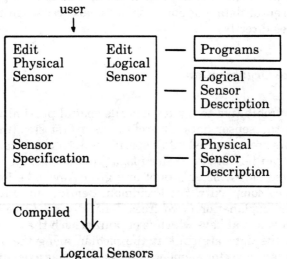

Figure 7.15. Sensor Specification.

sors can be defined in terms of other logical sensors. The compilation process involves producing a process which carries out the required computation on the data from the desired physical sensors.

The low-level model must be specified in that meanings must be provided for the elements of the k-dimensional vectors stored in the kd-tree. This basically amounts to formatting instructions (see Figure 7.16). Moreover, the number of neighbors and distance thresholds in the spatial proximity graph must be defined in terms of these meanings. For example, if one sensor returns (x,y,z) location and a measure of the "edgeness" at that location, while another sensor gives a measure of surface curvature at a point, then positions in the vector must be assigned for the various features measured. Another use of the kd-tree data structure is simply to organize locations where features are detected, that is (x,y,z) positions, and associate features measured at those locations with the position vectors. User-defined constants and functions necessary to build the kd-tree must be specified, too, such as the bucket size of the terminals.

Finally, the high-level models must be specified, along with some mechanism for matching the models to descriptions derived from the sensor data (see Figure 7.17). In principle any high-level modeling method could be used, but it is reasonable to choose methods that can better exploit the low-level representation. For example, any method based on the graphical representation of spatial relations between the features could correspond directly to the spatial proximity graph.

Thus, the system is configured by defining the sensors, the low-level, and the high-level representations, and the preceeding paragraphs have given the compile-time view of the system. The goal, though, is

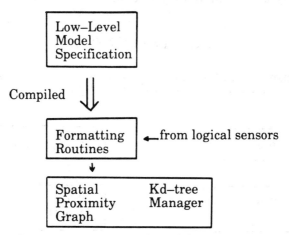

Figure 7.16. Low-Level Model Specification.

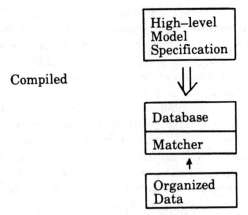

Figure 7.17. High-Level Model Specification.

the performance of some task. Our view is that the task ties the system together as shown in Figure 7.18. Thus, the given task description defines when new sensor data is required and how it should be obtained. Matching models to descriptions can take place in the task or can be incorporated directly into the sensor system. Based on the results of the analysis of the data, objects (or the environment) can be manipulated.

Although the development of task definition languages and high-level model techniques are important research topics, the main goal of this chapter is to provide a coherent and efficient method for obtaining a useful, low-level representation which can serve as the basis for a wide variety of such high-level systems.

4. HIGH-LEVEL MODELS

A wide range of high-level modeling techniques are available for use, and these divide naturally into two classes: feature models and struc-

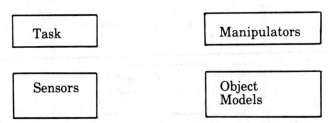

Figure 7.18. Relation of Task to Multisensor Kernel System.

tural models. Feature models involve mapping sensed data (or perhaps restricted portions of the data) into a single number or a vector which then represents the data, whereas structural methods provide a description of the parts of an object and the relations (usually spatial) between the parts.

Most of the current industrial vision systems model objects in terms of global features of objects (or regions), such as area, number of holes, hole area, etc. An object model is simply a set of feature values, and an unknown object is identified by how similar its feature measurements are to the reference values. This form of object modeling is supported quite easily by the MKS approach; namely, a logical sensor returns the location and feature vector of any object detected in the image (this generalizes to nonimage type sensors, too). Matching can be performed by standard methods, or the reference vectors can be stored as a *kd*-tree, and then matching merely requires a query on the tree.

Obviously, MKS also provides the basis for structural modeling. Features are detected and organized locally; they can then be analyzed directly (as suggested by Bolles and Cain, 1982), or they can be further grouped (for example, from surface points to faces) and then analyzed. We have investigated several high-level modeling techniques in terms of the MKS, and in particular, feature models and Hough shape models, both with great success. We are now exploring the use of constraint mechanisms for high-level modeling in the context of the MKS system.

REFERENCES

Barrow, H., & Tennenbaum, J. (1978, April). *Recovering Intrinsic Scene Characteristics from Images* (Tech. Rep. 157). Menlo Park, CA: Artificial Intelligence Center, SRI International.

Bolles, R.C., & Cain, R.A. (1982). Recognizing and locating partially visible objects: The local-feature-focus method. *International Journal of Robotics Research, 1*(3), 57–82.

Foley, J.D., & Van Dam, A. (1982). *Fundamentals of interactive computer graphics*. Reading, MA: Addison Wesley.

Friedman, J.H., Bentley, J.L., & Finkel, R.A. (1977). An algorithm for finding best matches in logarithmic expected time. *ACM Transactions on Mathematical Software, 3*(3), 209–226.

Henderson, T.C. (1982). An efficient segmentation method for range data. *Proceedings of the SPIE Conference on Robot Vision* (pp. 46–47). Arlington, VA.

Henderson, T.C., & Bhanu, B. (1982). Three-point seed method for the extraction of planer faces from range data. *Proceedings of the IEEE Workshop on Industrial Applications of Machine Vision* (pp. 181–186). Research Triangle Park, NC.

Henderson, T., & Triendl, E. (1982a). Storing feature tree descriptions as 2-D trees. *Proceedings of the Pattern Recognition and Image Processing Conference.* (pp. 555–556). Las Vegas, NV.

Henderson, T., & Triendl, E. (1982b). The k-d tree representation of edge descriptions. *Proceedings of the International Conference on Pattern Recognition.*

Hillis, D. (1982). A high-resolution image touch sensor. *International Journal of Robotics Research, 1*(2), 33–34.

Marr, D. (1975, December). *Early processing of visual information* (AI Memo 450). Cambridge, MA: MIT, AI Lab.

Pavilidis, T. (1977). *Structural pattern recognition.* New York: Springer Verlag.

Pfaff, G., Kuhlmann, H., & Hanusa, H. (1982). Constructing user interfaces based on logical input devices. *Computer, 15*(11), 62–69.

Raibert, M., & Tanner, R. (1982). VLSI implementation of tactile sensing. *Proceedings of the 12th International Conference on Industrial Robot Technology* (pp. 417–426).

Rosenthal, D.S., Michener, J.C., Pfaff, G., Kessener, R., & Sabin, M. (1982). The detailed semantics of graphics input devices. *Computer Graphics, 16*(3), 33–38.

Shneier, M., Nagalia, S., Albus, J., & Haar, R. (1982). Visual feedback for robot control. *Proceedings of the Workshop on Industrial Applications of Industrial Vision* (pp. 232–236).

Smith, R.G. (1981). *A framework for distributed problem solving.* Ann Arbor, MI: UMI Research Press.

Wesson, R., Hayes-Roth, F., Burge, J.W., Stasz, C., & Sunshine, C. (1981). Network structures for distributed situation assessment. *IEEE Transactions on Systems, Man, and Cybernetics,* SMC-11(1), 5–23.

Part II
Multisensor Fusion

8
Introduction to Part II

Ren C. Luo and
Michael G. Kay

Part II describes different methods that have been proposed for multisensor fusion. Discussion of additional fusion methods relating to specific applications is included in Parts III through V of the book. This chapter and the remaining chapters of Part II are organized based on the four different levels of multisensor fusion introduced in Section 1.3 of Chapter 1, namely, the signal, pixel, feature, and symbol levels of fusion. A number of different methods of signal-, pixel-, and symbol-level fusion are surveyed in this chapter. Feature-level fusion is discussed in Chapters 12 and 13 of this part, in Chapter 21 of Part IV, and in Part III where the subject is object recognition. (Feature-level fusion plays a fundamental role in most methods used to measure and recognize objects using multiple sensors.)

Clark and Yuille (1990) have used a Bayesian formulation of sensory processing to provide a mathematical foundation upon which multisensor fusion algorithms can be created and analyzed. Fusion algorithms are classified into two general types, distinguished by the manner in which information in the form of solution constraints is combined to obtain an overall solution to the multisensory processing problem: In "weakly coupled" algorithms the operation of the different sensory processing modules is not affected by the fusion process; in "strongly coupled" algorithms the output of a module does interact with the other modules and effects their operation. Examples are given of data fusion applied to feature-level stereo, binocular and monocular depth cue, and shape from shading algorithms.

1. SIGNAL-LEVEL METHODS

Multisensor fusion at the signal level can be considered as an estimation process when the signals from each sensor are modeled as random variables. Optimal estimation or fusion methods can be developed if certain assumptions concerning the nature of the sensory data are satisfied. Most methods of signal-level fusion make explicit assumptions concerning the nature of the sensory data. The most common assumptions include the use of a measurement model for the information from each sensor that includes a statistically independent additive Gaussian error or noise term (e.g., location data), and an assumption of statistical independence between the error terms for each sensor. Many of the differences between signal-level fusion methods presented in this section and in Chapters 9, 10 and 11 center on the particular techniques (e.g., calibration, thresholding) used for transforming raw sensory data into a form so that the above assumptions become valid and a mathematically tractable fusion method can result. Richardson and Marsh provide a thorough discussion of these assumptions in Chapter 9. Two different methods of signal-level fusion are presented in Chapters 10 and 11 by Luo, Lin, and Sherp, and Nakamura and Xu, respectively.

1.1. Weighted Average

One of the simplest and most intuitive methods of signal-level fusion is to take a weighted average of redundant information provided by a group of sensors and use this as the fused value. Whereas this method allows for the real-time processing of dynamic low-level data, in most cases the Kalman filter is preferred because it provides a method that is nearly equal in processing requirements and, in contrast to a weighted average, it results in an estimate for the fused data that is optimal in a statistical sense. A weighted average has been used for multisensor fusion in the mobile robot HILARE (see Section 4 of Chapter 19), after first thresholding the sensory information to eliminate spurious measurements.

The weighted average of n sensor measurements x_i with weights $0 \leq w_i \leq 1$ is

$$\bar{x} = \sum_{i=1}^{n} w_i x_i,$$

where $\Sigma_i w_i = 1$ and $w_i = 0$ if x_i is not within some specified thresholds. The weights can be used to account for the differences in accuracy between sensors, and a moving average can be used to fuse together a sequence of measurements from a single sensor so that the more recent measurements are given a greater weight.

1.2. Kalman Filter

The Kalman filter (see Maybeck, 1979, for a general introduction) is used in a number of multisensor systems when it is necessary to fuse dynamic low-level redundant data in real time. The filter uses the statistical characteristics of a measurement model to recursively determine estimates for fused data that are optimal in a statistical sense. If the system can be described with a linear model and both the system and sensor error can be modeled as white Gaussian noise, the Kalman filter will provide unique statistically optimal estimates for the fused data. The recursive nature of the filter makes it appropriate for use in systems without large data storage capabilities. Examples of the use of the filter for multisensor fusion include: object measurement using sequences of images from a sensor (see Section 1 of Chapter 16), robot navigation (see Section 4.6 of Chapter 19 and Chapter 21), multitarget tracking (see Section 4 of Chapter 22 and Chapter 24), inertial navigation (see Section 5 of Chapter 22), and remote sensing (see Section 6 of Chapter 22). In some of these applications the "U-D (unit upper triangular and diagonal matrix) covariance factorization filter" or the "extended Kalman filter" is used in place of the conventional Kalman filter if, respectively, numerical instability or the assumption of approximate linearity for the system model presents potential problems. An "adaptive Kalman filter" can be used if the parameters of the filter are not initially known. Durrant-Whyte, Rao, and Hu (1990) have used the extended Kalman filter in a decentralized fusion architecture, and Ayache and Faugeras (1989; see also Chapter 21, this volume) have used it for building and updating the three-dimensional world model of a mobile robot.

The measurements from a group of n sensors can be fused together using a Kalman filter to provide both an estimate of the current state of a system and a prediction of the future state of the system. The state being estimated may, for example, correspond to the current location of a mobile robot, the position and velocity of an object in the environment, features extracted from sensory data (e.g., edges in an image), or the actual measurements themselves. Given a system represented as a linear discrete Markov process, the "state-space model"

$$\mathbf{x}(t+1) = \mathbf{\Phi}(t)\mathbf{x}(t) + \mathbf{B}(t)\mathbf{u}(t) + \mathbf{G}(t)\mathbf{w}(t)$$

and the "measurement model"

$$\mathbf{z}(t) = \mathbf{H}(t)\mathbf{x}(t) + \mathbf{v}(t)$$

can be used to describe the system (see Figure 8.1),
where **x** : m state vector
$\quad\quad\quad$ **Φ** : $m \times m$ state transition matrix
$\quad\quad\quad$ **B** : $m \times p$ input transmission matrix
$\quad\quad\quad$ **u** : p input vector (e.g., position of sensor platform)
$\quad\quad\quad$ **G** : $m \times q$ process noise transmission matrix
$\quad\quad\quad$ **w** : q process noise vector
$\quad\quad\quad$ **z** : n measurement vector
$\quad\quad\quad$ **H** : $n \times m$ measurement matrix
$\quad\quad\quad$ **v** : n measurement noise vector.

The **w** and **v** are uncorrelated discrete-time zero-mean white Gaussian noise sequences with covariance kernels

$$E\{\mathbf{w}(t_i)\mathbf{w}^T(t_j)\} = \mathbf{Q}(t_i)\delta_{ij}$$
$$E\{\mathbf{v}(t_i)\mathbf{v}^T(t_j)\} = \mathbf{R}(t_i)\delta_{ij},$$

where $E\{\cdot\}$ denotes the expectation operator and δ_{ij} the Kronecker delta function.

When all of the parameters (the matrices **Φ, B, G, H, Q,** and **R**) of the models are known, the optimal filtering equations are:

$$\hat{\mathbf{x}}(t \mid t) = \hat{\mathbf{x}}(t-1) + \mathbf{K}(t)[\mathbf{z}(t) - \mathbf{H}(t)\hat{\mathbf{x}}(t \mid t-1)]$$
$$\hat{\mathbf{x}}(t+1 \mid t) = \mathbf{\Phi}(t)\hat{\mathbf{x}}(t \mid t) + \mathbf{B}(t)\mathbf{u}(t)$$

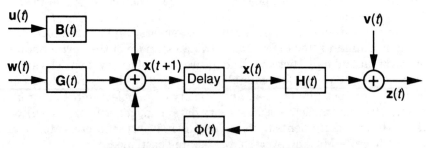

Figure 8.1. Kalman filter block diagram.

where $\hat{\mathbf{x}}(t \mid t)$ is the estimate of $\mathbf{x}(t)$ based on the measurements $\{\mathbf{z}(0), \ldots, \mathbf{z}(t)\}$, and $\hat{\mathbf{x}}(t+1 \mid t)$ is the prediction of $\mathbf{x}(t+1)$ based on the measurements $\{\mathbf{z}(0), \ldots, \mathbf{z}(t)\}$. The $m \times n$ matrix $\mathbf{K}$ is the "Kalman filter gain" and is defined as

$$\mathbf{K}(t) = \mathbf{P}(t \mid t-1)\mathbf{H}^T(t)[\mathbf{H}(t)\mathbf{P}(t \mid t-1)\mathbf{H}^T(t) + \mathbf{R}(t)]^{-1},$$

where $\mathbf{P}(t \mid t-1) = E\{(\mathbf{x}(t) - \hat{\mathbf{x}}(t \mid t-1))(\mathbf{x}(t) - \hat{\mathbf{x}}(t \mid t-1))^T\}$ is the $m \times m$ conditional covariance matrix of the error is predicting $\mathbf{x}(t)$ and is determined using

$$\mathbf{P}(t+1 \mid t) = \mathbf{\Phi}(t)\mathbf{P}(t \mid t)\mathbf{\Phi}^T(t) + \mathbf{G}(t)\mathbf{Q}(t)\mathbf{G}^T(t),$$

where

$$\mathbf{P}(t \mid t) = \mathbf{P}(t \mid t-1) - \mathbf{K}(t)\mathbf{H}(t)\mathbf{P}(t \mid t-1).$$

The initial conditions for the recursion are given by $\hat{\mathbf{x}}(0 \mid 0) = \hat{\mathbf{x}}_0$ and $\mathbf{P}(0 \mid 0) = \mathbf{P}_0$.

The application of Kalman filtering for multisensor fusion can be illustrated using the object recognition example given in Section 1.3 of Chapter 1. Sensors 1 and 2, $\mathbf{S}_1$ and $\mathbf{S}_2$, provide redundant information relative to each other concerning the shape of the objects to be recognized. The state to be estimated is the shape x of an object and can be assumed to remain constant over time, that is $x(t) = x$ for all t. The shape measurements z_1 and z_2 from $\mathbf{S}_1$ and $\mathbf{S}_2$, respectively, can be modeled as

$$z_1 = x + v_1 \text{ and } z_2 = x + v_2,$$

where v_1 and v_2 are independent zero-mean Gaussian random variables with variances σ_1^2 and σ_2^2, respectively. If the measurements from $\mathbf{S}_1$ and $\mathbf{S}_2$ are available simultaneously, batch processing can be used for fusion, where

$$\mathbf{z} = \begin{bmatrix} z_1 \\ z_2 \end{bmatrix} = \begin{bmatrix} 1 \\ 1 \end{bmatrix} x + \begin{bmatrix} v_1 \\ v_2 \end{bmatrix} = \mathbf{Hx} + \mathbf{v}.$$

If the measurements are available sequentially, recursive processing can be used to update the estimate of x as new measurements become available. Assuming that the measurement from $\mathbf{S}_1$ is available initially, $\hat{\mathbf{x}}_0 = \hat{x}_0 = z_1$ and $\mathbf{P}_0 = P_0 = \sigma_1^2$ can be considered the a priori information available about x before the receipt of the measurement from S_2. When z_2 becomes available, the optimal estimate of x is given by

$$\begin{aligned}
\hat{x} &= \hat{x}_0 + K[z_2 - H\hat{x}_0] \\
&= \hat{x}_0 + P_0 H^T (H P_0 H^T + R)^{-1}[z_2 - H\hat{x}_0] \\
&= z_1 + \sigma_1^2(\sigma_1^2 + \sigma_2^2)^{-1}[z_2 - z_1] \\
&= \frac{\sigma_2^2}{\sigma_1^2 + \sigma_2^2} z_1 + \frac{\sigma_1^2}{\sigma_1^2 + \sigma_2^2} z_2,
\end{aligned}$$

where $\mathbf{R} = \sigma_2^2$.

The variances σ_1^2 and σ_2^2 in the estimate of $\hat{x}$ can be interpreted as providing a means of weighing each measurement z_1 and z_2 so that the measurement with the least variance is given the greatest weight in the fused estimate. The variance of the estimate is $\sigma_1^2 \sigma_2^2/(\sigma_1^2 + \sigma_2^2)$, which is less than the variance of either measurement alone. The reduction in variance is shown in Figure 3(d) of Chapter 1 and represents the reduction in uncertainty due to the fusion of the measurements. $\hat{x}$ can be further updated as additional measurements become available from either sensor.

1.3. Statistical Decision Theory

Zeytinoglu and Mintz (1984, 1988) and McKendall and Mintz (1988) have used statistical decision theory to develop a general two-step method for the fusion of redundant location data from multiple sensors. ("Location data" refers to sensor measurements that are modeled as additive sensor noise translated by the parameter of interest being sensed.) Sensor noise is modeled as the ϵ-contamination of a variety of possible probability distributions. The use of ϵ-contamination in the sensor model serves to increase the robustness of the decision procedure by removing a certain outlying fraction ϵ of the distribution to account for heavy-tailed deviations from the assumed noise distribution which may have been caused by spurious sensor readings. Initially the data from different sensors is subject to a robust hypothesis test as to its consistency. Data that pass this preliminary test are then fused using a class of robust minimax decision rules.

2. PIXEL-LEVEL METHODS

The fusion of multisensor data at the pixel level can serve to increase the useful information content of an image so that more reliable segmentation can take place and more discriminating features can be extracted for further processing. Pixel-level fusion can take place at various levels of representation: the fusion of the raw signals from multiple sensors prior to their association with a specific pixel, the fusion of corresponding pixels in multiple registered images to form a composite or fused image, and the use of corresponding pixels or local groups of pixels in multiple registered images for segmentation and pixel-level feature extraction (e.g., an edge image). Fusion at the pixel level is useful in terms of total system processing requirements because use is made of the multisensor data prior to processing-intensive functions like feature matching, and can serve to increase overall performance in tasks like object recognition, because the presence of certain substructures like edges in an image from one sensor usually indicates their presence in an image from another sufficiently similar sensor. Duane (1988) has reported better object classification performance using features derived from the pixel-level fusion of TV and forward-looking infrared images as compared to the combined use of features derived independently from each separate image.

In order for pixel-level fusion to be feasible, the data provided by each sensor must be able to be registered and, in most cases, must be sufficiently similar in terms of its resolution and information content. The most obvious candidates for pixel-level fusion include sequences of images from a single sensor and images from a group of identical sensors (e.g., stereo vision). Many of the methods used for automatic target recognition (see Section 3 of Chapter 16) make extensive use of pixel-level fusion. Although it is possible to use many of the general multisensor fusion methods for pixel-level fusion (e.g., Bayesian estimation), four methods are discussed in this section that are particularly useful for fusion at the pixel level: logical filters, mathematical morphology, image algebra, and simulated annealing. What makes these four methods useful for pixel-level fusion is that (1) each method facilitates highly parallel processing because, at most, only a local group of pixels are used to process each pixel, and (2) each method can easily be used to process a wide variety of images from different types of sensors, because no problem or sensor specific probability distributions for pixel values are required, thus alleviating the need for either assuming a particular distribution or estimating a distribution through supervised training. (Only very general assumptions concerning pixel statistics are needed in simulated annealing to characterize the Markov random field used to represent an image.)

2.1. Logical Filters

One of the most intuitive methods of fusing the data from two pixels is to apply logical operators to their values; for example, if the values of both pixels are above particular thresholds, the resulting AND filter is assumed to be true. Features derived from an image to which the AND filter has been applied could then be expected to correspond to significant aspects of the environment. In a similar manner, an OR filter could be used to reliably segment an image because all of the sensory information would be available for use in the segmentation process. Ajjimarangsee and Huntsberger (1988) have made use of some of the results concerning the means by which rattlesnakes fuse visual and infrared information (see Section 2.2 of Chapter 1) to develop a set of logical filters that can be used for the unsupervised clustering of visual and infrared remote sensing information. Six logical filters are applied to the remote sensing information which correspond to the six types of bimodal neurons found in the optic tectum of the rattlesnake: AND, OR, visible enhanced infrared, infrared enhanced visual, visible inhibited infrared, and infrared inhibited visible filters. The two inhibitory filters implement, in effect, an exclusive OR filter.

2.2. Mathematical Morphology

Mathematical morphology (Giardina & Dougherty, 1988) is a method of image analysis that transforms each pixel of an image through the use of a set of morphological operators derived from the basic operations of set union, intersection, difference, and their conditional combinations; for example, dilation and erosion operators are used to expand and shrink regions in an image, respectively. Lee (1988) has used binary morphological processing for the fusion of registered images from a pair of millimeter-wave radars operating at different frequencies. The fused image was found to improve road and terrain boundary detection. The binary morphological processing starts with two pixel-level feature sets extracted from the images of both radars. A high-confidence "core" feature set is derived from both feature sets through set intersection if both sets support each other, and through set difference if both sets are competing. A "potential" feature set is derived from both feature sets through set union if the sets are supporting, and through the union of one set with the complement of the other if both sets are competing. The morphological operations of conditional dilation and conditional erosion are used to fuse the core and potential feature sets. Conditional dilation extracts only those connected components of the potential feature set that have a nonempty intersection with the core feature set and is especially useful in rejecting clutter when the potential feature set includes both good feature components and undesirable clutter components. Conditional erosion is useful for filling in missing segments of component boundaries in the core feature set.

2.3. Image Algebra

Image algebra (Ritter & Wilson, 1987) is a high-level algebraic language for describing image processing algorithms and is sufficiently complex to describe many pixel-level fusion algorithms. The four basic types of image algebra operands are coordinate sets, value sets, images, and templates. Coordinate sets can be defined as rectangular, hexagonal, or toroidal discrete arrays, or layers of rectangular arrays, and are used to provide a coherent approach to the representation of sensor images that may have different tessellations or resolutions. If the images from the multiple sensors used for pixel-level fusion have identical underlying coordinate systems, the coordinate set is called homogeneous; otherwise it is termed heterogeneous. Value sets usually correspond to the set of integers, real or complex numbers, or binary numbers of a fixed length, and have the usual arithmetical and logical operations defined on them. A value set is called homogeneous if all of its values come from the same set of numbers; otherwise it is termed heterogeneous. Images are the most fundamental of image algebra's operands and are defined as the graph of a function from a coordinate set to a value set. Templates and template operations are the most powerful tool of image algebra and serve to unify and generalize into one mathematical entity the concepts of templates, masks, windows, the structuring elements of mathematical morphology, and other functions defined on the neighborhood of a pixel. Template operations are used to transform images. They can also be used to define a particular image processing algorithm in an implementation and machine-independent way. The three basic template operations used to transform real-valued images are generalized convolution, multiplicative maximum, and additive maximum. Template operations can be used for local and global convolutions and for changing the dimensionality, size, and shape of images.

Ritter, Wilson, and Davidson (1988) have discussed the use of image algebra for multisensor pixel-level fusion. They have defined an image to be a "multisensor" image if its coordinate set is heterogeneous, and a "multivalue" image if its value set is homogeneous, or "multidata" if it is heterogeneous. A data fusion function is any function that maps a value set of higher dimension to one of lower dimension. The most common data fusion operation is the "reduce" operation where, for example, a vector-valued image is reduced to a real-valued image. A "multilevel" template is a stack of templates that can operate differently on the different levels of a multivalue or multisensor image.

Chen (1989) has extended the basic image algebra formalism to include incomplete and uncertain information. A stochastic image algebra is defined for image analysis that uses a three-dimensional Markov random field to model images. The use of a Markov random field allows relaxation techniques such as simulated annealing to be used for the processing of the images.

2.4. Simulated Annealing

Simulated annealing is a relaxation-based optimization technique which, when used in image processing applications (Geman & Geman, 1984; Wolberg & Pavlidis, 1985), amounts to viewing pixel values and the neighborhood in which they reside as states of atoms or molecules in a physical system. An energy function is assigned to the physical system and determines its Gibbs distribution. Due to the equivalence of the Gibbs distribution to a Markov random field, the energy function also determines an image model if the image can be represented as a Markov random field. Gradual temperature reductions in the energy function are used to relax or anneal the physical system towards a global minimum energy state which corresponds to the maximum a posteriori estimate of the true image given an initial image that is in some way corrupted. Local minima energy states are avoided during the relaxation process because changes in the system toward lower energy states are only favored and not strictly imposed.

The use of simulated annealing for pixel-level fusion reduces to the problem of finding energy functions that can adequately describe appropriate constraints on the final fused image. Wright (1989) has generalized the basic simulated annealing technique for image processing by creating a probability measure on a Markov random field which, in addition to modeling the information content of a single image, takes into consideration the information content of other registered images of the same view. Images from dissimilar sensors can be fused at the pixel level because the measure does not directly use the absolute values of the pixels in each image. Landa and Scheff (1987) and Clifford and Nasrabadi (1988) have used simulated annealing for the pixel-level binocular fusion of the images from two cameras in order to estimate depth. Clifford and Nasrabadi's fusion method uses intensity- and edge-based images together with optical flow data to compensate for partially occluded regions in images.

3. SYMBOL-LEVEL METHODS

Symbol-level methods of multisensor fusion are described in this section. The object recognition example given in Section 1.3 of Chapter 1 is used to illustrate the application of each method and to provide a means for their comparison. Additional discussion relating to symbol-level fusion methods can be found in Chapter 3 of Part I, in Chapters 14 and 15 of this part, and in Chapters 23 and 24 in Part V.

Henkind and Harrison (1988) have analyzed and compared four of the uncertainty calculi used in many symbol-level fusion techniques: Bayesian estimation, Dempster-Shafer evidential reasoning, fuzzy set theory, and the confidence factors used in production rule-based systems. The computational complexity of these calculi are compared and their underlying assumptions are made explicit. Cheng and Kashyap (1988) have compared the use of Bayesian estimation and Dempster-Shafer evidential reasoning for evidence combination.

3.1. Bayesian Estimation

Bayesian estimation provides a formalism for multisensor fusion that allows sensory information to be combined according to the rules of probability theory. Uncertainty is represented in terms of conditional probabilities $P(Y \mid X)$, where $P(Y) = P(Y \mid X)$ if X remains constant. Each $P(Y \mid X)$ takes a value between 0 and 1, where 1 represents absolute belief in proposition Y given the information represented by proposition X, and 0 represents absolute disbelief. Bayesian estimation is based on the theorem from basic probability theory known as Bayes's rule:

$$P(Y \mid X) = \frac{P(X \mid Y)P(Y)}{P(X)},$$

where $P(Y \mid X)$, the "posterior probability," represents the belief accorded to the hypothesis Y, given the information represented by X. The posterior probability is calculated by multiplying the "prior probability" associated with Y, $P(Y)$, by the "likelihood," $P(X \mid Y)$, of receiving X given that Y is true. The denominator $P(X)$ is a normalizing constant.

The redundant information from a group if n sensors, S_1 through S_n, can be fused together using the odds and likelihood ratio formulation of Bayes's rule. The information represented by X_i concerning Y from S_i is characterized by $P(X_i \mid Y)$ and the likelihood $P(X_i \mid \neg Y)$ given the negation of Y, or by the "likelihood ratio":

$$L(X_i \mid Y) = \frac{P(X_i \mid Y)}{P(X_i \mid \neg Y)}.$$

Defining the "prior odds" on Y as

$$O(Y) = \frac{P(Y)}{P(\neg Y)},$$

and assuming that the operation of each sensor is independent of the operation of the other sensors in the system, the "posterior odds" on Y, given the information $X_1, \ldots, X_n$ from the n sensors, are given by the product

$$O(Y \mid X_1, \ldots, X_n) = O(Y) \prod_{i=1}^{n} L(X_i \mid Y).$$

The posterior odds are related to the posterior probability by

$$P(Y \mid X_1, \ldots, X_n) = \frac{O(Y \mid X_1, \ldots, X_n)}{1 + O(Y \mid X_1, \ldots, X_n)}.$$

The above formulation can also be used to fuse together a sequence of information from a single sensor, provided that the uncertainty of the information can be assumed to be independent over time.

The application of Bayesian estimation for multisensor fusion can be illustrated using the object recognition example in Section 1.3 of Chapter 1. Sensors 1 and 2, S_1 and S_2, provide redundant information relative to each other concerning the shape of the objects to be recognized. Let the propositions S and R represent the hypotheses that the object being sensed is square or round, respectively, and let $S_1, R_1, S_2,$ and R_2 represent the shape indicated in the information provided by S_1 and S_2.

Given the information $P(S_1 \mid S) = 0.82$ and $P(S_2 \mid S) = 0.71$ from S_1 and S_2 concerning the hypothesis S, and assuming that square or round objects are equally likely to be encountered, that is, $P(S) = P(R) = 0.5$, the posterior odds on S given the fusion of the information from both sensors are

$$O(S \mid S_1, S_2) = \frac{P(S)}{P(\neg S)} \cdot \frac{P(S_1 \mid S)}{P(S_1 \mid \neg S)} \cdot \frac{P(S_2 \mid S)}{P(S_2 \mid \neg S)}$$

$$= \frac{0.5}{0.5} \cdot \frac{0.82}{0.18} \cdot \frac{0.71}{0.29} = 11.15,$$

which corresponds to a posterior probability of

$$P(S \mid S_1, S_2) = \frac{O(S \mid S_1, S_2)}{1 + O(S \mid S_1, S_2)} = \frac{11.15}{1 + 11.15} = 0.92.$$

In a similar manner, given the information $P(R_1 \mid R) = 0.12$ and $P(R_2 \mid R) = 0.14$, the posterior probability accorded the hypothesis R can be determined to be 0.02. The posterior probabilities of both hypotheses do not sum to unity in this example due to an assumed inherent uncertainty in the operation of S_1 and S_2 of six and fifteen percent, respectively. If, for example, it is known a priori that only a third of the objects likely to be encountered are square, the posterior odds on S would be reduced by half and the odds on R would double.

Durrant-Whyte (1986, 1987a, 1987b, 1988a, 1988b) has developed a model of a multisensor system that represents the task environment as a collection of uncertain geometric objects. Each sensor in the system is described by its ability to extract useful static descriptions of these objects. An "ϵ-contaminated" Gaussian distribution is used to represent the geometric objects. The sensors in the system are considered as a team of decision makers. Together, the sensors must determine a team-consensus view of the environment. A multi-Bayesian approach, with each sensor considered a Bayesian estimator, is used to combine the associated probability distributions of each respective object into a joint posterior distribution function. A likelihood function of this joint distribution is then maximized to provide the final fusion of the sensory information. The fused information, together with an a priori model of the environment, can then be used to direct the robotic system during the execution of different tasks.

3.2. Dempster-Shafer Evidential Reasoning

Dempster-Shafer evidential reasoning (Shafer, 1976; Zadeh, 1986) is an extension to the Bayesian approach that makes explicit any lack of information concerning a proposition's probability by separating firm belief for the proposition from just its plausibility. In the Bayesian approach all propositions (e.g., objects in the environment) for which there is no information are assigned an equal a priori probability. When additional information from a sensor becomes available and the number of unknown propositions is large relative to the number of known propositions, an intuitively unsatisfying result of the Bayesian approach is that the probabilities of known propositions become unstable. In the Dempster-Shafer approach this is avoided by not assigning unknown propositions an a priori probability (unknown propositions are assigned instead to "ignorance"). Ignorance is reduced (i.e., probabilities are assigned to these propositions) only when supporting information becomes available.

Garvey, Lowrance, and Fischler (Chapter 14) introduced the possibility of using Dempster-Shafer evidential reasoning for multisensor fusion. Bogler (1987), Waltz and Buede (Chapter 23), Blackman (Chapter 24), and Buede (1988) have explored the application of Dempster-Shafer evidential reasoning in, respectively, multisensor target identification and military command and control. Chatterjee and Huntsberger (1988), Yen (1990), and Tahani and Keller (1990) have explored a variety of fuzzy set theory modifications to the basic formalism.

In Dempster-Shafer evidential reasoning the set Θ, termed the "frame of discernment," is composed of mutually exclusive and exhaustive propositions termed "singletons." The level of detail represented by a singleton corresponds to the lowest level of information that is able to be discerned through the fusion of information from a group of sensors or other information sources, such as a knowledge base. Given n singletons, the power set of Θ, denoted by 2^Θ, contains 2^n elements and is composed of all the subsets of Θ including Θ itself, the empty set ϕ, and each of the singletons. The elements of 2^Θ are termed propositions and each subset is composed of a disjunction of singletons. The set of propositions $\{A_j \mid A_j \in 2^\Theta\}$ for which a sensor is able to provide direct information are termed its "focal elements." For each sensor S_i, the function

$$m_i: \{A_j \mid A_j \in 2^\Theta\} \to [0, 1],$$

termed a "basic probability assignment," maps a unit of probability mass or belief across the focal elements of S_i subject to the conditions

$$m_i(\Phi) = 0$$

and

$$\sum_{A_j \in 2^\Theta} m_i(A_j) = 1.$$

Any probability mass not assigned to a proper subset of Θ is included in $m_i(\Theta)$ and is assumed to represent the residual uncertainty of S_i that is distributed in some unknown manner among its focal elements.

A "belief" or "support" function, defined for S_i as

$$bel_i(A) = \sum_{A_j \subseteq A} m_i(A_j),$$

is used to determine the lower probability or minimum likelihood of each proposition A. In a similar manner, "doubt," "plausibility," and "uncertainty" functions are defined as

$$dbt_i(A) = bel_i(A^c),$$

$$pls_i(A) = 1 - dbt_i(A),$$

and

$$u_i(A) = pls_i(A) - bel_i(A).$$

The degree of doubt in A is the degree of belief in the complement of A. The plausibility function determines the upper probability or maximum likelihood of A and represents the mass that is free to move to the belief of A as additional information becomes available. The uncertainty of A represents the mass that has not been assigned for or against belief in A. The Bayesian approach would correspond to the situation where $u_i(A) = 0$ for all $A \in 2^\Theta$. The Dempster-Shafer formalism allows for the representation of total ignorance concerning the proposition A since $bel(A) = 0$ does not imply $dbt(A) > 0$, even though $dbt(A) = 1$ does imply $bel(A) = 0$. The interval $[bel(A), pls(A)]$ is termed a "belief interval" and represents, by its magnitude, how conclusive the information is for proposition A; for example total ignorance concerning A is represented as $[0, 1]$, whereas $[0, 0]$ and $[1, 1]$ represent A as being false and true, respectively.

"Dempster's rule of combination" is used to fuse together the propositions X and Y from the two sensors S_i and S_j:

$$m_{i,j}(A) = \frac{\sum_{X \cap Y = A} m_i(X) m_j(Y)}{1 - \sum_{X \cap Y = \phi} m_i(X) m_j(Y)},$$

whenever $A \neq \phi$, and where m_{ij} is the orthogonal sum $m_i \oplus m_j$ and $X, Y \in 2^\Theta$. The denominator is a normalization factor that forces the new masses to sum to unity, and may be viewed as a measure of the degree of conflict or inconsistency in the information provided by S_i and S_j. If the factor is equal to 0 the sensors are completely inconsistent and the orthogonal sum operation is undefined. The combination rule narrows the set of propositions by distributing the total probability mass into smaller and smaller subsets, and can be used to find positive belief for singleton propositions that may be embedded in the complementary information (i.e., focal elements composed of disjunctions of singleton propositions) provided by a group of sensors.

The application of Dempster-Shafer evidential reasoning to multisensor fusion can be illustrated using the object recognition example given in Section 1.3 of Chapter 1. Θ is composed of the four singleton propositions A, B, C, and D, corresponding to the four objects to be recognized. Each of the three sensors used to recognize the objects is only able to provide information to distinguish a particular class of objects, for example, square versus round objects. Sensors 1 and 2, S_1 and S_2, provide redundant information relative to each other concerning the shape of the objects, represented as the focal elements $A \lor C$ (square) and $B \lor D$ (round). The information from S_1 and S_2 is the same as that used to illustrate bayesian estimation in Section 3.1. Sensor 3, S_3, provides complementary information relative to S_1 and S_2 concerning the temperature of the objects, represented as the focal elements $A \lor B$ (cold) and $C \lor D$ (hot).

The mass assignments resulting from the fusion of the information from S_1 and S_2 using Dempster's rule are shown in Table 8.1. The probability mass assigned to each of the focal elements of the sensors reflects the difference in the sensors' accuracy indicated by the frequency distributions shown in Figure 1.3(b) and (c) of Chapter 1; for example, given that the object being sensed is most likely square, the greater mass attributed to $m_1(A \lor C)$ as compared to $m_2(A \lor C)$ reflects S_1's greater accuracy as compared to S_2. The difference in mass attributed to the object possibly being round reflects the amount of overlap in the distributions for each shape class. The mass attributed to $m(\Theta)$ for each sensor reflects the amount by which the focal element masses have been reduced to account for the inherent uncertainty in the information provided by each sensor. The normalization factor is calculated as 1 minus the sum of the two k's in the table, or $1 - 0.2 = 0.8$. As a result of the fusion, the belief attributed to the object being square has increased from $bel_1(A \lor C) = 0.82$ and $bel_2(A \lor C) = 0.71$ to $bel_{1,2}(A \lor C) = 0.93475$ (the sum of the $m_{1,2}(A \lor C)$'s in the table). This increase is also indicated by the narrower distribution shown for the fused information in Figure 3.1(d) of Chapter 1.

Table 8.2 shows the mass assignments resulting from the fusion of the combined information from sensors 1 and 2, $S_{1,2}$, with the focal elements of S_3. As a result of the fusion, positive belief can be

Table 8.1. Fusion using sensors 1 and 2

		S_2		
		$m_2(A \lor C) = 0.71$	$m_2(B \lor D) = 0.14$	$m_2(\Theta) = 0.15$
S_1	$m_1(A \lor C) = 0.82$	$m_{1,2}(A \lor C) = 0.72775$	$k = 0.1148$	$m_{1,2}(A \lor C) = 0.15375$
	$m_1(B \lor D) = 0.12$	$k = 0.0852$	$m_{1,2}(B \lor D) = 0.021$	$m_1(B \lor D) = 0.0225$
	$m_1(\Theta) = 0.06$	$m_{1,2}(A \lor C) = 0.05325$	$m_1(B \lor D) = 0.0105$	$m_{1,2}(\Theta) = 0.01125$

171

Table 8.2. Fusion using sensors 1, 2, and 3

	S_3		
	$m_3(A \vee B) = 0.92$	$m_3(C \vee D) = 0.06$	$m_3(\Theta) = 0.02$
$S_{1,2}$			
$m_{1,2}(A \vee C) = 0.93475$	$m_{1,2,3}(A) = 0.85997$	$m_{1,2,3}(C) = 0.056085$	$m_{1,2,3}(A \vee C) = 0.018695$
$m_{1,2}(B \vee D) = 0.054$	$m_{1,2,3}(B) = 0.04968$	$m_{1,2,3}(D) = 0.00324$	$m_{1,2,3}(B \vee D) = 0.00108$
$m_{1,2}(\Theta) = 0.01125$	$m_{1,2,3}(A \vee B) = 0.01035$	$m_{1,2,3}(C \vee D) = 0.000675$	$m_{1,2,3}(\Theta) = 0.000225$

attributed to the individual objects. The most likely object is A, as indicated by

$$bel_{1,2,3}(A) = m_{1,2,3}(A) = 0.85997$$

and

$$dbt_{1,2,3}(A) = m_{1,2,3}(B) + m_{1,2,3}(C) + m_{1,2,3}(D) + m_{1,2,3}(B \vee D) + m_{1,2,3}(C \vee D)$$
$$= 0.11076.$$

The evidence for this conclusion is quite conclusive as indicated by a small uncertainty and a narrow belief interval for A:

$$u_{1,2,3}(A) = pls_{1,2,3}(A) - bel_{1,2,3}(A) = 0.02927,$$
$$[bel_{1,2,3}(A), pls_{1,2,3}(A)] = [0.85997, 0.88924],$$

where the plausibility of A is

$$pls_{1,2,3}(A) = 1 - dbt_{1,2,3}(A) = 0.88924.$$

The least likely object is also quite conclusively D. If additional information becomes available, for example, that the object was stored inside a refrigerated room, it can easily be combined with the previous evidence to possibly increase the conclusiveness of the recognition process.

3.3. Fuzzy Logic

Fuzzy logic (Zadeh, 1965), a type of multiple-valued logic, allows the uncertainty in multisensor fusion to be directly represented in the inference (i.e., fusion) process by allowing each proposition, as well as the actual implication operator, to be assigned a real number from 0.0 to 1.0 to indicate its degree of truth. Consistent logical inference can take place if the uncertainty of the fusion process is modeled in some systematic fashion. Huntsberger and Jayaramamurthy (1987) have used fuzzy logic to fuse information for scene analysis and object recognition.

3.4. Production Rules with Confidence Factors

Production rules can be used to symbolically represent the relation between sensory information and an attribute that can be inferred from the information. Production rules that are not directly based on sensory information can be easily combined with sensory information-based rules as part of an overall high-level reasoning system, such as expert systems. The use of production rules promotes modularity in the multisensor integration process because additional sensors can be added to the system without requiring the modification of existing rules. Kamat (1985), Belknap, Riseman, and Hanson (1986), and Hanson, Riseman, and Williams (1988) have used production rule-based systems for object recognition using multisensor fusion.

The production rules used for multisensor fusion can be represented as the logical implication of a conclusion Y given a premise X, denoted as *if X then Y* or $X \rightarrow Y$. The premise X may be composed of a single proposition or the conjunction, disjunction, or negation of a group of propositions. The inference process can proceed in either a forward or backward chaining manner: in forward-chaining inference, a premise is given and its implied conclusions are derived; in backward-chaining inference, a proposition is given as a goal to be proven given the known information. In forward-chaining inference, the fusion of sensory information takes place both through the implication of the conclusion of a single rule whose premise is composed of a conjunction or disjunction of information from different sensors, and through the assertion of a conclusion that is common to a group of rules.

Uncertainty is represented in a system using production rules through the association of a "certainty factor" (CF) with each proposition and rule. Each CF is a measure of belief or disbelief and takes a value $-1 \leq CF \leq 1$, where $CF = 1$ corresponds to absolute belief, $CF = -1$ to absolute disbelief, and $CF = 0$ to either a lack of information or an equal balance of belief and disbelief concerning a proposition. Uncertainty is propagated through the system using a "certainty factor calculus," such as the EMYCIN calculus (Buchanan & Shortliffe, 1984).

Each proposition X and its associated CF is denoted as

$$X \; cf \; (CF[X]),$$

where $CF[X]$ is initially either known or assumed to be equal to 0. Given the set $\mathcal{R}$ of rules in a system, each rule $r_i \in \mathcal{R}$ and its associated CF is denoted as

$$r_i : X \rightarrow Y \; cf \; (CF_i[X, Y]).$$

The CF of the premise X in r_i can be defined as

Introduction to Part II   175

$$CF_i[X] = \begin{cases} CF[X] & \text{if } X = X_1 \\ \min(CF[X_1], \ldots, CF[X_n]) & \text{if } X = X_1 \wedge \ldots \wedge X_n \\ \max(CF[X_1], \ldots, CF[X_n]) & \text{if } X = X_1 \vee \ldots \vee X_n \\ -CF[\neg X] & \text{else,} \end{cases}$$

where each X_i is a proposition in X and $\neg X$ is the negation of X. The CF of the conclusion Y in r_i can be determined using

$$CF_i[Y] = \begin{cases} -CF_i[X] \cdot CF_i[X, Y] & \text{if both CF's} < 0 \\ CF_i[X] \cdot CF_i[X, Y] & \text{else.} \end{cases}$$

The $CF_i[X, Y]$ for r_i can be thought of as the $CF_i[Y]$ that would result if r_i is invoked and $CF_i[X] = 1$.

If there is only one rule, r_Y, for which the unknown proposition Y is its conclusion, then $CF[Y] = CF_Y[Y]$. If there is more than one rule, then $CF[Y]$ is determined by fusing together the $CF_i[Y]$'s of all the r_i for which Y is their conclusion. Let

$$\mathcal{R}_Y = \{r_i : x \to y \in \mathcal{R} \mid CF_i[x] \neq 0 \text{ and } y = Y\}$$

be the set of rules with known premises and Y as their conclusion. Given $N = |\mathcal{R}_Y|$ such rules,

$$CF[Y] = CF[Y]_{j=N},$$

where, for every $r_i \in \mathcal{R}_Y$, $CF[Y]_0 = 0$ and

$$CF[Y]_j = \begin{cases} CF[Y]_{j-1} + CF_i[Y] \cdot (1 - CF[Y]_{j-1}) & \text{both CF} > 0 \\ CF[Y]_{j-1} + CF_i[Y] \cdot (1 + CF[Y]_{j-1}) & \text{both CF} < 0 \\ \dfrac{CF[Y]_{j-1} + CF_i[Y]}{1 - \min(CF[Y]_{j-1}, CF_i[Y])} & \text{else} \end{cases}$$

for $j = 1$ to N.

The application of production rules with certainty factors for multi-sensor fusion can be illustrated using the object recognition example in Section 1.3 of Chapter 1. The information from the three sensors S_1, S_2, and S_3 is the same as that used in the illustrations of Bayesian estimation and Dempster-Shafer evidential reasoning in Sections 3.1 and 3.2, respectively. Let S_1 cf (0.87) and R_1 cf (-0.87) be the known propositions provided by S_1 concerning whether the objects being sensed are either square (S) or round (R), respectively. The two rules

$$r_1 : S_1 \to S \; cf \, (0.94) \text{ and}$$
$$r_2 : R_1 \to R \; cf \, (0.94)$$

account for an inherent uncertainty of six percent in the information provided by S_1. Using only S_1, the certainty that the object being sensed is square is $S \; cf \, (0.82)$ and that it is round is $R \; cf \, (-0.82)$. The information $S_2 \; cf \, (0.84)$ and $R_2 \; cf \, (-0.84)$ from S_2, together with the additional rules

$$r_3 : S_2 \to S \; cf \, (0.85) \text{ and}$$
$$r_4 : R_2 \to R \; cf \, (0.85),$$

can be fused with the redundant information from S_1 to increase the belief that the object is square to $S \; cf \, (0.9478)$ and to increase the disbelief that it is round to $R \; cf \, (-0.9478)$, where $CF[S] = 0.82 + 0.71(1 - 0.82)$ and $CF[R] = -0.82 - 0.71(1 - 0.82)$ corresponding to $\mathcal{R}_S = \{r_1, r_3\}$ and $\mathcal{R}_R = \{r_2, r_4\}$, respectively.

Let $C_3 \; cf \, (0.94)$ and $H_3 \; cf \, (-0.94)$ be the konwn propositions provided by S_3 concerning whether the objects are either cold (C) or hot (H), respectively. The two rules

$$r_5 : C_3 \to C \; cf \, (0.98) \text{ and}$$
$$r_6 : H_3 \to H \; cf \, (0.98)$$

account for the inherent uncertainty in S_3 and can be used together with the additional rules

$$r_7 : S \wedge C \to A \; cf \, (1.0),$$
$$r_8 : R \wedge C \to A \; cf \, (1.0),$$
$$r_9 : S \wedge H \to A \; cf \, (1.0), \text{ and}$$
$$r_{10} : R \wedge H \to A \; cf \, (1.0),$$

to enable the information from S_3 to be fused with the complementary information from S_1 and S_2 to determine the certainty factors associated with the propositions A, B, C, and D, corresponding to the four possible types of objects. Having determined that $C \; cf \, (0.92)$ and $H \; cf \, (-0.92)$,

$$\begin{aligned} CF[A] &= CF_7[S \wedge C] \cdot CF_7[S \wedge C, A] \\ &= \min(CF[S] \wedge CF[R]) \cdot 1.0 \\ &= \min(0.9478, 0.92) = 0.92. \end{aligned}$$

In a similar manner, $CF[B]$, $CF[C]$, and $CF[D]$ can be determined to be -0.9478, -0.92, and -0.9478, respectively.

The definition of a certainty factor calculus to use with production rules for multisensor fusion is ad hoc and will depend upon the particular application for which the system is being used. For example, the results of the object recognition example would more closely resemble the results found using Dempster-Shafer evidential reasoning in Section 3.2 if the definition of the CF of a conjunction of propositions in the premise of a rule was changed to correspond to the creation of a separate rule for each proposition, for example, $S \to A$ and $C \to A$ instead of $S \wedge C \to A$ in r_7. Using this definition, the resulting CF's for $A, B, C,$ and D would be 0.99, -0.014, 0.014, and -0.99, respectively (where a CF of 0 is assumed to correspond to a probability mass of 0.5).

4. OVERVIEW

This section presents an overview of the remaining chapters in Part II. Each of these chapters presents a different approach to the fusion of information from multiple sensors: signal-level fusion is the subject of Chapters 9 through 11, methods of feature-level fusion are introduced in Chapters 12 and 13, and symbol-level fusion is discussed in Chapters 14 and 15.

Chapter 9: Richardson and Marsh have provided an introduction to the conceptual problems inherent in any fusion method based on the common assumption that the measurement model for each sensor includes statistically independent additive Gaussian random noise. Their chapter provides a proof that the inclusion of additional redundant sensory information almost always improves the performance of any fusion method that is based on optimal estimation techniques. An example is given of the signal-level fusion of acoustical and optical information to estimate the elevation function of a solid object.

Chapter 10: Luo, Lin, and Sherp have developed a method for the fusion of redundant information from multiple sensors that can be used within their hierarchical phase-template paradigm for multisensor integration (see Section 1.1 of Chapter 2). The central idea behind the method is to first eliminate from consideration the sensor information that is likely to be in error and then use the information from the remaining "consensus sensors" to calculate a fused value. The information from each sensor is represented as a probability density function and the optimal fusion of the information is determined by finding the Bayesian estimator that maximizes the likelihood function of the consensus sensors.

Chapter 11: Nakamura and Xu have proposed a method for optimal signal-level fusion that minimizes the geometrical volume of the uncertainty ellipsoid corresponding to all possible linear combinations of the information from multiple sensors. The resulting equations used for the fusion are equivalent to those used for Bayesian estimation (see Section 3.1 of this chapter) and the Kalman filter (see Section 1.2 of this chapter).

Chapter 12: Porrill has used Gauss-Markov estimation together with geometric constraints for the feature-level fusion of multiple stereo views of a wireframe model of an object. A covariance matrix is used to store information concerning the constraints (e.g., the perpendicularity, intersection, parallelism, and equality of the lines in images) and can be used as a database for elementary geometric reasoning. Recent extensions of this research include Pollard, Pridmore, Porrill, Mayhew, and Frisby (1989).

Chapter 13: When information from multiple sensors is being used for classification and decision purposes some type of discrimination measure is needed so that perceived features of the environment can be compared to known features. Flachs, Jordan, Beer, Scott, and Carlson have developed a method of feature space mapping for multisensor fusion that is based on a new measure called the "tie statistic." The tie statistic allows an unknown sample probability density function to be quickly and efficiently classified. Their method is demonstrated through its application to the object location and texture recognition problems.

Chapter 14: Garvey, Lowrance, and Fischler introduce the possibility of using Dempster-Shafer evidential reasoning (see Section 3.2 of this chapter) for multisensor fusion. The use of evidential reasoning for fusion allows each sensor to contribute information at its own level of detail; for example, one sensor may be able to provide information that can be used to distinguish individual objects, whereas the information from another sensor may only be able to distinguish classes of objects. The Bayesian approach, in contrast, would not be able to fuse the information from both sensors.

Chapter 15: Stephanou and Lu have used the decrease in entropy associated with the use of Dempster's rule of combination as a measure of the effectiveness of the fusion of symbolic information from two knowledge sources. They have shown that, except in cases where the knowledge sources are in high conflict, entropy will decrease as a result of the fusion and will correspond to a focusing of knowledge. Several examples are used to illustrate the use of the effectiveness measure and a review is provided, from a set-theoretic perspective, of Dempster-Shafer evidential reasoning (cf. Section 3.2 of this chapter).

REFERENCES

Ajjimarangsee, P., & Huntsberger, T.L. (1988). Neural network model for fusion of visible and infrared sensor outputs. In P.S. Schenker (Ed.), *Proceedings of the SPIE, vol. 1003, Sensor Fusion: Spatial Reasoning and Scene Interpretation* (pp. 153–160). Cambridge, MA.

Ayache, N., & Faugeras, O. (1989). Maintaining representations of the environment of a mobile robot. *IEEE Transactions on Robotics and Automation, RA-5*(6), 804–819.

Belknap, R., Riseman, E., & Hanson, A. (1986). The information fusion problem and rule-based hypotheses applied to complex aggregations of image events. *Proceedings of the IEEE Conference on Computer Vision and Pattern Recognition* (pp. 227–234). Miami Beach, FL.

Bogler, P.L. (1987). Shafer-Dempster reasoning with applications to multisensor target identification systems. *IEEE Transactions on Systems, Man and Cybernetics, SMC-17*(6), 968–977.

Buchanan, B.G., & Shortliffe, E.H., (eds.). (1984). *Rule-based expert systems: The MYCIN experiments of the Stanford heuristic programming project*. Reading, MA: Addison-Wesley.

Buede, D.M. (1988). Shafer-Dempster and Bayesian reasoning: A response to "Shafer-Dempster reasoning with applications to multisensor target identification systems." *IEEE Transactions on Systems, Man and Cybernetics, SMC-18*(6), 1009–1011.

Chatterjee, P.S., & Huntsberger, T.L. (1988). Comparison of techniques for sensor fusion under uncertain conditions. In P.S. Schenker (Ed.), *Proceedings of the SPIE, vol. 1003, Sensor Fusion: Spatial Reasoning and Scene Interpretation* (pp. 194–199). Cambridge, MA.

Chen, S.S. (1989). Stochastic image algebra for multisensor fusion and spatial reasoning: A neural approach. In M.R. Weathersby (Ed.), *Proceedings of the SPIE, vol. 1098, Aerospace Pattern Recognition* (pp. 146–154). Orlando, FL.

Cheng, Y., & Kashyap, R.L. (1988). Comparison of Bayesian and Dempster's rules in evidence combination. In G.J. Erickson & C.R. Smith (Eds.), *Maximum-entropy and Bayesian methods in science and engineering* (vol. 2, pp. 427–433). Dordrecht, The Netherlands: Kluwer.

Clark, J.J., & Yuille, A.L. (1990). *Data fusion for sensory information processing systems*. Norwell, MA: Kluwer.

Clifford, S.P., & Nasrabadi, N.M. (1988). Integration of stereo vision and optical flow using Markov random fields. *Proceedings of the IEEE International Conference on Neural Networks* (pp. I-577–I-584). San Diego, CA.

Duane, G. (1988). Pixel-level sensor fusion for improved object recognition. In C.W. Weaver (Ed.), *Proceedings of the SPIE, vol. 931, Sensor Fusion* (pp. 180–185). Orlando, FL.

Durrant-Whyte, H.F. (1986). Consistent integration and propagation of disparate sensor observations. *Proceedings of the IEEE International Conference Robotics and Automation* (pp. 1464–1469). San Francisco, CA.

Durrant-Whyte, H.F. (1987a). Consistent integration and propagation of disparate sensor observations. *International Journal of Robotics Research,* 6(3), 3–24.

Durrant-Whyte, H.F. (1987b). Sensor models and multisensor integration. *Proceedings of the Workshop on Spatial Reasoning and Multisensor Fusion* (pp. 303–312). St. Charles, IL.

Durrant-Whyte, H.F. (1988a). *Integration, coordination and control of multisensor robot systems.* Boston: Kluwer.

Durrant-Whyte, H.F. (1988b). Sensor models and multisensor integration. *International Journal of Robotics Research,* 7(6), 97–113.

Durrant-Whyte, H.F., Rao, B.Y.S., & Hu, H. (1990). Toward a fully decentralized architecture for multi-sensor data fusion. *Proceedings of the IEEE International Conference on Robotics and Automation* (pp. 1331–1336). Cincinnati, OH.

Geman, S., & Geman, D. (1984). Stochastic relaxation, Gibbs distributions, and the Bayesian restoration of images. *IEEE Transactions on Pattern Analysis and Machine Intelligence,* PAMI-6(6), 721–741.

Giardina, C.R., & Dougherty, E.R. (1988). *Morphological methods in image and signal processing.* Englewood Cliffs, NJ: Prentice-Hall.

Hanson, A.R., Riseman, E. M., & Williams, T.D. (1988). Sensor and information fusion from knowledge-based constraints. In C.W. Weaver (Ed.), *Proceedings of the SPIE, vol. 931, Sensor Fusion* (pp. 186–196). Orlando, FL.

Henkind, S.J., & Harrison, M.C. (1988). An analysis of four uncertainty calculi. *IEEE Transactions on Systems, Man and Cybernetics,* SMC-18(5), 700–714.

Huntsberger, T.L., & Jayaramamurthy, S.N. (1987). A framework for multisensor fusion in the presence of uncertainty. *Proceedings of the Workshop on Spatial Reasoning and Multisensor Fusion* (pp. 345–350). St. Charles, IL.

Kamat, S.J. (1985). Value function structure for multiple sensor integration. *Proceedings of the SPIE, vol. 579, Intelligent Robots and Computer Vision* (pp. 432–435). Cambridge, MA.

Landa, J., & Scheff, K. (1987). Binocular fusion using simulated annealing. *Proceedings IEEE 1st International Conference on Neural Networks* (pp. IV-327–IV-334). San Diego, CA.

Lee, J.S.J. (1988). Multiple sensor fusion based on morphological processing. In P.S. Schenker (Ed.), *Proceedings of the SPIE, vol. 1003, Sensor Fusion: Spatial Reasoning and Scene Interpretation* (pp. 94–100). Cambridge, MA.

Maybeck, P.S. (1979). *Stochastic models, estimation, and control* (Vol. 1). New York: Academic.

McKendall, R., & Mintz, M. (1988). Robust fusion of location information. *Proceedings of the IEEE International Conference on Robotics and Automation* (pp. 1239–1244). Philadelphia, PA.

Pollard, S.B., Pridmore, T.P., Porrill, J., Mayhew, J.E.W., & Frisby, J.P. (1989). Geometrical modeling from multiple stereo. *International Journal of Robotics Research,* 8(4), 3–32.

Ritter, G.X., & Wilson, J.N. (1987). The image algebra in a nutshell. *Proceedings of the First International Conference on Computer Vision* (pp. 641–645). London.

Ritter, G.X., Wilson, J.N., & Davidson, J.L. (1988). Image algebra application to multisensor and multidata image manipulation. In M.R. Weathersby (Ed.), *Proceedings of the SPIE, vol. 933, Multispectral Image Processing and Enhancement* (pp. 2–7). Orlando, FL.

Shafer, G. (1976). *A mathematical theory of evidence*. Princeton, NJ: Princeton University Press.

Tahani, H., & Keller, J.M. (1990). Information fusion in computer vision using the fuzzy integral. *IEEE Transactions on Systems Man and Cybernetics, SMC-20*(3), 733–741.

Wolberg, G., & Pavlidis, T. (1985). Restoration of binary images using stochastic relaxation with annealing. *Pattern Recognition Letters, 3,* 375–388.

Wright, W.A. (1989). A Markov random field approach to data fusion and colour segmentation. *Image and Vision Computing, 7*(2), 144–150.

Yen, J. (1990). Generalizing the Dempster-Shafer theory to fuzzy sets. *IEEE Transactions on Systems Man and Cybernetics, SMC-20*(3), 559–570.

Zadeh, L.A. (1965). Fuzzy sets. *Informational Control, 8,* 338–353.

Zadeh, L.A. (1986). A simple view of the Dempster-Shafer theory of evidence and its implication for the rule of combination. *AI Magazine, 7*(3), 85–90.

Zeytinoglu, M., & Mintz, M. (1984). Optimal fixed size confidence procedures for a restricted parameter space. *Annals of Statistics, 12*(3), 945–957.

Zeytinoglu, M., & Mintz, M. (1988). Robust fixed size confidence procedures for a restricted parameter space. *Annals of Statistics, 16*(3), 1241–1253.

9
Fusion of Multisensor Data*

John M. Richardson and
Kenneth A. Marsh

This chapter treats two parts of the methodology of the fusion of multisensor data: conceptual and applied. In the conceptual part, we treat several basic questions including the fusionability of various kinds of signals derived from the different sets of raw data associated with separate sensor systems. We require that each derived signal has stand-alone significance. We also derive some general results pertaining to the desirability of augmenting the set of measurements. In the applied part, the general methodology established above is employed in a problem in robotic acquisition involving the determination of the geometry (i.e., the elevation function) of an object resting upon a flat surface. In the model, two types of measurements are assumed: (1) a single acoustical pulse–echo scattering measurement in which the incident wave propagates downward, and (2) a set of optical measurements involving a downward-looking TV camera imaging the object under sequentially pulsed light sources. In the second type, the raw image data are assumed to be preprocessed according to the principles of photometric stereo. The two types of measured data were combined in accordance with the general concepts discussed in Section 1 of the chapter. A computational example using synthetic data is presented and discussed.

---

*This investigation was supported by the Independent Research and Development funds of Rockwell International.

1. INTRODUCTION

In the last several years, there has been a significant increase in the development of data fusion methodologies with widespread military and commercial applications. For accounts of recent progress in this field, the reader is advised to consult papers by Foster and Hall (1981), and La Jeunesse (1986).

Data fusion is the process by which data from a multitude of sensors are used to yield an optimal estimate of a specified state vector pertaining to the observed system. There are several kinds of problems involved in this process: (1) the paper design of the data fusion process; and (2) the implementation of this design in terms of digital hardware without excessive reduction of performance below the optimal level.

In this chapter, we will deal exclusively with some of the problems of paper design. There are myriads of challenging problems in the implementation area, but to keep our scope within practical bounds we will not deal with them here. We will, within the conceptual domain, further restrict our scope by limiting our discussion to single-time estimation problems—more specifically, to problems in which the state changes negligibly during the time interval in which the various sensor data are taken.

Within this category, we will discuss in Section 2 some conceptual problems associated with fusion, and in Section 3 an application to the fusion of acoustical and optical data in the imaging of a solid object in a robotics context.

2. CONCEPTUAL PROBLEMS

2.1. Introduction

This section will deal with the following conceptual problems: (1) the proof that with optimal estimation procedures the inclusion of more sensor data almost always improves the estimation performance; and (2) the partitioning of the total estimation process into modules that have stand-alone significance. A particularly interesting question is how much processing can be done in the two information channels originating in two sensor systems before the final fusion process is carried out.

We cover the following topics: in Section 2.2, the formulation of the problem and a brief review of Bayesian decision theory; in Section 2.3, the desirability of using more sensors; that is, a quasi-rigorous proof of the assertion that the performance (defined in terms of a statistical ensemble of test data) is almost always improved by the addition of more sensors; in Section 2.4, the problem of decomposing the total decision system into modules, each of which has stand-alone significance; and finally in Section 2.5, we give a short summary of results obtained and a discussion of some problems worthy of further investigation.

In Section 3, these results are applied to the fusion of acoustical and optical data in the determination of the elevation junction of an object resting on a flat surface.

2.2. Formulation of the Problem

Let us assume the state of the system of interest at a given time to be represented by the m-dimensional vector x and the total set of measured quantities to be represented by the n-dimensional vector y. Unless otherwise specified, we will assume that both x and y are real and continuous-valued in the infinite Euclidean spaces of appropriate dimensionalities. Our problem is to estimate the value of x from a knowledge of y in accordance with some specified optimality criterion. Before proceeding with this task, it is necessary to specify (1) a model of the system of interest and the sensor system in the absence of experimental errors, and (2) the a priori statistical nature of x and y. (The random experimental errors are determined by the statistical nature of y when x is given.)

The most common procedure in this type of problem is to define a so-called measurement model, for example,

$$y = f(x) + v, \tag{1}$$

where the n-dimensional function $f(x)$ represents the ideal operation of the sensor system, and v is a random n-dimensional vector representing experimental error, model error, background signals, etc. The assumption that the experimental error is simply an additive term is clearly an idealization. It could be multiplicative (or convolutive), or it could be both additive and multiplicative. To achieve complete generality, we should replace $f(x) + v$ by $f(x, v)$; however, most problems involving this level of generality have not been solved in a practical sense.

The measurement model must include a specification of the a priori statistical properties of x and y from which we could deduce the a priori statistical properties of x and y. A common assumption is that x and v are statistically independent and that the probability densities (p.d.'s)

$P(x)$ and $P(v)$ are given. It is always assumed that $P(v)$ has a Gaussian form with zero mean; that is, v is a Gaussian random vector with the properties

$$Ev = 0, \qquad (2a)$$

$$Evv^T = C_v, \qquad (2b)$$

where E is the a priori averaging operator, the superscript T denotes the transpose, and C_v is the covariance matrix for v. We will adhere to this assumption in cases where an explicit consideration of v is involved. The a priori p.d. of x given by $P(x)$ is also often assumed to be Gaussian (i.e., x is also a Gaussian random vector), but with the different properties

$$Ex = \bar{x}, \qquad (3a)$$

$$E \, \Delta x \, \Delta x^T = C_x, \qquad (3b)$$

where Δ is the operator giving the deviation from the average, and C_x is the a priori covariance matrix for x. We will place considerable, but not exclusive, emphasis on this Gaussian case.

A measurement model of particular simplicity is obtained when $f(x)$ is a linear function of x; for example

$$f(x) = Ax, \qquad (4)$$

where A is an $n \times m$ matrix representing the characteristics of the sensor system in the linear regime. Here the measurement model is both linear and Gaussian, properties which enable one to obtain a closed-form solution to the estimation problem that is valid for several optimality criteria.

It is often argued that the a priori statistical properties of x (represented by $P(x)$) must be regarded as being subjective to some degree. On the other hand, the prior statistical properties of v (represented by $P(v)$) are usually assumed to be objective in the sense that an extensive set of experiments has been performed on the sensor system to establish a statistical model of the experimental errors with an adequate level of confidence. In the case of x, we could assume that a similarly extensive set of experiments was performed on the system of interest. However, for many reasons this is usually not done, and thus the onus of subjectivity cannot be totally avoided. A partial justification for the toleration of subjectivity can be based on the fact that, as we will see later, $P(x)$ is an intrinsic part of the optimality criterion. More precisely, the loss function and $P(x)$ occur as a product, and thus the intrinsic subjectivities of the loss function and $P(x)$ are commingled.

The p.d. $P(y|x)$ can be expressed in terms of the above measurement model in accordance with the expression

$$\log P(y|x) = -\tfrac{1}{2}(y - f(x))^T C_v^{-1}(y - f(x)) + \text{const.} \tag{5}$$

The joint p.d. $P(x, y)$ can be written in the form

$$P(x, y) = P(y|x)P(x) \tag{6}$$

and the a posteriori p.d. $P(x|y)$ can be written

$$\begin{aligned} P(x|y) &= P(x, y)P(y)^{-1} \\ &= P(x, y)\left[\int dx\, P(x, y)\right]^{-1}, \end{aligned} \tag{7}$$

where the second factor on the right-hand side is frequently ignorable because it depends only on y, which in the decision process can be regarded as fixed.

We turn now to the problem of estimating the value of x from the measured value of y. We consider an estimate $\hat{x}(y)$ whose optimal form is determined by an optimality criterion (i.e., a measure of the goodness of the estimate) involving a theoretical ensemble of test data. The first step in defining an optimality criterion is to define a loss function $(L(\hat{x}(y), x)$, which is the loss (penalty or cost) incurred when we estimate the state vector to be $\hat{x} = \hat{x}(y)$ when the actual value of the state vector is x. Then, the optimality criterion is given by the negative of the so-called risk R, given by

$$R = EL(\hat{x}(y), x) = \int dy \int dx\, P(x, y) L(\hat{x}(y), x). \tag{8}$$

Note that the argument of $\hat{x}$ is the random vector y given by the measurement model (Eq. (1)). When the optimal form of $\hat{x}$ is found, we use the actual measured value of y denoted by y as the argument of $\hat{x}$ to obtain the best estimate based on a particular set of measurements. It is to be emphasized that R is a functional of $\hat{x}(y)$; in other words it depends on the functional form of $\hat{x}(y)$ or equivalently on the procedure (the policy or rule) for estimating x from y and not on the actual value of $\hat{x}$ in a particular case. The procedure for determining the optimal form of $\hat{x}(y)$ is straightforward. We note that in Eq. (8) the integrand of the y-integration, that is,

$$\int dx\, P(x, y) L(\hat{x}(y), x), \qquad (9)$$

has the property that, for a given value of y, $\hat{x}(y)$ is a number, and furthermore two such numbers for different values of y are unrelated prior to the optimization process. Thus the optimal estimator is determined by minimizing the above expression with respect to $\hat{x}(y)$ with y fixed. If this can be done analytically for a general value of y, we then obtain the optimal functional form of the estimator. Since $P(y)$ is a constant in the above minimization process, we can divide the above expression by $P(y)$, thereby obtaining

$$\int dx\, P(x \mid y) L(\hat{x}(y), x) \equiv E(L(\hat{x}(y), x) \mid y) \triangleq R(\mid y), \qquad (10)$$

where the last quantity is called the a posteriori (conditional) risk, which depends on the value of $\hat{x}(y)$ at a specified value of y in contrast with R, which depends on the functional form of $\hat{x}(y)$.

We can also write the risk R in the slightly different form

$$R = \int dy \int dx\, P(y \mid x)[P(x) L(\hat{x}(y), x)], \qquad (11)$$

in which the entities involving some degree of subjectivity are isolated in the brackets. The factor $P(y \mid x)$ before the brackets is typically free of subjectivity to a satisfactory degree. In any case, $P(x)$ could be considered to be part of the loss function $L(\hat{x}(y), x)$ in the sense that a transformation in one factor could be compensated by another transformation in the other factor. The optimal estimator $\hat{x}_{opt}(y)$ and the corresponding optimal risk R depend only on the product of the two factors. Similar arguments cannot be applied to $P(y \mid x)$ since this quantity does not depend on y only through the estimator $\hat{x}(y)$, and thus cannot be regarded as part of a general loss function.

There is no end of conceivable loss functions that one can consider. However, we will present three such functions:

$$L(\hat{x}, x) = (\hat{x} - x)^T W(\hat{x} - x), \qquad (12a)$$

$$= [(\hat{x} - x)^T W(\hat{x} - x)]^{1/2}, \qquad (12b)$$

$$= -\delta(\hat{x} - x), \qquad (12c)$$

in which W is a symmetric positive definite weighting matrix, and $\delta(\cdot)$ is an m-dimensional Dirac δ-function. The optimal estimator corresponding to the first loss function is the posterior means; that is

$$\hat{x}_{opt}(y) = E(x \mid y), \qquad (13)$$

which, surprisingly, is independent of W. In the case of the second loss function, the optimal estimator is the conventional a posteriori median when x is one-dimensional and is a generalization thereof when x is multidimensional. Finally, in the case of the third loss function, the optimal estimator is the value of x with the maximum a posteriori probability; that is,

$$P(\hat{x}(y) \mid y) = \text{Max}_x P(x \mid y). \qquad (14)$$

This optimal estimator is sometimes called the a posteriori mode.

Our general problem is the determination of $\hat{x}(y)$, the posterior mean median, or mode of x, when the measurement vector represents the outputs of more than one type of sensor; for example,

$$y = (y_1/y_2), \qquad (15)$$

where y_i is an n_i-dimensional vector representing the outputs of sensors of type i ($i = 1, 2$) and where $n_1 + n_2 = n$. At the present level of abstraction, the problem of estimating x based on measured data from several types of sensors is no different from the problem involving one type of sensor, or even a single sensor. However, as we will see, the attempt to modularize the decision process will bring in some nontrivial problems.

2.3. Desirability of Using More Sensors

Before discussing the problem of modularization, we will first consider the basic question of the desirability of using more sensors. It seems self-evident that the use of additional sensors (of the same type or of different types) should give better estimates of the state vector x, or at least estimates that are no worse. However, some investigators have argued otherwise—that there is a finite optimal number of sensors of a given type in a specified estimation problem (Lee, Crane, & Moran, 1984). This could be true if the sensor data were processed suboptimally to yield an estimate of the state. It is to be stressed that we are not considering the cost of additional sensors in the optimality criterion.

Here, we will prove that the use of additional sensors can never reduce the performance of the corresponding optimal estimator, and we will present a quasi-proof that it will almost always improve the performance.

Let us consider the risk R defined by Eq. (8), which for convenience we repeat here with a minor modification of notation:

$$R = R(\{\hat{x}(y)\}) = EL(\hat{x}(y), x). \tag{16}$$

We have explicitly indicated that R is a functional of the estimator; that is, it depends on the entire set of vector values of $\hat{x}(y)$, one value for each value of y in the latter's domain of definition. Here, we will regard $L(\hat{x}, x)$ as a general loss function so that our conclusions will not be limited to a specific choice of $L(\hat{x}, x)$, for example Eq. (12a).

We are interested in the case where the measurement vector is partitioned into two parts as defined by Eq. (15), except that now y_1 corresponds to the original set of sensors and y_2 to an added set. We do not require in this section that y_1 and y_2 correspond to different types of sensors. We consider two kinds of estimates: $\hat{x}(y_1)$ and $\hat{x}(y_1, y_2)$ corresponding to the original and augmented sets of sensors. An essential assumption is that the same state vector x and the same $P(x)$ are used in both cases. Actually, we can consider the first estimator to be a special case of the second. Let us denote the set of all possible estimators $\hat{x}(y_1)$ by S_1 and the set of all possible estimated $\hat{x}(y_1, y_2)$ by S_2. Clearly, as shown in Figure 9.1, S_1 is a subset of S_2 (i.e., $S_1 \subset S_2$), and furthermore if we use some reasonable kind of bounded measure for S_2, S_1 is a set of zero measure.

We now consider the optimization of the two kinds of estimators, that is, the forms of the estimators $\hat{x}(y_1)$ and $(\hat{x}(y_1, y_2)$ that minimize R. Since $\hat{x}(y)$ is a special case of $\hat{x}(y_1, y_2)$, this is equivalent to the optimization of the form of $\hat{x}(y_1, y_2)$ that minimizes R when $\hat{x}(y_1, y_2)$ belongs to S_1 or S_2, respectively. Since the minimization in the first case is constrained, it is clear that

$$\underset{\hat{x}(y_1)}{\text{Min }} R(\{\hat{x}(y_1)\}) \geq \underset{\hat{x}(y_1, y_2)}{\text{Min }} R(\{\hat{x}(y_1, y_2)\}), \tag{17}$$

and thus the optimal risk in the second case is equal to or less than the optimal risk in the first. A typical configuration of points in function space is also depicted in Figure 9.1. Equality (i.e., the = in the above expression) is obtained if the optimal estimator $\hat{x}(y_1, y_2)$ lies in S_1 (i.e., $\hat{x}_{\text{opt}}(y_1, y_2)$ is identical to $\hat{x}_{\text{opt}}(y_1)$).

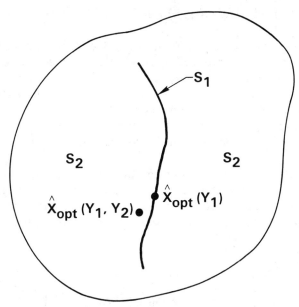

Figure 9.1. Nature of the sets S_1 and S_2 in the space of functions of y_1 and y_2 and the nature of the optimization problem.

We now present a plausibility argument that the probability of equality in the above expression is extremely small compared with the probability of inequality. Let us imagine a continuous statistical ensemble of various supplementary sensor systems (each of which corresponds to the measurement vector y_2), and let us suppose for the sake of simplicity that the dimensionality of y_2 is the same for all members of the ensemble. Since we have implied that the system of interest and the first sensor system (corresponding to the measurement vector y_1) are the same for all members of the ensemble, it follows that the dimensionalities and domains of x and y_1 should be the same for all members. If we further assume that the a priori p.d. $P(x)$ is the same for all members, then the sets S_1 and S_2 are the same for all members. Finally, it will then follow that, associated with the above statistical ensemble of supplementary sensor systems, there is another statistical ensemble of optimal estimates $\hat{x}_{opt}(y_1, y_2)$ in the function space S_2. If the relative probability density of points, representing $\hat{x}_{opt}(y_1, y_2)$, is bounded in some appropriate sense, then the relative probability of such an optimal estimator lying in S_1 is zero; that is, the relative probability of equality in Eq. (16) is zero.

2.4. The Modularization Problem

The primary problem is to estimate the state of the system of interest from two sets of data produced by two separate sensor systems involving, in the general case, different types of sensors. From an abstract point of view, this problem is the same as that involving one set of data. However, significant secondary problems emerge when one investigates the modularization of the estimation process, that is how to decompose the total process into parts that have stand-alone significance.

The nature of the modularization problem is illustrated in Figure 9.2. It is assumed that the information flows associated with y_1 and y_2 can proceed to a point where certain quantities z_1 and z_2 are produced by processors 1 and 2. It is further assumed that these quantities

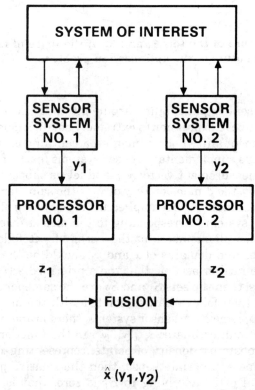

Figure 9.2. Information flows in data fusion.

provide sufficient information (other than a priori information) to enable the fusion processor to produce the optimal estimate $\hat{x}(y_1, y_2)$ based on the total set measured data (y_1, y_2). Two questions arise: (1) What requirement is necessary for any separation processing to be done? and (2) What forms of the variables z_1 and z_2 are sufficient?

The first step in the modularization of the estimation process is the imposition of a requirement on the state vector x, in addition to the requirement that x must contain information relevant to the user's interest. This requirement can be expressed in the form

$$P(y_1, y_2 \mid x) = P(y_1 \mid x) P(y_2 \mid x), \tag{18}$$

which means that y_1 and y_2 are statistically independent when x is given.[1] An alternative form of the above is the relation

$$P(y_1 \mid x, y_2) = P(y_1 \mid x), \tag{19}$$

which means that when the probability density of y_1 is conditioned on x (i.e., it is a posteriori relative to the specification of x), then the additional conditioning on y_2 is redundant. Of course, the same relation with y_1 and y_2 interchanged also holds.

In terms of measurement, models of the form (Eq. (1)) are translated into the present multisensor formalism; that is,

$$y_i = f_i(x) + v_i, \quad i = 1, 2. \tag{20}$$

The above requirement means simply that v_1 and v_2 are statistically independent. Although this might seem to be almost always true (perhaps because it is almost always assumed), it is not a sterile requirement. For example, there might exist a hidden (or neglected) "common cause" represented by random parameters that induce a correlation between v_1 and v_2. A rather commonplace common cause is the unknown ambient temperature of the environment in which the two sensor systems operate. The correlation between v_1 and v_2 can be eliminated by incorporating the parameters, defining the common cause, into the state vector.

The investigation of the modularization of the estimation process is conveniently based on the relation

---

[1] This requirement is reminiscent of the definition of state in systems theory, namely, that for a vector quantity to be a state it must make past and future quantities independent when such a quantity is given in the present.

$$P(x \mid y_1, y_2) = P(y_1 \mid x) P(y_2 \mid x) P(x) P(y_1, y_2)^{-1}$$
$$= \frac{P(x \mid y_1) P(x \mid y_2)}{P(x)} \cdot \frac{P(y_1) P(y_2)}{P(y_1, y_2)} \tag{21}$$

which can be derived from Eq. (18) with the use of general definitions discussed in Section 2.2.

In the following sections, we will investigate in more detail the nature of the information flows depicted in Figure 9.2. In particular, we will determine what kinds of outputs from the separate processors are required for the fusion module to produce the correct estimate of the state based upon the total set of multisensor data.

2.4.1. General case

Here, we consider a general situation in which, aside from the factorability assumption (Eq. (18)), no special assumptions are made about the structure of $P(y_1 \mid x)$, $P(y_2 \mid x)$, and $P(x)$. In this case, it is easily seen from Eq. (21) that the p.d.'s $P(x \mid y_1)$ and $P(x \mid y_2)$ must be the outputs of processors 1 and 2, respectively. The entity $P(y_1)P(y_2)P(y_1,y_2)^{-1}$ can be ignored, since it plays only the role of a normalization factor; if it is omitted, this factor can be recovered later (if necessary) by normalizing $P(x \mid y_1)P(x \mid y_2)P(x)^{-1}$ with respect to x. The p.d. $P(x)$ is not ignorable, but it is known a priori.

It is obvious that the p.d.'s $P(y_1 \mid x)$ and $P(y_2 \mid x)$ can be used as alternative outputs. This assertion follows from the fact that $P(y_1 \mid x) = P(x \mid y_1)P(y_1)P(x)^{-1}$, etc.

One might ask why we cannot make separate estimates of the state x, based first on y_1 and then on y_2, and then send these separate estimates to the fusion module which should compute the desired multisensor estimate $\hat{x}(y_1, y_2)$. It is clear that this cannot be done in the general case. Let us consider as an example the multisensor a posteriori mode given by the value of x that maximizes Eq. (21) or, alternatively, $P(x \mid y)$.

It is obvious that the maximum of $P(x \mid y_1)P(x \mid y_2)P(x)^{-1}$ has no relation to the maxima of $P(x \mid y_1)$ and $P(x \mid y_2)$ individually. One might ask the related question: "If the values of x that maximize $P(x \mid y_1)$ and $P(x \mid y_2)$, respectively, are sufficiently close together, can we average them to get a good approximation to the value of x that maximizes $P(x \mid y_1, y_2)$?" The answer is no, although this question has a certain relevance to the Gaussian case to be considered in Section 2.4.3.

2.4.2. Case in which the system of interest is separable

In this section, we consider the somewhat academic, but illustrative, case in which the system of interest is actually composed of two separate, noninteracting parts. It is assumed that the two sensor systems interact separately with these two parts.

It is perhaps worthy of note that Eq. (18) does not imply in general that

$$P(y_1, y_2) = P(y_1)P(y_2). \tag{22}$$

This can happen only in certain trivial cases. Suppose, for example, that x can be partitioned into two parts; that is,

$$x = (x_1/x_2), \tag{23}$$

where y_1 depends only on x_1, and y_2 depends only on x_2; that is, the two sensor systems observe independent parts of the system of interest. This assumption can be expressed in the form

$$P(y_1, y_2 \mid x_1, x_2) = P(y_1 \mid x_1, x_2)P(y_2 \mid x_1, x_2)$$
$$= P(y_1 \mid x_1)P(y_2 \mid x_2). \tag{24}$$

Let us make the further assumption that x_1 and x_2 are statistically independent a priori; that is

$$P(x_1, x_2) = P(x_1)P(x_2). \tag{25}$$

The two assumptions discussed above imply that

$$\begin{aligned}P(y_1, y_2) &= \int dx_1 \int dx_2\, P(y_1, y_2 \mid x_1, x_2) \\ &\quad \times P(x_1)P(x_2) \\ &= \int dx_1 \int dx_2\, P(y_1 \mid x_1)P(y_2 \mid x_2) \\ &\quad \times P(x_1)P(x_2) \\ &= P(y_1)P(y_2).\end{aligned} \tag{26}$$

If either or both of the above assumptions is violated, then this last relation does not hold. Thus, under assumption of Eq. (22), the factorability relation is a necessary condition for the statistical independence of the two subsystems of the system of interest, a condition defined by the relation

$$P(x_1, x_2, y_1, y_2) = P(x_1, y_1)P(x_2, y_2), \quad (27)$$

but it is not a sufficient condition.

Under the above assumption, Eq. (21) reduces to

$$P(x_1, x_2 \mid y_1, y_2) = P(x_1 \mid y_1)P(x_2 \mid y_2). \quad (28)$$

Thus, no matter what optimality criterion is used, we obtain

$$\hat{x}(y_1, y_2) = \hat{x}_1(y_1)/\hat{x}_2(y_2), \quad (29)$$

corresponding to the direct combination of the results of two separate estimation problems based on a common optimality criterion.

It is interesting to consider a variant of the present problem in which the nature of the separability is not known to the fusion module beyond the mere fact that it exists. The separate estimates of the total state vector, $\hat{x}(y_1)$ and $\hat{x}(y_2)$, are transmitted to the fusion module. Two questions arise in the attempt to deduce $\hat{x}(y_1, y_2)$: (1) Is this enough information (aside from a knowledge of $P(x)$)? (2) If the answer to the first question is affirmative, how are the separate estimates to be combined? We will answer both questions simultaneously in the following analysis.

Assuming that we know the nature of the separability, that is, Eqs. (18), (24), and (25) are satisfied, we can write

$$\hat{x}(y_1) = (\hat{x}_1(y_1)/\hat{x}_2), \quad (30)$$

$$\hat{x}(y_2) = (\hat{x}_1/\hat{x}_2(y_2)). \quad (31)$$

The quantities $\hat{x}_1$ and $\hat{x}_2$ are the best estimates based only on a priori statistical information; for example, in the case of the square deviation optimality criterion (Eq. (12a)), we have

$$\hat{x}_1 = Ex_1 = \int dx\, x_1 P(x) = \int dx_1\, x_1 P(x_1)$$

with a similar expression of $\hat{x}_2$. Actually, our arguments here hold for any conceivable optimailty criterion. We also define

$$\hat{x} = (\hat{x}_1/x_2), \quad (32)$$

where $\hat{x}$ is clearly the best estimate of x based only on a priori information.

Starting with Eq. (29), we obtain

$$\hat{x}(y_1, y_2) = \begin{pmatrix} \hat{x}_1(y_1) \\ \hat{x}_2(y_2) \end{pmatrix} \equiv \begin{pmatrix} \hat{x}_1(y_1) \\ \hat{x}_2 \end{pmatrix} + \begin{pmatrix} \hat{x}_1 \\ \hat{x}_2(y_2) \end{pmatrix} - \begin{pmatrix} \hat{x}_1 \\ \hat{x}_2 \end{pmatrix}, \quad (33)$$

a result that can be rewritten in the simple form

$$\hat{x}(y_1, y_2) = \hat{x}(y_1) + \hat{x}(y_2) - \hat{x}, \quad (34)$$

in which no explicit reference is made to the nature of the separability of the system of interest. Note that the simple averaging of estimates is very different from the above result.

2.4.3. Gaussian case

For the more restricted case in which $P(x \mid y_1)$ and $P(x \mid y_2)$ are both Gaussian in x, knowledge of the a posteriori means and covariances of x and y_1 and y_2 separately given suffices to determine $P(x \mid y_1)$ and $P(x \mid y_2)$, and hence $\hat{x}(y_1 y_2)$. However, even less information related to y_1 and y_2 is necessary. If we assume that both measurement models are linear and Gaussian in x, it is easy to show that the a posteriori covariances of x, that is $C_{x|y_1}$ and $C_{x|y_2}$, are independent of y_1 and y_2, although they depend on the fact that these quantities are measured. Thus, the quantities $z_1 = E(x \mid y_1) = \hat{x}(y_1)$ and $z_2 = E(x \mid y_2) = \hat{x}(y_2)$ provide sufficient information for the fusion module to produce the desired estimate $E(x \mid y_1, y_2) = \hat{x}(y_1, y_2)$. The explicit formula for combining the separate estimates is

$$\hat{x}(y_1, y_2) = [C_{x|y_1}^{-1} + C_{x|y_2}^{-1} + C_x^{-1}]^{-1} \\ \times [C_{x|y_1}^{-1} \hat{x}(y_1) + C_{x|y_2}^{-1} \hat{x}(y_2) - C_x^{-1} \hat{x}], \quad (35)$$

where $C_{x|y_1}$ and $C_{x|y_2}$ are the a posteriori covariances of x given y_1 and y_2, C_x is the a priori covariance matrix of x, and $\hat{x} = Ex$ is the a priori average of x. To obtain the explicit forms of the a posteriori covariances, we consider the measurement models

$$y_i = A_i x + v_i, \, i = 1, 2, \quad (36)$$

where A_i is a constant matrix, and y_i is a Gaussian random vector with zero mean and covariance C_{v_i}. *We also assume that v_1 and v_2 are statistically independent of each other.* The a posteriori covariances are now given by

$$C_{x|y_i} = [A_i^T C_{v_i}^{-1} A_i + C_x^{-1}]^{-1}, \; i = 1, 2. \tag{37}$$

The estimates $\hat{x}(y_i)$ are given by

$$x(y_i) = Ex + C_{x|y_i} A_i^T C_{v_i}^{-1} (y_i - A_i Ex), \; i = 1, 2, \tag{38}$$

a result that will be used later.

If the second set of measurements contains no information (i.e., $A_2 = 0$) we obtain

$$C_{x|y_2} = C_x \tag{39}$$

and

$$x(y_1, y_2) = x(y_1), \tag{40}$$

a result that provides a check on the validity of Eq. (35).

It is interesting to consider the case in which y_1 and y_2 are individually incomplete, but in which the combination (y_1, y_1) is complete. This means that the estimates $\hat{x}(y_1)$ and $\hat{x}(y_2)$ are heavily dependent on a priori information because of the rank deficiencies of the matrices $A_i^T C_{v_i}^{-1} A_i$. However, when $\hat{x}(y_1)$ and $\hat{x}(y_2)$ are combined in a correct manner using Eq. (35), the result $\hat{x}(y_1, y_2)$ is only weakly dependent on a priori information, at least for large signal-to-noise ratios.

The Gaussian result (35) has a certain formal similarity to (34) obtained for the case of separable systems, namely,

$$\hat{x}(y_1, y_2) = \hat{x}(y_1) + \hat{x}(y_2) - \hat{x}. \tag{41}$$

Of course, the Gaussian result reduces to the last expression if the system of interest is separable into two parts and if the two sensor systems relate separately to the two parts. In this case, it is obvious how the two incomplete data sets complement each other in the fusion process.

In the previous section, we made a few remarks about the possibility of averaging the optimal estimates based on the outputs of the two sensor systems. In the present Gaussian case, the result (Eq. (35)) approaches an averaging operation in the limit of very large a priori uncertainty. In more explicit mathematical terms, we obtain

$$\hat{x}(y_1, y_2) \to (C_{x|y_1\infty}^{-1} + C_{x|y_2\infty}^{-1})^{-1} \\ \times [C_{x|y_1\infty}^{-1} \hat{x}(y_1)_\infty + C_{x|y_2\infty}^{-1} \hat{x}(y_2)_\infty] \tag{42}$$

as $C_x \to \infty$ in some suitable sense. The reciprocal matrix weights $C_{x|y_{1,\infty}}$ and $C_{x|y_{2,\infty}}$ are the corresponding limiting forms of the a posteriori covariance matrices $C_{x|y_1}$ and $C_{x|y_2}$ defined by Eq. (37). The estimators $\hat{x}(y_1)_\infty$ and $\hat{x}(y_2)_\infty$ are the corresponding limiting forms of the estimates $\hat{x}(y_1)$ and $\hat{x}(y_2)$ given by Eq. (38). The above result (Eq. (41)) is reasonable in the sense that reciprocal matrix weights are measures of the degrees of uncertainty in the estimates based on y_1 and y_2, respectively. However, we hasten to emphasize that Eq. (42) collapses if the matrix inverses of $C_{x|y_{1,\infty}}$ and/or $C_{x|y_{2,\infty}}$ do not exist. The failure of a matrix inverse to exist is directly related to the incompleteness of the corresponding data set.

2.5. Discussion

We have considered the following problems at the conceptual level in the methodology of multisensor signal processing: (1) a proof of the assertion that with optimal estimation the use of more sensors never degrades the performance; (2) a quasi-proof that in the last case the performance is almost always improved; and (3) an extensive analysis of the problem of decomposing the total linference system into meaningful stand-alone modules. In items (1) and (2), it should be stressed that it is assumed that each estimate is optimal according to some uniform specified criterion for each set of sensors. This criterion involves the performance for a statistical ensemble of test data and thus does not pertain to performance for a small number of tests.

In item (3), dealing with modularization, we have concentrated mostly on the question of how much processing can be accomplished in the separate information channels, associated with individual sensor systems, before the final fusion (or aggregation) takes place. In the case of the a posteriori p.d.'s $P(x \mid y_1)$ and $P(x \mid y_2)$ of general structure, no further processing can be done before the final fusion process occurs. At the other extreme, in the case of linear Gaussian measurement models (which imply that $P(x \mid y_1)$ and $P(x \mid y_2)$ are Gaussian), it is only necessary to use the optimal estimates $\hat{x}(y_1)$ and $\hat{x}(y_2)$ as inputs to the fusion module.

The fusion of acoustical and optical data discussed in Section 3 represents an example of the first extreme; that is $P(x \mid y_1)$ and $P(x \mid y_2)$ are used as inputs to the fusion module. However, it could have been reformulated as a mixed case with $P(x \mid y_1)$ as the input from the acoustic channel and $\hat{x}(y_2)$ as the input from the optical channel. In this case, the state x represents the single-valued elevation function for an unknown solid object (for which the single-valuedness assumption is valid).

These results represent a small fraction of the conceptual problems worthy of further investigation. Even in the relatively limited domain of single-time estimation problems, at the conceptual level we can list the following possibilities:

1. The state vector x has components that are all discrete-valued or are partly discrete-valued.
2. The state vector has the structure $x = (x_1, x_{12}, x_2)^T$ where x_1 is unrelated to y_2, x_2 is unrelated to y_1, and x_{12} is related to both.
3. A mixed situation can occur in which the different information channels can accommodate different amounts of processing before fusion (e.g., the entities $P(x \mid y_1)$ and $\hat{x}(y_2)$ represent the maximal amount of processing in each channel).
4. Experimental error cannot be represented entirely by an additive term in the measurement model. Examples are sensor systems producing two images where one is out of registration with the other by an unknown displacement. Many more examples of this kind can be cited (e.g., inconsistent gray scales).

Clearly, when one enters the much larger domain of time-sequential estimation problems, the kinds of problems, listed above and discussed in earlier sections, become much more complex and ramified.

3. APPLICATION TO FUSION OF ACOUSTICAL AND OPTICAL DATA

3.1. Introduction

In this section, we treat the problem of combining acoustical and optical data in the estimation of the elevation function of a solid object resting on a solid surface, a typical problem arising in robotic acquisition. In the measurement model, the acoustical data re obtained from a single pulse-echo measurement in which the incident wave propagates downward through air. The optical data are obtained from a TV camera looking down at the object which is illuminated by sequentially pulsed light sources. In the last case, the raw image data are preprocessed according to the principles of photometric stereo (Horn 1986) under the assumption that the surface of the object is Lambertian. Using the concepts discussed in Section 2, we combine the two sets of data using the elevation function as the state vector. It is possible to formulate two separate measurement models for the two sets of data, with each depending only on the elevation function (aside from fixed experimental parameters and additive noise representing measurement error, extraneous signals, etc.), but on different aspects of this function.

3.2. Mathematical Preliminaries and Notation

The writing of equations will be simplified significantly by the introduction of a special notation that differentiates between two- and three-dimensional vectors. The desirability of this arises from the fact that the horizontal plane passing through the origin (i.e., xy-space) is a preferred geometrical entity, as we shall see in the later analysis.

The three-dimensional vector $\vec{r}$ in xyz-space is defined by the expression

$$\vec{r} = \vec{e}_x x + \vec{e}_y y + \vec{e}_z z \tag{43}$$

where x, y, and z are the usual Cartesian coordinates and $\vec{e}_x$, $\vec{e}_y$, and $\vec{e}_z$ are unit vectors pointing in the Cartesian coordinate directions. On the other hand, the two-dimensional position vector r in xy-space (i.e., in the xy-plane) is defined by

$$\underline{r} = \vec{e}_x x + \vec{e}_y y. \tag{44}$$

In general, we will denote any three-dimensional vector in xyz-space by an arrow over the symbol and any two-dimensional vector in xy-space by an underline. Clearly, $\vec{e}_x$ and $\vec{e}_y$ are equal to $\underline{e}_x$ and $\underline{e}_y$, but we will adhere to the arrow notation for the sake of clarity. The vector $\vec{r}$ and $\underline{r}$ are obviously related by the expression

$$\vec{r} = \underline{r} + \vec{e}_z z. \tag{45}$$

In the case of a general three-dimensional vector $\vec{u}$, we can write the relations

$$\vec{u} = \vec{e}_x u_x + \vec{e}_y u_y + \vec{e}_z u_z, \tag{46}$$

$$\underline{u} = \vec{e}_x u_x + \vec{e}_y u_y, \tag{47}$$

$$\vec{u} = \underline{u} + \vec{e}_z u_z. \tag{48}$$

We will use the vector magnitude operation $|\ |$ for both two- and three-dimensional vectors:

$$|\underline{u}| = (u_x^2 + u_y^2)^{1/2}, \tag{49}$$

$$|\vec{u}| = (u_x^2 + u_y^2 + u_z^2)^{1/2}. \tag{50}$$

It is also useful to consider the two- and three-dimensional unit tensors defined by

$$\underline{\underline{1}} = \vec{e}_x\vec{e}_x + \vec{e}_y\vec{e}_y, \tag{51}$$

$$\vec{\vec{1}} = \vec{e}_x\vec{e}_x + \vec{e}_y\vec{e}_y + \vec{e}_z\vec{e}_z, \tag{52}$$

in which the terms $\vec{e}_x\vec{e}_x$, etc., are dyadics.[2] The two-dimensional unit tensor $\underline{\underline{1}}$, along with $\vec{e}_z$, is useful in the decomposition of a three-dimensional vector into a two-dimensional vector and the z-component, namely

$$\underline{u} = \underline{\underline{1}} \cdot \vec{u}, \tag{53}$$

$$u_z = \vec{e}_z \cdot \vec{u}. \tag{54}$$

These results give the terms on the right-hand side of Eq. (48) in terms of the general three-dimensional vector on the left-hand side.

We close this subsection with a brief consideration of two- and three-dimensional gradiant operators defined by

$$\underline{\nabla} = \vec{e}_x \frac{\partial}{\partial x} + \vec{e}_z \frac{\partial}{\partial y}, \tag{55}$$

$$\vec{\nabla} = \vec{e}_x \frac{\partial}{\partial x} + \vec{e}_y \frac{\partial}{\partial y} + \vec{e}_z \frac{\partial}{\partial z}. \tag{56}$$

Other operators (e.g., the divergence and the curl) are related in an obvious way to the above definitions.

3.3. Representation of the Object

We assume that the object of interest (combined with part of its surroundings within the localization domain) is represented by a single-valued elevation function

---

[2] In indicial notation, a general dyadic $a\,b$ has the definition $(a\,b)_{ij} = a_i b_j$, where $i,j = 1, 2, 3$ correspond to the Cartesian coordinates x, y, z. In some notational systems, a would be regarded as a column vector and b as a row vector and, thus, the dyadic $a\,b$ might be represented by the expression ab^T. This is in contrast with the scalar (or dot product) $a \cdot b$ being represented by $a^\mathrm{T} b$.

$$z = Z(\underline{r}) \tag{57}$$

where z is the vertical coordinate and $\underline{r}$ is a two-dimensional position vector in the xy-plane. The points $\underline{r}$ are limited to the localization domain D_L defined by the inequalities

$$-\tfrac{1}{2}L_x \leq x < \tfrac{1}{2}L_x, \quad -\tfrac{1}{2}L_y \leq y < \tfrac{1}{2}L_y. \tag{58}$$

Outside of the localization domain, we assume that the elevation is, in effect, given by $z = -\infty$, or at least a negative number sufficiently large that its contribution to the acoustical measurement can be windowed out. In the optical model, the surface outside of D_L is at least partially visible, no matter how large and negative the elevation function is. We can handle this by requiring this part of the surface to be perfectly black (i.e., totally nonreflective). This assumption makes the shadow of the pedestal (associated with D_L), thrown onto the low-lying surface outside of D_L, totally invisible in most cases. It is understood that the object of interest need not fill all of D_L; the elevation function between the object and the boundaries of D_L could, for example, be part of the presentation surface. A typical setup is illustrated in Figure 9.3(a) and 9.3(b).

The single-valuedness of the elevation function requires further comment. Clearly, most objects involved in robotic assembly are not described faithfully by single-valued elevation functions. We can take two alternative points of view. The first is that we will, for the sake of simplicity, limit our investigation to objects that are actually described by single-valued elevation functions. The second is that, in the case of many objects described by multiple-valued elevation functions, it is possible in an approximate manner to confine attention to the so-called top elevation function (i.e., an elevation function that is equal to the maximum elevation wherever multiple elevations exist) if the lower branches contribute weakly to the measured data.

In the Kirchhoff approximation, the waveform from a pulse-echo scattering measurement with the incident wave propagating in the $-\vec{e}_z$ direction depends only on the single-valued elevation function, or on the top elevation function in the case of objects involving multiple-valued elevation functions. It is then clear that the elevation function constitutes an adequate state vector for the interpretation of acoustical measurements.

In general, the way in which the object scatters incident light should be regarded as part of the state of the object, along with the elevation function. However, to simplify the present problem as much as possible, we make the assumption that the surface has a matte finish that scatters light diffusely in accordance with Lambert's law. With a suffi-

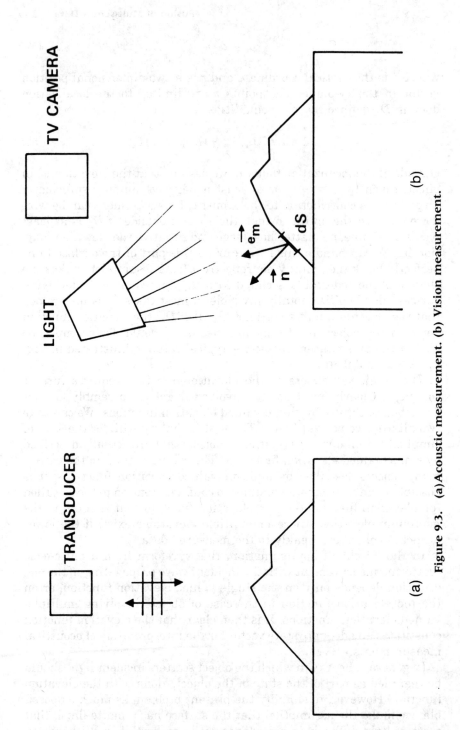

Figure 9.3. (a) Acoustic measurement. (b) Vision measurement.

cient number of illumination directions, one can, under the above assumption, derive a combination of directly measurable quantities that are independent of the local reflectivity. Thus, this measured combination is, in the absence of additive noise, directly related only to the elevation function $Z(\underline{r})$. Hence, $Z(\underline{r})$ constitutes an adequate state vector for interpreting optical measurements.

If the experimental errors in the two types of measurements are statistically independent, it is easy to see that, when $Z(\underline{r})$ is specified, the possible results of the two types of measurements are also statistically independent, a requirement in the general methodology.

It is expedient to decompose the elevation function $Z(\underline{r})$ into two parts: (1) a part $\bar{Z}$ that is the area average on the localization domain D_L, and (2) a part $\delta Z(\underline{r})$ that is the deviation from the above area average. To be explicit, we write

$$Z(\underline{r}) = \bar{Z} + \delta Z(\underline{r}), \tag{59}$$

where

$$\bar{Z} = A^{-1} \int_{D_L} d\underline{r}\, Z(\underline{r}), \tag{60}$$

where, in turn, $A = L_x L_y$ is the area of the localization domain D_L. It follows from the above equations that

$$\int_{D_L} d\underline{r}\, \delta Z(\underline{r}) = 0. \tag{61}$$

It is appropriate at this point to make a few remarks about the nature of the dependence of the two types of measurements upon $\bar{Z}$ and $\delta Z(\underline{r})$. The acoustical measurements depend on both $\bar{Z}$ and $\delta Z(\underline{r})$, but only on the horizontal cross-sectional area as a function of height; that is, $\int d\underline{r}\, 1(\bar{Z} + \delta Z(\underline{r}) - z^0)$ in which $1(\ )$ is the unit step function and z^0 is the height of the cross-section. The optical measurements depend only on $\delta Z(\underline{r})$; that is, they are independent of $\bar{Z}$.

3.4. Acoustical Measurement Model

We consider a single pulse-echo measurement of the scattering of acoustical waves from the object of interest. We of course assume that the host medium is ordinary air. We further assume that the transducer and the localization domain are in the far field of each other. The experimental setup is depicted schematically in Figure 9.3(a). The object is assumed to have a very high acoustical impedance and a very high density compared with the corresponding properties of air, and thus the surface of the object may be regarded as a rigid immovable boundary.

The appropriate measurement model is given (Richardson, Marsh, Schoenwald, & Martin, 1984) by the expression

$$f(t) = \alpha \int_{D_L} d\underline{r}\, p'(t + 2c^{-1} Z(\underline{r})) + \mu(t), \qquad (62)$$

where

$f(t)$ = a possible measured waveform.
$\mu(t)$ = experimental error and external noise.
$p'(t)$ = time derivative of $p(t)$, the measurement system response function. The latter is defined as the waveform produced by the measurement system if a fictitious scatterer with an impulse response function given by $R(t) = \delta(t)$ is positioned at the origin.
$Z(\underline{r})$ = elevation function discussed in the last section.
α = constant dependent upon the acoustical properties of air.
c = propagation velocity of acoustical waves in air.

It is appropriate to consider a discrete version of the above measurement model, namely

$$f(t) \propto \sum_{\underline{r}} \delta\underline{r}\, p'(t + 2c^{-1}Z(\underline{r})) + \mu(t), \qquad (63)$$

where $\underline{r}$ takes vector values on a suitable grid of points in the xy-plane spanning the localization domain D_L, $\delta\underline{r}$ is the area of one cell (or pixel) in the grid, and where the time t is now assumed to take a discrete set of values. The grid can be defined by setting $x = aq_x$, $y = aq_y$, where q_x and q_y are integers and where now $\delta\underline{r} = a^2$. The localization domain is defined by setting $L_x = Q_x a$ and $L_y = Q_y a$ in accordance with the assumptions that $q_x = -\tfrac{1}{2}Q_x + 1, \ldots, \tfrac{1}{2}Q_x$ and $q_y = -\tfrac{1}{2}Q_y + 1, \ldots, \tfrac{1}{2}Q_y$, in which Q_x and Q_y are even positive integers.

We turn now to a discussion of the a priori statistical aspects of the model. The random quantities $\mu(t)$ and $Z(\underline{r})$ are assumed to be statistically independent of each other. The noise $\mu(t)$ is assumed to be Gaussian with zero mean and with a covariance matrix given by

$$E\mu(t)\,\mu(t') = \delta_{u'}\,\sigma_\mu^2, \qquad (64)$$

where $\delta_{u'}$ is a Kronecker delta function generalized for the case of noninteger subscripts ($\delta_{u'} = 1$ if $t = t'$ and $= 0$ if $t \neq t'$), and where σ_μ is the standard deviation of $\mu(t)$. The above result is valid if the covariance function $C_\mu(t - t')$ associated with $\mu(t)$, temporarily regarded as a random process defined on a continuous time t, has a negligible amplitude when $|t - t'|$ is equal to or larger than the time-sampling interval pertaining to the discrete time case. Clearly, the standard deviation σ_μ is then given by $\sigma_\mu^2 = C_\mu(0)$.

We now assume that the set of quantities $\{\delta Z(\underline{r})\}$ is a Gaussian random vector with the properties

$$E\,\delta Z(\underline{r}) = 0, \qquad (65)$$

$$E\,\delta Z(\underline{r})\,\delta Z(\underline{r}') = C_{\delta z}\,(\underline{r} - \underline{r}'). \qquad (66)$$

At this point, we introduce the assumption of periodic (or cyclic) boundary conditions, an artifact that gives meaning to nonlocal quantities that depend, at least formally, on points beyond the boundary of D_L. This assumption necessitates the further assumption that $C_{\delta z}(\underline{r})$ is doubly periodic with period D_L. Because of Eq. (61), we must impose the requirement

$$\sum_{\underline{r}} C_{\delta Z}(\underline{r} - \underline{r}') = \sum_{\underline{r}} C_{\delta Z}(\underline{r}) = 0. \qquad (67)$$

The area average $\bar{Z}$ is assumed to be statistically independent of the $\delta Z(\underline{r})$. It is not unreasonable to assume that $\bar{Z}$ is a priori a Gaussian random vector with zero mean and variance $C_{\bar{z}}$.

3.5. Optical Measurement Model

In this case, we assume that a TV camera (or its equivalent) is situated at a high altitude (compared with the a priori range of the elevation function of the object) and is pointed straight down. As already noted, we assume that the surface is a diffuse Lambertian scatterer. We make the following additional assumptions: (1) Each light source is assumed to be equivalent to a point source at infinity, (2) Each element of surface is illuminated by each point source of light, and (3) Multiple scattering of light between different elements of surface can be neglected. This model is essentially identical to that treated by Ray, Birk, and Kelley (1983). The geometry of the experimental setup is depicted in Figure 9.3(b). We will first consider a noiseless model of the directly measurable quantities (i.e., the set of image intensities for each illumination direction) from which we ultimately obtain, using the concepts of photometric stereo (Horn, 1986), a set of derived quantities that depend only upon the local slopes. A noisy model is then formulated for these derived quantities. For the sake of completeness and in order to define notation, we present a short derivation below.

The noiseless direct optical measurement model can be expressed in the form

$$p(\underline{r}, \vec{e}_m) = \beta(\underline{r}) \vec{e}_m \cdot \vec{n}(\underline{r}), \tag{68}$$

where

$p(\underline{r}, \vec{e}_m)$ = possible image intensity at the position $\underline{r}$ in the xy-plane[3] with the illumination direction $\vec{e}_m$

$\vec{e}_m$ = unit vector pointing from an element of surface on the object toward illumination source (Since the distance from any part of the object to each light source is assumed to be very large compared with the size of the object and the localization domain, $\vec{e}_m$ is independent of $\underline{r}$.)

$\vec{n}(\underline{r})$ = outward-pointing normal vector for an element of surface above the position $\underline{r}$ in the xy-plane

$\beta(\underline{r})$ = factor associated with the surface reflectivity, characteristics of the imaging system and illumination intensity

The physical basis of Eq. (68) is discussed in a book edited by Kingslake (1965).

The local normal is easily shown to be

$$\vec{n}(\underline{r}) = \frac{\vec{\nabla}(z - Z(\underline{r}))}{|\vec{\nabla}(z - Z(\underline{r}))|} = (\vec{e}_z - \underline{\nabla} Z)(1 + |\underline{\nabla} Z|^2)^{-1/2}. \tag{69}$$

---

[3] Here, we assume that the two-dimensional coordinate system on the image plane and the two-dimensional coordinate systems used in the definition of the elevation function are in one-to-one correspondence.

In this model, we assume that the illumination direction $\vec{e}_m$ can assume several vector values.

The above model is suitable for continuous $\underline{r}$. For the case of discrete $\underline{r}$, defined on the xy-grid defined in the last section, certain modifications must be made. The above measurement model can stand as written, except that $\underline{r}$ is discrete. The most satisfactory approximation is obtained from an elevation function for continuous $\underline{r}$ obtained by Fourier interpolation applied to the discrete set of elevations defined on the above xy-grid. This procedure leads to the result

$$\underline{\nabla} Z(\underline{r}) = - \sum_{\underline{r}'} \underline{A}(\underline{r} - \underline{r}') Z(\underline{r}'), \tag{70}$$

where

$$-\underline{A}(\underline{r}) = Q^{-1} \operatorname{Re} \sum_{\underline{k}} i\underline{k} \, \exp(i\underline{k} \cdot \underline{r}). \tag{71}$$

The vector $\underline{k}$ takes the discrete set of values defined by

$$\underline{k} = 2\pi \left(\frac{p_x}{L_x} \vec{e}_x + \frac{p_y}{L_y} \vec{e}_y \right) \tag{72}$$

where p_x and p_y take the same integral values as q_x and q_y, respectively; namely, $p_x = \frac{1}{2}Q_x + 1, \ldots, \frac{1}{2}Q_x$ and $p_y = -\frac{1}{2}Q_y + 1, \ldots, \frac{1}{2}Q_y$. It should be stressed that the above results contain the implicit assumption that $\underline{A}(r)$ is periodic with a two-dimensional period D_L. This is consistent with the assumption of periodic boundary conditions or toroidal topology.

We turn next to the determination of $\underline{\nabla} Z(r)$ in the noiseless case. We assume that the illumination directions $\vec{e}_1, \vec{e}_2,$ and $\vec{e}_3$ are noncoplanar, and we then define a set of reciprocal vectors $\vec{e}_1^R, \vec{e}_2^R,$ and $\vec{e}_3^R$ by the relations

$$\vec{e}_m^R \cdot \vec{e}_{m^1} = \delta_{mm^1}, \quad m, m^1 = 1, 2, 3. \tag{73}$$

It is easily shown that

$$\sum_m \frac{\vec{e}_m^R \vec{e}_m}{e_m} = \overset{\leftrightarrow}{1} \tag{74}$$

where $\vec{1}$ is the three-dimensional unit tensor defined by Eq. (52). We now define a new observable quantity

$$\vec{\tau}(\underline{r}) = \sum_{m=1}^{3} \vec{e}_m^R \rho(\underline{r}, \vec{e}_m). \tag{75}$$

Using Eq. (68), we obtain

$$\begin{aligned}\vec{\tau}(\underline{r}) &= \beta(\underline{r}) \sum_{m=1}^{3} \vec{e}_m^R \vec{e}_m \cdot \vec{n}(\underline{r}) \\ &= \beta(\underline{r})\overset{\leftrightarrow}{1} \cdot \vec{n}(\underline{r}) = \beta \vec{n}(\underline{r}).\end{aligned} \tag{76}$$

We finally consider the ratio of the horizontal and vertical parts of $\vec{\tau}$ to obtain

$$\begin{aligned}\underline{\sigma}(r) &= \underline{\tau}(r)/\tau_z(r) = \underline{n}(r)/n_z(r) \\ &= -\underline{\nabla}\,\delta Z(\underline{r} = \sum_{\underline{r}} \underline{A}(\underline{r} - \underline{r}')\,\delta Z(\underline{r}'),\end{aligned} \tag{77}$$

where Z has been replaced by δZ since $\underline{\nabla}\,\bar{Z}$ vanishes. We have thus found a combination of observable quantities that is independent of the local reflectivity (i.e., albedo) and is dependent only upon the local slope. It should be reemphasized that, as stated earlier, the object and the illumination directions must be such that no part of the exposed body is in shadow. The value of β, which involves the reflectivity or as a factor, is simply obtained by taking the vector absolute value of both sides of Eq. (76) with the result $\beta = |\vec{\tau}|$.

We make the approximation that the experimental error (i.e., the combined effects of errors in the $\rho(\underline{r}, \vec{e}_m)$) can be represented by Gaussian additive noise, and thus the complete stochastic measurement model takes the form

$$\underline{\sigma}(r) = \sum_{\underline{r}'} \underline{A}(\underline{r} - \underline{r}')\,\delta Z(\underline{r}') + \underline{v}(\underline{r}). \tag{78}$$

The a priori statistical behavior of $\delta Z(\underline{r})$ has been described in the last subsection. The measurement error (or noise) $\underline{v}(\underline{r})$ is assumed a priori to be statistically independent of $\delta Z(\underline{r})$ and $\bar{Z}$. Also, it is assumed to be Gaussian with the properties

$$E\,\underline{v}(\underline{r}) = 0, \tag{79a}$$

$$E\underline{v}(\underline{r})\underline{v}(\underline{r}') = \underline{\underline{1}}\,\delta_{\underline{r}\underline{r}'}\,\sigma_v^2. \tag{79b}$$

The appearance of the two-dimensional unit tensor $\underline{\underline{1}}$ (see Eq. (50)) on the right-hand side of the last expression reflects an assumption of statistical isotropy in the xy-plane.

3.6. Procedure for Estimating the Elevation Function

Here, we treat the problem of combining the two types of measurements, acoustical and optical, in the estimation of the elevation function. With the best score optimality criterion, the best estimate of $Z(\underline{r})$ is the most probable $Z(\underline{r})$ given the results of the two types of measurements. In more explicit mathematical terms, this means the maximization of

$$P(Z \mid f, \sigma) = P(f, \sigma \mid Z)P(Z) \mid P(f, \sigma), \tag{80}$$

where Z, f, and σ are abbreviated symbols for the sets of values of $Z(\underline{r})$, $f(t)$, and $\underline{\sigma}(\underline{r})$. Using the relation

$$P(f, \sigma \mid Z) = P(f \mid Z)P(\sigma \mid Z), \tag{81}$$

expressing the assumption discussed in Section 3 regarding the statistical independence of f and σ when Z is given, we finally obtain the result that the best estimate of Z is given by the maximation of

$$\phi(Z \mid f, \sigma) = \log P(f \mid Z) + \log P(\sigma \mid Z) + \log P(Z), \tag{82}$$

which is a specialization of the first line of Eq. (18). In the above expression, an additive constant related to normalization has been ignored. We will use the same practice in all of the subsequent equations. The conditional probability densities are given by

$$\log P(f \mid Z) = -\frac{1}{2\sigma_\mu^2}\sum_t$$

$$\times \left[f(t) - \alpha \sum_{\underline{r}} \delta\underline{r}\, p'(t + 2c^{-1}Z(\underline{r})) \right]^2, \tag{83}$$

$$\log P(\sigma \mid Z) = -\frac{1}{2\sigma_v^2} \sum_{\underline{r}} \left[\sigma(\underline{r}) - \sum_{\underline{r}'} A(\underline{r} - \underline{r}') \, \delta Z(\underline{r}') \right]^2. \tag{84}$$

The a priori p.d. of $\bar{Z}$ and the $\delta Z(\underline{r})$ are given by the expression

$$\log P(Z) = -\frac{1}{2} \sum_{\underline{r},\underline{r}'} \delta Z(\underline{r}) C_{\delta z}(\underline{r} - \underline{r}')^+ \, \delta Z(\underline{r}')$$
$$- \frac{1}{2} \, C_{\bar{Z}}^{-1} \bar{Z}^2 \tag{85}$$

where $C_{\delta z}(\underline{r} - \underline{r}')^+$ is the pseudoinverse of $C_{\delta z}(\underline{r} - \underline{r}')$. The latter quantity is a singular matrix because of the constraint (61).

Our general task of finding the most probable elevation function $Z(\underline{r})$, given the measured values $\{f(t)\}$ and $\{\sigma(\underline{r})\}$, is tantamount to the maximization of $\phi(Z \mid f, \sigma)$ with respect to the set of elevations $Z(\underline{r})$ at the grid points $\underline{r}$.

It is of interest to consider the estimate of $\delta Z(\underline{r})$ based upon optical measurements alone. The linear estimator in two-dimensional spatial frequency space equals 0, if $\underline{k} = 0$, and takes the form

$$\delta \hat{Z}(\underline{k}) = [|\underline{k}|^2 + \sigma_v^2 C_{\delta z}(\underline{k})^{-1}]^{-1} i\underline{k} \cdot \sigma(\underline{k}), \text{ if } \underline{k} \neq 0 \tag{86}$$

In the above expression, all of the functions originally defined in $\underline{r}$-space have been transformed over to $\underline{k}$-space (the two-dimensional spatial frequency space). The relations between the two representations are

$$\delta Z(\underline{k}) = \sum_{\underline{r}} \exp(-i\underline{k} \cdot \underline{r}) \, \delta Z(\underline{r}), \text{ etc.,} \tag{87}$$

where it is understood that $\delta Z(\underline{k})$ is a different function (i.e., the function defined above), *not* simply $\delta Z(\underline{r})$ with $\underline{k}$ substituted for $\underline{r}$. It is easily shown from Eq. (71) that

$$\underline{A}(\underline{k}) = -i\underline{k} \tag{88}$$

a relation that was used in the derivation of Eq. (86). In the above expression, $\underline{k}$ takes the values given by Eq. (72).

3.7. Computational Example

As an illustrative example of the above procedure for estimating the elevation function of an object using a combination of acoustical and optical data, synthetic test data were generated based on an assumed tetrahedron resting on a flat table. A hidden representation of the assumed surface is shown in Figure 9.4. The surface was defined on a square grid of 16 × 16 points, with a length of 20 mm on each side. The length of one side of the tetrahedron was 15 mm. The coordinate system was chosen such that the table was in the xy-plane at $z = 0$. Optical and acoustical data were generated in accordance with the physical models outlined in the previous section. In the case of the optical data, the two-dimensional intensity distribution, as seen by a camera looking straight down, was calculated for three illumination directions, each having a polar angle of 15°, but with azimuthal angles of 0°, 90°, and 270°, respectively. Figure 9.5 shows gray-scale representations of the three synthetic optical images. In the case of the acoustic data, the assumed measurement system response function $p(t)$ was in the shape of a Hamming window in the frequency domain, whose bandpass between the zero points was 0–20 kHz.

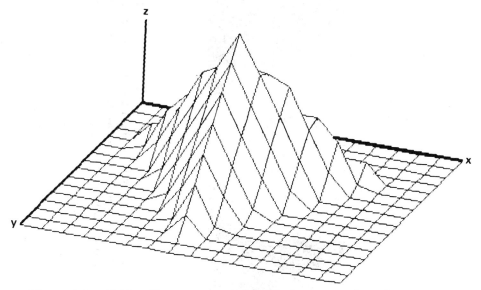

Figure 9.4. Hidden line representation of the assumed surface, corresponding to a tetrahedron whose sides are of length 15 mm placed on a flat table of width 20 mm.

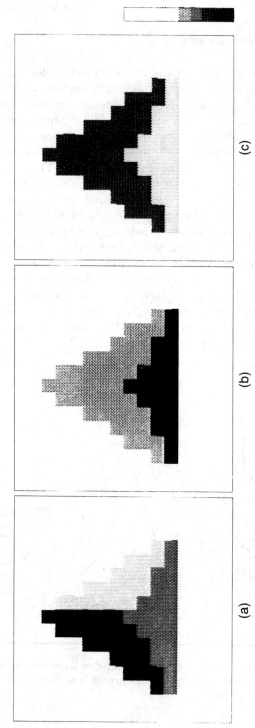

Figure 9.5. Synthetically generated optical data representing the intensity distribution which would be seen by a camera looking straight down. The illumination directions correspond to a polar angle of 15° in each case, and azimuth angles of (a) 0°, (b) 90°, and (c) 270°.

In the inversion procedure, the standard deviations of the measurement noise were assumed to be 0.01 and 0.1 for the acoustical and optical data, respectively, where the above quantities are relative to the peak absolute value of the synthetic measured data in both cases. The area average elevation $\bar{Z}$ was assumed to have an ensemble average of zero, and a covariance $C_{\bar{z}}$ of the square of half the width of the localization domain (i.e., 10 mm), thus providing a slight bias toward a spatial average height of zero in the reconstruction. The covariance of δZ was assumed here to be infinite.

The inversion was performed in three stages:

1. Determine $\delta Z(r)$ using the optical data alone.
2. Assuming $\delta Z(r)$ to be fixed at the above values, determine Z from the acoustic data alone.
3. Perform the final optimization using both acoustic and optical data by maximizing $P(Z \mid \sigma, f)$ with respect to δZ and $\bar{Z}$.

The results for the three stages are shown in Figure 9.6. In the case of stage 1 (Figure 9.6(a)), the reconstructed surface has a spatial mean elevation of zero, in accordance with our definition of δZ, and hence contains no absolute information on vertical position. In the case of stage 2 (Figure 9.6(b)), the acoustic data have brought the surface up to approximately the correct height. For the final image (Figure 9.6(c)), the vertical offset has been improved slightly, bringing the edges of the table (estimated) up to the level of the xy-plane. This represents the best estimate of the surface on the basis of the optical and acoustic data, and comparison with Figure 9.4 shows that the reconstruction is faithful. The height of the apex of the reconstructed pyramid above the table is 11.4 mm, compared with the true height of 12.2 mm. This

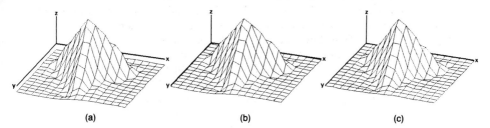

Figure 9.6. The results of the three stages of the inversion technique discussed in the text. (a) The relative profile $\Delta Z(x,y)$ deduced from optical data only. (b) An estimate of $Z(x,y)$ in which the acoustic data has been used only to adjust the vertical position offset. (c) The optimal image used from the combined optical and acoustical data.

discrepancy is probably due to the approximations involved in calculating gradients from measurements on a finite grid.

3.8. Discussion

The methodology for the probabilistic estimation of the state of a system from multisensor data has been applied to the estimation of a single-valued elevation function of a rigid object in air based upon a combination of acoustical and optical measurements, the nature of which we discussed in detail in earlier sections. The optical measurement system described here has the property that it provides complete information about the shape of the elevation function, but no information regarding the absolute elevation or vertical offset for the object and its immediate surroundings. On the other hand, the acoustical measurement system provides complete information about the vertical offset, but only incomplete information about the shape, that is, the horizontal cross-section as a function of altitude.

REFERENCES

Foster, J.L., & Hall, D.K. (1981). Multisensor analysis of hydrologic features with emphasis on the SEASAT SAR. *Photogrammetric Engineering and Remote Sensing* 47(5), 655–664.

Horn, B.K.P. (1986). *Robot vision.* Cambridge, MA: MIT Press.

Kingslake, R. (ed.) (1965). *Applied optics and optical engineering (Vols. I and II* New York: Academic Press.

La Jeunesse, T.J. (1986 September). Sensor fusion. *Defense Science and Electronics* 21–31.

Lee, D.A., Crane, R.L., & Moran, T.J. (1984). A practical method for viewing resolution-noise-bandwidth tradeoffs in NDE data reductions. In D.O. Thompson & D.E. Chimenti (Eds.), *Review of progress in quantitative nondestructive evaluation* (pp. 907–915). New York: Plenum.

Ray, R., Birk, J., & Kelley, R.B. (1983). Error analysis of surface normals determined by radiometry. *IEEE Transactions on Pattern and Analysis and Machine Intelligence PAMI-5* (6) 631–645.

Richardson, J.M., Marsh, K.A., Schoenwald, J.S., & Martin, J.F. (1984). *Proceedings of the IEEE Ultrasonics Symposium* (pp. 831–836).

10
Dynamic Multisensor Data Fusion System for Intelligent Robots

Ren C. Luo,
Min-Hsiung Lin, and
Ralph S. Scherp

The objective of this chapter is to develop an intelligent robot workstation capable of integrating data from multiple sensors.

The investigation is based on a Unimation PUMA 560 robot and various external sensors. These include overhead vision, eye-in-hand vision, proximity, tactile array, position, force/torque, cross-fire, overload, and slipsensing devices. The efficient fusion of data from different sources will enable the machine to respond promptly in dealing with the "real world." Towards this goal, a general paradigm of multisensor interaction has been developed, and some simulation results as well as results from the actual implementation of certain concepts of multisensor data fusion have been demonstrated.

1. INTRODUCTION

The next generation of industrial robots will require motion control based on feedback from the environment from visual, tactile, force/torque, and other types of sensors. This will allow these intelligent robots to accommodate changes in workpiece position/orientation and to perform complex operations such as automated assembly and sorting.

There has been increasing interest in recent years in upgrading robot intelligence using multiple visual and nonvisual sensors. For example, the concept of the Logical Sensor was introduced by Henderson and Shilcrat (Chapter 4), and the Multisensor Kernel system was introduced by Henderson and Fai (Chapter 7). Kak, Boyer, Chern, Safranek, and Yang (1986) have presented a concept of knowledge-based robotics assembly cells, using multiple sensors.

Several other approaches to multisensor integration have also been described, such as the use of sensor variables (Chern (1984), sensor data fusion (Harmon, Bianchini, & Pinz, 1986; Moravec & Elfes, 1985; Fostel & Sanderson, 1984), the integration and propagation of geometric sensor observations (Durrante-Whyte, 1986), parallel computing (Chiu, Morley, & Martin, 1986), active sensory processing (Lee & Goldwasser, 1985), and Control and Monitoring Systems (Lee, Barnes, & Hardy, 1983; Barbera, Fitzgerald, & Albus, 1982). Though many good individual ideas have been explored, several key issues remain to be resolved to make possible a more general multisensor system.

Basically, systems integration for advanced automation can be subdivided into three levels: 1) lowest level—sensors and control; 2) intermediate level—workcell and planning; 3) highest level—factory planning and integration. Since research on the lower two levels is essential to the success of the highest level, this chapter considers manufacturing activities at the "sensor and control level" and the "cell level." A general approach for data fusion and its information propagation is developed, and a multisensor-based intelligent robot system incorporating this fusion technique is presented.

2. BASIC CONCEPT

2.1. Phases Based on Sensing Distance

Robot sensors can be grouped into four stages of information acquisition, each distinctive for the type of sensors used and the nature of the information obtained. We have termed these four categories "Far Away," "Near To," "Touching," and "Manipulation." In the first stage, a scene is detected from far away to acquire macro information and a decision is made whether or not to acquire more information. If more information is required, the system zooms in and takes a closer look at the scene of interest, to obtain micro information. Again a decision is made. If more information is desired, the system proceeds to the

"Touching" phase, which can be considered the prepickup or premanipulation phase. The last stage would involve actual manipulation of the object.

2.2. The Contents of the Four Distinct Phases

More specifically, the phases of information acquisition are as follows

Phase I ("Far Away" Sensing): In this phase, the system acquires useful information about a scene from far away, typically consisting of 1) the position, orientation, visual texture, color, shape, and size of objects; and 2) ambient temperature, radiation level, etc. Sensors used in this phase would probably include an ambient temperature sensor, global vision sensors (cameras, etc.), and any other sensors which can perform adequately from a distance. If the specific scene is of sufficient interest for the performance of the particular task, the system proceeds to Phase II.

Phase II ("Near To" Sensing): The information acquired in Phase II will be somewhat different from that in Phase I. If we are near an object we may no longer be able to "see" all of it in one view, hence we can no longer determine the shape or size of the object. However, we can still measure its position, orientation, color, radioactivity, or visual texture, and update this information as obtained in Phase I. Sensors useful at close range could include a variety of proximity sensors, visual sensors, directional Geiger-counters, etc. If the information acquired is found to be of interest in the performance of the task, we proceed to Phase III.

Phase III ("Touch" Sensing): Clearly, several sensors are no longer useful in this phase and thus are no longer queried for information. Position and orientation information can still be acquired using tactile sensors to confirm this same information as obtained in Phase II. In addition, new types of sensors such as tactile sensors are introduced, and the system can obtain new, more detailed information through "sensing by touch." If performance of the task requires manipulating the object, Phase IV will then be performed.

Phase IV ("Manipulating"): In this phase, the system must keep track of all the information necessary to manipulate the object. Sensors to detect force/torque, slippage, and weight are useful in this phase.

As shown in the preceding paragraphs, each phase relies on a different subset of all the sensors available to the multisensor system. Furthermore, each phase results in common data (such as position/orientation), and phase-specific data, which, though not common to all the other phases, may be duplicated or refined in two or more phases. If we were to conveniently package the information obtained in each phase into a distinct template, a frame-type scheme for data representation would result. Figure 10.1 illustrates typical phase templates, where the common data x, y, z and α, β, γ define the object position and orientation, respectively.

Having established the general types of information we expect to obtain in each phase, we next consider the more specific issue of retrieving the information from all sensors used in a given phase.

3. SYSTEM CONFIGURATION AND ARCHITECTURE

The basic system architecture we have devised is shown in a functional block diagram in Figure 10.2. We divide the overall system into six distinct units, the functions of which are as follows.

1. *Data Acquisition Unit:* This unit is responsible for acquiring and storing the raw sensor information for later retrieval. It has as its inputs the multiple sensors which through an interface store their raw sensor data in a buffer acting as a storage medium. It runs independently of any of the other units.

2. *The Knowledge Base:* The knowledge base required here can be split into four major categories.

a) The Robot Database: This database has at its heart a robot controller which can be used for motion, position, and velocity calculations. The database also keeps track of any physical constraints on the robot for the purpose of path analysis.

b) The Sensor Database: This is the database containing all pertinent information about the sensors available to the system. It contains such information as: i) the types of sensors available and their respective output data formats; ii) the operating constraints on each sensor;

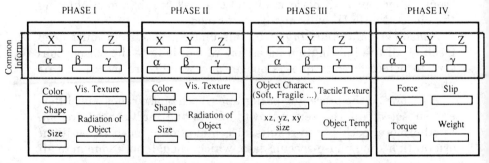

Figure 10.1. Schematic diagram of typical phase templates.

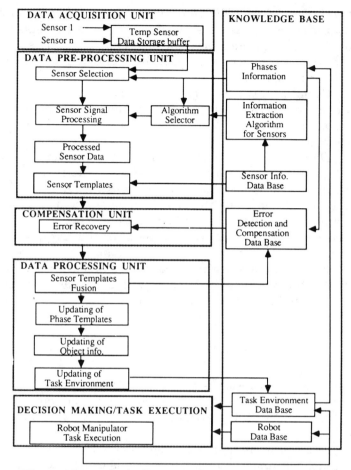

Figure 10.2. Block diagram of system configuration.

iii) the physical location of each sensor; iv) the time required to acquire information from each sensor; v) the characteristic parameters of the data from each sensor (e.g., standard deviation, etc.); and finally, vi) features of the algorithms required to convert raw sensor data into processed values.

c) Error Detection and Compensation Database: This database maintains information on all of the sensors and their respective performance. If a sensor is judged to be faulty, it is so labeled, and data from this sensor are further analyzed to allow error recovery. The error recovery compensation coefficients are stored in this database.

d) Environment Database: This database stores information concerning the task environment, as well as information from the four distinct phase templates described above.

3. *Data Preprocessing Unit:* Only appropriate sensor data, as determined by the current phase, are transferred to the arithmetic processing unit. The appropriate algorithms are simultaneously selected to convert raw sensor data into the data formats required to create the actual sensor templates.

4. *The Compensation Unit:* This unit compensates for those sensors which are known to give data that deviate from the actual values by a known relationship. It uses the coefficients calculated and stored in the Error Database.

5. *The Data Processing Unit:* This unit merges (or fuses) all appropriate sensor data into a coherent data unit (i.e., the phase template). The principle for sensor data fusion will be presented in a later section. By modifying and updating the phase template, the data processing unit modifies and updates the environment database.

6. *Decision Making/Task Execution:* Based on the task environment information, the desired tasks are decided upon, and consequently executed. Successful task performance requires knowledge of the characteristics of the robot manipulator as well as the task environment (as shown in the Environment Database).

4. FUSION OF SENSOR DATA

Effective sensor data fusion is critical to increasing robot capability. The more effectively and completely data from the various sensor resources are compiled, the greater the robot's ability to accomplish complex tasks.

The idea of fusion is to merge two or more separate items into a single entity. Our analysis indicates that this entity should be in the form of the current phase template and should be obtained by combining the appropriate sensor data templates into one representative template. Problems can arise in this fusion process if any of the sensing data specified are uncertain or in conflict, implying that an error in a sensor has occurred. Therefore, except in ideal circumstances in which all data are certain and in agreement, sensor data fusion will entail detection, verification, and recovery of sensor errors.

4.1. Definition of the "Distance Matrix" and "Confidence Distance Measures"

Data representing the same object properties (e.g., object position or orientation) will most likely deviate if acquired from different sensors. Consequently, "measures of confidence," that is, the description of sensors by probability distribution, represent a primary means of effective data fusion. Sensor deviations may be generated by 1) measurement, due to sensor characteristics (e.g., noise, accuracy, etc.) and 2) processing by the data interpretation algorithms.

Some of the many advantages of describing sensors by probability distributions include the ability to integrate a variety of information types in a consistent manner and to obtain a high degree of data compression. In addition, such statistical models have long been used in other areas, and well developed methodologies exist for analyzing optimality, uncertainty, and robustness. Here we will use a probability density function (pdf) curve as the sensor's characteristic function for analyzing the confidence measures. We will later define a "distance matrix" as a tool for obtaining confidence measures.

Upon obtaining a calibrated sensor's characteristic curve, we can use statistical estimation theory to define the error detection criterion. We will use a curve pdf as the sensor's characteristic function for the analysis, and will then define a "distance matrix" and use it as the criterion for detecting sensor errors.

The concept of a distance measure between two probability curves is widely used in statistics. For example, Grettenberg (1963), Kailath (1967), Kadota and Shepp (1967), and Hisashi (1970) discuss the application of some of these measures to communication problems.

An important class of distance measures frequently mentioned in the literature was surveyed by Ali and Silvey (1966), and includes, among others, the J-divergence (Kullback, 1959), Matsusita (Matsusita, Suzuki, & Hudimoto, 1954), and Bhattacharyya (Bhattacharyya, 1943) distances. These distance measures are defined as those which can be written in the general form

$$d(P_1, P_2) = f\{E_1\{C(L)\}\} \quad (1)$$

where $d(P_1, P_2)$ is the distance between the probability measures P_1 and P_2, f is an increasing function, C is a convex function on $(0, \infty)$, L is the likelihood ratio dP_2/dP_1, and E_1 denotes expectation with respect to P_1.

The three specific distance measures mentioned above are defined as follows:

a) J-divergence:

$$J = E_1\{(L - 1) \log L\}.$$

b) Matsusita's Distance:

$$d = \{E_1\{(\sqrt{L} - 1)^2\}\}^{1/2}.$$

c) Bhattacharyya's Distance:

$$B = -\log(1 - d^2)$$

where d is Matsusita's distance.

These functions were designed as distance measures between two probability distributions, that is, P_1 and P_2. However, they are not appropriate in the case of multiple sensor fusion.

For the multisensor case, we can define another useful distance measure as the criterion for the purpose of sensor error detection. Consider two probability distributions $P_i(x)$ and $P_j(x)$ as shown in Figure 10.3, where the variance measures are different, that is, $\sigma_i^2 \neq \sigma_j^2$, and where x_i, x_j represent sensor ith and sensor jth reading.

We can define the conditional probability function P_{ij} in the form

$$P_{ij} = P_i(x_j/x_i). \tag{2}$$

Similarly, we can define P_{ji} as

$$P_{ji} = P_j(x_i/x_j). \tag{3}$$

As an example, in Figure 10.3, P_{ij} is greater than P_{ji}, which can be interpreted as follows. For the probability distribution $P_i(x)$, x_i is sensor i's value. Based on x_i, the conditional probability function $P_{ij} = 0.75$, signifying that the probability of the jth sensor reading value (x_j) being accurate is 75 percent. In contrast, for the probability distribution $P_j(x)$, $P_{ji} = 0.3$, which means that the probability of the ith sensor reading value (x_i) being accurate is only 30 percent. Therefore, we can conclude that with respect to $P_i(x)$, sensor reading values x_i and x_j agree *more* closely. Similarly, based on $P_j(x)$ sensor reading value x_i and x_j agree *less* closely. Figure 10.3 thus demonstrates that the dis-

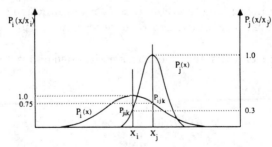

Figure 10.3. Two probability distributions $P_i(x)$ and $P_j(x)$ with different variance measures.

tance between two probability distributions $P_i(x)$ and $P_j(x)$ has two different values depending on which probability distribution $P_i(x)$ or $P_j(x)$ we chose as the reference.

Since uncertainties will exist in data derived from multiple sensors, we will need to find the interrelations among different sensors. If the sensor values are close to each other, we may fuse them together, but if the values vary greatly from each other, some values may be suspected to be incorrect and therefore not to be considered for fusion.

Based on this analysis, we will now define a new distance measure, either d_{ij} or d_{ji} as a criterion for detecting sensor errors. We call this new distance measure "confidence distance measure" d_{ij} or d_{ji} as shown in Figure 10.4(a) and (b).

$$d_{ij} = 2|F_i(x_i) - F_i(x_j)| = 2\left|\int_{x_i}^{x_2} P_i(x)dx\right| = 2A_{ij} \qquad (4)$$

and

$$d_{ji} = 2|F_j(x_i) - F_j(x_j)| = 2\left|\int_{x_i}^{x_j} P_j(x)dx\right| = 2B_{ji},$$

where $F_i(x)$ and $F_j(x)$ are cumulative distribution functions for sensor i and j, respectively. Here A or B is the area between sensor reading values x_i and x_j under probability distribution curve $P_i(x)$ or $P_j(x)$. In general, $d_{ij} \neq d_{ji}$ (unless the standard deviation $\sigma_i = \sigma_j$) and $0 \leq d_i, d_{ji} \leq 1$.

As an example of extreme cases of d_{ij}, such as

1. $x_i = x_j$, when $d_{ij} = 0$ (see Figure 10.5(a)).
2. x_i is far away from x_j, when $d_{ij} = 1$ (see Figure 10.5(b)).

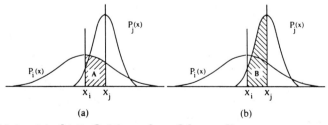

Figure 10.4. (a), (b) Definition of confidence distance measure d_{ij} or d_{ji}.

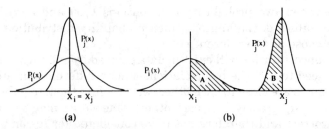

Figure 10.5. (a), (b) Illustrative example of extreme case of d_{ij}.

The advantages of this new confidence distance measure are twofold: Not only does it provide an abstract scale value as given by the aforementioned distance measures, but it also represents the relation of the distance versus confidence measures. For example if $d_{ij} = 0.6$, it means that if the sensor value x_i is correct, then the sensor value x_j is within 60 percent of confidence interval under the probability distribution of $P_i(x)$. Note that the higher the percentage of confidence interval, the larger the distance between x_i and x_j will be.

Basically, the Gaussian distribution is the most common and useful pdf. Furthermore, Fukunaga and Flick have developed a technique which allows for testing data to determine whether or not they are a Gaussian distribution. To clarify the analysis, we basically use the Gaussian distribution as the sensors' distribution model. Again, $P_i(x)$ = pdf of the ith sensor. As an example, we consider a Gaussian distribution in the one-dimensional case.

$$P_i(x) = \frac{1}{\sqrt{2\pi}\sigma_i} E^{-(1/2)(x-x_m/\sigma_i)^2} \quad (6)$$

where σ_i^2 is the variance of sensor i, x_i is the ith sensor's reading value, while in the multidimensional case

$$P_i(x) = \frac{1}{(2\pi)^{n/2}|C_i|^{1/2}} e^{-(1/2)[x-x_m]^T C_i^{-1}[x-x_m]} \quad (7)$$

where n is the dimensionality of the sensor data, C_i is covariance matrix of sensor i, and x_m is the mean vector of the n dimension.

Assume we have m sensors to measure the same object property whose measurements are $x_{11}, x_{21}, ..., x_{m1}$, where x_{ik} signifies the kth data measured by the ith sensor.

If sensor i and sensor j are measuring the kth object property, in a general case, the conditional probability function for one dimension can be defined as

$$P_{ijk} = P_i(x_{jk}/x_{ik}) = \frac{1}{\sqrt{2\pi}\,\sigma_{ik}(s)} \exp\left[-\frac{1}{2}\left(\frac{x_{jk} - x_{ik}}{\sigma_{ik}(s)}\right)^2\right] \quad (8)$$

$$P_{jik} = P_j(x_{ik}/x_{jk}) = \frac{1}{\sqrt{2\pi}\,\sigma_{jk}(s)} \exp\left[-\frac{1}{2}\left(\frac{x_{ik} - x_{jk}}{\sigma_{jk}(s)}\right)^2\right] \quad (9)$$

where $\sigma_{ik}(s)$ is the standard deviation of the distribution for the ith sensor in measuring the kth object property under the "s" phase. In general, the standard deviation of the sensors' pdf curves varies with the four distinct phases described previously. For example, in comparison with the eye-in-hand vision system in the "Far Away" phase, the overhead vision system will have a similar σ value. However, the eye-in-hand vision system in the "Near To" phase can have a smaller σ value than the overhead vision system.

The confidence distance measures can be computed by the use of an error function defined as

$$\text{erf}(\theta) = \frac{2}{\sqrt{\pi}} \int_0^\theta e^{-z^2} dz. \quad (10)$$

Letting

$$z = \frac{x - x_i}{\sqrt{2}\,\sigma_i} \quad dz = \frac{1}{\sqrt{2}\,\sigma_i} dx,$$

(10) becomes

$$\text{erf}(\theta) = \frac{\sqrt{2}}{\sqrt{\pi}\,\sigma_i} \int_{x_i}^{x_i + \sqrt{2}\theta\sigma_i} e^{-(1/2)(x - x_i/\sigma_i)^2} dx. \quad (11a)$$

Letting $x_j = x_i + \sqrt{2}\theta\sigma_i$, then

$$\theta = \frac{x_j - x_i}{\sqrt{2}\,\sigma_i}$$

and (11a) becomes

$$\text{erf}\left(\frac{x_j - x_i}{\sqrt{2}\,\sigma_i}\right) = 2 \int_{x_i}^{x_j} P_i(x/x_i)\, dx. \quad (11b)$$

Now, from (2), (3), and (11b) we can compute the confidence distance measures as shown in (12) and (13).

In the case of $x_{jk} > x_{ik}$

$$d_{ijk} = 2 \int_{x_i}^{x_j} P_i(x/x_i) P_i(x_i) \, dx = 2 P_i(x_i) \int_{x_i}^{x_j} P_i(x/x_i) \, dx$$

$$= \frac{1}{\sqrt{2\pi} \, \sigma_{ik}(s)} \cdot \text{erf}\left(\frac{x_{jk} - x_{ik}}{\sqrt{2} \, \sigma_{ik}(s)} \right) \tag{12}$$

$$d_{jik} = 2 \int_{x_i}^{x_j} P_j(x/x_j) P_j(x_j) \, dx = 2 P_j(x_j) \int_{x_i}^{x_j} P_j(x/x_j) \, dx$$

$$= \frac{1}{\sqrt{2\pi} \, \sigma_{jk}(s)} \cdot \text{erf}\left(\frac{x_{jk} - x_{ik}}{\sqrt{2} \, \sigma_{jk}(s)} \right). \tag{13}$$

Assuming we have m sensors for measuring the same object property, the general confidence distance measures can be described in a matrix format. To simplify the matrix, we neglect the object property index k for the following analysis:

$$D_k = \begin{bmatrix} d_{11} & d_{12} & \cdots & d_{1m} \\ d_{21} & d_{22} & \cdots & d_{2m} \\ \cdot & \cdot & \cdots & \cdot \\ \cdot & \cdot & \cdots & \cdot \\ d_{m1} & d_{m2} & \cdots & d_{mm} \end{bmatrix}. \tag{14}$$

4.2. Creation of the Relation Matrix and Directed Graph Representation

Having obtained the distance matrix ("D" matrix), we can determine the corresponding relationships of the sensors to one another. We can define a relation matrix "R" by thresholding the "D" matrices by some empirically found value. The relation matrix R is defined as

$$R_k = \begin{bmatrix} r_{11} & r_{12} & \cdots & r_{1m} \\ r_{21} & r_{22} & \cdots & r_{2m} \\ \cdot & \cdot & \cdots & \cdot \\ \cdot & \cdot & \cdots & \cdot \\ r_{m1} & r_{m2} & \cdots & r_{mm} \end{bmatrix} \tag{15}$$

where r_{ij} is the threshold value of d_{ij}, and

$$r_{ij} = \begin{cases} 1, & \text{if } d_{ij} \leq \text{threshold value} \\ 0, & \text{if } d_{ij} > \text{threshold value}. \end{cases}$$

The relational matrix R_k can be conveniently represented in the form of a directed graph (Deo, 1974) (or digraph for short). The graph is visualized by first representing all the sensors being used as nodes, and then drawing a directed arrow from node i to node j if r_{ij} equals one. The complete digraph will then represent a convenient way of visualizing the relationships among all of the used sensors, thus allowing us to look for consensus groups of sensors (i.e., with data in agreement).

The digraph concept can best be explained by means of an illustrated example. Suppose we generated an R_k matrix, with four different sensors, that is, $m = 4$, resulting from the thresholding of a D_k matrix.

$$R_k = \begin{bmatrix} 1 & 1 & 0 & 0 \\ 1 & 1 & 1 & 0 \\ 0 & 0 & 1 & 0 \\ 0 & 0 & 0 & 1 \end{bmatrix}. \tag{16}$$

Then the R_k matrix can be represented by the following digraph as shown in Figure 10.6.

Keeping in mind that each node represents a sensor value, we can say that sensor 1 and sensor 2 support each other and that sensor 3 is being supported by sensor 2. Sensor 4, on the other hand, is left unsupported and thus is suspected of being in error.

Next follows the identification of the largest connected group present in the digraph (or a clique). This represents the most likely group of sensors which yield an accurate representation of the actual data. All those sensors which are weakly supported by the largest connected group of sensors would then be suspected of being in error and thus would have to be subjected to either compensation (if possible) or complete dismissal (if compensation is not possible).

Figure 10.6. Digraph representation for R_k matrix in (16).

4.3. The Strategy for Determining the Optimal Fused Sensor Data

Having identified the largest connected subgraph, the next step will be to fuse all the sensors' data in this subgraph into one sensor node in the digraph. Furthermore, we want to develop a strategy for determining the optimal fused data as representative sensing data for an object property.

As an example, consider a robot with m sensors for sensing a set of object properties (e.g., distance, size, shape, color, etc.). Each sensor i will have its output vector x_i. Through Directed Graph analysis, we can find a consistent subset of l sensors which support each other's information. With this assumption, we are trying to determine the optimal estimated object properties θ by developing a consensus among our existing sensors and fusing all consistent sensor data.

Two methods for accomplishing effective data fusion have been developed. The first approach maximizes the total probability of all sensor data and can be formulated as follows: The optimal fused sensor data $\hat{\theta}$ should maximize the value of (17).

$$\sum_{i=1}^{l} P_i(\theta/x_i)P(x_i). \qquad (17)$$

In order to determine the optimal fused data value, we take the derivative of (17) with respect to theta, and set it to zero. That is

$$\frac{\partial}{\partial \theta} \sum_{i=1}^{l} P_i(\theta/x_i)P(x_i) \Big|_{\theta=\hat{\theta}} = 0$$

$$\sum_{i=1}^{l} \frac{1}{(2\pi)^{n/2}|C_i|^{1/2}} \{(C_i^{-1})[\hat{\theta} - x_i]\} e^{-(1/2)[\hat{\theta}-x_i]^T C_i^{-1}[\hat{\theta}-x_i]} = 0. \qquad (18)$$

Equation (18) is a transcendental equation, and it could be solved by iteration. Setting $\hat{\theta} = \hat{\theta}_1$ as a first iteration value, we obtain

$$d_i = \frac{e^{-(1/2)[\hat{\theta}_1 - x_i]^T C_i^{-1}[\hat{\theta}_1 - x_i]}}{(2\pi)^{n/2}|C_i|^{1/2}}. \qquad (19)$$

From (18) and (19)

$$\sum_{i=1}^{l} d_i(C_i^{-1})[\hat{\theta} - x_i] = 0$$

$$\hat{\theta} = \sum_{i=1}^{l} d_i(C_i^{-1})x_i \cdot \left[\sum_{i=1}^{l} d_i(C_i^{-1})\right]^{-1}. \tag{20}$$

This iteration procedure is continued until $\hat{\theta}$ converges.

Using the same example, we can show an alternative approach to determine the optimal fused sensor data as follows. Assume x and l sets of data vectors, $\chi = \{x_1, x_2, ..., x_l\}$. Then since the sensor vectors are measured independently,

$$p(\chi/\theta) = \prod_{k=1}^{l} p(x_k/\theta). \tag{21}$$

Viewed as a function of θ, $p(\chi/\theta)$ is called the likelihood of θ with respect to the set of measurements (Duda & Hart, 1973).

The maximum likelihood estimate of θ is, by definition, that value $\hat{\theta}$ that maximizes $p(\chi/\theta)$. Intuitively, it corresponds to the value of θ that in some sense best agrees with the actual measurements (i.e., the optimal fused sensor data).

For analytical purposes, it is usually easier to work with the logarithm of the likelihood than with the likelihood itself. Since the logarithm is monotonically increasing, the $\hat{\theta}$ that maximizes the log likelihood also maximizes the likelihood. If $p(\chi/\theta)$ is a well-behaved, differentiable function of θ, $\hat{\theta}$ can be found by the standard methods of differential calculus. Let θ be the p-component vector $\theta = (\theta_1, ..., \theta_p)^t$, let ∇_θ be the gradient operator

$$\nabla_\theta = \begin{bmatrix} \frac{\partial}{\partial \theta_1} \\ \cdot \\ \cdot \\ \cdot \\ \frac{\partial}{\partial \theta_p} \end{bmatrix} \tag{22}$$

and let $L(\theta)$ be the log-likelihood function; that is,

$$L(\theta) = \log p(\chi/\theta)$$
$$= \sum_{k=1}^{l} \log p(x_k/\theta) \tag{23}$$

and

$$\nabla_\theta L(\theta) \sum_{k=1}^{l} \nabla_\theta \log p(x_k \mid \theta). \tag{24}$$

Thus a set of necessary conditions for the maximum likelihood estimate for θ can be obtained from the set of p equations $\nabla_\theta L(\theta) = 0$.

To see how these results apply to a specific case, suppose that the measurements drawn from a set of sensors for the probability density distributions are all Gaussian.

$$L(\theta) = \log p(\chi/\theta) = \sum_{k=1}^{l} \log p(x_k/\theta)$$

$$= \sum_{k=1}^{l} \left\{ -\frac{1}{2} \log [(2\pi)^n |C_k|] - \frac{1}{2} (x_k - \theta)^t C_k^{-1} (x_k - \theta) \right\} \tag{25}$$

$$\nabla_\theta L(\theta) \mid_{\hat{\theta}} = \sum_{k=1}^{l} (C_k^{-1})(x_k - \hat{\theta})$$

$$= 0. \tag{26}$$

From (26)

$$\sum_{k=1}^{l} C_k^{-1} x_k = \sum_{k=1}^{l} C_k^{-1} \hat{\theta} \tag{27}$$

then

$$\hat{\theta} = \frac{\sum_{k=1}^{l} C_k^{-1} x_k}{\sum_{k=1}^{l} C_k^{-1}}. \tag{28}$$

Equations (20 and (28) represent the fused sensor data value a in a multidimensional situation. It is helpful to know the level of confidence we can have. Based on the linear interpolation technique, we can derive the covariance matrix value of the fused sensor data as indicated in (28).

$$\tilde{C} = \frac{1}{l-1} \cdot \sum_{i=1}^{l} \left[\frac{\sum_{i=1, j \neq i}^{l} |\hat{\theta} - x_j| C_i}{\sum_{k=1}^{l} |\hat{\theta} - x_k|} \right]. \quad (29)$$

Apparently, the larger the covariance matrix value of the fused sensor data is, the lower the confidence measures will be. After accomplishing the generation of the fused sensor template, we can update the current phase template by replacing it entirely with the fused sensor template.

4.4. Illustrative Example of Sensor Data Fusion

Consider a robot with eight sensors which have the digraph representation as shown in Figure 10.7. We will determine which of these sensor nodes should be used for the fusing process based upon the confidence measures.

First, we consider the simplest case for only two sensor nodes. Three cases can occur as shown in Figure 10.8. In the first case, the two sensors do not support each other. The best way is to select the sensor value which has the smaller variance (i.e., the higher confidence measure).

In the second case, sensor 1 supports sensor 2; however, sensor 2 does not support sensor 1. We choose sensor 2 as the resulting fused data and do not attribute to sensor 1 the status of being in error.

In the third case, sensors 1 and 2 support each other. It is highly probable that both sensors are near to the actual data value. We would then fuse two sensor data using the data fusion principle as described previously.

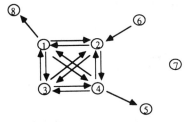

Figure 10.7. Digraph for illustrative example of sensor data fusion.

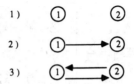

Figure 10.8. Relationship between two sensor nodes in a digraph.

Based on this concept, we can solve the data fusion problem in Figure 10.7 using the following procedures:

1. First, fuse the data which completely support each other (i.e., nodes 1, 2, 3, 4) to form a new sensor node f. The graph is then simplified to Figure 10.9. Here, the sensor data value f represents the node of highest confidence based solely upon those nodes which were fused to form it and will be henceforth called a "super" node. The remaining fusing procedures will then be based on the remaining nodes and the newly made "super" node.

2. Any sensor node which is supported by the super node (e.g., nodes 8, 5) will be considered as being correct and thus be fused with super node f. The resulting digraph is shown in Figure 10.10.

3. Any sensor node which is supporting the super node (e.g., node 6) will be considered to be slightly deviant from the actual data value and therefore is not to be labeled as faulty or in error.

4. Any isolated nodes (e.g., node 7) will result in the corresponding sensors to be labeled as faulty or erroneous. Therefore, the fused sensor data node f^* will be the highest confidence measure in this example.

5. EXPERIMENTATION

As described previously, we use a pdf curve as a sensor's characteristic function for the analysis. In addition, we developed a "distance matrix" and a "relation matrix" based on theory of the directed graphs to detect sensor errors and to fuse only the consistent sensors together.

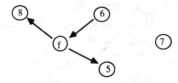

Figure 10.9. The fusion the completely supported sensor nodes.

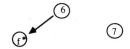

Figure 10.10. Further fusing with the "super" sensor node.

We have demonstrated a simulation based on Eqs. (12), (13), (15), (20), and (28) to verify the success of the sensor fusion concepts. The simulation procedure and results are described as follows.

Number of sensor data = 10

data[1] = 1.000000	variance[1] = 0.050000
data[2] = 0.990000	variance[2] = 0.070000
data[3] = 0.980000	variance[3] = 0.100000
data[4] = 0.970000	variance[4] = 0.200000
data[5] = 0.500000	variance[5] = 0.300000
data[6] = 0.650000	variance[6] = 0.250000
data[7] = 1.010000	variance[7] = 0.100000
data[8] = 1.020000	variance[8] = 0.100000
data[9] = 1.030000	variance[9] = 0.200000
data[10] = 1.500000	variance[10] = 0.300000

Using equation (12) and (13) to find the "distance" between any two sensor data

The Distance Matrix D =
```
0.000  0.036  0.071  0.107  0.975  0.882  0.036  0.071  0.107  0.975
0.030  0.000  0.030  0.060  0.936  0.801  0.060  0.090  0.120  0.946
0.050  0.025  0.000  0.025  0.871  0.703  0.076  0.101  0.126  0.900
0.053  0.036  0.018  0.000  0.707  0.526  0.071  0.089  0.107  0.764
0.639  0.629  0.619  0.609  0.000  0.216  0.648  0.658  0.667  0.932
0.516  0.503  0.491  0.478  0.236  0.000  0.528  0.541  0.553  0.911
0.025  0.050  0.076  0.101  0.893  0.745  0.000  0.025  0.050  0.879
0.050  0.076  0.101  0.126  0.900  0.758  0.025  0.000  0.025  0.871
0.053  0.071  0.089  0.107  0.764  0.605  0.036  0.018  0.000  0.707
0.639  0.648  0.658  0.667  0.932  0.879  0.629  0.619  0.609  0.000
```

Thresholding the "D" matrix to construct "R" matrix
Thresholding Value = 0.500000

The Relation Matrix $R =$

$$\begin{matrix} 1 & 1 & 1 & 1 & 0 & 0 & 1 & 1 & 1 & 0 \\ 1 & 1 & 1 & 1 & 0 & 0 & 1 & 1 & 1 & 0 \\ 1 & 1 & 1 & 1 & 0 & 0 & 1 & 1 & 1 & 0 \\ 1 & 1 & 1 & 1 & 0 & 0 & 1 & 1 & 1 & 0 \\ 0 & 0 & 0 & 0 & 1 & 1 & 0 & 0 & 0 & 0 \\ 0 & 0 & 1 & 1 & 1 & 1 & 0 & 0 & 0 & 0 \\ 1 & 1 & 1 & 1 & 0 & 0 & 1 & 1 & 1 & 0 \\ 1 & 1 & 1 & 1 & 0 & 0 & 1 & 1 & 1 & 0 \\ 1 & 1 & 1 & 1 & 0 & 0 & 1 & 1 & 1 & 0 \\ 0 & 0 & 0 & 0 & 0 & 0 & 0 & 0 & 0 & 1 \end{matrix}$$

****Finding the largest connected group****

The largest connected group has 7 nodes

7 1 2 3 4 8 9

Number of sensor data to be fused = 7

data[1] = 1.000000	variance[1] = 0.050000
data[2] = 0.990000	variance[2] = 0.070000
data[3] = 0.980000	variance[3] = 0.100000
data[4] = 0.970000	variance[4] = 0.200000
data[7] = 1.010000	variance[7] = 0.100000
data[8] = 1.020000	variance[8] = 0.100000
data[9] = 1.030000	variance[9] = 0.200000

—Method 1—
Using equation (19) to find the optimal fused data

—Method 2—
Using equation (27) to find the optimal fused data

Number of iteration = 1
The optimal fused data value = 9.991495$e - 01$

The optimal fused data value = 9.992641$e - 01$.

In order to test the aforementioned robot multisensor fusion system, a preliminary experimental setup has been established as shown in Figure 10.11.

In general, the overall experimental setup can be divided into three categories; robot, multisensors, and computer-support hardware. A Unimation PUMA 560 together with additional external multisensors are used to test the success of the multisensor data fusion algorithms.

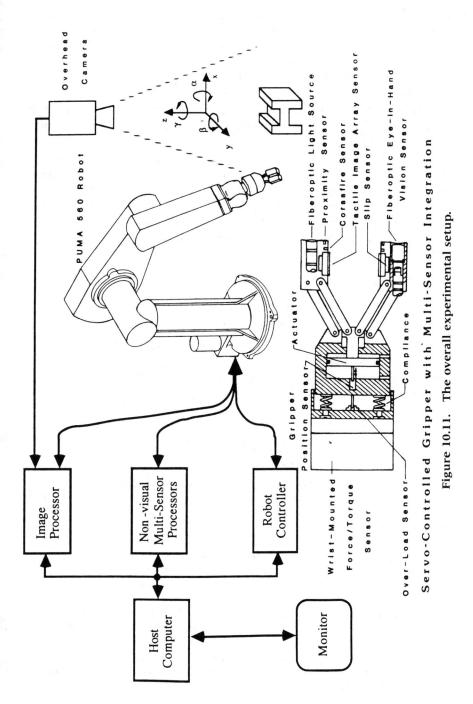

Figure 10.11. The overall experimental setup.

Several sensors are used including overhead vision, robot eye-in-hand vision, ultrasonic range sensor, tactile sensing array, wrist force/torque sensor, and finger-mounted force/slip sensors, etc. The supervisory system is a multiuser DEC VAX 11/785. Programs are also written in modular fashion in the C language. The Unimation PUMA robot is a six-axis articulated arm, with DEC 11/73 based controller; the programming language is VAL II. Vision processing is performed using a TRAPIX 5500 vision system with programs also written in a modular fashion in the C language.

The VAX acts as a supervisory system, providing an interface to the user and overall task control. The VAX is responsible for some portion of each sensor subsystem setup (i.e., calibration, communication, etc.). All sequences of adaptive commands generated for the PUMA by the VAX are communicated by the use of this extensive library. Subroutines are available to perform communication, logic, and movement commands as required.

6. CONCLUSION

The integration of multiple sensors in an intelligent robot system has been presented. The system is capable of performing multisensor data fusion and sensor data error detection, making it useful for industrial applications such as flexible manufacturing.

REFERENCES

Ali, S.M., & Silvey, S.D. (1966). A general class of coefficients of divergence of one distribution from another. *Journal of the Royal Statistical Society B, 28*, 131–142.

Barbera, A.J., Fitzgerald, M.L., & Albus, J.S. (1982). Concepts for a real time sensory-interactive control system architecture. *Conference Proceedings of the 14th Southeastern Symposium on System Theory.*

Bhattacharyya, A. (1943). On a measure of divergence between two statistical populations defined by their probability distributions. *Bulletin of the Calcutta Mathematical Society, 35*, 99–109.

Chern, M.Y. (1984). An efficient scheme for monitoring sensory conditions in robot systems. *IEEE International Conference on Robotics* (pp. 298–304). Atlanta, GA.

Chiu, S.L., Morley, D.J., & Martin, J.F. (1986). Sensor data fusion on a parallel processor. *IEEE International Conference on Robotics and Automation* (pp. 1629–1633). San Francisco, CA.

Deo, N. (1974). *Graph theory with applications to engineering and computer science.* Englewood Cliffs, NJ: Prentice-Hall.

Duda, R.O., & Hart, P.E. (1973). *Pattern classification and scene analysis.* New York: Wiley.

Durrant-Whyte, H.F. (1986). Consistent integration and propagation of disparate sensor observations. *IEEE International Conference on Robotics and Automation* (pp. 1464–1469). San Francisco, CA.

Fostel, N.J., & Sanderson, A.C. (1984). *Determining object orientation from a single image using multiple information sources* (Tech. Rep. CMU-RI-TR-84-15). Carnegie-Mellon University: Robotics Institute.

Fukunaga, K., & Flick, T.E. (1986). A test of the Gaussian-ness of a data set using clustering. *IEEE Transactions on Pattern Analysis and Machine Intelligence,* PAMI-8(2), 240–247.

Grettenberg, T.L. (1963). Signal selection in communication and radar systems. *IEEE Transactions on Information Theory,* IT-9(4), 265–275.

Harmon, S.Y., Bianchini, G.L., & Pinz, B.E. (1986). Sensor data fusion through a distributed blackboard. *IEEE International Conference on Robotics and Automation* (pp. 1449–1454). San Francisco, CA.

Kadota, T.T., & Shepp, L.A. (1967). On the best finite set of linear observables for discriminating two Gaussian signals. *IEEE Transactions on Information Theory,* IT-13(2), 278–284.

Kailath, T. (1967). The divergence and Bhattacharyya distance measures in signal selection. *IEEE Transactions on Communications Technology,* COM-15(1), 52–60.

Kak, A.C., Boyer, K.L., Chern, C.H., Safranek, R.J., & Yang, H.S. (1986). A knowledge-based robotics assembly cell. *IEEE International Conference on Robotics and Automation.* San Francisco, CA.

Kobayashi, H. (1970). Distance measures and asymptotic relative efficiency. *IEEE Transactions on Information Theory,* IT-16(3), 288–291.

Kullback, S. (1959). *Information theory and statistics.* New York: Wiley.

Lee, I., & Goldwasser, S.M. (1985). A distributed testbed for active sensory processing. *IEEE International Conference on Robotics and Automation* (pp. 925–930). St. Louis, MO.

Lee, M.H., Barnes, D.P., & Hardy, N.W. (1983). A control and monitoring system for multiple-sensor industrial robots. *Proceedings of the 3rd International Conference on Robot Vision and Sensory Controls.* Cambridge, MA.

Matsusita, K., Suzuki, Y., & Hudimoto, H. (1954). On testing statistical hypotheses. *Annals of the Institute of Statistical Mathematics* (Tokyo), 6, 133–141.

Moravec, H.P., & Elfes, A.E. (1985). High resolution maps from wide angle sonar. *IEEE International Conference on Robotics and Automation* (pp. 116–121). St. Louis, MO.

Ruokangas, C.C., Black, M.S., Martin,, J.F., & Schoenwald, J.S. (1986). Integration of multiple sensors to provide flexible control strategies. *IEEE International Conference on Robotics and Automation* (pp. 1947–1953). San Francisco, CA.

11
Geometrical Fusion Method for Multisensor Robotic Systems*

Yoshihiko Nakamura and
Yingti Xu

In this chapter, a general statistical fusion method motivated by the geometry of uncertainties is proposed for robotic systems with multiple sensors. The treatment of nonlinearity is generalized so as to include both the structural nonlinearity and the computational nonlinearity. First, assuming the Gaussian noise additive to the sensory data, an uncertainty ellipsoid is defined to be associated with the covariance matrix of the error of the sensory information. Second, optimal fusion is defined as that which minimizes the geometrical volume of the ellipsoid among all the possible linear combinations of sensory information. It is shown that the optimal fusion method results in a similar algorithm to the results obtained by Bayesian inference using a minimum variance estimate, Kalman filter theory, and the weighted least square estimate. Finally, the method is extended to include the fusion of partial information.

1. INTRODUCTION

Advanced applications of robotic systems require them to have various kinds of external sensors, such as force sensors, tactile sensors, prox-

---

*This material is based upon the work supported by the National Science Foundation under Contract number 8421415.

imity sensors, ultrasonic sensors, range sensors, vision sensors and so on, in addition to the basic internal sensors such as encoders and tachometers. As robotic applications expand not only towards advanced industrial fields where more adaptability is required, but also towards unknown environments such as space and underwater, robotic systems will naturally have to be equipped with more and more sensors to identify their environment and to determine their actions.

Sensor fusion is a technology to extract better information from multiple sensors. The primary aim is to pick up more accurate and less uncertain information by actively utilizing redundant information. For instance, a robot manipulator with a vision sensor and a set of joint sensors can identify its end effector location by either type of sensor. The conventional approach is to select one sensor when it looks more appropriate for the situation than the other. This selection procedure must be explicitly written as a program by knowing the detail of the measuring function of sensors and the moving function of robotic mechanisms. Although it does not seem to be significant when the degree of redundancy of sensors is relatively low, the load on programmers becomes heavier and heavier as the degree of redundancy increases. More importantly, this strategy is not taking advantage of the potential for improving the accuracy and suppressing the uncertainty that could be achieved by combining redundant sensory information. If we could combine both vision and joint information in an appropriate fashion in the above case, we would get better information than from either one of them. This fact becomes even more substantial as the degree of redundancy increases.

The goal of this chapter is to provide a general and systematic mathematical method of multisensor fusion for robotic systems that increases the accuracy and reduces the uncertainty by combining redundant sensory information.

2. BACKGROUND

Although research on sensor fusion has a relatively short history, many papers have been published in journals and conferences recently. In 1984, Henderson and Shilcrat (Chapter 4) discussed the framework of Logical Sensor Systems to treat multisensor systems in a coherent and efficient way, and Henderson, Fai, and Hansen (Chapter 7) developed the Multisensor Kernel System. On the other hand, Bajcsy and Allen (1985) proposed to fuse disparate sensory data for object recognition. The modeling of measurement uncertainty was addressed by

Brooks (1985) where he defined the Uncertainty Manifold for mobile robots and proposed back reasoning based on landmark information.

Statistical uncertainty modeling for multisensor systems was initiated by Durrant-Whyte (1985) when he assumed Gaussian distribution and applied Bayesian inference with minimum variance estimate to fuse linearly structured multisensor systems. This method was applied to a system which includes a stereo camera and a tactile array sensor mounted on a PUMA 560 (Durrant-Whyte, 1986). Luo, Lin, and Scherp (Chapter 10) defined the confidence distance measure using linear Gaussian models and proposed a hypothesis test to reject sensory data obtained by malfunction and discussed an iterative computational method of fusion. Hashimoto and Paul (1987) applied the approach introduced by Durrant-Whyte to integrating encoder data and tachometer data for the control of manipulators.

It is very interesting that similar statistical approaches have been proposed independently in the field of mobile robots. Chatila and Laumond (1985) proposed to use an average weighted by variances for the fusion of scalar data. Smith and Cheeseman (1985) discussed the uncertainty in mobile robot location caused by uncertain coordinate transformations where a nonlinear model was associated with the orientation of the coordinate frames. Although the fusion method was derived using Kalman filter theory, it is essentially equivalent to Bayesian inference with minimum variance estimate because the dynamics of the plant is the identity matrix and the state is static. On the other hand, Matthies and Shaper (1987) discussed the error modeling of stereo vision for mobile robots, where the fusion method was obtained by using the weighted least squares estimate with the inverse of the covariance matrix as the weight. It is well known that with this choice of weighting matrices and assuming a Gaussian distribution, the weighted least squares estimate is identical to Bayesian inference using a minimal variance estimate (Bryson & Ho, 1975).

It is an important property of robotic sensors that they are used to obtain various kinds of information. For instance, the joint sensors of robotic manipulators may be used to acquire the position and orientation of the end effector for operational space motion, to compute the position of the elbow for obstacle avoidance motion, and to obtain joint angles for joint motion. Therefore, the nonlinearity between the sensory data, which the low-level data from specific sensors, and the sensory information, which is the high-level information to be obtained by processing the sensory data, comes from both the inherent structural nonlinearity related to the mechanism used to generate the sensory data and the nonlinearity related to the computation used to obtain the desired sensory information. The generalization of nonlinearity should include the case where sensors contribute only partial information. This would make it possible to fuse, for example, joint sensors and a single-camera vision sensor to obtain the end effector position.

In this chapter, we propose a general statistical fusion method for multiple sensor systems which is directly motivated by the geometry of uncertainties. The treatment of nonlinearity is generalized so as to include both of the structural nonlinearity and the computational nonlinearity. First, assuming the Gaussian noise additive to the sensory data, the uncertainty ellipsoid is defined to be associated with the covariance matrix of the error of the sensory information. Second, the optimal fusion is defined as one that minimizes the geometrical volume of the ellipsoid among all the possible linear combinations of sensory informations. It is shown that the optimal fusion method results in an algorithm that is similar to those obtained by Bayesian inference using a minimum variance estimate, Kalman filter theory, and a weighted least squares estimate. Finally, the method is extended to include the fusion of partial information.

3. SENSING MODEL AND UNCERTAINTY ELLIPSOID

3.1. Nonlinear Sensing Model

We define $\theta^i \in R^{m_i}$ $i = 1, \ldots, p$, as sensory data from sensor unit i, where the sensory data are the low-level measurements inherent to a specific physical sensor and m_i is the number of the independent measurements. A sensor unit does not necessarily mean a single physical sensor, but may represent a set of similar sensors whose data is usually used simultaneously. p is the number of sensor units. $x^i \in R^n$, $i = 1, \ldots, p$, is called the sensory information which is computed from sensory data θ^i. n is the dimension of the sensory information. Therefore, x^1 can generally be represented as a nonlinear vector function of θ^i as follows:

$$x^i = f^i(\theta^i), \tag{1}$$

where we assumed $n \leq m_i$. When $n > m_i$, the relationship between the sensory data and the sensory information may not be represented as in Eq. (1) because sensory data have only partial information of the required sensory information. Modeling and fusion of partial information will be discussed in Section 5. Eq. (1) is used as a general model of sensors in this chapter. Some typical examples are given as follows:

1. **joint angles:** When the position and orientation of the end effector is computed using joint angles as shown in Figure 11.1, the joint angles are $\theta^i \in R^{m_i}$ and the position and the orientation of the end effector is $x^i \in R^n$. m_i is the number of joints and $n = 6$. It should be noted that x^i can be computed from θ^i even when $n > m_i$. This is an exceptional case of the sensing model.
2. **stereo vision:** Figure 11.2 is the sensing model of stereo vision. The position of point of reference P in the absolute coordinates is $x^i = (p_x\ p_y\ p_z)^T \in R^3$. x^i is computed from $\theta^i = (x_R\ y_R\ x_L\ y_L)^T \in R^4$ where $(x_R\ y_R)^T$ and $(x_L\ y_L)^T$ are the position of the image of P in the image frames of CAMERA-R and CAMERA-L, respectively. In this case, $n(=3) < m_i(=4)$ is satisfied. If only CAMERA-L is available, $n(=3) > m_i(=2)$ and, therefore, x^i cannot be computed in general.
3. **range sensor:** Figure 11.3 is the sensing model of a range sensor. The low-level measurements are the angles of sight α and β and the distance d from the origin of sensing frame $O - xyz$, and the point of reference is $P(p_x\ p_y\ p_z)$. Accordingly, the sensory data and the sensory information become $\theta^i = (\alpha\ \beta\ d)^T \in R^3$ and $x^i = (p_x\ p_y\ p_z)^T \in R^3$, respectively, and satisfy $n = m_i\ (=3)$.

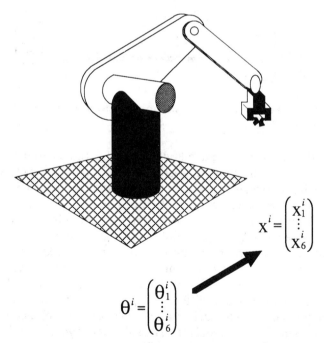

Figure 11.1. Sensing model: Joint angles.

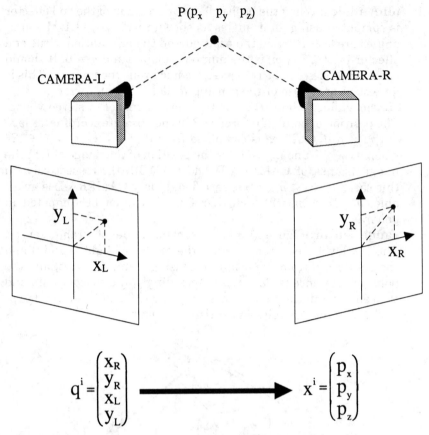

Figure 11.2. Sensing model: Stereo vision.

A nonlinear sensing model was used by Smith and Cheeseman (1986) to discuss the sensing uncertainty of a mobile robot, where the nonlinearity between the positions and orientations of neighboring coordinate frames is considered. Matthies and Shaper also used a nonlinear sensing model which is the same as Example 2. In these problems, the models were used to find a consensus from the same type of information; therefore, only one nonlinear model was considered at a time. The main interest of sensor fusion is to make a consensus from various different types of information. The nonlinear model of Eq. (1) intends to model various different types of nonlinear sensing structures in the same systematic manner. So far, sensor fusion has been discussed using linear models (Durrant-Whyte, 1985, 1986; Hashimoto & Paul, 1987; Luo, Lin, & Scherp, Chapter 10).

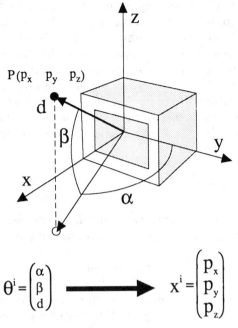

Figure 11.3. Sensing model: Range sensor.

Another distinctive point is that θ^i is defined as low-level information whose physical meaning is determined by the inherent structure of a specific sensor. In the next subsection, we will consider the statistical disturbances added to the low-level sensory data by assuming a Gaussian distribution. Although this assumption is not sufficient to strictly model disturbances caused by many kinds of sources, this makes the simple assumption more realistic than making the same assumption for processed information such as coordinate frames (Smith & Cheeseman, 1986). It would be acceptable to make this assumption in the sense that it can cover the random noise added to the output signals of the sensors. Therefore, defining θ^i as low-level information is important in making this assumption more realistic.

The third point to be remarked is that a sensor unit and sensory data should not necessarily be coupled with single sensory information. For example, the joint angle sensors of a manipulator can be used to measure the end effector location, the position of the elbow which is required to avoid obstacles, and, of course, the joint angles.

To fully integrate intelligence into the motion control of robotic systems so that they can decide their own motion, the motion controller of a robotic system should be intelligent enough to identify the necessary information and request it of the sensor system. The sensor system will compose and return the requested information if available from the low-level sensory signals; otherwise it will report unavailability. This suggests the separation of the motion controller and the sensor management system and bidirectional communication between them, while the conventional sensor system can only return the fixed sensory data to the controller. The sensor management system should be flexible so as to generate the appropriate nonlinear sensing model of Eq. (1) when the desired information is requested.

3.2. Uncertainty Ellipsoid

The disturbance or uncertainty included in the sensory data is assumed to be additive and can be represented as follows:

$$\boldsymbol{\theta}^i = \underline{\boldsymbol{\theta}}^i + \delta\boldsymbol{\theta}^i, \tag{2}$$

where $\boldsymbol{\theta}^i \in R^{m_i}$ $(i = 1, \ldots, p)$ is the undisturbed data or the true value, and $\delta\boldsymbol{\theta}^i \in R^{m_i}$ $(i = 1, \ldots, p)$ is the disturbance. Now, we assume Gaussian distribution for $\delta\boldsymbol{\theta}^i$. That is,

$$E(\delta\boldsymbol{\theta}^i) = \overline{\delta\boldsymbol{\theta}^i} = 0 \in R^{m_i} \tag{3}$$

$$\begin{aligned} V[\delta\boldsymbol{\theta}^i] &\triangleq E[(\delta\boldsymbol{\theta}^i - \overline{\delta\boldsymbol{\theta}^i})(\delta\boldsymbol{\theta}^i - \overline{\delta\boldsymbol{\theta}^i})^T] \\ &= \boldsymbol{Q}^i = diag.(\sigma_1^{i2}, \ldots, \sigma_{m_i}^{i2}) \in R^{m_i \times m_i}, \end{aligned} \tag{4}$$

where $E[*]$ means the expectation of $*$ and it is also assumed that $\delta\theta_j^i$ $(j = 1, \ldots, m_i)$, the j-th element of $\delta\boldsymbol{\theta}^i$, is not correlated and σ_j^{i2} is the variance of $\delta\theta_j^i$. $\boldsymbol{Q}^i$ is the covariance matrix of $\delta\boldsymbol{\theta}^i$.

Substituting Eq. (2) into (1) provides

$$\boldsymbol{x}^i = \boldsymbol{f}^i(\underline{\boldsymbol{\theta}}^i + \delta\boldsymbol{\theta}^i) \tag{5}$$

Now, if we assume $\delta\boldsymbol{\theta}^i$ is small enough, Eq. (5) is approximated by

$$\boldsymbol{x}^i = \boldsymbol{f}^i(\underline{\boldsymbol{\theta}}^i) + \boldsymbol{J}^i(\boldsymbol{\theta}^i)\delta\boldsymbol{\theta}^i \tag{6}$$

$$\boldsymbol{J}^i(\boldsymbol{\theta}^i) = \frac{\partial \boldsymbol{f}^i}{\partial \boldsymbol{\theta}^i} \in R^{n \times m_i}, \tag{7}$$

where $\boldsymbol{J}^i(\boldsymbol{\theta}^i)$ is the Jacobian matrix of $\boldsymbol{f}^i$ with respect to $\boldsymbol{\theta}^i$. From Eq. (3) the expectation and the covariance matrix of $\boldsymbol{x}^i$ become

$$E[\mathbf{x}^i] = \overline{\mathbf{x}^i} = \mathbf{f}^i(\mathbf{\theta}^i) \tag{8}$$

$$V[\mathbf{x}^i] = E[(\mathbf{x}^i - \overline{\mathbf{x}^i})(\mathbf{x}^i - \overline{\mathbf{x}^i})^T] = \mathbf{J}^i \mathbf{Q}^i \mathbf{J}^{iT}. \tag{9}$$

Eq. (8) implies that for the infinite number of measurements the average is equal to the true value of $\mathbf{x}^i$. This is because we are neglecting the calibration error. The calibration error is global and deterministic, while the disturbances we are discussing here are local and statistical. Although both of them are sources of uncertainty, they should be discussed separately. In this chapter, we focus on the statistical uncertainty and assume that the calibration error has been overcome. The same assumption was used by Smith and Cheeseman (1986).

In Eq. (9) the covariance matrix of $\mathbf{x}^i$ is not diagonal anymore since the Jacobian matrix is not diagonal in general. In other words, the correlation of x_j^i ($j = 1, \ldots, n$), the jth element of $\mathbf{x}^i$, is included in the model in spite of the fact that the $\delta\theta_j^i$ ($j = 1, \ldots, m_i$) are assumed to be uncorrelated. For a full rank $\mathbf{J}^i$, $\mathbf{J}^i \mathbf{Q}^i \mathbf{J}^{iT}$ is positive definite because $\mathbf{Q}^i$ is positive definite from Eq. (4).

Since $\mathbf{J}^i \mathbf{Q}^i \mathbf{J}^{iT}$ is symmetric, its singular value decomposition (Klema & Laub, 1980) is represented by

$$\mathbf{J}^i \mathbf{Q}^i \mathbf{J}^{iT} = \mathbf{U}^i \mathbf{D}^i \mathbf{U}^{iT} \tag{10}$$

$$\mathbf{U}^i = (e_1^i, \ldots, e_n^i) \in R^{n \times n}, \; e_j^{iT} e_k^i = \begin{cases} 1 \text{ for } j = k \\ 0 \text{ for } j \neq k \end{cases} \tag{11}$$

$$\mathbf{D}^i = diag.(d_1^i, \ldots, d_n^i), \; d_1^i \geq d_n^i \geq 0 \tag{12}$$

where $\mathbf{U}^i$ is an orthogonal matrix and d_j^i ($j = 1, \ldots, n$) are the singular values of $\mathbf{J}^i \mathbf{Q}^i \mathbf{J}^{iT}$. The scalar variance in the direction indicated by a unit vector e_j^i is given by

$$V[e_j^{iT} \mathbf{x}^i] = d_j^i. \tag{13}$$

Therefore, $\sqrt{d_j^i}$ represents the uncertainty of $\mathbf{x}^i$ in the direction of e_j^i. If we check the scalar variance in all directions using unit vectors, the distribution of the end points of the vectors (whose directions are those of the unit vectors and whose magnitudes are the corresponding scalar variances) forms an ellipsoid with e_j^i as the directions of the principal axes and $2\sqrt{d_j^i}$ as their lengths as shown in Figure 11.4 for the 3-D case. This ellipsoid is called the uncertainty ellipsoid. e_1^i and $\sqrt{d_1^i}$ correspond to the most uncertain direction, and e_n^i and $\sqrt{d_n^i}$ correspond to the least uncertain direction.

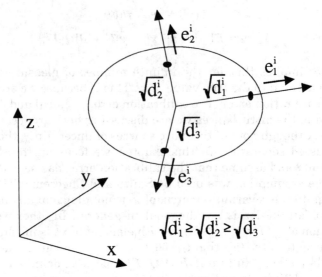

Figure 11.4. Uncertainty ellipsoid: 3D case.

4. GEOMETRICAL FUSION METHOD

4.1. Uncertainty of Fused Information

We propose to fuse the multiple sensory information x^i to get a consensus x in the scope of the linear combination, that is,

$$x = \sum_{i=1}^{p} W^i x^i \qquad (14)$$

where $W^i \in R^{n \times n}$ is the weighting matrix. The main objective is to determine W^i. The mean of x is computed from Eq. (8) as follows:

$$E[x] = \sum_{i=1}^{p} W^i E[x^i] = \sum_{i=1}^{p} W^i \overline{x^i}. \qquad (15)$$

Again, we assume no calibration errors and, therefore, $\bar{x}^i$ is equal to the true value $\bar{x}$ for all i. Accordingly,

$$E[x] = \left(\sum_{i=1}^{p} W^i \right) \bar{x}. \qquad (16)$$

Since $E[\mathbf{x}]$ should satisfy

$$E[\mathbf{x}] = \bar{\mathbf{x}}, \tag{17}$$

we have the following constraint on the weighting matrices:

$$\sum_{i=1}^{p} \mathbf{W}^i = \mathbf{I}, \tag{18}$$

where $\mathbf{I} \in R^{n \times n}$ is an identity matrix.

On the other hand, using $\bar{\mathbf{x}}^i = \bar{\mathbf{x}}$ and Eqs. (6), (8), (14), and (18), the covariance matrix of $\mathbf{x}$ is given by

$$V[\mathbf{x}] = E[(\mathbf{x} - \bar{\mathbf{x}})(\mathbf{x} - \bar{\mathbf{x}})^T] = \mathbf{W}\mathbf{Q}\mathbf{W}^T \in R^{n \times n} \tag{19}$$

$$\mathbf{W} \triangleq (\mathbf{W}^1 \mathbf{W}^2 \ldots \mathbf{W}^p) \in R^{n \times pn} \tag{20}$$

$$\mathbf{Q} \triangleq \begin{pmatrix} \mathbf{J}^1 \mathbf{Q}^1 \mathbf{J}^{1T} & \cdots & \mathbf{O} \\ \vdots & \ddots & \vdots \\ \mathbf{O} & \cdots & \mathbf{J}^p \mathbf{Q}^p \mathbf{J}^{pT} \end{pmatrix} \in R^{pn \times pn}. \tag{21}$$

In deriving Eq. (19) we assumed that $\delta\theta^i$ and $\delta\theta^j$ are uncorrelated. The shape and the size of the uncertainty ellipsoid of $\mathbf{x}$ depends on the choice of the weighting matrices.

4.2. Minimizing the Volume of Uncertainty Ellipsoid

In order to get more accurate and less uncertain information, we propose to determine the weighting matrix $\mathbf{W}$ so that it should minimize the volume of the uncertainty ellipsoid. The singular value decomposition of the covariance matrix of $\mathbf{x}$ becomes

$$\begin{aligned} \mathbf{W}\mathbf{Q}\mathbf{W}^T &= \mathbf{U}\mathbf{D}\mathbf{U}^T \\ \mathbf{U} &= (\mathbf{e}_1 \ldots \mathbf{e}_n) \in R^{n \times n}, \mathbf{e}_j \in R^n \\ \mathbf{D} &= diag.(d_1, \ldots, d_n), d_1 \geq \ldots \geq d_n > 0 \end{aligned} \tag{22}$$

where $2\sqrt{d_i}$ gives the length of the ith longest principal axis of the uncertainty ellipsoid of the fused information $\mathbf{x}$, and $\mathbf{e}_i$ represents its direction. The geometrical volume of an ellipsoid is computed as follows:

$$\text{volume} = \frac{\pi^{p/2}}{\Gamma(1+p/2)} \left(\prod_{i=1}^{p} d_i \right)^{1/2}$$

$$= \frac{\pi^{p/2}}{\Gamma(1+p/2)} \sqrt{det(\mathbf{WQW}^T)}, \qquad (23)$$

where $\Gamma(*)$ is the gamma function. Hence, minimizing the volume of the uncertainty ellipsoid is equivalent to minimizing the determinant of the covariance matrix of $\mathbf{x}$.

Now, our problem is to minimize

$$P.I. = det(\mathbf{WQW}^T) \qquad (24)$$

subject to the constraint of Eq. (18). This problem is solved using the Lagrange multipliers. The criterion of Eq. (24) is replaced with

$$P.I.^* = det(\mathbf{WQW}^T) + P \qquad (25)$$

$$P = \sum_{i=1}^{n} \sum_{j=1}^{n} \lambda_{ij} \left(\sum_{k=1}^{p} W_{ij}^k - \delta_{ij} \right) \qquad (26)$$

$$\delta_{ij} = \begin{cases} 1 & \text{for } i = j \\ 0 & \text{for } i \neq j \end{cases} \quad \Lambda = \begin{pmatrix} \lambda_{11} & \cdots & \lambda_{1n} \\ \vdots & \ddots & \vdots \\ \lambda_{n1} & \cdots & \lambda_{nn} \end{pmatrix}, \qquad (27)$$

where λ_{ij} are the Lagrange multipliers, W_{ij}^k is the (i,j) element of $\mathbf{W}^k$ and $(\Sigma_{k=1}^{p} W_{ij}^k - \delta_{ij})$ should be equal to zero from Eq. (18). In order to minimize $P.I.^*$, $\mathbf{W}$ must satisfy

$$\frac{\partial P.I.^*}{\partial \mathbf{W}} = \begin{pmatrix} \partial P.I.^*/\partial \mathbf{W}^1 \\ \vdots \\ \partial P.I.^*/\partial \mathbf{W}^p \end{pmatrix} = 0, \qquad (28)$$

where $\partial P.I.^*/\partial \mathbf{W}^i \in R^{n \times n}$ has an entry $\partial P.I.^*/\partial W_{jk}^i$ as the (k,j) element. Although the derivation will not be shown, using the condition of Eq. (30) the Lagrange multipliers are obtained by simple matrix computation as follows:

$$\Lambda = -2\, det(\mathbf{WQW}^T)(\mathbf{WQW}^T)^{-1} \left\{ \sum_{i=1}^{p} (\mathbf{J}^i \mathbf{Q}^i \mathbf{J}^{iT})^{-1} \right\}^{-1}. \qquad (29)$$

Finally, by substituting Eq. (29) into Eq. (36), we have the weighting matrices as follows:

$$W^i = \left\{ \sum_{i=1}^{p} (J^i Q^i J^{iT})^{-1} \right\}^{-1} (J^i Q^i J^{iT})^{-1}. \quad (30)$$

In addition, the covariance matrix of x can be computed by substituting Eq. (30) into Eq. (19) as follows:

$$V[x] = \left\{ \sum_{i=1}^{p} (J^i Q^i J^{iT})^{-1} \right\}^{-1}. \quad (31)$$

4.3. Relationship to Previous Work

Eq. (30) has the same form as the results of Smith and Cheeseman (1986) and Matthies and Shafer (1987), although the former used the Kalman filter theory, which is equivalent to Bayesian inference using minimum variance estimates because the dynamics are the identity matrix and the state is static in this case; the latter applied a weighted least squares estimate using the inverse of the covariance matrix.

In the Kalman filter theory or Bayesian inference, the weighting matrix W^i of Eq. (14) is determined that minimizes

$$a^T V[x] a = a^T W Q W^T a \quad (32)$$

for any constant vector $a \in R^n$.

On the other hand, the weighting least squares estimate using the inverse of the covariance matrix suggests that the weighting matrix be determined that minimizes the following scalar function:

$$\frac{1}{p} \sum_{i=1}^{p} (x - x^i)^T V[x^i]^{-1} (x - x^i). \quad (33)$$

It is known that the weighted least squares estimate using the inverse of the covariance matrix as the weighting matrix is identical to Bayesian inference with minimum variance estimate assuming a Gaussian distribution of disturbances (Bryson & Ho, 1975). The formulation we adopted in Section 4.2 is based on the geometrical motivation that the volume of the uncertainty ellipsoid should be minimized by choosing an appropriate weighting matrix, which is a new approach to this problem. The coincidence of the resultant weighting matrices provides one more reason to use Eq. (30) as the weighting matrix for multisensor fusion.

4.4. Comments on the Structure of the Computation

Consider the fusion of x and x^{p+1}. If we define H^i as the covariance matrix of x^i, the covariance matrix of x becomes, from Eq. (31),

$$H = \left\{ \sum_{i=1}^{p} (H^i)^{-1} \right\}^{-1}. \tag{34}$$

From Eqs. (14), (30), and (34), the fusion of x and x^{p+1} is given by

$$\begin{aligned} x^* &= \{H^{-1} + (H^{p+1})^{-1}\}^{-1}\{H^{-1}x + (H^{p+1})^{-1}x^{p+1}\} \\ &= \sum_{i=1}^{p+1} \left\{ \sum_{j=1}^{p+1} (H^i)^{-1} \right\}^{-1} (H^i)^{-1} x^i. \end{aligned} \tag{35}$$

Eq. (35) implies that the fusion of x and x^{p+1} is identical to that of $x^1, \ldots, x^p$, and x^{p+1}. This fact suggests the following recursive computation.

step 1. $x = 0$, $H^{-1} = 0$; *initialize*
step 2. $x^a = x$, $(H^a)^{-1} = H^{-1}$
            $x^b = x^i$, $(H^b)^{-1} = (H^i)^{-1}$
step 3. $x = \{(H^a)^{-1} + (H^b)^{-1}\}^{-1}((H^a)^{-1}x^a + (H^b)^{-1}x^b)$
            $H^{-1} = (H^a)^{-1} + (H^b)^{-1}$
step 4.   *go to step 2 for next i.*

The above procedure reveals the following interesting structural characteristics of the fusion method:

1. In the loop from step 2 to step 4, the order of i does not matter.
2. At every stage, x is the best estimate that can be obtained using x^i's which have already been used for fusion.
3. Since step 2 and step 3 require only x^i and $(H^i)^{-1}$ except for x and H^{-1}, the computation to fuse x^i can be done locally in parallel, that is, even in the sensor unit i.

Characteristics 1 and 2 imply that a sensor unit with a faster response can be fused earlier than ones with a slower response, and that a change of the number of sensor units does not cause any inconsistency. This fact allows asynchronous computation for fusion. Characteristic 3 suggests the distributed structure of the computation. These structural characteristics show that the computation for fusion is suitable for implementation in intelligent systems with blackboards or whiteboards (Shafer, Stentz, & Thorpe, 1986).

5. FUSING PARTIAL INFORMATION

5.1. Computation of Covariance Matrix

When sensor unit i measures only partial information, Eq. (1) cannot describe the relationship between θ^i and x^i. In this section, we discuss the fusion of partial information described by

$$\theta^i = g^i(x^i), \tag{36}$$

where $\theta^i \in R^{m_i}$, $x^i \in R^n$, and $m_i < n$. For example, when x^i is a point in the 3D space and θ^i is the location of its image in the image frame of a single-camera vision as shown in Figure 11.5, the relationship of θ^i and x^i is not governed by Eq. (1), but by Eq. (36).

Let $\underline{\theta}^i$ and $\underline{x}^i$ represent the true values of θ^i and x^i. Also let $\delta\theta^i$ and δx^i be the disturbance added to θ^i and the error of x^i caused by $\delta\theta^i$, respectively. By substituting $\theta^i = \underline{\theta}^i + \delta\theta^i$ and $x^i = \underline{x}^i + \delta x^i$, Eq. (36) becomes

$$\underline{\theta}^i + \delta\theta^i = g^i(\underline{x}^i + \delta x^i). \tag{37}$$

When δx^i is assumed to be small, subtracting $\underline{\theta}^i = g^i(\underline{x}^i)$ from Eq. (37) yields the following equation:

$$\delta\theta^i = K^i \delta x^i, \qquad K^i \triangleq \frac{\partial g^i}{\partial x^i} \in R^{m_i \times n} \tag{38}$$

where K^i is the Jacobian matrix of g^i with respect to x^i and a function of x^i. The covariance matrix of $\delta\theta^i$ is calculated as follows:

$$V[\delta\theta^i] = E[\delta\theta^i \delta\theta^{iT}] = K^i V[x^i] K^{iT} = Q^i. \tag{39}$$

In order to apply the fusion method defined by Eqs. (14) and (30),

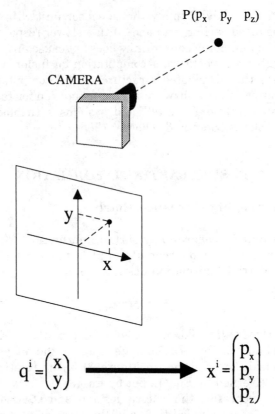

Figure 11.5. Sensing of partial information.

$V[\mathbf{x}^i]^{-1}$, which is identical with $(\mathbf{J}^i \mathbf{Q}^i \mathbf{J}^{iT})^{-1}$ in EQ. (30), must be prepared. Since $\mathbf{K}^i$ is an $m_i \times n$ ($m_i < n$) matrix, $V[\mathbf{x}^i]$ cannot be obtained from Eq. (39) in a straightforward manner.

Now, we add dummy measurements $\boldsymbol{\theta}_d^i \in R^{n-m_i}$ to $\boldsymbol{\theta}^i$ so that $\mathbf{K}^i$ becomes a nonsingular matrix. Eqs. (36) and (38) are modified by:

$$\boldsymbol{\theta}^{*i} = \mathbf{g}^{*i}(\mathbf{x}^i), \quad \mathbf{g}^{*i}(\mathbf{x}^i) \triangleq \begin{pmatrix} \mathbf{g}^i(\mathbf{x}^i) \\ \mathbf{g}_d^i(\mathbf{x}^i) \end{pmatrix}, \boldsymbol{\theta}_d^i = \mathbf{g}_d^i(\mathbf{x}^i) \qquad (40)$$

$$\delta\boldsymbol{\theta}^{*i} = \mathbf{K}^{*i} \delta\mathbf{x}^i, \quad \mathbf{K}^{*i} \triangleq \begin{pmatrix} \mathbf{K}^i \\ \partial \mathbf{g}_d^i / \partial \mathbf{x}^i \end{pmatrix} \in R^{n \times n}, \qquad (41)$$

where $\mathbf{K}^{*i}$ is nonsingular. If we assume that the additional dummy measurements are extremely uncertain, Eq. (39) becomes

$$V[\delta\theta^{*1}] = Q^{*i}, \quad Q^{*i} = \begin{pmatrix} Q^i & & & O & \\ & +\infty & \cdots & & 0 \\ & \vdots & \ddots & & \vdots \\ O & & & \ddots & \\ & 0 & \cdots & & +\infty \end{pmatrix}. \quad (42)$$

Since

$$(Q^{*i})^{-1} = \begin{pmatrix} (Q^i)^{-1} & & & O & \\ & +0 & \cdots & & 0 \\ & \vdots & \ddots & & \vdots \\ O & & & \ddots & \\ & 0 & \cdots & & +0 \end{pmatrix}, \quad (43)$$

the following equation is obtained:

$$V[x^i]^{-1} = K^{*iT}(Q^{*i})^{-1}K^{*i} = K^{iT}(Q^i)^{-1}K^i. \quad (44)$$

Eq. (44) can be used in the place of $(J^i Q^i J^{iT})^{-1}$ in the fusion method of Eqs. (14) through (30), when the i-th sensor unit measures only the partial information. Since $K^{iT}(Q^i)^{-1}K^i$ is a singular symmetric matrix, the uncertainty ellipsoid has infinitely long principle axes in the directions corresponding to its zero singular values.

In the case shown in Figure 11.5, this direction coincides with the line from the center of the lens of the camera to point P. When we call this line the sight line of P, the uncertainty is illustrated by the fact that the image of P on the image frame stays still even if P moves on the sight line of P.

5.2. Computation of x^i

x^i is required to evaluate Eq. (14) and compute K^i of Eq. (40). However, it is impossible to solve x^i from Eq. (36) because it is underdetermined. In this subsection, an approximate computation of x^i is proposed.

When the recursive computational method given in Section 4.4 is used, x^i can be computed taking advantage of x, which is the consensus obtained using the previous sensory data. In this case, x^i can be approximated by the point on the manifold determined by Eq. (36) that has the shortest distance from x; e.g., in Figure 11.5 this means the intersection of the sight line of P and its normal passing through x.

If the previous consensus of x is not available and only several pieces of partial information are available, a point of reference should be computed by the least squares method. It is generally obtained as the point that minimizes the sum of the squared distances from the point to the manifolds of partial information. And then, using the point as a previous consensus, x^i is obtained as the point on the manifold that has the shortest distance from the point.

When two cameras are considered not as a stereo vision sensor but as two sensor units which provide partial information, the point of reference is given as the centroid of the common normal between two sight lines of P. x^i is computed as the point of intersection of the corresponding sight line and the common normal.

6. CONCLUDING REMARKS

A general geometrical fusion method is proposed for multisensor robotic systems. This method is based on the geometrical analysis of the sensing uncertainty and motivated by the geometrical idea that the volume of the uncertainty ellipsoid should be minimized. The resultant fusion equation coincided with those which had been obtained by Bayesian inference, Kalman filter theory, and weighted least squares estimation. This fact provides another geometrical rationale to use the equation in the multisensor fusion.

Since the nonlinear sensing model used is general and covers most robotic sensors, the proposed fusion method works as a general fusion method for multisensor robotic systems. The fusion method was also extended to handle partial sensory information.

Although the proposed method is effective with a conventional robot controller, the fusion method will be more efficient when it is used with an intelligent robot controller which can decide and request by itself the necessary information. One of the most important future problems to develop a robotic system which includes an intelligent controller and a sensor management system with the function of sensor fusion. A future problem of fusion theory is to establish a method to relate and fuse sensory data with different physical dimensions.

REFERENCES

Bajcsy, R., & Allen, P. (1985). Converging disparate sensory data. In H. Hanafusa & H. Inoue (Eds.), *Robotics Research: The Second International Symposium* (pp. 81–86). Cambridge, MA: MIT Press.

Brooks, R.A. (1985). Visual map making for a mobile robot. *IEEE International Conference on Robotics and Automation* (pp. 1947–1953). St. Louis, MO.

Bryson, Jr., A.E., & Ho, Y.C. (1975). *Applied optimal control: Optimization, estimation, and control* (pp. 348–389). New York: Wiley.

Chatila, R., & Laumond, J. (1985). Position referencing and consistent world modeling for mobile robots. *IEEE International Conference on Robotics and Automation* (pp. 138–145). St. Louis, MO.

Durrant-Whyte, H.F. (1985). Integrating distributed sensor information, an application to a robot system coordinator. *Proceedings of the IEEE International Conference on Systems, Man, and Cybernetics* (pp. 415–419).

Durrant-Whyte, H.F. (1986). Consistent integration and propagation of disparate sensor observations. *IEEE International Conference on Robotics and Automation* (pp. 1464–1469). San Francisco, CA.

Englemore, R., & Moregan, A. (Eds.). (1987). *Blackboard systems: Application and framework*. Reading, MA: Addison-Wesley.

Harmon, S.Y., Bianchini, G.L., & Pinz, B.E. (1986). Sensor data fusion through a distributed blackboard. *IEEE International Conference on Robotics and Automation* (pp. 1449–1454). San Francisco, CA.

Hashimoto, M., & Paul, R.P. (1987). Integration of multi-sensor manipulator actuator information for robust robot control systems. *Proceedings of the Annual Conference of the Japan Robotics Society* (pp. 393–396). [In Japanese.]

Klema, V.C., & Laub, A.T. (1980). The singular value decomposition: Its computation and some applications. *IEEE Transactions on Automatic Control*, AC-25(2), 164–176.

Matthies, L., & Shafer, S.A. (1987). Error modeling in stereo navigation. *IEEE Journal on Robotics and Automation*, RA-3(3), 239–248.

Nii, H.P. (1986). Blackboard systems: Blackboard application systems from a knowledge engineering perspective (Part 1). *AI Magazine*, 7(2), 38–53.

Shafer, S.A., Stentz, A., & Thorpe, C.E. (1986, April). *An architecture for sensor fusion in a mobile robot* (Tech. Rep. 86-9). Carnegie-Mellon University: Robotics Institute.

Smith, R.C., & Cheeseman, P. (1986). On the representation and estimation of spatial uncertainty. *International Journal of Robotics Research*, 5(4), 56–68.

12
Optimal Combination and Constraints for Geometrical Sensor Data

John Porrill

A formalism is described in this chapter for the statistical combination of geometrical information from multiple sensors. This is illustrated by its applications to stereo vision, including the combination of multiple stereo views to increase the accuracy of a wire frame model and the consistent imposition of geometrical constraints on such a model.

1. INTRODUCTION

Many robotics applications involve the combination of error-prone information obtained from multiple sensors or from the same sensor at different times. A typical example would be a mobile robot that must combine information from vision or ultrasonic ranging with dead-reckoning information from position encoders to produce a usable map of its surroundings. Our aim is to develop a system (GEOMSTAT) that can deal with such sensor combination problems in complete generality, but whose main application will be to the refinement of the geometry delivered by the Sheffield AIVRU stereo vision system TINA. The main characteristics required of GEOMSTAT follow from this application.

The system must be able to deal naturally and in a uniform manner with measurements of a geometrical nature. Stereo observation delivers the positions in the world of such objects as points, lines, planes, and circles; we need to discuss these measurement primitives in a way that is convenient and independent of our choice of reference frame.

The system must be able to deal with anisotropic and correlated measurement errors, since to neglect these would lose a lot of the information which is a potential source of increased accuracy. For example, two main sources of error in stereo vision are inaccurate edge localization in the image plane, leading to depth errors which are much larger than lateral position errors, and inaccurate stereo rig calibration, which can cause large correlated errors in absolute position but much smaller errors in relative positions.

Geometrical constraints must be treated naturally, since a major use of the system will be as an aid to the kind of geometrical reasoning a wire frame completion module would have to do. For example, if two edges are hypothesized to meet at a vertex, one wants to test whether the lines do intersect in space within the known errors of measurement. If the vertex is accepted, then the data should be optimally corrected so that this intersection error is reduced to zero. The systematic imposition of such constraints is necessary not only to ensure geometric integrity of the wire frame but also to improve accuracy greatly, since inaccurate measurements will be corrected by the necessity of agreeing with more accurate ones.

Finally, sensor calibration parameters should be treated on the same footing as other measurement primitives. For example, in the combination of stereo views from a moving camera to produce a more accurate and complete world model, the exact transformation between subsequent views will not usually be known. This quantity is a "between sensor" calibration parameter, but it is also an interesting quantity in its own right.

We meet the first of the requirements by choosing convenient representations of geometrical measurement primitives and parameterizing their errors with respect to implicitly defined reference frames. The rest are satisfied by our choice of generalized Gauss-Markov estimation (where the singular covariance matrices required in the presence of constraints are allowed) as our basic formalism for sensor combination. It combines the generality required with mathematical simplicity and computational tractability. The theory is implemented in terms of a single algorithm for the recursive imposition of scalar constraints (a singular scalar Kalman filter). This has the advantage that constraint imposition and acquisition of measurements are treated by exactly the same process.

A typical robotics application of geometrical data combination is described by Crowley (1985). An approach to sensor combination and uncertain geometry based on assumptions of Gaussian errors is described in Durrant-Whyte (1985), where the need to impose a consistency constraint on the estimated transformations between the reference frames of multiple sensors is emphasized. The stationary Kalman filter has been applied to the data combination problem for stereo by Faugeras, Ayache, and Faverjon (1986 and in Chapter 23). This recursive approach is particularly useful when the data acquisition is serial in nature, as it will be in many applications. The treatment we give draws largely on these sources. A similar formalism is described by Smith and Cheeseman (1987). Recently, Bolle and Cooper (1986) have used maximum likelihood techniques to combine range data to estimate object positions. In practice, computational tractability requires the assumption of Gaussian errors, and so the data combination formalism, like ours and that of the other authors, is essentially that of Gauss-Markov estimation.

2. CONSTRAINT-FREE REPRESENTATIONS

Our first task is to describe the errors in geometrical primitives in a convenient and natural way. The major problem is that the natural descriptions of such primitives usually satisfy nonlinear constraints and are underdetermined, while unconstrained determinate descriptions have singularities, error "leverage," and inconvenient transformation properties. For example, a line in space is naturally described by its direction and any point on it. The direction is naturally described as a 3-vector y, which is constrained to be of unit length, $v \cdot v = 1$. We can use the unconstrained description given by the polar coordinates (θ, ϕ), but this has two singularities at the poles $\theta = 0, \pi$, and a terribly inconvenient transformation law under change of axes. Choosing a point p on the line is underdetermined. We can make a determinate choice by always taking that point on the line closest to the origin, $p \cdot v = 0$. However, this point may be far from the measurements which determined the line position, and the resulting leverage may mean that the errors in position p cannot be taken to be small.

Our approach is always to use the most convenient description of each primitive, but to introduce an unconstrained description for small perturbations of the primitive. These are referred to a frame attached to the primitive and so are invariant under change of axes. We will illustrate this by looking at point, line, plane, and rigid motion primitives. A more formal description can be found in Porrill, Pollard, and Mayhew (1987).

The basic measurement primitives returned by the AIVRU vision system are the straight-edge segments and circular arcs found in the scene. We consider here the straight edges only. The endpoints of the edge are not directly useful since the segmentation process often breaks up long edges. The basic result of the measurement is thus a line λ_0 on which the actual edge segment must lie. The convenient description of λ_0 by a point $\mathbf{p}_0$ in the observed segment and a unit vector $\mathbf{v}_0$ along the segment is chosen.

Now we extend the direction vector $\mathbf{y}_0$ to an orthonormal basis $(\mathbf{v}_0, \mathbf{v}_1, \mathbf{v}_2)$. Any line λ not perpendicular to λ_0 (in particular any line close to λ_0) can be described by $(\mathbf{p}, \mathbf{v})$ with

$$\mathbf{p} = \mathbf{p}_0 + p_1 \mathbf{v}_1 + p_2 \mathbf{v}_2, \quad \mathbf{v} = \mathbf{v}_0 + v_1 \mathbf{v}_1 + v_2 \mathbf{v}_2.$$

Note that the direction vector of the perturbed line $\mathbf{v}$ is not unity, but is so to linear order, in the perturbation; this is all we will need. The map $\lambda \to \mathbf{x} = (p_1, p_2, v_1, v_2)^t$ is then a C^∞ local coordinate chart on the line manifold near λ_0.

To describe the error of measurement in λ, we need only describe the error distribution of the perturbation 4-vector $\mathbf{x}$. If we have measured the position of the line as λ_0 and the true position is λ, we assume that the measurement process is adequately described by the measurement bias (expected error)

$$E[\mathbf{x}] = \bar{\mathbf{x}}$$

and the 4×4 measurement covariance matrix S, where

$$S = E[(\mathbf{x} - \bar{\mathbf{x}})(\mathbf{x} - \bar{\mathbf{x}})^t] = E[\mathbf{x}\,\mathbf{x}^t] - \bar{\mathbf{x}}\bar{\mathbf{x}}^t.$$

This would be the case if we were sampling $\mathbf{x}$ from a normal distribution

$$p(\mathbf{x}) = \frac{1}{(2\pi)^2 \det S} \exp\left(-\frac{1}{2}(\mathbf{x} - \bar{\mathbf{x}})^t S^{-1}(\mathbf{x} - \bar{\mathbf{x}})\right).$$

In this case, if the mean and variance of the distribution are small, we will say that the line measurement process is approximately normal. The appropriateness of such assumptions is discussed in more generality below.

Usually measurement processes are not (or at least are not known to be!) biased, and we can take $\bar{\mathbf{x}} = 0$. This leaves the task of determining S from the nature of the measurement process. The calculation of S for stereo edge data is described in Section 5. The line distribution is thus completely described by a composite structure (this is not a minimal representation) ($\mathbf{p}_0$, $\mathbf{v}_0$, $\mathbf{v}_1$, $\mathbf{v}_2$, $\bar{\mathbf{x}}$, S). Note that if we change axes, the transformation need only be applied to ($\mathbf{p}_0$, $\mathbf{v}_0$, $\mathbf{v}_1$, $\mathbf{v}_2$) since ($\bar{\mathbf{x}}$, S) are described intrinsically with respect to this frame.

To describe a point measurement, we choose an arbitrary basis ($\mathbf{v}_0$, $\mathbf{v}_1$, $\mathbf{v}_2$). A general perturbation of a point $\mathbf{r}_0$ can then be written as

$$\mathbf{r} = \mathbf{r}_0 + r_0 \mathbf{v}_0 + r_1 \mathbf{v}_1 + r_2 \mathbf{v}_2,$$

and the point mesaurement is described by the structure ($\mathbf{r}_0$, $\mathbf{v}_0$, $\mathbf{v}_1$, $\mathbf{v}_2$, $\bar{\mathbf{x}}$, S), where $\bar{\mathbf{x}}$ and S are the mean and covariance of the perturbation vector $\mathbf{x} = (r_0, r_1, r_2)^t$.

A plane is completely described by a point $\mathbf{p}_0$ on it and its normal $\mathbf{v}_0$. Again we extend the basis and describe nearby planes ($\mathbf{p}$, $\mathbf{v}$) by $\mathbf{x} = (p_0, v_1, v_2)^t$, where

$$\mathbf{p} = \mathbf{p}_0 + p_0 \mathbf{v}_0, \qquad \mathbf{v} = \mathbf{v}_0 + v_1 \mathbf{v}_1 + v_2 \mathbf{v}_2.$$

Finally, consider the case of a rigid motion; this might represent the motion of an object between two views. A convenient description is by a rotation matrix R_0 and a translation vector $\mathbf{t}$ so that the associated motion is

$$\mathbf{p}' = R_0 \mathbf{p} + \mathbf{t}.$$

A small correction to this motion can be represented by an additional infintesimal rotation ω and translation τ:

$$\mathbf{p}'' = \mathbf{p}' + \omega \times \mathbf{p}' + \tau.$$

These vectors can be expressed with respect to any basis ($\mathbf{v}_0$, $\mathbf{v}_1$, $\mathbf{v}_2$) as

$$\omega = \omega_i \mathbf{v}_i, \qquad \tau = \tau_i \mathbf{v}_i$$

(summation convention). The perturbed rigid motion is then the combination of these:

$$R = (I + \omega_0{}^*\mathbf{v}_0 + \omega_1{}^*\mathbf{v}_1 + \omega_2{}^*\mathbf{v}_2)R_0,$$
$$\mathbf{t}_0 = \mathbf{t}_0 + (\omega_0 \mathbf{v}_0 + \omega_1 \mathbf{v}_1 + \omega_2 \mathbf{v}_2) \times \mathbf{t}_0$$
$$+ \tau_0 \mathbf{v}_0 + \tau_1 \mathbf{v}_1 + \tau_2 \mathbf{v}_2.$$

(The operator * takes a vector $\mathbf{a}$ to the antisymmetric matrix $A = {}^*\mathbf{a}$ defined by $A\mathbf{x} = \mathbf{a} \times \mathbf{x}$.) In general, we assume that measurement primitives in three dimensions have a (probably underdetermined or constrained) description as an object ξ_0 in $\mathbf{R}^n$. The dimension n of this representation will usually be much larger than the intrinsic dimension m (number of degrees of freedom) of the primitive, so we attach a frame $B = (\mathbf{v}_0, \mathbf{v}_1, \mathbf{v}_2)$ to this primitive and assume that small perturbations can be described adequately and intrinsically with respect to this frame by a formula of the form

$$\xi = \xi_0 + F(B)\mathbf{x} + O(|\mathbf{x}|^2),$$

where $F(B)$ is a $n \times m$ matrix. The vector $\mathbf{x}$ then gives an unconstrained representation of perturbations of the primitive. The choice of representations ξ and $\mathbf{x}$ is made on the basis of convenience in calculation and the construction of $F(B)$ must be done separately for each type of primitive.

The error process can now be described in full generality (at least for error processes with support contained in the domain of the local coordinate chart $\xi \rightarrow \mathbf{x}$) by the probability distribution function $p(\mathbf{x})$. However, to do any useful calculations, we must assume approximate normality of $p(\mathbf{x})$ (or that it is adequately described by its mean and covariance). This assumption will only be justified in general for *small* errors of measurement. No representation will be adequate in general to describe large errors of measurement. For example, consider the process of measuring the position of a point in space by two range finders, one close and one distant. For the distant range finder the error will be described adequately by an ellipsoid centered on the point; for the close range finder this ellipsoid will have a conical distortion with its vertex at the range finder. Given small errors, these two error processes will be almost equivalent, but for large errors they are very different. No single scheme can successfully treat both error processes as Gaussian for large errors. We usually find that our errors of stereo measurement are small enough for the normality assumption to be valid; large errors are usually due to false matches, etc., which can be regarded as samples from a different error distribution and must be trapped and discarded as "flyers" (a discussion of the treatment of data, including flyers, can be found in Durrant-Whyte, 1985).

On the assumption of approximate normality of the error process a measurement of the primitive is then described by the structure (ξ_0, $\mathbf{v}_0$, $\mathbf{v}_1$, $\mathbf{v}_2$, $\bar{\mathbf{x}}$, S), where

$$\bar{\mathbf{x}} = E[\mathbf{x}], \quad S = \text{Cov}[\mathbf{x}].$$

A composite object has a description as a list of primitives $\Xi = (\xi_1,$

$\xi_2, \ldots, \xi_N$) with attached frames $B = (B_1, B_2, \ldots, B_N)$. Any small deformation of the object can be described by a list of the perturbation vectors of each constituent relative to these frames:

$$\mathbf{X} = (\mathbf{x}_1, \mathbf{x}_2, \ldots, \mathbf{x}_N)^t.$$

A measurement of the composite object is completely described by the expected value $\tilde{\mathbf{X}}$ and covariance S of this "state vector." In the case where all the constituents of the object have been independently measured, S will have block diagonal form with the covariances of the individual measurements down the diagonal. In general, this will not be the case since measurements, though independent in the sensor frame, will be correlated in the world through sensor calibration error. For example, the error in position of an edge in a stereo scene will not in general be affected by the presence of a second edge in the scene, but any stereo rig miscalibration will affect both their positions. We will show later how the required correlations in $\hat{S}$ can be set up.

3. GENERALIZED GAUSS-MARKOV ESTIMATION SIMPLIFIED

We will deal with the case where we have sufficient measurements of Ξ to determine it completely in the absence of errors, and where we can determine a good estimate Ξ_0 from a subset of these measurements. Our aim will be to calculate the optimal estimate of the state vector $\mathbf{X}$ representing the correction required.

At any stage in the calculation we can update the linearization point Ξ_0 by making the corrections found so far, and relinearizing about the new point. The new estimated correlation will be $\hat{\mathbf{X}} = 0$, and the estimated covariance $\hat{S}$ will be unchanged by the relinearization.

Given a good estimate Ξ_0 of the set of primitives of interest, we are interested in using our measurement devices to find the (assumed small) correction required, described by the state vector $\mathbf{X} \in \mathbf{R}^N$. Suppose previous measurements have told us that $E[\mathbf{X}] = \hat{\mathbf{X}}$ and Cov $[\mathbf{X}] = \hat{S}$. If there are no previous measurements, we can take $\hat{\mathbf{X}} = 0$ and let $\hat{S}$ be a large multiple of the unit matrix. Gauss-Markov estimation answers the problem of finding the optimal update of $\hat{\mathbf{X}}$ given a measurement of a quantity $\mathbf{z} \in \mathbf{R}^M$ related to $\mathbf{X}$ by a linear measurement equation

$$\mathbf{z} = H\mathbf{X} + \mathbf{u},$$

where the $M \times N$ plant matrix H is known, and **u** is a measurement error with mean zero and known covariance. An elegant description of the generalized (singular covariance) theory as an application of the Moore-Penrose pseudoinverse can be found in Albert (1972). A more conventional treatment of the statistics of linear models can be found in Morrison (1976).

In order to simplify the structure of the system, we have implemented our testbed programs in terms of a very simple but elegant result from Gauss-Markov theory, the optimal update rule after the imposition of a single scalar constraint (this is a singular scalar Kalman filter). We will show later that this is sufficient for all our purposes. It must be stressed that this is merely an implementations detail; more conventional implements such as a nonsingular Kalman filter (see, for example, Gelb, 1984) are available and entirely equivalent.

Suppose we are given a single further piece of information about the true correction **X**: It satisfied an exact linear constraint

$$z + \mathbf{h}^t \mathbf{X} = 0,$$

where z and **h** are known. The optimal update rule is then

$$\hat{S}' = \hat{S} - \frac{(\hat{S}\mathbf{h})(\hat{S}\mathbf{h})^t}{\mathbf{h}^t \hat{S} \mathbf{h}}, \quad \mathbf{k} = \frac{\hat{S}\mathbf{h}}{\mathbf{h}^t \hat{S} \mathbf{h}},$$

$$\hat{\mathbf{X}}' = \hat{\mathbf{X}} - \mathbf{k}(z + \mathbf{h}^t \hat{\mathbf{X}}).$$

(Note that the correction is described by an "innovation" term proportional to the error of the old estimate; this is typical of a Kalman filter.) The increase in residual (weighted mean square error) is

$$\epsilon' = \epsilon + \frac{(z + \mathbf{h}^t \hat{\mathbf{X}})^2}{\mathbf{h}^t \hat{S} \mathbf{h}}.$$

If we wanted to test the plausibility of the constraint, given the previous information, before imposing it, then the maximum likelihood test treats $\epsilon' - \epsilon$ as χ^2 on one degree of freedom. After imposition of the constraint, the relation

$$z + \mathbf{h}^t \hat{\mathbf{X}}' = 0.$$

holds exactly, and the presence of the exact correlation is signified by the singularity of the covariance matrix

$$\hat{S}'\mathbf{h} = 0.$$

We can impose as many of these constraints as we like as long as they are independent. A constraint is not independent of previous constraints if $\hat{S}\mathbf{h} = 0$. We must then check that $z + \mathbf{h}^t\mathbf{X} = 0$ holds. If this is true, then the constraint has already been imposed as a consequence of previous ones. If not, then the new constraint is inconsistent and cannot be imposed.

The method only guarantees the satisfaction of constraints to linearized order. If more accuracy is required, it can be obtained by iteration. The original estimate of the configuration was Ξ_0 with covariance $\hat{S}$. Applying the constraint to linear order generates a correction $\mathbf{X}$ which we can apply to Ξ_0 to get a new estimate Ξ_1. Relative to this new and more accurate solution the original measurement is described by $(\Xi_1, -\mathbf{X}, \hat{S})$, and if we apply the constraint $\mathbf{h}$ at about this new linearization point, it will hold to quadratic order. This can be iterated to obtain any desired accuracy.

4. MEASUREMENTS AND CONSTRAINTS

We now show that the above mechanism is sufficient to implement any kind of measurement or constraint. Suppose a sensor observes a measurement primitive ξ, its internal state (motion since last view, miscalibration, etc.) is described by another primitive σ, and it returns a third primitive ζ as measurement. For example, ξ could be the position of an edge in the world, σ the calibration parameters of a stereo rig, and ζ the position of the edge returned by the stereo system. If the measurement were exact, the relationship between the three would typically have the form

$$\mathbf{h}(\zeta, \sigma, \xi) = 0.$$

Choose local coordinates about the actual measurement ζ. On the assumption of small approximately normal errors, we know that the true measurement ζ is related to the actual measurement ζ_0 by

$$\zeta = \zeta_0 + F_z \mathbf{z}, \ \mathbf{z} = N(0, R).$$

If we have estimates σ_0 and ξ_0 of the other two quantities and introduce local coordinates about these estimates, we can linearize the equation (with obvious choice of notation) as

$$\mathbf{h}(\zeta_0, \sigma_0, \xi_0) + \left(\frac{\partial \mathbf{h}}{\partial \zeta} \cdot F_z, \frac{\partial \mathbf{h}}{\partial \sigma} \cdot F_s, \frac{\partial \mathbf{h}}{\partial \xi} \cdot F_x \right) \begin{pmatrix} \mathbf{z} \\ \mathbf{s} \\ \mathbf{x} \end{pmatrix} = 0.$$

Suppose previous measurements of the system of interest have provided us with a description (Ξ_0, $\hat{X}$, $\hat{S}$), and we are including measurements of this primitive from this sensor for the first time. We augment the description of the system to include a new observed primitive ξ_0, the sensor calibration primitive σ_0, and the primitive which is the result of the measurement ζ_0:

$$\Xi' = (\Xi_0, \xi_0, \sigma_0, \zeta_0).$$

The perturbation vector is augmented so that it describes the whole system

$$\mathbf{X}' = \begin{pmatrix} \hat{\mathbf{X}} \\ \hat{\mathbf{x}} \\ \hat{\mathbf{s}} \\ \hat{\mathbf{z}} \end{pmatrix}$$

with initially $\hat{\mathbf{x}} = 0$, $\hat{\mathbf{s}} = 0$, $\hat{\mathbf{z}} = 0$, and the extended system covariance is augmented by large multiples of the unit matrix to represent complete uncertainty in the estimates of $\hat{\mathbf{x}}$, $\hat{\mathbf{s}}$, and with the known covariance of the measurement result $\hat{\mathbf{z}}$. Our description of the sensor says that the linearized constraint equation above is satisfied exactly (at least to linearized order) by the true values of the corrections $\mathbf{x}$, $\mathbf{s}$, $\mathbf{z}$. Each component of the equation is thus a linear scalar constraint which can be applied by the method described in the last section.

The process above not only finds the optimal correction $\hat{\mathbf{x}}$ to the primitive ξ_0, but also gives a correction $\hat{\mathbf{z}}$ to the measurement ζ_0; that is, it tells us what this measurement *should have been*. In general, the measurement is only of interest insofar as it allows us to correct the original primitive, ξ; ζ itself is not of interest and so can be deleted from the system description, the state vector, and the state matrix at this point. This is very important if the state vector is not to grow to an impossible size, recording corrected values of every measurement we have made on the system.

If we make subsequent measurements with the same sensor, or of the same primitive, they will not need to be added to the system description since they are already present. This will automatically correlate measurements of different primitives through the same sensor.

If we have reason to believe our sensor may have malfunctioned, we can test the likelihood of the measurement equation being correct, given our previous measurements, before including the measurement in the estimate. This can be achieved by treating the total increase in residual as a result of imposing the constraint as a χ^2 variable, with the number of degrees of freedom given by the number of constraints imposed.

The imposition of constraints is similar. Suppose our system description contains two primitives ξ and ζ, and we have reason to believe that a constraint $\mathbf{h}(\xi, \zeta) = 0$ is satisfied by their exact values. The constraint can be linearized about the present system description to give

$$\mathbf{h}(\xi_0, \zeta_0) + \left(\frac{\partial \mathbf{h}}{\partial \xi} \cdot F_x, \frac{\partial \mathbf{h}}{\partial \zeta} \cdot F_z \right) \begin{pmatrix} \mathbf{x} \\ \mathbf{z} \end{pmatrix} = 0,$$

which is again a set of linear constraints to be applied to the state vector.

5. THE ACCURACY OF STEREO MEASUREMENT

From now on we will concentrate on applying the above formalism to the analysis of stereo data. TINA supplies a list (the geometrical descriptive base, GDB) of the straight edges and circles found in the scene. Here we will use only the straight-edge data. We need estimates of the measurement covariance associated with these data. Because of the complexity of the process of extracting these edge data, it is difficult to give a complete error analysis, so we will consider only an idealization of the process.

First we will consider an idealized situation where we are observing not lines but sets of n collinear points. The stereo rig is taken to be a parallel camera (in our system the edge maps are rectified from convergent to parallel camera geometry) with focal length f and inter-camera distance I. A point (x, y, z) in the world projects to a point (X_L, Y) in the left image and (X_R, Y) in the right image. We refer to (X_L, Y, X_R) as coordinates on *disparity space*. The map from world points to disparity space is then

$$X_L = \frac{fx}{z}, \quad Y = \frac{fy}{z}, \quad X_R = \frac{f(x-1)}{z}.$$

Small vectors can be projected from disparity space into the world by using the Jacobian matrix

$$J = \frac{I}{(X_L - X_R)^2} \begin{pmatrix} -X_R & 0 & X_L \\ -Y & X_L - X_R & Y \\ -f & 0 & f \end{pmatrix}.$$

Points are assumed to be matched without error between left and right images, and the imaging process is assumed to produce equal uncorrelated errors of variance σ^2 in the three image coordinates (X_L, Y, X_R). (σ is assumed constant over the image; if the image is rectified, it will actually vary slightly.) Fitting a line by orthogonal regression in (X_L, X_R, Y_L)-space (disparity space) is then optimal (Porrill, Pridmore, Mayhew, & Frisby, 1986) in that it minimizes the sum of squared perpendicular distances of the points from the fitted line. This produces position error in the centroid of the fitted line of variance σ^2/n and an angular error of variance $12\sigma^2/nl^2$, where l is the length of the line in disparity space. These two errors are uncorrelated. In terms of local line coordinates *in disparity space* the error covariance is thus

$$S_{disp} = \frac{\sigma^2}{n} \begin{pmatrix} I & 0 \\ 0 & \frac{12}{l^2}I \end{pmatrix},$$

where I is the 2×2 unit matrix.

We must transform this result to world coordinates. The lateral position error coordinates transform by

$$p_i = \mathbf{y}_i \cdot (\mathbf{p} - \mathbf{p}_0)_{world} = \mathbf{v}_i \cdot J(\mathbf{p} - \mathbf{p}_0)_{disparity}.$$

Since the Jacobian does not preserve the length of vectors, the lateral direction error has an extra scalar factor

$$v_i = \mathbf{v}_i \cdot (\mathbf{v} - \mathbf{v}_0)_{world} = \frac{\mathbf{v}_1 \cdot J(\mathbf{p} - \mathbf{p}_0)_{disparity}}{|J\mathbf{v}_0|}.$$

We can thus calculate the error covariance of the description in the world to be

$$S = \begin{pmatrix} \Sigma & 0 \\ 0 & \frac{12}{l^2|J\mathbf{v}_0|^2}\Sigma \end{pmatrix},$$

where

$$\Sigma_{ij} = \frac{\sigma^2}{n} \mathbf{v}_i^t J J^t \mathbf{v}_j, \quad i, j = 1, 2,$$

where the basepoint p_0 is taken as the projection of the disparity space centroid into the world. This covariance is adjoined to the description of the edge segment in the GDB.

The above idealization is unrealistic for two main reasons. (1) The stereo matching of *continuous* edges mixes horizontal errors with vertical errors; for edges making angles θ with the horizontal which are close to zero, depth values are highly inaccurate. (When $\theta = 0$, matching is impossible.) A crude way of compensating for this is to multiply J by a matrix, producing an expansion factor of $1/\sin \theta$ in depth before using the above formulae. (2) The points detected on continuous edges are not randomly scattered on the edges but wander slowly from one side to the other. This can be compensated for by replacing n by a smaller effective number of points on the line which counts these wanderings. Though crude, this model then captures most of the essential information about stereo errors.

As an alternative to the calculation of an a priori covariance, we can estimate the covariance directly from the data (Faugeras et al. 1986). Fit an approximate line (p_0, v_0) to the data. Suppose one of the data points (x, y, z) projects to $(X_L, Y) = (x/z, y/z)$ in the left image. Let $\mathbf{a} = (X, Y, 1)^t$. The condition that this image point lies on the projection of the true line into the image is $\mathbf{p} \cdot (\mathbf{a} \times \mathbf{v}) = 0$, which linearizes to

$$\mathbf{p}_0 \cdot (\mathbf{a} \times \mathbf{v}_0) + p_1 \mathbf{v}_1 \cdot (\mathbf{a} \times \mathbf{v}_0) + p_2 \mathbf{v}_2 \cdot (\mathbf{a} \times \mathbf{v}_0) + \nu_1 \mathbf{p}_0 \cdot (\mathbf{a} \times \mathbf{v}_1)$$
$$+ \nu_2 \mathbf{p}_0 \cdot (\mathbf{a} \times \mathbf{v}_2) = 0.$$

If we assume no prior knowledge, then by walking down the string of points imposing this constraint in each image, we can simultaneously correct our initial line and build up its covariance matrix.

6. GEOMETRICAL CONSTRAINTS

The use of GEOMSTAT as a knowledge source for a wire frame completion package was described in the introduction. For example, three edges that are close to intersecting at a common vertex and are almost mutually perpendicular might be hypothesized, in an environment of manufactured objects, to form a rectangular trihedral vertex. This hypothesis can be tested for its plausibility given the errors of observation, and, if accepted, the model can be optimally adjusted to satisfy the constraint.

The constraints we have implemented—perpendicularity, intersection, parallelism, and equality of lines—are given in linearized form in the appendix. Their use in wire frame completion has been investigated through two programs. GOFRIT uses some (very) simpleminded heuristics to propose likely constraints, then tests and imposes them. On test data it performs well. For example, Figure 12.1(a) shows a simple test object with Gaussian errors, and Figure 12.1(b) shows the result after cleaning. On real data the presence of accidental relationships and the occasional flyer in the data can lead to disaster. CLEANUP is an interactive program in which the user proposes constraints, sees the changes as they occur, and has the opportunity to recover from disasters. It is seen as a testbed for a knowledge source under intelligent control. An application of CLEANUP to real data is given in Section 7.

Since the covariance matrix stores information about all the constraints imposed, it can form a database for some elementary geometric reasoning. For example, if we have four lines forming an approximate square and we successively apply the constraint of perpendicularity at the vertices, the fourth application will be detected as nonindependent but consistent with the preceding ones. An attempt to make the last angle different from 90° would be rejected as inconsistent. Notice that the linearized nature of the constraint makes this reasoning incomplete; after imposition of perpendicularity, opposite sides of the square would not necessarily be parallel, since skewing the square out of plane changes the angles only at quadratic order; this constraint would have to be imposed separately.

Figure 12.2 is a computer-generated stereo pair illustrating our test object, the widget (though this image is artificial, all the subsequent work uses real images of this object). As a very simple test of the adequacy of our model of stereo errors for real data, the CLEANUP program was applied to real data (a view of the widget similar to Figure 12.2), and a sequence of about 40 constraints which were known to hold were applied, the residual increase for each being recorded. This should be a sample from a χ^2 distribution on one degree of freedom with mean 1 and variance 2. The sample mean was 0.95 and the variance was 4.0. The agreement is not startling, not surprisingly given our model of stereo errors, but we have the right order of magnitude. The techniques of analysis of covariance might allow us to eventually fit a more sophisticated multiparameter model to the data (Morrison, 1976).

7. MERGING MULTIPLE STEREO VIEWS

Another basic application of GEOMSTAT is to the acquisition of accurate and complete wireframe models of objects or environments from multiple stereo views. Suppose we have built up a model with an associated covariance matrix from previous views and now want to include

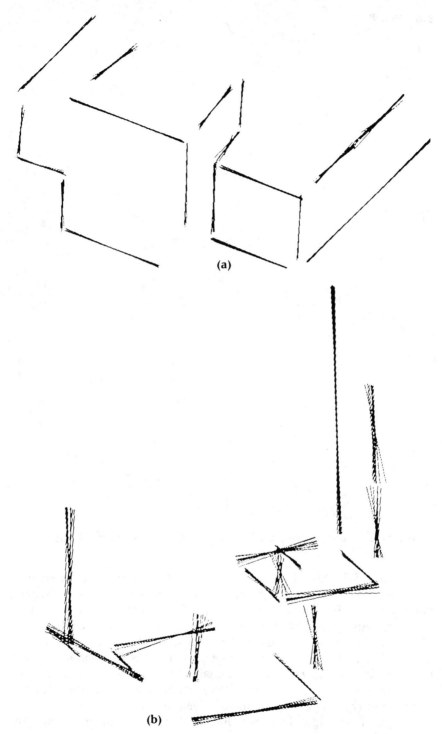

Figure 12.1. Wire frame completion (a) Result after cleaning. (b) Test object with Gaussian errors.

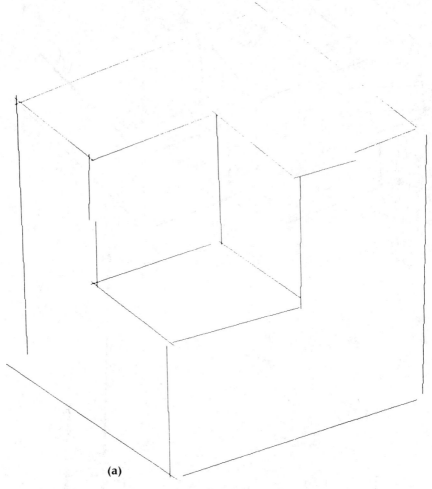

Figure 12.2. Computer-generated widget (a) Left view (b) Right view

a new view. Matching is automatic rather than hand held; consistent matches between lines are chosen by SMM (scene and model matcher: Pollard et al., 1986), which relates the old model to the new view and calculates an approximate transformation (R_0, t_0) between the two. This is used to transform all the elements of the old model into the new frame. This transformation is nonoptimal. The "calibration error" between model and view (ω, τ) is adjoined to the state vector of the model with infinite covariance. In a mobile robot application we might use an estimate of the motion and its error given by position encoders.

For each pair of matched lines the new view of the line is adjoined to

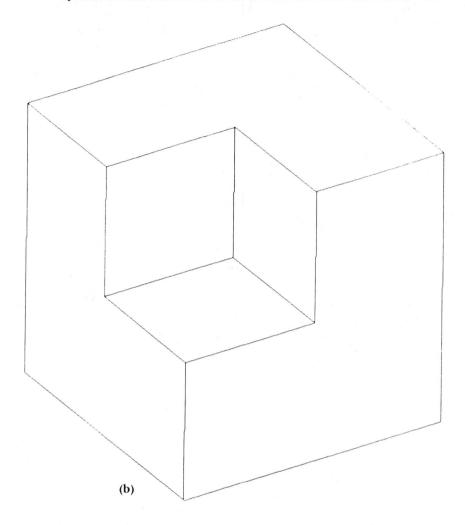

(b)

the state vector (or if a line in the model has no match in the new view, an identical "virtual" match is adjoined with infinite covariance). The constraint that they are related by the incremental rigid motion (ω, τ) is then imposed (see Appendix). (This merges the two lines in the first case, or performs the required transformation of the line and its statistics into the new frame in the second.) The old version of the line is deleted from the state vector.

Figure 12.3 (a–c) shows the long edges extracted from three images of the widget. (Extremal boundaries and line segments corresponding to the circular edge of the cylinder have been removed by hand so that

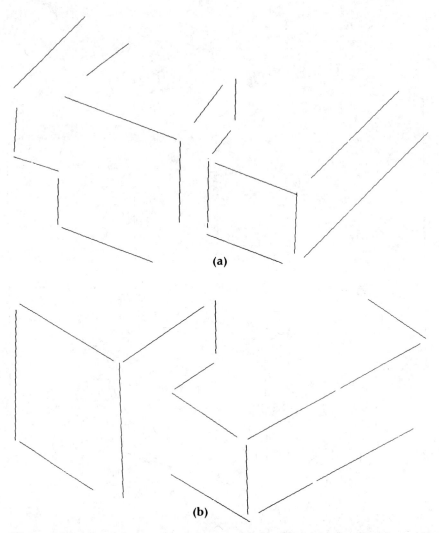

Figure 12.3. (a–c) Long edges extracted from three images of widget. (d) Result after cleaning.

the resulting figure would be relatively clean.) Figure 12.3(d) is the result of applying the matching and merging process and the CLEAN-UP program to the resulting model. All obvious relationships of incidence, orthogonality, and parallelism have been imposed (in fact, no others would be accepted at the 95% confidence level). Matched line segments are merged and "unioned"; that is, the most extreme pair of endpoints is used. Corners described by the referee as "too nice to be true" were produced by extending lines which intersect (if the exten-

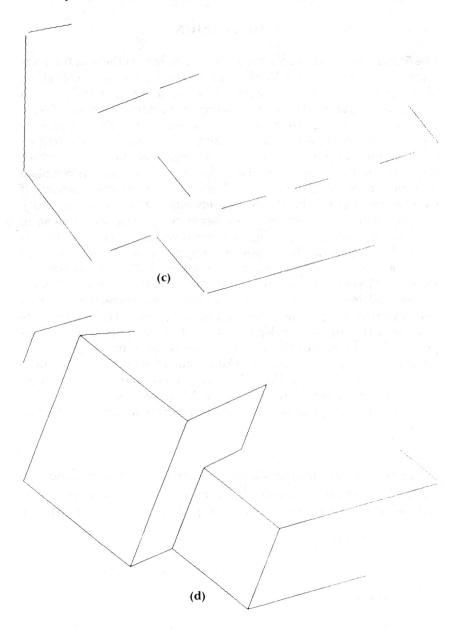

sion required is less than a few percent) up to their common intersection except when this would produce a three-dimensional T-junction (this is a "no surface markings" assumption).

8. DISCUSSION

The formalism we have presented is very similar to others in the literature in its use of Gauss-Markov estimation for sensor combination. (The implementation as a sequence of scalar constraints is only a technical difference.) There are two important differences. The first is the ability to treat constrained problems and to use the statistics to test and impose hypothesized constraints. The second is the retention of the error correlation between all elements of the model and all sensor calibration parameters. We believe that an essentially complete implementation of the theory is of interest in a testbed program, if only to see whether the theoretical advantage of increased accuracy actually exists. However, there is a heavy computational overhead in the maintenance and updating of large covariance matrices. This is acceptable at present, but a practical algorithm would need to avoid much of the calculation. One way to approach this is discussed in Durrant-Whyte (1985), where the calculation of the optimal estimator is arranged in such a way that it is clear when correlations are no longer contributing to the solution. Imposing geometrical constraints cuts down the number of degrees of freedom in the problem, but at present does not reduce the workload. This could be improved by occasionally locating highly constrained groups of primitives by using a singular value decomposition of the covariance matrix and treating these assemblies as primitive objects with lumped degrees of freedom (similar to the lumped systems in the finite element analysis of structures).

Appendix: Geometrical Constraints and their Linearizations

We give here some examples of conditions on the state vector resulting from geometrical constraints on the pair of lines $(\mathbf{p}, \mathbf{v})$ and $(\mathbf{p}', \mathbf{v}')$.

1. Orthogonality

$$\mathbf{v} \cdot \mathbf{v}' = (\mathbf{v}_0 + \nu_1 \mathbf{v}_1 + \nu_2 \mathbf{v}_2) \cdot (\mathbf{v}'_0 + \nu'_1 \mathbf{v}'_1 + \nu'_2 \mathbf{v}'_2) = 0$$

linearizes to

$$\mathbf{v}_0 \cdot \mathbf{v}'_0 + \nu_1 \mathbf{v}_1 \cdot \mathbf{v}'_0 + \nu_2 \mathbf{v}_2 \cdot \mathbf{v}'_0 + \nu'_1 \mathbf{v}_0 \cdot \mathbf{v}'_1 + \nu'_2 \mathbf{v}_0 \cdot \mathbf{v}'_2 = 0.$$

2. Intersection

$$(\mathbf{p} - \mathbf{p}') \cdot (\mathbf{v} \times \mathbf{v}') = 0$$

linearizes to

Optimal Combination and Constraints for Geometrical Sensor Data

$$\begin{aligned}
(\mathbf{p}'_0 - \mathbf{p}_0) \cdot (\mathbf{v}_0 + \mathbf{v}'_0) &+ p_1 \mathbf{v}_1 \cdot (\mathbf{v}_0 \times \mathbf{v}'_0) \\
+ p_2 \mathbf{v}_2 \cdot (\mathbf{v}_0 + \mathbf{v}'_0) &- p'_1 \mathbf{v}'_1 \cdot (\mathbf{v}_0 \times \mathbf{v}'_0) \\
- p'_2 \mathbf{v}'_2 \cdot (\mathbf{v}_0 \times \mathbf{v}'_0) &+ v_1(\mathbf{p}_0 - \mathbf{p}'_0) \cdot (\mathbf{v}_1 + \mathbf{v}'_0) \\
+ v_2(\mathbf{p}_0 - \mathbf{p}'_0) \cdot (\mathbf{v}_2 \times \mathbf{v}'_0) & \\
+ v'_1(\mathbf{p}_0 - \mathbf{p}'_0) \cdot (\mathbf{v}_0 \times \mathbf{v}'_1) & \\
+ v'_2(\mathbf{p}_0 - \mathbf{p}'_0) \cdot (\mathbf{v}_0 + \mathbf{v}'_2) &= 0.
\end{aligned}$$

3. Equality

$$\mathbf{v} = \mathbf{v}', \quad (\mathbf{p}' - \mathbf{p}) - (\mathbf{p}' - \mathbf{p}) \cdot \hat{\mathbf{v}}' \hat{\mathbf{v}}' = 0,$$

$$\hat{\mathbf{v}}' = \frac{\mathbf{v}}{|\mathbf{v}'|}.$$

Each of these represents only two independent constraints, which can be extracted by taking the scalar product with $\mathbf{v}'_1$ and $\mathbf{v}'_2$. The result linearizes to

$$\begin{aligned}
(\mathbf{p}'_0 - \mathbf{p}_0) \cdot \mathbf{v}'_1 - p_1 \mathbf{v}_1 \cdot \mathbf{v}'_1 - p_2 \mathbf{v}_2 \cdot \mathbf{v}'_1 + p_1 - v'_1(\mathbf{p}'_0 - \mathbf{p}_0) \cdot \mathbf{v}_0 &= 0, \\
(\mathbf{p}'_0 - \mathbf{p}_0) \cdot \mathbf{v}'_2 - p_1 \mathbf{v}_1 \cdot \mathbf{v}'_2 - p_2 \mathbf{v}_2 \cdot \mathbf{v}'_2 + p'_2 - v'_2(\mathbf{p}'_0 - \mathbf{p}_0) \cdot \mathbf{v}'_0 &= 0,
\end{aligned}$$

and

$$\begin{aligned}
\mathbf{v}_0 \cdot \mathbf{v}'_1 + v_1 \mathbf{v}_1 \cdot \mathbf{v}'_1 + v_2 \mathbf{v}_2 \cdot \mathbf{v}'_1 - v'_1 &= 0, \\
\mathbf{v}_0 \cdot \mathbf{v}'_2 + v_1 \mathbf{v}_1 \cdot \mathbf{v}'_2 + v_2 \mathbf{v}_2 \cdot \mathbf{v}'_2 - v'_2 &= 0.
\end{aligned}$$

(The last two constraints are sufficient to impose parallelism.)

4. The two lines are connected by the small rigid motion $(\boldsymbol{\omega}, \boldsymbol{\tau})$ if

$$(\mathbf{p}' - \mathbf{p} - \boldsymbol{\omega} \times \mathbf{p} - \boldsymbol{\tau}) - (\mathbf{p}' - \mathbf{p} - \boldsymbol{\omega} \times \mathbf{p} - \boldsymbol{\tau}) \cdot \hat{\mathbf{v}}' \hat{\mathbf{v}}' = 0,$$
$$\hat{\mathbf{v}}' - \hat{\mathbf{v}} - \boldsymbol{\omega} \times \hat{\mathbf{v}} = 0.$$

This linearizes to

$$\begin{aligned}
(\mathbf{p}'_0 - \mathbf{p}_0 - \mathbf{t}_{0_0}) \cdot \mathbf{v}'_1 + p'_1 - p_1 \mathbf{v}_1 \cdot \mathbf{v}'_1 - p_2 \mathbf{v}_2 \cdot \mathbf{v}'_1 & \\
- v'_1(\mathbf{p}'_0 - \mathbf{p}_0 - \mathbf{t}_{0_0}) \cdot \mathbf{v}_0 - (\mathbf{p}_0 \times \mathbf{v}'_1) \cdot \boldsymbol{\omega} & \\
- \mathbf{v}'_1 \cdot \boldsymbol{\tau} &= 0, \\
(\mathbf{p}'_0 - \mathbf{p}_0 - \mathbf{t}_{0_0}) \cdot \mathbf{v}'_2 + p'_2 - p_1 \mathbf{v}_1 \cdot \mathbf{v}'_2 - p_2 \mathbf{v}_2 \cdot \mathbf{v}'_2 & \\
- v'_2(\mathbf{p}'_0 - \mathbf{p}_0 - \mathbf{t}_{0_0}) \cdot \mathbf{v}_0 - (\mathbf{p}_0 \times \mathbf{v}'_2) \cdot \boldsymbol{\omega} & \\
- \mathbf{v}'_2 \cdot \boldsymbol{\tau} &= 0, \\
- \mathbf{v}_0 \cdot \mathbf{v}'_1 + v'_1 - v_1 \mathbf{v}_1 \cdot \mathbf{v}'_1 - v_2 \mathbf{v}_2 \cdot \mathbf{v}'_1 & \\
- (\mathbf{v}_0 \times \mathbf{v}'_1) \cdot \boldsymbol{\omega} &= 0, \\
- \mathbf{v}_0 \cdot \mathbf{v}'_2 + v'_2 - v_1 \mathbf{v}_1 \cdot \mathbf{v}'_2 - v_2 \mathbf{v}_2 \cdot \mathbf{v}'_2 & \\
- (\mathbf{v}_0 \times \mathbf{v}'_2) \cdot \boldsymbol{\omega} &= 0,
\end{aligned}$$

REFERENCES

Albert, A. (1972). *Regression and the Moore-Penrose pseudoinverse.* New York: Academic Press.

Bolle, R.M., & Cooper, D.B. (1986). On optimally combining pieces of information, with application to estimating 3-D complex-object position from range data. *IEEE Transactions on Pattern Analysis and Machine Intellience,* PAMI-8(5), 619-638.

Crowley, J.L. (1985). Navigation for an intelligent mobile robot. *IEEE Journal of Robotics and Automation,* RA-1(1), 31–41.

Durrant-Whyte, H.F. (1985). *Consistent integration and propagation of disparate sensor observations.* Unpublished doctoral dissertation, University of Pennsylvania, GRASP Lab.

Faugeras, O.D., Ayache, N., & Faverjon, B. (1986). Building visual maps by combining noisy stereo measurements. *Proceedings of the IEEE International Conference on Robotics and Automation* (pp. 1433–1438). San Francisco, CA.

Gelb, A. (1984). *Applied optimal estimation.* Cambridge, MA: MIT Press.

Morrison, D.F. (1976). *Multivariate statistical methods.* New York: McGraw-Hill.

Pollard, S.B., Porrill, J., Mayhew, J.E.W., & Frisby, J.P. (1987). Matching geometrical descriptions in three space. *Image and Vision Computing* 5(2), 73–78.

Porrill, J., Pridmore, T.P., Mayhew, J.E.W., & Frisby, J.P. (1986). Fitting planes, lines and circles to stereo disparity data (AIVRU Memo 017). University of Sheffield: Artificial Intelligence Vision Research Unit.

Porrill, J., Pollard, S.B., and Mayhew, J.E.W. (1987). Optimal combination of multiple sensors including stereo vision. *Image and Vision Computing* 5(2), 175–180.

Smith, R.C., & Cheeseman, P. (1985). On the representation and estimation of spatial uncertainty. *International Journal of Robotics Research* 5(4), 56–68.

13
Feature Space Mapping For Sensor Fusion*

Gerald M. Flachs,
Jay B. Jordan,
C.L. Beer,
D.R. Scott, and
Jeffrey J. Carlson

In the context of a random process scene environment model, a method is presented in this chapter for fusing data from multiple sensors into a simplified, ordered space for performing electronic vision tasks. The method is based on a new discriminating measure called the *tie statistic* that is introduced to quantify sensor/feature performance and to provide a mapping from sensor/feature measurement space to a simplified and ordered decision space. The mapping process uses the tie statistic to measure the closeness of an unknown sample probability density function (pdf) to a known pdf for a decision class. Theorems presented in this chapter relate the tie statistic to minimum probability of error decision making and to the well-known Kolmogorov–Smirnov distance. As examples of the sensor/feature fusion method, the tie mapping process is applied to the object location (cueing) and the texture recognition problems.

---

*The research reported in this chapter was primarily sponsored by the U.S. Army Research Office, Research Triangle Park, NC, Contract No. DAAL03-87-K-0106. Other sponsors were the U.S. Army Vulnerability Assessment Laboratory, U.S. Army Atmospheric Sciences Laboratory, and the AT&T foundation.

1. INTRODUCTION

Electronic vision systems are called upon to reduce scene data acquired from multiple sensors to control decisions. Typically, these systems are required to locate regions containing objects of interest, separate the objects from the background, classify objects and background scenes, and perform control functions. These electronic vision tasks are often referred to as the cuer, segmenter, recognizer and controller, respectively. The design of such systems requires the selection of sensors and features together with the development of processing algorithms to accomplish these tasks.

The performance of an electronic vision system depends heavily on the selected sensors and features. The selection of sensor/feature combinations together with the design of a fusion algorithm is often considered an art that depends on the experience of the designer. The crucial steps are to find sensor/feature combinations that perform well in the intended application environments and to develop fusion algorithms that map the measured features into an ordered decision space to achieve minimal probability of error performance.

A method is presented for evaluating measurements obtained from multiple sensors using multiple features and for fusing the sensor/feature information into an ordered space for performing vision tasks. A difference measure, called the *tie statistic,* is introduced to quantify sensor/feature performance and to provide a mapping from the feature measurement space to an ordered decision space. The mapping process uses the tie statistic to measure the closeness of an unknown sample probability density function (pdf) to a known pdf for a decision class.

Various measures have been established that measure this difference (Fukunaga & Krihe, 1967; Bhattacharyya, 1943; Kailath, 1967; Matusita, 1951; Kirmani, 1979; Carlson, Jordan, & Flachs, 1988; Smirnov & Tikheyeva, 1978). These include the divergence measure (J), Kolmogorov's variational distance (V), the Bhattacharyya coefficient (p), Matusita's distance (M), and the Kolmogorov-Smirnov (KS) distance. Toussaint (1972) has developed relationships between these measures and discussed their relative merits. The tie statistic has at least two advantages over most of these measures: 1) It is well suited for efficient machine computation, and 2) it is directly related to the error rate associated with minimum probability of error (MPE) statistical decision making.

In this chapter, a theorem is presented that relates the tie statistic directly to the decision probability of error under the conditions that the decision rule is optimal (i.e. MPE) and that the a priori probabilities of decision classes are equal. Also, another theorem is presented that relates the tie statistic (T) to the well-known Kolmogorov-Smirnov statistic (KS). Under certain conditions, the two statistics are directly related, implying that the T and KS have the same discriminating power. In situations where these conditions are not met, the T is more sensitive to small differences in the pdfs and hence can provide better separation between different decision classes.

In summary, the tie statistic provides a computationally simple method of evaluating and comparing probability distributions that is closely related to the expected upper bound on the performance of a system using sensor/feature data drawn from the distributions. The boundary surface separating the decision regions under a tie space mapping is unusually simple, allowing the decision boundary to be adaptively learned and altered using a priori knowledge and current information. This results in an effective method for fusing multisensor features into a simplified, integrated decision space.

The tie mapping process is applied to the cuer problem and texture recognition problem for multiple sensor environments. Experimental results are given to illustrate the power of the method.

2. BACKGROUND—MULTISENSOR SCENE MODEL

The methodology for multisensor fusion based on the tie statistic occurs within the mathematical framework of a random process model of the scene generating environment. Most electronic vision systems perceive their environment with sensors that make measurements in a multidimensional electromagnetic energy field. The observed values of these signals at any time are influenced by a myriad of factors in the energy field and the sensors. The overall effect of these factors makes it desirable to model the signals composing the scene as a stochastic or random process (Papoulis, 1965) in time, space and spectra. For multiple sensor systems, there is a dimension of the random process associated with each sensor. At any point in time, region of space and spectra, a multisensor system observes a single realization of the process.

In general, the joint distribution of the random variables composing the random process associated with the multisensor system is incredibly complex. However, in physical systems the random process describing the scene environment often contains small regions that are approximately wide sense stationary in space, time and spectra with relatively simple statistical properties (Jordan & Flachs, 1987). The existence of such regions allows one to obtain information about the random process by examining spatially and temporally proximate samples. These properties provide the fundamental justification for many of the techniques presented.

2.1. Object/Background and Object/Object Dichotomies

The object/background dichotomy representation of a scene environment that arises in the context of many vision systems is an implicit statement of a priori information concerning the random process modeling the scene environment. Specifically, the *a priori knowledge* that there are two classes, *objects* and *nonobjects*, allows us to partition the set of random variables comprising the random process into two subsets described by two random processes; the process giving rise to observations in the object class, C_1, and the process giving rise to observations in the background class, C_2.

In terms of the random process model of the scene environment, the tasks of detecting the object in the background and separating it from the background are naturally posed as statistical hypothesis tests to determine which of the sets of random variables gave rise to the observed measurement(s). Formulation of the hypothesis test requires that the joint distributions of the random variables composing the objects and background be estimated (Bendat & Piersol, 1966).

The object *recognition* problem—the object/object dichotomy—further partitions the set of random variables into several subsets of random variables comprising different object classes. The problem of identifying or classifying an object is an m-ary hypothesis test to determine which of the object classes gave rise to the observed value(s). Again, formulation of this test requires the estimation of the joint distributions of the random variables composing each object class.

2.2. Features and Feature Space

Although the statistical decision-making technique is conceptually simple, its application in practice can be quite difficult. The difficulty arises because in each scene, there is a continuum of random variables in the random process describing each class. It is not practical in real scenes to acquire enough information to fully characterize the complex joint distributions of the random variables composing the random processes. For this reason, it is necessary to use some function (or set of functions) of the random variables that transforms the continuum to a finite set of random variables, $\{X_1, X_2, \ldots, X_n\}$, called *features*. As the set is ordered, it is often denoted $\mathbf{X} = [X_1, X_2, \ldots, X_n]$ where $\mathbf{X}$ is termed the feature vector. This reduction in dimensionality of the problem (Duda & Hart, 1973), is essential for the implementation of an actual system.

To illustrate the statistical decision-making process, consider the object locating and segmenting tasks where the random variables X_1, $X_2, \ldots, X_n$, are features common to both object regions and background. The set $\mathbf{x} = \{x_1, x_2, \ldots, x_n\} = [x_1, x_2, \ldots, x_n]$ is the observed feature vector, $f_\mathbf{X}(x_1, x_2, \ldots, x_n \mid C_1) = f_\mathbf{X}(x \mid C_1)$ is the conditional joint probability density or mass function (pdf) of the random variables under the object hypothesis, and $f_\mathbf{X}(x_1, x_2, \ldots x_n \mid C_2) = f_\mathbf{X}(x \mid C_2)$ is the conditional joint pdf of the random variables under the background hypothesis.

The typical hypothesis test (Vantrees, 1968), based on observed values $x_1, x_2, \ldots, x_n$, is stated:

$H_0(C_1)$: $x_1, x_2, \ldots, x_n$ are observations from $f_\mathbf{X}(x_1, x_2, \ldots, x_n \mid C_1)$
$H_1(C_2)$: $x_1, x_2, \ldots, x_n$ are observations from $f_\mathbf{X}(x_1, x_2, \ldots, x_n \mid C_2)$

Decisions to classify the observations as being from object (H_0) or background (H_1) are typically made in such a manner that either a) the probability of making an error is minimized or b) the cost of making an error is minimized. A similar set of tests is constructed for the classification of objects into various object classes.

Elements of the feature vector $\mathbf{X}$ may come from transformations acting on measurements from a single sensor or acting on measurements from more than one sensor. Mathematically, the treatment of systems involving multiple sensors, multiple features, or multiple sensors and features is identical. The first step in sensor/feature fusion is determining the set of features that converts the raw sensor measurements into the feature measurements represented by $\mathbf{X}$. This chapter does not prescribe a way to find the best $\mathbf{X}$, but rather introduces the tie statistic and its associated properties to provide a means for evaluating the performance of a system once the transformations generating $\mathbf{X}$ have been chosen. It also provides a means of transforming the space of $\mathbf{X}$ into a simpler and more ordered space to simplify the decision process and enhance adaptive learning.

3. TIE STATISTIC

The tie statistic (T) is a discriminating measure between sample conditional probability density functions (pdfs) for two decision classes. The features common to each class are represented as a vector of random variables $\mathbf{X} = [X_1, X_2, \ldots, X_n]$ with the set $\mathbf{x} = \{x_1, x_2, \ldots, x_n\} = [x_1,$

$x_2, \ldots, x_n$], the observed feature vector. $f_X(x_1, x_2, \ldots, x_n \mid C_1) = f_X(x \mid C_1)$ and $f_X(x_1, x_2, \ldots, x_n \mid C_2) = f_X(x \mid C_2)$ are the conditional pdfs for the feature vectors under two decision classes, C_1 and C_2. For continuous random variables, the tie statistic is defined by

$$T = \int_{V_x} f_X(x \mid C_1) \wedge f_X(x \mid C_2) \, dx,$$

where the operator $\wedge$ selects the minimum. If the random variables are discrete, the statistic is defined in terms of probability mass functions

$$T = \sum_{V_x} f_X(x \mid C_1) \wedge f_X(x \mid C_2).$$

The tie statistic ranges from 0 to 1. A tie value of 0 indicates disjoint pdfs for decision classes C_1 and C_2, and a value of 1 indicates equality of the pdfs. Under a single feature common to two decision classes, C_1 and C_2, Figure 13.1 illustrates the value of the tie statistic as the shaded area. As shown, the T is inversely related to the distance between the pdfs. A low T indicates a large distance and a high T implies pdfs that are closer. Defined as such, T is useful in evaluating pdfs to determine the decision class they most closely represent and to determine if two pdfs come from the same class.

3.1. Minimum Probability of Error Relationship

An important characteristic of the tie statistic is its direct relationship to the minimum probability of error (MPE) associated with a two class decision rule.

Theorem 1. If the a priori probabilities of two decision classes C_1 and C_2 are equally likely (P(C1) = P(C2) = 0.5), then T = 2 MPE.

Proof. The probability of error associated with a two class decision rule is given as:

$$P_e = P(C_1) \int_{R_1} f_X(x \mid C_1) dx + P(C_2) \int_{R_2} f_X(x \mid C_2) \, dx,$$

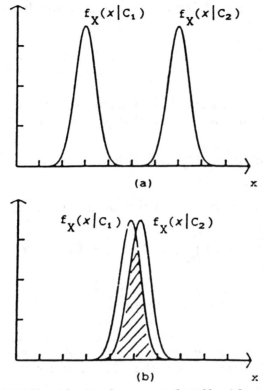

Figure 13.1. (a) Pdfs with a T value near 0. (b) Pdfs with a T value near 1.

where:

$R_1 = \{x: x \text{ is classified as belonging to } C_1\}$ and
$R_2 = \{x: x \text{ is classified as belonging to } C_2\}$.

The decision rule that minimizes the probability of error P_e is the likelihood ratio test

$$\frac{f_X(x \mid C_1)}{f_X(x \mid C_2)} \underset{C_2}{\overset{C_1}{\gtrless}} \frac{P(C_2)}{P(C_1)}.$$

Equivalently, $P(C_1)f_X(x \mid C_1) \underset{C_2}{\overset{C_1}{\gtrless}} P(C_2)f_X(x \mid C_2)$.

For a minimum probability of error decision rule, R_1 and R_2 are restricted as follows:

$$R_1 = \{x: P(C_1)f_X(x \mid C_1) > P(C_2)f_X(x \mid C_2)\}, \text{ and}$$
$$R_2 = \{x: P(C_1)f_X(x \mid C_1) \leq P(C_2)f_X(x \mid C_2)\}.$$

This restriction on R_1 and R_2 for minimizing the probability of error results in the following compact expression for the MPE:

$$\text{MPE} = \int_{V_x} P(C_1)f_X(\mathbf{x} \mid C_1) \wedge P(C_2)f_X(\mathbf{x} \mid C_2) \, d\mathbf{x}$$

Letting $P(C_1) = P(C_2) = 0.5$ leads to the desired result:

$$\text{MPE} = 0.5 \int_{V_x} f_X(\mathbf{x} \mid C_1) \wedge f_X(\mathbf{x} \mid C_2) \, d\mathbf{x} = 0.5T.$$

3.2. Kolmogorov Distance Measures

Two well-known measures often used to determine the distance between pdfs are the Kolmogorov variational distance, V, and the Kolmogorov–Smirnov distance (KS). The Kolmogorov variational distance is defined by

$$V = \int_{V_x} |f_X(\mathbf{x} \mid C_1) - f_X(\mathbf{x} \mid C_2)| \, d\mathbf{x}.$$

The KS distance measure is defined by

$$\text{KS} = \sup_x |F_X(\mathbf{x} \mid C_1) - F_X(\mathbf{x} \mid C_2)|,$$

where $F_X(\mathbf{x} \mid C_1)$ and $F_X(\mathbf{x} \mid C_2)$ are the joint conditional cummulative distribution functions (cdfs) for feature vector $\mathbf{X}$ under classes C_1 and C_2. The KS distance ranges from 0 to 1, where KS = 0 indicates equality of the two functions and KS = 1 indicates no overlap between them (See Figure 13.2). The KS statistic is considered a particularly valuable tool because its distribution is independent of the underlying defining distributions and its distribution in the case of the null hypothesis is known. The following section presents theorems that relate the tie statistic to the Kolmogorov distances.

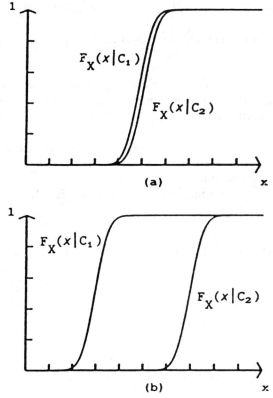

Figure 13.2. (a) Cdfs with a KS near 0. (b) Cdfs with a KS near 1.

3.3. Kolmogorov Distances and the Tie Statistic

The following theorems are presented to show some interesting and useful relationships between the tie statistic and the Kolmogorov distances. In the theorems, the feature space is represented by Ω.

Theorem 2:

$$T = 1 - V/2$$

Proof. The minimum of two quantities can be written $x \wedge y = (x + y - |x-y|)/2$. Similarly, the minimum of two functions

$$f_X(x \mid C_1) \wedge f_X(x \mid C_2) = [f_X(x \mid C_1) + f_X(x \mid C_2) - |f_X(x \mid C_1) - f_X(x \mid C_2)|]/2.$$

Integrating the last equation over all x and simplifying completes the proof.

Theorem 3: Let $F_X(x \mid C_1)$ and $F_X(x \mid C_2)$ be differentiable cummulative distribution functions on $\mathbb{R}^1$. Then $T + KS \leq 1$ with equality if there is only one point, p, such that $f_X(p \mid C_1) = f_X(p \mid C_2)$ and

$$f_X(x \mid C_1) > f_X(x \mid C_2) \text{ for } x > p \text{ and } f_X(x \mid C_1) < f_X(x \mid C_2) \text{ for } x < p.$$

Proof: Part 1: Show that $T + KS \leq 1$.

Let R and $\bar{R}$ be complementary sets, where $R \cup \bar{R} = \Omega$. It is known that

$$\left| \int_R (f_X(x \mid C_1) - f_X(x \mid C_2))dx \right| \leq \int_R |f_X(x \mid C_1) - f_X(x \mid C_2)|\, dx \text{ and}$$

$$\left| \int_{\bar{R}} (f_X(x \mid C_1) - f_X(x \mid C_2))dx \right| \leq \int_{\bar{R}} |f_X(x \mid C_1) - f_X(x \mid C_2)|\, dx.$$

So, it is also true that

$$\left| \int_R (f_X(x \mid C_1) - f_X(x \mid C_2))dx \right| + \left| \int_{\bar{R}} (f_X(x \mid C_1) - f_X(x \mid C_2))dx \right| \leq$$

$$\int_R |f_X(x \mid C_1) - f_X(x \mid C_2)|dx + \int_{\bar{R}} |f_X(x \mid C_1) - f_X(x \mid C_2)|\, dx.$$

The left-hand side of the inequality can be rewritten by observing that

$$\left| \int_R (f_X(x \mid C_1) - f_X(x \mid C_2))dx \right| = \left| \int_{\bar{R}} (f_X(x \mid C_1) - f_X(x \mid C_2))dx \right|$$

and the two integrals in the right hand side can be combined since R and $\bar{R}$ are a partition of Ω:

$$2\left| \int_R (f_X(x \mid C_1) - f_X(x \mid C_2))dx \right| \leq \int_\Omega |f_X(x \mid C_1) - f_X(x \mid C_2)|\, dx \text{ or}$$

$$\left| \int_R (f_X(x \mid C_1) - f_X(x \mid C_2))dx \right| \leq \frac{1}{2}\int_\Omega |f_X(x \mid C_1) - f_X(x \mid C_2)|\, dx. \quad (1)$$

Since the above inequality is true for any partition R and R̄, it is valid when R is restricted to

$$R = \{x \mid -\infty < x \le x^*\} \text{ and } KS = |F_X(x^* \mid C_1) - F_X(x^* \mid C_2)|.$$

Using this definition of R, the left hand side of (1) becomes the Kolmogorov–Smirnov distance. By Theorem 2, the right hand side is equivalent to $1 - T$. Hence, Eq. (1) becomes

$$T + KS \le 1.$$

Part 2:

Show that $T + KS = 1$ if $f_X(x \mid C_1) > f_X(x \mid C_2)$ for $x > p$ and $f_X(x \mid C_1) < f_X(x \mid C_2)$ for $x < p$. With this condition T can be expressed as

$$T = \int_{-\infty}^{p} f_X(x \mid C_1)dx + \int_{p}^{\infty} f_X(x \mid C_2)dx.$$

Now, to find the point where the KS occurs, evaluate the function

$$F_X(x \mid C_2) - F_X(x \mid C_1) = \int_{-\infty}^{x} (f_X(z \mid C_2) - f_X(z \mid C_1))dz. \tag{2}$$

For $x < p$, the integrand is positive so

$$\int_{-\infty}^{x} (f_X(z \mid C_2) - f_X(z \mid C_1))dz \tag{3}$$

is an increasing function.

For $x < p$,

$$\int_{-\infty}^{x} (f_X(z \mid C_2) - f_X(z \mid C_1))dz = \int_{-\infty}^{d} (f_X(z \mid C_2) - f_X(z \mid C_1))dz + \int_{p}^{x} (f_X(z \mid C_2) - f_X(z \mid C_1))dz.$$

The second term in the summation is negative. Hence, we know that

$$\int_{-\infty}^{x} (f_X(z \mid C_2) - f_X(z \mid C_1))dz \leq \int_{-\infty}^{p} (f_X(z \mid C_2) - f_X(z \mid C_1))dz \text{ for all } x.$$

Therefore, the supremum of (2) occurs at point p, that is

$$KS = \int_{-\infty}^{p} (f_X(x \mid C_2) - f_X(x \mid C_1))dz.$$

Since $f_X(x \mid C_1) > f_X(x \mid C_2)$ for $x > p$ and $f_X(x \mid C_1) < f_X(x \mid C_2)$ for $x < p$,

$$KS = \int_{-\infty}^{p} f_X(x \mid C_2)dx - \int_{-\infty}^{p} f_X(x \mid C_1)dx = 1 - \int_{-\infty}^{p} f_X(x \mid C_1)dx$$
$$- \int_{p}^{\infty} f_X(x \mid C_2)dx,$$

which can be rearranged and expressed as

$$T + KS = 1.$$

Similar arguments can be used to obtain the result for the case when $f_X(x \mid C_1) < f_X(x \mid C_2)$ for $x > p$ and $f_X(x \mid C_1) > f_X(x \mid C_2)$ for $x < p$. This completes the proof.

Theorem 2 can be extended to a multidimensional vector space by defining the KS distance for n dimensions. Let this new KS distance be designated as KS_n and defined as

$$KS^n = \sup_x |F_X(x \mid C_1) - F_X(x \mid C_2)|,$$

where $X \in \mathbb{R}_n$. A relationship between the tie statistic and KS_n is now presented in Theorem 4. A proof of this relationship can be found in Beer (in preparation).

Theorem 4:

Let $F_X(x \mid C_1)$ and $F_X(x \mid C_2)$ be differentiable cummulative distribution functions on $\mathbb{R}_n$. Then $T + KS_n \leq 1$, and if the feature space is partitioned into two complementary regions R and $\bar{R}$ where $R = \{x; x \leq x^* \text{ and } KS_n = |F_X(x^* \mid C_1) - F_X(x^* \mid C_2)|\}$, then $T + KS_n = 1$ if $f_X(x \mid C_1) - F_X(x \mid C_2) \leq 0$ for all x in a region R and

$$f_X(x \mid C_1) - f_X(x \mid C_2) < 0 \text{ for all } x$$

in a region $\bar{R}$ and

$$T + KS^n < 1 \text{ if } f_X(x \mid C_1) - f_X(x \mid C_2) \geq 0$$

is not true for all x in a region R, and

$$f_X(x \mid C_1) - f_X(x \mid C_2) > 0$$

is not true for all x in a region $\bar{R}$.

In the situations where T + KS = 1, the tie statistic, like the KS statistic, is independent of the underlying distributions; however, this independence does not hold in general. The relationship between T and KS gives a bound on KS that is easily computed and may enhance the determination of rejection regions during hypothesis testing. Figure 13.3 illustrates a situation in which the T differentiates between two pdfs after the KS has been determined at P. In general, the KS is a measure of the maximum difference between two distributions, but the T is more sensitive because it measures differences between distributions that do not affect the KS.

3.4. Tie Space Mapping

The selection of the features is an important part in the design of an electronic vision system. It is desirable to select a feature space that is well-ordered with the decision classes separated by simple decision boundaries. This is often difficult to achieve in real application environments. One approach to this problem is to transform the feature space into a space that is easier to dichotomize. Such an approach is taken by Fukunaga (1986). The Mahalanobis distance, $1/2(X - \mu_i)^T \sigma_i^{-1} (X - \mu_i)$, is used to create a distance mapping for feature vector X with mean μ_i and standard deviation σ_i. A distance is found between a sample feature vector and the feature vector representing the mean

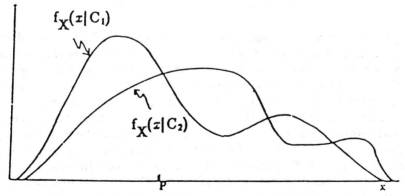

Figure 13.3. T and KS measures of pdf differences.

of each class. Thus a mapping to a distance space is created with dimensionality equivalent to the number of known classes. Decision boundaries between classes in the distance space are generally simpler than those in the feature space.

An alternative approach to this mapping process is provided by the tie statistic. A tie space can be created that is bounded between 0 and 1 and results in a well-ordered statistical representation of the difference between two class probability density functions, providing a decision theoretic basis for deciding whether a sample obtained from feature measurements belongs to a given decision class.

For any region R in a scene and feature vector $\mathbf{X}$, the tie mapping process is performed by using the tie statistic

$$T_i = \int_{V_x} f_\mathbf{X}(\mathbf{x} \mid R) \wedge f_\mathbf{X}(\mathbf{x} \mid C_i) d\mathbf{x}$$

to measure the difference between the pdf $f_\mathbf{X}(\mathbf{x} \mid R)$ for region R and the conditional pdf $f_\mathbf{X}(\mathbf{x} \mid C_i)$ for class C_i. Parametric or nonparametric techniques can be used to estimate $f_\mathbf{X}(\mathbf{x} \mid R)$ and $f_\mathbf{X}(\mathbf{x} \mid C_i)$. When estimates are used for $f_\mathbf{X}(\mathbf{x} \mid R)$ and $f_\mathbf{X}(\mathbf{x} \mid C_i)$, the tie value is itself a random variable, T, with values, t, ranging from 0 to 1 and having a pdf, $f_{T_{i_x}}(t \mid C_j)$, defined under the hypothesis that the region R belongs to class C_j.

Tie pdfs under several hypotheses were generated using various features. It was found that the tie random variable for feature $\mathbf{X}$, T_{i_x}, has a pdf $f_{T_{i_x}}(t \mid C_j)$ that can be parametrically approximated by a beta distribution with two parameters, α and β, with a high degree of confidence in terms of the Kolmogorov-Smirnov goodness of fit test. The beta density function can be expressed as

$$b(x) = \frac{\Gamma(\alpha + \beta)}{\Gamma(\alpha)\Gamma(\beta)} x^{\alpha-1}(1-x)^{\beta-1}, \quad 0 \le x \le 1.$$

Typical experimentally derived tie pdfs are given in Figure 13.4 along with their beta representations. Using the beta parametric representation, a rejection region can be established to decide whether a given region belongs to class C_i based on its tie value. In some applications it is useful to use the tie value as a measure of class membership.

Figure 13.5 illustrates the tie mapping process from an n dimensional feature vector $\mathbf{X}$ to a single dimensional tie space. For any region R, an estimate of $f_\mathbf{X}(\mathbf{x} \mid R)$ is obtained and compared to the decision class pdf $f_\mathbf{X}(\mathbf{x} \mid C_i)$ to obtain a tie value. The resulting tie value can be mapped into the tie pdf $f_{T_{i_x}}(t \mid C_j)$ to determine its membership value for class C_i.

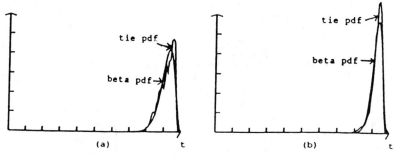

Figure 13.4. A tie pdf and its beta approximation.

The tie mapping procedure for two feature vectors, $\mathbf{X}_1$ and $\mathbf{X}_2$, into a two-dimensional tie space is shown in Figure 13.6. The pdfs, $f_{\mathbf{X}_1}(\mathbf{x}_1 \mid R)$ and $f_{\mathbf{X}_2}(\mathbf{x}_2 \mid R)$, for the given region R are obtained for each feature vector and compared to the pdf for the corresponding decision class C_i, $f_{\mathbf{X}_1}(\mathbf{x}_1 \mid C_i)$ and $f_{\mathbf{X}_2}(\mathbf{x}_2 \mid C_i)$, using the tie statistic. This yields two tie values, t_1 and t_2, which define a location in two-dimensional tie space. The shaded region in the upper right corner of the figure portrays a two-dimensional estimate of the joint pdf for the tie statistic when R came from C_j where $i = j$. The shaded region in the lower corner of the figure portrays the joint pdf when R came from C_j where $i \neq j$. The location of (t_1, t_2) in relation to $f_{T_{i_{\mathbf{X}_1}} T_{i_{\mathbf{X}_2}}}(t_1 t_2 \mid C_j)$ determines whether R is a member of C_i.

4. APPLICATIONS

Potential applications of the tie statistic can be found throughout a typical electronic vision system. The tie statistic is by nature a measure of the separability between two distributions and hence is a good measure for feature evaluation and selection. Also, since the T has the sensitivity needed to distinguish distributions, it provides a mecha-

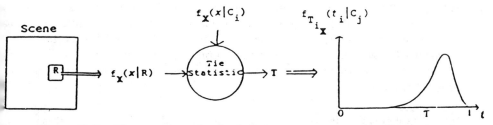

Figure 13.5. Tie mapping of a single feature vector to a one-dimensional tie space.

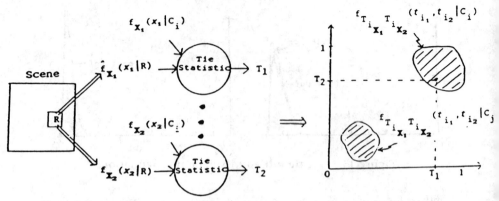

Figure 13.6. Tie mapping of two feature vectors to a two-dimensional tie space.

nism for selecting features for recognizing various textures, backgrounds, or objects using information from multiple sensors and/or features. The following two sections discuss applications of the tie statistic to the cuer problem and to texture recognition.

4.1. Cueing Application

The purpose of this section is to illustrate the ability of the tie mapping technique to fuse multisensor/multifeature scene descriptions into a simplified space suitable for locating regions that may contain objects of interest. Locating interesting regions, a process referred to as cueing, allows the computing power of the vision system to be focused on small regions rather than the entire scene for the more computationally intensive vision tasks of segmentation, recognition, and tracking. The tie statistic is useful in cueing because of its ability to map areas with distinguishable statistical properties from an n-dimensional feature space into distinguishable areas in a lower-dimensional space.

To demonstrate the tie fusion process for cueing applications in multisensor environments, measurements from two coaligned sensor images—laser radar range and amplitude—are utilized as features.[1] These images are shown in Figure 13.7(a) and 13.7(b). The method presented, however, could utilize any number of sensors or features to provide the necessary separability between objects of interest and the rest of the scene.

---

[1] Data provided by the Center for Night Vision and Electro-Optics, Fort Belvoir, Virginia, 1989.

Feature Space Mapping for Sensor Fusion 299

Figure 13.7. (a)Laser radar range, and (b) laser radar amplitude.

Coupled with the selection of cuer features, a strategy is necessary to locate enclosed regions in the scene with statistically different properties than the background. The strategy adopted here is to determine these regions by performing a tie mapping, utilizing estimates of the background class pdf, $f_X(x \mid B)$, and the search region, R, pdf, $f_X(x \mid R)$. The background class (B) is defined as any region not containing objects of interest. The boundary of the scene can often be utilized to estimate $f_X(x \mid B)$ when the objects of interest are completely contained within the scene. This approach is attractive because it requires no a priori knowledge of the objects of interest other than the fact that the scene encloses the objects. With this strategy the entire scene is searched for regions which are statistically separable from the background.

For each coaligned sensor, a background class pdf, $f_X(x \mid B)$, is estimated from a histogram of feature values accumulated from the boundary of the scene. Spatial stationarity is assumed along the boundary together with the a priori knowledge that there are no interesting regions present in the boundary area. A 12 by 12 neighborhood region R was chosen to scan across the scene to search for regions with characteristics distinguishable from the background. In order to obtain an estimate of the pdf of each search region, $f_X(x \mid R)$, a histogram of the feature vector is obtained from the neighborhood region. The 12 by 12 region size used here is a compromise between being large enough to obtain a good estimate of the pdf from a histogram yet small enough to obtain good resolution and preserve spatial stationarity within the region. For each region, R, in each sensor image, a tie statistic value is calculated using $f_X(x \mid R)$ and $f_X(x \mid B)$. At this point it is informative to view both the original feature space in Figure 13.8(a) and the tie space mapping in Figure 13.8(b). The original feature space is a plot of the ordered pairs of measurements obtained from corresponding locations on the sensor images. The tie space mapping is a plot of the tie statistic ordered pairs obtained from corresponding regions in the sensor images. Knowledge of the location of the object is used to show object points in black, background points in white and overlapping points in shades of gray. Observe the ordering that takes place when the original feature space is mapped using the tie statistic.

When the tie space mapping is complete, a membership distance,

$$d(\mathbf{T} \mid R) = \left[\sum_{i=1}^{n} T_i^2 \right]^{1/2},$$

is used to fuse the sensor information and produce a gray level image G identifying areas in the scene which may contain objects of interest. For each region R in the scene, $d(\mathbf{T} \mid R)$, is calculated and compared to the smallest membership distance from a boundary region, d_{min}. The gray-level value for each region R in the scene is determined as follows:

$$G(R) = 255 \qquad \text{if } d(\mathbf{T} \mid R) \geq d_{min}, \text{ or}$$
$$G(R) = \frac{255 \cdot d(\mathbf{T} \mid R)}{d_{min}} \qquad \text{if } d(\mathbf{T} \mid R) < d_{min}$$

Dark regions in G correspond to regions in the scene with low membership compared to the boundary. Figure 13.9 depicts the areas which may contain objects of interest as the darkest portions of the scene which were found to have statistical characteristics distinguishable

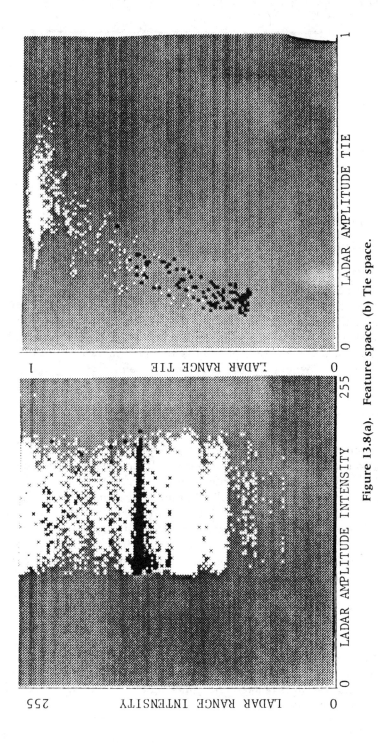

Figure 13.8(a). Feature space. (b) Tie space.

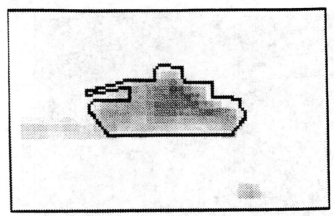

Figure 13.9. Gray level image of the cueing algorithm.

from the boundary. The location of the object is illustrated by the outline of the tank superimposed on the gray level mapping. Observe that both the tank and the road in front of the tank are identified as regions distinguishable from the boundary. It is important to note that the result of the tie fusion process is to combine two sensors into a composite scene where the object is clearly visible.

4.2. Texture Recognition

In computer vision, texture analysis plays an important role in segmentation and classification techniques. It provides cues for distinguishing objects in natural scenes and is useful for recognizing types of surfaces. To exploit textural differences it is necessary to select sensors and define and extract features that discriminate between textures. The resulting feature space is often cluttered and difficult to separate into regions. However, by using the tie statistic and the tie space mapping, textural regions can be dichotomized quickly and with a low probability of error. This section discusses an application of the tie statistic to the texture recognition problem. The features and the recognition algorithm used are briefly described. A summary of results is also presented.

Features and feature pdfs: The goal in the texture recognition problem is to classify a region as a member of a class based on its textural content. The features used to accomplish this goal are measures of gray level differences between neighboring pixels that are a fixed distance apart; that is,

$$x_d = |g(x,y) - g(x',y')| \text{ for } d = |x - x'| \text{ and/or } d = |y - y'|,$$
where $g(x,y)$ is the gray level at pixel location (x,y).

If it is assumed that the underlying random process is wide sense stationary in space over a region, R, each gray level difference feature measurement x_d is an observation from a random variable, X_d. The first order pdf of X_d can be estimated by the relative frequency histogram, called the difference histogram (Davis, 1981), of observed gray level differences in the region. This estimated pdf is denoted $f_{X_d}(x_d \mid R)$.

An estimate of the pdf for class C_i using feature X_d, $f_{X_d}(x_d \mid C_i)$ was established by analyzing several regions with texture C_i using several different rotations and depression angles.

Recognition algorithm: A single feature from a single sensor often does not provide sufficient information to adequately discriminate between classes because of the wide variations within the texture classes. Hence, the feature information from several sensors should be incorporated into the system for recognition and classification purposes. Depending on the number of features used, the feature space can become of such high dimensionality as to be quite cumbersome. The tie statistic can provide a solution to this problem by providing a mapping to a decision space that is of lower dimensionality than the feature space through the use of joint statistics. If the joint statistics are not available or are not easily estimated, the tie mapping can be used on the marginal pdfs to create ordered feature information. The tie mapped features can then be fused by applying various methods commonly used in classification problems.

The texture recognition algorithm described uses either one- or two-dimensional estimated feature pdfs mapped into a one-dimensional tie space. Decisions are made on the tie values by employing a sequential decision tree technique (Fu, 1968; Friedman, 1977; Gustafson, Gelfand, & Mitter, 1980; Meisel & Michalopoulos, 1973). In this implementation, a decision is made at each node of the tree between the two classes that are most easily separated in tie space in terms of the minimum probability of error. The tree is created as follows.

Estimates of $f_{T_{i_x}}(t \mid C_j)$ for all classes C_i and C_j and all X are found. These are used to determine the probability of error (PE) between classes. For example, the probability of error between class C_j and class C_k using feature vector X is obtained using the tie statistic and Theorem 1. For the root of the tree, the PE is found between all classes using all different feature vectors. The minimum PE is then determined and the information saved at that node is the indices of the two classes C_j and C_k that are most separable and the feature that yielded the minimum PE. This node then branches off into a left and right node, in which class C_k is eliminated from the list of possible classes in the left node and class C_j is eliminated from the list of possible classes in the right node. This same procedure is followed for each node of the tree until the node has only a single possible class remaining.

Once the tree is created, it can be used to classify a sample based on the tie values it generates. At each node of the tree, a likelihood ratio is found between the two classes saved at that node, C_j and C_k, using the designated feature $\mathbf{X}_d$. The decision rule

$$f_{T_{i_{\mathbf{X}_d}}}(t \mid C_j) \underset{C_k}{\overset{C_j}{\gtrless}} f_{T_{i_{\mathbf{X}_d}}}(t \mid C_k),$$

selects the most likely class. These probabilities are obtained from the beta representations of the tie pdfs. If the decision indicates that class C_k is not as likely as class C_j a branch to the left is taken. Otherwise a right branch is traversed. Hence, in this scheme classes are eliminated from the list of possibilities based on the likelihood of the sample coming from that class. If the sample is less likely to come from class C_j than from class C_k, class C_j is eliminated as a possible choice and likewise for class C_k.

Results: The decision tree algorithm was performed on unknown texture regions randomly chosen from a digital image. The unknown regions were classified as one of the eight texture classes shown in Figure 13.10.

To determine the misclassification error rates, the following experi-

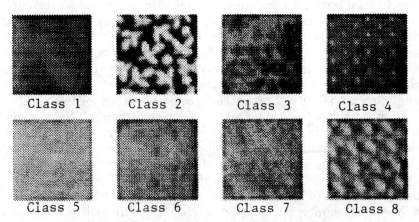

Figure 13.10. Samples of known texture classes.

ment was performed. A 16 × 16 pixel sample region R is randomly chosen from a texture image and the pdfs $f_{X_d}(x_d \mid R)$ in which $d \in \{2,4,6,8,10,12,14,16\}$ are estimated. In the situations where two-dimensional feature pdfs are used, a 64 × 64 pixel region is randomly chosen for the sample region and two-dimensional pdfs $f_{X_{d_1} X_{d_2}}(x_{d_1}, x_{d_2} \mid R)$ are estimated. The decision tree is then traversed to classify the region.

The results are presented in tabular form where each class is listed along with the number of times it was classified as any of the possible classes. There were 100 samples randomly drawn from each of the eight classes for a total of 800 samples. Hence, the total probability of error is estimated by dividing the total number of misclassifications over all classes by 800. The results using one-dimensional feature pdfs are presented in Table 13.1. An error rate of 8.625% resulted, with the most misclassifications made on class 7 and class 1 and no misclassifications made on classes 2, 4, and 8. The classification results using two-dimensional feature pdfs are shown in Table 13.2 Here, an error rate of 0.875% was obtained.

It can be seen that the accuracy of the classification decisions can be greatly improved by going to higher dimensions. However, when the sample size is limited such that higher dimensional pdfs are difficult to estimate, relatively low error rates can still be achieved by fusing together the feature information from the marginal pdfs.

5. CONCLUSION

The tie statistic presented here has the ability to quickly and efficiently classify probability density functions and has proven to be a useful tool for evaluating the performance of sensor feature combina-

Table 13.1. Classification results using 1-dimensional feature pdfs

	1	2	3	4	5	6	7	8
C 1:	80	0	0	0	2	18	0	0
C 2:	0	100	0	0	0	0	0	0
C 3:	0	0	90	0	0	0	10	0
C 4:	0	0	0	100	0	0	0	0
C 5:	2	0	0	0	98	0	0	0
C 6:	8	0	0	0	6	86	0	0
C 7:	2	0	16	0	0	5	77	0
C 8:	0	0	0	0	0	0	0	100

Total wrong = 69

Table 13.2. Classification results using 2-dimensional feature pdfs

	1	2	3	4	5	6	7	8
C 1:	100	0	0	0	0	0	0	0
C 2:	0	100	0	0	0	0	0	0
C 3:	0	0	97	0	0	0	3	0
C 4:	0	0	0	100	0	0	0	0
C 5:	0	0	0	0	100	0	0	0
C 6:	0	0	0	0	0	100	0	0
C 7:	0	0	4	0	0	0	96	0
C 8:	0	0	0	0	0	0	0	100

Total wrong = 7

tions and for simplifying the sensor/feature space of an electronic vision task. Encouraging experimental results from application of the statistic to the cuer and texture recognition problems should motivate further investigation of this novel statistical approach to other multiple sensor electronic vision problems.

REFERENCES

Beer, C. (in preparation). The tie statistic and texture recognition. Unpublished doctoral dissertation, New Mexico State University, Department of Electrical and Computer Engineering.

Bendat, J., & Piersol, A. (1966). *Measurement and analysis of random data*. New York: Wiley.

Bhattacharyya, A. (1943). On a measure of divergence between two statistical populations defined by their probability distributions. *Bulletin of the Calcutta Mathematical Society, 35*, 99–109.

Carlson, J., Jordan, J., & Flachs, G. (1988). Task specific complexity metrics for electronic vision. *Proceedings of the SPSE Conference on Imaging Technology*.

Davis, L. (1981). Image texture analyses techniques—A survey. In W.K. Pratt (Ed.), *Digital image processing* (pp. 189–201). New York: Wiley.

Duda, R.O., & Hart, P.E. (1973). *Pattern classification and scene analysis*. New York: Wiley.

Friedman, J. (1977). A recursive partitioning decision for nonparametric classification. *IEEE Transactions on Computers, C-26*(4), 404–408.

Fu, K.S. (1968). *Sequential methods in pattern recognition and machine learning*. New York: Academic Press.

Fukunaga, K. (1986). Statistical pattern classification. In T.Y. Young & K.S. Fu (Eds.), *Handbook of pattern recognition and image processing*. New York: Academic Press.

Fukunaga, K., & Krihe, T.F. (1967). An approximation to the divergence as a measure of feature effectiveness. *Proceedings of the National Electronics Conference, Vol. 23* (pp. 57–61).

Gustafson, D.E., and Gelfand, S., & Mitter, S.K. (1980). A nonparametric multiclass partitioning method for classification. *IEEE Proceedings.*

Jordan, J., & Flachs, G. (1987). Statistical segmentation of digital images. In H.K. Lin & P.S. Shenker (Eds.), *Proceedings of the SPIE, Vol. 754, Optical and Digital Pattern Recognition.* Los Angeles, CA.

Kailath, T. (1967). The divergence and Bhattacharyya distance measures in signal selection. *IEEE Transactions on Communications Technology,* COM-*15*(1), 52–60.

Kirmani, S. (1979). On the relation between Matusita's and Kolmogorov's measures of distance. *Annals of the Institute of Statistical Mathematics* (Tokyo), *31*, 289–291.

Matsusita, K. (1951). On testing statistical hypotheses. *Annals of the Institute of Statistical Mathematics* (Tokyo), *3*, 17–35.

Meisel, W.S., & Michalopoulos, D.A. (1973). A partitioning algorithm with applications in pattern classification and the optimization of decision trees. *IEEE Transactions on Computers,* C-22(1), 93–103.

Papoulis, A. (1965). *Probability, random variables, and stochastic processes.* New York: McGraw-Hill.

Smirnov, V., & Tikheyeva, A. (1978). *The connection between the Bayesian risk and the Kolmogorov distance and a modification of it in recognition problems.* Potomac, MD: Scripta Publishing Co.

Toussaint, G. (1972). Some inequalities between distance measures for feature evaluation. *IEEE Transactions on Computers,* C-21(4), 409–410.

Van Trees, H. (1968). *Detection, estimation, and modulation theory* (Vol. 1). New York: Wiley.

14
An Inference Technique for Integrating Knowledge from Disparate Sources*

Thomas D. Garvey,
John D. Lowrance, and
Martin A. Fischler

This chapter introduces a formal method for integrating knowledge derived from a variety of sources for use in "perceptual reasoning." The formalism is based on the "evidential propositional calculus," a derivative of Shafer's mathematical theory of evidence (1976). It is more general than either a Boolean or Bayesian approach, providing for Boolean and Bayesian inferencing when the appropriate information is available. In this formalism, the likelihood of a proposition A is represented as a subinterval, [s(A), p(A)], of the unit interval, [0,1]. The evidential support for proposition A is represented by s(A), while p(A) represents its degree of plausibility; p(A) can also be interpreted as the degree to which one fails to doubt A, p(A) being equal to one minus the evidential support for ~A. This chapter describes how evidential information, furnished by a knowledge source in the form of a probability "mass" distribution, can be converted to this interval representation; how, through a set of inference rules for computing intervals

---

* The work described here has been jointly supported by the Defense Advanced Research Projects Agency of the Department of Defense (monitored by the Air Force Avionics Laboratory under Contract No. F33615-80-C-1110) and the Office of Naval Research under Contract No. N00014-81-C-0115).

of dependent propositions, this information can be extrapolated from those propositions it directly bears upon, to those it indirectly bears upon; and how multiple bodies of evidential information can be pooled. A sample application of this approach, modeling the operation of a collection of sensors (a particular type of knowledge source), illustrates these techniques.

1. INTRODUCTION AND OVERVIEW

We are pursuing a program of research aimed at developing a computer-based capability for "perceptual reasoning" (Garvey & Fischler, 1980) that will make it possible to interpret important aspects of a situation from information obtained by a collection of disparate sensors. Situational assessment implies the need to integrate sensory information with a body of relevant "expertise," or prior knowledge. This integration poses a number of difficult technical problems that must be examined.

Among the problems focused upon in our work are the following:

- How to model sensors and other knowledge sources (KSs), so as to know which situations they can provide information about and how to interpret their responses.
- How to effectively combine (sometimes contradictory) information from multiple knowledge sources to compensate for their individual deficiencies.
- How to automatically devise a data-acquisition/sensor-utilization strategy to maximize overall system effectiveness.

In this chapter we shall concentrate on the approach to sensor modeling and knowledge integration that is currently under investigation. These form the core of the overall system.

1.1. Previous Work

Earlier research (Garvey & Fischler, 1979, 1980a, 1980b) led to a number of important conclusions regarding the integration of perceptual information. First, because of the variety of knowledge types required and the particular uses of each, it became apparent that a proliferation of specialized representations was inevitable. This is a departure from standard approaches that attempt to develop a representation of sufficient scope to encompass all of the knowledge needed by a system. Use of nonmonolithic representations allows KSs to perform efficient operations on widely diverse, locally appropriate data formats. However, the problem then becomes one of somehow connecting these KSs in a flexible, effective manner.

We formulated several requirements of a reasoning paradigm for the combination and extrapolation of evidential information from disparate KSs. Whereas earlier work has focused upon a Bayesian-based probabilistic scheme, we feel that this is too restrictive. A likelihood represented by a point probability value is usually an overstatement of what is actually known, distorting the available precision. In particular, there is no adequate, non–ad hoc representation of ignorance within a Bayesian framework.[1]

Another problem with a Bayesian approach to the modeling of belief is the difficulty of ensuring and maintaining consistency in a collection of interrelated propositions. This difficulty also stems from the need to assign point probability values, even when the underlying models from which these values are derived are incapable of supplying such precise data.

There are many occasions when the inference technique of choice is probabilistic reasoning (e.g., particularly when reasoning is done with data close to the signal level), and other occasions when a (Boolean) logical formalism is preferred (e.g., when trying to combine "higher-level" knowledge). To avoid an ad hoc approach to "global" knowledge integration, the inference paradigm should flow smoothly from a probabilistic technique to a logical one, as the propositions in question become more nearly true or false. In addition, whenever the underlying model is complete and consistent enough for traditional methods to be effective, the technique should reduce to a Bayesian paradigm.

1.2. The Shafer Representation

The representation we have adopted to satisfy the preceding requirements for the integration of global knowledge is based on the work of Shafer (1976). It expresses the belief in a proposition A by a subinterval [s(A), p(A)] of the unit interval, [0,1]. The lower value, s(A), represents the support for that proposition and sets a minimum value for its likelihood. The upper value, p(A), denotes the plausibility of that prop-

---

[1] For example, if no information is available concerning two initially exclusive and exhaustive possibilities, in a Bayesian framework they are usually assigned a probability of 0.5. This is quite different from specifying that nothing is known regarding such propositions.

osition and establishes a maximum likelihood. Support may be interpreted as the total positive effect a body of evidence has on a proposition, while plausibility represents the total extent to which a body of evidence fails to refute a proposition. The degree of uncertainty about the actual probability value for a proposition corresponds to the width of its interval. As will be shown, this representation with the appropriate inference rules satisfies the requirements established above.

In the remainder of this chapter, we shall demonstrate Dempster's rule of combination (Shafer, 1976) for pooling evidential information from independent knowledge sources, present an inference mechanism for updating proposition intervals based on other dependent proposition intervals, and demonstrate their use in sensor modeling and integration.

2. KNOWLEDGE REPRESENTATION AND INFERENCE

In what we call "evidential propositional calculus," we represent a proposition using the following notation:

$$A_{[s(A), p(A)]},$$

where A is the proposition, $s(A)$ is the support for the proposition, and $p(A)$ is its plausibility. $p(A)$ is equivalent to $1 - s(\sim A)$, the degree to which one fails to doubt A. The interval $[s(A), p(A)]$ is called the "evidential interval." The uncertainty of A, $u(A)$, corresponds to $p(A) - s(A)$. If $u(A)$ is zero for all propositions, the system is Bayesian.

The following examples illuminate some important points:

- $A_{[0,1]}$ → no knowledge at all about A.
- $A_{[0,0]}$ → A is false.
- $A_{[1,1]}$ → A is true.
- $A_{[.25,1]}$ → evidence provides partial support for A.
- $A_{[0,.85]}$ → evidence provides partial support for ~A.
- $A_{[.25,.85]}$ → probability of A is between .25 and .85; that is, the evidence simultaneously provides support for both A and ~A.

2.1. Dempster's Rule of Combination

Dempster's rule is a method of integrating distinct bodies of evidence. This is most easily introduced through the familiar formalism whereby propositions are represented as subsets of a given set, here referred

Inference Technique for Integrating Knowledge from Disparate Sources

to as the "frame of discernment" (denoted θ). When a proposition corresponds to a subset of the frame of discernment, it is said to be discerned. The primary advantage of this formalism is that it translates the logical notions of conjunction, disjunction, implication, and negation into the more graphic, set-theoretic notions of intersection, union, inclusion, and complementation. Dempster's rule combines evidential information expressed relative to those propositions discerned by θ.

2.1.1. Single Belief Functions

We assume that a knowledge source, KS_1, distributes a unit of belief across a set of propositions for which it has direct evidence[2], in proportion to the weight of that evidence as it bears on each. This is represented by a function:

$$m_1: \{A_i \mid A_i \subseteq \theta\} \rightarrow [0, 1],$$
$$m_1(\emptyset) = 0,$$
$$\sum_{A_i \subseteq \theta} m_1(A_i) = 1.$$

$m_1(A_i)$ represents the portion of belief that KS_1 has committed exactly to proposition A_i, termed its "basic probability mass." m_1 can be depicted as a partitioned unit line segment, the length of each subsegment corresponding to the mass attributed to one of its focal elements (Figure 14.1). Any mass assigned to θ represents the residual "uncertainty" of the KS directly. That is, $m_1(\theta)$ is the mass that could not be ascribed to any smaller subset of θ on the basis of the evidence at hand, but must instead be assumed to be distributed in some (unknown) manner among the propositions discerned by θ. A similar interpretation is given to mass assigned any (nonunit) set.

Once mass has been assigned to a set of propositions, the evidential interval can be determined directly. Support for a proposition A is the total mass ascribed to A and to its subsets; the plausibility of A is one minus the sum of the mass assigned to $\sim$A and to subsets of $\sim$A; the uncertainty of A is equal to the mass remaining, that is, that attributed to supersets of A, including θ.

$$s_1(A) = \sum_{A_i \subseteq A} m_1(A_i).$$
$$p_1(A) = 1 - s_1(\sim A).$$
$$u_1(A) = p_1(A) - s_1(A).$$

---

[2] Those propositions are referred to as the KS's "focal elements."

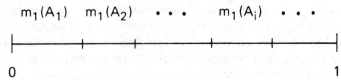

Figure 14.1. Probability mass assignment for KS_1

For example,

if $A = \{a\}$, $A \vee B = \{a, b\}$,
$\sim A = \{b, c\}$, $\theta = \{a, b, c\}$,
and $m_1(<A, \sim A, A \vee B, \theta>) = <.4, .2, .3, .1>$;
then $A_{[.4, .8]}$, $A \vee B_{[.7, .1]}$,
$\sim A_{[.2, .6]}$, $\theta_{[1, 1]}$.

2.1.2. Composition of Mass Functions

If the belief function of a second KS, KS_2, is also provided, the information supplied by these KSs can be pooled by computing the "orthogonal sum"; this computation is illustrated by the unit square in Figure 14.2.

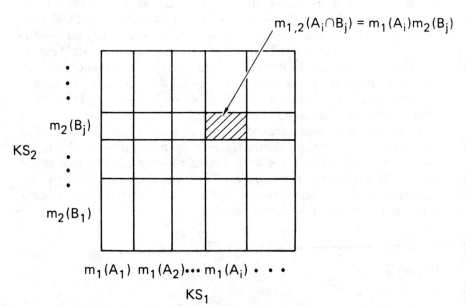

Figure 14.2. Composition of mass from KS_1 and KS_2

To combine the effects of KS_1, and KS_2, we consider the unit square as representing the combined probability mass of both KSs; KS_1 partitions the square into vertical strips corresponding to its focal elements, while KS_2 partitions it into horizontal strips that correspond to its focal elements. For example, Figure 14.2 shows a vertical strip of measure $m_1(A_i)$ that is exactly committed to A_i by KS_1, and a horizontal strip of size $m_2(B_j)$ committed precisely to B_j by KS_2. The intersection of these strips commits exactly $m_1(A_i)m_2(B_j)$ to the combination of $A_i \cap B_j$.

Accordingly, we can compute the area commitment of each rectangle comprising the square. A given subset of θ, C, may have more than one rectangle exactly committed to it; the total mass allocated to C is

$$\sum_{A_i \cap B_j = C} m_1(A_i)m_2(B_j).$$

This scheme is likely to commit a portion of mass to the empty set $\varnothing$. Every rectangle committed to $A_i \cap B_j$, where $A_i \cap B_j = \varnothing$, results in such a commitment. The remedy is to discard all such rectangles, proportionally increasing (i.e., normalizing) the size of the remaining rectangles by the following multiplicative factor:

$$N = (1 - k)^{-1},$$

where

$$k = \sum_{A_i \cap B_j = \varnothing} m_1(A_i)m_2(B),$$

thereby restoring the total probability mass to one.

There are several points of interest with respect to Dempster's rule of combination. The operation is commutative; therefore, the order of combination is immaterial. The operation is also associative, allowing the pairwise compositions of a sequence of KSs. When two Bayesian mass functions are combined, one associating its full unit of mass with a single proposition, the resulting support and plausibility values are the expected Bayesian conditionals. Yet when only less precise information is available, it too can be exploited.

The degree of conflict between two KSs can be measured intuitively by the size of the factor k. The greater the value of k, the greater the degree of conflict between the two KSs. When k is one, the KSs are irreconcilably different and the orthogonal sum does not exist.

2.2. Inference Rules

In addition to a technique for pooling distinct bodies of evidence, rules are needed that allow evidential information to be translated from those propositions it bears upon directly to those it bears upon indirectly. These rules are based on the following two principles of evidential support:

- The proposition corresponding to the frame of discernment always receives full support.
- Any support committed to a proposition is thereby committed to any other proposition it implies.

From the first principle we know that $s(\theta) = p(\theta) = 1$. The second principle dictates that any support committed to a subset of the frame of discernment is thereby committed to its supersets. This follows because one proposition implies another if it is a subset of that proposition in the frame of discernment. Of the total support committed to a given proposition A, some may be committed to one or more proper subsets of A, while the rest is committed exactly to A—and to no smaller subset, that is, m(A). If it is assumed that a knowledge source expresses itself in terms of support and plausibility estimates for a selected set of propositions from the frame of discernment, then a set of inference rules allows these estimates to be translated from proposition to proposition, thereby reducing uncertainty. A sampling of these rules follows. The statements above the line in each rule allow the statement below the line to be inferred.

$$\overline{\theta_{[1,1]}.}$$

$$\frac{A \subset \theta}{A_{[0,1]}.}$$

$$\frac{A_{[s1(A),p1(A)]}}{A_{[s2(A),p2(A)]}} \qquad s(A) = \mathrm{MAX}[s1(A),s2(A)],$$
$$\frac{}{A_{[s(A),p(A)]},} \qquad p(A) = \mathrm{MIN}[p1(A),p2(A)].$$

$$\frac{A_{[s(A),p(A)]}}{\sim A_{[s(\sim A),p(\sim A)]},} \qquad s(\sim A) = 1 - p(A),$$
$$p(\sim A) = 1 - s(A).$$

Inference Technique for Integrating Knowledge from Disparate Sources 317

$$\frac{A_{[s(A),p(A)]}}{B_{[s(B),p(B)]}}$$
$$A \lor B_{[s(A\lor B),p(A\lor B)]},$$
$$\qquad s(A\lor B) = MAX[s(A),s(B)],$$
$$\qquad p(A\lor B) = MIN[1,p(A)+p(B)].$$

$$\frac{A \lor B_{[s(A\lor B),p(A\lor B)]}}{A_{[s(A),p(A)]}}$$
$$\overline{B_{[s(B),p(B)]}}, \quad s(B) = MAX[0,s(A\lor B)-p(A)],$$
$$\qquad p(B) = p(A\lor B).$$

$$\frac{A_{[s(A),p(A)]}}{B_{[s(B),p(B)]}}$$
$$A \& B_{[s(A\&B),p(A\&B)]},$$
$$\qquad s(A\&B) = MAX[0,s(A)+s(B)-1],$$
$$\qquad p(A\&B) = MIN[p(A),p(B)].$$

$$\frac{A \& B_{[s(A\&B),p(A\&B)]}}{A_{[s(A),p(A)]}}$$
$$\overline{B_{[s(B),p(B)]}}, \quad s(B) = s(A\&B),$$
$$\qquad p(B) = MIN[1,1+p(A\&B)-s(A)].$$

As can be easily shown, when propositions are known to be true or false (that is, when their corresponding belief intervals become either [0,0] or [1,1]), these rules reduce to the corresponding rules of the propositional calculus. Thus, when appropriate knowledge exists, this method will enable an easy transition to take place from a probabilistic inference computation to the standard propositional calculus.

3. EXAMPLE: MODELING A KNOWLEDGE SOURCE

As our intention has been to treat sensors as specialized KSs, in this section we shall describe an approach to modeling such a KS. We shall begin by discussing the usual parameters measured by a (hypothetical) sensor, illustrating how, for this simple example, these measurements are converted to hypotheses by the inference mechanism.

3.1. Sensor Measurements

We assume that collections of electromagnetic signal emitters deployed in various configurations comprise the situation of interest. Measurements of characteristics of the signals emitted by these devices will be used to formulate hypotheses about their identities. In the complete system, these hypotheses will interact with those derived from other KSs to create a more comprehensive picture of the situation. Let us first concern ourselves with a single KS and then show how it may be composed with other KSs.

3.1.1. Emitter Characteristics

In this example, an emitter will radiate a pulsed radar signal whose pertinent characteristics will include the carrier frequency (rf) and the pulse width (pw), which are measured directly by the receiver. For the example we assume that the emitters of interest are of types E1, E2, E3, E4, or E5. The goal of the program is to identify a signal as having originated from one of those types.

The information about the parameter values likely to be exhibited by an emitter is presented in the form of parameter distribution graphs—for example, as shown in Figure 14.3. These curves indicate the probability that any given emitter (of the type indicated) will have a specific parameter value; the total area under each curve is one.

A typical approach to identifying an emitter is to look up the measured parameters in a table. In addition to difficulties traceable to the static nature of the table (e.g., emitter characteristics are not expected to remain stable and constant in actual operation), the technique gives little information regarding the relative likelihoods of ambiguous identifications.

3.1.2. Sensor Characteristics

A sensor (receiver) will specify a range of possible values for the measured emitter parameter, as determined by the resolution of the sensor's measurements. For example, the receiver may specify an emitter's frequency value as lying within a band of frequencies, for example, from 5.5 to 5.6 GHz. Similarly, other emitter parameters will also be specified as falling within a range of values.

Our previous work (Garvey & Fischler, 1979) described how sensor models were modified in the event of changing environmental conditions. In the approach described here, such environmental factors will instead determine the total mass a sensor may allocate to propositions other than θ. In effect, the uncertainty U of a receiver in the prevailing conditions is its minimal commitment to θ (i.e., $m(\theta) \geq U$), leaving only $(1 - U)$ of the mass to be freely distributed.

3.2. Modeling the Operation of a Sensor

The modeling process begins with the determination of a frame of discernment. If the task is to determine the true value of some vari-

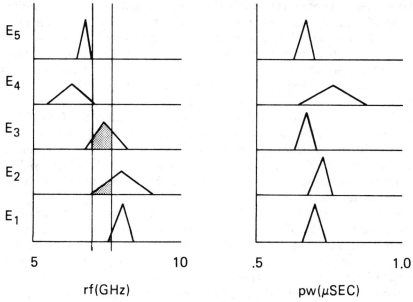

Figure 14.3. Examples of typical emitter parameter distributions

able, the frame of discernment is the set of all possible values for that variable. For the problem at hand, each element of the frame of discernment consists of an emitter type paired with a feature vector representing one possible electromagnetic signature that such an emitter might exhibit. Thus, θ is a subset of all of the combinations of emitter types (ET), radio frequencies (RF), and pulse widths (PW).

$$\theta \subseteq ET \times RF \times PW.$$

The key requirement of the frame of discernment is that all the propositions of interest be in correspondence with its subsets. In the current context the following propositions are some of those that might be of interest:

(The emitter is type E1)
  = $\{q \mid q \in \theta$ and $et(q) = E1\}$;
(The radio frequency (rf) is between 5.5 and 5.6 GHz)
  = $\{q \mid q \in \theta$ and $5.5 \leq rf(q) \leq 5.6\}$;
(The emitter is type E1 with pulse width (pw) between .68 and .7 μs)
  = $\{q \mid q \in \theta$ and $et(q) = E1$ and $.68 \leq pw(q) \leq .7\}$.

Once a frame of discernment has been determined, it can be represented as a dependency graph (Lowrance, 1982). In this formalism propositions are represented by nodes, and their interrelationships by arcs. These interrelationships can be interpreted either as set-theoretic notions relative to the frame of discernment (e.g., intersection, union, inclusion, and complementation), or as logical connectives (e.g., conjunction, disjunction, implication, and negation). The appropriate subset of propositions and relationships, so represented, depends on the preferred vocabulary of discourse among the KSs. Those propositions to which the KSs tend to assign mass need to be included, along with those relationships that best describe their interdependence. Once such a dependency graph has been established, it provides an integrated framework for both the combination and extrapolation of evidential information.

In the current context there is a subgraph for each emitter feature. At the lowest level of these subgraphs is a set of propositions representing the smallest bands into which that continuous feature has been partitioned—this partitioning being necessary within a propositional framework. These primitive bands form the basis of a hierarchy in each subgraph, relating larger bands to more primitive ones. The emitter types are similarly represented, the higher elements in the hierarchy corresponding to disjunctions of emitter types. All this is tied together by one last subgraph that relates the base elements of the hierarchies to elements of the frame of discernment, the frame of discernment consisting of the possible combinations of base elements. Figure 14.4 is a sketch of this dependency graph, with each node representing a proposition equal to the disjunction of those immediately below it, and the conjunction of those immediately above it.

This dependency graph contains all the information needed to determine the collective impact of several bodies of evidence on all the

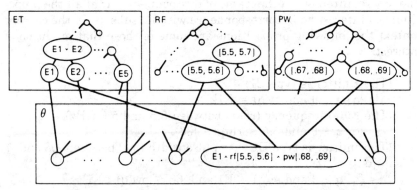

Figure 14.4. Dependency graph for sensor model

propositions of interest. Given several distinct bodies of evidential information extracted from the environment by several knowledge sources, repeated applications of Dempster's rule followed by repeated applications of the inference rules for support and plausibility propagation—all based on the information embodied in the dependency graph—result in a support and plausibility estimate for every proposition of interest (Lowrance, 1982). There are no restrictions regarding which propositions serve as premises or conclusions. Information about radio frequency and pulse width can be used to determine the most likely types of emitters—or information about emitters and pulse width can be used to predict the expected radio frequency. Inferencing is unconstrained.

3.3. Simplification of the Sensor Model

In the preceding discussions, we showed how inferences could be drawn in a formal system that modeled all relevant elements of θ. It is frequently inconvenient to model these elements individually. For example, too many elements may be needed to represent the resolution of any particular sensor. An obvious simplification is to *compute* new propositions in θ as they are needed. For example, when a receiver reports a signal in a specific frequency band, propositions can then be created which assert that the signal originated from one element of a subset of possible emitter types. The exact hypotheses and their associated mass allocations are determined by comparing receiver measurements with tabulated information about the emitters.

3.3.1. Initial Mass Computations

The first step is to convert sensory measurements into a probability mass distribution over propositions. In essence, the parameter measurement range is overlaid on the curves representing distributions of emitter parameters, as shown in Figure 14.3. The area of the distribution curve is computed for each emitter. (Propositions are created only for those emitters whose parameter ranges overlap the sensor's report.) A set of "basic mass numbers" is then computed by normalizing the resultant areas to bring their total area to one. This process is exactly equivalent to computing the probability of each emitter, conditioned upon the measured parameter's falling in the specified range (and assuming that only the tabulated emitter could radiate the received signal).

The uncertainty U of the receiver is accounted for through reducing each basic mass number by multiplying it by a factor equal to one minus U. This new set of mass numbers then represents the contribution of the receiver measurement to the support of the proposition.

3.3.2. Example

In this example we assume that there are five emitter types {E1, ..., E5}, whose rf and pw characteristics are shown graphically in Figure 14.3. The receiver has reported a frequency measurement of 7.6 to 7.7 GHz and a pulse width range of .68 to .7 μs. Assuming an uncertainty of .3 in the rf measurement and an uncertainty of .2 for pw, the resulting mass functions are

$$m_{rf}(<E1,E2,E3,E4,E5>) = <.13,.22,.35,0,0>$$

and

$$m_{pw}(<E1,E2,E3,E4,E5>) = <.26,.085,.17,.034,.26>.$$

Combining these with Dempster's rules gives the composite mass function,

$$m_{rf\&pw}(<E1,E2,E3,E4,E5>)$$
$$= <.25,.16,.33,.018,.14>,$$

with a resulting uncertainty of 0.11. This computation is illustrated in Figure 14.5, in which all rectangles attributed to $\emptyset$ are shaded and the remaining rectangles are labeled with the proposition receiving that mass. These values concert directly into the following intervals on the propositions:

$$E1_{[.25, .36]}$$
$$E2_{[.16, .27]}$$
$$E3_{[.33, .43]}$$
$$E4_{[.018, .13]}$$
$$E5_{[.14, .25]}$$

This information may be readily combined with information provided by other KSs. For example, a KS that indicated a high likelihood of encountering an E1 might produce the following mass function:

$$m_{prior}(<E1,E2,E3,E4,E5>)$$
$$= <.7,0,0,0,0>,$$

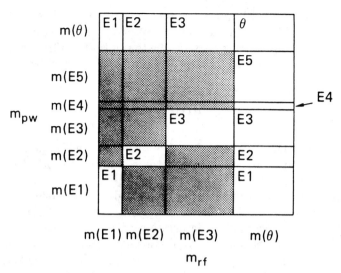

Figure 14.5. Composition of the mass assignments by sensor models

which, when integrated with the receiver measurements, would result in a mass function

$$m_{composite}(<E1,E2,E3,E4,E5>)$$
$$= <.59,.089,.18,.01,.076>,$$

with an uncertainty of .06. This leads to the following relevant hypotheses:

$$E1_{[.59,.65]} \text{ and } E3_{[.18,.24]}.$$

Based on sensor data alone, the method leads to two primary hypotheses, $E1_{[.25,.36]}$ and $E3_{[.33,.43]}$. E3 is slightly favored over E1. When external evidence is brought to bear, the support for E1 becomes significantly greater than for all others (and, in fact, all others except E3 drop to very low levels of support). Any other KS that provides a mass assignment over this set of propositions may also be combined.

This simplification of the formal method provides the ability to integrate information quickly from a variety of sources, even in those areas where the necessary propositions have not already been extracted from θ. The technique does not yet allow the propagation of evidence to arbitrarily selected propositions from the network. For example, it is not possible to take the structure defined for this problem and use it to determine what radio frequency values should be expected on the basis of pulse width data—a process easily carried out by the full representation. This is an area of current research. A related computational technique, restricted to evidence that either confirms or denies a single proposition, is also being investigated (Barnett, 1981).

4. SUMMARY

We have briefly described an inference technique that appears to satisfy many of the requirements for reasoning in perceptual domains. In particular, the method provides the capability for (Bayesian) probabilistic reasoning when the appropriate underlying models are available (e.g., at the lowest levels of the system), (evidential) subjective reasoning when incomplete descriptions must be used (e.g., at the "middle" levels of the system), and (Boolean) logical reasoning when the truth values of propositions are true and false. This technique allows us to augment a static, incomplete model with current sensory information.

The approach provides a formal technique for updating the likelihoods of propositions in a consistent manner. In effect, by simultaneously performing computations over a collection of propositions, the method maintains global consistency without the problems frequently plaguing techniques that perform iterative updating by means of local rules. Most importantly, besides offering an inference technique that can be used within a KS (as illustrated), the method provides a "language" for KSs to communicate with one another, as well as furnishing the means for linking disparate sources of information.

In our previous work on perceptual-reasoning systems, we evolved a number of effective generic (e.g., terrain, weather, etc.) and domain-specific (e.g., sensor) KSs. Our current research, focusing on the evidential propositional calculus as the integrating medium, aims at developing a general framework for linking these KSs together smoothly and flexibly.

REFERENCES

Barnett, J.A. (1981). Computational methods for a mathematical theory of evidence. *Proceedings of the Seventh International Joint Conference on Artificial Intelligence* (pp. 868–875). Vancouver, BC, Canada.

Garvey, T.D., & Fischler, M.A. (1979, October). *Machine-intelligence-based multisensor ESM system* (Tech. Rep. AFAL-TR-79-1162). Wright-Patterson Air Force Base, OH: Wright Avionics Lab.

Garvey, T.D., & Fischler, M.A. (1980a). Perceptual reasoning in a hostile environment. *Proceedings of the First Annual Proceedings of the National Conference on Artificial Intelligence* (pp. 253–255). Stanford, CA.

Garvey, T.D., & Fischler, M.A. (1980b). The integration of multi-sensor data for threat assessment. *Proceedings of the Fifth Joint Conference on Pattern Recognition* (pp. 343–347). Miami Beach, FL.

Lowrance, J.D. (1982). Dependency-graph models of evidential support. Unpublished doctoral dissertation, University of Massachusetts, Amherst.

Shafer, G. (1976). *A Mathematical Theory of Evidence*. Princeton, NJ: Princeton University Press.

15
Measuring Consensus Effectiveness by a Generalized Entropy Criterion*

Harry E. Stephanou, and
Shin-Yee Lu

This chapter introduces a quantitative criterion for measuring the effectiveness of the consensus obtained by pooling evidence from two knowledge sources. We begin with a brief review of the Dempster-Shafer theory of mathematical evidence, which is based on a set-theoretic description of subjective uncertainty. We then introduce the concept of generalized entropy as a measure of the uncertainty in a knowledge source. We also prove that the pooling of evidence by Dempster's rule of combination decreases the total amount of generalized entropy in the knowledge sources. The decrease of entropy corresponds to the focusing of knowledge, and is used as a measure of consensus effectiveness. Several examples are used to illustrate this measure.

---

* The authors are grateful to the late Professor King-Sun Fu of Purdue University for first bringing the Dempster-Shafer theory to their attention, and to Y. C. Cheng of Exxon Production Company for his assistance in deriving Lemma 5.4.

TABLE OF SYMBOLS

Symbol	Definition	Equation
pbf	partial belief function	(3.1)
pcf	partial certainty function	(3.3)
Q	core	(3.3)
q	focal element	(3.4)
scf	simple certainty function	(3.6)
C	total certainty function	(3.7)
D	disbelief	(3.8)
L	lack of belief	(3.9)
P	plausibility	(3.10)
H_b	belief entropy	(4.1)
H_q	core entropy	(4.2)
H_t	total entropy	(4.4)
I	partial ignorance	(4.6)
H	generalized entropy	(4.7)

1. MOTIVATION

The methodology proposed in this chapter is motivated by the need to design expert systems for applications that involve: 1) subjective and/or incomplete knowledge provided by a group of domain experts, and 2) inaccurate or incomplete information obtained by integrating several datasets. The knowledge bases in such systems include a mixture of procedural knowledge based on rules of thumb, and declarative knowledge derived from a basic understanding of the fundamental phenomena relevant to the specific application. This situation is rather common in soft science applications (e.g., social sciences, geology, medicine) where the extremely complex underlying phenomena are only partially understood, and cannot be adequately described by rigorous mathematical models. The domain experts must therefore make extensive use of subjective knowledge in the form of their collective judgment, experience, or intuition. Furthermore, decision makers in these types of applications typically have to rely on inaccurate and/or incomplete data that cannot be adequately modeled by probabilistic methods.

2. INTRODUCTION

The Dempster-Shafer (D-S) theory of mathematical evidence (Dempster, 1968; Shafer, 1976) provides a powerful tool for the mathematical representation of this type of subjective (as opposed to probabilistic) uncertainty, mainly by virtue of its explicit definition of the concept of ignorance. The D-S theory, which is basically a set-theoretic generalization of Bayes's theory, is currently a topic of increasing interest among researchers in expert systems (Lowrance & Garvey, 1983; Barnett, 1981; Ishizuka, Fu, & Yao, 1981; see also chapter 14, this volume). It provides a powerful tool for attacking two key problems in the design of expert systems: collective reasoning, and reasoning under bounded (nonprobabilistic) ignorance. Yager (1983) has extended the concept of entropy from probability distributions to belief functions. In Lu and Stephanou (1984), the authors have outlined a set-theoretic approach to expert systems design. In this approach, knowledge is represented as a collection of mappings from *knowledge sources* (or *bodies of evidence*) in an *observation space to knowledge sinks* in a *conclusion space*. The D-S theory provides the necessary tools for the mathematical representation of knowledge sources and knowledge sinks. In Lu and Stephanou (1984), Dempster's rule is used to pool evidence from multiple knowledge sources in the observation space. Dempster's rule is also used to pool the support provided by the different mappings to the set of knowledge sinks in the conclusion space.

In this chapter, we introduce an information-theoretic criterion to quantitatively measure the quality of the consensus generated by pooling evidence from two knowledge sources, or by pooling support for two knowledge sinks. The criterion is based on the heuristic generalization of the concept of entropy from a point-theoretic to a set-theoretic framework. Since the consensus quality criterion is the same for both knowledge sources and knowledge sinks, we will confine our discussion to knowledge sources.

Several potential application areas of the D-S theory are currently being investigated, but are somewhat limited by the lack of computationally efficient reasoning algorithms. Such applications include sensor fusion (Chapter 23) and sensor-based control (Erkmen & Stephanou, 1987). Other approaches to the combination of uncertain or imprecise information are surveyed in a comprehensive review (Prade, 1985). Links with Bayesian, heuristic (e.g., MYCIN) and possibilistic approaches are stressed in that paper. In particular, it is shown that, in general, the combination of two possibility distributions is not a possibility distribution.

Section 3 of the chapter is a review of the fundamental concepts in the D-S theory. The review follows Shafer (1976) rather closely, although we have modified and generalized some of Shafer's terminology for the sake of simplicity and also for consistency with later sections in this chapter. Section 4 introduces the concept of generalized entropy in a set-theoretic framework. In Section 5 we prove that the generalized entropy of the knowledge sources (via Dempster's rule) is generally smaller than the sum of the individual entropies of the knowledge sources. The combined knowledge can thus be thought of as being more focused. Several examples and their intuitive interpretation are given in Section 6. The amount by which the combination (or consensus) reduces the entropy of the knowledge sources (i.e., sharpens their focus) is used as our criterion for consensus quality.

3. THE MATHEMATICAL THEORY OF EVIDENCE

This section is a brief review of the Dempster-Shafer theory (Shafer, 1976).

3.1. Partial Belief Function

Let a *frame of discernment* F be the set of all possible values of some numerical or symbolic variable x. Let $b(q)$ denote the degree of belief that the true value of x is in the subset q of set F, and in no smaller subset of q. It is convenient to visualize x as a mass of weight $b(q)$ which is confined to q, but can move anywhere inside q.

A function $b: 2^F \to [0, 1]$ is called a *partial belief function* (pbf) if:

$$b(\emptyset) = 0 \tag{3.1a}$$

$$0 < b(q_i) \leq 1 \tag{3.1b}$$

$$\sum_{i=1,n} b(q_i) = 1 \tag{3.1c}$$

where $\emptyset$ is the empty set, q_i, $1 \leq i \leq n$ are subsets of F, and 2^F denotes the set of all subsets of F. $b(q_i)$ is a measure of the belief committed exactly to q, and to no proper subset of q_i.

An important special case is the vacuous partial belief function given by:

$$b(F) = 1 \tag{3.2a}$$

$$b(q_i) = 0 \text{ for all } q_i \neq F. \tag{3.2b}$$

This function describes total ignorance since no portion of one's belief is committed to any proper subset of F. Thus the true value of x can be anywhere inside F.

Measuring Consensus Effectiveness by a Generalized Entropy Criterion

The definition of a partial belief function establishes a one-to-one correspondence between subsets of F and logical propositions. Thus the notions of conjunction, disjunction, implication, and negation are equivalent to the set-theoretic notions of intersection, union, inclusion, and complementation.

3.2. Partial Certainty Function

A *partial certainty function* (pcf) denoted by $c(b, Q)$ consists of:

1. a core $Q = \{q_1, ..., q_n\}$ (Figure 15.1) \hfill (3.3a)
   where $q_i \subset F$ for $1 \leq i \leq n$.

2. a partial belief function $b: Q \to [0, 1]$ where

$$0 < b(q_i) \leq 1 \qquad (3.3b)$$

$$\sum_{i=1,n} b(q_i) = 1 \qquad (3.3c)$$

The subsets $q_1, ..., q_n$ of F are called the *focal elements* of the pcf $c(b, Q)$. Thus the core of a pcf is the set of all its focal elements.

A subset q_i of F is a focal element if

$$q_i \neq \emptyset \qquad (3.4a)$$

$$b(q_i) \neq 0. \qquad (3.4b)$$

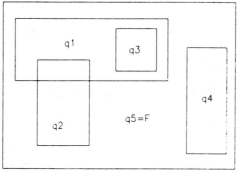

Figure 15.1. The core $Q = \{q_1, q_2, q_3, q_4, q_5\}$ of a pcf.

There are no other restrictions on Q. In particular, it should be emphasized that the following situations are possible, but not necessary:

1. $q_i = F$ for some value of i, $1 \le i \le n$ (3.5a)
    that is, one of the focal elements can (but need not) be the entire frame of discernment.

2. $q_i \cap q_j \ne \varnothing$ $1 \le i, j \le n$ (3.5b)
    that is, the focal elements need not be disjoint.

3. $\underset{i=1,n}{\cup} q_i \ne F$ (3.5c)

    that is, the union of all focal elements need not cover the entire frame of discernment.

It follows from (3.5) that a pcf corresponds to the intuitive idea that a portion of one's belief can be committed to a set, but need not be committed to either the set or its complement.

3.3. Simple Certainty Function

A *simple certainty function* (scf) is a special pcf $c(b, Q)$ that consists of:

1. a core $Q = \{q, F\}$
    where $q \ne 0$ and $q \ne F$ (3.6a)

2. a pbf b such that
    $b(q) + b(F) = 1$.   (3.6b)

3.4. Total Certainty Function

A *total certainty function* is denoted by $C(B, Q)$ and consists of:

1. a core $Q = \{q_1, \ldots, q_n\}$ (3.7a)

2. a total belief function $B: Q \to [0, 1]$ where

    $$B(q_i) = \sum_{q_j \subset q_i} b(q_j) \quad 1 \le i, j \le n \quad (3.7b)$$

where $B(q_i)$ is a measure of the total belief committed to q_i and to all its subsets.

A *disbelief function* $D: \mathbf{Q} \to [0, 1]$ is defined by:

$$D(\mathbf{q}_i) = B(\mathbf{F} - \mathbf{q}_i) \tag{3.8}$$

where $\mathbf{F} - \mathbf{q}_i$ is the complement of $\mathbf{q}_i$ in $\mathbf{F}$.
A *lack of belief function* $L: \mathbf{Q} \to [0, 1]$ is defined by:

$$L(\mathbf{q}_i) = 1 - B(\mathbf{q}_i). \tag{3.9}$$

A *plausibility function* $P: \mathbf{Q} \to [0, 1]$ is defined by:

$$P(\mathbf{q}_i) = 1 - B(\mathbf{F} - \mathbf{q}_i). \tag{3.10}$$

It follows from (3.7) that in general:

$$\sum_{i=1,n} B(\mathbf{q}_i) \neq 1 \tag{3.11a}$$

and

$$B(\mathbf{q}_i) + B(\mathbf{F} - \mathbf{q}_i) \neq 1. \tag{3.11b}$$

Therefore, the disbelief $B(\mathbf{F} - \mathbf{q}_i)$ that the true value of x is in $\mathbf{q}_i$ is not in general equal to the lack of belief $1 - B(\mathbf{q}_i)$ that the true value of x is in $\mathbf{q}_i$. The definition of a total certainty function thus supports the intuitive idea that the existence of evidence leading to the disbelief of a hypothesis should, in general, be differentiated from the lack of evidence leading to the belief of that hypothesis.

3.5. Demptser's Rule of Combination

Dempster's rule (Shafer, 1976) is the basic mechanism for combining several partial belief functions. Its use can be interpreted as the generation of a consensus. Let $c_1(b_1, \mathbf{Q}_1)$ and $c_2(b_2, \mathbf{Q}_2)$ be two partial certainty functions, with cores $\mathbf{Q}_1 = \{\mathbf{q}_{11}, \ldots, \mathbf{q}_{1n1}\}$, and $\mathbf{Q}_2 = \{\mathbf{q}_{21}, \ldots, \mathbf{q}_{2n2}\}$, and with pbf's $b_1: \mathbf{Q}_1 \to [0, 1]$ and $b_2: \mathbf{Q}_2 \to [0, 1]$. The consensus of c_1 and c_2 is denoted by:

$$c(b, \mathbf{Q}) = C_1(b_1, \mathbf{Q}_1) \oplus c_2(b_2, \mathbf{Q}_2) \tag{3.12}$$

and is generated by applying Dempster's rule:

$$b(\mathbf{q}_k) = \frac{\sum\sum_{q_k=\mathbf{q}_{1i}\cap\mathbf{q}_{2j}} b_1(\mathbf{q}_{1i}) b_2(\mathbf{q}_{2j})}{1 - \sum\sum_{\mathbf{q}_{1i}\cap\mathbf{q}_{2j}} b_1(\mathbf{q}_{1i}) b_2(\mathbf{q}_{2j})}. \tag{3.13}$$

4. SET-THEORETIC GENERALIZATION OF ENTROPY

4.1. Definitions

Let $c(b, \mathbf{Q})$ be a partial certainty function with partial belief function b and core $\mathbf{Q} = \{\mathbf{q}_1, \ldots, \mathbf{q}_n\}$.

Definition 4.1: The *belief entropy* of the pcf $c(b, \mathbf{Q})$ is defined by:

$$\mathbf{H}_b(c) = \sum_{i=1,n} b(\mathbf{q}_i) \log b(\mathbf{q}_i) \tag{4.1}$$

Definition 4.2: The *core entropy* of the pcf $c(b, \mathbf{Q})$ is defined by:

$$\mathbf{H}_q(c) = \sum_{i=1,n} h(\mathbf{q}_i) \log h(\mathbf{q}_i) \tag{4.2}$$

where

$$\mathbf{h}(\mathbf{q}_i) = k(\mathbf{q}_i) / \sum_{j=1,n} k(\mathbf{q}_j) \quad \text{for } n > 1 \tag{4.3a}$$

$$= 1 \quad \text{for } n = 1 \tag{4.3b}$$

and $k(\mathbf{q}_i)$ is equal to the cardinality (i.e., the number of elements) of $\mathbf{q}_i$ minus 1. Thus, $k(\mathbf{q}_i)$ is equal to zero if $\mathbf{q}_i$ is a singleton.

Definition 4.3: The *total entropy* of the pcf $c(b, \mathbf{Q})$ is defined by:

$$H(c) = \mathbf{H}_b(c) + \mathbf{H}_q(c). \tag{4.4}$$

It is straightforward to show that:

$$\mathbf{H}_t(c) = \sum_{i=1,n} \sum_{j=1,n} b(\mathbf{q}_i) h(\mathbf{q}_j) \log [b(\mathbf{q}_i) h(\mathbf{q}_j)]. \tag{4.5}$$

Definition 4.4: The *partial ignorance* of the pcf $c(b, \mathbf{Q})$ is defined by:

$$I(c) = \sum_{i=1,n} b(q_i) \, q_i^\# \quad (4.6a)$$

where

$$q_i^\# = k(q_i)/k(F) \quad \text{if } k(F) > 0 \quad (4.6b)$$
$$= 1 \quad \text{if } k(F) = 0. \quad (4.6c)$$

Definition 4.5: The *generalized entropy* of the pcf $c(b, Q)$ is defined by:

$$H(c) = H_t(c) + \beta I(c) \quad (4.7)$$

where the weight $\beta > 0$ is a problem-dependent scaling factor. For simplicity, we set $\beta = 1$ in the sequel without any loss of generality.

4.2. Interpretation

The belief entropy is a measure of the degree of confusion in one's knowledge about the exact fraction of belief that should be committed to each focal element in Q. It is equal to zero if $n = 1$, that is, if one's entire belief is committed to a single focal element (i.e., if $b(q_1) = 1$). The maximum belief entropy is equal to log n, and occurs when one's belief is divided in equal fractions among the focal elements of Q.

The core entropy is a measure of the degree of confusion in one's knowledge of which possible subset(s) of F the true value of the variable x might be in. It is equal to zero if $n = 1$, that is, if one's entire belief is committed to a single focal element (the belief entropy, and therefore the total entropy are also equal to zero in this case). The maximum core entropy is equal to log n, and occurs when one's belief is divided among a number of focal elements having the same cardinality.

The partial ignorance $I(c)$ is a measure of one's inability to confine the true value of x within a small subset of the frame of discernment. It is small when the two functions $b(q_i)$ and $q_i^\#$ are weakly correlated, that is, when large belief is committed to focal elements with small cardinality numbers.

Similarly, $I(c)$ is large when large belief is committed to large focal elements. $I(c)$ is equal to zero if one's entire belief is committed to a singleton, since for this case $b(q) = 1$, and $q^\# = 0$. $I(c) = 1$ if one's entire belief is committed to the frame of discernment, since for this case $q = F$, and therefore $b(q) = 1$ and $q^\# = 1$. It should be noted, that although this last instance corresponds to maximum ignorance, the confusion (as measured by the total entropy) is equal to zero, indicating full awareness about the state of one's ignorance.

5. REDUCING ENTROPY BY CONSENSUS

Consider two simple certainty functions $s_1(b_1, q_1)$ and $s_2(b_2, q_2)$ where:

$$Q_1 = \{q_1, F\} \tag{5.1a}$$

$$b_1(q_1) = m_1 \tag{5.1b}$$

$$b_1(F) = 1 - m_1 \tag{5.1c}$$

and

$$Q_2 = \{q_2, F\} \tag{5.2a}$$

$$b_2(q_2) = m_2 \tag{5.2b}$$

$$b_2(F) = 1 - m_2. \tag{5.2c}$$

From (4.1), the belief entropy functions are:

$$H_b(s1) = -m_1 \log m_1 - (1 - m_1) \log (1 - m_1) \tag{5.3a}$$

$$H_b(s_2) = -m_2 \log m_2 - (1 - m_2) \log (1 - m_2). \tag{5.3b}$$

Let

$$g_1 = k(q_1)/[k(q_1) + k(F)] = q_1^{\#}/(q_1^{\#} + 1) \tag{5.4a}$$

$$g_2 = k(q_2)/[k(q_2) + k(F)] = q_2^{\#}/(q_2^{\#} + 1) \tag{5.4b}$$

so that

$$1 - g_1 = k(F)/[k(q_1) + k(F)] = 1/(q_1^{\#} + 1) \tag{5.5a}$$

$$1 - g_2 = k(F)/[k(q_2) + k(F)] = 1/(q_2^{\#} + 1). \tag{5.5b}$$

From (4.2), the core entropy functions are:

$$H_q(s_1) = -g_1 \log g_1 - (1 - g_1) \log (1 - g_1) \tag{5.6a}$$

$$H_q(s_2) = -g_2 \log g_2 - (1 - g_2) \log (1 - g_2). \tag{5.6b}$$

From (4.6a), the partial ignorance functions are:

$$I(s_1) = m_1 q_1^\# + (1 - m_1) \tag{5.7a}$$

$$I(s_2) = m_2 q_2^\# + (1 - m_2). \tag{5.7b}$$

From (4.4), the generalized entropy functions are:

$$H(s_1) = H_b(s_1) + H_q(s_1) + I(s_1) \tag{5.8a}$$

$$H(s_2) = H_b(s_2) + H_q(s_2) + I(s_2). \tag{5.8b}$$

Let $c(b, \mathbf{Q}) = s_1(b_1, \mathbf{Q}_1) \otimes s_2(b_2, \mathbf{Q}_2)$ be the consensus of the two simple support functions, as computed by Dempster's rule. Let $H(c)$ be the generalized entropy of $c(b, \mathbf{Q})$. We will now show that under certain conditions, the generation of a consensus reduces generalized entropy, that is,

$$H(c) \leq H(s_1) + H(s_2). \tag{5.9}$$

The four different cases shown in Figure 15.2 need to be examined.

5.1. Case 1: $q_1 = q_2$

The two scf's have the same core, indicating that there are two bodies of evidence that support the same proposition $q = q_1 = q_2$, but with different beliefs.

From Dempster's rule, we get:

$$\mathbf{Q} = \{q, F\} \tag{5.10a}$$

$$b(q) = 1 - (1 - m_1)(1 - m_2) \tag{5.10b}$$

$$b(F) = (1 - m_1)(1 - m_2). \tag{5.10c}$$

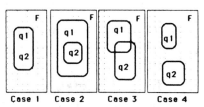

Figure 15.2. Two simple certainty functions (4 cases).

It is interesting to note that for this case:

$$b(q) > b_1(q) \text{ and } b(q) > b_2(q); \tag{5.11a}$$

that is, the consensus of two concordant scf's reinforces the belief committed to their common focal element. It is also easy to show that:

$$L(q) = L_1(q)L_2(q); \tag{5.11b}$$

the postconsensus lack of belief function is the product of the preconsensus lack of belief functions. Note that this result is similar to the one obtained in Duda, Hart, and Nilsson, (1976) by using a "subjective Bayesian method."

The belief entropy, core entropy, ignorance, and generalized entropy functions of $c(b, Q)$ are given by:

$$\begin{aligned}H_b(c) = &-[1 - (1 - m_1)(1 - m_2)] \\ &\cdot \log\,[1 - (1 - m_1)(1 - m_2)] \\ &- (1 - m_1)(1 - m_2) \log\,(1 - m_1)(1 - m_2)\end{aligned} \tag{5.12}$$

$$\begin{aligned}H_q(c) = &- h_1 \log h_1 - h_2 \log h_2 - (1 - h_1 - h_2) \\ &\cdot \log\,(1 - h_1 - h_2)\end{aligned} \tag{5.13a}$$

where

$$\begin{aligned}h_1 &= k(q_1)/[k(q_1) + k(q_2) + k(F)] \\ &= q_1^\#(q_1^\# + q_2^\# + 1)\end{aligned} \tag{5.13b}$$

and

$$\begin{aligned}h_2 &= k(q_2)/[k(q_1) + k(q_2) + k(F)] \\ &= q_2^\#/(q_1^\# + q_2^\# + 1)\end{aligned} \tag{5.13c}$$

$$\begin{aligned}I(c) = &[1 - (1 - m_1)(1 - m_2)]q^\# \\ &+ (1 - m_1)(1 - m_2)\end{aligned} \tag{5.14}$$

$$H(c) = H_b(c) + H_q(c) + I(c). \tag{5.15}$$

Lemma 5.1: The following inequalities are true:

$$H_b(c) \le H_b(s_1) + H_b(s_2) \tag{5.16a}$$

$$H_q(c) \le H_q(s_1) + H_q(s_2) \tag{5.16b}$$

$$I(c) \le I(s_1) + I(s_2) \tag{5.16c}$$

$$H(c) \le H(s_1) + H(s_2). \tag{5.16d}$$

Lemma 5.1 implies that the pooling of two concordant bodies of evidence reduces entropy. The proof is given in the Appendix.

5.2. Case 2: $q_2 \subset q_1$

The focal element q_2 of $s_2(b_2, Q)$ is included in the focal element q_1 of $s_1(b_1, Q)$. This indicates that the proposition corresponding to q_2 is a special case of the proposition corresponding to q_1.

From Dempster's rule:

$$Q = \{q_1, q_2, F\} \quad (5.17a)$$

$$b(q_1) = m_1(1 - m_2) \quad (5.17b)$$

$$b(q_2) = m_2 \quad (5.17c)$$

$$b(F) = (1 - m_1)(1 - m_2). \quad (5.17d)$$

It can be easily shown that for this case:

$$B(q_1) > B_1(q_1) \quad (5.18a)$$

$$B(q_2) = B_2(q_2); \quad (5.18b)$$

that is, the consensus reinforces the total belief committed to q_1, but the total belief committed to q_2 remains unchanged.

The belief entropy, focal entropy, ignorance, and generalized entropy functions of the consensus pcf $c(b, q)$ are:

$$\begin{aligned} H_b(c) = &- m_1(1 - m_2) \log [m_1(1 - m_2)] - m_2 \log m_2 \\ &- (1 - m_1)(1 - m_2) \\ &\cdot \log [(1 - m_1)(1 - m_2)] \end{aligned} \quad (5.19)$$

$$\begin{aligned} H_q(c) = &-h_1 \log h_1 - h_2 \log h_2 \\ &- (1 - h_1 - h_2) \log (1 - h_1 - h_2) \end{aligned} \quad (5.20)$$

where h_1 and h_2 are given by (5.13b) and (5.13c)

$$I(c) = m_1(1 - m_2) q_1^\# + m_2 q_2^\# + (1 - m_1)(1 - m_2) \quad (5.21)$$

$$H(c) = H_b(c) + H_q(c) + I(c). \quad (5.22)$$

Lemma 5.2: Inequalities (5.16) from Lemma 5.1 are also true for case 2. The proof is outlined in the Appendix.

5.3. Case 3: $q_{12} = q_1 \cap q_2 \neq \emptyset$

From Dempster's rule:

$$Q = \{q_1, q_{12}, q_2, F\} \quad (5.23a)$$

$$b(q_1) = m_1(1 - m_2) \quad (5.23b)$$

$$b(q_{12}) = m_1 m_2 \quad (5.23c)$$

$$b(q_2) = m_2(1 - m_1) \quad (5.23d)$$

$$b(F) = (1 - m_1)(1 - m_2). \quad (5.23e)$$

It can easily be shown that for this case:

$$B(q_1) = B_1(q_1) \quad (5.24a)$$

$$B(q_2) = B_2(q_2) \quad (5.24b)$$

$$B(q_1 \cup q_2) < B_1(q_1) + B_2(q_2); \quad (5.24c)$$

that is, the consensus does not change the total belief committed to either q_1 or q_2. It does, however, decrease the total belief committed to their union.

The belief entropy, core entropy, partial ignorance, and generalized entropy functions of $c(b, Q)$ are given by:

$$\begin{aligned} H_b(c) = &-m_1(1 - m_2) \log [m_1(1 - m_2)] \\ &- m_2(1 - m_1) \log [m_2(1 - m_2)] \\ &- m_1 m_2 \log (m_1 m_2) - (1 - m_1)(1 - m_2) \\ &\cdot \log [(1 - m_1)(1 - m_2)] \end{aligned} \quad (5.25)$$

$$\begin{aligned} H_q(c) = &- h_1 \log h_1 - h_{12} \log h_{12} - h_2 \log h_2 \\ &- [1 - (h_1 + h_{12} + h_2)] \\ &\cdot \log [1 - (h_1 + h_{12} + h_2)] \end{aligned} \quad (5.26a)$$

where

$$h_1 = k(q_1)/[k(q_1) + k(q_{12}) + k(q_2) + k(F)] \quad (5.26b)$$

$$h_{12} = k(q_{12})/[k(q_1) + k(q_{12}) + k(q_2) + k(F)] \quad (5.26c)$$

$$h_2 = k(q_2)/[k(q_1) + k(q_{12}) + k(q_2) + k(F)] \quad (5.26d)$$

$$\begin{aligned} I(c) = &m_1(1 - m_2) \, q_1^\# + m_1 m_2 q_{12}^\# \\ &+ m_2(1 - m_1) \, q_2^\# + (1 - m_1)(1 - m_2) \end{aligned} \quad (5.27)$$

$$H(c) = H_b(c) + H_q(c) + I(c). \quad (5.28)$$

Lemma 5.3: The following relations are true:

$$H_b(c) = H_b(s_1) + H_b(s_2) \tag{5.29a}$$

$$H_q(c) \le H_q(s_1) + H_q(s_2) \tag{5.29b}$$

$$I(c) \le I(s_1) + I(s_2) \tag{5.29c}$$

$$H(c) \le H(s_1) + H(s_2). \tag{5.29d}$$

The proof of this lemma is also outlined in the Appendix.

5.4. Case 4: $q_1 \cap q_2 = \varnothing$

Sets q_1 and q_2 are disjoint. This indicates that there are two bodies of evidence supporting two conflicting propositions (corresponding to q_1 and q_2, respectively).

From Dempster's rule:

$$Q = \{q_1, q_2, F\} \tag{5.30a}$$

$$b(q_1) = m_1(1 - m_2)/(1 - m_1 m_2) \tag{5.30b}$$

$$b(q_2) = m_2(1 - m_1)/(1 - m_1 m_2) \tag{5.30c}$$

$$b(F) = (1 - m_1)(1 - m_2)/(1 - m_1 m_2). \tag{5.30d}$$

It can be easily shown that for this case:

$$B(q_1) \le B_1(q_1) \tag{5.31a}$$

$$B(q_2) \le B_2(q_2); \tag{5.31b}$$

that is, the consensus erodes the original amount of total belief committed to q_1 or q_2, because of the conflicting nature of the two disjoint propositions.

The belief entropy, core entropy, partial ignorance, and generalized entropy functions of the consensus pcf $c(b, Q)$ are given by:

$$\begin{aligned}
H_b(c) = -\{ & m_1(1 - m_2) \\
& \cdot \log[m_1(1 - m_2)/(1 - m_1 m_2)] \\
& + m_2(1 - m_1) \\
& \cdot \log[m_2(1 - m_1)/(1 - m_1 m_2)] \\
& + (1 - m_1)(1 - m_2) \log[(1 - m_1) \\
& \cdot (1 - m_2)/(1 - m_1 m_2)]\}(1 - m_1 m_2)
\end{aligned} \tag{5.32}$$

$$H_q(c) = -h_1 \log h_1 - h_2 \log h_2 - (1 - h_1 - h_2)$$
$$\cdot \log(1 - h_1 - h_2) \qquad (5.33\text{a})$$

where

$$h_1 = k(\boldsymbol{q}_1)/[k(\boldsymbol{q}_1) + k(\boldsymbol{q}_2) + k(\boldsymbol{F})] \qquad (5.33\text{b})$$

$$h_2 = k(\boldsymbol{q}_2)/[k(\boldsymbol{q}_1) + k(\boldsymbol{q}_2) + k(\boldsymbol{F})] \qquad (5.33\text{c})$$

$$\boldsymbol{I}(c) = [m_1(1 - m_2)\boldsymbol{q}_1^{\#} + m_2(1 - m_1)\boldsymbol{q}_2^{\#}$$
$$+ (1 - m_1)(1 - m_2)]/(1 - m_1 m_2) \qquad (5.34)$$

$$\boldsymbol{H}(c) = \boldsymbol{H}_b(c) + \boldsymbol{H}_q(c) + \boldsymbol{I}(c). \qquad (5.35)$$

Lemma 5.4: The following inequalities are true:

$$\boldsymbol{H}_b(c) \le \boldsymbol{H}_b(c_1) + \boldsymbol{H}_b(c_2) + \log 2 \qquad (5.36\text{a})$$

$$\boldsymbol{H}_q(c) \le \boldsymbol{H}_q(c_1) + \boldsymbol{H}_q(c_2) \qquad (5.36\text{b})$$

$$\boldsymbol{I}(c) \le \boldsymbol{I}(c_1) + \boldsymbol{I}(c_2) \qquad (5.36\text{c})$$

$$\boldsymbol{H}(c) \le \boldsymbol{H}(c_1) + \boldsymbol{H}(c_2) + \log 2. \qquad (5.36\text{d})$$

Inequalities (5.36a) and (5.36b) are generally not true without the log 2 term on the right-hand side. This term is needed to prevent the inequalities from reversing when m_1 and/or m_2 are large, since for high conflict situations, the consensus can result in a bounded increase (as opposed to the usual decrease) of belief entropy. The upper bound of this increase is equal to log 2. Lemma 5.4 is derived in the Appendix.

6. EXAMPLES

6.1. Belief Entropy

6.1.1. Preconsensus Belief Entropy

Figure 15.3 shows a plot of the preconsensus belief entropy (i.e., the sum of the belief entropy of s_1 and s_2 as given by (5.3)) as a function of the beliefs m_1 (Horizontal axis) and m_2 (vertical axis), respectively, committed to $\boldsymbol{q}_1$ and $\boldsymbol{q}_2$ by knowledge sources Σ_1 and Σ_2. This function is given by:

$$\textbf{PRE}b(m_1, m_2) = H_b(s_1) + H_b(s_2). \qquad (6.1)$$

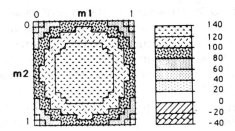

Figure 15.3. Preconsensus belief entropy.

The range of m_1 is from 0 (left) to 1 (right). Similarly, the range of m_2 is from 0 (top) to 1 (bottom). To facilitate the interpretation of the examples in the sequel, we will say that Σ_1 (Σ_2) is confident when $m_1(m_2)$ is large, confused when m_1 (m_2) is medium, and ignorant when m_1 (m_2) is low. The maximum value of the preconsensus belief entropy occurs for $m_1 = m_2 = 0.5$, and is equal to **PRE** b (0.5, 0.5) = 2 log 2. The minima are **PRE**b (0, 0) = **PRE**b (0, 1), = **PRE**b (1, 0) = **PRE**b (1, 1) = 0.

Figure 15.3 also shows the texture assigned to each quantization level of **PRE**b. The same textures are used in Figure 15.4–15.8.

6.1.2. Postconsensus Belief Entropy—Case 1 ($q_1 = q_2$)

Figure 15.4(a) shows a plot of the postconsensus belief entropy (as a function of m_1 and m_2) from (5.12),

$$\textbf{POST}b_1(m_1, m_2) = H_b(c). \tag{6.2}$$

Figure 15.4(b) shows a plot of the postconsensus decrease in entropy:

$$\Delta b_1(m_1, m_2) = \textbf{PRE}b(m_1, m_2) - \textbf{POST}b_1(m_1, m_2). \tag{6.3}$$

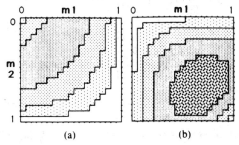

Figure 15.4. Postconsensus belief entropy: case 1. (a) POST b_1 (m_1, m_2). (b) $\Delta b_1(m_1, m_2)$.

Large values of Δb_1 occur when m_1 and m_2 are moderately high, indicating that for the case of concordant evidence, the maximum decrease of entropy occurs when the amounts of belief, respectively, committed to q_1 and q_2 by knowledge sources Σ_1 and Σ_2 are moderately high. In this case, Σ_1 and Σ_2 are in good agreement, and therefore reinforce each other's belief. The maximum reduction in entropy does not, however, occur at the highest values of belief. The reason is that although **POSTb_1** is low for such values, **PREb** is also relatively low. Also note that **POSTb_1** is small for low values of either m_1 or m_2, indicating that the consensus is not very effective when either Σ_1 or Σ_2 is ignorant, and therefore commits a low amount of belief to their common focal element.

6.1.3. Post-Consensus Entropy—Case 2 ($\mathbf{q}_2 \subset \mathbf{q}_1$)

Figures 15.5(a) and (b) show plots of the postconsensus entropy function **POSTb_2** (m_1, m_2) given by (5.19), and the difference entropy function Δb_2 (m_1, m_2) (i.e., **PREb-POSTb_2**), respectively.

Large values of Δb_2 occur if m_2 is high and m_1 is medium, indicating that Σ_2 is confident, but Σ_1 is confused. Thus, the consensus is most effective when a confident Σ_2 helps Σ_1 by committing a large fraction of belief to a subset of the focal element q_1 to which the more confused Σ_1 commits only a small fraction of belief. Small values of Δb_2 occur if: 1) m_2 is low (i.e., if Σ_2 is ignorant and can therefore not effectively help Σ_1) or 2) if m_1 is low (i.e., if Σ_1 is so ignorant that it cannot effectively utilize the additional knowledge provided by Σ_2) or 3) if m_1 is large (i.e., if Σ_1 is already so confident that it cannot effectively utilize the additional knowledge offered by Σ_2.)

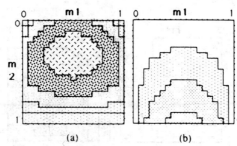

Figure 15.5. Postconsensus belief entropy: case 2. (a) POST b_2 (m_1, m_2). (b) $\Delta b_2(m_1, m_2)$.

6.1.4. Post-Consensus Belief Entropy—Case 3 ($q_1 \cap q_2 \neq \emptyset$)

It follows from Lemma 5.3 that:

$$\mathbf{POST}b_3(m_1, m_2) = \mathbf{PRE}b(m_1, m_2) \tag{6.4}$$

and therefore

$$\Delta b_3(m_1, m_2) = 0 \quad \text{for } 0 \leq m_1, m_2 \leq 1. \tag{6.5}$$

Consensus has no effect in this case, as the postconsensus belief entropy is identical to the preconsensus belief entropy. The moving mass analogy introduced in Section II suggests that for this case neither Σ_1 nor Σ_2 confines the true value of x to a subset of F which was not initially accessible to it. Σ_1 and Σ_2 are not providing each other with additional knowledge, and their consensus is therefore ineffective.

6.1.5. Postconsensus Belief Entropy—Case 4 ($q_1 \cap q_2 = \emptyset$)

Figures 15.6(a) and (b) show the postconsensus entropy function $\mathbf{Post}b_4(m_1, m_2)$ as given by (5.32), and the difference entropy function $\Delta b_4(m_1, m_2)$ (i.e., $\mathbf{PRE}b - \mathbf{POST}b_4$). Note that Σ_1 and Σ_2 are now in conflict as they each commit nonzero belief to two conflicting propositions corresponding to the disjoint sets q_1 and q_2.

Large values of Δb_4 occur if m_1 is large and m_2 is moderately low. The consensus is effective because a confused Σ_2 is helped by the additional knowledge provided by a confident Σ_1. This observation is of course symmetric; that is, large values of Δb_4 also occur if m_2 is large and m_1 is moderately low. Also note that the consensus is still effective (i.e., Δb_4 is reasonably large) when m_1 and m_2 are medium (i.e., Σ_1 and

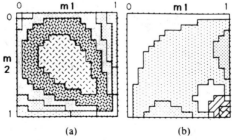

Figure 15.6. Postconsensus belief entropy: case 4. (a) $\mathrm{POST}b_4(m_1, m_2)$. (b) $\Delta b_4(m_1, m_2)$.

Σ_2 are still helping each other by pooling their knowledge when they are both confused).

It is also interesting to note that if both m_1 and m_2 are large (i.e., Σ_1 and Σ_2 are confident in their conflicting knowledge), $\Delta \boldsymbol{b}_4(m_1, m_2)$ becomes very small, and even negative. Thus, for high conflict situations, the consensus not only becomes ineffective, but it results in a bounded increase of the belief entropy. The maximum increase in belief entropy is $-\Delta \boldsymbol{b}_4 (0.5, 0.5) = \log 2$ from (A.27). This occurs when both Σ_1 and Σ_2 are very confident in their conflicting beliefs.

6.2. Core Entropy (Case 4)

Figure 15.7(a) shows the preconsensus core entropy, that is, the sum of the core entropy of the scf's s_1 and s_2 as given by (5.6). Let

$$\textbf{PRE}q\ (q_1^\#, q_2^\#) = H_q(s_1) + H_q(s_2). \qquad (6.6)$$

The range for both $q_1^\#$ (horizontal axis) and $q_2^\#$ (vertical axis) is from 0 to 1. Figure 15.7(b) shows the postconsensus core entropy for case 4 (i.e., q_1 and q_2 are disjoint), as given by (5.33). The core entropy is only displayed in the $q_1^\# + d_2^\# \leq 1$ range since the two sets are disjoint.

$$\textbf{POST}\ q_4\ (q_1^\#, q_2^\#) = H_q(c). \qquad (6.7)$$

Both $\textbf{PRE}q$ and $\textbf{POST}q_4$ are monotonically increasing functions of $q_1^\#$ and $q_2^\#$, indicating that as $q_1^\#$ and/or $q_2^\#$ tend toward 1 (i.e., as $k(q_1)$ and/or $k(q_2)$ tend toward $k(F)$), the core entropy increases. This increase results from the distribution of one's belief among focal elements having increasingly similar cardinality numbers (as discussed in Section 4.2). It should be noted, however, that $\textbf{POST}q_4$ increases

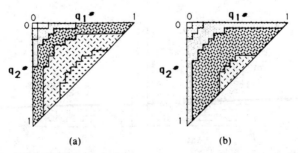

Figure 15.7. Pre- and postconsensus core entropy: case 4. (b) $\text{PRE}q(q_1^\#, q_2^\#)$. (b) POST $q_4(q_1^\#, q_2^\#)$.

less rapidly than **PRE**q, indicating that the consensus is effective in reducing the core entropy for all values of $q_1^\#$ and $q_2^\#$.

6.3. Partial Ignorance (Case 4)

The preconsensus partial ignorance, that is, the sum of the partial ignorance of the scf's s_1 and s_2, is given by:

$$\mathbf{PRE}i(m_1, m_2, q_1^\#, q_2^\#) = I(s_1) + I(s_2) \tag{6.8}$$

where $I(s_1)$ and $I(s_2)$ are given by (5.7).

Figure 15.8(a) shows the preconsensus partial ignorance **PRE**$i(m, q^\#)$, where it was assumed (for the sake of simplicity and clarity of the example, but without loss of generality) that:

$$m_1 = m_2 = m \tag{6.9a}$$

$$q_1^\# = q_2^\# = q^\#. \tag{6.9b}$$

Figure 15.8(b) shows the postconsensus partial ignorance function **POST**$i_4(m, q^\#)$ for case 4 (i.e., when q_1 and q_2 are disjoint). The range of $q^\#$ is from 0 to 0.5, since the two sets cannot be disjoint if $q_1^\# + q_2^\# \geq 1$.

$$\mathbf{POST}i_4(m, q^\#) = I(c) \tag{6.10}$$

where $I(c)$ is given in (5.34).

As suggested by the discussion in Section 4.2, partial ignorance is small when m is large and $q^\#$ is small (upper right corner). Similarly, partial ignorance is large when m is small and $q^\#$ is large (lower left corner). It should be noted here that both plots in Figure 15.8 have been rescaled to avoid cluttering. The values on the texture chart in Figure 15.3 should be multiplied by a factor of 1.5 when used to read **PRE**i and **POST**i_4 from Figure 15.8.

A comparison of Figures 15.8(a) and (b) shows that for any point in

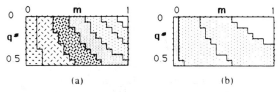

Figure 15.8. Pre- and postconsensus partial ignorance: case 4. (a) PRE$i(m, q^\#)$. (b) POST $i_4(m, q^\#)$.

the $m - q^\#$ plane, **POST**i_4 is smaller than **PRE**i, indicating again that the consensus is effective in reducing partial ignorance.

7. SUMMARY

The pooling of knowledge from multiple sources is an important practical problem in the design of expert systems. The knowledge sources can correspond to different bodies of evidence, and/or sets of rules contributed by different experts. In this chapter, we have defined a criterion to measure the quality of the consensus generated by pooling two knowledge sources. This criterion is based on the generalization of the concept of entropy from point functions to set functions. We have shown that, except in cases where the two knowledge sources are in high conflict, the postconsensus entropy is smaller than the preconsensus entropy. Further work is needed to extend these results to the pooling of knowledge from more than two sources. This will require the generalization of our results from knowledge sources that are represented by simple certainty functions to knowledge sources represented by partial certainty functions.

Appendix

A. *Proof of Lemma 5.1 (Case 1)*

1. *Belief Entropy:* From (5.3) and (5.12):

$$\begin{aligned}
\boldsymbol{H}_b(s_1) + \boldsymbol{H}_b(s_2) &= -m_1 \log m_1 - (1 - m_1) \\
&\quad \cdot \log (1 - m_1) \\
&\quad - m_2 \log m_2 - (1 - m_2) \\
&\quad \cdot \log (1 - m_2) \\
\boldsymbol{H}_b(c) &= -(m_1 + m_2 - m_1 m_2) \\
&\quad \cdot \log (m_1 + m_2 - m_1 m_2) \\
&\quad - (1 - m_1)(1 - m_2) \\
&\quad \cdot \log [(1 - m_1)(1 - m_2)].
\end{aligned} \quad (A.2)$$

Note that

$$\begin{aligned}
-(m_1 + m_2 - m_1 m_2) &\log (m_1 + m_2 - m_1 m_2) \\
&\leq -(m_1 + m_2) \log (m_1 + m_2 - m_1 m_2) \\
&\leq -m_1 \log [m_1 + m_2(1 - m_1)] - m_2 \\
&\quad \cdot \log [m_2 + m_1 (1 - m_2)] \\
&\leq -m_1 \log m_1 - m_2 \log m_2 \qquad (A.3)
\end{aligned}$$

and

$$-(1-m_1)(1-m_2)\log[(1-m_1)(1-m_2)]$$
$$= -(1-m_1)(1-m_2)\log(1-m_2)$$
$$- (1-m_1)(1-m_2)\log(1-m_2)$$
$$\leq -(1-m_1)\log(1-m_1) - (1-m_2)$$
$$\cdot \log(1-m_2). \qquad (A.4)$$

Combining (A.3) and (A.4), we get (5.16a).

2. *Core Entropy:* From (5.6) and (5.13),

$$\boldsymbol{H}_q(s_1) + \boldsymbol{H}_q(s_2) = -g_1 \log g_1 - (1-g_1)$$
$$\cdot \log(1-g_1) - g_2$$
$$\cdot \log g_2 - (1-g_2)\log(1-g_2) \qquad (A.5)$$

$$\boldsymbol{H}_q(c) = -h_1 \log h_1 - h_2$$
$$\cdot \log h_2 - (1-h_1-h_2)$$
$$\cdot \log(1-h_1-h_2). \qquad (A.6)$$

Noting that

$$g_1 \log g_1 \geq -h_1 \log h_1 \qquad (A.7a)$$

$$g_2 \log g_2 \geq -h_2 \log h_2 \qquad (A.7b)$$

$$-(1-g_1)\log(1-g_1) - (1-g_2)\log(1-g_2)$$
$$\geq -(1-h_1-h_2)\log(1-h_1-h_2) \qquad (A.7c)$$

and summing both sides of (A.7), it follows that (5.16b) is true.

3. *Partial Ignorance:* From (5.7) and (5.14),

$$\boldsymbol{I}(s_1) + \boldsymbol{I}(s_2) = m_1 \boldsymbol{q}_1^\# + (1-m_1) + m_2 \boldsymbol{q}_2^\#$$
$$+ (1-m_2) \qquad (A.8)$$

$$\boldsymbol{I}(c) = [1 - (1-m_1)(1-m_2)]\boldsymbol{q}^\#$$
$$+ (1-m_1)(1-m_2). \qquad (A.9)$$

Combining (A.7) and (A.8), and rearranging terms,

$$\boldsymbol{I}(s_1) + \boldsymbol{I}(s_2) - \boldsymbol{I}(c) = m_1 m_2 \boldsymbol{q}^\# + (1-m_1 m_2) \geq 0. \qquad (A.10)$$

This proves (5.16c). Equation (5.16d) follows directly from the addition of (5.16a) to (5.16c).

B. *Proof of Lemma 5.2 (Case 2)*

1. *Belief Entropy:* From (5.19)

$$H_b(c) = -m_1(1 - m_2) \log [m_1(1 - m_2)] - m_2 \log m_2$$
$$-(1 - m_1)(1 - m_2)$$
$$\cdot \log [(1 - m_2)(1 - m_2)]. \quad (A.11)$$

Using (5.3) to rewrite (A.10), we get:

$$\begin{aligned}H_b(c) &= H_b(s_2) - m_1 (1 - m_2) \log m_1 - (1 - m_1) \\ &\quad \cdot (1 - m_2) \log (1 - m_1) \\ &\leq H_b(s_2) - m_1 \log m_1 - (1 - m_1)(1 - m_2) \\ &\quad \cdot \log (1 - m_1) \\ &\leq H_b(s_2) - m_1 \log m_1 - (1 - m_1) \\ &\quad \log (1 - m_1) \\ &\leq H_b(s_2) + H_b(s_1). \end{aligned} \quad (A.12)$$

This proves (5.16a) for case 2 (Lemma 5.2).

2. *Core Entropy:* $H_q(s_1)$, $H_q(s_2)$, and $H_q(c)$ are the same for case 1 (Lemma 5.1). Inequality (5.16b), therefore, also holds for case 2 (Lemma 5.2).

3. *Partial Ignorance:* From (5.21),

$$I(c) = m_1(1 - m_2)q_1^\# + m_2 q_2^\# + (1 - m_1)(1 - m_2). \quad (A.13)$$

Subtracting (A.13) from (A.8), we get

$$I(s_1) + I(s_2) - I(c) = m_1 m_2 q_1^\# + (1 - m_1 m_2) \geq 0 \quad (A.14)$$

which proves (5.16c) for case 2 (Lemma 5.2).

Again, (5.16d) follows directly from the addition of (5.16a) to (5.16c).

C. *Proof of Lemma 5.3 (Case 3)*

1. *Belief Entropy:* From (5.25)

$$\begin{aligned}H_b(c) = &-m_1 (1 - m_2) \log [m_1 (1 - m_2)] \\ &-m_2 (1 - m_1) \log [m_2 (1 - m_1)] \\ &-m_1 m_2 \log (m_1 m_2) - (1 - m_1)(1 - m_2) \\ &\cdot \log [(1 - m_1)(1 - m_2)]. \end{aligned} \quad (A.15)$$

Rewriting the logarithms of products as sums of logarithms, regrouping, and then comparing to (A.1), we get:

$$\begin{aligned}H_b(c) &= -m_1 \log m_1 - m_2 \log m_2 - (1 - m_1) \\ &\quad \cdot \log (1 - m_1) - (1 - m_2) \log (1 - m_2) \\ &= H_b(s_1) + H_b(s_2). \end{aligned} \quad (A.16)$$

This proves (5.29a).

2. *Core Entropy:* From (5.26),

$$H_q(c) = -h_1 \log h_1 - h_{12} \log h_{12} - h_2 \log h_2 \\ -[1 - (h_1 + h_{12} + h_2)] \\ \cdot \log [1 - (h_1 + h_{12} + h_2)]. \quad \text{(A.17)}$$

Noting that

$$-g_1 \log g_1 \geq -h_1 \log h_1 \quad \text{(A.18a)}$$

$$-g_2 \log g_2 \geq -h_2 \log h_2 \quad \text{(A.18b)}$$

$$-(1 - g_1) \log (1 - g_1) \geq -h_{12} \log h_{12} \\ \text{(since } \boldsymbol{q}_{12}^\# \leq 1 \text{ and } \boldsymbol{q}_1^\# + \boldsymbol{q}_{12}^\# + \boldsymbol{q}_2^\# \\ \geq \boldsymbol{q}_1^\#\text{), and} \quad \text{(A.18c)}$$

$$-(1 - g_2) \log (1 - g_2) \geq -(1 - h_1 - h_{12} - h_2) \\ \cdot \log (1 - h_1 - h_{12} - h_2). \quad \text{(A.18d)}$$

Now add both sides of the inequalities in (A.18), and compare it to (A.5) and (A.7). It follows that

$$H_q(s_1) + H_q(s_2) \geq H_q(c). \quad \text{(A.19)}$$

This proves (5.29b).

3. *Partial Ignorance:* From (5.27)

$$I(c) = m_1(1 - m_2)\boldsymbol{q}_1^\# + m_1 m_2 \boldsymbol{q}_{12}^\# + m_2(1 - m_1)\boldsymbol{q}_2^\# \\ + (1 - m_1)(1 - m_2). \quad \text{(A.20)}$$

Subtracting (A.20) from (A.8), we get

$$I(s_1) + I(s_2) - I(c) = m_1 m_2(\boldsymbol{q}_1^\# + \boldsymbol{q}_2^\# - \boldsymbol{q}_{12}^\#) \\ + (1 - m_1 m_2) \\ = m_1 m_2 \boldsymbol{q}_3^\# + (1 - m_1 m_2) \geq 0 \quad \text{(A.21)}$$

where $q_3 = q_1 \cup q_2$.

This proves (5.29c). Equation (5.29d) follows directly from the addition of (5.29a) to (5.29c).

D. Derivation of Lemma 5.4 (Case 4)

1. Belief Entropy: From (5.32),

$$\begin{aligned}H_b(c) = \{&-m_1(1-m_2) \\ &\cdot \log[m_1(1-m_2)/(1-m_1m_2)] \\ &-m_2(1-m_1)\log[m_2(1-m_1)/ \\ &(1-m_1m_2)] \\ &-(1-m_1)(1-m_2)\log[(1-m_1) \\ &\cdot (1-m_2)/(1-m_1m_2)]\}/(1-m_1m_2).\end{aligned} \quad (A.22)$$

(A.22) can be rewritten as

$$\begin{aligned}H_b(c) = [&-m_1(1-m_2)\log m_1 - m_2(1-m_2)\log m_2 \\ &-(1-m_1)\log(1-m_1) - (1-m_2) \\ &\cdot \log(1-m_2)]/(1-m_1m_2) \\ &+ \log(1-m_1m_2).\end{aligned} \quad (A.23)$$

Subtracting (A.23) from (A.1), we get

$$\begin{aligned}\Delta H_b &= H_b(s_1) + H_b(s_2) - H_b(c) \\ &= -m_1m_2\{(1-m_1)\log[m_1/(1-m_1)] \\ &\quad + (1-m_2)\log[m_2/(1-m_2)]\}/(1-m_1m_2) \\ &\quad - \log(1-m_1m_2).\end{aligned} \quad (A.24)$$

The partial derivatives of ΔH_b with respect to m_1 and m_2 are

$$\begin{aligned}\partial \Delta H_b/\partial m_1 = &-m_2\{(1-m_2)\log[m_2/(1-m_2)] \\ &+ [1-m_1(2-m_1m_2)] \\ &\cdot \log[m_1/(1-m_1)]\}/(1-m_2m_2)^2\end{aligned} \quad (A.25a)$$

$$\begin{aligned}\partial \Delta H_b/\partial m_2 = &-m_1\{(1-m_1)\log[m_1/(1-m_1)] \\ &+ [1-m_2(2-m_2m_1)] \\ &\cdot \log[m_2/(1-m_2)]\}/(1-m_2)^2.\end{aligned} \quad (A.25b)$$

Figure 15.9 shows three regions of the m_1m_2 plane for which one or both of the partial derivatives are negative. The minimum value of ΔH_b occurs at $m_1 = m_2 = 1$. The value of this minimum is obtained by setting $m_1 = m_2 = m$ in (A.24), and taking the limit as m tends toward 1:

$$\begin{aligned}\Delta H_b(m,m) &= -2m^3\{(1-m)\log[m/(1-m)]\}/ \\ &\quad (1-m^2) - \log(1-m^2) \\ &= -2m^2[\log m - \log(1-m)]/(1+m) \\ &\quad -\log(1-m^2).\end{aligned} \quad (A.26)$$

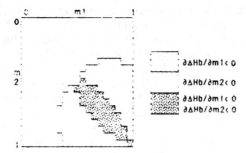

Figure 15.9. Partial derivatives of $\Delta H_b(m_1, m_2)$.

Therefore,

$$\lim_{m \to 1} = 2m^2 [\log(1-m)]/(1+m)$$
$$-\log(1-m) - \log 2$$
$$= (2m^2 - m - 1)[\log(1-m)]/(1+m) - \log 2$$
$$= (2m+1)[(m-1)\log(1-m)]/(1+m) - \log 2$$
$$= -\log 2. \tag{A.27}$$

2. *Core Entropy:* $H_b(c_1)$, $H_b(c_2)$, and $H_b(c)$ are given by the same expressions as for case 2 (Lemma 5.2). Inequality (5.36b) is therefore true.

3. *Partial Ignorance:* From (5.34)

$$I(c) = -[m_1(1-m_2)q_1^\# + m_2(1-m_1)q_2^\# + (1-m_1)(1-m_2)]/(1-m_1m_2). \tag{A.28}$$

Subtracting (A.27) from (A.8), we get:

$$I(s_1) + I(s_2) - I(c)$$
$$= \{m_2(1-m_1)q_1^\# + m_1(1-m_2)q_2^\# + [(1-m_1)^2 m_2/(1-m_1m_2) + (1-m_2)]\}/(1-m_1m_2) \geq 0. \tag{A.29}$$

This proves (5.36c). Equation (5.36d) follows directly from the addition of (5.36a) to (5.36c).

REFERENCES

Barnett, J.A. (1981). Computational methods for a mathematical theory of evidence. *Proceedings of the Seventh International Joint Conference on Artificial Intelligence* (pp. 868–875). Vancouver, BC, Canada.

Dempster, A.P. (1968). A generalization of Bayesian inference. *Journal of the Royal Statistical Society B, 30,* 205–247.

Duda, R.O., Hart, P.E., & Nilsson, N.J. (1976). Subjective Bayesian methods for rule-based inference systems. *Proceedings of the National Computer Conference, Vol. 45, AFIPS* (pp. 1075–1082). New York, NY.

Erkmen, A.M., & Stephanou, H.E. (1987). Evidential control of dextrous grasps. *Proceedings of the IEEE International Conference on Systems, Man, and Cybernetics.* Alexandria, VA.

Ishizuka, M., Fu, K.S., & Yao, J.P.T. (1981, August). *Inference procedure with uncertainty for problem reduction method* (Tech. Rep. TR-EE 81-33). Purdue University: School of Electrical Engineering.

Lowrance, J.D., & Garvey, T.D. (1983, December). *Evidential reasoning: An implementation for multisensor integration* (Tech. Note 307). Menlo Park, CA: Artificial Intelligence Center, SRI International.

Lu, S.Y., & Stephanou, H.E. (1984). A set-theoretic framework for the processing of uncertain knowledge. *Proceedings of the Fourth National Conference on Artificial Intelligence* (pp. 216–221). Austin, TX.

Prade, H. (1985). A computational approach to approximate and plausible reasoning with applications to expert systems. *IEEE Transactions on Pattern Analysis and Machine Intelligence,* PAMI-7(3), 260–283.

Shafer, G. (1976). *A Mathematical Theory of Evidence.* Princeton, NJ: Princeton Univ. Press.

Shortliffe, E.H. (1976). *Computer based medical consultation: MYCIN.* New York: American Elsevier.

Yager, R.R. (1983). Entropy and specificity in a mathematical theory of evidence. *International Journal of General Systems, 9,* 249–260.

PART III
Object Recognition

16
Introduction to Part III

Ren C. Luo and
Michael G. Kay

Part III describes a variety of approaches to object recognition using the integration and fusion of information from combinations of different types of sensors. Object recognition is an important function required in most multisensor intelligent machines and systems. In addition to the actual recognition of an object, information gathered during the recognition process can be used for the measurement and manipulation of the object and for scene understanding. An effort is made in this part to present approaches to object recognition that exploit the specific characteristics of the information provided by a variety of different types of sensors and have the potential for broad application. Vision and thermal sensors are used in Chapter 17 for object measurement and recognition, and vision and tactile sensors are used for object recognition in Chapter 18. A wide variety of additional sensor combinations are presented in Parts IV and V that have been used for object recognition in mobile robot and other applications, respectively.

Figure 16.1 shows a diagram of the typical functions found in many object (or, in general, pattern) recognition systems. In contrast to object recognition using just a single sensor, data from multiple sensors may enter into the system at any stage of the processing. During the "signal processing" function the data from multiple sensors may be fused at either the signal or pixel level (see Section 1.2 of Chapter 1) and can be used to increase the accuracy of the signals sent to the feature extraction function. During "feature extraction," feature-level fusion using the data from multiple sensors can help to eliminate spurious

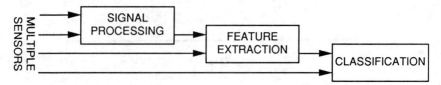

Figure 16.1. Functional diagram of object recognition using multiple sensors.

features from being sent for classification. Either statistical pattern recognition or model (e.g., template) matching techniques are generally used to implement the "classification" function in object recognition. In statistical pattern recognition the features provided by the use of additional complementary sensors serve to increase the dimensionality of the feature space so that patterns can be more easily separated for classification purposes. In model matching, symbol-level fusion can serve to reduce the uncertainty measures of symbols representing possible objects.

Pau (1982, 1988a, 1988b, 1990) describes a number of statistical pattern recognition techniques that are appropriate for multisensor fusion. All of these techniques could be used to reduce the error in classifying objects through the use of multiple sensors to provide redundant information concerning features of the objects. To avoid an exponential increase in complexity as sensors are added to a system, a key requirement is that the number of features and levels in the recognition process increase at a slower rate than the number of sensors. To meet this requirement it becomes necessary to improve the overall methods of feature extraction and selection—two major areas of interest in pattern recognition. Thus, multisensor fusion becomes a problem within the context of statistical pattern recognition. Pau describes a number of operators and techniques that can fuse the features perceived by the sensors to limit their growth as additional sensors are added (Pau, 1982), and has introduced a representation for multisensor fusion that is based on "context truth maintenance" (Pau, 1988a) and a behavioral control formalism (Pau, 1990) that can be used to model the fusion process in man–machine systems. In his formalism the cognitive states of the components or actors in a system are used to more realistically model complex interactions.

1. VISION

Visual information is the most powerful single source of sensory information available to a system for object recognition and measurement. Many different types of nonvisual sensors are used in combination with vision sensors to compensate for some of the difficulties encountered in the machine processing of visual information. Tasks such as object recognition can sometimes require the aid of additional types of sensors to approach the capabilities of a human, using visual information alone. This section will not describe in detail the many integration and fusion techniques that use only vision sensors because there already is an extensive literature, including many reviews and book-length treatments (e.g., Ballard & Brown, 1982; Horn, 1986) covering the various aspects of computational vision.

Magee and Aggarwal (1985) provide a review of research efforts aimed at combining intensity and range features derived from visual images to determine the structure of three-dimensional objects. In some of the work reviewed, information from one feature is used to guide the acquisition of information concerning another feature when the second feature either requires a much longer processing time or is in some other way less desirable. Other research in this area includes: intensity-guided range sensing for object recognition (Magee, Boyter, Chien & Aggarwal, 1985) and the determination of motion parameters (Aggarwal & Magee, 1986), and automatic model generation from range and intensity images (Bastuscheck, 1988; Wang & Aggarwal, 1989). Delcroix and Abidi (1988) provide an analytic method for the fusion of intensity and range information to detect edges in a scene. Their paper also provides a review of other intensity and range fusion methods. Hackett and Shah (1989) have used intensity and range information for image segmentation.

Research related to the fusion of sequences of images has used the "optical flow" of the images to determine the motion of objects in the image (see Hildreth, 1986, for a review, and Moezzi and Weymouth, 1990, for an object-centered representation that can be used for "dynamic vision"). A Bayesian (Hung, Cooper & Cernuschi-Frias, 1988) and an extended Kalman filter (Ayache & Faugeras, 1988; Faugeras, Ayache & Faverjon, 1986) have been used to determine the surfaces of three-dimensional objects using sequences of images. Many researchers have used stereoscopic processing to determine range information using multiple visual sensors (see Barnard & Fischler, 1986, for a stereo vision review, Hong & Brzakovic, 1990, for 3-D scene reconstruction, and Hansen, Ayache, and Lustman, 1988, 1990, for the use of passive "trinocular" stereo).

In robotics, overhead and "eye-in-hand" vision sensors have been combined for use in three-dimensional object recognition (Luo & Lin, 1987). Many of these techniques, originally developed to fuse both sequences of images from a single vision sensor and images derived simultaneously from multiple sensors, have significantly influenced subsequent work in nonvisual fusion.

2. VISION AND TACTILE

The integration of visual and tactile information gives a robot, together with its own manipulation capabilities, a wide range over which to receive sensory information. Combined vision and tactile sensors have been used to a great extent by industrial robots to perform object recognition, measurement, and manipulation. Additional information concerning the integration of visual and tactile information for object recognition can be found in Chapter 18 of this part.

2.1. Integration Using a Decision Tree

Luo and Tsai (1986) have developed a system that uses two-dimensional vision, together with two tactile sensing arrays mounted on a gripper of a robot, to recognize objects. Moment invariants of an object's shape are used as features for recognition and to calculate the centroid of a region of the object needed for determining the proper grasping position for the gripper. During the initial learning phase, the system creates a decision tree by first presenting all of the objects to be recognized to the vision sensor so that their top-view silhouette boundaries can be determined. If there still exist groups of objects that are indistinguishable in terms of this visual information, tactile information concerning the objects' lateral shape is obtained to make the objects in each group more distinguishable. Different predetermined lateral directions are used until all of the objects are able to be distinguished. The final result of this clustering process is a hierarchical decision tree with each leaf representing a single discriminable object, each nonterminal node corresponding to a group of objects that are indistinguishable at that level of sensory processing, and each arc associated with the effective lateral direction used by the tactile sensor to distinguish the child from the parent node. The first level below the root node in the tree corresponds to the initial visual sensing; levels below the first represent successive stages of tactile sensing. Finally, the recognition phase proceeds by traversing the decision tree in the same direction as the tree was created until the object is able to be recognized.

2.2. Object Apprehension

Stansfield (1986, 1987, 1988a, 1988b) has presented a system which uses vision and tactile sensors for object apprehension. "Apprehension" is defined as the determination of the properties of an object and the relationships among these properties without, as in recognition, going on to attach a label to the object as a whole. The system is structured as a modularized hierarchy of knowledge-based experts, each responsible for either the execution of an exploratory procedure or for the further processing of information from other exploratory procedures. An exploratory procedure extracts information concerning a predefined general-purpose primitive (e.g., compliance, elasticity, texture, etc.) or feature (e.g., edges, surface patches, holes, cavities, etc.) that is related to some aspect of the object's form, substance, or function (Stansfield, 1986). Each feature is composed of one or more primitives or features. Modules in the lower portion of the hierarchy are responsible for processing the information from each sensory system, while the upper-level modules integrate the information coming from the different sensor systems. Many of the higher-level modules are able to function with information from a variety of different lower-level modules. Spatial polyhedrons have been proposed recently by Stansfield (1988a) as a generic object representation that can extend the capabilities of the system to include recognition.

2.3. Conductivity Measure

Stephanou and Erkmen (1990) describe a model-based evidential pattern classifier for visual and tactile information. Patterns are classified using a conductivity measure. Conductivity measures the strength of the interactions between a belief function representing the current sensory information and the belief functions of known features which comprise the antecedents of rules in a knowledge base containing object classes.

2.4. Range and Tactile

Grimson and Lozano-Pérez (1984) describe a technique that uses tactile and range sensors to provide measurements of position and surface normals that can be used to identify and locate objects from among a group of known objects. The objects are modeled as polyhedrons, and constraints are used to keep the number of hypotheses as to an object's identity small. The only assumptions made about the sensors required are that they be able to provide information concerning an object's surface points and surface normals; as a result, the technique should be applicable to a wide variety of different types of sensors besides range and tactile sensors.

3. AUTOMATIC TARGET RECOGNITION

Automatic target recognition (ATR) using multiple complementary sensors located on a single sensor platform has been an active area of research over the past decade. Most ATR systems are capable of both the detection of a target (see Section 4 of Chapter 22) and, to some degree, the recognition of the target. In some cases the target can only be classified as being a possible threat or as belonging to a particular class of target, for example, a tank, while in more advanced systems operating under favorable conditions it is sometimes possible to identify the particular model of a target, such as an M1 tank. Many ATR systems are intended for use in military applications and, as such, entail the consideration of a number of additional requirements beyond those of a general-purpose object recognition system (see Section 2 of Chapter 22 and Chapter 23 in Part V). In military applications the use of multisensor integration and fusion allows an ATR system to address many of these additional requirements. For example, suites of active and passive sensors can be used by a system to foil possible enemy countermeasures; in time-critical situations, most of the processing of each sensor's data can be done in parallel; different groups of sensors can be used in response to changing environmental conditions; and the use of distributed sensor platforms can overcome possible target occlusion limitations as compared to the use of a single platform. A number of reviews of the present and future needs for ATR research have appeared in recent years (Bhanu, 1986; Brown & Swonger, 1989; Delashmit, 1989; Science Appl. Int. Corp., 1988) and each has emphasized the important role that multisensor integration and fusion will play in the development of smart, and even "brilliant" (Klein & Kassis, 1989), ATR systems.

Given the goal of actually identifying a target under a variety of environmental conditions, multiple sensors are almost always used in ATR systems to provide complementary information. The time-critical performance requirements of many systems make signal- or pixel-level fusion especially attractive due to its lower processing requirements as compared to higher-level methods of fusion. Signal- or pixel-level fusion is feasible in many instances if the information provided by the sensors in a system is sufficiently similar and the sensors are located on a single platform so that communication bandwidth limitations are not as much of a problem as they are for distributed platform target detection and tracking systems (see Section 4 of Chapter 22). Registration for pixel-level fusion is facilitated if the sensors on a platform are either coaligned or share a common aperture (Benser, Cox and French, 1989). Symbol-level fusion can be used in conjunction with expert systems and other AI techniques to allow high-level context-dependent information to be included in the ATR process—information that is critical in order to make an ATR system robust. Dempster-Shafer evidential reasoning (see Section 3.2 of Chapter 8, and Chapters 14, 23, and 24) has proved to be a useful means of handling high-level sensor fusion for ATR.

Figure 16.2 shows a functional diagram of a typical automatic target recognition and multitarget tracking system. What is most notable in the diagram is the manner in which the partial processing results of both the recognition and tracking subsystems are used at various stages in the other subsystem's processing. An imaging sensor (e.g., infrared or visual), together with a sensor providing target range information, is mounted on a single sensor platform (e.g., a helicopter). Platform motion measurements are used to keep the image fixed in earth coordinates so that potential targets can be detected in the image. Target range information is used to size detection windows. Kinematic features of potential targets (e.g., velocity and position) are used to establish tracks in the multitarget tracking subsystem, while nonkinematic target features (e.g., number of pixels, invariant moments, and target-to-background intensity ratios) are used in the recognition subsystem for target classification. Nonkinematic features can be used in the tracking subsystem to upgrade the status of existing target tracks, and kinematic features (e.g., velocity) can be used in the recognition subsystem to aid in target classification. The final result of the recognition and tracking processing is a symbol indicating the type of target and its position relative to the platform.

3.1. Neural Networks

The use of neural networks for ATR offers the possibility of a highly parallel means of processing that is robust to noise and other factors (Castelaz, 1988). A major problem with the use of neural networks in many object recognition applications is that they require a large number of training samples that may be difficult to acquire. This problem is ameliorated in many ATR applications because high-level CAD-like models of possible targets can be created for training purposes. Baran (1989) has developed an approach to multisensor integration and fusion for ATR that uses an associative memory (see Section 1.3 of Chapter 2). An analysis is provided of the required size of a network needed to reach a particular level of recognition performance given the level of quantization and noise of a sensor. Cain, Stewart, and Morse (1989) have used a neural network for target classification using a multi-

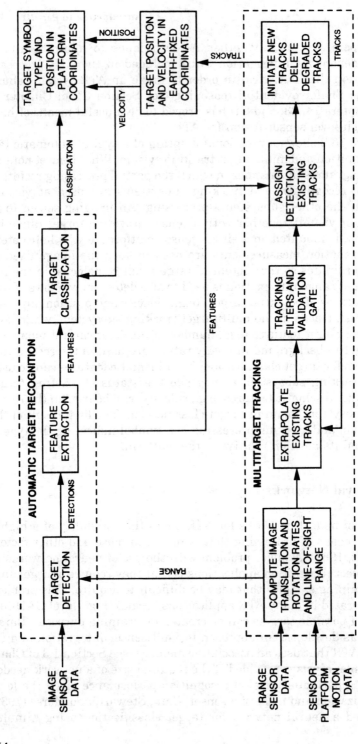

Figure 16.2. Functional diagram of an automatic target recognition and multitarget tracking system that uses an imaging and a range sensor mounted on a single platform. (Adapted from Mitzel (1990, Figure 9.1).)

spectral IR sensor and an ultraviolet laser radar (LADAR). Competitive learning was used in the network to learn the correlation between a variety of multisensor features and target classes. The use of features derived from the fusion of individual features resulted in the greatest improvement in classification performance as compared to the use of just a combination of the separate features.

3.2. Sensor Combinations

Three functional categories of sensors are used in most ATR systems: microwave radar (Eaves & Reedy, 1987), millimeter-wave (MMW) radar (Currie & Brown, 1987), and electro-optical sensors. The electro-optical category includes sensors such as active laser radar (LADAR) (Bachman, 1979), passive infrared (IR or forward-looking infrared (FLIR)) (Pau & El Nahas, 1983), and cameras operating in the visible region of the spectrum. Table 16.1 provides a qualitative comparison of these categories with respect to a variety of their characteristics that are important, in most operational scenarios, for ATR. As can be seen from the table, there is no single type of sensor that clearly dominates the others with respect to all characteristics. Although ATR systems have been designed that use a single sensor (e.g., microwave radar (Ezquerra, 1987)), it is usually desirable to consider the use of two or more complementary sensors in the design of an ATR system so that a large number of desirable characteristics can be obtained.

The major distinguishing desirable and undesirable features of the three different categories of sensors with respect to ATR are as follows: Microwave radar is superior to the other sensors in terms of its detection range and immunity to attenuation in the atmosphere, but is limited in its usefulness for recognition purposes in ATR systems (and is usually limited to detection and tracking functions) due to its poor classification and identification capabilities and the large size of its antenna. MMW sensors fall midway between microwave and electro-optical sensors with respect to most characteristics. Their major advantage in comparison to microwave radar is their smaller size and better resolution; their major advantage in comparison to electro-optical sensors is their greater immunity to attenuation. Electro-optical sensors are superior to the other sensors in terms of their classification and identification capabilities due to their much higher resolution; their major disadvantages are their greater susceptibility to atmospheric attenuation and their greater processing demands.

MMW radar and IR: The principal benefits of integrating the information from MMW radar and IR sensors for ATR, as compared to the

Table 16.1. Automatic target recognition sensor comparison[1]

Characteristic	Microwave Radar	Millimeter-Wave Radar	Electro-Optical Sensors
Frequency	MHz (10^6 Hz)	GHz (10^9 Hz)	10^{13} Hz
Wavelength	cm (10^{-2}m)	mm (10^{-3}m)	μm (10^{-6}m)
Characteristic frequency or wavelength	6000 MHz (C-band)	35 or 94 GHz	10.6μm
Mode of operation	active (radar)	active (radar) or passive (radiometric)	active (LADAR) or passive (FLIR)
Aperture (angular resolution)	large antenna (degrees)	small antenna (mr)	small aperture (μr)
Components	large and rugged	small and rugged	small and fragile
Processing requirements	moderate	heavy	very heavy
Detection range[2]	unlimited	10km	5-15km
Attenuation:			
fog and clouds	none	some	high
rain	none	high	high
dust and smoke	none	some	high
Imaging	impractical	possible	excellent
Typical target recognition features	radar cross section polarization	radar cross section polarization range profile[3] velocity[4]	intensity[5] range (LADAR) velocity[4] (LADAR)
Classification or identification	poor	fair	good
Tracking accuracy	fair	fair	good
Search volume	large	medium	small
Covertness	poor	fair	good

[1] Portions adapted from Seashore (1983, Table 1), Hovanessian (1988, Tables 1.1 and 1.6), and Reedy (1987, Table 2.4).
[2] Maximum range in the atmosphere.
[3] High-resolution range and angular profile achieved through the use of pulse compression and monopulse techniques.
[4] The Doppler shift of a signal can be used to determine recognition features such as the characteristic vibrations of a target.
[5] IR provides thermal intensity while LADAR provides signal intensity.

use of only electro-optical sensors, are the increased resistance to atmospheric attenuation and the larger search volume provided by the MMW radar. Hoschette and Seashore (1988) have detailed the design tradeoffs in the configuration of MMW radar and IR sensors used for signal-level fusion on precision-guided munitions. Given current technology, a side-by-side coaligned common boresight configuration of the sensors is easier and less costly to build than a configuration where the sensors share a common aperture, but the latter configuration allows for a smaller packaging volume which is desirable in precision-guided munitions. Eggleston and Kohl (1988) have described a blackboard architecture for the fusion of MMW radar and IR imagery at the symbolic level. Separate tokens are created from the radar and IR feature sets for each potential target. The tokens are passed to the blackboard where they are used to invoke high-level rule-based interpretation strategies that generate target hypotheses using additional a priori knowledge. A master controlling schema is then used to direct the sensors to focus attention on particular regions of interest so that additional information can be obtained.

LADAR and FLIR: The principal advantages of integrating the information from LADAR and FLIR sensors for military ATR applications are the mixture of active and passive modes of operation that this combination provides. In contrast to the integration of MMW radar and FLIR, both of these sensors can operate at the same frequency to provide registered information of equal resolution that can be more easily fused at the pixel level (with the potential for both sensors to share the same optical hardware). Although LADAR alone may be sufficient for accurate recognition due to the high resolution of the three-dimensional target information that it can provide, its active mode of operation makes it more susceptible to enemy countermeasures as compared to a passive FLIR sensor. In most LADAR and FLIR ATR systems the FLIR sensor is used initially to search and detect potential targets due to its passive mode of operation and faster processing speed. A combination of FLIR and LADAR information is then used for recognition, with the LADAR providing information that, unlike FLIR, is independent of a target's changing thermal state.

Hannon and Shapiro (1990) have addressed the problem of optimal target detection through the use of generalized likelihood ratio tests. Quantitative results were obtained through the simulation of pixel-level statistics that prove that the fusion of LADAR and FLIR data nearly always provides for better performance than the exclusive use of either for detection. Nettleson, Fox, Rohde, and Buser (1989) describe the Tri Service Laser Radar (TSLR) developed through the cooperation of the US Army, Navy, and Air Force. The TSLR is an active/passive target acquisition sensor that produces pixel-level registered range, velocity, active signal intensity, and passive thermal intensity (FLIR) images. Filtering followed by pixel-level fusion has been used to provide reliable cues for the detection of transmission wires—a critical task for a low-flying helicopter operating under poor visibility conditions. Selzer and Gutfinger (1988) have developed techniques for recognition using target edges derived from LADAR and FLIR images.

The edges are correlated to a wireframe target model and the resulting correlation coefficients are fused using either Bayesian or Dempster-Shafer methods (see Sections 3.1 and 3.2 of Chapter 8). Experimental results were obtained using an image database containing targets at a variety of different orientations.

Tong, Rogers, Mills, and Kabrisky (1987), Roggemann, Mills, Rogers, and Kabrisky (1988), Rogers, Tong, Kabrisky, and Mills (1989), and Roggemann, Mills, Kabrisky, Rogers, and Tatman (1989) have developed a method of fusing the complementary information provided by LADAR and FLIR sensors to segment and enhance features of man-made objects such as tanks and trucks in a cluttered background. Once separated from the background, these features can then be used by other methods to identify the objects. The LADAR image provides range information for areas within a particular field of view and the FLIR image shows special features of the area. The gradients of both images are used for both object enhancement and segmentation. Boundaries enclosing areas of small range gradient can be used to identify possible objects because natural backgrounds such as mud, grass, and trees exhibit large range differences from one pixel to another that can be modeled as random noise. The gradient of the FLIR image is used to sharpen the infrared signature and temperature characteristics of objects that are infrared sources, and can also serve to identify cold objects in a hot background because only temperature differences are noted. Initially, a binary mask of the LADAR image is created that indicates the location, area, and boundary of possible objects. Assuming objects exhibit small gradients relative to the background and occupy a small percentage of the overall image, the first derivative of the histogram of the gradient magnitudes in the image is used to estimate a threshold for the binary mask. The threshold alone is not discriminatory enough to separate every pixel in the image. To further distinguish object from background pixels, both the segmented infrared and segmented range gradient images are first "anded" pixel to pixel with the mask. The resulting images are then multiplied to produce a final image that shows where the range and infrared gradients match, emphasizing object features and de-emphasizing the background.

FLIR and vision: The integration of the information from FLIR and visual sensors for ATR, like the integration of LADAR and FLIR, offers the possibility of improved registration through the sharing of the same optical hardware, but, unlike LADAR and FLIR, the sensors will necessarily be operating at different frequencies so that simple pixel-by-pixel fusion is not possible. The fusion of thermal (FLIR) and visual images can provide information that is not available in either image alone; for example, targets that have a low visual contrast can sometimes be easily seen in thermal images, whereas visual images can sometimes provide more target details as compared to thermal images if there are larger temperature gradients within the target or the background has a low thermal contrast.

Duane (1988) has discussed the different levels of fusion available for ATR and has demonstrated the potential of pixel-level fusion to improve recognition performance through the fusion of FLIR and TV images of military vehicles. Toet, van Ruyven, and Valeton (1989) have introduced a hierarchical thermal and visual image fusion method that is based on a multiresolution contrast pyramid. The resulting fused images preserve perceptually important details that are characterized by high local luminance contrast. The use of a multiresolution pyramid structure allows corresponding regions in the thermal and visual images to be combined.

4. OVERVIEW

This section presents an overview of the remaining chapters in Part III.

Chapter 17: Nandhakumar and Aggarwal have presented a technique for the classification of objects in outdoor scenes using thermal and visual sensors. A thermal camera is used to acquire an infrared image of a scene and a vision camera is used to acquire an intensity image. Both cameras are adjusted so that their images are in spatial correspondence. Three features are used in a decision tree to label the objects in a scene. The first, the conductive heat flux of each region in the scene, is determined by integrating complementary information provided by both sensors. Although this feature, characterizing the intrinsic thermal behavior of the imaged object, provides the greatest amount of discriminatory information, two additional features are used to identify the objects unambiguously: the surface reflectance of a region as determined from the visual image and the average region temperature as derived from the thermal image. Production rules are used to implement the decision tree. An object label is assigned in the consequent of each rule and logical combinations of heuristically determined intervals for the value of each feature are used in the antecedent. Recent extensions of their work include Nandhakumar and Aggarwal (1988, 1990).

Chapter 18: Allen has developed a robotic object recognition system that uses three-dimensional vision together with active exploratory tactile sensing. The system was developed to recognize common kitchen items like mugs, plates, pitchers, and bowls that had no discernible textures and were homogeneous in color. Recognition of objects like these pose a serious problem for many vision-only recognition systems because of the lack of features that can be used for matching and depth analysis. Through the integration of tactile information with vision, the system is able to obtain information concerning any holes, cavities, or curved surfaces of an object that can be used for its identification.

The model database represents each object in a hierarchical manner that allows the sensory devices to match the models at different levels of detail. The models are independent of viewpoint and scale, and contain relational information that can be used to reduce the searching of the database. Each object is modeled as a collection of components and features: The components correspond to the discernable differences in the surface of the objects, and the features correspond to the objects' holes or cavities. At the lowest level, each surface component is modeled as a grid of bicubic spline curves that form a surface patch. Both holes and cavities are modeled as right cylinders of a constant cross-sectional area—cavities having the additional tribute of depth. The operation of the system includes a five-step recognition cycle and provides for robust viewer-independent object recognition because no a priori viewpoint or orientation of the object is assumed; for example, any identifiable part of the model of an object can be used to invoke a search to verify the remaining surfaces or features of the model needed for recognition. More information concerning the system can be found in Allen (1987).

REFERENCES

Aggarwal, J.K., & Magee, M.J. (1986). Determining motion parameters using intensity guided range sensing. *Pattern Recognition, 19*(2), 169–180.

Allen, P.K. (1987). *Robotic object recognition using vision and touch.* Boston, MA: Kluwer.

Ayache, N., & Faugeras, O.D. (1988). Building, registrating, and fusing noisy visual maps. *International Journal of Robotics Research, 7*(6), 45–65.

Bachman, C.G. (1979). *Laser radar systems and techniques.* Dedham, MA: Artech House.

Ballard, D., & Brown, C. (1982). *Computer vision.* Englewood Cliffs, NJ: Prentice-Hall.

Baran, R.H. (1989). A collective computation approach to automatic target recognition. *Proceedings of the International Joint Conference on Neural Networks,* (pp. I-39–I-44). Washington, DC.

Barnard, S.T., & Fischler, M.A. (1986). Stereo vision. *Encyclopedia of Artificial Intelligence* (pp. 1083–1090). New York: Wiley.

Bastuscheck, C.M. (1988). Automatic model generation from range and intensity images of an object. In P.S. Schenker (Ed.), *Proceedings of the SPIE, vol. 1003, Sensor Fusion: Spatial Reasoning and Scene Interpretation* (pp. 44–51). Cambridge, MA.

Benser, E.T., Cox, J.A., & French, H.B. (1989). Infrared/millimeter wave common-aperture optics. *Optical Engineering, 28*(1), 14–19.

Bhanu, B. (1986). Automatic target recognition: State of the art survey. *IEEE Transactions on Aerospace and Electronic Systems,* AES-22(4), 364–376.

Brown, W.M., & Swonger, C.W. (1989). A prospectus for automatic target recognition. *IEEE Transactions on Aerospace and Electronic Systems,* AES-25(3), 401–410.

Cain, M.P., Stewart, S.A., & Morse, J.B. (1989). Object classification using multispectral sensor data fusion. In C.B. Weaver (Ed.), *Proceedings of the SPIE, vol. 1100, Sensor Fusion II* (pp. 53–61). Orlando, FL.

Castelaz, P.F. (1988). Neural networks in defense applications. *Proceedings of the IEEE International Conference on Neural Networks* (pp. II-473–II-480). San Diego, CA.

Currie, N.C., & Brown, C.E. (Eds.). (1987). *Principles and applications of millimeter-wave radar.* Norwood, MA: Artech House.

Delashmit, W.H. (1989). Present status and future needs for automatic target recognizers. In Y. Lin & R. Srinivassan (Eds.), *Proceedings of the SPIE, vol. 1075, Digital Image Processing Applications* (pp. 373–383).

Delcroix, C.J., & Abidi, M.A. (1988). Fusion of range and intensity edge maps. In P.S. Schenker (Ed.), *Proceedings of the SPIE, vol. 1003, Sensor Fusion: Spatial Reasoning and Scene Interpretation* (pp. 145–152). Cambridge, MA.

Duane, G. (1988). Pixel-level sensor fusion for improved object recognition. In C.W. Weaver (Ed.), *Proceedings of the SPIE, vol. 931, Sensor Fusion* (pp. 180–185). Orlando, FL.

Eaves, J.L., & Reedy, E.K. (Eds.). (1987). *Principles of modern radar.* New York: Van Nostrand.

Eggleston, P.A., & Kohl, C.A. (1988). Symbolic fusion of MMW and IR imagery. In P.S. Schenker (Ed.), *Proceedings of the SPIE, vol. 1003, Sensor Fusion: Spatial Reasoning and Scene Interpretation* (pp. 20–27). Cambridge, MA.

Ezquerra, N.F. (1987). Target recognition considerations. In J.L. Eaves & E.K. Reedy (Eds.), *Principles of modern radar* (pp. 646–677). New York: Van Nostrand.

Faugeras, O.D., Ayache, N., & Faverjon, B. (1986). Building visual maps by combining noisy stereo measurements. *Proceedings of the IEEE Conference on Robotics and Automation* (pp. 1433–1438). San Francisco, CA.

Grimson, W.E.L., & Lozano-Pérez, T. (1984). Model-based recognition and localization from sparse range or tactile data. *International Journal of Robotics Research, 3*(3), 3–35.

Hackett, J.K., & Shah, M. (1989). Segmentation using intensity and range data. *Optical Engineering, 28*(6), 667–674.

Hannon, S.M., & Shapiro, J.H. (1990). Active-passive detection of multipixel targets. In R.J. Becherer (Ed.), *Proceedings of the SPIE, vol. 1222, Laser Radar V* (pp. 2–23). Los Angeles, CA.

Hansen, C., Ayache, N., & Lustman, F. (1988). Efficient depth estimation using trinocular stereo. In P.S. Schenker (Ed.), *Proceedings of the SPIE, vol. 1003, Sensor Fusion: Spatial Reasoning and Scene Interpretation* (pp. 124–131). Cambridge, MA.

Hansen, C., Ayache, N., & Lustman, F. (1990). High speed trinocular stereo for mobile-robot navigation. In J.T. Tou & J.G. Balchen (Eds.), *Highly redundant sensing in robotic systems* (pp. 127–146). Berlin: Springer-Verlag.

Hildreth, E. (1986). Optical flow. *Encyclopedia of artificial intelligence* (pp. 684–687). New York: Wiley.

Hong, L., & Brzakovic, D. (1990). Distributed algorithm for multi-sensor integration applied to 3-D scene reconstruction. *Proceedings of the IEEE International Conference on Robotics and Automation* (pp. 2024–2031). Cincinnati, OH.

Horn, B.K.P. (1986). *Robot vision*. Cambridge, MA: MIT Press.

Hoschette, J.A., & Seashore, C.R. (1988). IR & MMW sensor fusion for precision guided munitions. In C.W. Weaver (Ed.), *Proceedings of the SPIE, vol. 931, Sensor Fusion* (pp. 124–130). Orlando, FL.

Hovanessian, S.A. (1988). *Introduction to sensor systems*. Norwood, MA: Artech House.

Hung, Y.P., Cooper, D.B., & Cernuschi-Frias, B. (1988). Bayesian estimation of 3-D surfaces from a sequence of images. *Proceedings of the IEEE International Conference on Robotics and Automation* (pp. 906–911). Philadelphia, PA.

Klein, L.A., & Kassis, S.Y. (1989). Processing requirements for multi-sensor, low-cost brilliant munitions. In C.B. Weaver (Ed.), *Proceedings of the SPIE, vol. 1100, Sensor Fusion II* (pp. 97–108). Orlando, FL.

Luo, R.C., & Lin, M. (1987). 3-D object recognition using combined overhead and robot eye-in-hand vision system. *Proceedings of the SPEI, vol. 856, IECON: Industrial Applications of Robots and Machine Vision* (pp. 682–689. Cambridge, MA.

Luo, R.C., & Tsai, W. (1986). Object recognition using tactile array sensors. *Proceedings of the IEEE International Conference on Robotics and Automation* (pp. 1248–1253). San Francisco, CA.

Magee, M.J., & Aggarwal, J.K. (1985). Using multisensory images to derive the structure of three-dimensional objects—A review. *Computer Vision, Graphics, and Image Processing, 32*, 145–157.

Magee, M.J., Boyter, B.A., Chien, C., & Aggarwal, J.K. (1985). Experiments in intensity guided range sensing recognition of three-dimensional objects. *IEEE Transactions on Pattern Analysis and Machine Intelligence,* PAMI-7(6), 629–636.

Mitzel, J.H. (1990). Multitarget tracking applied to automatic target recognition with an imaging sensor. In Y. Bar-Shalom (Ed.), *Multitarget-multisensor tracking: Advanced applications* (pp. 297–320). Norwood, MA: Artech House.

Moezzi, S., & Weymouth, T.E. (1990). A model for fusion of spatial information in dynamic vision. *Proceedings of the IEEE International Conference on Robotics and Automation* (pp. 1148–1153). Cincinnati, OH.

Nandhakumar, N., & Aggarwal, J.K. (1988). Thermal and visual information fusion for outdoor scene perception. *Proceedings of the IEEE International Conference on Robotics and Automation* (pp. 1306–1308). Philadelphia, PA.

Nandhakumar, N., & Aggarwal, J.K. (1990). A phenomenological approach to thermal and visual sensor fusion. In J.T. Tou & J.G. Balchen (Eds.), *Highly redundant sensing in robotic systems* (pp. 87–101). Berlin: Springer-Verlag.

Nettleson, J.E., Fox, C.S., Rohde, R.S., & Buser, R.G. (1989). Active/passive infrared imaging. In C. Werner & J.W. Bilbro (Eds.), *Proceedings of the SPIE, vol. 1181, Coherent Laser Radar: Technology and Applications* (pp. 274–284). Munich, FRG.

Pau, L.F. (1982). Fusion of multisensor data in pattern recognition. In J. Kittler, K.S. Fu & L.F. Pau (Eds.), *Pattern recognition theory and applications* (pp. 189–201). Dordrecht, The Netherlands: Reidel.

Pau, L.F., & El Nahas, M.Y. (1983). *An introduction to infrared image acquisition and classification systems.* Letchworth, UK: Research Studies Press.

Pau, L.F. (1988a). Knowledge representation for three-dimensional sensor fusion with context truth maintenance. In A.K. Jain (Ed.), *Real-time object measurement and classification* (pp. 391–404). Berlin: Springer-Verlag.

Pau, L.F. (1988b). Sensor data fusion. *Journal of Intelligent Robots and Systems, 1*, 103–116.

Pau, L.F. (1990). Behavioral knowledge in sensor/data fusion systems. *Journal of Robotic Systems, 7*(3), 295–308.

Reedy, E.K. (1987). Fundamentals of MMW radar systems. In N.C. Currie & C.E. Brown (Eds.), *Principles and applications of millimeter-wave radar* (pp. 19–71). Norwood, MA: Artech House.

Rogers, S.K., Tong, C.W., Kabrisky, M., & Mills, J.P. (1989). Multisensor fusion of ladar and passive imagery for target segmentation. *Optical Engineering, 28*(8), 881–885.

Roggemann, M.C., Mills, J.P., Kabrisky, M., Rogers, S.K., & Tatman, J.A. (1989). An approach to multiple sensor target detection. In C.B. Weaver (Ed.), *Proceedings of the SPIE, vol. 1100, Sensor Fusion II* (pp. 42–52). Orlando, FL.

Roggemann, M.C., Mills, J.P., Rogers, S.K., & Kabrisky, M. (1988). Multisensor information fusion for target detection and classification. In C.W. Weaver (Ed.), *Proceedings of the SPIE, vol. 931, Sensor Fusion* (pp. 8–13). Orlando, FL.

Science Applications International Corp. (1988). *Automatic Target Recognition Panel Report* (Tech. Rep. ET-TAR-002). San Diego, CA.

Seashore, C.R. (1983). mm-wave sensors for missile guidance. *Microwave Journal, 26*(9), 133–144, Sep. 1983.

Selzer, F., & Gutfinger, D. (1988). LADAR and FLIR based sensor fusion for automatic target classification. In P.S. Schenker (Ed.), *Proceedings of the SPIE, vol. 1003, Sensor Fusion: Spatial Reasoning and Scene Interpretation* (pp. 236–246). Cambridge, MA.

Stansfield, S.A. (1986). Primitives, features, and exploratory procedures building a robot tactile perception system. *Proceedings of the IEEE International Conference on Robotics and Automation* (pp. 1274–1279). San Francisco, CA.

Stansfield, S.A. (1987). Visually-aided tactile exploration. *Proceedings of the IEEE International Conference on Robotics and Automation* (pp. 1487–1492). Raleigh, NC.

Stansfield, S.A. (1988a). Representing generic objects for exploration and recognition. *Proceedings of the IEEE International Conference on Robotics and Automation* (pp. 1090–1095). Philadelphia, PA.

Stansfield, S.A. (1988b). A robotic perceptual system utilizing passive vision and active touch. *International Journal of Robotics Research, 7*(6), 138–161.

Stephanou, H.E., & Erkmen, A.M. (1990). Model-based sensory pattern fusion. *Journal of Robotic Systems, 7*(3), 395–418.

Toet, A., van Ruyven, L.J., & Valeton, J.M. (1989). Merging thermal and visual images by a contrast pyramid. *Optical Engineering, 28*(7), 789–792.

Tong, C.W., Rogers, S.K., Mills, J.P., & Kabrisky, M.K. (1987). Multisensor data fusion of laser radar and forward looking infrared (FLIR) for target segmentation and enhancement. In R.G. Buser & F.B. Warren (Eds.), *Proceedings of the SPIE, vol. 782, Infrared Sensors and Sensor Fusion* (pp. 10–19). Orlando, FL.

Wang, Y.F., & Aggarwal, J.K. (1989). Integration of active and passive sensing techniques for representing three-dimensional objects. *IEEE Transactions on Robotics and Automation*, RA-5(4), 460–471.

17
Integrated Analysis of Thermal and Visual Images for Scene Interpretation*

**N. Nandhakumar and
J.K. Aggarwal**

This chapter presents a new approach for computer perceptions of outdoor scenes. The approach is based on integrating information extracted from thermal images and visual images, which provides new information not available by processing either type of image alone. The thermal image is analyzed to provide estimates of surface temperature. The visual image provides surface absorptivity and relative orientation. These parameters are used together to provide estimates of heat fluxes at the surfaces of viewed objects. The thermal behavior of scene objects is described in terms of surface heat fluxes. Features based on estimated values of surface heat fluxes are shown to be more meaningful and specific in distinguishing scene components.

1. INTRODUCTION

We present a new approach for computer perception of natural scenes containing man-made objects. The approach is based on the integra-

---

* It is a pleasure to acknowledge the comments of Dr. K.R. Diller, C.H. Chien, Dr. J.A. Pearce, Z. Ryu, and Dr. A. Mitiche in the preparation of this chapter.

tion of information obtained from thermal (infrared) images and that obtained from visual intensity images. This makes available information that cannot be obtained by processing visual images alone or thermal images alone, and which is useful for the interpretation of images of outdoor scenes. The approach developed identifies the type of information to be extracted from each image and establishes a way of combining this information for this general class of applications.

The task of interpreting images, either visual images alone or thermal images alone, is an underconstrained problem. The thermal image can at best yield estimates of surface temperature, which, in general, is not specific in distinguishing between object classes. The features extracted from visual intensity images also lack the specificity required for uniquely determining the identity of the imaged object. The interpretation of each type of image thus leads to ambiguous inferences about the nature of the objects in the scene. The use of thermal data gathered by an infrared camera, along with the visual image, is seen as a way of resolving some of these ambiguities.

Thermal images are obtained by sensing radiation in the infrared spectrum. The radiation sensed is that which is either emitted by an object, which is at a nonzero absolute temperature, or is reflected by it. The mechanisms that produce thermal images are different from those that produce visual images. The thermal image produced by an object's surface can be interpreted to identify these mechanisms. Thus, thermal images can provide information about the object being imaged which is not available from a visual image.

A great deal of effort has been expended on automated scene analysis using visual images, and some work has been done in recognizing objects in a scene using infrared (IR) images. However, there has been little effort at interpreting thermal images of natural scenes based on a study of the mechanisms that give rise to the differences in the thermal behavior of object surfaces in the scene, nor has there been any effort to integrate information extracted from the two modalities of imaging.

In the new approach presented in this chapter, the principles of heat transfer have been applied to estimate heat fluxes at the surfaces of the objects. Features based on heat flux estimates are shown to describe the thermal behavior of the objects in a more meaningful manner when compared to those (such as shape features and moments) that have traditionally been used. The features are also specific and may be used for delineating classes of objects, such as buildings, pavements, vegetation, and automobiles.

Thermal images are used to deduce temperature at the surface of viewed objects. Visual images are used to provide information about absorptivity and relative orientation of the viewed surface which is needed for correct estimation of the surface heat fluxes.

The remainder of this chapter is organized as follows. In the next section, we review the current literature that discusses related research which is directed towards applying thermal image analysis (viz. thermography) to the detection of objects in a scene. The salient features of the various techniques presented in recent literature are discussed. In Section 3, we establish a quantitative model for measuring object surface temperature using an IR camera. Various factors such as surface absorptivity and emissivity, characteristics of the radiation source, imaging geometry, atmospheric effects, etc., are discussed with the perspective of applying thermography for the perception of outdoor scenes illuminated by bright sunlight. Section 4 contains a discussion of the thermal behavior of various classes of objects in the scene. The thermal behavior is modeled using surface heat fluxes. The estimation of the absorbed, convective, and conductive heat fluxes is described and shown to be useful for distinguishing components of a scene. In Section 5, we describe how information such as surface absorptivity and relative surface orientation is extracted from the visual image. This information is combined with temperature, which is estimated from the thermal image to produce estimates of the surface heat fluxes. Preliminary results of applying the developed approach to labeling regions of segmented thermal images with the aid of information extracted from the corresponding (registered) visual images are presented in Section 6. Real data gathered from naturally occurring scenes are used for the example. Finally, we conclude with a summary and indicate the directions for future work required to extend and implement the approach in an automated system for scene perception.

2. SURVEY OF RELATED RESEARCH

We examine some of the salient features of related research that has recently been reported. The new approach described in this chapter is motivated by the need to overcome some of the failings of the existing techniques.

There have been no reports of research which deals with the integration of information from thermal and visual images for scene interpretation. A great deal of research has been conducted in interpreting visual intensity images of scenes. This work is not reviewed here; instead, the reader is referred to the many books and journals that discuss the state of the art of this field. In contrast, thermographic techniques have been developed only during the past few years and have only recently found use in a variety of applications of image analysis. These include military applications such as autonomous vehicle guidance and surveillance, and civil applications such as home energy audits, fault detection in components, medical diagnoses, astronomy, monitoring of industrial affluents, etc. Most of the work done in automated scene interpretation using thermal images has been of limited scope. It has been directed at the identification of one among a set of tactical military vehicles in a scene. We review below some of the work done in this area.

The development of a system which analyzes thermal images of natural scenes containing man-made objects has been reported (Kim, Payton, & Olin, 1984). The system uses thermal images alone, and visual information is not incorporated into the analysis. The knowledge-based vision system developed uses frames for the representation of knowledge and uses an object-oriented approach. The system is designed to recognize man-made objects from sequential frames of thermal imagery. The approach taken in designing the system, however, does not take into account the unique nature of information available in thermal images. The resulting system therefore resembles one developed for visual image analysis. Features used in the system are based directly on image gray levels. Features and rules for hypothesis generation focus on geometric and spatial information. The thermal behavior of the objects and features arising from the differences in their behavior are ignored. The system thus fails to exploit an important source of knowledge.

A comparison of the design and performance of several algorithms used for the identification of tactical vehicles can be found in several sources (Burton & Benning, 1981; Sevigny, 1981; Sevigny, Hvedstrup-Jensen, Bohner, Ostevold, & Grinaker, 1983; Hinderer, 1981). These algorithms typically use features such as contrast, intensity histograms, magnitude and phase angles of gradient operators, target area, shape features, contour smoothness functions, moments, etc., and Bayesian and nearest neighbor classifiers. The techniques used are simple and straightforward, but suffer from many drawbacks, the performance of the techniques being sensitive to relative orientation of the viewed object, whether or not the object is partially occluded, average scene radiance, etc.

The analysis of IR images of oceanic scenes containing ships is described in Casasent, Pauly, and Felterly (1981) and Keng (1981). The features used for classification are computed directly from image intensity values and include gray level histograms and higher order moments of the thresholded image. A tree classifier has been used for discriminating among tanks, jeeps, armored personnel carriers, and "burning hulks" in IR images (Lin, 1981). The classifier uses two intensity-based features, nine geometric features, and six texture features. A special class of discriminant functions has been proposed for the identification of M-60 tanks in IR images (Hester & Casasent, 1981). The authors claim that the classifier is insensitive to object intensity and geometric difference, but no proof (neither experimental nor theoretical) has been presented to validate the claim. Another algorithm developed to detect tanks in IR images uses features such as contrast, centroid and area of thresholded image, and a template matching scheme (Aguilera, 1980).

We observe that the past research in IR image analysis has dealt mainly with the use of statistical pattern recognition techniques and with features that are computed directly from the image pixel values. This approach suffers from many limitations, a major factor being the minimal amount of information that can be extracted from the image (Nandhakumar & Aggarwal, 1985). In the survey conducted by Sevigny (1981), this factor is presented as the main criticism against the existing IR image analysis systems. One of the conclusions arrived at was the need for a fusion of data from many different sources, and a more general artificial intelligence (AI)-based approach for overcoming the limitations of the existing approach to IR image analysis (Sevigny, 1981).

The approach described in this chapter meets these needs in several ways. The use of principles of heat transfer allows for an analysis of the thermal images that identifies features (such as surface heat fluxes) that are more meaningful when compared to those (such as moments and shape features) that have traditionally been used. Visual images provide additional information not only to complement that extracted from thermal images, but also to supply important parameters needed for correct interpretation of the thermal image. This knowledge-based approach is warranted here due to the complexity in modeling the mechanism that generate the thermal image, and in representing their relationship with the mechanisms that generate the visual image. It is a pragmatic approach for incorporating the large amount of knowledge that is available about the thermal behavior of the objects in the scene, and it facilitates the efficient use of this knowledge for scene analysis. Such an approach, when implemented as a rule-based system, will produce a region classification scheme possessing the advantages of a flexible context-based approach.

3. ESTIMATING TEMPERATURE FROM THERMAL IMAGES

In this section, a quantitative model is established for estimating the surface temperature of a viewed object using the thermal image. The model is based on observations that are unique to the situation where outdoor scenes are illuminated by bright sunlight. The model allows for the use of a simple method for estimating temperature. Later sections will explain how these temperature values are used to estimate surface heat fluxes which are useful in distinguishing scene objects.

It is well known that the spectral distribution of the intensity of radiation emitted by a blackbody is given by Planck's equation (Incropera & De Witt, 1981).

$$I_{\lambda,b}(\lambda, T, \theta, \phi) = \frac{C_1}{\lambda^5(\exp(C_2/\lambda T) - 1)}$$

where $I_{\lambda,b}$ is the spectral intensity of emitted radiation which has units $W/m^2 \cdot sr \cdot \mu m$; λ is the wavelength of the radiation in μm; T is the absolute temperature (K); $C_1 = 3.742 \times 10^8 \ W \cdot \mu m/m^2$; and $C_2 = 1.439 \times 10^4 \ \mu m \cdot K$. Since a blackbody is a diffuse emitter, the emissive power contained in a spectral band (λ_1, λ_2) is given by

$$E_{b_{\lambda_1,\lambda_2}}(T) = \int_{\lambda_1}^{\lambda_2} \frac{C_1}{\lambda^5(\exp(C_2/\lambda T) - 1)} d\lambda$$

and has the units W/m^2.

The thermal camera used has an HgCdTe detector which senses radiation in the 8–12 μm band. The detector, which subtends a nonzero solid angle (ω_c), scans the scene along rasters, and the camera produces a standard RS330 composite video signal.

The radiation received by the IR camera depends not only on object surface temperature, but also on surface emissivity. It has been shown (Incropera & De Witt, 1981) that for conductors, the range of the ratio $r = \epsilon(\theta)/\epsilon_n$ rarely lies outside $1.0 \leq r \leq 1.3$ (where ϵ denotes the emissivity, θ denotes the viewing angle, and ϵ_n denotes the total normal emissivity). The range of r for nonconductors is $0.95 \leq r \leq 1.0$. Hence, surfaces viewed in scenes may be approximated quite reasonably as diffuse emitters. Further, with reference to Table 17.1, a constant value of 0.9 may be chosen for the emissivity of any imaged surface.

Figure 17.1 illustrates the various components that constitute the radiosity J_o of an object's surface in a natural scene. The components are surface emission W_{EM}, reflected solar radiation W_{RS}, and reflection (W_{RO}) of radiation that emanates from other surfaces. The corresponding components of irradiation at the IR detector are given by G_{EM}, G_{RS}, and G_{RO}. The sun may be considered to be a blackbody radiator with a surface temperature of 5672 K (Howell, Bannerot, & Vliet, 1982). Only 0.1 percent of its energy lies in the 8–12 μm band. G_{RS}

Table 17.1. Emmissivity of surfaces commonly found in natural scenes (Incropera & DeWitt, 1981)

Surface Material	Emissivity	Surface material	Emissivity
Asphalt Pavement	0.85 - 0.93	Red Brick	0.93 - 0.96
Wood	0.82 - 0.92	Concrete	0.88 - 0.93
Window Glass	0.90 - 0.95	Black Parson's Paint	0.98
White Acrylic Paint	0.90	White Zinc Oxide Paint	0.92
White Paper	0.92 - 0.97	Sand	0.90
Skin	0.95	Soil	0.93 - 0.96
Rocks	0.88 - 0.95	Vegetation	0.92 - 0.96
Water	0.96		

comprises the portion of this energy which is reflected by the object. The surfaces listed in Table 17.1 are opaque to IR radiation. Therefore, since reflectivity $\rho = 1 - \epsilon$, the surface reflectivities to IR are very low. On the other hand, a large percentage of emission from scene objects lies in the 8–12 μm band since their surface temperatures lie typically between 250 and 350 K. Also, emmissivities are high, and therefore $W_{EM} \gg W_{RS}$. Using a similar argument we have $W_{EM} \gg W_{RO}$, whence $G_{EM} \gg G_{RS}, G_{RO}$.

The above discussion along with Planck's law yields the following expression for object surface radiosity (in W/m^2):

$$J_o = \epsilon_o \int_{\lambda_1}^{\lambda_2} \frac{C_1}{\lambda^5 (\exp(C_2/\lambda T) - 1)} d\lambda \tag{1}$$

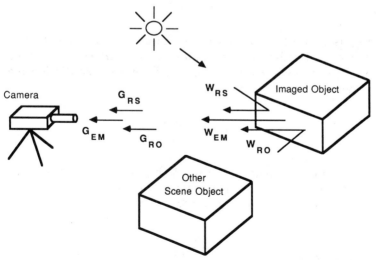

Figure 17.1. Heath exchange between imaged object and camera.

where λ is the wavelength (μm) which is in the range $\lambda_1 = 8$ μm to $\lambda_2 = 12$ μm, and $\epsilon_o = 0.9$ is the emissivity of the surface of the object at temperature T (Kelvin).

The above assumption will not hold in a few special cases, such as where an object in a scene has an internal heat source that produces a high surface temperature. A significant amount of emitted radiation may reflect off surrounding surfaces. Such situations form small regions in the image and can be treated as exceptions to the rule.

If W'_c denotes the radiation (in watts) absorbed by the thermal camera's detector due to imaging the object's surface, we have

$$W'_c = A_c(\alpha_c G'_c - J_c) \tag{2}$$

where A_c, α_c, G_c, and J_c denote the detector's surface area, absorptivity, irradiation (W/m^2), and radiosity (W/m^2), respectively.

In the thermal camera used for our experiments, the radiation from the viewed object is compared to that from an internal reference blackbody target at room temperature. If the irradiation due to the reference target is G''_c and the radiation absorbed by the detector due to this effect is W''_c, then we have

$$W''_c = A_c(\alpha_c G''_c - J_c). \tag{3}$$

The net radiation absorbed by the detector is hence

$$\begin{aligned} W_c &= W'_c - W''_c \\ &= A_c \alpha_c (G'_c - G''_c). \end{aligned} \tag{4}$$

Since ω_c is very small, we have collimated radiation incident on the detector, and therefore we may assume that G'_c arises solely due to the viewed object's surface ratiosity J_o. The detector irradiation may be expressed as

$$G'_c = \frac{J_o A_o F_{oc}}{A_c} \tag{5}$$

Where F_{oc} is the view factor between the detector and the portion of the object's surface that is viewed. In an analogous manner, the irradiation due to the reference target is given by

$$G''_c = \frac{J_r A_r F_{rc}}{A_c} \tag{6}$$

whence we have

$$W_c = \alpha_c(J_o A_o F_{oc} - J_r A_r F_{rc}). \tag{7}$$

We note that for a particular camera, we have complete knowledge of A_r and F_{rc}. Further, while imaging a scene, J_r is constant for all pixels if the reference target is maintained at a constant temperature.

The effect of viewed surface orientation relative to the IR detector has heretofore been ignored in quantitative thermography. We consider this factor in the following analysis. The view factor F_{oc} is, in general, difficult to compute since it depends on the viewing geometry and it involves the evaluation of complex integrals (Siegel & Howell, 1981). It is, however, possible to arrive at a reasonable approximation of F_{oc} by making the following observations with reference to Figure 17.2. Let A_o be the projection of the detector's area onto the surface viewed at a distance d. Let θ_c be the angle between the normal to the viewed surface and the viewing direction. Since the solid angle subtended by the detector θ_c is usually very small (on the order of 2 mrad), we can approximate A_o to be a planar patch. Hence, we have

$$A_o = d^2 \cdot \omega_c/\cos\theta_c. \tag{8}$$

The view factor F_{co} for a circular disk of area A_o with diameter D and at a distance d from an elemental area c has been evaluated to be (Incropera & De Witt, 1981)

$$F_{co} = D^2/(D^2 + 4d^2). \tag{9}$$

When the disk makes an angle of θ_c with the axis drawn to the elemental area and when $d \gg D$, we may make the following first approximation:

$$F_{co} = D^2 \cos\theta_c/4d^2. \tag{10}$$

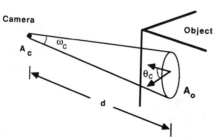

Figure 17.2. View factor between camera and imaged surface.

Using the reciprocity theorem (Incropera & De Witt, 1981) which states that $A_o F_{oc} = A_c F_{co}$, we have

$$F_{oc} = A_c \cos \theta_c / (\pi d^2). \tag{11}$$

Substituting the above results in Eq. 1 and rearranging the terms, we have

$$\int_{\lambda_1}^{\lambda_2} \frac{C_1}{\lambda^5 (\exp(C_2/\lambda T) - 1)} d\lambda = \frac{\pi}{0.9} \frac{(W_c + \alpha_c J_r A_r F_{rc})}{A_c \alpha_c \omega_c}. \tag{12}$$

We observe that on the right-hand side of the above expression, all quantities are known, except for the radiation W_c absorbed by the camera and the radiosity J_r of the reference target. The known quantities remain constant while imaging the scene. If the camera has internal level compensation, then J_r is also constant over time.

The thermal camera produces a voltage output which is directly proportional to the net radiation (W_c) absorbed by the detector. If L_t denotes the resulting gray level of the digitized thermal image, then we have the following relationship:

$$L_t = K_1 W_c + K_2 \tag{13}$$

where K_1 represents the overall gain of the imaging system and K_2 denotes the offset. Combining Eqs. 12 and 13, we can relate the temperature of the imaged surface to the corresponding pixel gray level as

$$\int_{\lambda_1}^{\lambda_2} \frac{C_1}{\lambda^5 (\exp(C_2/\lambda T) - 1)} d\lambda = K_a L_t + K_b \tag{14}$$

where $K_a = \pi/0.9 K_1 A_c \omega_c$ and $K_b = (\pi/0.9 A_c \omega_c)(J_r A_r F_{rc} - K_2/\alpha_c K_1)$. We note that neither the distance from object to camera nor the view factor between the two appear in the above relationship between object temperature and thermal image gray level. The absence of these parameters in the above model allows for the use of a simple method for estimating the scene temperature. The form of Eq. 14 is similar to that used by Ryu and Pearce (1985) for practical measurement of temperatures, and hence their algorithm has been used to measure temperatures in the outdoor scenes imaged in our experiments. At the outset, a table of values of $0.9 \int_{\lambda_1}^{\lambda_2} (C_1/\lambda^5(\exp(C_2/\lambda T) - 1))d\lambda$ is created for various values of T. During the calibration phase, the scene being imaged contains two surfaces at different temperatures, the emissivities and the temperatures of which are known. Eq. 14 is then solved for the two unknowns K_a and K_b. Having thus calibrated the system, the temperature of any visible surface in the scene can be obtained by using the corresponding gray level to evaluate Eq. 14 and looking up the table of values created above for a match.

We have ignored the effect of atmospheric attenuation while deriving the above model. The magnitude of atmospheric attenuation is greatly dependent on the spectral range of the detector. It has been shown that for sensing radiation in the 8–12 μm band, the attenuation is negligible up to a distance of a few hundred meters (Ohman, 1981). If distances are greater, then attenuation may be accounted for by available models (Ohman, 1981; Schott & Biegel, 1983; Jarem, Pierluissi, & Ng, 1984).

4. ESTIMATING AND USING HEAT FLUXES

In this section, the various heat fluxes at the surface of the object are identified and the relationship between them is specified. A method for estimating these heat fluxes is then presented. This method uses values of surface temperature deduced from the thermal image (as described above) and surface reflectivity and relative orientation deduced from the visual image. A feature based on the estimated values of heat fluxes is shown to be meaningful in delineating object classes which differ in their thermal behavior.

The heat exchange at the surface of the object is represented by Figure 17.3 where W_i is the incident solar radiation, θ_i is the angle between the direction of irradiation and the surface normal; the surface temperature is T_s; and W_{abs} is that portion of the irradiation that is absorbed by the surface. W_{cv} denotes the heat convected from the surface to the air which has temperature T_{amb} and velocity V. W_{rad} is the heat lost by the surface to the environment via radiation, and W_{cd} denotes the heat conducted from the surface into the interior of the object. Irradiation at the object surface also includes that emanating from other scene components. The magnitude of this absorbed irradiation is small when compared to total solar irradiation absorbed (in visible and IR bands). The contribution of the former may therefore be ignored. This assumption is violated for surfaces in shadow which are inherently difficult to analyze.

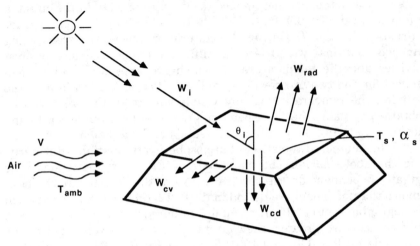

Figure 17.3. Surface heat balance.

At any given instant, an equilibrium is assumed to exist between the heat fluxes flowing into the surface of the object and those flowing out from the surface. We therefore have

$$W_{abs} = W_{cd} + W_{cv} + W_{rad} \tag{15}$$

where $W_{rad} = \epsilon_0 \sigma (T_s^4 - T_{amb}^4)$,

$$W_{abs} = W_i \alpha_s \cos \theta_i, \tag{16}$$

σ denotes the Stefan-Boltzmann constant, and α_s denotes the solar absorptivity of the surface. The convection heat transfer is given by

$$W_{cv} = h(T_s - T_{amb}) \tag{17}$$

where h is the average convection heat transfer coefficient, and depends on the properties of the surrounding air (e.g., velocity, viscosity, temperature, etc.), and on the geometry and the nature of the object's surface. We note that W_{rad} is immediately available when T_{amb} is known since T_s is deduced from the thermal image as discussed in the previous section.

The conduction heat transfer W_{cd} depends on surface conductivity and temperature profile (both spatial and temporal), which, in general, are unknown. However, since W_{cd} is highly dependent on the properties of the object surface, we expect it to be a useful feature for distinguishing objects from each other. We discuss below a method for estimating W_{abs}, W_{cv}, and thence W_{cd}.

In order to estimate the heat flux absorbed by the surface, it is first necessary to determine the magnitude of the incident radiation. The variation of the intensity of solar radiation incident on a horizontal surface on the ground has been modeled by Thepchatri, Johnson, and Matlock (1977) based on the data presented by Strock and Koral (1965). The empirical model accounts for diurnal and seasonal variations. This model is used for specifying W_i. In order to determine W_{abs} from Eq. 16, we need to also know the values of $\cos \theta_i$ and α_s. These values are not available from the thermal image and need to be derived from other sources. We have, for an opaque surface, $\alpha_s = 1 - \rho_s$ where ρ_s is the solar reflectivity of the surface. Since the visual image is produced by differences in surface solar reflectivity and surface orientation, we can obtain $\cos \theta_i$ and α_s from the visual image. In the next section, we describe a method for evaluating these quantities from the visual image. By substituting these values in Eq. 16, W_{abs} can be estimated.

The convective heat flux is obtained by using Eq. 17. The temperature for the object's surface is obtained from the thermal image as described in the previous section. The ambient temperature T_{amb} is known. The problem therefore lies in estimating the average convection heat transfer coefficient h. A plethora of empirical correlations have been established for computing h for various thermal and hydrodynamic conditions (Incropera & De Witt, 1981). In our case, we make the simplifying assumption that the portion of the surface being viewed is flat. This is valid since typical wind velocities are low, 5–15 miles per hour and the flow tends to be mostly laminar. We can therefore use the convection correlations developed for external flow over flat plates (Incropera & De Witt, 1981). The procedure for estimating the convection heat flux is as follows: Knowing the wind velocity and the air temperature, the Reynolds number is computed where the characteristic length of the object is assumed to be 1 m. The value of the Reynolds number determines whether laminar or mixed flow conditions exist. Accordingly, the appropriate correlation is used. The Nusselt number is thus obtained, and thence the convection heat transfer coefficient h. Eq. 17 is now used to provide the estimate of convection heat flux.

Having estimated the convection heat flux, the radiated heat flux, and the absorbed irradiation as described above, the conduction heat flux is then deduced using Eq. 15. We now discuss the thermal behavior of the surfaces of various objects in a natural scene and show how conduction heat flux relates to the type of the object imaged.

We study four broad classes of objects: buildings, vehicles, vegetation, and pavement (both asphalt and concrete). We first outline the mechanisms that determine the magnitude of the conduction heat flux in the different surfaces and then discuss the results of experiments conducted to substantiate the arguments. We show that the ratio W_{cd}/W_{abs} is both a sensitive and a specific feature for categorizing the thermal behavior of objects in outdoor scenes.

The conductive heat flux in pavements depends on many factors. Pavements possess great thermal mass, and consequently, with an increase in depth, the diurnal and seasonal variations in temperature decrease. It has been shown that during periods of strong daylight (10 A.M.–5 P.M.), there exists a large temperature gradient between the surface and the interior of the pavement (Bukowski, Tucker, & Fowler, 1983). This supports large conductive heat flux into the pavement during this period.

The walls of buildings also possess large thermal masses, resulting in considerable lag between the time of maximum irradiation at the outer surface and the time of maximum heat flow into the building from the inner surface (Stamper & Koral, 1979). The large thermal mass of the wall results in large conductive surface heat flux into the wall during periods of strong sunlight.

The bodies of automobiles possess relatively low thermal mass when compared to walls of buildings and pavements. Change in intensity of irradiation results in faster changes in surface temperature. The body of the automobile quickly attains a temperature distribution that is uniform with depth into the metal surface. Hence, during periods of strong solar irradiation, the conduction heat flux is relatively small except momentarily when the surface enters into or leaves a shadow.

While plants absorb a significant percentage of the incident solar radiation, the absorbed energy is not transported via conduction into the leaf structure. The energy absorbed is used for photosynthesis and also for transpiration. Therefore, when we estimate the absorbed solar radiation and subtract from this the convected heat flux, we are left not with the conductive heat flux, but with the flux used for other processes in the plant. Freely transpiring vegetation was found to have a temperature close to the ambient air temperature (Kumar, 1980). Absorptivity to radiation in the visual spectrum (in which solar radiation is concentrated) is high, typically 0.85. This implies that a only a small amount of the absorbed radiation is convected into the air. Therefore, if Eq. 15 is used, the estimate of the conductive heat flux will be almost as large (typically 95 percent) as that of the absorbed heat flux.

In order to verify the expected thermal behavior of surfaces as discussed above, experiments were conducted to estimate the heat fluxes at the surfaces of various objects in outdoor scenes. The temperatures and orientations of the surfaces of building walls, pavements, automobile bodies, and plants were measured at widely spaced intervals of time during bright daylight. The measurements were made with a digital thermometer possessing an accuracy of $\pm 1°C$. The wind velocity was obtained from the daily weather report; the values of solar absorptivity were obtained from Incropera and De Witt (1981), Roshenaw and Hartnett (1973), and Clifford (1984), and the intensity of solar radiation was estimated using the model developed by Thepchatri et al. (1977). These parameters were used to compute the absorbed, radiated, convective, and thence the conductive heat fluxes. The ratio W_{cd}/W_{abs} was computed. The results of the experiments are shown in Tables 17.2, 17.3, and 17.4. The quantity W_{lost} includes the heat loss by

Table 17.2. Temperatures and heat fluxes at 10:30 A.M.*

Surface	Temperature (Centigrade)	Heat Flux (W/m²)			$R =$ Cond. heat Abs. Heat
		Absorbed	Lost	Conducted	
Car					
L. Door	33.4	0	18	−18	
R. Door	39.0	293	90	203	0.69
Roof	42.0	277	129	148	0.53
Front	45.0	195	168	27	0.14
Back	32.7	0	9	−9	
Brick Wall					
Facing North	28.6	0	−39	39	
South	34.8	85	24	61	0.71
East	40.5	413	84	329	0.80
West	31.0	0	−15	15	
Concrete Wall					
Facing North	28.1	0	−44	44	
South	34.4	42	21	21	0.50
East	35.5	206	32	174	0.85
West	30.8	0	−17	17	
Pavement					
Asphalt	42.0	554	129	425	0.77
Concrete	37.0	485	64	421	0.87
Plant Leaf					
Facing North	31.8	0	−6	6	
South	32.5	99	1	98	0.99
East	39.0	482	69	413	0.86
West	31.5	0	−10	10	
Up	32.6	441	1	440	1.0

*The temperatures of the car and pavement were measured in July, the other readings were taken in August.

Table 17.3. Temperatures and heat fluxes at 1:30 P.M.*

Surface	Temperature (Centigrade)	Heat Flux (W/m²)			$R =$ Cond. heat Abs. Heat
		Absorbed	Lost	Conducted	
Car					
L. Door	40.5	0	64	−64	
R. Door	47.0	110	151	−41	−0.37
Roof	55.0	379	270	109	0.29
Front	41.0	0	71	−71	
Back	51.5	82	212	−130	−1.60
Brick Wall					
Facing North	33.5	0	−26	26	
South	41.5	209	64	145	0.69
East	42.0	20	62	−42	−2.10
West	34.9	0	−11	11	
Concrete Wall					
Facing North	33.3	0	−28	28	
South	40.5	104	53	51	0.49
East	39.2	10	38	−28	−2.80
West	34.0	0	−20	20	
Pavement					
Asphalt	51.0	759	205	554	0.73
Concrete	46.5	664	145	519	0.78
Plant Leaf					
Facing North	35.3	0	−6	6	
South	36.0	244	2	242	0.99
East	36.2	24	4	20	0.82
West	36.0	0	2	−2	
Up	36.0	635	2	633	1.0

*The temperatures of the car and pavement were measured in July, the other readings were taken in August.

the surface to the environment via convection W_{cv} and via radiation W_{rad}.

We observe that when the surface is in shadow, the absorbed heat flux is zero and the value of the ratio becomes indeterminate. Also, the ratio W_{cd}/W_{abs} when positive is lowest for the surfaces on the body of the automobile and highest for vegetation. When this ratio is negative, that is, when the surfaces are losing heat due to near grazing angles of incident solar irradiation, the magnitude of this ratio is again lower for surfaces on the body of the automobile and higher for walls of buildings. The values of this ratio for pavements are similar to those for walls of buildings. In short, there is a high degree of correlation between the expected thermal behavior of the components of the scene and the experimentally obtained values. We note also that the ratio

Table 17.4. Temperatures and heat fluxes at 4:30 P.M.*

Surface	Temperature (Centigrade)	Heat Flux (W/m²)			R = Cond. heat / Abs. Heat
		Absorbed	Lost	Conducted	
Car					
L. Door	51.5	200	193	7	0.04
R. Door	40.0	0	39	−39	
Roof	51.7	258	196	62	0.24
Front	37.5	0	6	−6	
Back	54.2	337	230	107	0.32
Brick Wall					
Facing North	34.2	0	−31	31	
South	42.7	142	70	72	0.51
East	36.9	0	4	−4	
West	46.0	326	108	218	0.67
Concrete Wall					
Facing North	33.0	0	−39	39	
South	39.5	71	33	38	0.53
East	35.6	0	−10	10	
West	40.9	163	50	113	0.70
Pavement					
Asphalt	54.0	516	229	287	0.56
Concrete	46.0	451	118	333	0.74
Plant Leaf					
Facing North	37.6	0	12	−12	
South	39.0	165	27	138	0.83
East	36.3	0	−2	2	
West	42.0	380	62	318	0.84
Up	34.8	417	−19	436	1.0

*The temperatures of the car and pavement were measured in July, the other readings were taken in August.

W_{cd}/W_{abs} provides significant information about surfaces studied and is useful for discriminating between the types of objects in the scene.

In Section 6, we present several examples where the segmented thermal images of brightly illuminated outdoor scenes are labeled with values of the above ratio. The specificity of this feature in distinguishing between scene components will be demonstrated.

5. INFERRING SURFACE REFLECTIVITY AND RELATIVE ORIENTATION

The estimation of surface heat fluxes requires the determination of surface temperature which is achieved using the thermal image as described in Section 3. We also need to know for each region the surface solar absorptivity (α_s) and for each pixel the projection of the surface normal along the direction of the irradiation, namely $\cos \theta_i$, where θ_i is the angle between the surface normal and the direction of irradiation. We describe below a method of computing these quantities from the visual image. In the following discussion, we assume that the thermal and visual images are spatially registered; that is, a pixel at location (m, n) in the thermal image and the pixel at location (m, n) in the visual image correspond to the same portion of the viewed surface in the scene.

A smooth opaque object gives rise to a shaded image in which brightness varies spatially, even though the object is illuminated evenly and the surface color and texture are uniform. The use of shading information to recover the shape of the object has been exploited in machine vision by Horn and Sjoberg (1979), Horn (1981), Woodham (1981), and others. Ikeuchi has proposed a numerical relaxation algorithm which obviates the additional view required by Woodham's technique (Ikeuchi & Horn, 1981). The above techniques can be applied only if certain conditions are satisifed. The bidirectional reflectance distribution function (Nicodemos, Richmond, Hsia, Ginsberg, & Limperis, 1977) of the surface must be known a priori. Ikeuchi's algorithm further requires that the image resolution be high enough to allow the rendition of several surface patches near the occluding boundary. These conditions are difficult to satisfy when imaging objects in a natural scene. We also note that while the aforesaid efforts attempt the problem of determining the surface normals of the object in 3-D space, our problem is to arrive at an accurate estimate of $\cos \theta_i$ which contains less information when compared to the surface normal. We therefore use a simple, more direct method for computing α_s and $\cos \theta_i$.

Real surfaces, in general, exhibit a combination of diffuse and specular reflectivity. The Lambertian surface is a good approximation for nonglossy surfaces such as those typically found in natural scenes. Hence, if L_v represents the digitized value of the intensity of the visual image, we have

$$L_v = K_o \cos \theta_i + C_v \tag{18}$$

and

$$K_\rho = \rho K_v \tag{19}$$

where ρ is the reflectivity of the surface to visual radiation, $\rho = 1 - \alpha_s$, and K_v and C_v are the overall gain and offset of the visual imaging system. Both K_v and C_v are fixed for a given camera calibration. These quantities are determined experimentally as follows. The camera aperture, system gain, and black level offset are first set for the scene being imaged. The digitized gray-level value is noted for two surfaces of known reflectivity and orientation. Substituting these values in Eq. 18, we solve for K_ρ and C_v. Eq. 19 then gives us K_v. Having calibrated the visual imaging system, we now proceed to analyze the imaged scene.

It is possible to obtain, either via active methods such as laser/sonar ranging (Besl & Jain, 1985) or via passive methods such as stereoscopy (Kim & Aggarwal, 1985), the orientation of one elemental surface patch in the entire surface that is represented by a given image region. We assume that this orientation for one elemental patch (such as at one pixel in the image) is given for each image region. We use this to compute the value of $\cos \theta_i$ for the remaining pixels in the image region as follows. Given $\cos \theta_i$ for an elemental area of the surface represented by a region in an image where the elemental area corresponds to a particular pixel in that region, the gray level of the pixel is used to compute the value of K_ρ from Eq. 18. ρ is then evaluated from Eq. 19, and therefore $\alpha_s = 1 - \rho$ is obtained for the entire region. Once K_ρ is known for the region, we use Eq. 18 at each pixel in that region to compute the corresponding value of $\cos \theta_i$. This procedure is repeated for each region in the image.

The assumption that viewed surfaces are opaque and Lambertian is sometimes violated by the presence of transparent objects (e.g., glass windows) or regions of specular reflection (e.g., a polished surface). however, as illustrated in the following section, such regions in the image are usually small, and the misinterpretation of these regions (or portions of these regions) will not lead to gross errors in image interpretation.

We note here that the problem lies primarily in estimating the reflectivity of a region. Once the reflectivity is known, the value of $\cos \theta_i$ for every pixel in that region may easily be obtained from Eq. 18. The above approach may be substituted by any other known technique for estimating region reflectivity.

6. SCENE INTERPRETATION USING THERMAL AND VISUAL IMAGES

We discuss the application of the approach developed in previous sections for the interpretation of the thermal image and the corresponding visual image of an outdoor scene. The usefulness of estimating the various heat fluxes and of determining the ratio W_{cd}/W_{abs} is illustrated by applying the techniques developed to several examples. Real data are used for each example. The data were gathered from naturally occurring scenes and were obtained at different times of the day and during different seasons of the year.

The developed approach which integrates information from the thermal and visual images of a scene is represented schematically by the block diagram in Figure 17.4. The various components represent the techniques developed in the previous sections. Surface temperature of the viewed object is inferred using the thermal image. This information, along with knowledge of ambient air temperature, allows for the estimation of the radiation heat loss at the surface. Convection heat loss is computed with the knowledge of wind speed, air temperature, and surface temperature. Knowledge of the time and date of data acquisition allows for the determination of the magnitude and direc-

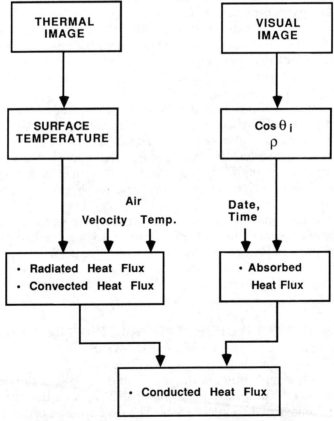

Figure 17.4. Overview of the developed approach.

tion of solar irradiation. The visual image provides surface reflectivity and relative orientation, which, when combined with solar irradiation information, allows for the estimation of the absorbed heat flux. Finally, using the surface heat balance model, the conductive heat flux and thence the ratio W_{cd}/W_{abs} is computed.

Figure 17.5 shows the visual image of a scene (henceforth referred to as Scene-X) imaged at 3:30 P.M. in July. The ambient air temperature was 32.5°C. The scene consists of a car parked on an asphalt pavement in front of a building. The building is constructed of brick walls joined by concrete pillars at the corners. Figure 17.6 shows the thermal image and Figure 17.7 shows the result of the segmented image which is generated by an interactive computer program.

While acquiring the thermal and visual images, an attempt was made to spatially register the two images as closely as possible. This was effected by choosing a set of fiducial points that were visible both in the thermal and visual images and then ensuring that their positions coincided. As can be seen, the registration is not perfect. This was due to the low contrast and the amorphous nature of the thermal image which precludes the discernment of distinct fiducial points for registration. The situation was worsened by the low contrast of the

Figure 17.5. Visual image of Scene-X.

Figure 17.6. Thermal image of Scene-X.

Figure 17.7. Interactively segmented thermal image of Scene-X.

monitor which was placed in the brightly lit environment. However, the error in registration does not cause serious problems, and is acceptable, especially in the interior of a region.

The direction of solar irradiation, the surface normal at selected ponts on objects, and the direction of the camera axis were measured manually. The thermal imaging system was first calibrated using the procedure outlined in Section 3. The temperatures at a point on the asphalt surface and at a point on the concrete pillar were measured with a digital thermometer and these points served as the reference target areas. The temperatures and the corresponding gray levels of the thermal image at these points were used in Eq. 14 to solve for K_a and K_b. The temperatures of the regions were computed at every point in the thermal image by substituting the corresponding gray level into Eq. 14.

The visual gray levels at the selected reference target areas were used to calibrate the visual imaging system. From known values of $\cos \theta_i$ and ρ at these points, Eqs. 18 and 19 were solved for K_v and C_v. The value of $\cos \theta_i$ was manually determined for one point in each region of the segmented thermal image. Eqs. 18 and 19 give the value of ρ and therefore α_s for each region. Determining the value of $\cos \theta_i$ at every pixel in the thermal image involved the use of the value of α_s determined above for that region and the substitution of this value and the corresponding visual gray level into Eqs. 18 and 19.

The values of scene temperature, $\cos \theta_i$, and α_s are thus available at every pixel of the thermal image. The various heat fluxes are estimated using the methods outlined in previous sections. The ratio W_{cd}/W_{abs} is then computed. The values obtained at various pixels of the thermal image are shown in Figure 17.8. The lowest values of this ratio are those obtained on the surface of the car, and they range from 0.02 to 0.33, which are as expected. The values for the asphalt pavement and the building wall are considerably higher. The concrete pillar produces values between 0.86 and 0.87. The brick wall produces slightly lower values, ranging from 0.76 to 0.81, and the asphalt pavement produces values that are even lower, ranging between 0.71 and 0.73. The values of the above ratio are not available in regions that are in shadow and interpretation of these regions must be based on other sources of information.

Figures 17.9, 17.10, and 17.11 represent Scene-Y imaged at 12:30 P.M. in early March when ambient temperature was only 18.5°C. Figure 17.12 shows the result of computing the values of W_{cd}/W_{abs} at the different pixels of the thermal image. Although Scene-X and Scene-Y were imaged in widely differing ambient conditions, the results are similar. The lowest values of the ratio for Scene-Y are also found on

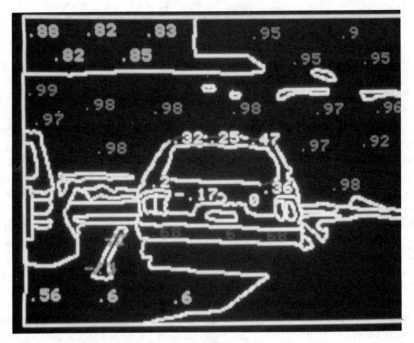

Figure 17.8. Ratio of conducted heat flux to absorbed heat flux for Scene-X imaged at 3:30 P.M. in July.

Figure 17.9. Visual image of Scene-Y.

Figure 17.10. Thermal image of Scene-Y.

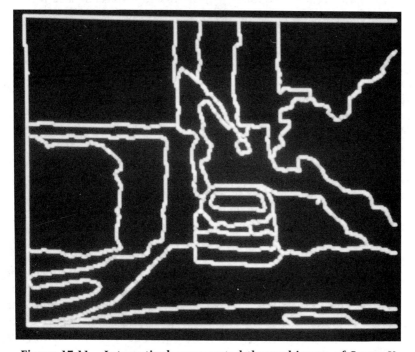

Figure 17.11. Interactively segmented thermal image of Scene-Y.

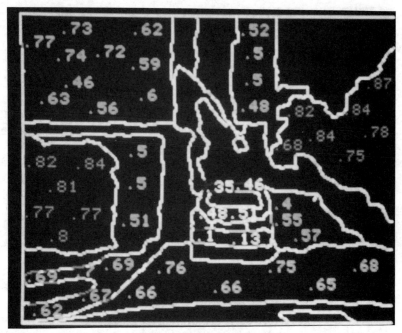

Figure 17.12. Ratio of conducted heat flux to absorbed heat flux for Scene-Y imaged at 12:30 P.M. in early March.

the body of the automobile. Vegetation produces the highest values, while building walls and pavement produce medium values of the ratio. We also note that there exists a narrow band of specular reflection on the body of the automobile. This violates the assumption of Lambertian behavior and hence produces relatively high values of W_{cd}/W_{abs}. However, this will not lead to a wrong inference about the nature of the object since the majority of the pixels in that region have very low values of the ratio. When inference is based on the mode of the distribution of the computed values, small areas such as these which violate the assumptions will not cause wrong interpretations.

Figures 17.13, 17.14, and 17.15 represent Scene-Z imaged at 1:30 P.M. in March when ambient temperature was 19.5°C. Figure 17.16 shows values of the ratio W_{cd}/W_{abs} at various pixels of the thermal image. As before, regions representing vegetation produce the largest values of the ratio, while the surface of the automobile produces the smallest values. The building walls and pavement produce medium values. Some of the values are negative. The rationale presented in Section 4 is tenable here; that is, the magnitudes of the negative values are lower for automobile bodies and higher for the pavement. Note

Analysis of Thermal and Visual Images for Scene Interpretation 401

Figure 17.13. Visual image of Scene-Z.

Figure 17.14. Thermal image of Scene-Z.

Figure 17.15. Interactively segmented thermal image of Scene-Z.

also in this example the relatively high values obtained on the rear bumper (which is chrome plated). Here again, the assumption regarding Lambertian behavior of the surface is violated. The region is, however, relatively small and will not produce serious (viz. pervasive) errors in interpretation.

The examples show that the estimation of surface heat fluxes is indeed a useful approach in interpreting thermal and visual images of outdoor scenes, and makes available features such as the ratio defined above that are meaningful discriminants of thermal behavior. Although the ranges for the values of W_{cd}/W_{abs} for the various object classes do not significantly overlap with each other, the limits of each range vary with the time of the day and the season of the year. The specification of the limits of these ranges and the establishment of rules to use the value of the ratio W_{cd}/W_{abs} for automated scene interpretation will be areas of future research.

7. CONCLUSION

We have described research that will provide a new dimension for systems that implement automatic perception of natural scenes. A

Analysis of Thermal and Visual Images for Scene Interpretation 403

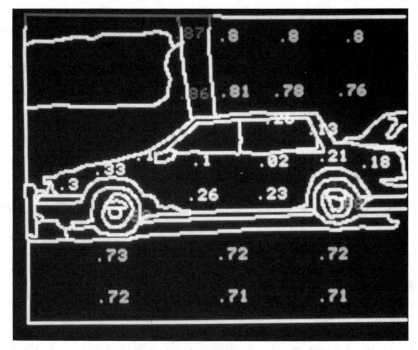

Figure 17.16. Ratio of conducted heat flux to absorbed heat flux for Scene-Z imaged at 1:30 P.M. in March.

general approach has been developed based on the integration of information obtained from thermal images and that obtained from visual images. The mechanisms that produce thermal images are seen to be very different from those that produce visual images. Thus, thermal images provide information about the object being imaged which is not available from a visual image. Also, combining information from the two modalities provides information that was heretofore unavailable.

The approach developed uses features based on estimates of heat fluxes at the surface of scene components. The estimation of heat fluxes involved modeling heat exchange between object, the scene, and the camera. Suitable simplifying assumptions were made about parameters such as object–surface emissivity and radiosity. The assumptions used were for outdoor scenes illuminated by bright sunlight. This related in a simple method for measuring the temperature. The thermal behavior of various classes of objects in the scene were studied. The measurement of the absorbed, convective, radiated, and conductive heat fluxes was shown to be useful for distinguishing components of a scene, such as vehicles from roads and buildings.

The determination of the various heat fluxes at the surface of an object requires the knowledge of, among other parameters, the surface absorptivity and the surface orientation relative to the source of illumination. A method was described for obtaining surface absorptivity and surface orientation from the visual image. The suggested method requires that the relative surface orientation of one elemental surface patch (corresponding to a pixel) be provided a priori, for example, by stereoscopic or active lighting techniques. If the application domain does not facilitate accurate estimation of this value, then the region reflectivity will have to be estimated by other means. The development of heursitic methods to estimate surface reflectivity is one promising avenue that needs to be explored.

The approach outlined above requires registered thermal and visual images. Also, the thermal image was assumed to be segmented into regions. This immediately raises the issue of how segmentation of the thermal image is related to the visual image. We note that large differences in surface radiosity arise either due to different temperatures or due to significant differences in surface absorptivity or both. Consider two adjacent surfaces that exhibit markedly different radiosity resulting in their segmentation in the thermal image. It is unlikely that these are physically connected surfaces which possess identical surface properties but different temperatures. These two surfaces are either physically distinct or possess different surface absorptivities. Therefore, segmentation in the thermal domain is also meaningful when examined from the visual domain, especially because both images are spatially registered. The problem of automatic segmentation of the thermal image has not been addressed in this chapter since it is a major topic of research in itself. Any reliable segmentation algorithm may be used.

To illustrate the application of the approach, the techniques developed for scene interpretation using the thermal and visual images of the scene were applied to real data gathered from brightly lit outdoor scenes. This produced labeled images in which the scene components were distinguishable. The preliminary work reported above opens several avenues for further research. In the examples shown above, the scenes were labeled with the values of one feature, that is, the ratio W_{cd}/W_{abs}. The variation with the time of the day and with the season of the year in the value of this ratio for a particular class of objects needs to be analyzed and accounted for in the scheme for classification. Other sources of information also need to be incorporated, such as color, position, size, etc. Future work will also focus on the implementation of the above approach as a rule-based system. This will facilitate the use of different types of information, extracted from thermal and visual images, and provide an integrated system for scene perception.

We finally conclude by observing that the research described above has shown the usefulness of integrating thermal and visual information for scene analysis and has addressed many issues involved in the suggested approach. Several issues remain to be addressed in the design of a general-purpose system for automated scene perception using such an approach. We have indicated these issues and suggested directions for future research in this area.

REFERENCES

Aguilera, R.A. (1980). Advanced IR image seeker program. *Proceedings of the SPIE, vol. 253* (pp. 58–64).

Besl, P., & Jain, R. (1985). Range image understanding. *Proceedings of the IEEE Conference on Computer Vision and Pattern Recognition* (pp. 430–449). San Francisco, CA.

Bukowski, M.E., Tucker, R.L., & Fowler, D.W. (1983, April). *Detection of voids underneath concrete pavements using infrared thermography* (Tech. Rep. 246-2). University of Texas, Austin: Center for Transportation Research.

Burton, M., & Benning, C. (1981). Comparison of imaging infrared detection algorithms. *Proceedings of the SPIE 25th International Symposium, vol. 302* (pp. 26–32). San Diego, CA.

Casasent, D., Pauly, J., & Felterly, D. (1981). Infrared ship classification using a new moment pattern recognition concept. *Proceedings of the SPIE 25th International Symposium, vol. 302* (pp. 126–133). San Diego, CA.

Clifford, G.E. (1984). *Heating, ventilating and air conditioning.* Reston, VA: Reston Publishing.

Hester, C.F., & Casasent, D. (1981). Interclass discrimination using synthetic discriminant functions (SFDs). *Proceedings of the SPIE 25th International Symposium, vol. 302* (pp. 108–116). San Diego, CA.

Hinderer, J. (1981). Model for generating synthetic 3-D images of small vehicles. *Proceedings of the SPIE, vol. 302* (pp. 8–13). San Diego, CA.

Horn, B.K.P. (1981). Hill shading and the reflectance map. *Proceedings of the IEEE, 69*(1), 14–47.

Horn, B.K.P., & Sjoberg, R.W. (1979). Calculating the reflectance map. *Applied Optics, 18*(1), 1770–1779.

Howell, J.R., Bannerot, R.B., & Vliet, G. C. (1982). *Solar thermal energy systems: Analysis and design.* New York: McGraw-Hill.

Ikeuchi, K., & Horn, B.K.P. (1981). Numerical shape from shading and occluding boundaries. *Artificial Intelligence, 17,* 141–184.

Incropera, F.P., & De Witt, D.P. (1981). *Fundamentals of heat transfer.* New York: Wiley.

Jarem, J.M., Pierluissi, J.H., & Ng, W.W. (1984). A transmittance model for atmospheric methane. In I.J. Spiro & R.A. Mollicone (Eds.), *Proceedings of the SPIE, vol. 510, Infrared Technology X* (pp. 94–99). San Diego, CA.

Keng, J. (1981). Automatic ship recognition using a passive radiometric sensor.

Proceedings of the SPIE 25th International Symposium, vol. 302 (pp. 122–125). San Diego, CA.

Kim, J.H., Payton, D.W., & Olin, K.E. (1984). An expert system for object recognition in natural scenes. *Proceedings of the 1st Conference on Artificial Intelligence Applications* (pp. 170–175). Denver, CO.

Kim, Y.C., & Aggarwal, J.K. (1985). Finding range from stereo images. *Proceedings of the IEEE Conference on Computer Vision and Pattern Recognition* (pp. 289–294). San Francisco, CA.

Kumar, M. (1980). Use of reflectivity ratios to measure light interception by crops. *Proceedings of the SPIE, vol. 234* (pp. 77–81).

Lin, Y.J. (1981). Feature analysis for forward looking infrared (FLIR) target identification. *Proceedings of the SPIE 25th International Symposium, vol. 302* (pp. 117–121). San Diego, CA.

Nandhakumar, N., & Aggarwal, J.K. (1985). The artificial intelligence approach to pattern recognition—A perspective and an overview. *Pattern Recognition, 18*(6), 383–389.

Nicodemus, F.E., Richmond, J.C., Hsia, J.J., Ginsberg, I.W., & Limperis, T. (1977). *Geometrical considerations and nomenclature for reflectance* (NBS Monograph 160). U.S. National Bureau of Standards.

Ohman, C. (1981). Practical methods for improving thermal measurements. *Proceedings of the SPIE, vol. 313* (pp. 204–212).

Roshenaw, W.M., & Hartnett, J.R. (1973). *Handbook of heat transfer.* New York: McGraw-Hill.

Ryu, Z.M., & Pearce, J.A. (1985, June). Private communications.

Schott, J.R., & Biegel, J.D. (1983). Comparison of modelled and empirical atmospheric propagation data. In I.J. Spiro & R.A. Mollicone (Eds.), *Proceedings of the SPIE, vol. 430, Infrared Technology IX* (pp. 45–52). San Diego, CA.

Sevigny, L. (1981). *Evaluation of a class of segmenters for IR imagery* (Tech. Rep. DREV R-4172/80). Valcartier, Canada: Defense Research Establishment.

Sevigny, L., Hvedstrup-Jensen, G., Bohner, M., Ostevold, E., & Grinaker, S. (1983). Discrimination and classification of vehicles in natural scenes from thermal imagery. *Computer Vision, Graphics, and Image Processing, 24,* 229–243.

Siegel, R., & Howell, J.R. (1981). *Thermal radiation heat transfer* (2nd ed.). New York: McGraw-Hill.

Stamper, E., & Koral, L. (Eds.). (1979). *Handbook of air conditioning, heating and ventilating* (3rd ed.). New York: Industrial Press.

Strock, C., & Koral, R.L. (1965). *Handbook of air conditioning, heating and ventilating* (2nd ed.). New York: Industrial Press.

Thepchatri, T., Johnson, C.P., & Matlock, H. (1977). *Prediction of temperature and stresses in highway bridges by a numerical procedure using daily weather reports* (Tech. Rep. 23-1). University of Texas, Austin: Center for Highway Research.

Woodham, R.J. (1981). Analysing images of curved surfaces. *Artificial Intelligence, 17,* 117–140.

18
Integrating Vision and Touch for Object Recognition Tasks*

Peter K. Allen

A robotic system for object recognition is described in this chapter that uses passive stereo vision and active exploratory tactile sensing. The complementary nature of these sensing modalities allows the system to discover the underlying 3-D structure of the objects to be recognized. This structure is embodied in rich, hierarchical, viewpoint-independent 3-D models of the objects which include curved surfaces, concavities and holes. The vision processing provides sparse 3-D data about regions of interest that are then actively explored by the tactile sensor mounted on the end of a six-degree-of-freedom manipulator. A robust, hierarchical procedure has been developed to integrate the visual and tactile data into accurate 3-D surface and feature primitives. This integration of vision and touch provides geometric measures of the surfaces and features that are used in a matching phase to find model objects that are consistent with the sensory data. Methods for verification of the hypothesis are presented, including the sensing of visually occluded areas with the tactile sensor. A number of experiments have been performed using real sensors and real, noisy data to demonstrate the utility of these methods and the ability of such a system to recognize objects that would be difficult for a system using vision alone.

---

* This work was supported in part by: NSF grant MCS 82-07294, Air Force grant AFOSR 82-NM-299, NIH grant 5-RO1-HL-29985-02, DEC Corp., Lord Corp. and IBM Corp.

1. INTRODUCTION

There is at present much work going on in the area of sensor design for robotics. Range finders, tactile sensors, force/torque sensors, and other sensors are actively being developed. The challenge to the robotic system builder is to incorporate these sensors into a system and to make use of the data provided by them. Much of the sensor-related work in robotics has tried to use a single sensor to determine the structure of objects in an environment (Agin, 1972; Shapiro, Moriarty, Haralick, & Mulgaonkar, 1981; Hillis, 1982; Bolles, Horaud, & Hannah, 1983; Fisher, 1983; Grimson & Lozano-Perez, 1983; Oshima & Shirai, 1983; Overton, 1984; Tomita & Kanade, 1984). This strategy seems unduly restrictive given the availability of multiple sensing devices. For robotic tasks such as object recognition, in which shape determination of 3-D objects is required, multiple sensors can be used in a complementary fashion to extract more information, in a more reliable way, than with a single sensor (e.g., machine vision) strategy (Nitzan, 1981; Shneier, Nagalia, Albus, & Haar, 1982). If vision sensing can be supplemented with other sensing information that directly measures shape, more robust and error-free descriptions of object structure can result (Allen, 1985).

Many important issues are involved in sensor integration for robotics. Among these are establishing a framework to include new and different sensors, establishing communication and control pathways between the various sensor subsystems, methods for dealing with noise, error, and conflict in sensory data, and planning strategies for intelligent use of the sensors. This chapter is an examination of these issues within the context of integrating vision and tactile sensing for the task of object recognition. Vision sensing was chosen because of its great promise as a robotic sensor and its use by humans in recognition tasks. Tactile sensing was chosen because it is a low-cost robotic sensor that can directly sense the position and orientation of objects we desire without regard to visual occlusion. It is a necessary component of any manipulation or assembly system, and this chapter motivates touch as a natural companion of vision for object recognition.

The paradigm used in this work is model-based object recognition in which one of a particular set of known object models is chosen based upon sensory feedback. Figure 18.1 is an overview of the system. The system is divided into six main modules: vision sensing, tactile sensing, sensor integration, matching, verification, and the model database. The control flow in the recognition cycle is as follows:

1. The vision system images the scene and analyzes all identifiable regions of interest.

2. The tactile system explores each region identified from vision.
3. The results of the tactile and visual sensing are integrated into surface and feature descriptions.
4. The surface and feature descriptions are matched against the model database, trying to invoke a model consistent with the sensory information.
5. The invoked model is verified by further sensing to see if it is correct.

The experimental hardware is shown in Figure 18.2. The objects to be recognized are rigidly fixed to a work-table and imaged by a pair of CCD cameras. The tactile sensor is mounted on a six-degree-of-freedom PUMA 560 manipulator that receives feedback from the tactile sensor and is further controlled by a host processor. The experimental object domain is made up of common kitchen items: mugs, plates, bowls, pitchers, and utensils. The objects are planar as well as volumetric, contain holes, and have concave and convex surfaces. These are fairly complex objects which test the modeling and recognition abilities of most existing systems. The objects are homogeneous in color with no discernible textures. The lack of surface detail on these objects poses serious problems for many visual recognition systems,

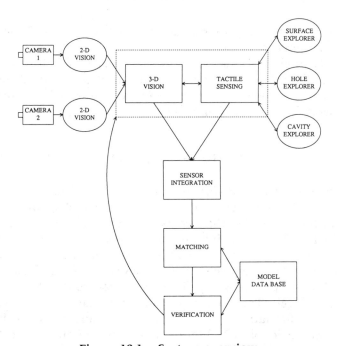

Figure 18.1. System overview.

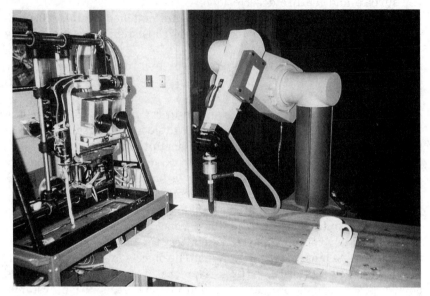

Figure 18.2. Experimental hardware.

since there is a lack of potential features that can be used for matching and depth analysis.

The remainder of this paper is organized as follows: Sections 2 through 7 describe the system's modules in detail, and Section 8 reports experimental results from sensing and recognizing a number of real objects from the kitchen domain.

2. MODEL DATABASE

The model database encodes the high-level knowledge about the objects which is needed for recognition. The global structure of the objects which is encoded in the models is used to understand and place in context the low-level sensing information. Objects are modeled as collections of surfaces, features, and relations organized into four distinct hierarchic levels. A hierarchic model allows us to do matching on many different levels, providing support or inhibition for a match from lower and higher levels. The models are viewpoint independent and contain relational information that further constrains matches between sensed and model objects. Figure 18.3 shows the hierarchical model

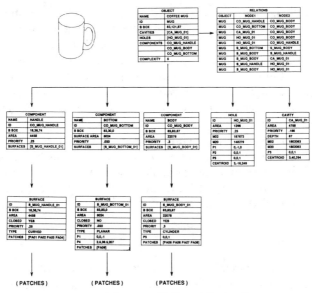

Figure 18.3. Object modeling of a coffee mug.

structure for a coffee mug, outlining the decomposition and structure of the models.

The top level of the hierarchy is composed of a list of all object nodes in the database. An object node corresponds to an instance of a single rigid object. Associated with this node is a list of all the components (subparts) and features (holes, cavities) of this object which make up the next level of the hierarchy. For gross shape classification, a bounding box volumetric description of the object is included. A complexity attribute is also included for each object. This is a measure of the number of features and components that comprise an object, and it is used by the matching rules to distinguish competing matches.

2.1. Components

The component nodes are the result of a functional and geometric decomposition of an object. The components of a coffee mug are the body of the mug, the bottom of the mug, and the handle. A teapot consists of a body, bottom, spout, handle, and lid. Each component has an attribute list consisting of its bounding box, surface area, and priority. The priority field is an aid for recognition in which the components are ordered as to their likelihood of being sensed. High priorities are assigned large components or isolated components in space that protrude (handles, spouts). The protruding parts may show up as outliers from the vision analysis. Obscured components, such as a coffee mug bottom, when in a normal pose, are assigned lower priorities. If the object is in a regular pose, then certain parts of the object are more prominent, which can aid the matching process. Each component node contains a list of one or more surfaces that make up this functional component and that constitute the next level of the hierarchy.

The subdivision of an object by function as well as geometry is important. In some sense, what determines a coffee mug is that it holds a hot liquid, in addition to having some familiar geometric shape. While no explicit attempt has been made here to exploit the semantic structure of objects, the model maintains a node level in the hierarchy should this be attempted.

2.2. Features

Rock (1983) has shown that features are important in recognition tasks for humans. The features modeled in the database are holes and cavities. Holes are modeled as right cylinders with constant arbitrary cross-section occupying a negative volume. Holes can be thought of as having an approach axis which is perpendicular to the hole's planar cross-section. Modeling holes as a negative volumetric entity has implications in matching. Volumetric elements have an object-centered coordinate system that contains an invariant set of orthogonal axes (inertial axes). If the sensors can discover these axes, a transformation between model and world coordinates is defined, which is a requirement of viewpoint-independent matching.

Each hole node contains a coordinate frame that defines the hole. This frame contains a set of orthogonal axes which are the basis vectors for the frame. The hole coordinate frame is defined by the homogeneous matrix H:

$$H = \begin{bmatrix} P_{1x} & P_{2x} & P_{3x} & C_x \\ P_{1y} & P_{2y} & P_{3y} & C_y \\ P_{1z} & P_{2z} & P_{3z} & C_z \\ 0 & 0 & 0 & 1 \end{bmatrix},$$

where

$\mathbf{P}_1$ is the axis of maximum inertia of the hole's planar cross-section.

$\mathbf{P}_2$ is the axis of minimum inertia of the hole's planar cross-section.

P_3 is the normal to the hole's planar cross-section.
C is the centroid of the hole's planar cross-section.

Besides the coordinate frame, each feature has a set of moments of order 2 that are derived from the planar cross-section of the feature's opening.

Cavities are features that are similar to holes but may only be entered from one direction, whereas holes can be entered from either end along their axis. An example is the cavity in the coffee mug where the liquid is poured. Cavities have the additional attribute of depth, which is the distance along the cavity's approach axis from the cavity's opening to the surface below.

2.3. Surface Level

The surface level consists of surface nodes that embody the constituent surfaces of a component of the object. The object's components are decomposed by continuity constraints into a number of smooth, continuous surfaces. Each surface contains as attributes a list of bicubic patches that further subdivide it; bounding box, surface area, a flag indicating whether the surface is closed, and a symbolic description of the surface as planar, cylindrical, or curved. For planar surfaces, a partial coordinate frame is described which consists of the centroid of the plane and the plane's outward-facing unit normal vector. For a cylinder, the partial frame consists of the cylinder's axis.

2.4. Patch Level

The particular form of surface patch used in this research is a bicubic patch known as a Coons' patch (Faux & Pratt, 1979). A Coons' patch P is a parametric surface that can be defined as

$$P(u, v) = \sum_{i=0}^{3} \sum_{j=0}^{3} A_i(u)B_j(v)Q_{ij},$$

where A_i and B_j are the blending functions of the patch and Q_{ij} are coefficients computed from patch data. This patch has been used extensively in computer graphics, computer-aided design systems, and object modeling (York, 1981; Potmesil, 1982). It possesses important features which make it desirable as a 3-D primitive for modeling and for synthesizing surfaces from sensory data. They are interpolating patches constructed from sparse sets of data defined on an arbitrary rectangular parametric mesh. The patches can be joined with C^2 continuity to form axis-independent, complex, composite curved surfaces, and their analytic representation allows simple and efficient computation of surface patch attributes. The object domain contains many curved surfaces which are difficult or impossible to model accurately by polygonal networks or quadric surfaces.

Each surface is represented by a grid of bicubic spline patches. Each patch contains its parametric description as well as an attribute list for the patch. Patch attributes include surface area, mean normal vector (Potmesil, 1982), symbolic form (planar, cylindrical, curved), and bounding box. Patches constitute the lowest local matching level in the system.

2.5. Relational Constraints

One of the more powerful approaches to recognition is the ability to model relationships between object components and to successfully sense them. Relational consistency enforces firm criteria that allow incorrect matches to be rejected. This is especially true when the relational criteria are based on 3-D entities which exist in the physical scene, as opposed to two-dimensional projective relationships which vary with viewpoint.

Each component contains a list of adjacent components, where adjacency is simple physical adjacency between components. The features (holes and cavities) also contain a list of the components that comprise their cross-sectional boundary curves. Thus, a surface sensed near a hole will be related to it from low-level sensing, and in a search for model consistency, this relationship should also hold in the model.

At the surface level each surface contains a list of physically adjacent surfaces that can be used to constrain surface matching. These relations are all built by hand, since the geometric modeling system being used has no way of computing or understanding this relationship. The patch relations are implicit in the structure of the composite surface patch decomposition being used. Each patch's neighbors are directly available from an inspection of the composite surface's defining knot grid.

The models have been created by a combination of hand and computer modeling techniques. Figure 18.4 shows the surfaces that were generated from modeling a plate, a pitcher, and a coffee mug. The plate consists of one surface containing 25 patches. The pitcher is made from 24 patches on the handle and 18 on the body. The mug has 4 patches on the body and 24 on the handle.

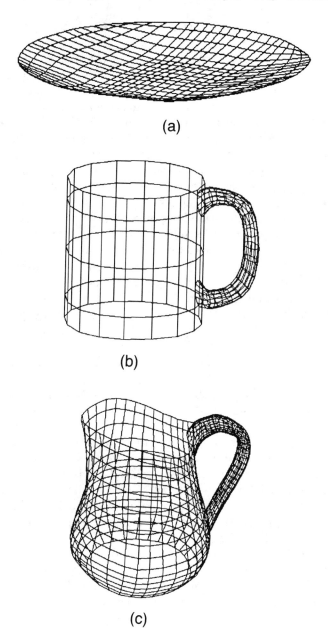

Figure 18.4. Modeled surfaces. (a) Plate. (b) Coffee mug. (c) Pitcher.

3. VISION SENSING

The vision processing described here is an attempt to take what is useful and reliable from machine vision and to supplement it with active, exploratory tactile sensing. There is no attempt to try to understand the full structure of an object from vision alone, but to use low- and medium-level vision processing to guide further tactile exploration, thereby invoking consistent hypotheses about the object to be recognized. The vision processing consists of two distinct phases. The first phase is a series of two-dimensional vision routines that are performed on each of the camera images. The second phase is a stereo matching process that yields sparse depth measurements about the object. The output of these modules is combined with active exploratory tactile sensing to produce hypotheses about objects.

Static images of a single object placed on a homogeneous black background are acquired from two CCD cameras which are calibrated with the robotic work-space. The lighting consists of the overhead fluorescent room lights and a quartz photographic lamp to provide enough illumination for the CCD elements. The Marr-Hildreth edge operator (Marr & Hildreth, 1979) is applied to each of the images, and zero-crossings of the convolved images are found. These zero-crossings define homogeneous regions in the image from which region contours are extracted.

The matching phase uses the region contours as input. Isolated zero-crossings not on a contour are discarded, leaving sparse but stable contour match pixels. The matcher then attempts to match contour pixels using the constraints of scan line coherence and zero-crossing orientation and sign. The candidate match pixels are then correlated with regions of small window size centered on each candidate. Only those matches fulfilling the criteria above and having a correlation confidence level above 95% are accepted as match points. The outcome of this matching phase is a sparse set of match points on the contours of regions isolated from vision.

There are limitations to the amount and accuracy of the data provided by the vision system. Stereo matching suffers from three main problems. The first is the inability of stereo to handle many candidate match points, such as are found in regularly textured objects. By using only sparse contour data, the matcher becomes more accurate, with few if any false matches. The second is the error due to quantization on a discrete pixel grid. For the camera geometry used here this can be 4 mm. The location of zero-crossings to subpixels reduces this error to 2 mm. The last problem is the inability of stereo to match horizontally oriented zero-crossings. There is no basis for distinction between locally horizontal matches in a small region. Zero-crossings whose orientations are more than 60° from vertical yield incorrect match results and are not used by the matcher.

The outcome of stereo matching for a set of digital images of a coffee mug is shown in Figure 18.15 below. There are sparse 3-D depth data on the contours, containing no horizontal matches. These are clearly not enough data to try to recreate surfaces and understand the object's structure. However, the data are accurate and reliable because they have been thinned and abstracted. They allow us to proceed to the next level of sensing with confidence, having sparse but accurate regions identified that can be used for further sensing. Attempts to drive the vision modules beyond this capability will invariably lead to a potentially serious error. The key idea is that *less is more* in the case of multiple sensing. We do not have to rely on this single modality for all our sensory inputs, only those it can reliably produce. The matches provided by the stereo algorithms are reliable because they are based on contour tokens as opposed to pixels. High confidence levels are established for the matches in order to reduce error. The sparse and conservative matches produced are sufficient to allow tactile sensing to further explore the regions in space.

4. TACTILE SENSING

Tactile sensing is a relatively new and underutilized sensing modality (Harmon, 1982). Previous work in tactile sensing for recognition tasks has emphasized traditional pattern recognition paradigms on arrays of sensor data, similar to early machine vision work (Kinoshita, Aida & Mori, 1975; Hillis, 1982; Ozaki, Waku, Mohri, & Takata, 1982; Overton, 1984). Most sensing has been static in that the sensor is larger than the object and a single touch or "handprint" is used for recognition. Very little has been done on dynamic sensing and integrating multiple touch frames into a single view of an object.

Touch is different from vision in that it is an active, exploratory sensing modality. Active touch sensing provides accurate and robust shape information, but it extracts its price for this information by demanding powerful control of the medium, which makes it difficult to use. Blind groping on a surface with a tactile sensor is a poor and inefficient way of understanding 3-D structure. Touch needs to be guided to be useful, and the vision data can provide guidance to an active touch sensor.

The experimental tactile sensor used in this research was developed at Laboratoire d'Automatique et d'Analyse des Systèmes du CNRS in

Toulouse, France (Figure 18.5). It consists of a rigid plastic core covered with 133 conducting surfaces that is roughly the size and shape of a human index finger. The geometry of the sensor is an octagonal cylinder of length 228 mm and radius 20 mm. On each of the eight sides of the cylinder there are 16 equally spaced conducting surfaces. The tip of the sensor contains one conducting surface, and there are four other sensors located on alternate tapered sides leading to the tip. The conducting surfaces are covered by a conductive elastomeric foam. The sensor is connected to an A/D converter that outputs the readings on all sensors in an 8-bit gray value, and the entire array of sensors may be read in a few milliseconds.

Figure 18.5. Tactile sensor.

The organization of tactile sensing is on three distinct hardware and software levels (Figure 18.6). The highest level consists of programs on a VAX host that provide high-level control information about the regions in space that are to be explored with the sensor. Algorithms have been developed to explore the regions isolated from the vision processing and determine if they are surfaces, holes, or cavities. Once a region is identified by tactile sensing, it can be further explored by tactile surface following algorithms that report contact points on surfaces and boundary contours of holes and cavities to the controlling host process. These contacts can be integrated with the 3-D contours from vision to build robust surface and feature descriptions. The intermediate level consists of programs written in VAL-II (Unimation, 1983) that run on the PUMA and move the robotic arm based upon feedback from the tactile sensor. The intermediate level receives region exploration parameters via the VAL-II's host control mechanism which then allows it to invoke a surface exploration, hole exploration, or cavity exploration procedure. These procedures use the feedback from the tactile sensor contacts to control arm motion along the exploration path determined by the high-level host control. The intermediate level communicates with the low-level sensor system via commands that set thresholds for contacts, request contact interrupts, and request gray level outputs from arbitrary subsets of the sensor's elements. The low-level system is implemented on a microprocessor that samples, digitizes, conditions, and localizes the data coming from the tactile sensor, interrupting the intermediate level if a contact of a certain nature occurs.

The classification of a region isolated by the vision system into surface, hole, or cavity is performed by an intermediate-level tactile exploration program. This program controls the motion of the robotic arm and wrist-mounted tactile sensor as it explores the region. The program needs as input an approach vector toward the region which establishes the sensor's orientation. The vector is computed by calculating the least squares plane P_{lsq} with unit normal $\mathbf{N}_{lsq}$ from the matched 3-D stereo points that form the contour of the region. $\mathbf{N}_{lsq}$ then becomes the approach vector for the sensor. The arm control routines will orient the arm so that the tactile sensor's long axis is aligned with $\mathbf{N}_{lsq}$, pointing in the direction of the region's centroid as determined from the vision processing.

The arm is then moved along the sensor's long axis until it makes contact with a surface or it moves beyond plane P_{lsq}, implying the presence of a hole or a cavity. If the sensor is able to travel its full length beyond P_{lsq} without contact, then a hole has been found. If it travels beyond a specified cavity threshold T_{cav} before contact, then the region is a cavity. If the region is a surface, a surface exploration program will trace the surface. If it is a hole or cavity, a boundary

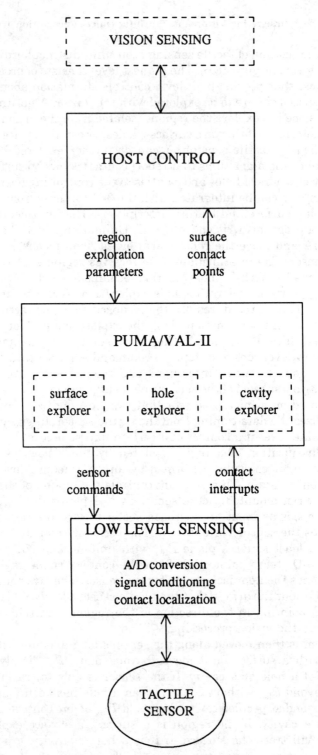

Figure 18.6. Tactile sensing system.

curve will be traced. The output of these exploration programs will be integrated with the 3-D vision data to form surface and feature primitives (described below) that are used in the matching phase.

5. SENSOR INTEGRATION

Once the tactile system has classified a visually detected region as a surface or a feature, integration procedures are invoked to further sense and quantify the region, allowing the formation of 3-D primitives that can be used by the matching phase.

5.1. Building Surface Descriptions

The integration of vision and touch data for a sensed surface is done by building a Coons' patch description of the surface. The sparse 3-D contours from vision form the initial patch grid, and the description is refined by tactile sensing in the interior of the region. Level 0 surfaces are surfaces comprised of a single surface patch. The information needed to compute a level 0 by surface is a two by two rectangular know set consisting of points on the surface boundary, the tangents in each of the parametric directions at the knots, and the twist vectors (cross derivatives) at the knots (Figure 18.7). The knot points should be chosen at points of high curvature on the boundary curve and need to be spaced uniformly in each of the parametric directions. The algorithm for choosing points of high curvature on a contour is a modification of an algorithm originally proposed by Rosenfeld and Johnston (1973). This algorithm analyzes the boundary contour's curvature at different scales, choosing local maxima along the contour. The knot points are then chosen by maximum curvature and distance along the boundary contour in order to preserve equal parametric length for opposite boundary curves.

The tangent vectors in each of the parametric directions must also be calculated. The contour of the region contains a series of 3-D data points obtained from stereo matching that define four boundary curves on the surface. These curves are approximated by a least squares cubic polynomial parameterized by arc length, which is then differentiated and scaled to yield tangent vector values at the knots.

The twist vectors are more difficult to estimate. If the parametric directions on the surface are along the lines of curvature of the surface, then there is no twist in the surface and the twist vectors are zero. In practice, these vectors can be set to zero with minor effects on the surface. This assumes that the parameterization of the surface has

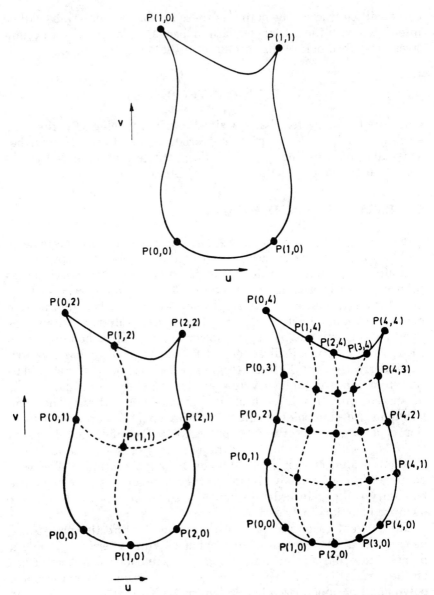

Figure 18.7. Level 0, 1, and 2 composite surfaces.

been chosen wisely, with corner knot points chosen at places of high curvature or discontinuity along the boundary and spaced uniformly in both parametric directions.

A level 0 surface is built from vision data only and is not an accurate description of the underlying surface since it lacks information about the interior of the surface. The tangents which are estimated from stereo match points are inaccurate along contours that are horizontal due to the lack of stereo match points. Figure 18.7 describes the method of building higher-level surfaces. A level 1 surface is formed by adding tactile traces across the single surface patch defined in level 0, and a level 2 surface is formed by adding tactile traces to each of the four patches defined by level 1, thus creating a new surface with 16 patches. This method is hierarchical, allowing surfaces of arbitrary level to be computed. The only restriction is that the new composite surface is globally computed.

The traces begin at the point of surface contact found in the initial exploration of the region found from vision processing. The sensor then traces in the direction of the midpoints of the level 0 boundary curves, using the surface contacts from the tactile sensor to control the robot arm motion.

The movement vector **M** along the surface is determined by

$$= \sum_{i=1}^{3} w_i G_i,$$

where

w_i are the weights for each of the vectors G_i.
G_1 is the unit vector in the direction of the boundary curve midpoint.
G_2 is the unit vector formed from the previous two contact points.
G_3 is the unit vector that preserves equal parameterization.

G_1 is needed to make progress towards the boundary edge. We will want to make progress towards the boundary at each movement step. However, with concave and convex surfaces, cycles can occur as the trace progresses. G_2 is used to maintain a path's direction. Once we start moving in a certain direction, we do not want to stray too far too fast from that path. This vector is an "inertia" vector helping the sensor stay on a steady course. G_3 is needed to keep the parameterization of the surface patches uniform, and this vector moves the trace in the direction to preserve equal parameterization. This vector is the unit resultant of the vectors from the present contact point on the surface to the endpoints of the boundary curve that the trace is approaching.

The points reported during these traces are combined into cubic least squares polynomial curves that are differentiated and scaled to calculate the tangential information needed at the boundaries. The boundary-curves tangents computed from vision data are updated to include the new tactile information, which fills in areas that lack horizontal detail from the stereo process.

Figure 18.8 shows the level 1 surface that results from active tactile sensing of the front surface region of a pitcher. The surfaces are accurate and built from sparse amounts of data. The analytic nature of these surfaces allows stable and accurate symbolic descriptions based upon the Gaussian curvature of the surface, classifying these surfaces as planar, cylindrical, or curved.

The vision processes are supplying the justification for building smooth curvature continuous surfaces from a region. If the region were not a smooth surface, then zero-crossings would have appeared inside the region, precluding the assumption of smoothness. The lack of zero-crossings, or the "no news is good news" criteria established by Grimson (1981) supports this method and is the reason why it succeeds in interpolating the surfaces well.

5.2. Building Feature Descriptions

If the region-exploring algorithm determines that the region is a hole or cavity, a different tactile-tracing routine is used to determine the boundary curve of the feature. The algorithm begins by moving the sensor just beyond the least squares plane P_{lsq} of a region's contour points, aligned with $\mathbf{N}_{lsq}$. It then proceeds to move in a direction perpendicular to $\mathbf{N}_{lsq}$ until it contacts a surface. Once the surface is contacted, the sensor moves along the bounding surface, staying perpendicular to $\mathbf{N}_{lsq}$ and recording the contact points until it reaches the starting point of the trace.

This can be a noisy procedure because many of the tactile sensor's contacts become activated in a small tight area such as the hole in the handle of a coffee mug. The spatial resolution of the sensor contacts also contributes to this phenomenon. The data are not continuous, but are a set of ordered contact points that need to be smoothed; this is done by approximating the series of linked contour points with a periodic spline curve which matches derivatives at the endpoints. Figure 18.17 above shows the smoothed boundary curve created from sensing the hole in the coffee mug. This boundary can then be used to compute cross-sectional area and moments for matching against the model database of objects.

6. MATCHING

The low-level vision and tactile algorithms provide a set of 3-D surface and feature primitives that are used by the matching routines to deter-

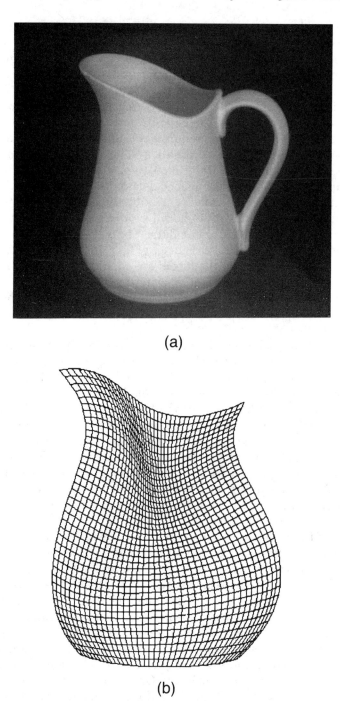

Figure 18.8. (a) Digital image of a pitcher. (b) Level 1 surface.

mine what the object is and its orientation. The matching routines try to find an object in the model database that is consistent with the surface and feature information discovered by the sensors. The intent is to invoke a uniquely consistent model from the 3-D surface and feature primitives discovered. If more than one consistent object is found in the database, a probabilistic measure is used to order the interpretations. Once a consistent interpretation is found, a verification procedure is begun. This requires the matcher to calculate a transformation from the model coordinate system to the sensed-world coordinate system. This transformation is then used to verify the model by reasoning about the slots in the model database that are not filled. The initial choice of a model is made easier by the 3-D nature of the primitives, allowing matching of higher-level attributes rather than sets of confusing and noise-filled point data. The rules used for invoking a model are such that no a priori choice of features or surfaces is needed; all the structural parts of the model are candidates for matching. The object recognition system has no way of knowing what features or surfaces will be sensed from a particular viewpoint. It must be able to invoke a model based upon any identifiable part of the model (Allen & Bajcsy, 1985).

The matching phase is the most difficult of all the modules since it requires the system to do high-level reasoning about objects and their structure based upon incomplete and partial sensor information. The approach taken here is to develop a rule-based system that will allow experimentation and modification of sensing strategies. Some of the rules and strategies implemented are discussed below, and development of new rules and strategies are a focus of our current work.

Model instantiation is done by first pruning the space of object models that are not consistent with two global criteria: physical size and gross shape. All objects in the model database consistent with these criteria are then further matched according to features and surface attributes as determined by the integration of vision and touch sensing.

One of the benefits of using active tactile exploration is that physical size constraints can be used for global discrimination. Nevatia and Binford (1977) and Brooks (1981) have shown the utility of using physical size constraints in recognition tasks. The tactile sensor can be moved into the workspace to trace the global outline of the object to determine its bounding box. This procedure also puts coarse bounds on the location of the object which can be used by the verification procedures later. Gross shape is able to prune based upon the number of features discovered and whether surfaces are classified as planar, cylindrical, or curved based upon the Gaussian curvature of the sensed surface (Hilbert & Cohn-Vossen, 1952). Sensed surfaces constrain the set of consistent object models less tightly because the sensors discover patches of possibly larger surfaces (the aperture problem). A curved surface in the model may have cylindrical regions, which may be sensed as a cylindrical partial patch. Therefore, gross shape discrimination must be conservative in matching curved surfaces.

Feature attributes are used as a discrimination tool to invoke a consistent model. The constant cross section of the feature can be used to define a set of moments that can be used to match the cross section with a sensed feature. Moment matching was first described by Hu (1962), who described a set of seven moment invariants involving moments of up to third order. At the instantiation level the moment M_{00} which measures the area of the planar cross-section, and the second order moments $M_{02} + M_{20}$ are matched between the sensed and model systems. The latter measure is scaled to reflect the difference in M_{00} when it is matched. In the case of cavities, the depth attribute is also used as a matching criteria.

Surface matching tries to match on two attributes: area and type of surface. The sensor is not capable of sensing accurately parts of the model with fine structure, such as the handle of the mug. The area criteria effectively culls out small feature matching and leaves the task of larger shape correspondence. The set of possible consistent interpretations is restricted further by maintaining relational consistency between the sensed rations and the model nodes. The relational constraint used is adjacency. If two sensed regions in space are physically adjacent, then the model nodes that these regions match with must also be adjacent.

7. VERIFICATION

Verification can be viewed as slot filling, where the instantiated model's nodes are either filled, representing a sensed match, or unfilled. Verification then becomes a process of reasoning about unfilled slots. Once a model is instantiated, a transformation between model coordinates and sensed-world coordinates must be computed. This transformation will allow the knowledge embedded in the model-coordinate frame to be used in the sensed-world frame. By transforming model surfaces and features to the sensed-world frames, verification of unrecognized slots in the model can proceed, since their assumed location is now computable with this transformation. This knowledge enables the sensors to explore regions that were not seen in the initial sensing and to explore visually occluded areas with tactile sensing. The transformation may be computed with feature information or surface information. In some cases, a partial transformation may be computed that will allow further verification sensing.

7.1. Matching Feature Frames

Each feature in the database is associated with an object-centered coordinate frame. Once the models and their frames are developed, mappings from one feature frame to another are readily computable. Figure 18.9 shows the frames C_m and H_m, which are object-centered frames defined for a coffee mug's cavity and a hole in the model coordinate system. The relative transformation between the hole frame and the cavity frame R_{hcm} can be defined as

$$C_m = H_m : R_{hcm},$$
$$R_{hcm} = H_m^{-1} : C_m.$$

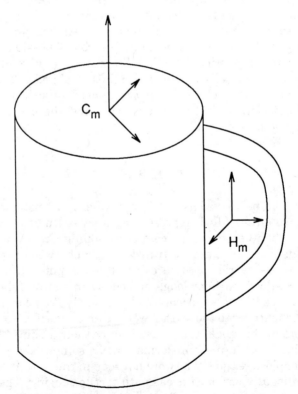

Figure 18.9. Relative feature frames for a coffee mug.

Similarly, the transformation from modeled cavity to modeled hole R_{chm} is

$$R_{chm} = C_m^{-1} : H_m.$$

Because these are relative frames, discovering one of the model frames in the sensed coordinate space will define the other feature in the sensed coordinate space. Assuming we know the match between the hole in sensed-world coordinates with frame H_s and the model hole with frame H_m, then the cavity in sensed-world coordinates is defined by frame C_s:

$$C_s = H_s : R_{hcm}.$$

The determination of the new feature frame in sensed-world coordinates is important to the verification process. If an unfilled feature slot is seen, then the feature's frame in sensed coordinates is available through the relative frame mapping. The frame for a feature defines the axis of the hole or cavity in sensed-world coordinates, which is then used as an approach vector to sense the unseen feature even if it is occluded.

Feature frames may be only partially defined as is the case with rotationally symmetric features such as a circular cavity or hole. The approach axis of these features is well defined, but the principal axis of these features is well defined, but the principal axes of inertia of the cross-sectional opening are not. However, the frame-matching technique discussed above can still determine within this rotational parameter the new sensed frame. An example of this is given in Section 8, where the tactile sensor is able to sense a visually occluded hole.

7.2. Matching Surface Frames

Matching of surfaces is more difficult because a unique surface frame is not as easily sensed as a feature frame. Planar and cylindrical surfaces have one well-defined frame vector which is the plane's normal and the cylinder's axis. Curved surfaces in general do not have any such natural embedded frame. In the case of planar and cylindrical surfaces, the one axis which is defined will allow defining the transformation up to a rotational parameter about that axis and a translation. In the case of the plane, the plane's centroid is also computable, and this will supply the translational component of the transformation. This can be used in conjunction with other feature and surface matches to constrain the sensed frame.

The analytic nature of the surfaces created from vision and touch allows computation of differential geometry measures, such as lines of curvature, principal directions, and Gaussian curvature. Brady, Ponce, Yuille, and Asada (1985) have suggested that certain lines of curvature that are planar might be significant in terms of recognizing structure. For example, the only planar lines of curvature on an ellipsoid are the lines formed by the intersection of the symmetry planes with the surface. Discovery of lines such as these is feasible with the representation used and may lead to more robust recognition methods for curved surfaces.

8. EXPERIMENTAL RESULTS

This section details the experiments that were conducted to test out the approaches developed in the previous sections. The experiments show that integrating vision and touch is a viable method for recognition, particularly when compared to standard vision processing. The experiments reported have been run using real objects and real noisy sensors. In addition, the tactile sensor being used is relatively crude in terms of spatial resolution compared with newer devices. Despite these shortcomings, the approaches to matching discussed previously work well in a number of important cases. The implementation of the matcher consists of a set of PROLOG goals that match sensed regions with model nodes. The model database is implemented as a set of PROLOG facts that are indexed in a hierarchical manner. The database consists of eight kitchen objects: pitcher, mug, spoon, teapot, plate, bowl, drinking cup, pot. Four of these objects (pitcher, mug, plate, bowl) were used in experiments to test the matcher and its ability to correctly identify the objects. The main intent of these experiments is to show (1) the utility of the methods presented and (2) the ability of touch and vision to succeed in situations that vision alone would find difficult.

The first experiment tried to recognize a planar salad plate. The digital images and stereo matches are shown in Figure 18.10. The images yielded few feature points that could be matched to determine depth as expected with a smooth homogeneous surface. The stereo matcher was only accurate in matching zero-crossings up to 65° from vertical, yielding sparse and incomplete depth information. An image such as this would pose large problems for a vision system alone; the data are too sparse to support a consistent visual hypothesis. The region analysis revealed only a single region to be explored which was the central area of the plate. The tactile system explored the plate and built the surface description shown in Figure 18.11 by integrating the touch and vision data into a level 1 surface description. The surface

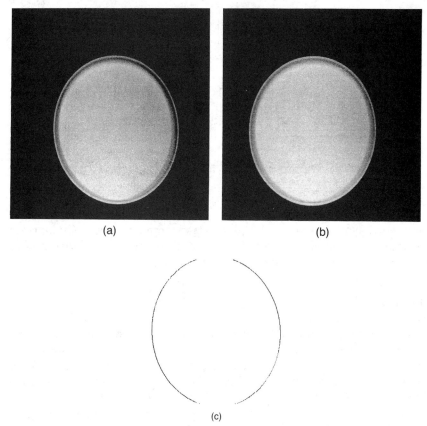

Figure 18.10. (a) Left image of plate. (b) Right image of plate. (c) Stereo matches for plate.

was sampled at small intervals in parameter space calculating the Gaussian curvature and confirming its planar nature. Figure 18.12 shows the computed surface normals on the plate, verifying its planar appearance.

The normal of the least squares plane fitted to the surface was the

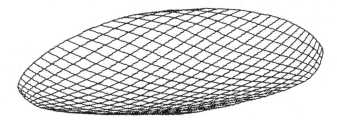

Figure 18.11. Level 1 surface for the plate.

Figure 18.12. Sensed surface normals for the plate.

estimate for the orientation of the object. No other orientation parameters were available since the plate was symmetric about the surface normal. The sensed plate's estimated surface normal was within 6° of the actual plate orientation on the table.

8.1. Experiment 2

The second object imaged was a cereal bowl. The digital images and stereo matches are shown in Figure 18.13. The images are similar to the plate in experiment 1. The only depth cues are monocular, where small shading gradients exist but elude the zero-crossing edge detector. This is an excellent example of the discriminatory power when tactile sensing is added to vision. The region analysis yields one region to explore with the tactile sensor. Upon exploration, a level 1 surface of the bowl was computed and is shown in Figure 18.14. The tactile sensor did not find a surface until it had passed 40 mm beyond the plane of the region's contour determined from vision. This prompted a cavity trace in addition to the surface trace.

The matcher tried to match the surface and the cavity with an object in the database. The combination of the curved surface and cavity (with measured feature moments and depth) was sufficient to invoke the correct model. The estimate of the object's orientation in space was the angular difference between the actual cavity axis and the sensed axis, which was approximately 5°.

The initial visual data for experiments 1 and 2 were almost identical. Only by using touch sensing did the surface's depth become apparent. The discovery of a cavity allowed the system to discriminate between two potential surface matches. The combination of surface and feature information reduces the likelihood of multiple consistent models being found.

Integrating Vision and Touch for Object Recognition Tasks   433

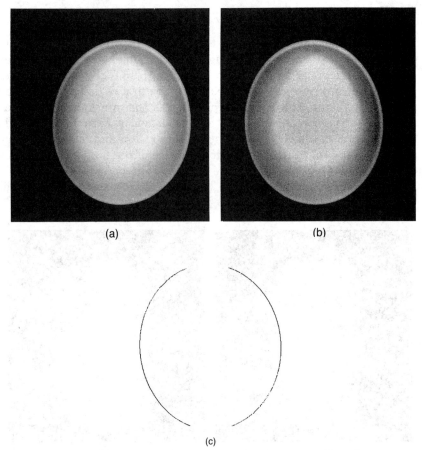

Figure 18.13. (a) Left image of bowl. (b) Right image of bowl. (c) Stereo matches for bowl.

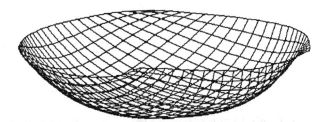

Figure 18.14.   Level 1 surface for bowl.

8.2. Experiment 3

The third experiment imaged a coffee mug. In this image the hole, cavity, handle, and body of the mug were all visible. The digital images and the stereo matches are shown in Figure 18.15. The region analysis yielded four separate regions to explore. The first region explored was the cavity. The second region explored was the mug's main body for which a surface patch was built and is shown in Figure 18.16. This surface patch is a level 1 patch built from vision and touch and very closely approximates the cylindrical surface of the mug. The analysis of the patch's Gaussian curvature classified the patch as a cylinder.

The hole was found after the region exploration algorithm pene-

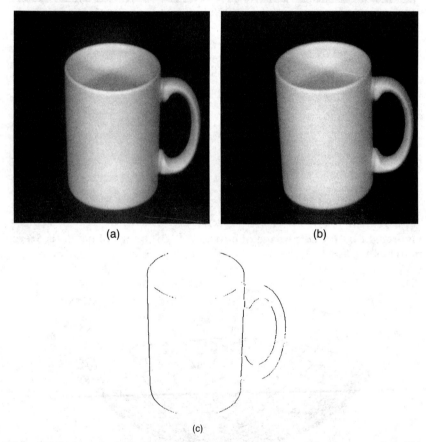

Figure 18.15. (a) Left image of coffee mug. (b) Right image of coffee mug. (c) Stereo matches for coffee mug.

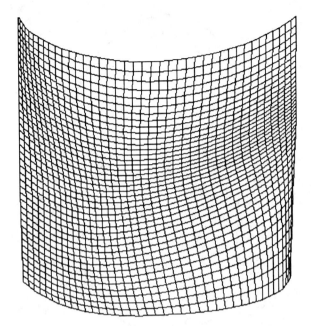

Figure 18.16. Level 1 surface for the coffee mug.

trated the region defined from vision processing and did not contact a surface. The hole was traced by the tactile sensor and the smoothed boundary curve shown in Figure 18.17 was computed from the contact points on the hole's boundary.

The matcher was presented with an abundance of sensed region information to try to instantiate a model. The cylindrical surface that was computed matched a number of objects in the database (pot, coffee mug, drinking glass) as did the cavity (drinking glass, coffee mug). The hole was not found in the drinking glass (an identical object in the data base to the mug but without a hole or a handle) but matched with the coffee mug, yielding a unique choice of object. The cylindrical surface axis and the cavity axis are parallel in the model, and the agreement between these two axes and the actual orientation was quite close ($<5°$).

The handle of the mug is too small and fine for the sensor to adequately build a patch description. It can be verified as a surface with the sensor, but attempts at building a patch description failed due to the sensor's much larger size. This experiment shows the many ways an object can be recognized. Holes, cavities and surfaces are all able to be used to both recognize and correctly identify orientation parameters for the objects. This is important in that certain viewing angles may

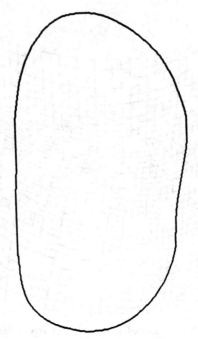

Figure 18.17. Smooth boundary curve of mug handle hole.

present a confusing region that cannot be sensed accurately. However, if one of the regions is able to be sensed accurately, then a partial match can be established, leading to later recognition.

8.3. Experiment 4

In this experiment, the coffee mug was imaged with the handle occluded. The objects in the database that will match with these two regions (body surface and cavity) are the drinking glass without a handle and a mug with a handle. From this visual angle there is no way that the two objects can be distinguished. The instantiation module will pick both objects to be verified.

It can be determined that the object is a mug by verifying the occluded hole. If it is a mug, the hole lies in the occluded area shown in Figure 18.18. The bounds on this volume are known from the vision and touch sensing that has already been performed. The handle can be located by knowing the relative feature frames between the sensed cavity and the hole. The cavity, however, does not possess a unique frame; it is rotationally symmetric, leaving a degree of freedom in its

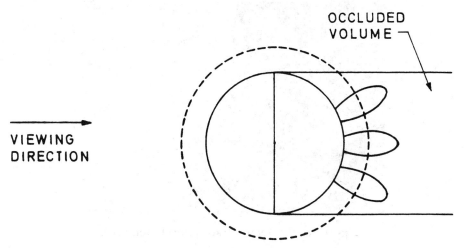

Figure 18.18. Occluded volume of coffee mug.

internal frame which is the rotation about its approach axis. This degree of freedom can be exploited to reason about the location of the hole. The fixing of the cavity's approach axis in space means that the hole centroid is confined to lie in a circle centered at the cavity and swept out about the cavity's axis. Computing this circle gives a set of 3-D points which represent possible locations of the hole's centroid. Intersecting this circle with the known occluded volume yields a possible set of locations of the hole. Each of these locations is associated with a particular fixing of the rotationally symmetric axes about the cavity's axis. The approach is to fix the cavity's rotationally symmetric axes at an angle of rotation that is midway between the angles that bring the hole into occlusion and bring it out. Once this is defined, it yields an approach axis for the hole which the tactile sensor can then use to probe the hole. In the experiment, the hole was found this way, rejecting the drinking glass match and accepting the mug match. Figure 18.19 shows the sensor searching for and finding the hole in the visually occluded area.

This last experiment shows the power of this approach to object recognition. Multiple sensors were used synergistically to invoke a possible set of objects. High-level reasoning about the object's structure that is encoded in 3-D models allowed further verification sensing to successfully discriminate between the objects. The knowledge about the three-dimensional world (the occluded volume) and the object's geometry (which is encoded in the model) can be used to perform active sensing in occluded areas.

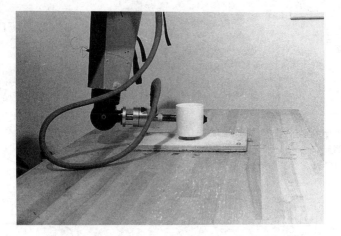

Figure 18.19. Tactile trace of occluded hole.

9. SUMMARY

The research presented in this chapter has attempted to improve robotic performance in a real noisy object domain by integrating multiple sensors. The use of multiple sensors has provided more robust and accurate sensory data that can be combined into three-dimensional primitives that facilitate matching and an understanding of the underlying structure of the objects. The ability to sense actively demands higher levels of control than with passive sensors, including the ability to reason at a high level about object structure. This reasoning capability needs to be further developed and is a natural extension of this work, allowing tasks beyond recognition to be attempted in a multisensor environment.

REFERENCES

Agin, G. (1972, October). *Representation and description of curved objects* (AI Memo 173). Stanford University: Artificial Intelligence Laboratory.

Allen, P. (1985). Object recognition using vision and touch. Unpublished doctoral dissertation. University of Pennsylvania, Department of Computer and Information Science.

Allen, P., & Bajcsy, R. (1985). Converging disparate sensory data. In H. Hanafusa & H. Inoue (Eds.), *Robotics research: The second international symposium* (pp. 81–86). Cambridge, MA: MIT Press.

Bolles, R.C., Horaud, P., & Hannah, M.J. (1983). 3DPO: A three-dimensional part orientation system. *Proceedings of the Eighth International Confer-*

ence on *Joint Artificial Intelligence,* (pp. 1116–1120). Karlsruhe, Germany.

Brady, M., Ponce, J., Yuille, A., & Asada, H. (1985). Describing surfaces. In H. Hanafusa & H. Inoue (Eds.), *Robotics research: The second international symposium.* Cambridge, MA: MIT Press.

Brooks, R. (1981). Symbolic reasoning among 3-D models and 2-D images. *Artificial Intelligence, 17,* 285–349.

Faux, I.D., & Pratt, M.J. (1979). *Computational geometry for design and manufacture.* New York: Wiley.

Fisher, R.B. (1983). Using surfaces and object models to recognize partially obscured objects. *Proceedings of the Eighth International Conference on Artificial Intelligence.* (pp. 989–995). Karlsruhe, Germany.

Grimson, W.E.L. (1981). *From images to surfaces: A computational study of the human early visual system.* Cambridge, MA: MIT Press.

Grimson, W.E.L., & Lozano-Perez, T. (1983, August). *Model based recognition and localization from sparse three dimensional sensory data* (AI Memo 738). MIT AI Laboratory.

Harmon, L. (1982). Automated tactile sensing. *International Journal of Robotics Research* 1(2), 3–32.

Hilbert, D., & Cohn-Vossen, S. (1952). *Geometry and the imagination.* New York: Chelsea.

Hillis, W.D. (1982). A high resolution imaging touch sensor. *International Journal of Robotics Research* 1(2), 33–44.

Hu, M.K. (1962). Visual pattern recognition by moment invariants. *IEEE Transactions on Information Theory,* IT-8, 179–187.

Kinoshita, G., Aida, S., & Mori, M. (1975). A pattern classification by dynamic tactile sense information processing. *Pattern Recognition 7,* 243–250.

Marr, D., & Hildreth, E. (1979). Theory of edge detection. *Proceedings of the Royal Society of London, 204,* 301–328.

Nevatia, R., & Binford, T. (1977). Description and recognition of curved objects. *Artificial Intelligence, 8,* 77–98.

Nitzan, D. (1981). Assessment of robotic sensors. *Proceeding of the First International Conference on Robot Vision and Sensory Controls,* (pp. 1–12). Stratford-upon-Avon, UK.

Oshima, M., & Shirai, Y. (1983). Objects recognition using three-dimensional information. *IEEE Transactions on Pattern Analysis and Machine Intelligence,* PAMI-5(4), 353–361.

Overton, K.J. (1984). *The acquisition, processing and use of tactile sensor data in robot control.* Unpublished doctoral dissertation, University of Massachusetts, Department of Computer and Information Science.

Ozaki, H., Waku, S., Mohri, A., & Takata, M. (1982). Pattern recognition of a grasped object by unit vector distribution. *IEEE Transactions on Systems, Man and Cybernetics,* SMC-12(3), 315–324.

Potmesil, M. (1982). *Generating three-dimensional surface models of solid objects from multiple projections* (Tech. Rep. 033). Rensselaer Polytechnic Institute: Image Processing Laboratory.

Rock, I. (1983). *The logic of perception.* Cambridge, MA: MIT Press.

Rosenfeld, A., & Johnston, E. (1973). Angle detection on digital curves. *IEEE Transactions on Computers, C-22,* 875–878.

Shapiro, L., Moriarty, J.D., Haralick, R., & Mulgaonkar, P. (1981). Matching three-dimensional models. *Proceedings of the IEEE Conference on Pattern Recognition and Image Processing* (pp. 534–541). Dallas, TX.

Shneier, M., Nagalia, S., Albus, J., & Haar, R. (1982). Visual feedback for robot control. *Proceedings of the IEEE Workshop on Industrial Applications of Industrial Vision* (pp. 232–236).

Tomita, F., & Kanade, T. (1984). A 3-D vision system: Generating and matching shape descriptions in range images. *Proceedings of the IEEE Conference on Artificial Intelligence Applications* (pp. 186–191).

Unimation. (1983). *User's guide to VAL-II.* Danbury: Unimation Inc.

York, B. (1981). Shape representation in computer vision. Unpublished doctoral dissertation, University of Massachusetts, Department of Computer and Information Science.

PART IV
Multisensor-Based Mobile Robots

19
Introduction to Part IV

Ren C. Luo and
Michael G. Kay

Part IV describes the role of multisensor integration and fusion in the operation of mobile robots. The mobility of robots and other vehicles is required in a variety of applications. In simple well-structured environments automatic control technology is sufficient to coordinate the use of the required sensor systems (e.g., automatic guided vehicles, missiles, etc.) (Harmon, 1986a). When a vehicle must operate in an uncertain or unknown dynamic environment—usually in close to real time—it becomes necessary to consider integrating or fusing the data from a variety of different sensors so that an adequate amount of information from the environment can be quickly perceived. Because of these factors, mobile robot research has proved to be a major stimulus to the development of concrete approaches to multisensor integration and fusion. This chapter first describes different control architectures used for multisensor integration on mobile robots. Different world model representations and sensor combinations are then surveyed, and the chapter concludes with a number of examples of existing multisensor-based mobile robots. The three remaining chapters of Part IV describe in detail different high-level representations that are suitable for multisensor integration and fusion on a mobile robot.

Luo and Kay (1988) have reviewed the role of multisensor integration and fusion in the operation of mobile robots, and Levi (1987) has discussed some of the multisensor fusion techniques appropriate for mobile robot navigation and has reviewed their use in a number of applications. Multiple sensors have been used in mobile robots to enable them to operate in environments ranging from roadways (Goto & Stentz, 1987; Turk, Morgenthaler, Gremban & Marra, 1987) to unstructured indoor environments (Giralt, Chatila, & Vaisset, 1984) to unknown natural terrain (Daily et al., 1988; Harmon, 1987) and even underwater (Oskard, Hong & Shaffer, 1988; Rigaud & Marce, 1990) and on Mars (Hebert, Caillas, Krotkov, Kweon & Kanade, 1989).

1. CONTROL STRATEGIES

A number of different strategies used to control the operation of multisensor-based mobile robots are described in this section within the context of the role of perception in a typical control architecture.

1.1. The Role of Perception

Figure 19.1 illustrates the role of the perception function in a typical architecture for the control of a multisensor mobile robot. Perception,

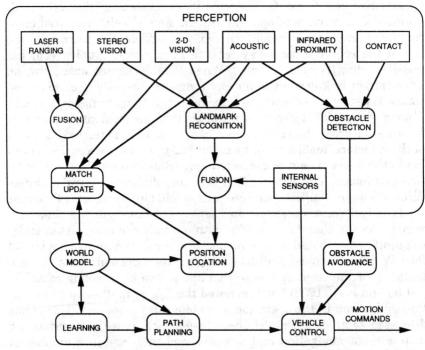

Figure 19.1. The role of the perception function in a hypothetical architecture for a mobile robot.

together with vehicle control, obstacle avoidance, position location, path planning, and learning, are generic functions necessary for intelligent autonomous mobility (Harmon, 1986a). Six different external sensor types are shown in the figure as part of the perception function. Subsets of these sensors are used to perform three tasks that usually comprise the perception function: the matching of sensory data to a world model (or map) representing the environment and then updating the model to reflect the matching results, the recognition of landmarks in the environment for use in determining the location of the robot, and the detection of obstacles so that they can be avoided. The degree of integration and fusion of the sensory data required for each of these tasks can differ. In a simple system, each sensor used for obstacle detection might operate independently of the other sensors if the detection of nearby obstacles is required; in a more complex system, some of the sensor data might be also fused so as to extend the range and accuracy of possible detection (Harmon, 1987). One of the simplest techniques used for position location is trajectory integration, where the location is calculated from the accumulated rotational and translational motion of the vehicle as determined by internal sensors like an odometer. Due to the inherent inaccuracies in any sensor, locational error continues to accumulate as the robot moves. In order to reduce this cumulative error most mobile robots periodically determine the location of some external landmark. As shown in the figure, the results from landmark recognition are sometimes fused with the location determined by internal sensors after each has been transformed to common coordinates. Any of the techniques of multisensor object recognition presented in Part III may be used to first recognize the landmark. The world model matching and updating task requires that the sensor information and any associated measure of its uncertainty correspond to the representation used in the world model so that integration can take place. Depending on the representational format used in the world model, the information will in most cases have to be made commensurate by applying appropriate space and time transformations. Information from the different sensors might be fused or otherwise transformed before reaching the matching task in order to reduce the communication bandwidth required or the complexity of the matching process. In the figure, information from the laser ranging and stereo vision sensors are fused before being matched to the world model.

1.2. Animal Behavior Paradigm

While the typical architecture described represents in broad outline most current approaches to the design of mobile robots, a number of researchers have suggested the use of animal behaviors as a paradigm for the development of control strategies for multisensor-based mobile robots (Anderson & Donath, 1990; Beer, Chiel & Sterling, 1990). They argue that many simple animals already exhibit most of the control properties required by an autonomous mobile robot and should serve as the starting point for future research. Nagata, Sekiguchi, and Asakawa (1990) have used a structured hierarchical neural network to control a mobile robot that can be taught different behaviors by changing the patterns of sensory information presented to the robot. An instinct network is used to determine the correspondence between sensory input and behavioral patterns.

Subsumption architecture: The MIT mobile robot project has adopted a layered approach for autonomous control that is termed a "subsumption" architecture (Brooks, 1986, 1987, 1989, 1990). Each layer in this architecture consists of a complete control system similar to that in Figure 19.1 for a simple task-achieving behavior such as avoiding obstacles or wandering. Starting with low-level tasks, new task-achieving behaviors can be added incrementally because the layers operate asynchronously, communicating over low-bandwidth lines without a central locus of control, central data structure, or global plan. Rosenblatt and Payton (1989) have modified the subsumption architecture so that task behaviors at each level are separated into a number of smaller and simpler decision-making units. The interactions between the units are easier to control because each unit has complete access to the internal state of all existing behaviors. Bestavros, Clark, and Ferrier (1990) have developed an architecture that is based on an "input-output timed automata" abstract model of a robot's sensorimotor activity that can deal with behaviors that have dynamically changing priorities, whereas the subsumption architecture must create a static hierarchy of dominant and inferior behaviors.

Behavioral schemata: Behavioral schemata are a useful means of implementing animal-like behaviors for robotic control because single schemata that correspond to a primitive behavior can be combined with other simple schemata to yield more complex behaviors. Arkin (1989, 1990) has used motor and perceptual schemata to implement a control system for mobile robot navigation. The perceptual schemata are embedded within motor schemata and provide only the sensory information needed by the motor schema to react to the world. In contrast to most traditional architectures, computational demands are reduced because no world model is created using sensory data; only a priori knowledge of objects and adaptive models of previous sensing are utilized.

2. HIGH-LEVEL REPRESENTATIONS

Considerable research has been directed at the development of either a single representation or multiple hierarchical levels of representations suitable for use by a mobile robot to perform the reasoning required for its control, path planning, and learning functions. The representations are usually at a high enough level so as not to be sensor specific. As mentioned before, information from different sensors is usually transformed to the common high-level representation and then added to a world model. The function of the world model and the particular form of the high-level representation depend both on the control architecture used in the robot and the complexity of the required reasoning —extremes range from road-following vehicles where sensor information is dynamically processed using feedback loops to produce control commands without ever using a world model, to pure production rule-based representations that assume a static and perfect model of the world that is difficult to modify (Crowley, 1986). In practice, the representations used for robots operating in unknown or unstructured environments allow for their world models to be dynamically modified and updated with uncertain sensor information. Except for explicit learning procedures used in many production rule-based representations, learning takes place implicitly as the world model is updated with new information as the robot traverses the environment.

Included below are examples of different high-level representations. Many of the papers referenced are distinguished by a discussion of the multisensor integration and fusion issues relevant to their proposed representation. Other representations are discussed in Section 4 of this chapter and in the remaining chapters of this part.

2.1. Grids

Multisensory information can be represented in a multidimensional grid of cells. Each cell in the grid corresponds to a region of space from which the sensor information is assumed to have originated. A grid is attractive as a means of representing multisensory information because the data from each sensor is automatically in spatial correspondence as long as each sensor can correctly map its data to the grid. It may also be possible for fusion and other processing to take place within each cell before any further high-level processing is required— a feature that is important in many real-time applications. A possible disadvantage of a grid representation is that it usually requires a large amount of memory to store the grid. Dean (1988) has explored the computational complexity of integrating uncertain spatial information in a two-dimensional grid representation, and has found that the problem is potentially intractable unless the relative position of every location in the environment is distinguishable; that is, there are known reference landmarks in the environment.

Occupancy grids (Elfes, 1986, 1987, 1989) were one of the first grid representations used for sensory processing on mobile robots. An occupancy grid world model representation is a 2-D or 3-D lattice of random variables (i.e., a random field) that divides the environment into equal-sized cells. An occupancy grid can be either vehicle or world centered. The distribution of each random variable represents the probability that the corresponding cell contains some attribute of the environment, such as whether or not the cell is occupied by an object. Once sensory information has been converted into a probability corresponding to the presence of some attribute in the cell, general Bayesian estimation techniques are used to fuse together both information from multiple sensors and sequences of sensor readings taken as a robot moves in the environment. The resulting grid can then be used for many robot control functions, such as path planning and obstacle avoidance. Differences in the resolution required for different parts of the environment are handled in an *ad hoc* manner through the creation of a nested hierarchy of maps with different resolutions. Many of the processing operations on an occupancy grid have a direct correspondence to familiar image processing techniques; for example, obstacle growing for path planning corresponds to region growing in image processing. As a result of this correspondence, off-the-shelf special-purpose image processing boards could be used directly for much of the sensory processing on board the mobile robot.

Waldron and Meystel (1988) and Meystel (1990) provide a thorough discussion of many of the problems encountered in developing a representation of spatial knowledge for multisensor-based mobile robots and have described a multiresolutional grid representation that is able to account for many of these problems in an efficient manner. Raw sensory data corresponding to, for example, the boundary of an object, is represented at a high level of resolution as a set of cells in a grid which is at the lowest level in a hierarchy of grids of decreasing resolution. The raw data is transformed to grids at higher levels in the hierarchy through a process of generalization in which any number of clustering-like heuristics are applied to the raw data. A level in the hierarchy is eventually reached at which the original set of cells is represented as a single cell with an associated estimate as to the identity of the object being represented. Object identification takes place during the process of generalization when the transformed sensory information is matched to objects in memory using a matched filter and heuristics. In cases where there are partial matches, the expected perception of a known object from memory is used to focus attention to a particular region of a grid at a lower level in the hierarchy so that additional data can be obtained to further aid the identification process.

Jorgensen (1987) has proposed dividing the environment into equal-sized volumetric cells and associating each cell with a neuron. In a manner similar to the occupancy grid the magnitude of each neuron's activation corresponds to the probability that the cell it represents is occupied. The neurons are trained using sensory information from different perspectives. Associative recall (see Section 1.3 of Chapter 2) can then be used to recognize objects in the environment and simulated annealing (see Section 2.4 of Chapter 8) can be used to find optimal global paths for navigation. In many respects, Jorgensen's approach is a reformulation of the occupancy grid representation in terms of a neural network that enables standard neural network techniques to be applied to multisensor mobile robot processing tasks.

2.2. Graphs

Graph structures have been used to represent the local and topological features of the environment in order not to have to define a global metric relation between nonadjacent nodes (or points) in the graph. When landmarks or beacons are not used to correct cumulative position error, a global metric would contain too much uncertainty to be useful. Graph structures allow the topological features to be represented and reasoned with in an efficient manner. Kak, Roberts, Andress, and Cromwell (1987) and Andress and Kak (1988) use an attributed graph and Dempster-Shafer evidential reasoning (see Section 3.2 of Chapter 8) to integrate sensory information for hierarchical spatial reasoning. Brooks (1985) has proposed the use of a graph to represent regions of potential collision-free motion termed "freeways" and "meadows." Each point in the graph, represented as an "uncertainty manifold," corresponds to the location of a robot in configuration space at which sensory information was acquired; each arc is labeled with a local measurement of the distance travelled between endpoints. The cumulative uncertainty of the robot as it moves from point to point in the graph is taken into account through the cascading of successive uncertainty manifolds.

2.3. Labeled Regions

Sensory information can be used to segment the environment into regions with properties that are useful for spatial reasoning. The known characteristics of different types of sensory information can be used to label some useful property of each region so that symbolic reasoning can be performed at higher levels in the control structure. Asada (1988) has proposed a method for building world models that uses the range images from sensors to create height maps of the local environment. Gray levels represent the height of points in the map with respect to an assumed ground plane. The map is then segmented into regions and labeled. Sequences of maps, created as a robot moves, are integrated into a global map by overlaying pairs of height maps and then replacing the labels of corresponding regions in the height maps with a label determined according to a precedence procedure (e.g., if a region is labeled as unexplored in one height map and as an obstacle in another, the global map might label the region as an obstacle). The global map is then used for obstacle detection and path planning. Miller (1985) has developed a spatial representation that divides a map of an indoor environment into labeled regions. Each label is one of four possible types—each type referring to the number of degrees of freedom in the region (i.e., the two planar dimensions and the robot's orientation) that information from a sensor could be used to eliminate (e.g. the empty space in the center of the room is of type zero, a region near a corner is of type three, etc.). Voronoi diagrams are then used to group the regions into areas that correspond to a specific edge (or wall) in the environment.

2.4. Production Rules

The use of production rules in a control structure allows for a wide range of well-known artificial intelligence methods to be used for path planning and learning purposes. Lawton, Levitt, McConnell, and Glicksman (1986) have used production rules to create schemata to represent both objects in terrain models and certain generic object types. Network hierarchies are created from the schemata that allow inference and matching procedures to take place at multiple levels of abstraction, with each level using an appropriate combination of the sensors that are available. Isik and Meystel (1986) have used fuzzy-valued linguistic variables to represent the attributes of objects as part of fuzzy logic-based (see Section 3.3 of Chapter 8) production system for mobile robot control.

3. SENSOR COMBINATIONS

Due to the advantages and limitations of each type of sensor, most mobile robots use some combination of different sensor types to perform each task of the perception function described in Section 1.1. Some sensors cannot be used in a particular environment due to their inherent limitations (e.g., acoustic sensors in space), while others are limited due to either technical or economic factors. Obstacle detection with contact sensors necessarily limits the speed of a robot because contact must be made before detection can take place (Harmon, 1986b); laser sensors require an intense energy source, and they have a short range and slow scan rate (their use can also cause eye problems (Harmon, 1988)); vision sensors are critically dependent on ambient lighting conditions, and their scene analysis and registration procedures can be complex and time-consuming (Harmon, 1986b). SHAKY, one of the first multisensor-based mobile robots, used vision together with tactile sensors for obstacle detection (Nilsson, 1969). JASON, another early robot, combined acoustic and infrared proximity sensors for obstacle detection and path planning (Smith, Sobek, Coles, Hodges, Robb, & Sinclair, 1975), and the Stanford University Cart (Moravec, 1983) used acoustic and infrared sensors together with stereo vision for navigating over a flat terrain while avoiding obstacles. Bixler and Miller (1987) used simple low-resolution vision in their autonomous mobile robot to locate the direction of an obstacle, and then used an ultrasonic range finder to determine its depth and shape. Other combinations of sensors used in mobile robot systems have included contact, infrared, and stereo vision (Everett, 1985); sonar and infrared (Flynn, 1988); contact and acoustic (Berry, Loebbaka, & Hall, 1983); acoustic and stereo vision (Wallace, Stentz, Thorpe, Moravec, Whittaker, & Kanade, 1985); and stereo vision and laser range finding (Miller, 1977).

4. SELECTED EXAMPLES

Short descriptions of a number of different multisensor-based mobile robots are provided in this section. Emphasis is given to the role of multisensor integration and fusion in their navigation and control. Table 19.1 summarizes for comparison the relevant multisensor integration and fusion features of each mobile robot. Included under the name of each mobile robot in the table is the year the initial publication appeared. In cases where there have been major modifications to the mobile robot, the features listed in the table correspond to the most recent published research.

Table 19.1. Selected examples of multisensor-based mobile robots

Mobile Robot	External Sensors	Operating Environment	World Model Representation	Fusion Method
HILARE (1979)	vision acoustic laser range finder	unknown man-made	polygon objects in graph of locations	weighted average
Crowley's mobile robot (1984)	rotating ultrasonic tactile	known man-made	connected sequences of line segments in two dimensions	best correspondence using integer valued confidence factors
Ground surveillance robot (1984)	high-resolution grey level vision low-resolution color vision acoustic laser range finder	unknown natural terrain	triangular segments in blackboard	variety possible (data put in spatial and temporal correspondence)
DARPA ALV (1985)	color vision sonar laser range finder	unknown natural terrain	Cartesian elevation maps (CEM's)	average elevation change over small CEM areas
CMU's ALV's NAVLAB and Terregator (1986)	color vision sonar laser range finder	unknown roadway	polygon tokens with attribute-value pairs in whiteboard	variety possible (data put in spatial and temporal correspondence)
Stanford mobile robot (1987)	stereo vision tactile ultrasonic	unknown man-made	hierarchical sensor measurements and symbols	Kalman filter
HERMIES (1988)	multiple cameras sonar array laser range finder	unknown man-made	node network graph structure	production rules

452

4.1. HILARE

The mobile robot HILARE combines contact, acoustic, two-dimensional vision, and laser range finding sensors to enable it to operate in unknown environments (Bauzil, Briot & Ribes, 1981; Briot, Talou & Bauzil, 1981; Chatila & Laumond, 1985; de Saint Vincent, 1986; Ferrer, Briot & Talou, 1981; Giralt, Chatila & Vaisset, 1984; Giralt, Sobek & Chatila, 1979; Grandjean & de Saint Vincent, 1989; Noreils & Chatila, 1989). HILARE was the first mobile robot to create a world of an unknown environment using information from multiple sensors (Harmon, 1986a). Acoustic and vision sensors are used to create a graph that is partitioned into a hierarchy of locations. Vision and laser range finding sensors are then used to develop an approximate three-dimensional representation of different regions in the environment—constraints being used to eliminate extraneous features in the representation. The laser range finder is then used to obtain more accurate range information for each region. To provide a robust and accurate estimation of the robot's position, three independent methods are used: absolute position referencing by use of a beacon, trajectory integration without external reference, and relative position referencing with respect to landmarks in the environment (Chatila & Laumond, 1985). Each of these methods is used in a complementary fashion to correct or reduce errors and uncertainties in the other methods. The information from the various sensors is combined to provide the position of known objects and places relative to the robot. The shape of each object is represented as a polygon. Depending on the features of an object and its distance from the robot, an appropriate group of redundant sensors is selected to measure the object. The uncertainty of each sensor is modeled as a Gaussian distribution. If the standard deviations of all the sensor's measurements have the same magnitude, a weighted average of their values is used as the fused estimate of a vertex of the object (see Section 1.1 of Chapter 8); otherwise, the measurement from the sensor with the smallest standard deviation is used. The estimated vertices of the object can then be matched to known regions of the world model by finding an object in the model that minimizes the weighted sum of the distance between corresponding vertices.

4.2. Crowley's Mobile Robot

Crowley (1984, 1985a, 1985b, 1989) describes a mobile robot with a rotating ultrasonic range sensor and a touch sensor that is capable of autonomous navigation in a known domain. Information from a pre-learned global world model is integrated with information from both sensors to maintain dynamically a composite model of the local environment. Obstacles and surfaces are represented as connected sequences of line segments in two dimensions. Confidence as to the actual existence of each line segment is represented by an integer ranging from one (transient) to five (stable and connected). The uncertainty as to the position, orientation, and length of each segment is accounted for by allowing tolerances in the values of these attributes. Information from the global model and the sensors is matched to the composite local model by determining which line segment in the local model has the best correspondence with a given line segment from either the global model or the sensors. The best correspondence is found by performing a sequence of tests of increasing computational cost based on the position, orientation, and length of the line segments relative to each other. The results of the matching process are then used to update the composite local model by either adding newly perceived line segments to the model or adjusting the confidence value of the existing segments. The local model can then be used for obstacle detection, local path planning, path execution, and learning.

4.3. Ground Surveillance Robot

The ground surveillance robot described by Harmon (1987, 1990) is an autonomous vehicle designed to transit from one known location to another over unknown natural terrain. Vision and acoustic ranging sensors are used for obstacle detection. A laser range finder together with a high-resolution gray-level camera and a low-resolution color camera are used for distant terrain and landmark recognition. The information from the obstacle detection sensors is fused into a single estimate of the position of nearby obstacles by superpositioning distributions that represent each sensor's a priori probability of detection. A distributed blackboard is used both to control the various subsystems of the vehicle and as a mechanism through which to integrate and fuse various types of sensor data. As part of the blackboard, a world model is used to organize the data into a class tree with inheritance properties. Each element in the world model has a list of properties to which values are assigned, some values being determined by sensory data. Terrain data are represented as triangular segments with the properties of absolute position, orientation, adjacency, and type of ground cover. In order to allow a variety of fusion methods to be used, each element in the world model includes a time stamp and measures of its accuracy and confidence. When two or more sensor values are functionally dependent, changes in one value will propagate throughout the blackboard so that the dependent values reflect its change. When sensor values refer to the same property of an element, either a decision is made as to which of the competing values is to be used (e.g., the most recent value of the most accurate sensor) or the values are fused together.

4.4. The DARPA Autonomous Land Vehicle

The Autonomous Land Vehicle (ALV) (Daily et al., 1988; Dunlay, 1988; Linden, Marsh & Dove, 1986; Lowrie, Thomas, Gremban & Turk, 1985; Turk et al., 1987) built by Martin Marietta is part of the Defense Advanced Research Projects Agency's (DARPA) Strategic Computing Program. The ALV is intended to be a testbed designed for demonstrating the state of the art in autonomous vehicle research (Dunlay, 1988). A number of companies and universities are currently working on different research aspects of the project. In the initial stages of the project, the ALV was used in road-following applications (Lowrie et al., 1985; Turk et al., 1987; Waxman et al., 1987); in more recent stages, obstacle avoidance (Dunlay, 1988) and autonomous cross-country navigation capabilities (Dunlay, 1988; Payton, 1986) have been demonstrated. Future research is aimed at enhancing the operational speed and robustness of the ALV, and adding capabilities such as landmark recognition (Dunlay, 1988).

In road-following applications (Dunlay, 1988; Turk et al., 1987), the ALV uses sonar to determine its height, tilt, and roll with respect to road surfaces directly beneath it. Complementary information from a laser range scanner and two color video cameras is used for obstacle detection. Color video information is used to locate roads because the laser range information can easily be confused if there is very little difference in depth between the road and surrounding areas. Laser range information is used to obtain accurate descriptions of the geometrical features of obstacles on the road because, unlike the video information, it is not sensitive to poor lighting conditions and shadows. After being transformed to a common world coordinate system, the video information is used both the determine the boundaries of the road for path planning and, after being integrated with similarly transformed laser range information, for obstacle recognition.

In autonomous cross-country navigation applications (Daily et al., 1988), a hierarchical control system is used to provide the ALV with the flexibility needed for operation over natural terrain. At the lowest level in the hierarchy, "virtual sensors" and "reflexive behaviors" are used as real-time operating primitives for the rest of the control system (Payton, 1986). Functioning in a similar transparent manner as the logical sensors described in Chapter 4, virtual sensors combine information from physical sensors with appropriate processing algorithms to provide specific information to associated reflexive behaviors. Combinations of behaviors and virtual sensors are used to handle specific subproblems that are part of the overall navigation task. In these applications the laser range scanner, together with orientation sensors to determine the pitch, roll, and x and y position of the vehicle, were used to provide information needed to create overhead map-view representations of the terrain called "Cartesian elevation maps" (CEMs); other range sensors such as stereo vision could also be used to create CEMs. Smoothing procedures are applied to the CEMs to fill in detail not provided by the sparse laser range information. As the ALV travels over the terrain, CEMs are fused together to provide a means for selecting traversable trajectories for the vehicle.

4.5. CMU's Autonomous Land Vehicles

The NAVLAB and Terregator are two vehicles developed at Carnegie-Mellon University's Robotics Institute as part of their research on autonomous land vehicles (Goto & Stentz, 1987; Shafer, Stentz & Thorpe, 1986). Each vehicle is equipped with a color TV camera, laser range finder, and sonar sensors. The sonar sensors are used to detect nearby obstacles. The design of an architecture able to support parallel processing and the development of multisensor integration and fusion techniques have been major goals of the research. The current system consists of several independently running modules that are tied together in what is termed a "whiteboard" control structure, which differs from a blackboard in that each module continues to run while synchronization and data retrieval requests are made. Data in a local world model are represented as tokens with attribute–value pairs. Tokens representing physical objects and geometric locations consist of a two-dimensional polygonal shape, a reference coordinate frame that can be used to transform the location to other frames, and time stamps that record when the token was created and the time at which sensor data were received that led to its creation. When range data, measured by the camera and laser range finder at different times and locations on the vehicle, are to be fused, the coordinate frames of the tokens created by each sensor for these data are first transformed to a common vehicle frame and then transformed forward to the same point in time. The data are now fused, resulting in the creation of a new token representing the fused data.

4.6. Stanford Mobile Robot

The Stanford Mobile Robot (Kriegman, Triendl & Binford, 1987, 1989) uses tactile, stereo vision, and ultrasonic sensors for navigation in unstructured man-made environments. A hierarchical representation is used in its two-dimensional world model, with features close to the actual sensor measurements at the lowest level and more abstract or symbolic features at the higher levels. The uncertainty as to the location of the robot and the features in the environment is modeled with a Gaussian distribution. A Kalman filter (see Section 1.2 of Chapter 8) is used to fuse the measurements from a sensor as the robot moves. An example of the application of this method is shown in Figure 19.2. Figure 19.2(a) shows two points **a** and **b** as measured by the stereo vision sensor—first at location $\mathbf{p}_1$ and then at location $\mathbf{p}_2$. The uncertainty ellipses around the point measurements are elongated towards the sensor because the uncertainty due to distance is much greater than the angular uncertainty when calculated using stereo vision. The uncertainty due to distance is also greater for points further away from the robot (i.e., **b** is more uncertain than **a**). The two measurements of each point (e.g., $\mathbf{a}_1$ and $\mathbf{a}_2$) are not coincident because of the inherent error in the internal odometer sensor of the robot. In Figure 19.2(b), the uncertainty of the points and location $\mathbf{p}_2$ are shown with respect to $\mathbf{p}_1$. The uncertainty ellipse around $\mathbf{p}_2$ is elongated perpendicular to the direction of motion of the robot because the angular error of the odometer sensor is greater than the error in determining distance of $\mathbf{p}_2$. The uncertainty with respect to $\mathbf{p}_1$ of measurements $\mathbf{a}_2$ and $\mathbf{b}_2$ has increased because their uncertainty with respect to $\mathbf{p}_2$ has been compounded with $\mathbf{p}_2$'s locational uncertainty. In Figure 19.2(c), the Kalman filter is used to determine new fused estimates for both points (**a*** and **b***) that have a reduced uncertainty with respect to $\mathbf{p}_1$ and $\mathbf{p}_2$. The uncertainty of $\mathbf{p}_2$ with respect to $\mathbf{p}_2$ has also been reduced.

4.7. HERMIES

A series of HERMIES (hostile environment robotic machine intelligence experimental series) mobile robots have been developed at the Oak Ridge National Laboratory (Burks, de Saussure, Weisbin, Jones & Hamel, 1987; Mann, Hamel & Weisbin, 1988; Weisbin, Burks, Einstein, Feezell, Manges & Thompson, 1990; Weisbin, de Saussure, Einstein, Pin & Heer, 1989). The HERMIES-IIB (Burks et al., 1987; Weisbin et al., 1989) and the HERMIES-III (Weisbin et al., 1990) mobile robots have been developed as research platforms capable of autonomous navigation and manipulation in complex secured environ-

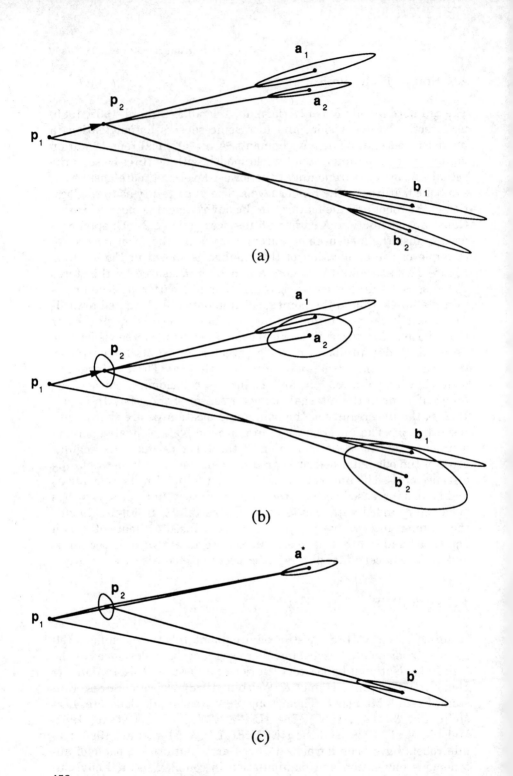

ments such as those found inside nuclear reactor buildings. A network graph structure is used as an a priori world model and a sonar array is used to detect unexpected obstacles in the path of the robot. If an unknown obstacle is blocking a planned movement along a link in the network, the robot returns to the most recently visited node and then autonomously determines a new path. Time constraints are included in the path-planning process. Multiple cameras are used to first search for known objects in the environment (e.g., control panels) and then to aid in the manipulation of the objects; no use is made of the cameras for depth determination. HERMIES-III includes a laser range finder for more accurate range information. Production rules are used within an expert system for high-level planning and decision making, including the integration and fusion of sensor information.

5. OVERVIEW

This section presents an overview of the remaining chapters in Part IV.

Chapter 20: Chen has proposed a "spherical octree" representation for use in mobile robot navigation. A spherical octree is an 8-ary tree structure that at its first level separates a spherical perspective view of the environment into eight octants corresponding to the children of the root node (the entire spherical environment perceived by a robot). Objects in the environment can be represented in the octree by recursively subdividing octants containing part of the object into eight more octants at the next lowest level and merging octants that are completely contained by the object into one octant at the next highest level, repeating this process to represent the object at increasingly finer resolution. The use of a spherical perspective view eliminates some of the limitations of the typical orthographic and planar perspectives used in optical sensing. It is also appropriate for sensors providing range information because range values can be represented as the radial distances from the sensor to the object. Information from each different sensor is used to reconstruct three-dimensional surfaces using a knowledge base of typical patterns for the sensor. The reconstructed

---

Figure 19.2. Reduction in uncertainty as to the location of a robot (p) and two points (a and b) in the environment through the use of the Kalman filter to fuse measurements as the robot moves from p_1 to p_2. (a) Uncertainty before fusion of points a and b as measured from p_1 and p_2. (b) Uncertainty of a, b, and p_2 with respect to p_1. (c) Fused estimates for a, b, and p_2 with respect to p_1. (Adapted from Figure 10 in Kriegman, Triendl, and Binford (1987).)

surfaces are then fused together as part of the process of being represented in the octree structure. Recent extensions of this work can be found in Chen (1988a, 1988b, 1988c, 1990).

Chapter 21: Ayache and Faugeras describe the means by which three-dimensional world models called "visual maps" can be created for mobile robots using passive visual information. Sequences of visual maps are fused together at the feature level using an extended Kalman filter (see Section 1.2 of Chapter 8). The use of the extended Kalman filter allows for the efficient registration of the sequences of visual maps and enables the overall uncertainty as to the location of objects in the environment to be reduced in the presence of environmental and sensor noise.

REFERENCES

Anderson, T.L., & Donath, M. (1990). Animal behavior as a paradigm for developing robot autonomy. *Robotics and Autonomous Systems, 6,* 145–168.

Andress, K.M., & Kak, A.C. (1988). Evidence accumulation & flow of control in a hierarchical spatial reasoning system. *AI Magazine, 9*(2), 75–94.

Arkin, R.C. (1989). Motor schema-based mobile robot navigation. *International Journal of Robotics Research, 8*(4), 92–112.

Arkin, R.C. (1990). Integrating behavioral, perceptual, and world knowledge in reactive navigation. *Robotics and Autonomous Systems, 6,* 105–122.

Asada, M. (1988). Building a 3-D world model for a mobile robot from sensory data. *Proceedings of the IEEE International Conference on Robotics and Automation* (pp. 918–923). Philadelphia, PA.

Bauzil, G., Briot, M., & Ribes, P. (1981). A navigation sub-system using ultrasonic sensors for the mobile robot HILARE. *Proceedings of the 1st Conference on Robot Vision and Sensory Controls.* Stratford-upon-Avon, UK.

Beer, R.D., Chiel, H.J., & Sterling, L.S. (1990). A biological perspective on autonomous agent design. *Robotics and Autonomous Systems, 6,* 169–186.

Berry, R., Loebbaka, K., & Hall, E. (1983). Sensors for mobile robots. *Proceedings of the 3rd Conference on Robot Vision and Sensory Controls* (pp. 584–588). Cambridge, MA.

Bestavros, A.A., Clark, J.J., & Ferrier, N.J. (1990). Management of sensorimotor activity in mobile robots. *Proceedings of the IEEE International Conference on Robotics and Automation* (pp. 592–597). Cincinnati, OH.

Bixler, J.P., & Miller, D.P. (1987). A sensory input system for autonomous mobile robots. *Proceedings of the Workshop Spatial Reasoning and Multisensor Fusion* (pp. 211–219). St. Charles, IL.

Briot, M., Talou, J.C., & Bauzil, G. (1981). The multisensors which help a mobile robot find its place. *Sensor Review, 1*(1), 15–19.

Brooks, R.A. (1985). Visual map making for a mobile robot. *Proceedings of the IEEE International Conference on Robotics and Automation* (pp. 824–829). St. Louis, MO.

Brooks, R.A. (1986). A robust layered control system for a mobile robot. *IEEE Journal of Robotics Automation*, RA-2(1), 14–23.

Brooks, R.A. (1987). A hardware retargetable distributed layered architecture for mobile robot control. *Proceedings of the IEEE International Conference on Robotics and Automation* (pp. 106–110). Raleigh, NC.

Brooks, R.A. (1989). A robot that walks; emergent behaviors from a carefully evolved network. *Proceedings of the IEEE International Conference on Robotics and Automation* (pp. 692–696). Scottsdale, AZ.

Brooks, R.A. (1990). Elephants don't play chess. *Robotics and Autonomous Systems, 6*, 3–15.

Burks, B.L., de Saussure, G., Weisbin, C.R., Jones, J.P., & Hamel, W.R. (1987, Winter). Autonomous navigation, exploration, and recognition using the HERMIES-IIB robot. *IEEE Expert*, 18–27.

Chatila, R., & Laumond, J. (1985). Position referencing and consistent world modeling for mobile robots. *Proceedings of the IEEE International Conference on Robotics and Automation* (pp. 138–145). St. Louis, MO.

Chen, S. (1988a). Adaptive control of multisensor systems. In C.W. Weaver (Ed.), *Proceedings of the SPIE, vol. 931, Sensor Fusion* (pp. 98–102). Orlando, FL.

Chen, S. (1988b). Fusion of multisensor data into 3-D spatial information. In P.S. Schenker (Ed.), *Proceedings of the SPIE, vol. 1003, Sensor Fusion: Spatial Reasoning and Scene Interpretation* (pp. 80–85). Cambridge, MA.

Chen, S. (1988c). A geometric approach to multisensor fusion. In C.W. Weaver (Ed.), *Proceedings of the SPIE, vol. 931, Sensor Fusion* (pp. 22–25). Orlando, FL.

Chen, S. (1990). A spherical model for navigation and spatial reasoning. *Proceedings of the IEEE International Conference on Robotics and Automation* (pp. 776–781). Cincinnati, OH.

Crowley, J.L. (1984). Dynamic world modeling for an intelligent mobile robot. *Proceedings of the 7th International Conference on Pattern Recognition* (pp. 207–210). Montreal, PQ, Canada.

Crowley, J.L. (1985a). Dynamic world modeling for an intelligent mobile robot using a rotating ultra-sonic ranging device. *Proceedings of the IEEE International Conference on Robotics and Automation* (pp. 128–135). St. Louis, MO.

Crowley, J.L. (1985b). Navigation for an intelligent mobile robot. *IEEE Journal of Robotics and Automation*, RA-1(1), 31–41.

Crowley, J.L. (1986). Path planning and obstacle avoidance. *Encyclopedia of artificial intelligence* (pp. 708–715). New York: Wiley.

Crowley, J.L. (1989). World modeling and position estimation for a mobile robot using ultrasonic ranging. *Proceedings of the IEEE International Conference on Robotics and Automation* (pp. 674–680). Scottsdale, AZ.

Daily, M., Harris, J., Keirsey, D., Olin, K., Payton, D., Reiser, K., Rosenblatt, J., Tseng, D., & Wong, V. (1988). Autonomous cross-country navigation with the ALV. *Proceedings of the IEEE International Conference on Robotics and Automation* (pp. 718–726). Philadelphia, PA.

de Saint Vincent, A.R. (1986). A 3D perception system for the mobile robot HILARE. *Proceedings of the IEEE International Conference on Robotics and Automation* (pp. 1105–1111). San Francisco, CA.

Dean, T. (1988). On the complexity of integrating spatial measurements. In P.S. Schenker (Ed.), *Proceedings of the SPIE, vol. 1003, Sensor Fusion: Spatial Reasoning and Scene Interpretation* (pp. 358–365). Cambridge, MA.

Dunlay, R.T. (1988). Obstacle avoidance perception processing for the Autonomous Land Vehicle. *Proceedings of the IEEE International Conference on Robotics and Automation* (pp. 912–917). Philadelphia, PA.

Elfes, A. (1986). A sonar-based mapping and navigation system. *Proceedings of the IEEE International Conference on Robotics and Automation* (pp. 1151–1156). San Francisco, CA.

Elfes, A. (1987). Sonar-based real-world mapping and navigation. *IEEE Journal of Robotics and Automation*, RA-3(3), 249–265.

Elfes, A. (1989). Using occupancy grids for mobile robot perception. *Computer*, 22(6), 46–57.

Everett, H.R. (1985, April). A second-generation autonomous sentry robot. *Robotics Age*, 29–32.

Ferrer, M., Briot, M., & Talou, J.C. (1981). Study of a video image treatment system for the mobile robot HILARE. *Proceedings of the 1st Conference on Robot Vision and Sensory Control*. Stratford-upon-Avon, UK.

Flynn, A.M. (1988). Combining sonar and infrared sensors for mobile robot navigation. *International Journal of Robotics Research*, 7(6), 5–14.

Giralt, G., Chatila, R., & Vaisset, M. (1984). An integrated navigation and motion control system for autonomous multisensory mobile robots. In M. Brady & R. Paul (Eds.), *Robotics research: The first international symposium* (pp. 191–214). Cambridge, MA: The MIT Press.

Giralt, G., Sobek, R., & Chatila, R. (1979). A multilevel planning and navigation system for a mobile robot: A first approach to HILARE. *Proceedings of the 6th International Joint Conference on Artificial Intelligence* (pp. 335–337). Tokyo, Japan.

Goto, Y., & Stentz, A. (1987). The CMU system for mobile robot navigation. *Proceedings of the IEEE International Conference on Robotics and Automation* (pp. 99–105). Raleigh, NC.

Grandjean, P., & de Saint Vincent, A.R. (1989). 3-D modeling of indoor scenes by fusion of noisy range and stereo data. *Proceedings of the IEEE International Conference on Robotics and Automation* (pp. 681–687). Scottsdale, AZ.

Harmon, S.Y. (1984). USMC Ground Surveillance Robot: A testbed for autonomous vehicle research. *Proceedings of the 4th University of Alabama Robotics Conference*. Huntsville, AL.

Harmon, S.Y. (1986a). Autonomous vehicles. *Encyclopedia of artificial intelligence* (pp. 39–45). New York: Wiley.

Harmon, S.Y. (1986b). Robots, mobile. *Encyclopedia of artificial intelligence* (pp. 957–963). New York: Wiley.

Harmon, S.Y. (1987). The Ground Surveillance Robot (GSR): An autonomous vehicle designed to transit unknown terrain. *IEEE Journal of Robotics Automation,* RA-3(3), 266–279.

Harmon, S.Y. (1988). A report on the NATO Workshop on Mobile Robot Implementation. *Proceedings of the IEEE International Conference on Robotics and Automation* (pp. 604–610). Philadelphia, PA.

Harmon, S.Y. (1990). Tools for multisensor data fusion in autonomous robots. In J.T. Tou & J.G. Balchen (Eds.), *Highly redundant sensing in robotic systems* (pp. 103–125). Berlin: Springer-Verlag.

Hebert, M., Caillas, C., Krotkov, E., Kweon, I.S., & Kanade, T. (1989). Terrain mapping for a roving planetary explorer. *Proceedings of the IEEE International Conference on Robotics and Automation* (pp. 674–680). Scottsdale, AZ.

Isik, C., & Meystel, A. (1986). Decision making at a level of a hierarchical control for unmanned robots. *Proceedings of the IEEE International Conference on Robotics and Automation* (pp. 1772–1778). San Francisco, CA.

Jorgensen, C.C. (1987). Neural network representation of sensor graphs in autonomous robot path planning. *Proceedings of the IEEE 1st International Conference on Neural Nets* (pp. IV-507–IV-515). San Diego, CA.

Kak, A.C., Roberts, B.A., Andress, K.M., & Cromwell, R.L. (1987). Experiments in the integration of world knowledge with sensory information for mobile robots. *Proceedings of the IEEE International Conference on Robotics and Automation* (pp. 734–740). Raleigh, NC.

Kriegman, D.J., Triendl, E., & Binford, T.O. (1987). A mobile robot: sensing, planning and locomotion. *Proceedings of the IEEE International Conference on Robotics and Automation* (pp. 402–408). Raleigh, NC.

Kriegman, D.J., Triendl, E., & Binford, T.O. (1989). Stereo vision and navigation in buildings for mobile robots. *IEEE Transactions on Robotics and Automation,* RA-5(6), 792–803.

Lawton, D.T., Levitt, T.S., McConnell, C., & Glicksman, J. (1986). Terrain models for an autonomous land vehicle. *Proceedings of the IEEE International Conference on Robotics and Automation* (pp. 2043–2051). San Francisco, CA.

Levi, P. (1987). Principles of planning and control concepts for autonomous mobile robots. *Proceedings of the IEEE International Conference on Robotics and Automation* (pp. 874–881). Raleigh, NC.

Linden, T.A., Marsh, J.P., & Dove, D.L. (1986). Architecture and early experience with planning for the ALV. *Proceedings of the IEEE International Conference on Robotics and Automation* (pp. 2035–2042). San Francisco, CA.

Lowrie, J.M., Thomas, M., Gremban, K., & Turk, M. (1985). The autonomous land vehicle (ALV) preliminary road-following demonstrations. In D.P. Casasent (Ed.), *Proceedings of the SPIE, vol. 579, Intelligent Robots and Computer Vision* (pp. 336–350).

Luo, R.C., & Kay, M.G. (1988). The role of multisensor integration and fusion in the operation of mobile robots. *Proceedings of the IEEE International Workshop on Intelligent Robots* (pp. 259–264). Tokyo, Japan.

Mann, R.C., Hamel, W.R., & Weisbin, C.R. (1988). The development of an intelligent nuclear maintenance robot. *Proceedings of the IEEE International Conference on Robotics and Automation* (pp. 621–623). Philadelphia, PA.

Meystel, A. (1990). On the phenomenon of high redundancy in robotic perception. In J.T. Tou & J.G. Balchen (Eds.), *Highly redundant sensing in robotic systems* (pp. 177–250). Berlin: Springer-Verlag.

Miller, D. (1985). A spatial representation system for mobile robots. *Proceedings of the IEEE International Conference on Robotics and Automation* (pp. 122–127). St. Louis, MO.

Miller, J. (1977). A discrete adaptive guidance system for a roving vehicle. *Proceedings of the IEEE Conference Decision and Contr.* (pp. 566–575). New Orleans, LA.

Moravec, H.P. (1983). The Stanford Cart and the CMU Rover. *Proceedings of the IEEE, 71*(7), 872–884.

Nagata, S., Sekiguchi, M., & Asakawa, K. (1990). Mobile robot control by a structured hierarchical neural network. *IEEE Control Systems Magazine, 10*(3), 69–76.

Nilsson, N.J. (1969). A mobile automaton: An application of artificial intelligence techniques. *Proceedings of the 1st International Joint Conference Artificial Intelligence* (pp. 509–520). Washington, DC.

Noreils, F.R., & Chatila, R.G. (1989). Control of mobile robot actions. *Proceedings of the IEEE International Conference on Robotics and Automation* (pp. 701–707). Scottsdale, AZ.

Oskard, D.N., Hong, T.H., & Shaffer, C.A. (1988). In P.S. Schenker (Ed.), *Proceedings of the SPIE, vol. 1003, Sensor Fusion: Spatial Reasoning and Scene Interpretation* (pp. 439–450). Cambridge, MA.

Payton, D.W. (1986). An architecture for reflexive control. *Proceedings of the IEEE International Conference on Robotics and Automation* (pp. 1838–1845). San Francisco, CA.

Rigaud, V., & Marce, L. (1990). Absolute location of underwater robotic vehicles by acoustic data fusion. *Proceedings of the IEEE International Conference on Robotics and Automation* (pp. 1310–1315). Cincinnati, OH.

Rosenblatt, J.K., & Payton, D.W. (1989). A fine-grained alternative to the subsumption architecture for mobile robot control. *Proceedings of the International Joint Conference on Neural Networks,* (pp. II-317–II-323). Washington, DC.

Shafer, S.A., Stentz, A., & Thorpe, C.E. (1986). An architecture for sensory fusion in a mobile robot. *Proceedings of the IEEE International Conference on Robotics and Automation* (pp. 2002–2011). San Francisco, CA.

Smith, M.H., Sobek, R.P., Coles, L.S., Hodges, D.A., Robb, A.M., & Sinclair, P.L. (1975). The design of JASON, a computer controlled mobile robot. *Proceedings of the International Conference of the Cybernetics Society* (pp. 72–75). New York, NY.

Turk, M.A., Morgenthaler, D.G., Gremban, K.D., & Marra, M. (1987). Video road-following for the Autonomous Land Vehicle. *Proceedings of the IEEE International Conference on Robotics and Automation* (pp. 273–279). Raleigh, NC.

Waldron, S., & Meystel, A. (1988). Multiresolutional representation of spatial knowledge in intelligent control. In J.S. Gero (Ed.), *Artificial intelligence in engineering: Robotics and processes* (pp. 99–119). Amsterdam: Elsevier.

Wallace, R., Stentz, A., Thorpe, C., Moravec, H., Whittaker, W., & Kanade, T. (1985). First results in robot road-following. *Proceedings of the 9th International Joint Conference on Artificial Intelligence* (pp. 1089–1095). Los Angeles, CA.

Waxman, A.M., LeMoigne, J.J., Davis, L.S. Srinivasan, B., Kushner, T.R., Liang, E., & Siddalingaiah. (1987). A visual navigation system for autonomous land vehicles. *IEEE Journal of Robotics Automation*, RA-3(2), 124–141.

Weisbin, C.R., Burks, B.L., Einstein, J.R., Feezell, R.R., Manges, W.W., & Thompson, D.H. (1990). HERMIES-III: A step toward autonomous mobility, manipulation and perception. *Robotica, 8,* 7–12.

Weisbin, C.R., de Saussure, G., Einstein, J.R., Pin, F.G., & Heer, E. (1989). Autonomous mobile robot navigation and learning. *IEEE Computer, 22*(6), 29–35.

20
Multisensor Fusion and Navigation of Mobile Robots

Su-shing Chen

Navigation and motion control of autonomous mobile robots require an on-line, real-time sensory feedback system to guide robots to stay on planned paths, to avoid unexpected obstacles, to return to the planned path if a detour is necessary, and even to replan the path. This problem is a difficult one because of incomplete world knowledge and unknown obstacles. A spherical sensory model similar to human perception is presented. Its spherical octree data structure provides an efficient and unified representation scheme for multisensor fusion, navigation, motion control, and spatial reasoning.

1. INTRODUCTION

In the endeavor of developing AMRs (autonomous mobile robots), navigation and motion control are two basic issues. If AMRs are to emulate human-operated vehicles, an on-line, real-time sensory feedback system is essential to guiding robots to stay on course, to avoid unknown obstacles, to return to a planned path from a detour, and even to replan the path. This is a difficult problem because of dynamic and incomplete world knowledge and unknown obstacles. So preprocessing world knowledge and using brutal computing power may not be able to solve the problem. It is desirable to develop an efficient model and representation scheme that captures some human cognitive and subcognitive characteristics and yet is implementable in current computer technology.

Since navigation and motion control are determined by sensory data, a theoretical foundation of multisensor fusion is needed. A spherical sensory model similar to human perception has been investigated (Chen, 1985a, 1985b, 1986). Its spherical data structure provides an efficient and unified representation scheme for multisensor fusion, navigation, motion control, and spatial reasoning. This model is independent of different sensor types. Images of sonar sensing, optical sensing, radar sensing, infrared sensing, and others may be integrated in the same model to enhance image understanding and object recognition capabilities. The spherical model eliminates some limitations of the usual orthographic and planar perspective models in optical sensing. It is also the natural model for range data, because range values are radial distances from a sensor to an observed object.

The main question of multisensor fusion is to integrate many numerical and spatial sensory data to yield useful information about an object (or environment). One approach is to integrate different images (considered as partial and incomplete information) by artificial intelligence and evidential reasoning methods. Our approach is to gather 3-D spatial information about an object by partial surface reconstruction from sensory data. Then the integration is performed in the spherical model into a single set of spatial data about the object.

Multisensor families may be homogeneous or heterogeneous. Multisensor fusion may be classified into two categories: static and dynamic. "Static multisensor fusion" deals with the situation in which both the robot and the environment are static. Although it is not of interest to mobile robots, it is basic to the dynamic case. In static multisensor fusion, we integrate different sensory data from possibly heterogeneous sensors. There are two possibilities—a single robot or a distributed system of robots or surveillance stations communicating sensory data among themselves. In the static case, they and the environment are assumed to be static. "Dynamic multisensor fusion" deals with situations in which robots and/or the environment may be moving. Dynamic multisensor fusion is temporal, for it integrates sensory data over time. The spherical model is very useful and efficient for dynamic fusion, because we may integrate temporal images on the same sphere.

The spherical data structure of the model is a generalization of the octree data structure (Ahuja & Nash, 1984; Samet, 1984), which is gaining popularity in computer graphics, computer vision, robotic navigation, and planning. The octree structure divides the world space into eight octants. Each octant is again divided into eight octants. This recursive scheme provides a fine structure of the world space. For instance, collision avoidance may be treated as an intersection problem of two shaded regions in a sufficiently fine octree subdivision. This approach is more efficient than the configuration space approach (e.g., in Brooks & Lozano-Perez, 1985). One disadvantage of the octree representation is that it is not rotation invariant. For each rotation, we must recalculate the octree representation. The spherical octree representation avoids this difficulty.

In this chapter we shall not be concerned with robotic planning. We shall provide a navigation strategy that is based on local sensory data. Then we shall present an algorithm for collision avoidance of unknown obstacles. We are not assuming that our robotic sensors have a very accurate view of the environment. They only need to detect unknown obstacles at a reasonable distance. At such a distance, we require real-time response. In reality, image understanding and object recognition require too much processing time (including all the low-level image processing for edge detection, segmentation, etc.) to be of practical use.

Our approach to navigation and collision avoidance in the spherical model employs human cognitive skills described as follows. Imagine that we are running in a forest. We are able to avoid any obstacle in a split-second by simply changing our direction of movement. There is no need to understand images of the obstacle. When an AMR observes an obstacle in a viewing cone which is a sector of the spherical data structure, it simply changes its motion direction by a suitable angle to avoid the obstacle.

In general, navigation is performed by making sure that the radial direction of the robot motion coincides with the direction of the planned path. Any error in movement is corrected by this scheme. As a subtask of navigation, collision avoidance means not just avoiding the obstacle but also returning to the planned path after a detour. We have derived an efficient algorithm, the walk-around algorithm, which guides the robot returning to its planned path. This algorithm depends on the spherical data structure of the model.

In a more complicated environment such as narrow corridors, hallways, or mountain passes, an obstacle may imply retreat of the AMR and replanning of the path. Even though we have complete world knowledge, replanning may take a significant amount of time, so the robot has to stand still until a path is found. Our approach includes a learning scheme in which, during the course of its motion, an AMR is observing the environment and building a 2-D or 3-D map. Its system of multisensors dynamically creates and updates world knowledge in the spherical model which is stored in system memory. We note that a spherical model can be established at each position in space wherever the AMR may be. Here temporal and spatial fusion, discussed earlier, play an important role in this dynamic spatial information system. If retreat of the AMR is necessary, it returns to a position where an alternative path is plausible using the learning scheme.

Motion control refers to the changing of the steering angle of an AMR. Since the steering angle is compatible with the spherical data structure, motion control is unified with navigation. Implicitly, the walk-around algorithm is also a motion-control algorithm with a sensory feedback system to guide the "walk-around." In Chen (1990), we shall investigate motion control of AMRs in the mathematical system-theoretic framework of Kalman, Falb, and Arbib (1969).

Spatial reasoning involves reasoning and decision-making about spatial information and knowledge. In the above, we have depicted a spherical model and its representation of spatial sensory data. Spatial knowledge and reasoning are also representable in the spherical model. For instance, closeness between objects is determined by the elevation and azimuth angles θ, ϕ and the radial distance (depth value) ρ. The angles θ and ϕ represent whether an object is on the top (or bottom) and to the right (or left) of another object, respectively. The size of an object is represented by the solid angle and the radial scaling (Chen, 1986) of its enclosing region.

Finally, we classify AMRs into three categories—ALRs (autonomous land robots), ASRs (autonomous sea robots), and AARs (autonomous air robots). ALRs move on 2-D or $2 + 1/2$-D maps, while ASRs and AARs move in 3-D maps. Our spherical system offers a single, unified model for all three kinds of robots. In the case of 2-D maps, our spherical data structure (spherical octree) is reduced to a circular data structure (circular quadtree).

2. A SPHERICAL SENSORY MODEL

For simplicity, we shall consider generic sensors that yield range and shading data. Since optical sensing gives the most detailed information under normal situations, we present this spherical model here in the context of optical sensing. The relevance of this model to radar, thermal, and range sensing will be discussed in Section 4.

The world space is the 3-D Euclidean space R^3 whose origin 0 is assumed to be the position of a family of sensors. In most vision systems, a point $p(x, y, z)$ in R^3 is projected to the image point $Q(X, Y)$ by the formulas $X = x/z$ and $Y = y/z$, where the focal length is 1 and the z-axis is the optical axis. This projection is the perspective projection onto the flat image plane (X, Y). A problem with the flat perspective is distortion over a wide viewing angle. As a consequence, numerical computation becomes unstable. In image processing and computer vision, the orthographic model is often used. It also has its limitations. For instance, a robot viewing a straight hallway at a certain distance will only see the end wall and will not see the two side walls. It is a good approximation for remote sensing but not for AMRs. (See Figure 20.1.)

The spherical model uses the unit sphere as the image sphere on which all sensory data are represented. One improvement over the flat model is that we may represent sensory data of not only 360 degrees, but also the whole spherical solid angle around the robot (see Figure 20.2). It is feasible to implement many different sensor families on the robot in a spherical manner. There have been robots built with sonar sensors covering 360 degrees of viewing angle. The unit sphere is parameterized by the two parameters θ and ϕ, where $0 \leq \theta \leq \pi$, $0 \leq \phi < 2\pi$. Explicitly, an arbitrary point on the sphere is given by ($\cos \theta \cos \phi$, $\cos \theta \sin \phi$, $\sin \theta$). The angle θ is called the elevation angle which measures the angle from the ray OA to the ray OP. The angle ϕ is called the azimuth angle which measures the angle from the x-axis to the ray OA. (See Figure 20.3.)

The image point $Q(X, Y)$ is related to the spherical image point $S(\theta, \phi)$ by

$$X = x/z = \cot \theta \cos \phi,$$

$$Y = y/z = \cot \theta \sin \phi.$$

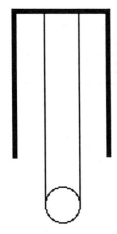 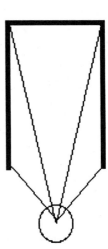

Figure 20.1. Robotic vision.

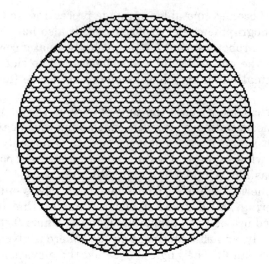

Figure 20.2. A spherical sensor family.

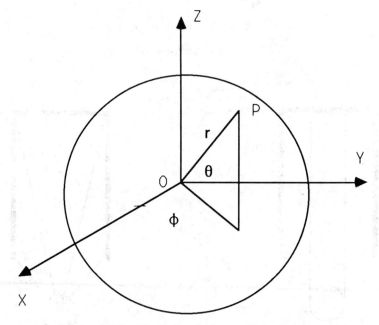

Figure 20.3. The spherical coordinate system.

This relation is a nonlinear transformation between the image plane and the image hemisphere (the half of the sphere tangent to the image plane). If we place sensors over a sphere on an AMR, we shall receive sensory data in all directions. There are several image planes tangent to the same sphere. Under different nonlinear transformations described above, image data on different image planes are transformed to the same image sphere. (See Figure 20.4.)

The rotation group SO(3) (of 3 by 3 orthogonal matrices) transforms (or shuffles) these image planes tangent to the sphere. In fact, given two arbitrary points on the sphere, we are able to find a rotation which transforms one to the other and transforms an image plane at the first point to an image plane at the second point. This idea is useful to dynamic (temporal) fusion of several frames over time (see Section 4.2).

Vanishing points are often annoying to computer vision researchers. Under the perspective projection, parallel lines intersect at a vanishing point which is far out in the image plane. Computation of vanishing points can be done easily using the sphere. Any two parallel lines in R^3 are projected onto two intersecting arcs on the sphere. The inter-

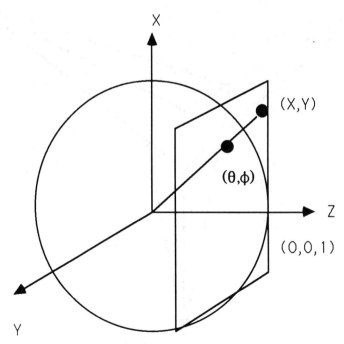

Figure 20.4. Relation between spherical and flat imaging systems.

section point is a vanishing point. Since finite and vanishing points are treated equally on the image sphere, knowledge about vanishing points allows us to constrain certain elements of an image in an efficient way. (See Figure 20.5.)

The shading of an optical image is based on the Lambertian model. Under the natural transformation from the flat image coordinates (X, Y) to the spherical coordinates (θ, ϕ) of elevation and azimuth angles θ and ϕ, the image intensity $i(\theta, \phi)$ at (θ, ϕ) is defined as $i(X(\theta, \phi), Y(\theta, \phi))$ which is given by the usual Lambertian law.

In the spherical coordinates (ρ, θ, ϕ) of R^3, the radial value (depth value) $\rho = \rho(\theta, \phi)$ depends on θ and ϕ. As (θ, ϕ) varies, $\rho(\theta, \phi)$ sweeps out the object that is sensed. Thus, geometric information about the object can be determined by the radial value (depth value) $\rho(\theta, \phi)$ and its derivatives $\partial \rho / \partial \theta$ and $\partial \rho / \partial \phi$ with respect to (θ, ϕ). The quantities $(1/\rho)(\partial \rho / \partial \theta)$ and $(1/\rho)(\partial \rho / \partial \phi)$ are the tangents $\tan \sigma$ and $\tan \tau$ of slant angles σ and τ (Brooks & Lozano-Prerz, 1985). They determine the orientation (normal vector) at the point of $\rho(\theta, \phi)$ on the object surface. By calculating further derivatives, we can determine the complete

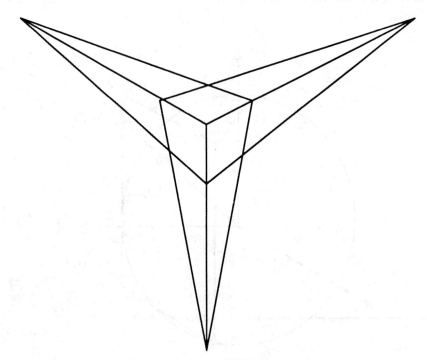

Figure 20.5. Vanishing points.

local geometry of the object surface (Chen & Penna, 1986b, 1987; Penna & Chen, 1986).

Now we describe how to relate rigid motions of objects to the spherical model. In the world space, a rigid motion is given by $(x', y', z')' = R(x, y, z)' + (x_0, y_0, z_0)'$, where R is a rotation around the origin and (x_0, y_0, z_0) is the translation vector. We want to find the projection of this motion onto the image sphere located at the origin and to show that motion analysis is easily understood in the spherical model. By decomposing the vector $(x', y', z')'$ into $R'R(x, y, z)'$ and a radial vector from the end point of $R'R(x, y, z)'$ to the end point of $(x', y', z')'$, we see that the motion is decomposed into two rotations R and R' and a scaling of constant factors indicating whether the object is moving away or towards the robot (see Figure 20.6). A scaling either shrinks or expands a region radially. The effect on a region A under a translation is depicted in Figure 20.7.

In Chen (1986) spherical harmonics are used to expand intensity functions on the sphere into many bands for edge detection and object identification. This scheme is a generalization of the usual Fourier

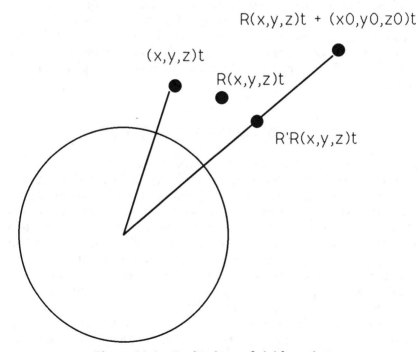

Figure 20.6. Projections of rigid motions.

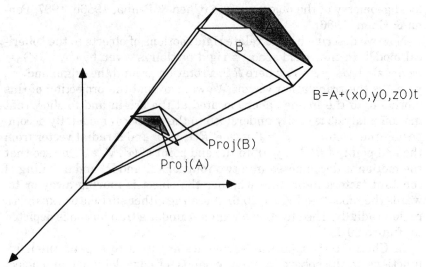

Figure 20.7. Scaling effect.

descriptor method for boundary curves to intensity functions. This method is also useful for representing infrared and radar information because it can also be expanded in spherical harmonics. This Fourier analysis is different from the 3-D approach presented and will not be pursued here; however, it offers another approach to multisensor fusion.

3. SPHERICAL DATA STRUCTURES

There are several 3-D data structures that have been used for spatial reasoning, robotic planning, and sensory image understanding, including constructive solid geometry, sweep representation, boundary representation, spatial enumeration, primitive instancing, and octree encoding. The octree encoding approach represents arbitrary objects to a limited precision in hierarchical tree structures. The higher-resolution details are represented by the lower-level nodes. Algorithms for manipulating these data structures are of linear growth and are easily implementable in parallel VLSI processors. For robotics, the spherical octree representation is more efficient than the rectangular octree representation. The spherical octree (an 8-ary hierarchical tree) is described as follows. The nodes represent spherical sector volumes generated by a recursive subdivision of a finite universe which can occupy any portion of a solid shell excluding the origin. A robot and its sensors are located at the origin. (See Figure 20.8.)

For simplicity, we examine the 2-D case where we have a sector of a circular ring. The outer radius can be as far as we wish and the inner radius depends on speed and other features of the robot.

In an octree, the root node (a spherical sector or a whole shell) represents the entire finite universe. A cut sphere separates the universe into two equal parts (see Figure 20.9). Additional cut spheres separate the universe into eight octants corresponding to the eight children of the root. Lower-level nodes correspond to the eight octants of the parent node. Recursively, a hierarchical tree is constructed to a certain resolution scale. An empty node (spherical sector) is shaded in white. A full node is completely enclosed by the object and is shaded in black. A partial node is partially intersecting the object and is shaded in gray (see Figure 20.10). The representation scheme is a recursive application of a 7 to 0 traversal sequence in the following manner. (See Figure 20.11.)

For AMRs moving on a 2-D map, a 2-D circular quadtree is used to represent obstacles and robots. The usual octree data structure represents orthographic views of any number of objects from any point in

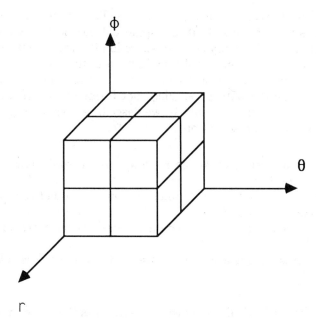

Figure 20.8. Spherical octree.

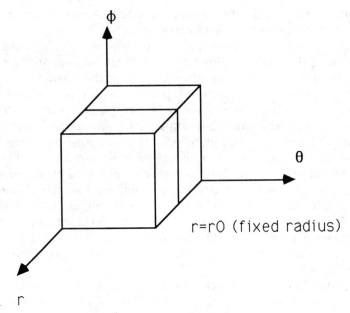

Figure 20.9. A spherical sector.

space in one direction (see Figure 20.12). The spherical octree data structure is used to represent the spherical perspective view of any number of objects from any point in space in all directions (full field-of-view). It is quite clear that a spherical octree is the right data structure to represent the behavior of AMRs. Collision avoidance is easily performed by finding a path which does not intersect any of the shaded sectors (see Figure 20.13). Finally, we describe a display algorithm for spherical octree representation.

1. Set up a spherical quadtree representing a front view at a fixed radius (depth value).
2. Project octree nodes (black and gray) onto the quadtree in front to back traversal order.
3. Write into the quadtree if a location has not been previously displayed.
4. If an octree node is completely obscured, it and its descendants are deleted.

The result is a spherical image which represents the surroundings of a robot. If we use planes tangent to the sphere to capture projected flat images, we generate the usual panorama view of the world around us.

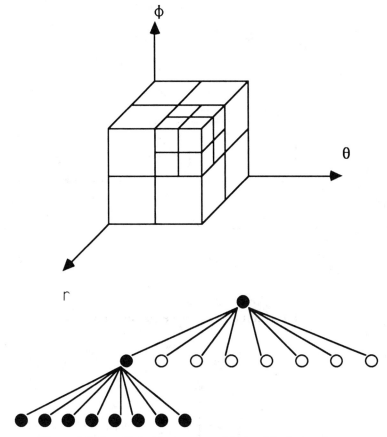

Figure 20.10. Spherical octree hierarchical structure.

4. MULTISENSOR FUSION

There are different kinds of sensors for an AMR: sonar, radar, optical, thermal (infrared), laser range-finding sensors, and shaft encoders. We have been successful in developing more sophisticated and less expensive sensors. A key question is how to integrate various sensory data into 3-D spatial information for semantic and high-level processing. So far we know very little about (heterogeneous) multisensor fusion. Only multiple sensors of the same family are successfully used in dealing with motion and dynamic scene analysis. We know very well that a single image cannot provide complete information about static as well as dynamic scene analysis. So multiple sensors are needed for perception and cognition.

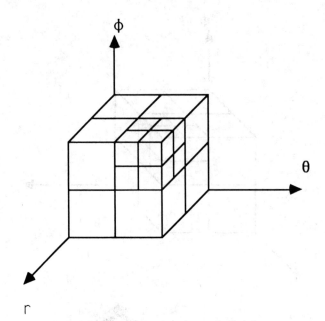

Figure 20.11. Recursive subdivision.

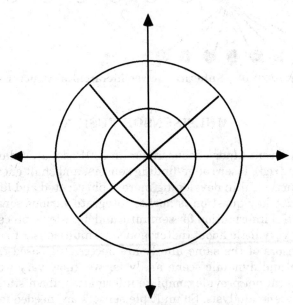

Figure 20.12. Circular quadtree.

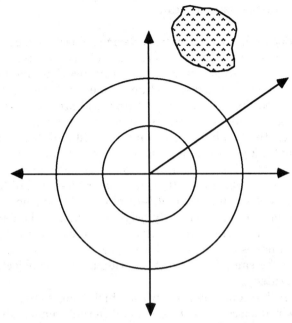

Figure 20.13. Collision avoidance.

In this section, we shall consider generic sensors, each of which may be a different type. Thus, they may be considered as heterogeneous without loss of generality. Multisensor fusion is classified into two categories: (1) static multisensor fusion and (2) dynamic multisensor fusion. Static multisensor fusion refers to the integration of all sensory data observed by different sensors at one point or in a distributed environment. Dynamic multisensor fusion refers to the temporal integration of static multisensor fusions at different time instants. If static fusion is integration over space, then dynamic fusion is double integration over space and time.

A key problem of multisensor fusion is correspondence (or registration). The correspondence problem of optical sensing is to establish the correlation of different images in either stereopsis (and its generalization to multiframe viewing, Martin & Aggarwal, 1983) or motion analysis (or dynamic scene analysis, Chen & Penna, 1986b). The correspondence problem is essential to other types of sensing such as thermal and radar. The problem is much more complex for images from different sensing mechanisms. Some known results include integration of shading data with range data. In this section, we present some ideas about multisensor fusion of shading, range, thermal, and radar data.

4.1. Static Multisensor Fusion

The main idea is first to reconstruct various object surfaces from various sensory data and then to integrate the object surfaces in the world space. This new approach is different from previous methods which mostly are trying to integrate at the image level. Different kinds of sensory data require different algorithms and provide different kinds of image data. For instance, infrared sensing uses hot spots. Any object whose temperature is above a certain threshold radiates thermal energy. A moving tank generates a great deal of heat; a building or machinery also generates heat. From different radiation profiles, we have different images of objects. So thermal images are quite different from optical images of shading data. Thermal emitters are not necessarily good visual reflectors and visually bright objects may be dark in thermal scenes. Consequently, it is extremely difficult to integrate these two kinds of images at the image level. However, in a 3-D object model, they provide the same kind of information about the object, and thus can be integrated.

Now, I mention some previous work which leads to the idea of using the single world space model instead of different images. In Chen and Penna (1986b, 1987) and Penna and Chen (1986), we have investigated object recovery from shading data under structured lighting environments. Under multiple light sources (or photometric stereopsis), we are able to recover the surface patch completely if the depth value is known at one object point (Penna & Chen, 1986). Using stripe lighting, we may further gather global information about a pile of objects. In Chen and Penna (1986a, 1986c), 3-D geometric features are computed from range data so that an object recognition scheme can be derived.

In an unstructured environment, these results are no longer valid. In Chen (1988a, 1988b) a geometric theory of multisensor fusion and perception based on the spherical perspective is developed. The spherical model and its data structure provide an efficient scheme for integrating different sensory data and for spatial reasoning.

Range and shading data: In the spherical model, range data are easily represented by spatial points in spherical coordinates (ρ, θ, ϕ). In Chen and Penna (1986a), geometric features about the 3-D approximating surface can be calculated efficiently. Two features—Gaussian curvature and mean curvature—characterize the local shape at each point. Other features can be calculated from these two, including principal curvatures and averages of different curvatures. From shading data, we also get geometric features of the surface which is to be reconstructed. Using models depending on sets of parameters of the desired surface, geometric features obtained from range data are used to guide the search in the model space (Chen, 1988b).

Multiframe optical viewing: It is known that a single image does not give complete information about 3-D objects and their environment. In the image intensity equation $i(X, Y) = R(x, y, z)\bar{n} \cdot \bar{s}$, where r is the reflectance, $\bar{n}$ is the unit normal vector, and $\bar{s}$ is the known direction of light source, there are two unknown components of the unit normal vector n. Intuitively, this is the reason why a single image does not provide complete 3-D information. Stereopsis and its generalization, multiframe viewing, employ at least two sensors to determine the depth values, orientations, and 3-D shapes. Over the intersection of two corresponding images we may solve the image intensity equation and its differentiated equations. The spherical model at the object provides a nice model for the integration of multiframes and for shape recovery. In Chen (1988b), we shall extend previous research results on multiframe views to the spherical model (see Figure 20.14).

Fusion of thermal and shading data: Thermal imaging systems extend our vision beyond the short-wavelength red into the far infrared by making visible the light naturally emitted by warm objects. While natural visual images are produced by reflection and by reflectivity

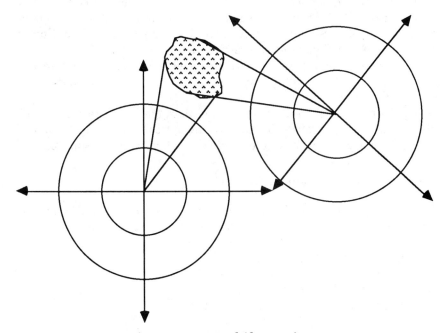

Figure 20.14. Multiframe views.

differences, thermal images are produced by self emission and by emissivity differences. The scene temperature produces the measured irradiance. The variations in the temperature correspond to the details in the visual scene, so a thermal image provides a visible analog of the thermal scene. The spatial patterns in the displayed thermal scene resemble those of the corresponding visible scene. There are significant differences in thermal and optical sensing. Thermal scenes have fewer shadows than visible scenes and 3-D contour information is lost. But all surfaces radiate energy so that all forward surfaces tend to be visible. Thermal emitters are not necessarily good visual reflectors, thus visually bright objects may be dark in the thermal scenes and vice versa. With a knowledge-base of thermal patterns, we are able to reconstruct a 3-D surface from thermal data (Chen, 1988b). This 3-D information is used to match with the reconstructed 3-D object from shading data of multiframe images or to guide the search in the model space of a single-frame image.

Fusion of radar and shading data: In radar sensing, shapes of aircraft, missiles, and satellites are determined by their radar cross section (RCS). The RCS of an object characterizes its scattering properties. The object is considered to be an ensemble of components, each of which can be geometrically approximated by a simple shape in such a way that the RCS of the simple shape approximates that of the component it models. After calculation of the RCSs, a proper combination of the component RCSs yields the estimate of the RCS of the entire object. In radar sensing, the spherical model has been adopted in the near-zone to study spherical wave fronts. In the far-zone, the flat model is used to study plane wave fronts.

The 3-D shape determined by radar data is again used to match with the 3-D shape determined by multiframe optical data, or to guide the search in model space by single-frame optical data. (See Figure 20.15.)

4.2. Dynamic Multisensor Fusion

For simplicity, we consider the relationship between a robot and an object, each of which may be in motion. There are four cases:

1. Static robot and static object.
2. Static robot and dynamic object.
3. Dynamic robot and static object.
4. Dynamic robot and dynamic object.

The first case is not interesting to us. If motions are constant, all three remaining cases are equivalent to each other. The robot undergoing a

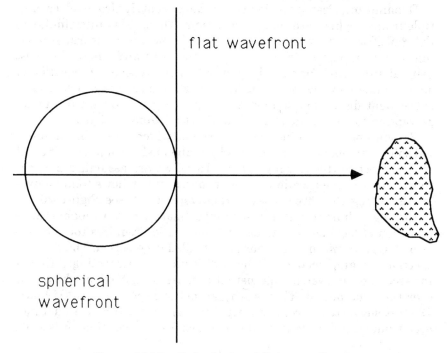

Figure 20.15. Spherical and flat wave fronts.

rigid motion M should be equivalent to the object undergoing the inverse rigid motion of M. Similarly, the robot undergoing motion M and the object undergoing motion M' may be considered as the robot undergoing composite motion $(M')^{-1} * M$ while the object remains static. If motions are time dependent, then the situation is much more complicated. (See Figure 20.16.)

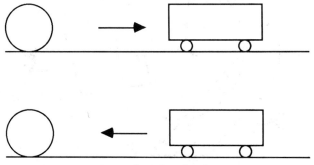

Figure 20.16. Relative robotic movements.

Dynamic multisensor fusion is time dependent. It also involves multiple frames, which are images over time. Thus, it is quite similar to the multiframe viewing discussed above. However, multiframe viewing over time is double integration over space and time—the most general situation. For simplicity, we shall only discuss integration of single-frame viewing over time and leave the more general case for a subsequent discussion. Temporal integration is important in human perception to determine shape and structure from motion.

We shall propose an incremental scheme which maintains an internal spherical model of the moving object and modifies it at each instant with respect to the viewing sphere. Here, we are assuming that the robot remains fixed while the object moves (this follows from equivalences among the three cases of relative motion) (see Figure 20.17). According to human visual research (Ullman, 1983), a reliable interpretation of local surface structure from motion requires the integration of spatial information over an extended time period. The flat perspective imaging model will have difficulty in integrating different internal models over a time period because of distortions that arise over the time period. This is why an optimization process (Ullman, 1983) is suggested to recover a rigid motion over a time period. Since each frame is not directly related to other frames over time, it is quite

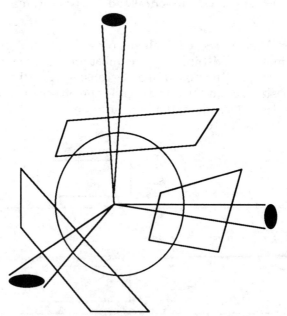

Figure 20.17. Temporal fusion.

hard to see how this process works. We can maintain an internal model $M(t)$ over time t on the sphere. The transformation of $M(t)$ to $M(t')$ is performed by a rotation that represents the time variation from t to t'.

5. LOCAL MAPS AND COLLISION AVOIDANCE

As an AMR moves along a planned path, its multisensor system is constructing a local map of the surroundings which are not completely known to the AMR. The spherical multisensor system supports a full field of view and creates a complete local map. This system detects obstacles that are unknown to the global path planner. While the AMR moves along the path, the global map is updated. In particular, each alternative path on the global map can be checked for feasibility and new alternative paths may be discovered (see Figure 20.18).

If the AMR meets a dead end or is trapped in a complex maze, the updated map is very useful in enabling the AMR to retreat to a position where it can move along an alternative path. The spherical vision system sees all 360 degrees around the AMR so that it can easily find a suitable direction to retreat. In existing systems, only a limited field-of-view is used (due to the usual flat vision system). Thus, the overhead is significant to integrate local maps at different points. One must keep track of what angles have been scanned and what remains to be scanned.

Navigation of AMRs is concerned with finding free pathways and choosing a suitable one for the next period of motion. We assume that

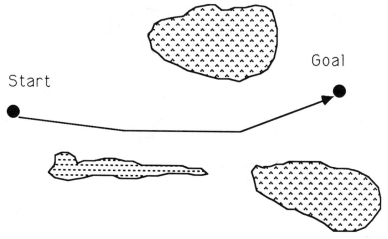

Figure 20.18. A global map.

the planned path is polygonal. Free pathways are represented by clear sectors which span angles of varying degrees at the origin (the AMR) between obstacles. They are assumed to be maximal in the sense that they are not contained in any larger sector satisfying the same conditions. At each position, there is a spherical octree (or circular quadtree) structure representing obstacles and free pathways (see Figure 20.19).

If the diameter of an AMR is D, then we can use a cone with the disk of diameter D as its base to estimate whether a free pathway is suitable for the planned path. The AMR finds the suitable free pathway whose clear sector intersects with the planned path as the direction of the next period of motion (see Figure 20.20). If there is no suitable free pathway intersecting the planned path, a detour is searched and an effort is made to return to the planned path (see Figure 20.21). We describe here an algorithm called the "walk-around" algorithm which performs the detour and looks for the planned path. This algorithm will also navigate the robot to walk around any nonconvex obstacle, such as a cul-de-sac. Moreover, it will navigate the robot to walk around a maze, although the orbit may not be the shortest. The robot will be able to leave the maze eventually by continuously moving around the connected wall. If returning to the planned path is impossible (the global map will be used here), the AMR has to replan the path by using stored information about the environment which has been collected along the path (see Figure 20.22).

In this chapter, we shall not pursue replanning. In the following, we describe the "walk-around" algorithm. The key idea is to look continuously for the planned path while the AMR is moving to avoid obstacles.

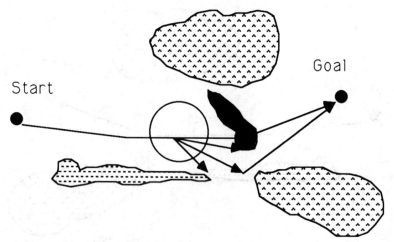

Figure 20.19. Free pathways in the spherical model.

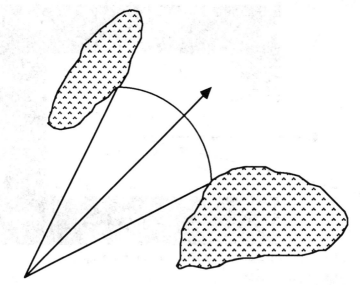

Figure 20.20. A suitable free pathway for the planned path.

At each position, the AMR uses the clear sector nearest to the planned path as the orientation of its movement. In the 2-D circular case, the most natural orientation is given by the bisector. The AMR may continuously follow the bisector to guide its motion. The motion is quite

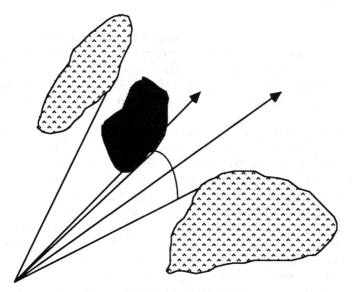

Figure 20.21. An easy detour.

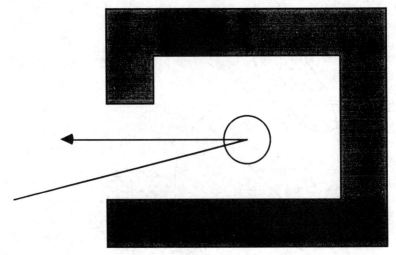

Figure 20.22. Turn-around in a trap.

random because it is influenced by the environment. In order to return to the planned path, we should modify this approach.

Walk-Around Algorithm. Following the planned path, the AMR may find an obstacle intersecting the path. The following algorithm will guide the AMR to move around the obstacle provided that the planned path is not completely blocked off (thus any replanning is not necessary).

1. Find a suitable free pathway nearest to the planned path.
2. Find a sector whose base has diameter $D + d$ (a small quantity) which is tangent to the obstacle.
3. Use its bisector as orientation of the next period of movement.
4. This process is carried out on a finite number of instants.

It can be proved that the AMR will reach the other side of the obstacle and will intersect the planned path again if the AMR continuously walks around a connected obstacle (see Figure 20.23).

For a dense configuration of obstacles, this algorithm may not work well. For example, the AMR may get into a trap of many obstacles as follows (see Figure 20.24). A better approach is to avoid the configuration completely. First we enclose it by a larger connected obstacle. Then we apply the "walk-around" algorithm to this enclosure. Now the question is to decide when to enclose several obstacles. Clearly, a larger enclosure will imply a longer detour. We should find the minimal enclosure so that there is a suitable free pathway tangent to the enclo-

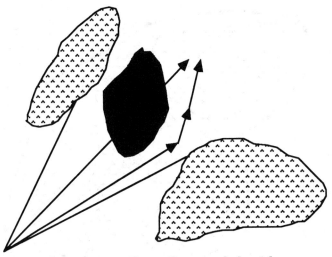

Figure 20.23. The walk-around algorithm.

sure. The spherical multisensor system is again more useful than the usual flat sensor system here. The full field-of-view does not miss any obstacle unless it is hidden behind observed obstacles. While the AMR walks around the enclosure, more obstacles may be observed and may be added in the enclosure. Thus the enclosure is dynamically updated and enlarged (see Figure 20.25).

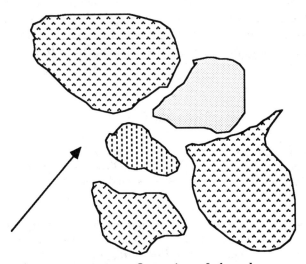

Figure 20.24. A configuration of obstacles.

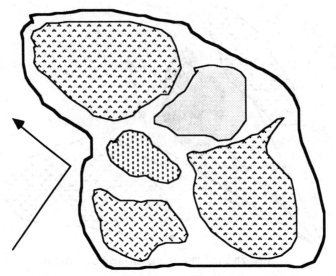

Figure 20.25. Enclosing a collection of obstacles.

6. CONCLUSION

We have presented an efficient computational model for multisensor fusion, robotic navigation, robotic motion control, and spatial reasoning. All these tasks may be performed in a single and unified framework so that overhead of computing is significantly reduced.

A theoretical foundation of multisensor fusion has also been established. The main idea is that we may integrate 3-D spatial information derived from various images in the world model. This idea has other applications in industry, medicine, and the military besides sensing for mobile robots.

REFERENCES

Ahuja, N., & Nash, C. (1984). Octree representation of moving objects. *Computer Vision, Graphics, and Image Processing, 26,* 207–216.

Brooks, R.A., & Lozano-Perez, T. (1985). A subdivision algorithm in configuration space for findpath with rotation. *IEEE Transactions on Systems, Man, and Cybernetics,* SMC-15(2), 224–233.

Chen, S. (1985a). A new vision system and the Fourier descriptor method by group representation theory. *Proceedings of the IEEE Conference on Computer Vision and Pattern Recognition* (pp. 106–110). San Francisco, CA.

Chen, S. (1985b). Spherical data structures and visual feedback for robotic control. *Proceedings of the First Annual Workshop on Intelligent Control.*
Chen, S. (1986). An intelligent computer vision system. *International Journal of Intelligent Systems, 1,* 15–28.
Chen, S. (1988a). Fusion of multisensor data into 3-D spatial information. In P.S. Schenker (Ed.), *Proceedings of the SPIE, vol. 1003, Sensor Fusion: Spatial Reasoning and Scene Interpretation* (pp. 80–85). Cambridge, MA.
Chen, S. (1988b). A geometric approach to multisensor fusion. In C.W. Weaver (Ed.), *Proceedings of the SPIE, vol. 931, Sensor Fusion* (pp. 22–25). Orlando, FL.
Chen, S. (1990). A spherical model for navigation and spatial reasoning. *Proceedings of the IEEE International Conference on Robotics and Automation* (pp. 776–781). Cincinnati, OH.
Chen, S., & Penna, M. (1986a). *An efficient algorithm for computing features of parametrized surfaces* (Tech. Rep. 86-2). University of North Carolina-Charlotte: Department of Computer Science.
Chen, S., & Penna, M. (1986b). Shape and correspondence. *Proceedings of the SPIE Symposium on Advances in Intelligent Robotics Systems.*
Chen, S., & Penna, M. (1986c). *Three-dimensional object recognition using range data* (Tech. Rep. 86-1). University of North Carolina-Charlotte: Department of Computer Science.
Chen, S., & Penna, M. (1987). Motion analysis of deformable objects. In T. Huang (Ed.), *Advances in computer vision and image processing* (Vol. 3). JAI Press.
Kalman, R.E., Falb, P.L., & Arbib, M.A. (1969). *Topics in mathematical system theory.* New York: McGraw-Hill.
Martin, W.N., & Aggarwal, J.K. (1983). Volumetric descriptions of objects from multiple views. *IEEE Transactions on Pattern Analysis and Machine Intelligence,* PAMI-5(2), 150–158.
Penna, M., & Chen, S. (1986). *Spherical perspective in computer vision and image understanding* (Tech. Rep. 86-4). University of North Carolina-Charlotte: Department of Computer Science.
Samet, H. (1984). The quadtree and related hierarchical data structures. *ACM Computing Surveys, 6,* 187–260.
Ullman, S. (1983). *Maximizing rigidity: The incremental recovery of 3-D structure from rigid and rubbery-motion* (Lab. Memo 721). MIT: AI Laboratory.

21
Building, Registrating, and Fusing Noisy Visual Maps*

Nicholas Ayache and
Olivier D. Faugeras

This chapter deals with the problem of building three-dimensional descriptions (we call them *visual maps*) of the environment of a mobile robot using passive vision. These maps are local (i.e., attached to specific frames of reference). Since noise is present, they incorporate information about the geometry of the environment and about the uncertainty of the parameters defining the geometry. This geometric uncertainty is directly related to its source (i.e., sensor uncertainty). We show how visual maps corresponding to different positions of the robot can be registered to compute a better estimate of its displacement between the various viewpoint positions, assuming an otherwise static environment. We use these estimates to fuse the different visual maps and reduce locally the uncertainty of the geometric primitives which have found correspondents in other maps. We propose to perform these three tasks (building, registering, and fusing visual maps) within the general framework of extended Kalman filtering, which allows efficient combination of measurements in the presence of noise.

---

* The authors acknowledge the contribution of Bernard Faverjon to an earlier version of this work (Faugeras et al., 1986) and stimulating discussions with Francis Lustman, Giorgio Toscani, and Pierre Tournassoud. Also, the help of Chantal Chazelas and Nathalie Rocher in preparing this chapter is much appreciated.

1. INTRODUCTION

The problem of dealing with noise in three-dimensional vision and mobile robots is one of the first to be tackled in order to make both things useful. We believe that it cannot be engineered away and that its solution has to be found, first, by representing explicitly the uncertainty in the world model used by the robot and, second, by combining a large number of measurements and/or sensors.

In this chapter, we propose a partial solution along those lines in the case where passive stereo is used to collect three-dimensional information. This work continues the one presented in Ayache, Faugeras, Faverjon, and Toscani (1985) and Faugeras, Ayache, and Faverjon (1986) and is connected to that of Brooks (1985), Bolle and Cooper (1985), Laumond and Chatila (1985), Crowley (1986), Smith and Cheeseman (1986), and Durrant-Whyte (1986).

The goals to be reached include the establishment of a three-dimensional description of the environment in which the vehicle moves, which includes both geometric information and information about the uncertainty attached to the corresponding geometric primitives. This description can then be used for various tasks, such as the definition of a sensing strategy—where to look next in order to increase the accuracy of the model—and a navigation strategy—how to go from here to there given our present state of knowledge: it can also be used to detect changes in the environment or recognize places. These applications are not incorporated in this chapter.

The key points of our approach are the use of a powerful tool for dealing with large numbers of noisy measures, the extended Kalman filter (Darmon, 1982; Jazwinsky, 1970), which we found extremely useful in some of our previous work (Ayache & Faugeras, 1986; Faugeras & Hebert, 1986), and the way we represent three-dimensional rotations to relate frames of reference.

The latest developments of this work and new results are presented in Ayache and Faugeras (1988, 1989) and Ayache (1989, 1990).

2. LINEARIZING THE PROBLEM

In all the cases we discuss, we deal with an observation $\mathbf{x}$ in $\mathbf{R}^m$ that depends on a parameter $\mathbf{a}$ in $\mathbf{R}^n$ in a nonlinear fashion that can be expressed as a relation $\mathbf{f}(\mathbf{x}, \mathbf{a}) = \mathbf{0}$, where $\mathbf{f}$ maps $\mathbf{R}^m \times \mathbf{R}^n$ into $\mathbf{R}^p$. We assume that the observation $\mathbf{x}$ is corrupted with noise, which we model as an additive zero mean Gaussian noise:

$$\mathbf{x} = \mathbf{x}' + \boldsymbol{\epsilon} \text{ with } E(\boldsymbol{\epsilon}) = \mathbf{0} \text{ and } E(\boldsymbol{\epsilon}\boldsymbol{\epsilon}') = \Lambda.$$

The problem is, given a number of observations $\mathbf{x}_i$, to find the parameter vector $\mathbf{a}$ that best satisfies the relations $\mathbf{f}_i(\mathbf{x}_i, \mathbf{a}) = \mathbf{0}$. "Best" is to be made more precise in a moment.

Let us drop the i indices for a while. Supposing that we know a "good" estimate $\mathbf{a}^*$ of $\mathbf{a}$, we can use the idea of linearization and expand $\mathbf{f}$ in the vicinity $(\mathbf{x}', \mathbf{a})$:

$$\mathbf{f}(\mathbf{x}', \mathbf{a}) = \mathbf{0} \approx \mathbf{f}(\mathbf{x}, \mathbf{a}^*) + \frac{\partial \mathbf{f}}{\partial \mathbf{x}}(\mathbf{x}, \mathbf{a}^*)(\mathbf{x}' - \mathbf{x})$$
$$+ \frac{\partial \mathbf{f}}{\partial \mathbf{a}}(\mathbf{x}, \mathbf{a}^*)(\mathbf{a} - \mathbf{a}^*).$$

As usual, $\partial \mathbf{f}/\partial \mathbf{x}$ is a $p \times m$ matrix and $\partial \mathbf{f}/\partial \mathbf{a}$ is a $p \times n$ matrix. This expression can be rewritten as (dropping the $\approx$ sign):

$$-\mathbf{f}(\mathbf{x}, \mathbf{a}^*) + \frac{\partial \mathbf{f}}{\partial \mathbf{a}}(\mathbf{x}, \mathbf{a}^*) = \frac{\partial \mathbf{f}}{\partial \mathbf{a}}(\mathbf{x}, \mathbf{a}^*)\mathbf{a} - \frac{\partial \mathbf{f}}{\partial \mathbf{x}}(\mathbf{x} - \mathbf{a}^*)\boldsymbol{\epsilon},$$

which is a linear measurement equation:

$$\mathbf{y} = \mathbf{M}\mathbf{a} + \mathbf{u},$$

where

$$\mathbf{y} = -\mathbf{f}(\mathbf{x}, \mathbf{a}^*) + \frac{\partial \mathbf{f}}{\partial \mathbf{a}}(\mathbf{x}, \mathbf{a}^*)\mathbf{a}^*,$$

$$\mathbf{M} = \frac{\partial \mathbf{f}}{\partial \mathbf{a}}(\mathbf{x}, \mathbf{a}^*) \quad \text{and} \quad \mathbf{u} = -\frac{\partial \mathbf{f}}{\partial \mathbf{x}}(\mathbf{x}, \mathbf{a}^*)\boldsymbol{\epsilon}.$$

Notice that $\mathbf{y}$ and $\mathbf{M}$ are known because we know $\mathbf{f}$, $\mathbf{x}$, and $\mathbf{a}^*$; since we also know Λ, we know $\mathbf{u}$'s second-order statistics:

$$E(\mathbf{u}) = \mathbf{0},$$

$$\mathbf{W} = E(\mathbf{u}\mathbf{u}^t) = \frac{\partial \mathbf{f}}{\partial \mathbf{x}}(\mathbf{x}, \mathbf{a}^*) \Lambda \frac{\partial \mathbf{f}}{\partial \mathbf{x}}(\mathbf{x}, \mathbf{a}^*)^t.$$

Let us now come back to our n observations $\mathbf{x}_i$; for each of them, knowing the function $\mathbf{f}_i$ and the covariance Λ_i of $\mathbf{x}_i$, one can form a linear measurement equation

$$\mathbf{y}_i = \mathbf{M}_i \mathbf{a} + \mathbf{u}_i$$

and compute the noise covariance matrix $\mathbf{W}_i$ attached to it. If we start with an initial estimate $\hat{\mathbf{a}}_0$ of $\mathbf{a}$ and its associated covariance matrix $\mathbf{S}_0 = E((\hat{\mathbf{a}}_0 - \mathbf{a})(\hat{\mathbf{a}}_0 - \mathbf{a})^t)$, we can use the Kalman filtering approach to deduce recursively an estimate $\hat{\mathbf{a}}_n$ of $\mathbf{a}$ and its covariance matrix $\mathbf{S}_n((\hat{\mathbf{a}}_n - \mathbf{a})(\hat{\mathbf{a}}_n - \mathbf{a})^t)$ after taking into account n observations. The corresponding recursive equations are the standard Kalman equations and are given in Appendix A. We can now give a precise meaning to the word "best." $\hat{\mathbf{a}}_n$ is the parameter vector that minimizes the criterion

$$(\mathbf{a} - \hat{\mathbf{a}}_0)^t \mathbf{S}_0^{-1}(\mathbf{a} - \hat{\mathbf{a}}_0) + \sum_{i=1}^{n} (\mathbf{y}_i - \mathbf{M}_i \mathbf{a})^t \mathbf{W}_i^{-1}(\mathbf{y}_i - \mathbf{M}_i \mathbf{a}).$$

This equation is important because it shows how the Kalman filtering explicitly takes into account noise in the measurements and weighs them accordingly. The more noise we have on the ith measurement, the smaller the inverse covariance matrix $\mathbf{W}_i^{-1}$ is, and therefore the less the ith term in the above criterion contributes to the final estimate.

Let us now study in detail the application of this technique to some previously mentioned problems.

3. STEREO RECONSTRUCTION

In a standard, two-camera, stereo system, such as the one depicted in Figure 21.1, we can relate the (x, y, z) coordinate space to the (u_1, v_1) and (u_2, v_2) retina spaces linearly in projective spaces:

$$\begin{bmatrix} s_i u_i \\ s_i v_i \\ s_i \end{bmatrix} = \mathbf{P}_i \begin{bmatrix} x \\ y \\ z \\ 1 \end{bmatrix}, \quad i = 1, 2,$$

where matrices $\mathbf{P}_i$ are obtained by calibration (Faugeras & Toscani, 1986). When we match a point of coordinates (u_1, v_1) in retina 1 to a point of coordinates (u_2, v_2) in retina 2, we can compute by triangulation the coordinates (x, y, z) of the corresponding point in three-dimensional space. To cast this in the previous formalism, let us write (dropping the indexes for the moment)

$$\mathbf{x} = [u, v]^t, \quad \mathbf{a} = [x, y, z]^t = \mathbf{OM}.$$

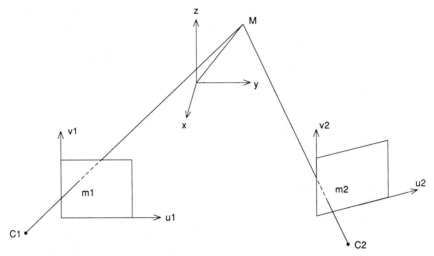

Figure 21.1. Geometry of a standard, two-camera, stereo system.

Rewriting the 3 × 4 matrix **P** as

$$\mathbf{P} = \begin{bmatrix} \mathbf{l}_1 & l_{14} \\ \mathbf{l}_2 & l_{24} \\ \mathbf{l}_3 & l_{34} \end{bmatrix},$$

where $\mathbf{l}_1, \mathbf{l}_2, \mathbf{l}_3$ are 3 × 1 row vectors, and eliminating s, we have the following relationships:

$$(\mathbf{l}_3 \mathbf{OM} + l_{34})u - \mathbf{l}_1 \mathbf{OM} - l_{14} = 0,$$
$$(\mathbf{l}_3 \mathbf{OM} + l_{34})v - \mathbf{l}_2 \mathbf{OM} - l_{24} = 0.$$

Therefore,

$$\mathbf{f}(\mathbf{x}, \mathbf{a}) = \begin{bmatrix} (\mathbf{l}_3 \mathbf{OM} + l_{34})u - \mathbf{l}_1 \mathbf{OM} - l_{14} \\ (\mathbf{l}_3 \mathbf{OM} + l_{34})v - \mathbf{l}_2 \mathbf{OM} - l_{24} \end{bmatrix}. \quad (2)$$

From the above formalism we can deduce an estimate $\hat{\mathbf{a}}_2$ of **a** after two measurements (i.e. of the position in three-dimensional space of the point M) as well as the covariance matrix of this estimate, which is an indication of the uncertainty of our knowledge. This is a function of our uncertainty on the pixel coordinates (u_1, v_1) and (u_2, v_2) and of our initial estimate $\hat{\mathbf{a}}_0$ of the position of M and its covariance matrix $\mathbf{S}_0$.

The equations are in Appendix B. In practice, S_0 is diagonal with very large diagonal terms, so the first term in Eq. (1) is very small.

This shows how the uncertainty on points obtained by stereo can be computed. In practice, we consider points, lines, and planes. The uncertainty of these primitives depends first on how they have been extracted and, second, on how they are represented. Let us look at representations first.

A possible way to represent lines is to use a vector parallel to the line and a point on the line. A line D is represented by two vectors (**l**, **m**) defined as follows. Given two points M_1 and M_2 on L, we have

$$\mathbf{l} = \mathbf{OM}_2 - \mathbf{OM}_1, \quad \mathbf{m} = (\mathbf{OM}_1 + \mathbf{OM}_2)/2.$$

Planes are represented by their normal **n** and their distance to the origin d. See Faugeras and Hebert (1986) for an application of this representation to the recognition and localization of three-dimensional objects.

The description built by the stereo system consists of two parts. It produces, first, the parameters of the geometric elements represented and second, the uncertainty on these parameters. This uncertainty is represented by a set of covariance matrices.

We have treated the case of points in this section. The case of lines can be deduced very simply from the above representation, as shown in the next section. The interested reader can find an analysis for the case of planes in Faugeras and Lustman (1986).

The resulting description of the environment, including the geometric and uncertainty aspects is called a *realistic uncertain description of the environment*.

4. REGISTRATING STEREO PAIRS

The problem is the following: Suppose that the analysis of a first stereo pair yields a partial three-dimensional description of the environment in terms of points, lines, and planes, each with some uncertainty attached to it. The problem of obtaining this uncertainty has been treated in the previous section for points.

Now suppose that the vehicle on which the cameras are mounted moves (let us say in three-dimensions) by an imperfectly known displacement **D**. We then acquire a second stereo pair, analyze it, and obtain another three-dimensional description of another part of the environment. If the displacement **D** is not too large, it is likely that some of the geometric primitives identified in position 1 will also be identified in position 2. By matching such primitives we should be able to recover a better estimate of the displacement **D** and to construct a better estimate of the position and orientation of these primitives (this is done in Section 6) which have been identified in the two positions; that is, we should be able to improve the description of the environment.

We must also say something about the way we represent three-dimensional displacements. Every such displacement can be decomposed in an infinite number of ways as the product of a translation characterized by a vector **t** and a rotation **R** characterized by its angle θ, its origin, and its axis **u** (a unit vector). Fixing the origin of the rotation makes the decomposition unique.

For our next purpose we can therefore consider the group of three-dimensional displacements as the product of the group SO(3) of rotations and the group of translations $\mathbf{R}^3$. How we parameterize SO(3) is also important. For an excellent review of the different parameterizations of SO(3), see Stuelpnagel (1964). In our previous work (Faugeras & Hebert, 1986) we used quaternions. This has the disadvantage of imposing the constraint that the quaternions dealt with are of unit norm. In this chapter we propose to use the exponential form of a rotation matrix **R**. Indeed, for every orthogonal matrix **R**, there exists a unique antisymmetric matrix **H** such that $\mathbf{R} = e^{\mathbf{H}}$, where matrix exponentials are defined as usual as $e^{\mathbf{H}} = \mathbf{I} + \mathbf{H}/1! + \mathbf{H}^2/2! + \cdots$. The matrix **H** can be written as

$$\mathbf{H} = \begin{bmatrix} 0 & -c & b \\ c & 0 & -a \\ -b & a & 0 \end{bmatrix}.$$

The three-dimensional vector $\mathbf{r} = [a, b, c]^t$ has some useful properties. Its direction is that of the axis of rotation, and its squared norm is equal to the rotation angle squared. Proofs of that and other properties of this representation are presented in Appendix C. Moreover, matrix **H** represents the cross product with vector **r**, which we denote by $c(\mathbf{r})$. By this we mean

$$\mathbf{Hx} = c(\mathbf{r})\mathbf{x} = \mathbf{r} \wedge \mathbf{x}.$$

We can now deal with the problem of estimating the displacement **D** and its uncertainty by matching geometric primitives detected in positions 1 and 2 of the vehicle. Let us start with points first. If the same physical point is represented in the coordinate system associated with the first position by **OM** and in the coordinate system associated with the second position by **O'M'** then

$$\mathbf{O'M'} - \mathbf{ROM} - \mathbf{t} = 0. \tag{3}$$

This equation is of the form $\mathbf{f}(\mathbf{x}, \mathbf{a})$, if we let $\mathbf{x} = [\mathbf{O'M'}^t, \mathbf{OM}^t]^t$ and $\mathbf{a} = [\mathbf{r}^t, \mathbf{t}^t]^t$ with **r** defined as above. Therefore, the previous formalism can again be used and an estimate of both **r** and **t** can be built by matching a number of points in positions 1 and 2. The uncertainty on **r** and **t** can also be computed if we have a model of the uncertainty on **OM** and **O'M'**, which we have after Section 3. The equations are presented in Appendix D.

The problem of matching straight lines is very similar. Let the two lines be defined by two points $(M_1 M_2)$ and $(M'_1 M'_2)$ defining representations $(\mathbf{l}, \mathbf{m})$ and $(\mathbf{l'}, \mathbf{m'})$. When a line is submitted to a rotation **R** and a translation **t**, it is fairly easy to show that its representation becomes $(\mathbf{RL}, \mathbf{RM} + \mathbf{t})$. We can then write that

$$\mathbf{l'} \times \mathbf{Rl} = 0 \tag{4}$$

and

$$\mathbf{Rl} \times (\mathbf{m'} - \mathbf{Rm} - \mathbf{t}) = 0$$

or, using Eq. (3),

$$\mathbf{l'} \times (\mathbf{m'} - \mathbf{Rm} - \mathbf{t}) = 0. \tag{5}$$

The geometric interpretation of Eq. (3) is that the transformed line is parallel to the second line. The geometric interpretation of Eq. (4) is that the line joining the midpoints of the transformed segment and the second segment is parallel to the second line (see Figure 21.2).

Letting $\mathbf{x} = (\mathbf{l'}^t, \mathbf{m'}^t, \mathbf{l}^t, \mathbf{m}^t)$ and **a** as before, this is again of the form $\mathbf{f}(\mathbf{x}, \mathbf{a}) = 0$, where $\mathbf{f}(\mathbf{x}, \mathbf{a})$ is a vector. But in fact the measurement equations produced by a cross product are not independent: The knowledge of two of them is sufficient to derive the third one. Therefore one must keep only four measurements out of six, the first two coming from the first cross product, the last two coming from the second cross product. Then $\mathbf{f}(\mathbf{x}, \mathbf{a})$ becomes a 4-vector. The equations are presented in Appendix E.

The case of planes can be treated similarly. Letting the same physi-

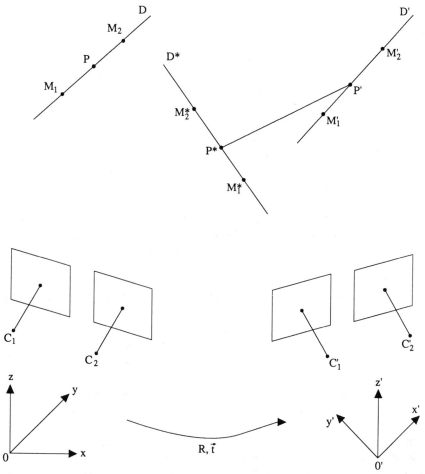

Figure 21.2. D is a line reconstructed by stereo in the coordinate system (0xyz), D' is a line reconstructed by stereo in the coordinate system (0' x' y' z') and D* is D displaced by the rotation R and the translation $\vec{t}$. We can write that D* is the same as D'.

cal plane be represented by $(\mathbf{n}', d')$ and $(\mathbf{n}, d)$ in coordinate systems 1 and 2, we can write

$$\mathbf{n}' - R\mathbf{n} = 0 \tag{6}$$

and

$$d' - d + \mathbf{t}^t R\mathbf{n} = 0$$

or

$$d' - d - \mathbf{t}^t\mathbf{n}' = 0. \qquad (7)$$

Letting $x = (\mathbf{n}'^t, \mathbf{n}^t, d', d)^t$ and $\mathbf{a}$ as before, we can again put this equation in the form $\mathbf{f}(\mathbf{x}, \mathbf{a}) = \mathbf{0}$. Equations are presented in Appendix F.

5. REGISTRATING STEREO PAIRS AND IMAGES

In order to avoid solving the stereo matching problem too often, it may be useful, once a three-dimensional estimation of the scene has been constructed, to track the projections in one image of the geometric features used to compute the three-dimensional displacement. This is similar in spirit to the work of Lowe, who does not use our formalism (Lowe, 1985). Let us first derive the case of points. We assume that we know the image coordinates u', v' of point M' such that $\mathbf{O'M'} = \mathbf{ROM} + \mathbf{t}$. Therefore, letting $\mathbf{x} = [\mathbf{OM}^t, u', v']^t$ and $\mathbf{a} = [\mathbf{r}^t, \mathbf{t}^t]^t$, we can use a combination of Eqs. (2) and (3):

$$\mathbf{f}(\mathbf{x}, \mathbf{a}) = \begin{cases} (\mathbf{l}_3(\mathbf{ROM} + \mathbf{t}) + l_{34})u' - \mathbf{l}_1(\mathbf{ROM} + \mathbf{t}) - l_{14}, \\ (\mathbf{l}_3(\mathbf{ROM} + \mathbf{t}) + l_{34})v' - \mathbf{l}_2(\mathbf{ROM} + \mathbf{t}) - l_{24}. \end{cases} \qquad (8)$$

The equations for $\partial \mathbf{f}/\partial \mathbf{x}$ and $\partial \mathbf{f}/\partial \mathbf{a}$ are presented in Appendix G.

Let us now derive the case of lines. Let D be a three-dimensional line defined by two points M_1 and M_2. After rotation and translation, the transformed line D' is defined by M'_1 and M'_2 such that $\mathbf{O'M'_1} = \mathbf{ROM}_1 + \mathbf{t}$ and $\mathbf{O'M'_2} = \mathbf{ROM}_2 + \mathbf{t}$. The projection d' of D' in the regina of one of the cameras is defined by the two points m'_1 and m'_2, projections of M'_1 and M'_2. If we denote by $[U'_1, V'_1, T'_1]$ and $[U'_2, V'_2, T'_2]$ the projective coordinates of the points m'_1 and m'_2, the projective equation of the line d' is given by the determinant

$$\begin{vmatrix} U & U'_1 & U'_2 \\ V & V'_1 & V'_2 \\ T & T'_1 & T'_2 \end{vmatrix}$$

or

$$U(V'_1 T'_2 - V'_2 T'_1) + V(T'_1 U'_2 - T'_2 U'_1) + T(U'_1 V'_2 - U'_2 V'_1) = 0.$$

If we match d' to a line d'' in the focal plane defined by two points p_1 and p_2 (see Figure 21.3) with projective coordinates $[u_1, v_1, 1]$ and $[u_2,$

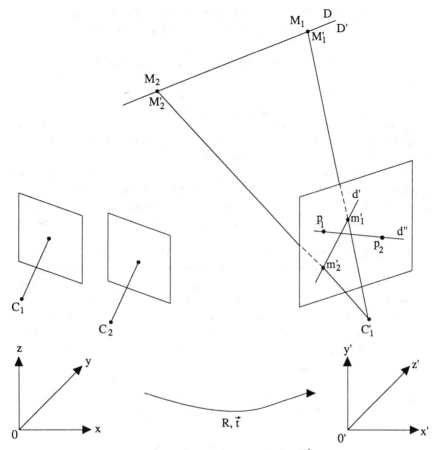

Figure 21.3. After the rotation R and translation $\vec{t}$, the line D in coordinate system (0xyz) becomes line D' in coordinate system (0' x' y' z'). D' projects as d' in retina 1 and is matched to d''.

v_2, 1], the necessary and sufficient condition for the two lines to be the same is $\mathbf{h}_1 \times \mathbf{h}_2 = \mathbf{0}$, where $\mathbf{h}_1 = [V'_tT'_2 - V'_2T'_1, T'_1U'_2 - T'_2U'_1, U'_1V'_2 - U'_2V'_1]^t$ and $\mathbf{h}_2 = [v_1 - v_2, u_2 - u_1, u_1v_2 - u_2v_1]^t$. Now, with $\mathbf{x} = [\mathbf{OM}^t_1, \mathbf{OM}^t_2, u_1, v_1, u_2, v_2]^t$ and $\mathbf{a}$ as before, the measurement equation is

$$\mathbf{f}(\mathbf{x}, \mathbf{a}) = \mathbf{h}_1 \times \mathbf{h}_2 = \mathbf{0},$$

where the components of $\mathbf{h}_1$ can be easily computed as functions of $\mathbf{x}$ and $\mathbf{a}$. Here again, $\mathbf{f}(\mathbf{x}, \mathbf{a})$ is a 3-vector, but the measurements are correlated and only two measurements can be kept. The details are presented in Appendix G.

6. FUSING VISUAL MAPS OR UPDATING THE MODEL OF THE ENVIRONMENT

What we have done so far is, first, to build, associated with each position of the mobile robot, a three-dimensional description of the environment in terms of its geometry (the positions and orientations of points, lines, and planes) and the uncertainty of the parameters describing these primitives. Each such description is attached to a local coordinate frame. Second, when there exist physical primitives which are common to two frames of reference, and we do not know exactly (perhaps even not at all) the relative position and orientation of the two frames, we have shown that, by matching primitives across frames, we were capable of building estimates of the three-dimensional transformation between the frames and a measure of the uncertainty of this transformation.

The last step is to close the loop and use this information to update, in each local frame, the description of the geometry and uncertainty of the primitives corresponding to parts of physical objects visible in another frame. This situation corresponds to that depicted in Figure 21.4, where m is a physical point represented by the vector $\mathbf{O}_i\mathbf{M}_i$ and the covariance matrix cov $\mathbf{M}_i$ in frame $\mathbf{F}_i (i = 1, \ldots, n)$, and by the vector $\mathbf{OM}$ and the covariance matrix Cov $\mathbf{M}$ in a frame $\mathbf{F}$ in which we want to update the position and uncertainty of m.

Frame $\mathbf{F}$ is related to frame i by rigid displacements $\mathbf{D}_1, \ldots, \mathbf{D}_n$, each represented by a vector $[\mathbf{r}_i^t, \mathbf{t}_i^t]^t$ and its covariance matrix Λ_i in frame i. We therefore have the following n measurement equations:

$$\mathbf{OM} - \mathbf{R}_i\mathbf{O}_i\mathbf{M}_i - \mathbf{t}_i = 0,$$

which are of the form $\mathbf{f}_i(\mathbf{x}, \mathbf{a}) = 0$ with $\mathbf{a} = [\mathbf{O}_n\mathbf{M}_n]$ and $\mathbf{x}_i = [\mathbf{r}_i^t, \mathbf{t}_i^t, \mathbf{O}_i\mathbf{m}_i^t]^t$. We can apply the artillery developed in Section 2 and obtain a new estimate of $\mathbf{OM}$ and Cov $\mathbf{M}$. Therefore, using the notations of Appendix C, we get

$$\partial \mathbf{f}_i / \partial \mathbf{x} = [-\mathbf{K}(\mathbf{R}_i, \mathbf{O}_i\mathbf{M}_i) - \mathbf{I} - \mathbf{R}_i] \quad \text{a } 3 \times 9 \text{ matrix}$$

and

$$\partial \mathbf{f}_i / \partial \mathbf{a} = \mathbf{I} \quad \text{a } 3 \times 3 \text{ matrix.}$$

Similarly, in the case of lines, we could try to use Eqs. (4) and (5) to

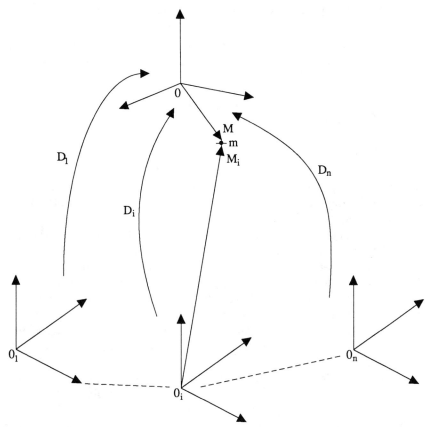

Figure 21.4. The physical point m is represented by $M, M_1, \ldots, M_n$ in the various coordinate systems.

update the estimate of the representation of a given line and its associated uncertainty:

$$l \times R_i l_i = 0 \quad \text{and} \quad l \times (m - R_i m_i - t_i) = 0,$$

which are of the form $f_i(x, a) = 0$ (with $a = [l^t, m^t]^t$ and $x = [r_i^t, t_i^t, l_i^t, m_i^t]^t$), keeping only four independent measurements out of six. But it is better to use minimal representations of primitives updated by the Kalman filter (i.e., four-parameter representations of lines). This is discussed and experimented with in Ayache and Faugeras (1987, 1988).

7. IMPLEMENTATION AND RESULTS

We have implemented the theoretical results developed in the previous sections and run the programs on a number of real sequences of stereo pairs.

7.1. Grid Example

7.1.1. Stereo Reconstruction

We show in Figure 21.5 the lines detected in an image of vertical and horizontal lines painted on the wall of the laboratory at INRIA. We took four stereo triplets of this pattern with the cameras mounted on the mobile robot at distances of 3, 3.5, 4, and 4.5 m. The stereo program described in Ayache and Faverjon (1987) was then used to compute the positions in three-dimensional space of the points of intersection of the horizontal and vertical lines of the pattern using only cameras 2 and 3.

The results are shown in Figure 21.6(a) projected in a vertical plane and in Figure 21.6(b) projected in a horizontal plane. The sets of points give an indication of the spread of the reconstruction results. Figure 21.7 is a representation of the covariance matrices computed from the measurement Eq. (1) in a vertical plane (21.7a), and in a horizontal plane (21.75). The value of the corresponding quadratic form is equal to 1, and the pixel noise was taken to be of variance 1 pixel. There is an excellent qualitative agreement between Figures 21.6 and 21.7, indicating that the extended Kalman filtering approach is compatible with experimental evidence.

7.1.2. Matching

Figure 21.8 shows the result of the estimation of the displacement between views 1 and 2 using the previous points and measurement equation, Eq. (3). Figure 21.8(a) shows the points corresponding to view 1 as crosses and the points corresponding to view 2 as plus signs. The displacement between the two views is mostly a translation perpendicular to the plane of the wall (see Table 21.1). Figure 21.8(b) shows the result of applying the estimated displacement to the points in view 2 and superimposing them to the points in view 1. The displacement is estimated by the method described in Section 5; that is, we are here combining a stereo pair and an image. The correspondence is seen to be quite good.

A more quantitative description of what is happening can be found in Table 21.1. The first row shows the initial estimates of the rotation

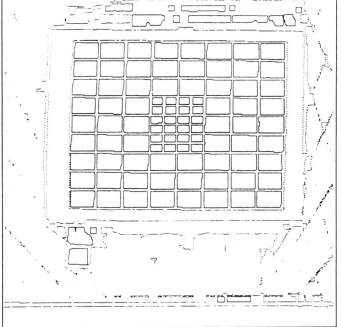

(a)

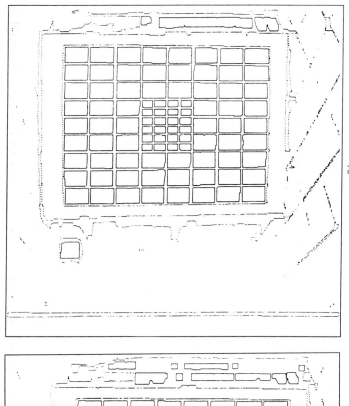

(b)

Figure 21.5. Edges extracted from a stereo view of the grid pattern. (a) (b)

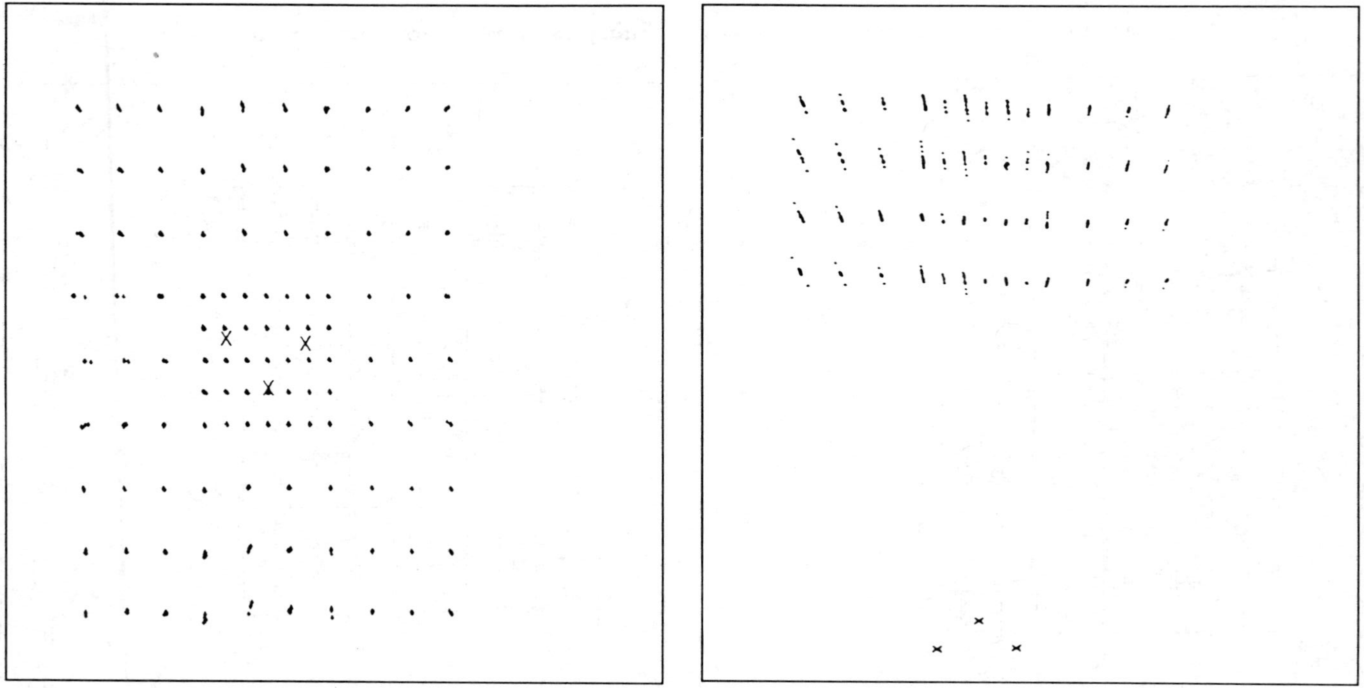

Figure 21.6. Horizontal and vertical projection of the reconstructed intersections of the grid pattern observed in four positions. (a) (b)

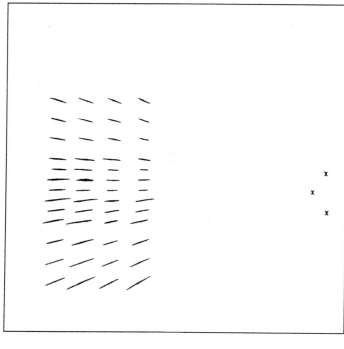

Figure 21.7. Covariance matrices attached to the points shown in Figure 21.6. (a) (b)

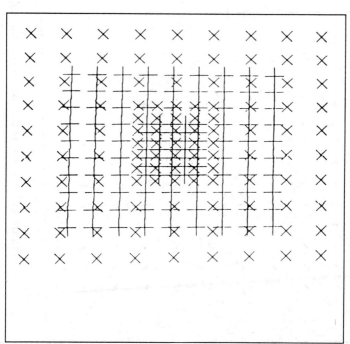

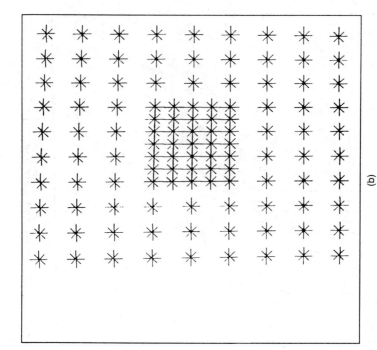

Figure 21.8. Images of the grid pattern observed in two different positions before and after application of the estimated displacement. (a) (b)

Table 21.1. Motion between two grid patterns.

	r_x (rad)	r_y (rad)	r_z (rad)	t_x (cm)	t_y (cm)	t_z (cm)	Angle (°)
Motion initial estimate	0	0	0	0	0	0	0
Initial covariance	1.0	1.0	1.0	100	100	100	
Motion iteration 1	0.009	−0.002	−0.000	4.41	1.94	−154.01	1.40
Motion iteration 2	0.002	−0.001	−0.002	0.88	1.03	−150.39	0.21
Real motion manually computed	0	0	0	0	0	−150.00	0

and translation, the second row the corresponding covariance matrices, and the third and fourth rows the estimates found by running the extended Kalman filter twice over a set of 113 points. The fifth row shows the actual displacement between the first and fourth positions. The final covariance matrices are very small and are not shown.

Figure 21.9 shows a similar example where a rotation has been added to the translation. Figure 21.9(a) shows the points in views 1 and 2, and Figure 21.9(b) shows the points after the estimated displacement has been applied to the points in view 2. In both cases, similar results for the estimated displacement are obtained when stereo pairs are combined. Table 21.2 details the results in the same format as Table 21.1.

7.1.3. Fusion

Figures 21.10 and 21.11 show the results of the integration of two different kinds of information. First, the points are reconstructed in each plane using the third camera (this is just adding one more measurement equation of the type (2)). Second, the method of Section 6 has been applied to the points in each of the four coordinate systems associated with views 1 to 4. The results are presented in the same format as the one in Figure 21.6 and 21.7.

Two facts can be inferred from Figure 21.10 and 21.11. First, the uncertainty has been greatly decreased, and, second, the new computed uncertainty still seems to be in excellent agreement with the spread of the updated data, thus yielding more credibility to the whole scheme. In all these figures, the positions of the three cameras are represented by triplets of crosses.

7.2. Office Example

7.2.1. Stereo Reconstruction

We have applied the same programs to a different set of images. Figures 21.12 and 21.13 show the polygonal approximations of the edge points in two stereo pairs of an office scene taken from different viewpoints, and Figures 21.14 and 21.15 show the segments which have been matched by the stereo program described in Ayache and Faverjon (1987).

Figures 21.16 and 21.17 have the same format as Figure 21.6; that is, we show the projection of the reconstructed three-dimensional segments in a vertical plane (Figure 21.6(a) and 21.17(a)) and in a

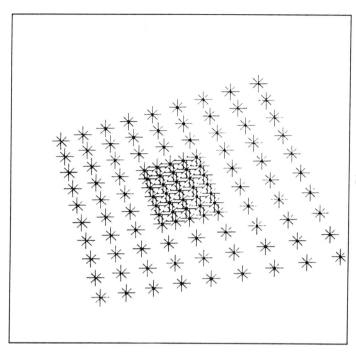

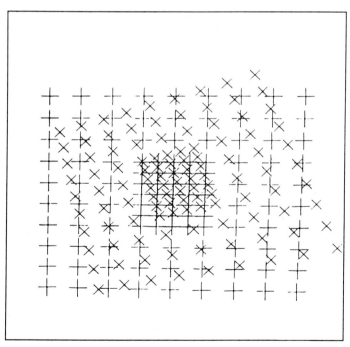

Figure 21.9. Images of the grid pattern observed in two different positions before and after application of another estimated displacement. (a) (b)

Table 21.2. Motion between two grid patterns.

	r_x (rad)	r_y (rad)	r_z (rad)	t_x (cm)	t_y (cm)	t_z (cm)	Angle (°)
Motion initial estimate	0	0	0	0	0	0	0
Initial covariance	1.0	1.0	1.0	100	100	100	
Motion iteration 1	0.32	0.55	−0.26	−60.70	35.90	20.38	39.82
Motion iteration 2	0.29	0.31	−0.30	−50.90	49.62	49.16	30.27
Real motion manually computed	0.3	0.3	−0.3	−50.00	50.00	50.00	29.77

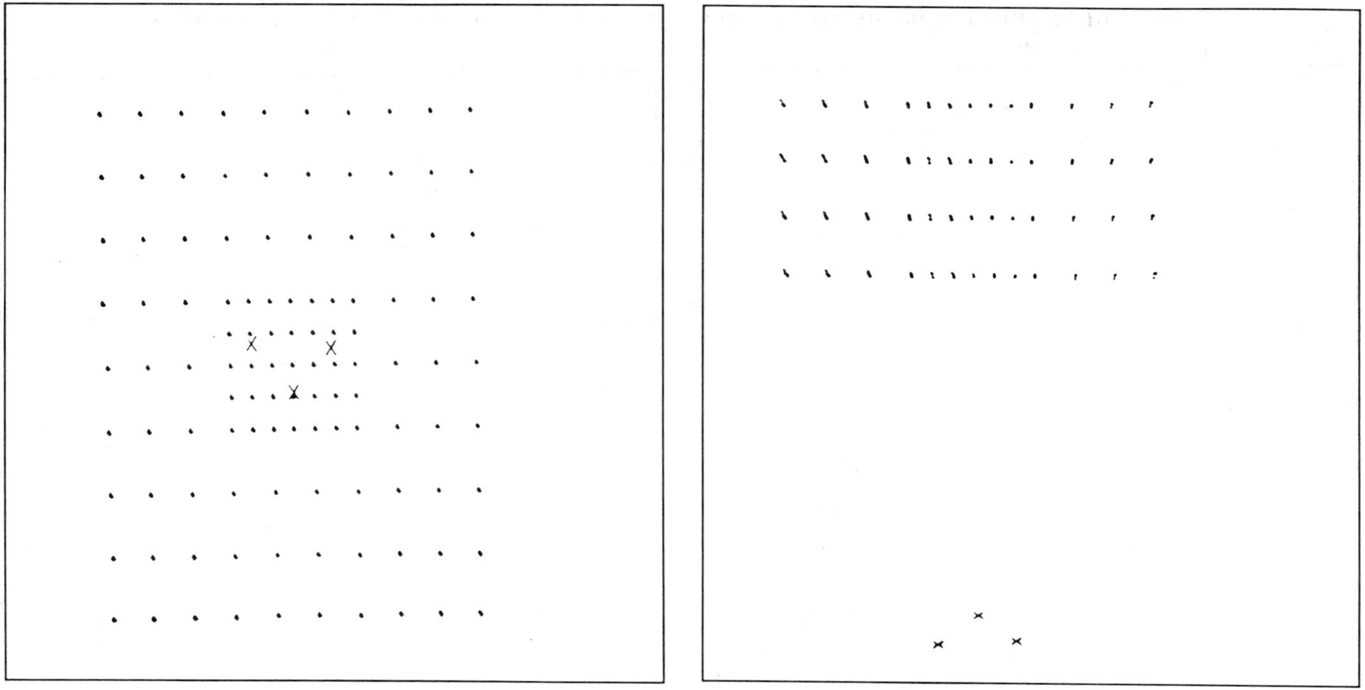

Figure 21.10. Fusion of the reconstructed intersections of the grid pattern. (a) (b)

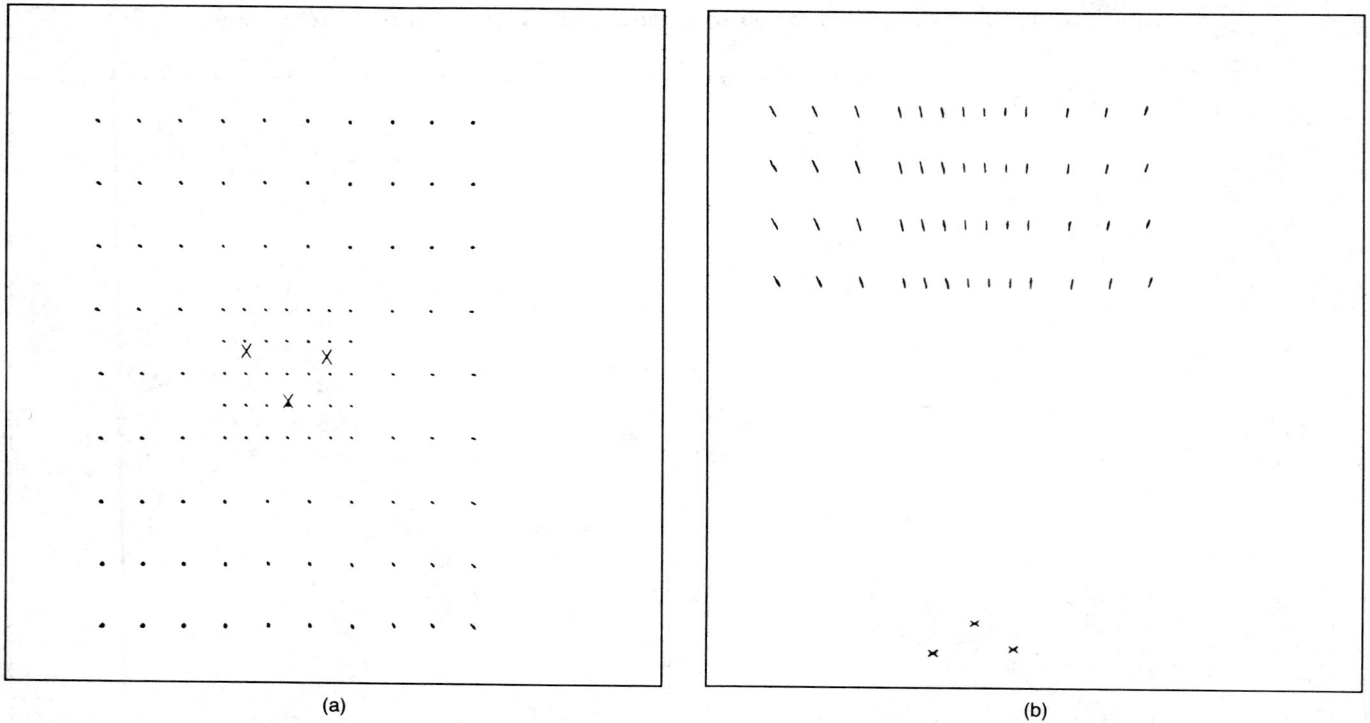

(b)

(a)

Figure 21.11. Covariance matrices attached to the points shown in Figure 21.10. (a) (b)

Figure 21.12. Polygonal approximation of the edge points of a stereo pair of an office room observed in position 1. (a) (b)

519

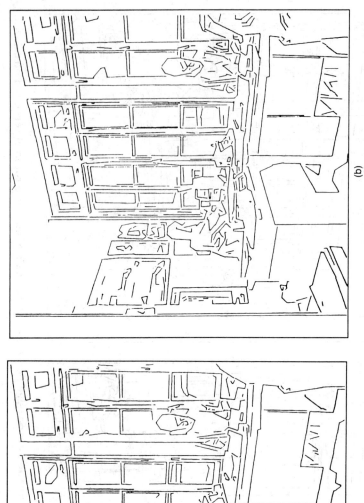
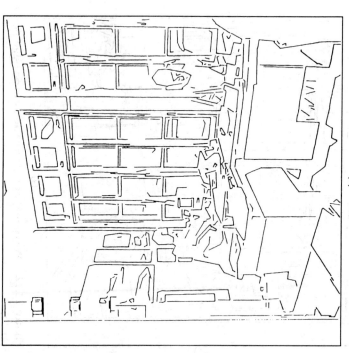

Figure 21.13. Polygonal approximation of the edge points of a stereo pair of the office room in Figure 21.12 observed in position 2. (a) (b)

(a)

(b)

Figure 21.14. Edge segments matched in stereo pair of Figure 21.12. (a) (b)

Figure 21.15. Edge segments matched in stereo pair of Figure 21.13. (a) (b)

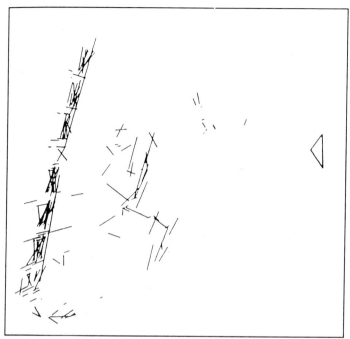

Figure 21.16. Horizontal and vertical projection of the reconstructed segments of the office room observed in position 1. (a) (b)

Figure 21.17. Horizontal and vertical projection of the reconstructed segments of the office room observed in position 2. (a) (b)

horizontal plane (Figures 21.16(b) and 21.17(b)). The position of the cameras mounted on the robot are shown by a triangle. Figures 21.18 and 21.19 have the same format as Figure 21.7; that is, we show a representation of the covariance matrices of the endpoints of the reconstructed line segments computed from Eq. (2) in a vertical plane (21.18(a) and 21.19(a)), and in a horizontal plane (21.18(b) and 21.19(b)).

7.2.2. Matching

Figure 21.20 shows the results of the estimation of the displacement of the robot from view 1 to view 2 by matching three-dimensional lines using Eqs. (4) and (5). Figure 21.20(a) shows a view from above of the segments in view 1 which are matched in view 2; Figure 21.20(b) shows the corresponding segments in view 2; and Figure 21.21(a) shows the result of applying the estimated displacement to the segments in view 1. The result looks much like Figure 21.20(b) (as it should). The position of the cameras is shown as a triangle.

Figure 21.21(b) is yet another way of displaying the results: After applying to them the estimated displacement, the matched segments in view 1 are projected (as continuous lines) in one of the images corresponding to view 2 where the segments are displayed as dotted lines. Again, the agreement is seen to be quite good.

A more quantitative description of what is happening can be found in Table 21.3. The first row shows the initial estimates of the rotation and translation, the second row the corresponding covariance matrices. These covariance matrices contain the knowledge that the motion is close to a horizontal plane. The third row shows the estimate of the displacement obtained by matching manually two lines in views 1 and 2, thus yielding two measurement equations of types (4) and (5).

The fourth and fifth rows show the estimates found by running the extended Kalman filter twice over a set of 79 and 84 pairs of lines, respectively. Notice that the matches are found automatically by the matcher after the first two matches have been given manually.

7.2.3. Fusion

Experiments concerning fusion of straight lines can be found in Ayache and Faugeras (1987).

8. CONCLUSIONS AND DISCUSSION

We have proposed some ideas related to the construction, by a mobile robot using stereo, of a three-dimensional model of its environment. In

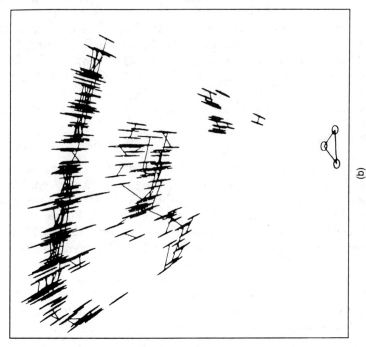

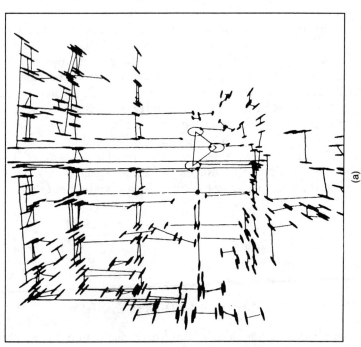

Figure 21.18. Covariance matrices attached to the endpoints of the reconstructed segments of the office room observed in position 1. (a) (b)

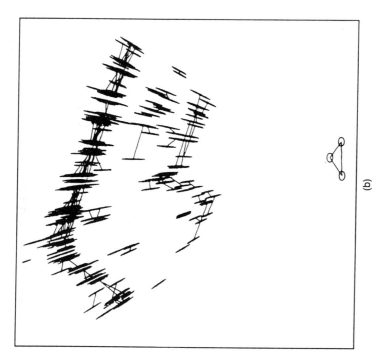

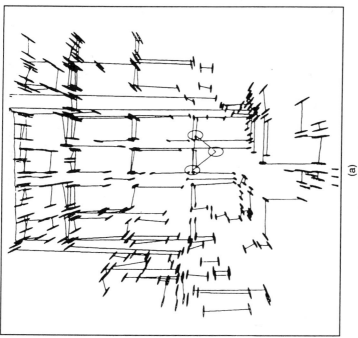

Figure 21.19. Covariance matrices attached to the endpoints of the reconstructed segments of the office room observed in position 2. (a) (b)

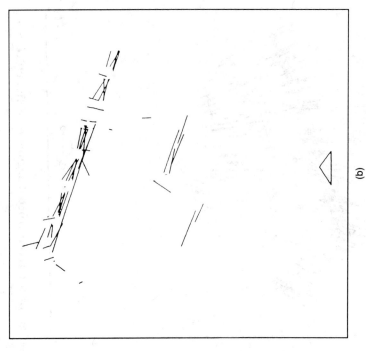

Figure 21.20. Reconstructed segments matched between positions 1 and 2. (a) (b)

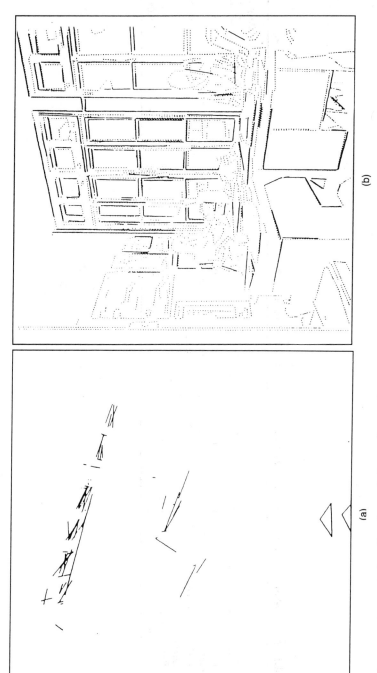

Figure 21.21. (a) Application of the estimated motion to the segments of position 1: the triangles show the estimated motion of the robot. (b) Application of the estimated motion to the segments of position 1 followed by a perspective projection (solid lines) on one of the images actually observed in position 2 (dotted lines).

Table 21.3. Motion computed between two stereo views of an office.

	r_x (rad)	r_y (rad)	r_z (rad)	t_x (cm)	t_y (cm)	t_z (cm)	Angle (°)
Motion initial estimate	0	0	0	0	0	0	0
Initial covariance	0.01	2.0	0.01	500	1	500	
Motion: 2 lines man. matched	0.03	0.17	0.02	42.03	0.32	−24.49	10.17
Motion iteration 1	0.01	0.137	−0.01	47.84	−2.58	−35.01	7.89
Motion iteration 2	0.01	0.138	0.008	47.56	−2.54	−33.56	8.06

this effort we have been following two guiding lights. The first one is that of linearizing the measurement equations of our processes in order to apply the powerful Kalman filter (extended Kalman filtering). The second one is that of using a representation of three-dimensional rigid displacements which is adapted to such a linearization, and we have come up with the exponential representation of orthogonal matrices. From there, our reflections have pursued three ideas.

The first idea is that the model of the environment must contain not only a geometric characterization of the geometric primitives it uses (here points, lines, and planes), but also a characterization of the uncertainty on the parameters of these primitives (uncertainty caused by the noisy measurements). We have used a characterization of this uncertainty by covariance matrices and have shown that it could be traced all the way to the sensor noise (in our case the pixel noise). We call such a description a realistic uncertain description of the environment.

The second idea is that of using local coordinate frames attached to the various positions of the robot to describe the environment and to relate the various representations obtained from several stereo pairs taken from those different viewpoints whose spatial relationships are unknown or imperfectly known, to obtain an estimate of the three-dimensional displacements which relate the positions of the robot and a characterization of the uncertainty of these displacements.

The third idea is to use the previous characterization of their relationships to update the various representations. Indeed, if a given geometric primitive in some coordinate frame has been identified as corresponding to the same part of a physical object as another geometric primitive in another coordinate frame, then we can use our knowledge of the relation between the two frames to update the geometric and uncertainty descriptions of these primitives in their respective coordinate frames.

Several questions remain open. The first one is related to the representation of uncertainty of the geometric primitives such as lines and planes. We have considered that lines were defined by two points. In practice, this is not so since three-dimensional lines are reconstructed by intersecting planes defined by the focal center of the cameras and two-dimensional line segments obtained by mean square approximation of edge points. Therefore the uncertainty on three-dimensional lines is more complex than the uncertainty on pairs of three-dimensional points. Second, the fact that we are assuming Gaussian distributions on the parameters of the representations of lines, planes, and rotations is also subject to criticism for two reasons. The first one is unavoidable and is related to the linearization of the measurement equations; the second one is deeper and related to the fact that we have to be careful when defining probability densities on geometric sets. Despite these problems, the results that we have obtained are quite encouraging, and we think that the basic approach is promising and worth more investigation. New developments and results are presented in Ayache and Faugeras (1987, 1988, 1989).

Appendix A: Kalman Filter Equations

The equation

$$\mathbf{y}_i = \mathbf{M}_i \mathbf{a} + \mathbf{u}_i$$

of Section 2 is, in the terminology of the Kalman filter (Jazwinsky, 1970), a measurement equation on the process $\mathbf{a}$ constant with respect to i: $\mathbf{a}_i = \mathbf{a}_{i-1}$. Using the equations of the Kalman filter, we write the new estimate and estimation covariance matrix as

$$\hat{\mathbf{a}}_i = \hat{\mathbf{a}}_{i-1} + \mathbf{K}_i(\mathbf{y}_i - \mathbf{M}_t \hat{\mathbf{a}}_{i-1}),$$

$$\mathbf{K}_i = \mathbf{S}_{i-1} \mathbf{M}_i^t (\mathbf{W}_i + \mathbf{M}_i \mathbf{S}_{i-1} \mathbf{M}_i^t)^{-1},$$

$$\mathbf{S}_i = (\mathbf{I} - \mathbf{K}_i \mathbf{M}_i) \mathbf{S}_{i-1},$$

or, equivalently,

$$\mathbf{S}_i^{-1} = \mathbf{S}_{i-1}^{-1} + \mathbf{M}_i^t \mathbf{W}_i^{-1} \mathbf{M}_i,$$

where

$$\mathbf{W}_i = E(\mathbf{u}_i \mathbf{u}_i^t).$$

When all measurements have been processed, parameter $\mathbf{a}$ is known by its a posteriori estimate $\hat{\mathbf{a}}_n$ and the corresponding covariance matrix $\mathbf{S}_n$.

Appendix B: Stereo Reconstruction

Remembering that $\mathbf{x} = [u, v]^t$ and $\mathbf{a} = \mathbf{OM}$, we can easily derive from Eq. (2) that

$$\frac{\partial \mathbf{f}}{\partial \mathbf{a}} = \begin{bmatrix} u\mathbf{l}_3 - \mathbf{l}_1 \\ v\mathbf{l}_3 - \mathbf{l}_2 \end{bmatrix} \quad \text{a } 2 \times 3 \text{ matrix}$$

and

$$\frac{\partial \mathbf{f}}{\partial \mathbf{x}} = \begin{bmatrix} \mathbf{1}_3 \mathbf{OM} + l_{34} & 0 \\ 0 & \mathbf{1}_3 \mathbf{OM} + l_{34} \end{bmatrix}.$$

Appendix C: Exponential Representation of Rotation Matrices

A simple justification of the fact that every matrix $e^\mathbf{H}$, with $\mathbf{H}$ an antisymmetric matrix, is orthogonal, is the following:

$$(e^\mathbf{H})^t = e^{\mathbf{H}^t} = e^{-\mathbf{H}} = (e^\mathbf{H})^{-1}.$$

This follows from the formula $e^\mathbf{H} = \mathbf{I} + \mathbf{H}/1! + \mathbf{H}^2/2! + \cdots$. We also know (Gantmacher, 1977) that the eigenvalues a and b of $\mathbf{R}$ and $\mathbf{H}$ are related by $a = e^b$. Since it is well known that the eigenvalues of $\mathbf{R}$ are 1, $e^{i\theta}$, and $e^{-i\theta}$, where θ is the rotation angle, the eigenvalues of $\mathbf{H}$ are easily found to be 0, $i(a^2 + b^2 + c^2)^{1/2}$, and $-i(a^2 + b^2 + c^2)^{1/2}$. Therefore

$$\theta = \pm(a^2 + b^2 + c^2)^{1/2}.$$

Let us now consider an eigenvector of $\mathbf{H}$ associated with eigenvalue 0. Since $\mathbf{H}$ represents the vector product with vector $\mathbf{v} = [a, b, c]^t$, $\mathbf{v}$ is such a vector:

$$\mathbf{Hv} = 0.$$

$\mathbf{v}$ is also an eigenvector of matrix $\mathbf{R}$ associated with eigenvalue 1, as can be easily verified by the formula

$$\mathbf{R} = e^\mathbf{H} = \mathbf{I} + \mathbf{H}/1! + \mathbf{H}^2/2! + \cdots.$$

Therefore

$$\mathbf{Rv} = \mathbf{v},$$

and $\mathbf{v}$ gives the direction of the axis of rotation. $\mathbf{H}$ is thus a very compact representation of the rotation in terms of its axis and angle. Another property of this representation can be deduced from a theorem in Gantmacher (1977, p. 158), which states that if we compute the Lagrange-Sylvester polynomial p of the exponential function for the eigenvalues of $\mathbf{H}$—that is, the polynomial such that

$$p(0) = e^0 = 1, p(i\theta) = e^{i\theta}, p(-i\theta) = e^{-i\theta},$$

—then we have the nice relationship

$$e^{\mathbf{H}} = p(\mathbf{H}).$$

It can be easily verified that

$$p(\mathbf{H}) = \mathbf{I} + ((\sin \theta)/\theta)\mathbf{H} + ((1 - \cos \theta)/\theta^2)\mathbf{H}^2,$$

which is precisely the well-known Rodrigues formula (Rodrigues, 1840).

We finish with a property of this representation that is heavily used in the rest of the paper and related to the derivative of $e^{\mathbf{H}}$ with respect to $\mathbf{r}$. The corresponding computation is a little painful but is certainly worth doing. We refer the interested reader to the INRIA internal report corresponding to this chapter. We give only the result. We want to compute the 3 × 3 matrix

$$\mathbf{K}(\mathbf{R}, \mathbf{OM}) = \frac{\partial(\mathbf{ROM})}{\partial \mathbf{r}}$$

or, more simply, the 3-vector $\mathbf{K}(\mathbf{R}, \mathbf{OM})\mathbf{v}$, where $\mathbf{v}$ is an arbitrary 3-vector.

Letting $f(\theta) = (\sin \theta)/\theta$ and $g(\theta) = (1 - \cos \theta)/\theta^2$, one obtains

$$\begin{aligned}\mathbf{K}(\mathbf{R}, \mathbf{OM})\mathbf{v} = &\, f'(\theta)/\theta (\mathbf{r} \cdot \mathbf{v})\mathbf{r} \times \mathbf{OM} \\ &+ g'(\theta)/\theta (\mathbf{r} \cdot \mathbf{v})\mathbf{r} \times (\mathbf{r} \times \mathbf{OM}) \\ &+ f(\theta)(\mathbf{v} \times \mathbf{OM}) \\ &+ g(\theta)(\mathbf{v} \times (\mathbf{r} \times \mathbf{OM}) \\ &+ \mathbf{r} \times (\mathbf{v} \times \mathbf{OM})),\end{aligned} \quad \text{(C.1)}$$

where $f'(\theta)$ and $g'(\theta)$ are the derivatives of $f(\theta)$ and $g(\theta)$ with respect to θ. A special case occurs when $\mathbf{v}$ is collinear to $\mathbf{r}$ (i.e., when $\mathbf{v} = \mathbf{r}$). In this case one has

$$\mathbf{K}(\mathbf{R}, \mathbf{OM})\mathbf{v} = \alpha \mathbf{r} \times \mathbf{ROM}.$$

Appendix D: Matching Three-Dimensional Points

Using Eq. (3), remembering that $\mathbf{x} = [\mathbf{O'M'}^t, \mathbf{OM}^t]^t$, and $\mathbf{a} = [\mathbf{r}^t, \mathbf{t}^t]^t$, and taking into account Eq. (C.1), we have, with the notations of Section 1,

$$\partial f/\partial x = [I - R] \quad \text{a } 3 \times 6 \text{ matrix}$$

and

$$\partial f/\partial a = [-K(R, OM) - I] \quad \text{a } 3 \times 6 \text{ matrix.}$$

Appendix E: Matching Three-Dimensional Lines

We use Eqs. (4) and (5). From these equations, we can take $x = [l'^t, m'^t, l^t, m^t]^t$ and, as in the case of points, $a = [r^t, t^t]^t$. From these, we can deduce

$$\frac{\partial f}{\partial l'} = \begin{bmatrix} -c(Rl) \\ -c(m' - Rm - t) \end{bmatrix},$$

$$\frac{\partial f}{\partial m'} = \begin{bmatrix} 0 \\ c(l') \end{bmatrix},$$

$$\frac{\partial f}{\partial l} = \begin{bmatrix} c(l')R \\ 0 \end{bmatrix},$$

$$\frac{\partial f}{\partial m} = \begin{bmatrix} 0 \\ -c(l')R \end{bmatrix},$$

which completes the computation of $\partial f/\partial x = [\partial f/\partial m', \partial f/\partial l', \partial f/\partial m, \partial f/\partial l]$, a 6×12 matrix. We also have

$$\frac{\partial f}{\partial r} = \begin{bmatrix} c(l')K(R, l) \\ -c(l')K(R, m) \end{bmatrix},$$

$$\frac{\partial f}{\partial t} = \begin{bmatrix} 0 \\ -c(l') \end{bmatrix},$$

which completes the computation of $\partial f/\partial a = [\partial f/\partial r, \partial f/\partial t]$, a 6×6 matrix. But, as we said before, only four measurement equations can be kept instead of six; therefore, one must keep for $\partial f/\partial x$ (and $\partial f/\partial a$) only the 4×12 (resp. 4×6) matrix obtained by keeping the four rows corresponding to the four independent measurements.

Appendix F: Matching Planes

We use Eqs. (6) and (7). Remembering that $x = [n'^t, n^t, d', d]^t$ and $a = [r^t, t^t]^t$ and taking into account Eq. (C.1), we have, with the notations of Section 2,

$$\frac{\partial \mathbf{f}}{\partial \mathbf{x}} = \begin{bmatrix} \mathbf{I} & -\mathbf{R} & 0 & 0 \\ -\mathbf{t}^t & \mathbf{0}^t & -1 & 1 \end{bmatrix} \quad \text{a } 4 \times 8 \text{ matrix}$$

and

$$\frac{\partial \mathbf{f}}{\partial \mathbf{a}} = \begin{bmatrix} -\mathbf{K}(\mathbf{R}, \mathbf{n}) & 0 \\ \mathbf{0}^t & -\mathbf{n}'^t \end{bmatrix} \quad \text{a } 4 \times 6 \text{ matrix,}$$

where $\mathbf{0}$ is a 3×1 vector of zeros.

Appendix G: Matching Three-Dimensional and Two-Dimensional Points and Lines

We treat the case of points first. From Eq. (8), and remembering that $\mathbf{x} = [\mathbf{OM}^t, u', v']^t$ and $\mathbf{a} = [\mathbf{r}^t, \mathbf{t}^t]^t$, we have

$$\frac{\partial \mathbf{f}}{\partial \mathbf{a}} = \begin{bmatrix} (u'\mathbf{l}_3 - \mathbf{l}_1)\mathbf{K}(\mathbf{R}, \mathbf{OM}) & u'\mathbf{l}_3 - \mathbf{l}_1 \\ (v'\mathbf{l}_3 - \mathbf{l}_2)\mathbf{K}(\mathbf{R}, \mathbf{OM}) & v'\mathbf{l}_3 - \mathbf{l}_2 \end{bmatrix} \quad \text{a } 2 \times 6 \text{ matrix,}$$

$$\frac{\partial \mathbf{f}}{\partial \mathbf{x}} = \begin{bmatrix} (u'\mathbf{l}_3 - \mathbf{l}_1)\mathbf{R} & \mathbf{l}_3(\mathbf{ROM} + \mathbf{t}) + l_{34} & 0 \\ (v'\mathbf{l}_3 - \mathbf{l}_2)\mathbf{R} & 0 & \mathbf{l}_3(\mathbf{ROM} + \mathbf{t}) + l_{34} \end{bmatrix}$$

a 2×5 matrix.

Let us now tackle the case of lines. Remembering that $\mathbf{x} = [\mathbf{OM}_1^t, \mathbf{OM}_2^t, u_1, v_1, u_2, v_2]^t$ and $\mathbf{a} = [\mathbf{r}^t, \mathbf{t}^t]^t$, we can compute the components of $\mathbf{h}_1$:

$$h_{11} = (\mathbf{l}_2(\mathbf{ROM}_1 + \mathbf{t}) + l_{24})(\mathbf{l}_3(\mathbf{ROM}_2 + \mathbf{t}) + l_{34})$$
$$\quad - (\mathbf{l}_2(\mathbf{ROM}_2 + \mathbf{t}) + l_{24})(\mathbf{l}_3(\mathbf{ROM}_1 + \mathbf{t}) + l_{34}),$$

$$h_{12} = (\mathbf{l}_1(\mathbf{ROM}_2 + \mathbf{t}) + l_{14})(\mathbf{l}_3(\mathbf{ROM}_1 + \mathbf{t}) + l_{34})$$
$$\quad - (\mathbf{l}_1(\mathbf{ROM}_1 + \mathbf{t}) + l_{14})(\mathbf{l}_3(\mathbf{ROM}_2 + \mathbf{t}) + l_{34}),$$

$$h_{13} = (\mathbf{l}_1(\mathbf{ROM}_1 + \mathbf{t}) + l_{14})(\mathbf{l}_2(\mathbf{ROM}_2 + \mathbf{t}) + l_{24})$$
$$\quad - (\mathbf{l}_1(\mathbf{ROM}_2 + \mathbf{t}) + l_{14})(\mathbf{l}_2(\mathbf{ROM}_1 + \mathbf{t}) + l_{24}).$$

Using standard rules of differential calculus, we can write

$$\frac{\partial \mathbf{f}}{\partial \mathbf{x}} = \begin{bmatrix} \dfrac{-c(\mathbf{h}_2)\partial \mathbf{h}_1}{\partial \mathbf{OM}_1} & \dfrac{-c(\mathbf{h}_2)\partial \mathbf{h}_1}{\partial \mathbf{OM}_2} & \dfrac{c(\mathbf{h}_1)\partial \mathbf{h}_2}{\partial [u_1, v_1]} & \dfrac{c(\mathbf{h}_1)\partial \mathbf{h}_2}{\partial [u_2, v_2]} \end{bmatrix}^t,$$

which is a 3×10 matrix, and

$$\frac{\partial \mathbf{f}}{\partial \mathbf{a}} = \begin{bmatrix} \dfrac{-c(\mathbf{h}_2)\partial \mathbf{h}_1}{\partial \mathbf{r}} & \dfrac{-c(\mathbf{h}_2)\partial \mathbf{h}_1}{\partial \mathbf{t}} \end{bmatrix}^t,$$

which is a 3 × 6 matrix. The various partial derivatives can be easily computed by using the expressions for h_1 and h_2 and Eq. (C.1). Of course, as in the case of line matching, one eventually keeps for $\partial f/\partial \mathbf{x}$ (resp. $\partial f/\partial \mathbf{a}$) the 2 × 10 matrix (resp. 2 × 6) obtained by keeping the two rows corresponding to the two independent measurements.

REFERENCES

Ayache, N. (1989). *Vision stéréoscopique et perception multisensorielle—Applications à la robotique mobile.* Paris: InterEditions.

Ayache, N. (1990). *Stereovision and multisensor perception—Application to mobile robots.* Cambridge, MA: MIT Press.

Ayache, N., & Faugeras, O.D. (1986). Hyper: A new approach for the recognition and positioning of two-dimensional objects. *IEEE Transactions on Pattern Analysis and Machine Intelligence,* PAMI-8(1), 44–54.

Ayache, N., & Faugeras, O.D. (1987). Building a consistent 3D representation of a mobile robot environment by combining multiple stereo views. *Proceedings of the International Joint Conference on Artificial Intelligence* (pp. 808–810). Milano, Italy.

Ayache, N., & Faugeras, O.D. (1988). Maintaining representations of the environment of a mobile robot. In R.C. Bolles & B. Roth (Eds.), *Robotics research: The fourth international symposium* (pp. 337–350). Cambridge, MA: MIT Press.

Ayache, N., & Faugeras, O.D. (1989). Maintaining representations of the environment of a mobile robot. *IEEE Transactions on Robotics and Automation,* RA-5(6), 804–819.

Ayache, N., Faugeras, O.D., Faverjon, B., & Toscani, G. (1985). Matching depth maps obtained by passive stereo. *Proceedings of the Third Workshop on Computer Vision: Representation and Control* (pp. 197–204). Bellaire, TX.

Ayache, N., & Faverjon, B. (1987). Efficient registration of stereo images by matching graph descriptions of edge segments. *International Journal of Computer Vision,* 107–131.

Bolle, R.M., & Cooper, D.B. (1985). On parallel bayesian estimation and recognition for large data sets, with application to estimating 3-D complex-object position from range data. *Proceedings of the SPIE Conference on Vision for Robots.* Cannes, France.

Brooks, R. (1985). Aspects of mobile robot visual map making. In H. Hanafusa & H. Inone (Eds.), *Robotics research: The second international symposium* (pp. 369–376). Cambridge, MA: MIT Press.

Crowley, J.L. (1986). Representation and maintenance of a composite surface model. *Proceedings of the International IEEE Conference on Robotics and Automation* (pp. 1455–1462). San Francisco, CA.

Darmon, C.A. (1982). A recursive method to apply the Hough transform to a set of moving objects. *Proceedings of the International Conference on Acoustics, Speech, and Signal Processing* (pp. 825–829). Paris, France.

Durrant-Whyte, H.F. (1986). Consistent integration and propagation of disparate sensor observations. *Proceedings of the International IEEE Conference on Robotics and Automation* (pp. 1464–1469). San Francisco, CA.

Faugeras, O.D., & Toscani, G. (1986). The calibration problem for stereo. *Proceedings of the IEEE Conference for Computer Vision and Pattern Recognition* (pp. 15–20). Miami Beach, FL.

Faugeras, O.D., Ayache, N., & Faverjon, B. (1986). Building visual maps by combining noisy stereo measurements. *Proceedings of the IEEE International Conference on Robotics and Automation* (pp. 1433–1438). San Francisco, CA.

Faugeras, O.D., & Hebert, M. (1986). The representation, recognition, and localisation of 3D shapes from range data. *International Journal of Robotics Research, 5*(3), 27–52.

Faugeras, O.D., & Lustman, F. (1986). Inferring planes by hypothesis prediction and verification for a mobile robot. *European Conference on Artificial Intelligence* (pp. 143–147). Brighton, UK.

Gantmacher, F.R. (1977). *Matrix theory.* New York: Chelsea.

Jazwinsky, A.M. (1970). *Stochastic processes and filtering theory.* New York: Academic Press.

Laumond, J.P., & Chatila, R. (1985). Position referencing and consistent world modeling for mobile robots. *Proceedings of the IEEE International Conference on Robotics and Automation* (pp. 138–145). St. Louis, MO.

Lowe, D. (1985). *Perceptual organization and visual recognition.* Boston: Kluwer Academic.

Rodrigues, O. (1840). Des lois géométriques qui régissent les déplacements d'un système solide dans l'espace, et de la variation de coordonnées provenant de ces déplacements condidérés indépendamment des causes qui peuvent les produire. *Journal of Mathematical Pures Applications, 5*(1), 380–440.

Smith, R.C., & Cheeseman, P. (1986). On the representation and estimation of spatial uncertainty. *International Journal of Robotics Research, 5*(4), 54–68.

Stuelpnagel, J. (1964). On the parameterization of the three-dimensional rotation group. *SIAM Review, 6*(4), 422–430.

PART V
Applications

22
Introduction to Part V

Ren C. Luo and
Michael G. Kay

Part V describes a variety of intelligent systems in different areas of application to illustrate the role of multisensor integration and fusion in their overall operation. Industrial applications are surveyed first in this chapter. The applications are categorized into the four general areas of material handling, part fabrication, inspection, and assembly. Military applications are surveyed next. A detailed example of the role of multisensor integration and fusion in military command and control is provided in Chapter 23. Space applications are then surveyed, followed by target detection and tracking. Chapters 24 through 27 describe both the theoretical aspects of multitarget tracking and practical algorithms that can be used for the fusion of information from networks of distributed sensors, with Chapters 26 and 27 discussing parallel and distributed decision fusion. This chapter concludes with a discussion of the application of multisensor integration and fusion in the areas inertial navigation and the remote sensing of coastal waters. A description of the use of multisensor-based mobile robots in different areas of application can be found in Part IV.

1. INDUSTRIAL

The addition of sensory capabilities to the control of industrial robots can increase their flexibility and allow for their use in the production of products with a low volume or short design life (Groen, Komen, Vreeburg & Warmerdam, 1986). In many industrial applications, the use of multiple sensors is required in order to provide the robot with sufficient sensory capabilities. Most of the multisensor integration and fusion techniques discussed in this book are suitable for industrial applications because the industrial environment is well-structured as compared to most other areas of application, and descriptions of many of the objects in the environment are usually available from the databases of computer-aided design systems.

Nitzan, Barrouil, Cheeseman, and Smith (1983) divide industrial robot applications into four general areas: material handling, part fabrication (e.g., spot and arc welding, forging, etc.), inspection, and assembly. Material handling is usually the simplest area of application and assembly the most complex (Albus, 1990).

1.1. Material Handling

Industrial robots can be used for in-process workpiece handling, and the loading and unloading of industrial trucks (e.g., automatic guided vehicles, tow tractors, etc.) and conveyors—the two major material handling equipment types. Much of the multisensor integration and fusion research for mobile robots applications (see Part IV) can readily be applied to existing industrial trucks to increase their capabilities in areas such as route planning and obstacle avoidance. Choudry, Duinker, Hertzberger, and Tuijnman (1985) have developed a simulation system to test designs for the sensory control of autonomous material handling vehicles. Their sensory control designs take advantage of the relatively well structured shop floor environment to avoid having to use the more cumbersome hierarchical control structures used in most mobile robots. The hierarchical phase-template paradigm (see Section 1.1 of Chapter 2 and Chapter 10) summarizes the integration and fusion issues resulting from the use of a multisensor robot for handling workpieces. Sensory capabilities can enable a robot to grasp workpieces that are randomly oriented in a bin or on a conveyor. Hitachi Ltd. (Mochizuki, Takahashi & Hata, 1985) has developed a robot which uses three-dimensional vision and force sensors to pick up randomly positioned connectors and mount them on a printed circuit board. One of the projects of the ESPRIT program (the European Strategic Programme for Research and Development into Information Technology) is developing a system that combines vision and tactile sensors for real-time applications in material handling (Ikonomopoulos, 1986). Miller (1986, 1987, 1989), Miller, Glanz, and Kraft (1987), Hewes and Miller (1988), and Miller, Hewes, Glanz, and Kraft (1990) have applied adaptive learning (see Section 2.4 of Chapter 2) to an experiment involving having a robot use sensory feedback to track and intercept an object on a moving conveyor. Results of the experiment showed that, by the tenth attempt to teach the robot to follow the object to the end of the conveyor, the gripper was able to approach the object to within a small (1 to 4 cm) degree of accuracy. In experiments using this approach the performance accuracy was limited by the resolution of the sensor feedback information rather than by any limitations in the control structure. Luo and Mullen (1988, 1989) have used vision and ultrasonic sensors for the robotic tracking of multidimensional planar objects on a conveyor.

1.2. Part Fabrication

As of 1985, almost half of the robots in U.S. industry were being used for welding (Porter & Rossini, 1987)—the majority being used in spot welding applications because arc welding robots without sensory capabilities cannot track a seam with randomly variable gaps. Kremers et al. (1983) have developed a robot that uses both a vision sensor and wrist-mounted laser range sensors to guide the arm of the robot during the one pass arc welding of workpiece joints that had random gaps along their seams. Howarth and Guyote (1983) describe work being done at Oxford that uses eddy current and ultrasonic sensors for robot arc welding. Nitzan et al. (1983) provide a plan for a sensor guided arc welding system as a specific example to illustrate the use of generic robot functions (e.g., "recognize," "place," "grasp," etc.) and their associated high-level properties (e.g., "identity," "location," etc.) determined from sensory information.

Ruokangas, Black, Martin, and Schoenwald (1986) describe an experimental hierarchically controlled multisensor robot workstation that has been developed using Rockwell's Automation Sciences Testbed. Vision, acoustic, and force/torque sensors, all mounted on the end effector of a robot, were used both separately and in different combinations to demonstrate the limitations of the information each sensor was able to provide and the advantages to be gained when two or more sensors are integrated. In one demonstration, distance information from the acoustic sensor was used to position the end effector so that the camera was at the correct focal distance for the visual inspection of workpieces. In another demonstration, the force/torque sensors were used to provide modifications during task execution to the measurement of hole positions that were initially determined by the integrated range information provided by stereo cameras and an acoustic sensor —the acoustic information being used to provide redundancy to the distance information provided by the cameras. Ruokangas (1990) has recently developed a prototype workstation for the robotic welding of aerospace components.

1.3. Inspection

Inspection can be divided into two different types (Nitzan et al., 1983): explicit and implicit. Explicit inspection verifies the integrity of workpieces, as a separate operation, either during or after the manufacturing process. Depending on the nature of the workpieces involved, any of the multisensor integration and fusion techniques described in this book could be of potential use for explicit inspection. Implicit inspection verifies the integrity of workpieces while handling them during the manufacturing process. Many of the object-recognition approaches that combine vision with tactile sensors (see Chapters 16 and 18 in Part III) would be especially appropriate if applied to implicit inspection (as well as assembly) operations because the manipulator would already be in position to grasp and inspect the workpieces. Manufacturing research at Georgia Tech (Didocha, Lyons & Thompson, 1987) is focused on integrating vision and tactile information for the adaptive control of a robot manipulator that would be useful in just such applications.

1.4. Assembly

Assembly is the most complex area of industrial robot application because, in addition to operations like insertion that are unique to assembly, different aspects of the other three application areas can be part of the overall assembly process. Raczkowsky and Rembold (1990, Table 2) describe the different types of sensor functions required to support assembly operations where the position of workpieces in the workspace is constrained to particular degrees of freedom, for example, from no sensor function for fixtured workpieces to the use of multiple sensors when the position of a workpiece is unconstrained in three dimensions. Smith and Nitzan (1983) describe an assembly station consisting of two robots with wrist-mounted vision and force sensors, overhead cameras, and a general-purpose parts feeder. Printer carriages were assembled by first locating components on the feeder using the overhead cameras, and then transporting them to the carriage and snapping them in place using the robots. The force and wrist-mounted vision sensors were used to verify that the components were correctly in place. One of the projects of the ESPRIT program is to develop vision and tactile sensors that can be used in an integrated manner for assembly operations (Ikonomopoulos, 1986). Rembold (1988) describes a mobile robot that can be used for assembly operations.

Groen, Petriu, Vreeburg, and Warmerdam (1985) and Groen et al. (1986) describe a multisensor robotic assembly station equipped with vision, ultrasonic, tactile, and force/torque sensors. The ass mbly process is represented as a sequence of stages that are entered when certain sensor-determined conditions are satisfied. A hierarchical control structure, modeled after the NBS control hierarchy (see Section 2.2 of Chapter 2), is used to enable the entire process to be executed using a set of modular low-level peripheral processes that perform dedicated tasks such as sensory processing, robot control, and data communication. The system has been applied to the assembly of three different types of hydraulic lift assemblies for gas water heaters. In operation, vision sensors are used to recognize different parts of the assemblies as they arrive in varying order and at undefined positions. Feedback information from the force/torque sensors and the passive compliance of the robot's gripper are used for bolt insertion operations and to transport and place, with great precision, assembly housings on work spots so that the housing can be used as a reference for the remaining assembly operations. Final inspection is performed with the vision sensors.

Malcolm and Smithers (1990) describe an autonomous assembly system that is able to use an assembly planning system that is simpler in comparison to most assembly planning systems due to the incorporation of a more intelligent plan execution agent. The plan execution agent achieves its greater intelligence through the use of a single hierarchy of behavioral modules, instead of the more traditional twin hierarchies of sensing and action (cf. the NBS hierarchy described in Section 2.2 of Chapter 2). Each behavioral module controls its own sensing and action operations necessary for the motion of a part.

Kelley, Sood, and Repko (1990) have used an integrated sensing approach to the problem of printed circuit board insertion. Their system operates in real-time and is designed to first locate circuit boards and then insert them into slots. Overhead stereo vision is used to determine the gross location of the boards and then a fingertip light-beam sensor is used to obtain more accurate position information. A fuzzy logic–based controller is used to handle the uncertainty inherent in the insertion process.

2. MILITARY

As the complexity, speed, and scope of warfare has increased, the military has increasingly turned to automated systems to support many activities that have traditionally been performed manually (Fowler & Nesbit, 1980). The use of large numbers of diverse sensors as part of these systems has resulted in the issues of multisensor integration and fusion assuming critical importance. As an example of the need for highly automated systems, the typical average information requirements for the command and control of tactical air warfare have been estimated to be 25–50 decisions/min based on 50,000–100,000 reports from 156 separate sensor platforms concerning as many as 1000 hostile targets being tracked up to an altitude of 20 km over an area of 800 km^2 (see Chapter 23). As part of a comprehensive survey of the possible military applications of artificial intelligence technologies, Franklin, Davis, Shumaker, and Morawski (1986) listed multisensor integration and fusion were listed in 20 of the 25 areas of application. Given this wide scope, multisensor integration and fusion will be one of the technologies necessary for the development of the Autonomous Land Vehicle (see Section 4.4 of Chapter 19), an intelligent Pilot's Associate, and a command and control system for naval battle management—three of the initial projects supported by DARPA's Strategic Computing Program aimed at exploring the potential of AI-based solutions to important military problems (Klass, 1985).

2.1. Unique Aspects of Military Applications

The use of multisensor integration and fusion for object recognition in military applications requires that consideration be given to some additional factors that are not present in nonmilitary applications (cf. Chapter 16). Object recognition can be considered as a two-person zero-sum statistical game played against nature by the system performing the recognition (Tou & Gonzalez, 1974, pp. 111–112). In the terms of game theory, at each move in the game both players select a strategy. Associated with each pair of possible strategies is a pay-off. In a zero-sum game, the gain of one player is equal to the loss of the other. The system's strategies are the possible decisions as to the identity of an object; nature's strategies are the a priori probabilities corresponding to the occurrence of each of the possible classes to which an object can belong. In most nonmilitary applications, nature can be considered to be indifferent (i.e., the strategies it selects are based upon the a priori probability of each object and they remain constant even though they may not be optimal in the game-theoretic sense); in military applications, by contrast, it is possible that the moves of the other player (e.g., the design or operation of the hostile aircraft being recognized) are being selected with the goal of maximizing the potential payoff.

The possibility of a game against a "malevolent nature" (i.e., the enemy) highlights the necessity of being able to make decisions through the use of a variety of different sensors. Any system relying on the information provided by just a single sensor type could be more vulnerable to what might be called "meta-sensor error": Although the sensor might be functionally providing correct information, it could be spoofed as to the true identity of an object being sensed (e.g., a hostile aircraft using a friendly radar signature). Through the use of redundant information provided by sensors of different types together with the ability to integrate this information intelligently, the system can minimize the effect of the spoofed sensor in the overall determination of the object's identity. Garvey and Fischler (1980) discuss the use of multiple sensors for inductive and interpretative perceptual reasoning in hostile environments; Comparato (1988) describes the potential role of multisensor fusion in the next generation of tactical combat platforms; and Mayersak (1988) reviews the multisensor fusion aspects of munition (e.g., guided missile) design.

2.2. ANALYST

ANALYST (Bonasso, 1984, 1985) is a prototype expert system developed for the U.S. Army that generates real-time battlefield tactical situation descriptions using the information provided by multiple sensor sources. ANALYST determines as output a situation map showing the suspected location of enemy units through the use of intelligence input from battlefield sensors, photographs, and intercepted enemy communications and radar transmissions. Each intelligence report input is represented as a frame. The use of frames allows default values to be attached to the slots of the frame in the case where the intelligence report was incomplete. Each frame is then applied simultaneously to production rules contained in the first two of six different knowledge bases. The initial fusion of the sensor information is performed by these rules in the process of inferring a possible battlefield entity (also represented as a frame). Associated with each entity frame is a slot containing a likelihood factor to indicate the strength of the evidence used to infer the presence of the entity. The third knowledge base eliminates possible multiple frames corresponding to the same entity that may have been created from the reports of different sensors. The fourth and fifth knowledge bases refine and reinforce the entity frames through the use of tactical and terrain data together with the presence of other possible related entities in the knowledge bases. The sixth knowledge base serves to remove from consideration those entities that have not been reinforced with additional information for a sufficient length of time. Each knowledge base is applied sequentially to each piece of sensor information as it becomes available, enabling ANALYST to continuously provide the most current estimate of the battlefield situation.

3. SPACE

NASA's permanently manned space station may be the United States' major space program in coming years (Culbert, Boarnet & Savely, 1988; Krishen, de Figueiredo & Graham, 1987). Previous NASA programs, including the space shuttle, have used a high degree of participation by both the crew and ground-based personnel to perform the sensing and perception functions required for many tasks. In order to both increase productivity and allow tasks beyond the capability of the crew to be performed, the space station will make increasing use of autonomous systems for the servicing, maintenance, and repair of satellites, and the assembly of large structures for use as production facilities and commercial laboratories. Probably the most important factor promoting the use of autonomous systems for these applications is the cost of having a human in space. In addition to these economic factors, aspects of the space environment can make the use of multiple sensors an especially important part of these systems; for example, the sensing of objects in space using just optical sensors is difficult because the lack of atmosphere invalidates some of the common assumptions concerning surface reflectance used in many visual recognition methods. Also, images in space frequently have deep shadows, missing edges, and intense specular reflections (Shaw, de Figueiredo & Krishen, 1988a).

Lumia and Albus (1988) have reviewed some of the applications for which multisensor-based robots can be used in space and have suggested a system architecture standard based on the NBS hierarchy (see Section 2.2 of Chapter 2) that would allow the control of robots in space to evolve from teleoperation to increasing degrees of autonomy.

Abidi and Gonzalez (1990) describe a robotic system that autonomously performs manipulation operations useful for space applications. The system uses vision and touch sensing, in addition to force, torque, and proximity sensing, to identify, remove, and replace a variety of different modules typically found on space vehicles.

Shaw et al. (1988a, 1988b) have presented a system that uses TV images to guide a microwave radar unit in the determination of the shape of objects in space. Microwave radar information serves to complement optical information for a number of important features of objects typically found in space. Scattering cross-sectional data from radar can be used to determine the shape of the metallic surfaces typically found on satellites; optical sensors and even laser range scanners have difficulty with metallic surfaces because they reflect light in a specular direction. Optical sensors would be more useful in determining the shape of the slightly matte surfaces found on the space shuttle because these surfaces reflect light more equally in all directions. As compared to optical wavelengths, the longer wavelength of radar can be used both to penetrate the solar blankets on space objects that sometimes cover important surface details needed by a robot for grasping and, in some cases, to diffract around objects that are occluded along the optical sensor's line of sight. The optical image is used to provide an initial estimate of the shape of a surface that serves to reduce the ambiguity inherent when interpreting narrow-band radar-scattering cross-sectional data. In operation, the system uses equations defining the orthogonal directions of the polarized radar-scattering cross section to determine surface shapes. Initially, occluding contours are derived from the optical image of the surface by thresholding and a partial surface shape description is derived from shape-from-shading or stereo. The surface is then either matched to some simple geometric shape or, if no match is found, a grid is constructed over the surface. If a simple match is found, a closed-form expression can be used for the scattering equations; if no match is found, an iterative nonlinear least squares technique is used to approximate the equations.

4. TARGET DETECTION AND TRACKING

Target detection and tracking using a single sensor are well understood and used in many aerospace applications. The use of multiple sensors can increase the performance level of a tracking system and make it less sensitive to sensor failure (Bullock & Boudreaux, 1989), but the use of multiple sensors presents a number of unique problems including data association or correspondence, sensor allocation, and the various types of fusion schemes that are possible when sensors are distributed over a large geographical area. Many of these problems are common to any method of multisensor integration and fusion (see Chapter 1), but target detection and tracking applications provide a valuable testbed to address many of these problems because the targets being sensed can be considered point sources and mathematical models of the targets' dynamics are available; in contrast to many other areas of application, realistic and sometimes optimal analytical approaches to the fusion problem are possible (see, e.g., Chapters 26 and 27 in this part). Blackman (Chapter 24), Drummond and Blackman (1989), and Blackman and Broida (1990) have provided thorough summaries of the issues and methods of tracking multiple targets using multiple sensors. In their papers a detailed discussion is provided of analytical methods of evaluating and bounding the performance characteristics of multisensor tracking systems based on the amount and quality of the sensory information. Iverson, Chang, and Chong (1989) have described a means of assessing the performance of multisensor target surveillance systems in terms of technical requirements and an estimate of the cost of a system over its life cycle. The assessment includes factors such as the adaptive allocation of sensor resources, sensor suite optimization, sensor modeling, and the type of fusion method used.

A variety of different filtering techniques, together with radar, optical, and sonar sensors, have been used for the detection and tracking of targets (e.g., missiles, planes, submarines, etc.) in the air, space, and under water. Bar-Shalom (1978) and Bar-Shalom and Fortmann (1988) have surveyed a number of tracking methods that can be used when there are multiple targets in the environment, and Blackman (1986) has provided a textbook treatment of the subject. Recently, researchers have been developing methods of multitarget tracking that integrate and/or fuse the information (or measurements) provided by a number of distributed sensors (Bar-Shalom, 1990). Nahin and Pokoski (1980), in a delightfully written early paper, question the notion that the information from multiple sensors can always be synergistically fused; that is, is more always better? Many of the open questions mentioned in their paper concerning sensor fusion have been the subject of much subsequent research. A key problem in multitarget tracking in general, and in multisensor multitarget tracking in particular, is "data association"—the association or registration of sensor information to a single target (Blackman, 1990; Brown, Pittard & Martin, 1989; Deb, Pattipati, Bar-Shalom, & Washburn, 1989; Dana, 1990; Pattipati, Deb, Bar-Shalom & Washburn, 1990).

4.1. Fusion Schemes

In target detection and tracking, the information from a network of sensors can be fused using three general schemes (Krzysztofowicz & Long, 1990):

1. the signal-level fusion of the actual or partially processed observations or measurements from each sensor at a processing site,

2. symbol-level fusion at the processing site using only the detection probabilities sent to the site by each sensor, and
3. the symbol- (or decision-) level fusion at the processing site of detection decisions provided by each sensor (each decision may also include additional information as to its quality).

The three fusion schemes present a tradeoff in terms of the smaller bandwidth required for communication within the network and the possible loss of information for fusion when only a decision or a probability is being sent, versus the larger bandwidth but more complete information provided when full measurements are being sent. Two different architectures have been developed for the processing of the information provided by each sensor in a network. In the first, the measurements, probabilities, or decisions of all the sensors are transmitted to a centralized site for processing; in the second, the processing is distributed to local nodes in the network. The second architecture is typically referred to as a "distributed network" (Chong, Mori, & Chang, 1985, 1990) and offers the possibility of using a combination of the different fusion schemes; for example, full measurements could be sent to a local node for fusion and the resulting decisions could then be transmitted to a central site where they could be fused with the decisions from other nodes in the network. As compared to the first, the second architecture provides the benefits of increased redundancy, reliability, and survivability.

Measurement fusion: Demirbas (1988, 1989) has presented a nonparametric target recognition method that sends only target feature measurements to a central processing site for fusion. This method does not assume a probability density function for any observations and requires a much smaller bandwidth for communication as compared to sending raw measurements to the processing site. In most multisensor fusion schemes used in multitarget tracking, each sensor usually provides the fusion processing site with highly redundant information concerning each target. An example of a situation in which it is necessary to transmit full measurements to the processing site for fusion is when the position and velocity of targets can be derived through the use of the complementary information provided by the time of arrival and frequency of the signals arriving at each sensor can be used to determine the tracks of targets. Arnold, Bar-Shalom, Estrada, and Mucci (1983) and Mucci, Arnold, and Bar-Shalom (1985) have used the Fisher information matrix to evaluate the performance of this approach and have found that a single pair of omnidirectional sensors are sufficient to determine the location of moving targets when they are in the vicinity (near field) of the sensors; three sensors are required when they are distant or stationary.

Probabilistic fusion: Buede and Waltz (1989) have described and analyzed the benefits of using probabilistic fusion for target detection and recognition as compared to decision fusion. Their analysis has shown that probabilistic fusion allows "soft decisions" to be made that can increase the range at which recognition can take place by 30 percent as compared to the "hard decisions" made with decision fusion. Krzysztofowicz and Long (1990) have formulated a Bayesian detection model in which each sensor provides the central fusion processor with a detection probability rather than measurements or detection decisions. The detection probabilities are used within parametric models of likelihood functions at the central processor for detection decisions.

Decision fusion: The majority of the research on multisensor fusion for target detection and tracking has focused on the formulation of optimal decision rules. Much of this research is based on Tenney and Sandell's (1981) extension of detection theory to the case of distributed sensors. Their extension is based on a formulation of the problem in terms of the classical team decision problem. Many researchers have determined optimal decision rules and fusion techniques for distributed decision fusion under a wide variety of assumptions and conditions (see, e.g., Chapters 26 and 27 in this part, and Chair & Varshney, 1986, 1988)). Tsitsiklis and Athans (1985) have determined that one necessary assumption for any optimal decision rule is the conditional independence between the measurements of each sensor; without this assumption the problem is NP-complete. Kam, Naim, Labonski, and Guez (1989) have formulated the decision fusion problem in terms of a two-layered neural network that is able to adapt to sudden changes in the quality of the information from a sensor.

5. INERTIAL NAVIGATION

The inertial system used in spacecraft and many advanced aircraft for navigation consists of a gyroscope mounted on a platform suspended in a gimbal structure that allows the vehicle to change its angular orientation while maintaining the platform fixed with respect to a reference coordinate frame (Britting, 1971; Maybeck, 1979). The position and velocity of the vehicle can be determined by integrating the signals from accelerometers mounted on the platform. Due to inherent gyro characteristics that cause errors in position and velocity to grow unbounded slowly over time (i.e., low-frequency noise), the inertial navigation system requires the aid of other external navigation sensors to bound or dampen these errors. Typical external sensors used to aid the inertial system include on-board or ground-based radar, radio, navigation satellites, landmarks or star sightings, laser ranging, and altimeters. As opposed to the inertial system which accurately follows the high-frequency motions of the vehicle, each of these external sensors provides information which is good on average (i.e., its error does not increase over time) but is subject to considerable high-frequency noise (i.e., each measurement has considerable error). A Kalman filter (see Section 1.2 of Chapter 8) can be used to determine the signal-level fusion of inertial system and external sensor information that will statistically minimize the error in the estimate of the vehicle's position.

Figure 22.1 shows a typical external sensor-aided inertial navigation system configuration. In the figure, the Kalman filter is used in an indirect (error state space) feedback configuration to generate estimates of the errors in the inertial system and then feed these estimates back into the inertial system to correct it. The indirect feedback filter configuration is used in most inertial navigation systems because

1. as opposed to the direct formulation where the vehicle's actual position is estimated, the indirect formulation increases the overall reliability of the navigation system because the inertial system can still operate if the filter should fail due to a temporary computer or external navigation sensor failure;
2. the feedback, as opposed to feedforward, mechanization is used so that inertial errors do not grow unchecked; and
3. the sample rate for this filter is low because only low frequency linear dynamics are modeled.

Brumback and Srinath (1987) have presented a design for a multisensor inertial navigation system that can still provide accurate position estimates after a navigation sensor has failed, thus eliminating the need to reinitialize the navigational system during operation. During the initial detection interval, data from the normal sensors and the failed sensor are fused to form the filter estimate resulting in an estimate that is contaminated with bad data. Multiple Kalman filter estimates from different subsets of sensors are used to isolate the information provided by the normal sensors so that a reliable estimate can be obtained.

6. REMOTE SENSING

In aerial photo mapping over land, known ground points can be used to establish the orientation of photographs; in aerial mapping over water,

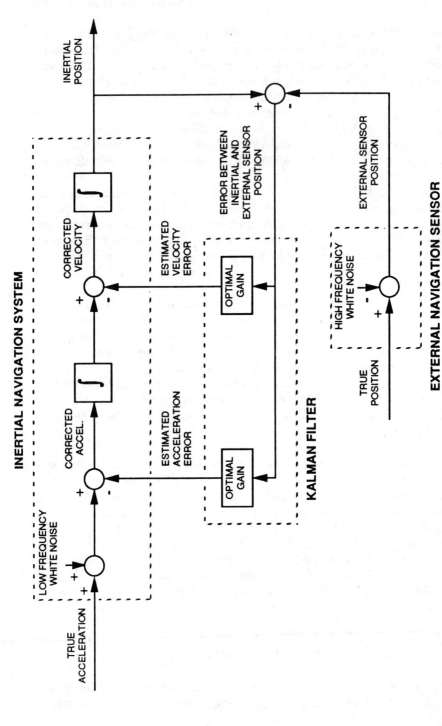

Figure 22.1. External sensor–aided indirect feedback inertial navigation system configuration. (Adapted from Figure 6.9(a) in Maybeck, 1979.)

the orientation must be determined by accurately knowing the position and attitude of the camera at the time the photograph is taken because known ground points are not generally available. Gesing and Reid (1983) describe a system that fuses information from multiple navigation sensors to estimate an aircraft's position and attitude accurately enough for use in the mapping of shallow coastal waters. An inertial navigation system is mounted to the top of the aerial survey camera in the aircraft used for mapping. During flight, information is recorded from a number of auxiliary navigation sensors, including a laser bathymeter to measure water depth, a microwave ranging system, barometric and radar altimeters, a radio navigation system, and a Doppler radar. A U-D covariance factorization filter (see Section 1.2 of Chapter 8) and a modified Bryson-Frazier smoother are then used for postflight processing to produce time-correlated sensor error estimates that can be subtracted from the recorded inertial system data to yield highly accurate position and attitude information that serves to orient the photographs taken during the flight.

7. OVERVIEW

This section presents an overview of the remaining chapters in Part V.

Chapter 23: Waltz and Buede proposed an architecture for a generic command and control system that includes multisensor integration and fusion functions as one of its two major subsystems. The operation of the system can be divided into four main steps of a feedback loop. First, a variety of different sensors collect data from the combat environment and then transmit these data on to the multisensor integration and fusion subsystem. The functions comprising this subsystem integrate and fuse the data so that any targets or events can be located and identified. The process of data fusion starts with each sensor or network of sensors in the combat environment sending detection reports or target tracks to a queue from which they are made commensurate by being transformed to a common space and time coordinate system. A local target track is maintained by a sensor if the measurement time of the sensor is small relative to the ability of the system to process the data. Because the system is generic, the common spatial reference (e.g., X-Y-Z; latitude/longitude, range/azimuth/elevation, etc.) depends on the specific environment, and the methods of transforming the sensed data depend on the differing locations, resolutions, fields of view, and measurement times of the particular sensors used. The fused information, representing the possible targets or events that comprise the current situation, is then sent to the decision support subsection where it is used to create, analyze, and rank alternative courses of action. A human commander completes the feedback loop by selecting a course of action which possibly changes the environment. The system initiates operation with a query from the human commander to the decision support subsystem for recommended courses of action. Using certain key parameter values supplied by the human commander and the system's assessment of current situation, the decision support subsystem analyzes alternative courses of action, possibly querying the multisensor integration and fusion subsystem for additional information, to select those actions to recommend to the human commander. The human commander can then either select one of the current recommended actions or query the system for additional information. Although the human commander can always make the final decision, certain routine or time-critical actions can automatically be determined by the system.

Chapter 24: Blackman presents a survey of the issues involved in the association and fusion of data from multiple sensors for target tracking and recognition. Issues discussed include the use of nearest-neighbor versus all-neighbor and sequential versus deferred decision logic methods for data association, central- versus sensor-level tracking, estimation of a target's kinematic quantities (e.g., its position and velocity), the symbol-level fusion of target attributes, and sensor allocation. The use of Bayesian estimation (see Section 3.1 of Chapter 8) and Dempster-Shafer evidential reasoning (see Section 3.2 of Chapter 8) for target attribute fusion is described, and a utility theory-based method of sensor allocation is introduced. Additional information concerning the use of multiple sensors for target recognition can be found in Section 3 of Chapter 16.

Chapter 25: Chang, Chong, and Bar-Shalom have presented a distributed processing version of the Joint Probabilistic Data Association algorithm, first applied in a centralized processing architecture (Fortmann, Bar-Shalom and Scheffe, 1983), which reduces the network's bandwidth requirements by fusing, at each local node in the network, measurements from a small number of sensors. The compressed higher-level fused information is then propagated to the other local nodes in the network. Each local node can use the fused information it receives from the other nodes to arrive at a solution to the global tracking problem. The algorithm used for fusion was developed by Speyer (1979). It is based on the use of a Kalman filter (see Section 1.2 of Chapter 9) at each local node, and requires the propagation of an additional data-dependent vector beyond the usual filter equations.

Chapters 26 and 27: Chapters 26 and 27 discuss parallel and distributed decision fusion. Dr. Stelios C.A. Thomopoulos has graciously provided the following introductory remarks:

These two chapters, together with Thomopoulos, Viswanathan, and Bougoulias (1987), constitute a trilogy in decision fusion and can be organized into two parts. The first part deals with the distributed decision fusion problem in parallel topology sensor networks. It consists of two papers (Thomopoulos et al. (1987) and Chapter 26) that have appeared separately in the *IEEE Transactions on Aerospace and Electronic Systems* in vol. AES-23, no. 5, 1987, and vol. AES-25, no. 5, 1989, respectively. The first paper deals with the problem of optimal decision fusion, in the Neyman-Pearson sense, when the peripheral sensors operate at fixed false alarm and detection probabilities. The optimal fusion scheme, in the Neyman-Pearson sense, is derived, and it is shown both analytically and numerically that performance improvement results from distributed decision fusion. In the second paper (Chapter 26), "Optimal distributed decision fusion" that appeared in 1989, the performance of the distributed decision fusion scheme, in the Neyman-Pearson sense, consists of Likelihood Ratio tests at the sensors, and a Neyman-Pearson test (or a randomized Neyman-Pearson test) at the fusion center. In a companion paper (not included in the trilogy) "Optimal partitioning of observations in distributed detection," which has appeared in the *Proceedings of the 1988 Information Theory Symposium* held in Japan, the results of the previous two papers are extended in the multilevel data quantization case. In this companion paper, it is shown that the optimal, in the Neyman-Pearson sense, multilevel quantization of observations for the distributed decision fusion problem is achieved when the data at the sensors are partitioned in the different levels according to Likelihood Ratios.

The second part of this contribution deals with the problem of distributed decision fusion in serial topology sensor networks. This part consists of the paper (Chapter 27) "Optimal serial distributed decision fusion" that has appeared in the *IEEE Transactions on Aerospace and Electronic Systems*, vol. AES-24, no. 4, 1988, and considers the problem of optimal, in the Neyman-Pearson sense, decision fusion when the sensors are connected in a serial topology. The optimal fusion scheme is derived, and a performance comparison between the parallel and serial topologies is carried out.

REFERENCES

Abidi, M.A., & Gonzalez, R.C. (1990). The use of multisensor data for robotic applications. *IEEE Transactions on Robotics and Automation,* RA-6(2), 159–177.

Albus, J.S. (1990). Robotics: Where has it been? Where is it going? *Robotics and Autonomous Systems, 6,* 199–219.

Arnold, J.F., Bar-Shalom, Y., Estrada, R., & Mucci, R.A. (1983). Target parameter estimation using measurements acquired with a small number of sensors. *IEEE Journal of Oceanic Engineering,* OE-8(3), 163–171.

Bar-Shalom, Y. (1978). Tracking methods in a multitarget environment. *IEEE Transactions on Automatic Control,* AC-23(4), 618–626.

Bar-Shalom, Y. Ed. (1990). *Multitarget-multisensor tracking: Advanced applications.* Norwood, MA: Artech House.

Bar-Shalom, Y., & Fortmann, T.E. (1988). *Tracking and data association.* New York: Academic.

Blackman, S.S. (1986). *Multiple target tracking with radar applications.* Dedham, MA: Artech House.

Blackman, S.S. (1990). Association and fusion of multiple sensor data. In Y. Bar-Shalom (Ed.), *Multitarget-multisensor tracking: Advanced applications* (pp. 187–218). Norwood, MA: Artech House.

Blackman, S.S., & Broida, T.J. (1990). Multiple sensor data association and fusion in aerospace applications. *Journal of Robotic Systems, 7*(3), 445–485.

Bonasso, Jr., R.P. (1984). *ANALYST: An expert system for processing sensor returns* (Tech. Rep. MTP-83W 00002). McLean, VA: The MITRE Corp.

Bonasso, Jr., R.P. (1985). *ANALYST II: A knowledge-based intelligence support system* (Tech. Rep. MTP-84W 00220). McLean, VA: The MITRE Corp.

Britting, K.R. (1971). *Inertial navigation system analysis.* New York: Wiley.

Brown, D.E., Pittard, C.L., & Martin, W.N. (1989). Neural network implementation of data association algorithms for sensor fusion. In C.B. Weaver (Ed.), *Proceedings of the SPIE, vol. 1100, Sensor Fusion II* (pp. 126–135). Orlando, FL.

Brumback, B.D., & Srinath, M.D. (1987). A fault-tolerant multisensor navigation system design. *IEEE Transactions on Aerospace and Electronic Systems,* AES-23(6), 738–756.

Buede, D.M., & Waltz, E.L. (1989). Benefits of soft sensors and probabilistic fusion. In D.E. Drummond (Ed.), *Proceedings of the SPIE, vol. 1096, Signal and Data Processing of Small Targets* (pp. 309–320). Orlando, FL.

Bullock, T.E., & Boudreaux, E.J. (1989). Sensor fusion in a nonlinear dynamical system. In C.B. Weaver (Ed.), *Proceedings of the SPIE, vol. 1100, Sensor Fusion II* (pp. 109–116). Orlando, FL.

Chair, Z., & Varshney, P.K. (1986). Optimal data fusion in multiple sensor detection systems. *IEEE Transactions on Aerospace and Electronic Systems,* AES-22(1), 98–101.

Chair, Z., & Varshney, P.K. (1988). Distributed Bayesian hypothesis testing with distributed data fusion. *IEEE Transactions on Systems, Man and Cybernetics,* SMC-18(5), 695–699.

Chong, C.Y., Mori, S., & Chang, K.C. (1985). Information fusion in distributed sensor networks. *Proceedings of the American Control Conference* (pp. 830–835). Boston, MA.

Chong, C.Y., Mori, S., & Chang, K.C. (1990). Distributed multitarget multisensor tracking. In Y. Bar-Shalom (Ed.), *Multitarget-multisensor tracking: Advanced applications* (pp. 247–295). Norwood, MA: Artech House.

Choudry, A., Duinker, W., Hertzberger, L.O., & Tuijnman, F. (1985). Simulating the sensory-control of an autonomous vehicle. *Proceedings of the 5th International Conference on Robot Vision and Sensory Controls* (pp. 147–154). Amsterdam, The Netherlands.

Comparato, V.G. (1988). Fusion—The key to tactical mission success. In C.W. Weaver (Ed.), *Proceedings of the SPIE, vol. 931, Sensor Fusion* (pp. 2–7). Orlando, FL.

Culbert, C., Boarnet, M., & Savely, R.T. (1988). AI applications for the space station. *Robotics, 4,* 35–40.

Dana, M.P. (1990). Registration: A prerequisite for multiple sensor tracking. In Y. Bar-Shalom (Ed.), *Multitarget-multisensor tracking: Advanced applications* (pp. 155–185). Norwood, MA: Artech House.

Deb, S., Pattipati, K.R., Bar-Shalom, Y., & Washburn, R.B. (1989). Assignment algorithms for the passive sensor data association problem. In D.E. Drummond (Ed.), *Proceedings of the SPIE, vol. 1096, Signal and Data Processing of Small Targets* (pp. 231–243). Orlando, FL.

Demirbas, K. (1988). Maximum a posteriori approach to object recognition with distributed sensors. *IEEE Transactions on Aerospace and Electronic Systems,* AES-24(3), 309–313.

Demirbas, K. (1989). Distributed sensor data fusion with binary decision trees. *IEEE Transactions on Aerospace and Electronic Systems,* AES-25(5), 643–649.

Didocha, R.J., Lyons, D.W., & Thompson, J.C. (1987). Integration of tactile sensors and machine vision for control of robotic manipulators. *Robots 9 Conference Proceedings* (pp. 37–71). Detroit, MI.

Drummond, O.E., & Blackman, S.S. (1989). Challenges of developing algorithms for multiple sensor, multiple target tracking. In D.E. Drummond (Ed.), *Proceedings of the SPIE, vol. 1096, Signal and Data Processing of Small Targets* (pp. 245–255). Orlando, FL.

Fortmann, T.E., Bar-Shalom, Y., & Scheffe, M. (1983). Sonar tracking of multiple targets using joint probabilistic data association. *IEEE Journal of Oceanic Engineering,* OE-8(3), 173–184.

Fowler, C.A., & Nesbit, R.F. (1980, November). Tactical C^3, counter C^3 and C^5. *Journal of Electronics and Defense.*

Franklin, J., Davis, L., Shumaker, R., & Morawski, P. (1986). Military applications. *Encyclopedia of artificial intelligence* (pp. 604–614). New York: Wiley.

Garvey, T.D., & Fischler, M.A. (1980). Perceptual reasoning in a hostile environment. *Proceedings of the 1st Annual National Conference on Artificial Intelligence* (pp. 253–255). Stanford Univ., CA.

Gesing, W.S., & Reid, D.B. (1983). An integrated multisensor aircraft track recovery system for remote sensing. *IEEE Transactions on Automatic Control,* AC-28(3), 356–363.

Groen, F.C.A., Komen, E.R., Vreeburg, M.A.C., & Warmerdam, T.P.H. (1986). Multisensor robot assembly station. *Robotics, 2,* 205–214.

Groen, F.C.A., Petriu, E.M., Vreeburg, M.A.C., & Warmerdam, T.P.H. (1985). Multisensor robot assembly station. *Proceedings of the 5th International Conference on Robot Vision and Sensory Controls* (pp. 439–448). Amsterdam, The Netherlands.

Hewes, R.P., & Miller, III, W.T. (1988). Practical demonstration of a learning control system for a five-axis industrial robot. In D.P. Casasent (Ed.), *Proceedings of the SPIE, vol. 1002, Intelligent Robots and Computer Vision: Seventh in a Series* (pp. 679–685). Cambridge, MA.

Howarth, M.P., & Guyote, M.F. (1983). Eddy current and ultrasonic sensors for robot arc welding. *Sensor Review, 3*(2), 90–93.

Ikonomopoulos, A. (1986). Trends in computer vision research for advanced industrial automation. In V. Cappellini & R. Marconi (Eds.), *Advances in image processing and pattern recognition*. New York: Elsevier.

Iverson, D.E., Chang, K.C., & Chong, C.Y. (1989). Performance assessment for airborne surveillance systems incorporating sensor fusion. In D.E. Drummond (Ed.), *Proceedings of the SPIE, vol. 1096, Signal and Data Processing of Small Targets* (pp. 269–283). Orlando, FL.

Kam, M., Naim, A., Labonski, P., & Guez, A. (1989). Adaptive sensor fusion with nets of binary threshold elements. *Proceedings of the International Joint Conference on Neural Networks,* (pp. II-57–II-64). Washington, DC.

Kelley, R.B., Sood, D., & Repko, M.C. (1990). Integrated sensing for circuit board insertion. *J. Robotic Systems, 7*(3), 487–505.

Klass, P.J. (1985). DARPA envisions new generation of machine intelligence technology. *Aviation Week and Space Technology, 122*(16), 46–84.

Kremers, J.H., Blahnik, C., Brain, A., Cain, R., DeCurtins, J., Mesegner, J., & Peppers, N. (1983). Development of a machine-vision based robotic arc-welding system. *Proceedings of the 13th International Symposium on Industrial Robots and Robots* (pp. 14.19–14.33). Chicago, IL.

Krishen, K., de Figueiredo, R.J.P., & Graham, O. (1987). Robotic vision/sensing for space applications. *Proceedings of the IEEE International Conference on Robotics and Automation* (pp. 138–150). Raleigh, NC.

Krzysztofowicz, R., & Long, D. (1990). Fusion of detection probabilities and comparison of multisensor systems. *IEEE Transactions on Systems, Man and Cybern.*, SMC-20(3), 665–677.

Lumia, R., & Albus, J.S. (1988). Teleoperation and autonomy for space robotics. *Robotics, 4,* 27–33.

Luo, R.C., & Mullen Jr., R.E. (1988). Combined vision/ultrasonics for multidimentional robotic tracking. In P.S. Schenker (Ed.), *Proceedings of the SPIE, vol. 1003, Sensor Fusion: Spatial Reasoning and Scene Interpretation* (pp. 113–121). Cambridge, MA.

Luo, R.C., & Mullen Jr., R.E. (1989). A modified optical flow approach for robotic tracking and acquisition. *Journal of Robotic Systems, 6*(5), 489–508.

Malcolm, C., & Smithers, T. (1990). Symbol grounding via a hybrid architecture in an autonomous system. *Robotics and Autonomous Systems, 6,* 123–144.

Maybeck, P.S. (1979). *Stochastic models, estimation, and control* (Vol. 1). New York: Academic.
Mayersak, J.R. (1988). An alternate view of munition sensor fusion. In C.W. Weaver (Ed.), *Proceedings of the SPIE, vol. 931, Sensor Fusion* (pp. 64–73). Orlando, FL.
Miller, III, W.T. (1986). A nonlinear learning controller for robotic manipulators. *Proceedings of the SPIE, 579, Intelligent Robots and Computer Vision* (pp. 416–423). Cambridge, MA.
Miller, III, W.T. (1987). Sensor-based control of robotic manipulators using a general learning algorithm. *IEEE Journal of Robotics and Automation*, RA-*3*(2), 157–165.
Miller, III, W.T. (1989). Real-time application of neural networks for sensor-based control of robots with vision. *IEEE Transactions on Systems, Man and Cybern.*, SMC-*19*(4), 825–831.
Miller, III, W.T., Glanz, F.H., & Kraft, III, L.G. (1987). Application of a general learning algorithm to the control of robotic manipulators. *International Journal of Robotics Research*, *6*(2), 84–98.
Miller, III, W.T., Hewes, R.P., Glanz, F.H., and Kraft, III, L.G. (1990). Real-time dynamic control of an industrial manipulator using a neural-network-based learning controller. *IEEE Transactions on Robotics and Automation*, RA-*6*(1), 1–9.
Mochizuki, J., Takahashi, M., & Hata, S. (1985). Unpositioned workpieces handling robot with visual and force sensors. *Proceedings of the IEEE International Conference on Industrial Electronics, Control, and Instrumentation* (pp. 299–302). San Francisco, CA.
Mucci, R., Arnold, J., & Bar-Shalom, Y. (1985). Track segment association with a distributed field of sensors. *Journal of the Acoustic Society of America*, *78*(4), 1317–1324.
Nahin, P.J., & Pokoski, J.L. (1980). NCTR plus sensor fusion equals IFFN or can two plus two equal five? *IEEE Transactions on Aerospace and Electronic Systems*, AES-*16*(3), 320–337.
Nitzan, D., Barrouil, C., Cheeseman, P., & Smith, R. (1983). Use of sensors in robot systems. *Proceedings of the International Conference on Advanced Robotics* (pp. 123–132). Tokyo, Japan.
Pattipati, K.R., Deb, S., Bar-Shalom, Y., & Washburn, R.B. (1990). Passive multisensor data association using a new relaxation algorithm. In Y. Bar-Shalom (Ed.), *Multitarget-multisensor tracking: Advanced applications* (pp. 219–246). Norwood, MA: Artech House.
Porter, A.L., & Rossini, F.A. (1987, June). Robotics in the year 2000. *Robotics Today*, 27–28.
Raczkowsky, J., & Rembold, U. (1990). The multisensory system of the KAMRO robot. In J.T. Tou & J.G. Balchen (Eds.), *Highly redundant sensing in robotic systems* (pp. 45–54). Berlin: Springer-Verlag.
Rembold, U. (1988). The Karlsruhe autonomous mobile assembly robot. *Proceedings of the IEEE International Conference on Robotics and Automation* (pp. 598–603). Philadelphia, PA.

Ruokangas, C.C. (1990). Dynamic control of robotic welding: On-going research. In M.M. Trivedi (Ed.), *Proceedings of the SPIE, vol. 1293, Applications of Artificial Intelligence VIII* (pp. 332–343). Orlando, FL.

Ruokangas, C.C., Black, M.S., Martin, J.F., & Schoenwald, J.S. (1986). Integration of multiple sensors to provide flexible control strategies. *Proceedings of the IEEE International Conference on Robotics and Automation* (pp. 1947–1953). San Francisco, CA.

Shaw, S.W., de Figueiredo, R.J.P., & Krishen, K. (1988a). Fusion of radar and optical sensors for robotic vision. *Proceedings of the IEEE International Conference on Robotics and Automation* (pp. 1842–1846). Philadelphia, PA.

Shaw, S.W., de Figueiredo, R.J.P., & Krishen, K. (1988b). Microwave and camera sensor fusion for the shape extraction of metallic 3D space objects. In P.S. Schenker (Ed.), *Proceedings of the SPIE, vol. 1003, Sensor Fusion: Spatial Reasoning and Scene Interpretation* (pp. 28–37). Cambridge, MA.

Smith, R.C., & Nitzan, D. (1983). A modular programmable assembly station. *Proceedings of the 13th International Symposium on Industrial Robots and Robots* (pp. 5.53–5.75). Chicago, IL.

Speyer, J.L. (1979). Computation and transmission requirements for a decentralized Linear-Quadratic-Gaussian control problem. *IEEE Transactions on Automatic Control*, AC-24(2), 266–269.

Tenney, R.R., & Sandell, Jr., N.R. (1981). Detection with distributed sensors. *IEEE Transactions on Aerospace and Electronic Systems*, AES-17(4), 501–510.

Thomopoulos, S.C.A., Viswanathan, R., & Bougoulias, D.K. (1987). Optimal decision fusion in multiple sensor systems. *IEEE Transactions on Aerospace and Electronic Systems*, AES-23(5), 644–653.

Tou, J.T., & Gonzalez, R.C. (1974). *Pattern recognition principles*. Reading, MA: Addison-Wesley.

Tsitsiklis, J.N., & Athans, M. (1985). On the complexity of decentralized decision making and detection problems. *IEEE Transactions on Automatic Control*, AC-30(5), 440–446.

23
Data Fusion and Decision Support for Command and Control

**Edward L. Waltz and
Dennis M. Buede**

In this chapter the problems and benefits of integrated data fusion and decision support are discussed across the spectrum of antisubmarine, tactical air, and land warfare. Then a general architecture of activities is proposed. This architecture includes data association, multitarget tracking, data combination, sensor management, situation assessment, and alternative analysis.

1. INTRODUCTION

An important development in the automation of command and control (C^2) functions is the implementation of systems which collect and merge information from diverse sources into an accurate representation of the tactical situation. They must also provide the commander with recommended alternative military actions and expected outcomes. These systems, often called battle management systems or combat decision aids, require the interaction of the following two primary functions.

1. *Data fusion* collects information from a variety of sensors and sources to develop the best possible perception of the military situation. This situation includes the orders of battle of friendly and hostile

forces; locations of material, equipment, weapons, and their movements; events of tactical interest; and intelligence data as it relates to the past, present, and predicted future behavior of the enemy. The fusion process includes the collection, association, aggregation, and merging of data to create and display current (and past) situations.

2. *Decision support* performs the creation and quantitative evaluation of alternative estimates of the real military situation and responses available to the commander. This evaluation process includes the consideration of target selection options, resource allocations, and employment timing for both autonomous and coordinated force actions. Candidate response options and predicted results are provided to the human commander, requiring modeling and evaluation of the effects of optional actions that can be taken.

As tactical and strategic warfare has increased in speed, complexity, and scope (Fowler & Nesbit, 1980), the requirements imposed on data fusion and decision support techniques have exceeded the capabilities of traditional manual techniques (plot boards, cross-check lists, display overlays, etc.). The increase in information flow from multiple sensors and reduced reaction time requirements have dictated the automation of the collection and merging of information as well as the generation of candidate actions and modeling of their expected outcomes.

Table 23.1 depicts the magnitude of data and decisions required to be processed by the C^2 function in three tactical warfare areas. In each case, the volume of information to be collected, sorted, and acted upon

Table 23.1. Typical information requirements in three tactical C^2 areas.

Parameter	ASW	TACAIR	Land Battle
C^2 command level	Battle Group Commander	Air Component Commander	Division Commander
Surveillance volume sensor systems	2000 × 2000 km 4 surveillance aircraft 12 ASW ships 2 ASW subs	800 km² × 20 km 6 airborne warning system aircraft 50 ground radars 100 fighter A/C	500 × 200 km 4 surveillance aircraft 20 outposts 6 ground radars 1 RPV battalion
Targets in track (max)	100–200	500–1000	100–250
Reports/min	1000–5000	50,000–100,000	100–500
c^2 decisions/min	1–5	25–50	10–25

imposes a formidable task for the area commander and staff. Automation of the fusion of data, and quantitative evaluation of alternative actions are necessary tools for the decisionmakers, the human commanders.

2. A MODEL OF THE C^2 FUSION/DECISION SUPPORT FUNCTIONS

The paradigm for C^2 decisionmaking proposed by Wohl (1981) includes four elements as depicted in Figure 23.1.

1. *Stimulus:* The initiation of the decision-making process is the data fusion function which provides information on the current situation with associated uncertainties. These uncertainties result from lack of sensor coverage, ambiguities in reports, conflicts in reports, or inaccuracies in measured data.

2. *Hypothesis:* Because of uncertainties in the correlated sensor data, the data fusion and decision support processes must jointly create hypotheses (perception alternatives) that are the best candidate real-world military situations that explain the fused data.

3. *Option:* For each hypothesis, options (response alternatives) are created and expected military results are modeled. These options and results are provided to the human decisionmaker for selection and action.

4. *Response:* Finally, the selected military response (action) is taken by the forces under command. This, in turn, creates new stimuli to the overall system.

The feedback and feedforward loops in the Wohl model emphasize the complexity of real-world, dynamic C^2 systems. Figure 23.1 adds an additional feedback loop to the Wohl model: the ability of the hypothesis process to query the data fusion process to search for data that may support candidate hypotheses under consideration. It is this interface between data fusion and decision support that must be carefully considered in the design of both functions to ensure that all available information is available to support timely and accurate decisions. This interface also must be able to couple the data fusion and decision support processes as current sensor systems, characterized by hard-decision signal processors and visual displays, giving way to soft-decisions data fusion techniques. The human interfaces will remain at the outputs of both functions: (1) combined sensor data will be displayed to the commander as the perception of the military situation, and (2) response options will also be enumerated to the commander.

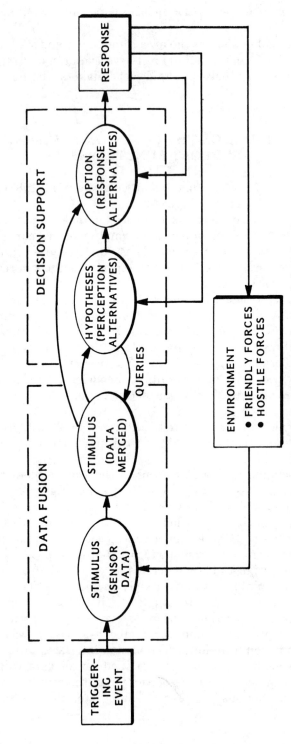

Figure 23.1. Dynamic relationships in tactical decision process.

3. BENEFITS OF DATA FUSION/DECISION AIDS IN C² SYSTEMS

In addition to the obvious improvement in the rate of information processing accrued by automation, several other benefits are provided by integrated data fusion/decision support systems. Table 23.2 summarizes the inherent benefits of multiple sensor systems over traditional single-sensor approaches. The fusion of multiple sensors can include multiple, different sensors (e.g., fire control radar, IR search and track, electro-optical imager, and passive electronic support mea-

Table 23.2. Benefits provided by multiple-sensor systems over single-sensor systems.

Improvement Category	Specific Characteristics	Tactical Benefits
Improved spatial/ temporal coverage	extended spatial coverage provided by multiple, overlapping sensor fields-of-regard	increased probability of threat detection
	increased detection probability due to synergy of multiple sensors	enhanced situation awareness and mutual support
Improved measurement performance	reduced ambiguity in data with multiple measurements	target acquisition, track and ID at longer ranges
	improved detection, tracking, identification when data is integrated from multiple looks at the target	accurate descrimination of target type and military capability (threat)
	reduced uncertainty in data when multiple independent measurements are integrated	
Enhanced operational robustness	redundancy of multiple sensors may increase mission reliability	reduced vulnerability to denial of a single sensor's data
	degraded (sensor subset) modes available	availability of alternate sensor modes to reduce observability
	robust performance provided by multi-spectral sensors	

sures) or multiple, common sensors (e.g., surveillance network of identical radars). In both cases, the use of multiple sensors may enhance overall C^2 performance in terms of spatial/temporal coverage, measurement performance, and operational robustness. These performance benefits, of course, must be weighed against the additional cost, complexity, and interface requirements introduced in any given application.

The benefits of automated decision support extend beyond the obvious benefits of rapid evaluation of multiple complex alternatives. Objective evaluation and consistent performance that is independent of battle stress is provided to the commander. As addressed by Wohl (1981) these objective outputs may require output tailoring to suit the decisionmaking style of individual commanders.

4. DATA FUSION/DECISION AIDS IN C^2 SYSTEMS APPLICATIONS

Virtually every C^2 application employs a variety of sensors (e.g., radar, sonar, IR/EO detectors, seismometers) and sources (e.g., humint, photoint, data-linked reports) to collect information necessary to develop a perception of the military situation. In each C^2 application, the fusion requirements may vary widely because of the unique characteristics of sensors, collection system and target or event behavior. The primary mission-unique parameters that characterize each application include the following.

1. Target quantities (number of targets to individually detect/identify/track) and categories (levels of distinction between targets) vary for each application. These factors influence the size of the target database and processing requirements to update the database with new data.

2. Detection and decision rate requirements are a function of the relative temporal behavior of targets (speed, rate of fire, rate of activities, etc.) and reaction time requirements of the C^2 system. These requirements dictate the necessary update rates for sensors to acquire and track target behavior.

3. Quantity and variety of sensors greatly influence the architecture and processing requirements on the data fusion algorithm. Sensors may be collocated on a single weapon platform or they may be distributed. Differences in sensor characteristics (e.g., resolution, FOV, range, target revisit rates) influence the data association and sensor management functions.

Figures 23.2–23.4 characterize three different C^2 applications that employ automated data fusion techniques to combine information

Data Fusion and Decision Support for Command and Control   569

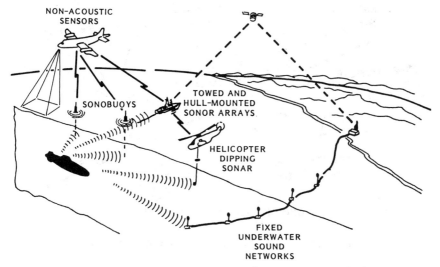

Figure 23.2. Antisubmarine warfare (ASW) C² mission.

from multiple sensors and sources. The diverse requirements and characteristics of each mission area are highlighted in the figures.

4.1. Antisubmarine Warfare

The antisubmarine warfare (ASW) mission is crucial to the survival of the Navy task force. The coordination of numerous sensor systems is

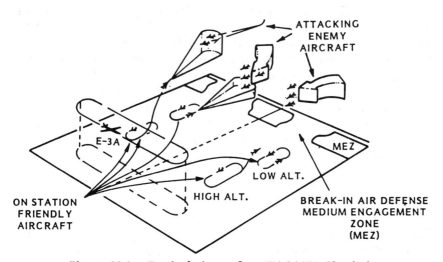

Figure 23.3. Tactical air warfare (TACAIR) C² mission.

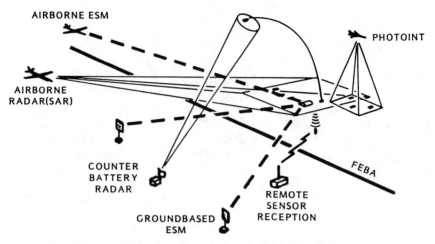

Figure 23.4. Landbattle battlefield C² mission.

necessary to ensure that hostile attack submarines do not enter the outer defense zone undetected or unidentified. Aircraft (carrier-based and land-based) provide the over-the-horizon ASW sensing capability of the fleet, using air-dropped sonobuoys and nonacoustic sensors (Stone, 1979; Starkey, 1981; Wohl, 1984) to detect and track submarines. (See Figure 23.3.) Towed array and hull-mounted sonars of ASW destroyers, deployed at the perimeter of the task force, form the outer surveillance barrier.

The task force commander must also rely on probable target tracks relayed by other naval forces and ground-based centers to predict threats approaching the outer perimeter. These reports, combined from fixed underwater sonar sensors (deployed at necessary passage points), along with visual sightings, periscope detections, emitter detections, national intelligence sources, and other task force detections are used to cue the local task force's sensors. The fusion of data from these external sources, from organic sensors detecting possible coordinated hostile force movements, and from the task force's own ASW sensors is a difficult task. It requires the coordination of a wide variety of platforms to detect, track, and identify elusive targets hidden in such a vast surveillance volume.

4.2. Tactical Air Warfare

The defensive counterair mission depicted in Figure 23.3 shows fighter aircraft flying "lanecap" patrol with long-range surveillance support from airborne warning and control system (AWACS) aircraft (Anderegg & Payne, 1983). Two sources of data are available for data fusion on each fighter aircraft:

1. ownership sensors may include fire control radar, infrared search and track, radar/IR/EO warning sensors, identification friend or foe (IFF), and EO sensors, and
2. tactical data links provide the ability to pass target tracks and identities from AWACS to fighters or fighter-to-fighter.

The fighter requires a moderate volume (10–30 tracks) data fusion/decision support capability to rapidly acquire, track, identify, and hand off targets as well as recommend attack options to the pilot. Such air battle management systems require the ability to operate independently or in a cooperative mode, in which cooperating fighters share sensor data and coordinate a multiple target attack. In this case, the data fusion/decision support function is effectively distributed among the air battle management algorithms, located in separate fighters, and interconnected by the tactical data link.

4.3. Landbattle Battlefield Warfare

Only the land battle portion of the total airland battlefield scenario is depicted in Figure 23.4, emphasizing the sensors and fusion necessary to detect and locate ground-based targets. These targets include C^2 modes, weapon systems (stationary and moving), troops, transportation systems, material, and geographical features (e.g., bridges, roads, railways, and terrain features influencing troop movement). Detection and identification of these targets are achieved by a variety of phenomena of which the most significant are movement, RF/EO/IR emissions, and weapon engagement-related events (battlefield targets are characterized as "movers," "emitters," and "shooters," respectively). The wide variety of sensors employed (Mahaffey, 1979) include the following.

1. Airborne radars detect and locate stationary and moving targets (MTI radar) at slant ranges extending well beyond the FLOT (Forward Line of Own Troops).
2. Airborne passive emitter detection/location systems provide the location of RF emitters (e.g., air defense and surveillance radars, communication nodes) beyond the FLOT.
3. Ground-based counter-battery radars track incoming rounds and compute the source weapon location.

4. Airborne remotely piloted vehicles (RPV) as well as manually piloted reconnaissance aircraft provide targeting beyond the FLOT using TV/IR imaging (photoint).
5. Remotely deployed ground sensors (magnetics, seismic, acoustic) report the detection of ground events (e.g., troop movements, formation, and assembly activities) beyond the FLOT.

In addition, verbal reports from field commanders, outposts, patrols, and intelligence reports from interrogation of prisoners or exploitation of captured communication, are used to develop a comprehensive picture of the battlefield situation.

Table 23.3 summarizes the differing characteristics of these three areas of warfare, and highlights the similarity in the basic requirements imposed on the C^2 data fusion/decision support functions.

5. USE OF SENSED INFORMATION

Data fusion uses a combination of sensors and sources to collect information on the tactical situation. This information includes reports of events or target detections, target tracks (location plus derivatives to predict future behavior), or factual statements. These data are used to detect, locate, and discriminate between tactical targets and events.

Discrimination between targets of a similar type or discrimination between targets of different types (i.e., identification) can be achieved by any one or a combination of sensed variables. The discrimination process can infer identity by measured target attributes, target behavior, or contextual clues provided by multiple sensors.

Directly measured features include attributes of the target (e.g., spectral signatures, spatial characteristics) or of phenomena that can be associated with the target (e.g., effects on the environment, secondary effects, or events linked to the target). These attributes are measured by the sensor directly or result from preprocessing operations (filtering, integration, clustering), which refine and combine the raw measurements into a single attribute.

Behavior of the target includes temporal behavior (velocity, acceleration, maneuvering, direction of travel, etc.) and tactical activities (emitter status/mode, and hostile or friendly acts such as jamming, deceptive, or engagement actions). In most cases, it can be used to discriminate an identity only when performance of a target exhibits unique characteristics. Doctrinal procedures, however, can be established to permit behavior to be independent of target performance and to allow unique target discrimination. Air corridors and restricted

Table 23.3. Characteristics of three C² mission areas.

Characteristics	Antisubmarine Warfare	Offensive/Defensive Tactical Air Warfare	Battlefield
Targets	submarines submersibles mines	aircraft missiles	vehicles (movers) C² centers (emitter) air defense units missile, artillery units (shooters)
Events	surface activity torpedo launch missile surface broach	aircraft maneuvers missile engagements ECM (jamming)	weapon firing nuclear bursts engagements troop assembly, movement
Sensors	sonar signature —land based —towed array —hull mount —sonobuoy —helo dipping passive ESM satellite surveillance nonacoustic sensors —Magnetometers	radar —fighter fire control —airborne surveillance IR search/track IFF passive ESM EO imager	airborne surveillance —SAR/SLAR —passive ESM emitter location —photorecon recon teams counter-battery radar ground-based ESM (DF) remote ground sensors

(continued)

Table 23.3. (Continued)

Characteristics	Antisubmarine Warfare	Offensive/Defensive Tactical Air Warfare	Battlefield

	—IR/EO
	visual sightings
		visual sightings	—acoustic
			—seismic
			RPV
			  —EO/FLIR
			  —ESM

Sources	intelligence
	national sources
		pre-flight intel
		tactical data link
		  —passed tracks
		  —friend locations
			intelligence
			national sources

Command/control decisions	submarine
	  —which tactical approach
	  —when to initiate tactical approach
	  —when to engage
		DCA
		  —air order of battle aggregation
		  —allocation of A/C
		  —assignment of A/C to raids
		  —weapons choice
		OCA target prioritization
		OCA route planning
		C³ CM planning
			central battle
			  —which avenue of approach
			second echelon attack
			  —where, when
			  —which targets
			  —with what weapon

zones are examples of procedures used in tactical air warfare to provide discrimination of foes by restricting the behavior of friends. These procedures must be maintained secure, of course, to achieve friend-foe discrimination.

Context includes the total spatial, spectral, and temporal situation in which the target (or event) is found. Spatial context includes location and relationship to other targets or participants in the scenario. The spectral context may include sensed attributes in relationship to other activities in the same spectrum (e.g., communication exchanges, countermeasure activities, levels of noise). Temporal contextual information includes the relative timing of sensed events or target activities and their implications of coordinated group behavior.

Table 23.4 provides typical examples of measured features, behavioral characteristics, and contextual information that can be used to

Table 23.4. Examples of measurable discriminants for antisubmarine and tactical air warfare missions.

Discriminant Categories	Tactical C² Mission Areas	
	ASW	TACAIR
Directly measured features	acoustic signatures magnetic signatures diesel fume spectra measurable phenomenologies —surface wafe effects —biological effects —atmospheric effects —nuclear effects	radar signatures IR signature electronic emissions (PRF, pulse characteristics) IFF replies acoustic signature imagery shape/size signature (IR/EO)
Behavioral characteristics	speed sustained speed depth maneuverability hostile act (cruise missile launch, torpedo launch) communication activities with hostile forces	velocity/altitude envelope maneuverability operation within an air corridor (friend) or a restricted volume (foe) hostile act (ECM, missile engagement against a friend, etc.) flight path tactics executed
Contextual information	origin of mission (homeport) or ports of call location relative to friendly surface vessels	origin of flight from hostile or friendly base flight path ECM activities relative formation with other knowns

discriminate submarine and aircraft targets in the ASW and TACAIR missions, respectively.

6. DATA FUSION/DECISION SUPPORT ARCHITECTURES

The functional elements of the data fusion and decision support subsystems (DFS and DSS, respectively) of a generic C^2 system (Waltz, 1986) are depicted in Figure 23.5, and closely follow the Wohl model. A variety of sensors collect data from the combat environment and pass them on to the DFS. The sensors may provide different kinds of data: (1) detections (reports) may include time-tagged events or targets with available location or identity information; (2) tracks include temporal models of target behavior (position plus time history or derivatives of position) and may include identity information; and (3) statements of fact are typically provided by intelligence sources and usually are related to current or predicted (probable) behavior of hostile forces.

The raw sensor data must be associated, that is, correlated in space and time, to form common files for each sensed event or target. As these reports are accumulated in time, temporal tracks are maintained to model the dynamic behavior of each target. These tracks of targets, histories of events/detections, and statements of fact form the situation database that is used to develop a perception of the combat environment.

Numerical data combination algorithms and symbolic reasoning processes refine the data in the database to a model of the real-world conditions. This model includes

- locations of all targets and events (and the uncertainty associated with each),
- identification of targets (if known),
- predicted behavior of targets (tracks),
- situations of military importance resulting from individual target locations, behavior (e.g., threat weapon systems in attack positions), or aggregate behavior of multiple targets.

The DFS passes this model to the DSS for further analysis. The modeled situation includes, of course, uncertainty arising from limitations in the sensor measurements and coverage. As a result this uncertainty allows for multiple hypotheses concerning many of the elements of the situation model (e.g., target locations, identities, behaviors). The situation assessment function refines these hypotheses using doctrinal tem-

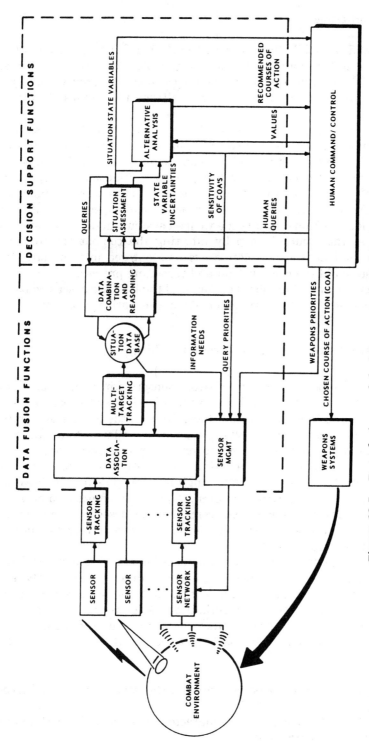

Figure 23.5. Data fusion and decision support architecture.

plates and probabilistic inference to select a finite set of important alternatives for analysis. The set of possible situations, plus uncertainties of the state variables are passed to the alternatives analysis function to create, analyze, and rank alternative courses of military action.

The human commander (e.g., pilot, division commander, task force commander, or tactical air control commander) views the situation display (range/azimuth display, map display, etc.) with symbology overlaying target identities, velocity vectors, weapons envelopes, and other information relevant to each target. In addition, the commanders may view the alternative courses of action and expected results. The commander's action commits the weapon systems under command and completes the feedback loop by affecting the combat environment. Planned actions and procedures are also entered into the situation database to aid the combination and reasoning process.

The three major functional elements of the DFS are described below, summarizing the major implementation alternatives available.

6.1. Data Association and Target Tracking

Detections (reports) and tracks (from sensors which maintain local track files of targets) must be associated in time and space to assign sensed data to individual target files. Because the reports and tracks arrive from sensors with differing geometries (relative to the targets), resolutions, fields of view, measurement spaces, and measurement times, it is necessary to transform all measurements to a common spatial reference (i.e., latitude/longitude, range/azimuth/elevation, X-Y-Z, etc.) and temporal reference. Once the measurements are transformed to a common measurement space, association hypotheses can be developed and scored to determine probable report–report or report–track assignments.

Figure 23.6 depicts the typical association/tracking functions for a DFS which includes both tracking and nontracking (report-only) sensors. Each new report on track is first transformed to a common spatial coordinate system before hypothetical assignments (pairings) are formed to existing reports or tracks in the situation database. Each hypothesis is scored on the basis of a metric which can include the following:

1. spatial distance measures between the sensed report and hypothetical assignment and
2. feature data measures that characterize the sensed report and hypothetical assignment.

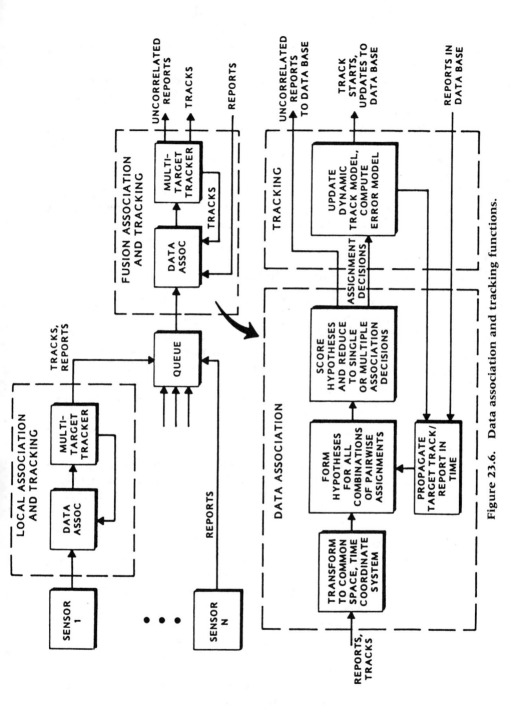

Figure 23.6. Data association and tracking functions.

These hypotheses are then evaluated to select a single pairing or to minimize the set of acceptable pairs if multiple hypotheses are to be saved for further iterations when more data are available.

When unique assignments of new report data are made to existing tracks, the dynamic tracking filter is updated to improve the estimate of the targets' behavior. Uncorrelated reports are passed to the situation database for possible association in the future. Because of the uncertainty in sensor measurements and density of targets, probabilistic methods are often required to score and evaluate the many hypotheses that can result in multiple sensor systems (Fortmann, Bar-Shalom, & Scheffe, 1980; Goodman, 1982; Kosaka et al., 1983). Hypothesis management over time and dynamic tracking of maneuvering targets are the most difficult challenges to the association/tracking function.

6.2. Data Combination and Inferencing

The core function of the DFS is the process of combining the collected sensor data on a single target to infer its identity and even higher-order attributes (e.g., intent, future behavior, threat capability). Conventional, structured algorithms and expert systems are both candidates to mechanize these combination/inference functions.

Expert system implementations offer the advantages of partitioning the discriminating information into a distinct knowledge base and providing powerful reasoning capabilities using any combination of directly measured features, behavioral characteristics, and contextual information.

Expert system reasoning functions employ a variety of categories of knowledge to combine multisensor data and infer higher levels of information about targets than contained in any individual element of the raw data.

1. *Structural models* are maintained to define the relationships between measured target attributes (e.g., acoustic/IR/radar signatures, RF emissions, kinematic envelopes, and component parts) and targets or target classes. These relationships between attributes and entities are defined by the so-called IS-A and IS-A-PART-OF hierarchical connectives in a frame-like database.

2. *Behavioral models* relate the temporal behavior (e.g., aircraft velocity/altitude flight envelopes, ground troop assembly/attack profiles) as well as spatial behavior (e.g., target formations, weapon ranges) of targets or events.

3. *Heuristic inference rules,* including simple IF-THEN and Boolean (AND, OR, COMPLEMENT) relationships, provide a general structure to

construct inference templates. These rules include an antecedent (the IF conditions that must be satisfied by the sensor data) and consequent (the THEN inference that can be concluded when the antecedent conditions are present).

4. *Numerical algorithms* combine incomplete, ambiguous sensor data by computing composite hypothesis scores which use the independence of multiple measurements to reduce the ambiguity in the measurement data.

The focus of much of the recent data fusion work has been to develop these numerical combination algorithms. When sensors provide hard decisions (declarations), the numerical combination may be a simple algorithm to sort declarations to search for a unique target or target set which describes the set of data, or accumulate declarations for combination by "as majority vote" or "weighted summation" decision rule.

Because sensor measurements and intelligence data are often characterized by uncertainty, a number of methods may be employed to quantitatively represent the uncertainty in sensor and intelligence data. Probabilities (Nahin & Pokoski, 1980), fuzzy variables (Ruspini, 1982), and probability intervals (Bonasso, 1985; Cohen, 1985; Rauch, 1984; Shafer, 1976) are candidates for representation of the uncertainty associated with sensor data. Numerical combination algorithms may be used to provide a more accurate composite estimate of the measurements, reducing uncertainty in target identity or location.

Figure 23.7 compares the structures of two numerical combination algorithms that mergemultiple hypothesis data vectors from N sensors. In each case, the sensors include statistical classifiers that classify measured features into a vector of parameters. These parameters quantify the certainty (likelihood, degree of fit, etc.) that the measurements represent each hypothesis. For the Bayesian inference case, these parameters are forward-conditional probabilities. Bayes's rule is applied to compute a composite a posteriori probability. A decision rule, such as the maximum a posteriori (MAP), is then applied to select the most likely hypothesis.

Because probabilities mathematically represent events of chance rather than events measured with uncertainty, the alternative Dempster-Shafer representation uses probability intervals to describe sensor data. Each hypothesis is represented by two parameters:

1. a supportability variable ($0 \leq S(x) \leq 1$) that describes the degree to which measurements support the hypothesis and
2. a plausibility variable ($0 \leq P(x) \leq 1$) that represents the degree to which the evidence fails to refute the hypothesis.

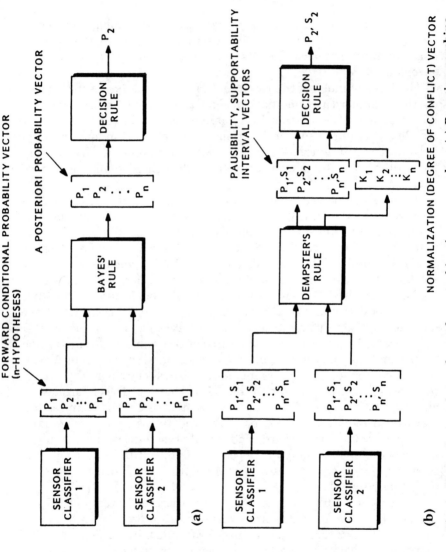

Figure 23.7. Comparison of two data combination approaches: (a) Bayesian combination. (b) Dempster-Shafer combination.

The difference, $P(x) - S(x)$, is a measure of ignorance about the hypothesis. When $P(x) = S(x)$, the probability interval collapses to a single probability equivalent to a forward conditional probability.

Dempster's rule of combination, analogous to Bayes's rule, provides a means of computing composite supportability/plausibility intervals (credibility intervals) for each hypothesis, reducing the uncertainty in the measured data. An appropriate decision rule is then applied on the basis of both supportability and plausibility.

The inference process can be driven by the arrival of new sensor data or by queries fed back from the DSS. The process of combining new data with the existing situation data to determine if ambiguity is reduced or consequents can be achieved is referred to as *forward-chaining*. The arrival of new associated report data (antecedents) on a given target will cause the combination algorithm to be iterated to refine the estimate of target state and determine if new inferences (consequents) can be drawn. The situation database is then updated with any new consequents. In contrast, the queries from the DSS cause a *backward-chaining* process that searches to determine if the antecedents in the database support a hypothetical consequent supplied by the query. The DDS query may request, for example, the degree of support for a consequent: "What is the certainty that multiple hostile bombers with fighter support (a strike package) are enroute to attach the airfield at location X within ten minutes?" Such a query may use each of the types of knowledge to verify the consequent. This process could be as follows.

- Behavioral models define airfield attack profiles and airspace regions in which potential strike packages must be located.
- Situation database is then searched to locate hostile and unknown aircraft meeting the strike criteria, and any related events that may indicate the presence of a strike.
- Structural models can then be compared with target identities or attributes, flight patterns, related electronic warfare events, etc. from the database to determine if a strike package can be located.
- Numerical combination algorithms compute the certainty for each hypothesis (each candidate strike package located).

The DFS responds to the queries with multiple hypotheses, each represented by state variables (target locations, identities, etc.) and associated certainties. These are formatted as vectors, with the degree of belief for each hypothesis being an element of the vector.

6.3. Sensor Management

The allocation of sensors to targets refers to the ability to control the pointing and dwell time of sensors on detected targets or regions of the surveillance volume. Management of the sensors is based upon the following driving functions.

- Information needs include detected or tracked targets that require additional data to refine the track, resolve ambiguity in target location, or discriminate target identity. These needs may be ranked by degree of threat to friendly forces.
- Query priorities are data required for situation assessment. For example, this may include sensor searches to reinforce developing hypotheses.
- Weapons priorities affect those sensors which directly support weapon systems, such as fire control sensors. These priorities result from C^2 decision to engage targets.

The sensor management function merges these (possibly conflicting) requirements to allocate sensors to targets. The functions also include sensor cueing, handoff and human override.

7. CHARACTERISTICS OF FUSED INFORMATION

The information provided by the data fusion function is characterized by multiple levels of information content and a representation of the degree of certainty (confidence) in the information provided. Figure 23.8 depicts an example of the levels of identification information needed by a TACAIR decision support system. The hierarchy of aircraft identification includes four general levels of information content.

1. Detection and tracking of a target is the first level of information provided. Detection information can include three-dimensional spatial coordinates (e.g., range, azimuth, elevation) or single-dimensional data only (e.g., passive detection of an emitter with azimuth information only). When repeated detections are associated and a time-series representation of the target's dynamic behavior can be determined, a track can be established.

2. Aircraft allegiance is the traditional friend–foe–neutral identity which provides the first and most important level of situation awareness. If foe, the aircraft is a potential threat and a candidate to engage.

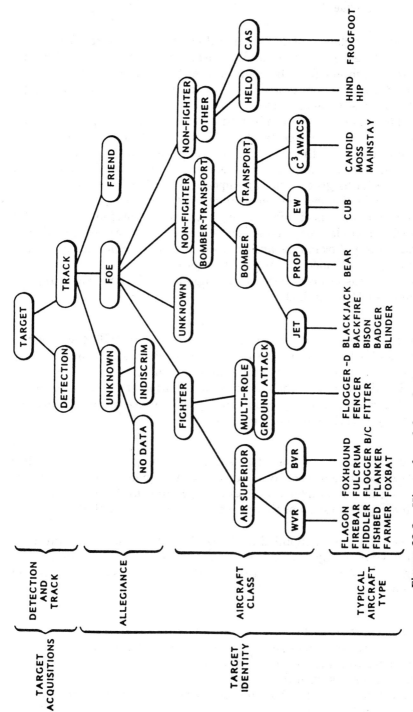

Figure 23.8. Hierarchy of data fusion information on sensed aircraft target.

3. Aircraft class provides a general identity of the aircraft mission, weapons (degree of threat), and performance capability. The discrimination of fighters from bombers is a critical capability for friendly fighters to allow them to avoid threats (hostile fighters) and to engage strike targets (bombers) selectively.

4. The highest level of information is the discrimination of aircraft type. Soviet aircraft selected from Taylor (1984) are depicted in the figure to illustrate the variety of aircraft types that are desired to be discriminated. For an identified foe, this information will aid the DSS to assess the degree of threat imposed by a fighter or to select the highest-value bomber/fighter-bomber to attack.

Additional levels of information that may be provided on targets by the DFS include weapons status (stores remaining), estimated fuel status (inferred from type and point-in-mission) and predicted mission intent (e.g., intended targets, next-action).

The various levels of information supplied to the DSS can be reported in one of two methods.

1. Hard decisions (declarations) are statements of fact where the combined evidence exceeds a predefined threshold of certainty (i.e., greater than 0.99 probability of occurrence).
2. Soft decision data includes a representation of uncertainty in the information using probabilities, possibilities/supportabilities, or fuzzy variables for each hypothesis.

Hard decisions are reported as single statements or ambiguity lists (lists of possible alternatives, each with an equal likelihood of occurrence) and soft decisions are provided as multiple hypotheses, each with a representation of the uncertainty associated with the hypothesis.

The information supplied to the DSS results from queries initiated by the DSS and by new sensor reports which result in changes in the knowledge of the tactical situation. For example, such changes can include

- new targets detected;
- refined/revised identities, unknown targets identified;
- changes in target behavior or location;
- loss of targets from track; and
- detection of events or aggregate target behavior that infers opponents' tactics or future behavior.

8. C² DECISION SUPPORT AND FUSION

As described earlier, the two major functions of decision support are situation assessment and alternative analysis. The relationships among these two decision-support functions, the fusion system and the human-based command and control are depicted in the IDEF diagram of Figure 23.9 (IDEF terminology is as follows: processes are encapsulated in boxes, inputs to the process enter from the left side of the box and outputs exit from the right, guidance for performing the process enters from the top, and a mechanism that is needed to support the process enters the box from below.)

Fused data from the fusion system are the primary input for situation assessment. Also utilized are the results of sensitivities derived from the analysis of alternatives and the chosen course of action determined by the commander. Outputs include the situation state variables (the descriptors necessary to define the situation for decision purposes, e.g., the identification of all aircraft); certainty vectors for the possible values of the state vectors (e.g., the measure of certainty or probability that a given aircraft is friend, foe, or neutral); and additional queries of the fusion system that help determine the priorities for management. These queries may be needed to determine the degree of belief of specific hypotheses or to distinguish between two competing hypotheses of the entire situation. The major mechanism of this process is a goal-driven (backward-chaining) expert system that probes the fusion database to define the situation, its state variables, and their probabilities.

The analysis of alternatives operates on three inputs: the state variables and their certainties from the situation assessment and the values expressed by the commander and his subordinates for specific situations. The generic course of action that has been chosen by the commander provides guidance for this analysis process. The analysis of alternatives will generate and analyze alternatives for microdecisions within the generic course of action, but will also review the generic course of action and recommend when it should be revised. These inputs, coupled with a decision analysis mechanism, produce recommended alternatives and associated sensitivity analyses for the decision-makers to review and accept or reject.

The commander and his subordinates receive the recommendations and sensitivity analyses of the analysis function, use the state variables of the situation assessment function as guidance, and have the ultimate say in alternatives chosen. There will be provisions for the analysis process to make some automatic decisions which are either routine in low periods of stress or time-critical in high periods of stress.

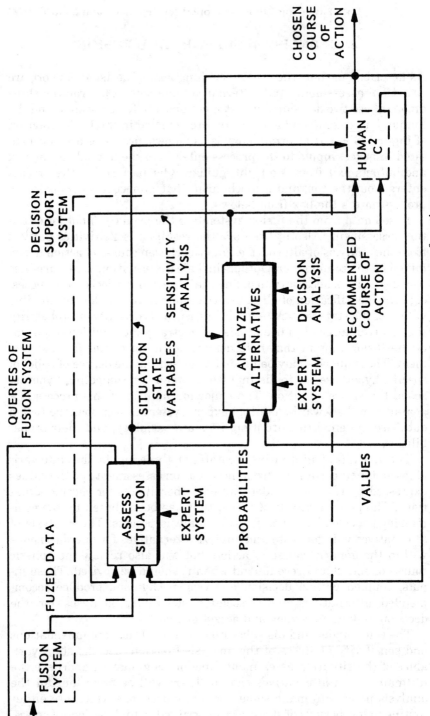

Figure 23.9. IDEF diagram of decision support functions.

To observe the situation assessment and alternative analysis processes more objectively, it is necessary to look at a lower level of detail. Figure 23.10 depicts the four processes that comprise situation assessment:

1. define state variables,
2. quantify probabilities of state variables,
3. hypothesize situation assessment weaknesses, and
4. generate queries of the fusion system.

The backward-chaining expert system serves as a mechanism to all of these processes. Backward-chaining is a general strategy used in expert systems when it is more efficient to choose a possible answer or proposition (e.g., as "the enemy's course of action is . . ."), and then to select those rules whose conclusions deal with this situation.

By accessing DFS, antecedents of these conclusions can be examined to determine which enemy course of action is most likely from this conclusion. Data from the fusion system are used to produce the state variables of the situation, and also, with the state variables as guidance, to estimate probabilities for the state variables. However, there will be many uncertainties for which there are few and weak data for the estimates of the hypotheses. These weaknesses would be established by the third process within situation assessment. This process of hypothesis generation and evaluation would also be implemented by a goal-driven expert system. The inputs for this process would arrive from the alternative analysis outputs or recommendation and sensitivity analysis. These analysis outputs guarantee that the potential weaknesses of situation assessment that are probed via backward-chaining are important in the overall decision process and not trivial items of interest that have no impact. Finally, the query generation process uses the state variables as input and the weaknesses as guidance to specify sensor collection requests that are output to the fusion system.

The alternative analysis process also contains four processes: generate alternatives, quantify situation values, analyze alternatives, and conduct sensitivity analyses (see Figure 23.11). The alternative generation process uses an expert system with inputs from the state variables to generate alternatives within the context of the developing situation. This expert system can apply forward-chaining, with potential state variables as the antecedents followed by possible alternatives as conclusions. The quantification of values can be accomplished either via decision analytic assessment questions directed at the commander or his subordinates for critical decisions or through the execution of

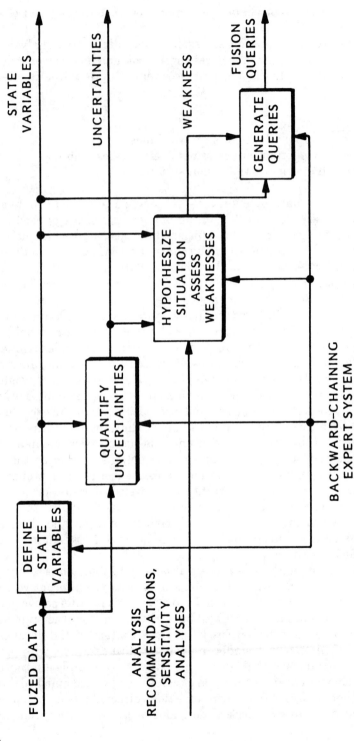

Figure 23.10. IDEF diagram of situation assessment.

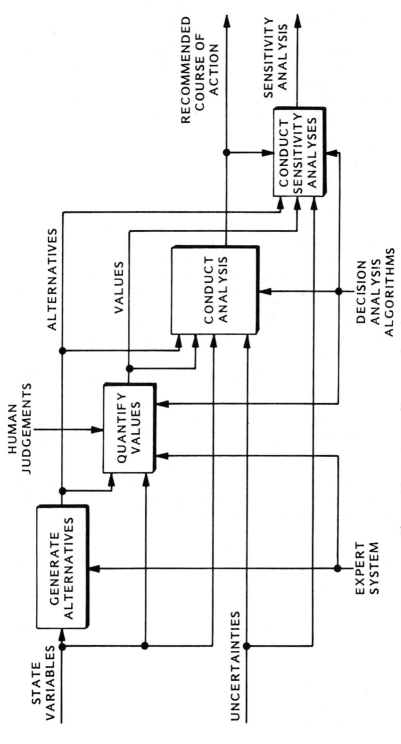

Figure 23.11. IDEF diagram of analysis of alternatives.

rules embedded in an expert system. The state variables and alternatives would be necessary inputs to this quantification in either case. The actual analysis of alternatives would use the alternatives, state variables, probabilities, and values within the decision analysis paradigm of maximum expected value to produce a recommended alternative. The sensitivity analysis would vary probabilities and values to find those key factors in the decision context that would change the decision-maker's choice. Algorithms have been developed to vary up to three parameters at a time in conducting policy region analyses of the available alternatives.

It is necessary to examine specific situations and decisions in which this combination of fusion and decision support could operate. Three time-phased sequences for the decision dimension are used: initiation of engagement tactics, choice of weapon or tactic for engagement, and the timing of the attack. Overlaid on this decision sequence are diverse examples from Army, Navy, and Air Force situations: the corps' attack of the second echelon, submarine versus submarine, and the fighter aircraft's defensive counter air mission. Figure 23.12 shows this matching of decision sequence with specific applications (Bromage, Brown, Chinnis, Cohen, & Ulvila, 1983; Garvey & Strat, 1985; Gossard & Linsenmayer, 1985; Slagle et al., 1982; Technology Corp., 1984; Ulvila & Brown, 1983; Wanner, 1984).

The first decision in this sequence involves the balancing of a need for more information combined with the potential of tipping one's hand versus waiting too long and jeopardizing the survival of key elements of one's force and/or losing key opportunities. In looking across the three applications of this decision in Figure 23.12, information regarding location of the threat is present in every situation. Other information for specific applications ranges from speed to direction and intent to friend/foe identification.

Information regarding the capability of the enemy force is more relevant for the second decision in the sequence: choice of weapon or engagement tactic. In choosing between smart antitank and area weapons for attacking the second echelon, the size and composition of the enemy force at key locations as well as the choice between delay versus destroy missions are key components of the decision process. The choice of the approach tactic by the friendly submarine depends on the course and capability of the enemy submarine. The fighter pilot will have a choice between long and short range missiles and would like to know if the foe aircraft is a high performance fighter or bomber in making this decision. Information about the speed of the foe aircraft can be conclusive about this distinction.

Finally, the timing decision of when to fire balances survival versus

	ARMY ATTACK OF 2ND ECHELON	NAVY SUBMARINE VS. SUBMARINE	AIR FORCE DEFENSIVE COUNTER AIR
BEGIN ENGAGEMENT TACTICS OR GATHER MORE INFORMATION	ISSUE ORDERS TO ARTY/AIR ASSETS / INFO: LOCATION SPEED	BEGIN APPROACH TACTIC / INFO: LOCATION DIRECTION	ASSIGN F-15 TO SPECIFIC TARGET / INFO: LOCATION FRIEND/FOE
CHOICE OF WEAPON TACTIC FOR ENGAGEMENT	SMART ANTI-TANK VS. AREA WEAPONS / INFO: SIZE COMPOSITION	LEAD/LAG VS. DIRECT APPROACH / INFO: COURSE CAPABILITY	LONG VS. SHORT RANGE MISSILE / INFO: FIGHTER/BOMBER
FIRE OR CONTINUE TO IMPROVE POSITION	FUTURE VS. CURRENT FORCE SURVIVABILITY / P_k (TARGET)	OWN-SHIP SURVIVAL / P_k (TARGET)	OWN-SHIP SURVIVAL / P_k (TARGET)

Figure 23.12. Decision sequence examples.

expectations of kill probability. For individual platforms (such as the submarine and fighter) opportunities for reattack are included in this decision. For larger force considerations such as the attack of the second echelon, the opportunity cost of diverting the attack resources from the first echelon to the second echelon must be balanced in terms of immediate impact versus future impact.

9. CONCLUSION

The integration of automated data fusion and decision support systems holds the promise of more effectively refining and analyzing the military meaning of the vast amounts of information collected by modern C^2 systems. The benefits of such automation, however, will not eliminate the central element of command control: the human commander. The real role of data fusion and decision support is that of converting data into meaningful and timely information that will enhance the process of human judgment. The current concerns that such automated systems will be vulnerable to deception are based, in fact, on the premise that countermeasures and tactics often rely on unpredictable behavior. The human commander is best suited to cope with these higher-order reasoning processes and is the appropriate authority to commit lethal weapons to engage the adversary.

REFERENCES

Anderegg, D., & Payne, B. (1983, September). Tactical relevance—A fighter pilot's view. *Defense Systems Review,* 36–40.

Bonasso, Jr., R.P. (1985). *ANALYST II: A knowledge-based intelligence support system* (Tech. Rep. MTP-84W 00220). McLean, VA: The MITRE Corp.

Bromage, R.C., Brown, R.V., Chinnis, J.O., Cohen, M.S., & Ulvila, J.W. (1983, March). *Decision aids for submarine C^2, phase III concept implementation* (Tech. Rep.). Falls Church, VA: Decision Science Consortium, Inc.

Cohen, P. (1985). Representativeness and uncertainty in classification systems. *AI Magazine,* 6(3), 136–149.

Fortmann, T., Bar-Shalom, Y., & Scheffe, M. (1980). Multitarget tracking using probabilistic data association. *Proceedings of the 19th IEEE Conference on Decision and Control* (pp. 807–812).

Fowler, C.A., & Nesbit, R.F. (1980, November). Tactical C^3, counter C^3 and C^5. *Journal of Electronics and Defense.*

Garvey, T., & Strat, T.M. (1985). AI for command decision-making. *Proceedings of the ADPA Artificial Intelligence and Robotics Symposium.*

Goodman, I.R. (1982). An approach to the data association problem through possibility theory. *Proceedings of the 5th MIT/ONR Conference.*

Gossard, W.H., & Linsenmayer, G.R. (1985, April). C^3I systems requirements to support C^3CM. *Signal,* 18–28.

Greenwood, D. (1984). Strengthening conventional deterrance. *NATO Review, 32*(4), 8–12.

Kosaka, M. et al. (1983). A track correlation algorithm for multisensor integration. *Proceedings of the Digital Avionics Systems Conference* (DASC) (pp. 10.3.1–10.3.8).

Mahaffey, F.K. (1979, October). Intelligence, surveillance and target acquisition in the 80's—The army concept. *Signal,* 39–42.

Nahin, P.J., & Pokoski, J.L. (1980). NCTR plus sensor fusion equals IFFN. *IEEE Transactions on Aerospace and Electronic Systems,* AES-*16*(3), 320–337.

Rauch, H.E. (1984). Probability concepts for an expert system used for data fusion. *AI Magazine, 5*(3), 55–60.

Ruspini, E.H. (1982, September). Possibility theory approaches for advanced information systems. *Computer, 15*(9), 83–91.

Shafer, G. (1976). *A Mathematical Theory of Evidence.* Princeton, NJ: Princeton Univ. Press.

Slagle, J.R. et al. (1982). BATTLE: An expert decision aid for fire support command and control. *Proceedings of the 49th Military Operations Research Symposium.*

Starkey, Jr., R.J. (1981, July). Anti-submarine warfare oceanography. *Military Electronics/Countermeasures,* 67–72.

Stone, N.L. (1979, June). ASW, the Soviet view. *Military Electronics/Countermeasures,* 34–73.

Taylor, J.W.R. (Ed.). (1984). *Jane's all the world's aircraft 1983–84.* London: Jane's Publishing Co. Ltd.

Technology Corp. (1984, May). *Decision aids for target aggregation* (Tech. Rep. TR-84-108 PAR). Decisions and Designs Inc., Systems Control Technology.

Ulvila, J.W., & Brown, R.V. (1983, October). *Attack planning decision aid for submarine C^2* (Tech. Rep. 83-4). Falls Church, VA: Decision Science Consortium, Inc.

Waltz, E.L. (1986). Data fusion for C^3I systems. *International C^3I handbook.* Palo Alto, CA: EW Communications.

Wanner, E. (1984, March). The application of decision aid technology to command and control. *Signal,* 43–46.

Wohl, J.G. (1981). Force management decision requirements for air force tactical command and control. *IEEE Transactions on Systems, Man, and Cybernetics,* SMC-*11*(5), 618–639.

Wohl, R. (1984, February). Ocean transparency: Impossible or inevitable? *Defense Science,* 20–28.

24
Theoretical Approaches to Data Association and Fusion

Samuel S. Blackman

This chapter presents a survey of the issues and methods for the association and fusion of data from multiple sensors. It will cover three broad areas. The first, data association, refers to the problem of partitioning the sensor data into tracks according to source. We next discuss the techniques used for kinematic and attribute estimation after data association has been performed. In particular, we will discuss the philosophies associated with alternative techniques for attribute and target-type estimation, with an emphasis upon the Dempster-Shafer approach. The third major topic discussed is sensor allocation.

1. INTRODUCTION

There exists a rather well developed theory for the design and analysis of individual sensors. However, the methods required to utilize efficiently the data from multiple sensors for such tasks as tracking and identifying targets are not nearly as well developed. The goal of this chapter is to present a broad overview of the many methods that are commonly in use and to discuss the relative merits of these methods for future advanced systems.

There are two basic areas of multiple sensor data fusion. The first area is concerned with the process of track formation and estimation of target quantities, such as position and velocity, and certain attributes, such as engine type. The second area, which typically involves the use of artificial intelligence methods, refers to making higher order inferences, such as target intent, enemy order of battle, etc., given the estimated track quantities. This chapter will be primarily concerned with the first area.

An important area in the field of multiple sensor tracking is the allocation of sensors to obtain new data. This important topic has only recently begun to be addressed in a theoretical, rather than an *ad hoc* manner. This chapter will outline the utility theory and expert system approaches to sensor allocation.

2. DATA ASSOCIATION

Data association, with the goal of partitioning observations into tracks, is the key function of any surveillance system. The importance of this subject has led to the recent publication of three books (Farina & Studer, 1985; Blackman, 1986; Bar-Shalom & Fortmann, 1987) and numerous papers that extensively discuss the issues. This section will summarize the philosophies and methods in current application.

2.1. Nearest-Neighbor versus All-Neighbors Data Association

The "nearest-neighbor" approach to data association determines a unique pairing so that at most one observation can be paired with a previously established track. Also, a given observation can only be used once, either to update an existing track or to start a new track. This method is based upon the likelihood theory and the goal is to minimize an overall distance function that considers all observation-to-track pairings that satisfy a preliminary gating test. However, since for a dense target environment there may be many sets of pairings that are computed to have similar likelihoods, the probability of error is typically large for this approach.

The alternative "all-neighbors" approach incorporates all observations within a gated region about the predicted track position into the update of that track. Also, a given observation can be used to update multiple tracks. Track update is then based on a probabilistically determined weighted sum of all observations within the gated region.

The all-neighbors approach, in effect, performs an averaging over observation-to-track data association hypotheses that have roughly comparable likelihood. This approach has been shown to be very effective for the tracking of single targets, using single or multiple sensors, against a background of clutter or noise. However, when considering multiple target environments, it may be necessary to devise special logic for a particular application so that new target track initiation and target resolution capabilities are maintained (Fitzgerald, 1986).

2.2. Sequential versus Deferred Decision Logic

An ideal, batch processing approach that would process all observations (from all time) together is typically not computationally feasible. Thus, a more standard approach has been to perform processing in a recursive (or sequential) manner as data are received. For example, a set of observations from a time frame (or scan) of a scanning radar may be collected and observation-to-track data association performed on these observations during the time period when the sensor is collecting the next frame of data. When this approach is used, once data association decisions are made, they are irrevocable.

A deferred decision approach to data association, as exemplified by the multiple hypothesis tracking (MHT) method (Reid, 1979), allows the final decision on difficult data association alternatives to be postponed until more data are received. Alternative hypotheses are formed and re-evaluated when later data are received. This approach clearly has the potential for ultimately achieving a much higher correct decision probability than does the sequential decision method. However, in order to maintain computational feasibility, an intricate logic to delete (prune) unlikely hypotheses and to combine similar hypotheses is required.

2.3. Issues in Multiple Sensor Data Association

The use of multiple sensor data has the potential, through the inclusion of more varied data, to greatly improve data association. For example, the combined use of accurate range data from a radar and accurate angle information from an optical sensor can lead to accurate track position estimates so that data association uncertainty is reduced. However, the problem of initially combining radar and optical sensor data into a track when the latter does not contain any range information is a difficult one.

An additional problem with the association of multiple sensor data occurs with sensors of different resolution. For example, an optical sensor may resolve closely spaced targets that appear as a single target to the radar. A similar problem occurs when data from a radar and an electronic support measures (ESM) sensor are combined because the platform being tracked may contain multiple emitters that are detected independently by the ESM.

The special problems involved in data association with multiple sensors typically require a complex logic utilizing the deferred decision approach. An example is the logic which has been developed for combining radar and ESM data (Trunk & Wilson, 1987). Using this method, the ESM observation data are compared with radar track estimates. Then, a set of rules are applied so that three levels of tentative decision are included. In addition to tentative decisions, the firm decisions to pair an ESM track with one of the radar tracks or to determine the ESM track not to have a corresponding radar track are available.

3. LEVEL OF DATA ASSOCIATION: CENTRAL- VERSUS SENSOR-LEVEL TRACKING

A key issue when developing a multiple sensor surveillance system is to decide where data association is to occur first. One alternative is to have each sensor maintain its own track file, based only upon the observations received by that sensor. Eventually these sensor-level tracks must be combined to form a central-level track. The alternative to sensor-level tracking is for all observation data to be sent directly to a central processor where a master track file is formed using all the observation data. For the latter approach, no track fusion is required.

There are a number of tradeoffs involved in the choice of sensor- versus control-level tracking. The central-level tracking approach is more accurate because all data are processed at the same place resulting in less track uncertainty and a corresponding decrease in misassociation. Also, mean tracking errors for dynamic targets are decreased because of the effective higher data rate. When track fusion occurs for the sensor-level tracking method, there is a reduction in the random error, but a mean error (for example, due to target maneuver) cannot be averaged out.

The major objection to central-level tracking is the high potential data transfer rate. Note that the periodic transmission of tracks, which is required for sensor-level tracking, typically involves much less data transmission than if all the observations that formed the tracks were transferred. Other potential problems with central-level tracking relate to the military environment where vulnerability to central-level failure (or destruction) and corrupted sensor data are important practical issues.

A major difficulty associated with the use of sensor-level tracking arises in the ultimate combining of the sensor tracks. First, an extensive track-to-track association logic must be defined. This may be difficult if deferred-decision data association logic is used, because multiple-hypothesis logic must be manipulated at both sensor and combined tracking levels. Finally, even if correct track association is performed, the combining logic must account for common error sources due to potential target maneuvers (Bar-Shalom & Campo, 1986).

Since both the sensor- and central-level approaches suffer from potential problems, a combined approach may be proposed where both central- and sensor-level tracks are maintained. One technique is to form initially central-level tracks from sensor-level tracks and then to send selected observations to the central-level for track updating. Another potential saving associated with this method occurs if observations from different sensors, but from the same target, can be precombined before inclusion in the processing.

4. KINEMATIC ESTIMATION

Kinematic filtering and prediction is used to determine such quantities as target position and velocity. Kinematic filters are required to determine the weighting to be applied to incoming measurement data and to estimate future target position and velocity.

4.1. Kalman versus Suboptimal Filtering

Kalman filtering provides a convenient means for determining the weightings (denoted as gains) to be given to input measurement data. It also provides an estimate of the target tracking error statistics, through the covariance matrix. The Kalman filter covariance matrix can then be used, along with measurement error statistics, for gating and for determining the final observation-to-track assignment.

The complexity of Kalman filtering has often led to the use of fixed-coefficient filters where some set of best filter gains are precomputed and used in place of the Kalman gains. However, since the Kalman gains vary adaptively in accordance with the input measurement rate and accuracy and with the target geometry, the use of fixed-gain filters typically leads to highly suboptimal performance.

4.2. Passive (Angle-Only) Sensor Tracking

The design of tracking filters for radar data is relatively straightforward, because the radar, through range and angular measurements, provides a three-dimensional target position. However, passive sensors such as infrared search and track sets (IRST) and radar warning receivers (RWR) only provide angular measurements. Thus, the full three-dimensional target position information may not be available with a single passive sensor.

One approach is to tracking with a passive sensor is merely to be content with angle information, and, for example, just track angle and angle rate. Alternatively, it may be possible to estimate a full three-dimensional target state vector if there is an ownership maneuver and if the target does not maneuver (Stallard, 1987). A third alternative is to use multiple angular position estimates from sensors at different locations to calculate target range through triangulation. However, for the case where there are multiple targets in a common plane with the sensors, a major problem with triangulation is the occurrence of false intersections or "ghosts."

4.3. Combining Active and Passive Sensor Data

In military applications, it is often necessary to restrict active transmission in order to avoid alerting the enemy to one's presence and position. One approach to this problem is to limit active sensor transmission providing sporadic active sensor data to augment the passive data. A typical application of this approach uses a radar to aid in a system where an infrared search and tracking (IRST) system is the primary sensor for track initiation and maintenance. The performance associated with this approach is highly dependent upon the target range and maneuver capability. However, for typical airborne target tracking problems, results have indicated that little angle tracking degradation occurs even when the rate of active sensor data (range and range rate) is as low as one-tenth the rate of the passive angle measurement data.

5. FUSION OF MULTIPLE SENSOR ATTRIBUTE AND TARGET TYPE DATA

Future multisensor systems will provide a variety of target attribute data, and a major current research area is the development of techniques to combine (or fuse) these data. Typically the ultimate goal of this fusion process is to determine target type and identity.

Pattern recognition is one method of using multiple sensor data to determine target identification. Using this approach, one would determine the appropriate set of features to be formed from multiple sensor observation data and the best weighting (confidence level) to be used with these data. This, however, is a complex process and is probably only feasible for a limited number of sensors. Also, a redefinition of the features and weightings will be required when another sensor is added to the system.

An alternative to the pattern recognition approach is for each sensor to first process its own data and to then output its current best estimate of a target's attributes. Here, the term attribute will include both target characteristics, such as engine type, and the actual target ID type. The confidence associated with each output must also be transmitted or assumed to be known from previous experience. Thus, the problem becomes one of combining multiple sensor attribute data to specify target type and the associated confidence level.

The simplest approaches to combining multiple sensor data are heuristic methods, such as voting and the use of possibility theory. The latter approach starts with unity possibility for all possible target types. Then, there is effectively a process of elimination as the possibilities are decreased when sensor data are inconsistent with particular target types. Two alternative mathematical approaches for fusion are the Bayesian (Nahin & Pokoski, 1980) and Dempster-Shafer methods (Bogler, 1987).

5.1. Bayesian Approach

The application of a Bayesian approach to the attribute and target identification problem requires a priori information and conditional probabilities. First, the measurement process is defined by $P(X_m|X)$ which is the (assumed known) probability of receiving measurement X_m given that the true quantity is X. Then, whenever measurement data are received, the updated probabilities for quantities X are computed using Bayes's rule.

To summarize, Bayes's rule is solved recursively as new data are received. This relatively simple relationship provides the estimated probabilities of target attribute based directly on the measurements of involved quantities. However, to initiate the process, before any measurements are received, an initial estimate of the probability of X is required. Also, the estimated probabilities can be improved using known interrelationships, as expressed by conditional probabilities, between attributes and target types.

Target type estimates can be used to update target attribute estimates and vice versa. This can be accomplished by virtue of the fact that certain types of targets utilize specific types of equipment. For example, the radars used in passenger-type aircraft are different than the radars used in military fighters. In order to relate attribute and target-type estimation, it is first necessary to specify conditional probability relationships between expected attributes and target types. Then the problem of jointly estimating target type and attribute values can be formulated as a special case of a general inference net (Blackman, 1986).

5.2. Dempster-Shafer Evidential Reasoning

Considerable interest has recently arisen regarding the application of the Dempster-Shafer method to the problem of multiple sensor fusion for the purpose of target identification (Bogler, 1987). This approach has a number of unique features and advantages that are probably best illustrated by an example.

Assume that an imaging electro-optical (EO) sensor declares a given target to be of a shape category that is consistent only with targets types T_1 and T_2, which are hostile and friendly, respectively. Further, assume the confidence on this declaration to be 0.9. According to this declaration, there will be a mass $M_1(T_1 \lor T_2) = 0.9$ assigned to the disjunction of T_1 and T_2 (either T_1 or T_2). Also, a mass $M_1(\theta) = 0.1$, corresponding to one minus the confidence of 0.9, is assigned to θ, which represents the disjunction of all propositions (all target types).

Next, assume that an IFF (Interrogation Friend or Foe) sensor does not receive a response from the target in question. This implies a hostile (or at least nonfriendly) target type, but since there are conditions under which a friend may not respond to an IFF interrogation, the confidence on the hypothesis of a hostile target is only 0.6 and the remainder is assigned to θ, $M_2(\theta) = 0.4$.

Note that the Dempster-Shafer method has allowed each sensor to contribute information on its own terms, or more formally at its own level of abstraction. Probability mass can be assigned to individual propositions or to the disjunction of propositions. For example, there is no need to arbitrarily force the target type probability mass associated with the shape declaration into equal probabilities for types T_1 and T_2.

Dempster's rule is used to combine sensor information by effectively determining the intersection of the sensor statements. For example, taking the product of $M_1(T_1 \lor T_2)$ and $M_2(H)$ results in a mass declaration of 0.54 to the proposition that the target type is T_1 (a hostile target). Similarly, the product of $M_1(\theta)$ and $M_2(H)$ results in a declaration of 0.06 to hostile. The resulting probability mass vector is:

$$M = \begin{bmatrix} M(T_1) = 0.54 \\ M(T_1 \vee T_2) = 0.36 \\ M(H) = 0.06 \\ M(\theta) = 0.04 \end{bmatrix} \quad (1)$$

The mass vector given in Eq. (1) illustrates the Dempster-Shafer concept of a probability interval, defined by the support and plausibility for a given proposition. The support for a given proposition is that mass assigned directly to that proposition. For example, the support for the proposition that the target type is T_1 is 0.54. The plausibility of a given proposition is the sum of all masses not assigned to its negation. For example, noting that θ contains all propositions, the plausibility of the type T_1 proposition is 1.0. On the other hand, the support and plausibility for the proposition that the target is the friendly type T_2 are 0.0 and 0.4, respectively.

Dempster's rule also conveniently handles the condition of inconsistency between sensor declaration. For example, if T_1 and T_2 were both friendly, the above example would have assigned the value of 0.54 to inconsistency (denoted k),

$$M_1(T_1 \vee T_2) M_2(H) = 0.54 = k$$

Then, before final mass values are declared, a normalization by the factor $1 - k$ is required (Blackman, 1986; Bogler, 1987).

6. DISTRIBUTED SENSOR SYSTEMS

The discussion so far has been basically for local sensor fusion which can be defined as the integration of data from sensors on board a single platform. Next, we briefly consider the issues involved in the fusion of data from sensors that are spatially distributed so that they see the targets from different locations and viewing angles.

An important consideration for a distributed sensor system is the communication involved in transfer of information between the sensors. This can lead to a tradeoff between allocating system resources for computation versus communications. Also, the potential cost of transferring all observations and the desirability of performing local data processing tends to favor the sensor-level tracking approach. However, techniques have been proposed in which selected observations are passed between sensor sites, so the central-level tracking accuracy can be achieved by distributed data processing (Deley, 1978).

Another important issue is that of sensor control. Here, based upon survivability considerations, it is desirable that each individual sensor system have the capability to operate autonomously. This implies that each site will determine, based upon locally available information, where its sensors should point and what targets should be tracked.

Another important question involves track maintenance. Should all tracks be maintained at all sites or should each site only maintain a selected subset of target tracks? One common approach to this problem has each site maintaining two sets of track files. The first (global) track file contains tracks on all targets, with track information being communicated from other sites. The second (local) track file contains tracks on those targets that are being actively tracked by that site. Thus, the global track file is a composite of the local track files which give each site an overview of the entire situation. It aids in local sensor allocation and in the determination of which targets should be included in the local track file.

7. SENSOR ALLOCATION

The simplest approach to sensor allocation uses one sensor to cue another. For a typical scenario, a low angular resolution sensor with a large field of view obtains a preliminary estimate of target position. Then, a second high (angular) resolution sensor is slewed to the predicted target position. This approach may be appropriate if the number of tracks requiring sensor allocation is limited. However, for a dense target environment, more sophistictated approaches are required.

A modern sensor allocation algorithm will be required to adaptively direct multisensor systems:

1. to search for new targets,
2. to update target positions,
3. to obtain target identification, and
4. to remain covert and thus evade detection by the enemy.

This algorithm should be adaptive to varying target densities and dynamics, to sensor capabilities, and to the overall situation and mission objectives.

There are two general approaches to sensor allocation in a dense target environment. The first is based upon longer-term planning and involves computing the expected frequency at which the many required tasks should be performed. For example, a regular update rate would be computed for each target track. The next step will involve bin or time slot packing to accommodate long-term objectives to be performed by each sensor.

An alternative approach is to perform allocation more dynamically based upon current conditions. For example, rather than adhering to some predetermined track update rate, the desirability of updating each track is regularly computed based upon current conditions and compared with the desirability of performing other tasks, such as search or communication. Then short-term objectives are formed and frequently updated. We will next discuss two techniques available for implementing the dynamic sensor allocation approach.

7.1. Utility Theory-Based Allocation

Sensor allocation can be based upon the minimization of some cost function or equivalently the maximization of a utility function. The basic approach here is to determine the usefulness of the state of knowledge before and after the potential application of a sensor to a given task. For example, considering the track update allocation option, the usefulness, or the utility of the estimate of track position can be measured by the Kalman covariance matrix. Then, the utility of track update can be computed from the present covariance matrix and the computed covariance matrix if an observation was received. For example, a typical adaptive filtering scheme will operate by increasing the Kalman filter covariance matrix upon maneuver detection. Then the utility theory allocation method will automatically favor the update of maneuvering targets because of the anticipated utility gain associated with decreasing the covariance matrix. Similarly, the utility of search can be determined from the expected value of the targets to be detected in search.

7.2. Sensor Allocation Using an Expert System

The use of expert system techniques for sensor allocation offers several important advantages. First, a rule-based system readily allows for expansion through the inclusion of additional rules. The use of rules also makes it easier to interpret and to explain the behavior of an expert system, as opposed to analyzing the properties of utility functions. Finally, the expert system technique conveniently allows for sensor allocation to be closely related to situation assessment, since concepts such as target hostile intent are an integral part of both the situation assessment and sensor allocation functions.

As an example of the expert system approach to sensor allocation, the method of Popoli and Blackman (1987) starts by defining quantitative (root) concepts such as distance, closing rate, and target bearing which are determined from encounter geometry. Following this, qualitative (higher order) concepts, such as target identification (ID) and danger posed by the target, are defined. The membership of each target in the "fuzzy set" defined by these concepts is computed. For example, a simple relationship of time-to-go ($R/\dot{R}$) can be used for the root concept "close." Then using a set of "IF-THEN" rules the membership of each target in the fuzzy set defined by higher-order concepts, such as dangerous, is computed. Finally, using a combination of root and higher-order concepts, the membership, as well as priorities, in the set of tracks to be updated is computed and the allocation of sensors is made.

8. CONCLUSIONS

It is anticipated that in the future increased computational capabilities will allow the use of improved methods for data association and estimation in order to effectively utilize the wide variety of data that will be available in multiple sensor systems. This means that the all-neighbors and deferred decision methods, such as MHT, should replace the current emphasis upon sequential nearest-neighbor methods. Similarly, the many advantages of Kalman filtering should make the use of fixed-gain filtering approaches essentially obsolete for future systems. Finally, the use of Bayesian and Dempster-Shafer techniques for target identification should replace the more *ad hoc* methods presently in common practice.

In order to effectively utilize the capability of multiple sensor systems, an efficient allocation method is required. Also there will be an increasing use of AI techniques for interpreting the track file information (see, e.g., Chapter 23 of this book). Thus, it is likely that expert systems approaches will be widely applied for sensor allocation.

REFERENCES

Bar-Shalom, Y., & Campo, L. (1986). The effect of common process noise on the two-sensor fused-track covariance. *IEEE Transactions on Aerospace and Electronic Systems*, AES-22, 803–805.

Bar-Shalom, Y., & Fortmann, T.E. (1987). *Tracking and data association*. New York: Academic.

Blackman, S.S. (1986). *Multiple target tracking with radar applications*. Dedham, MA: Artech House.

Bogler, P.L. (1987). Shafer-Dempster reasoning with applications to multisensor target identification systems. *IEEE Transactions on Systems, Man, and Cybernetics*, SMC-17(6), 968–977.

Deley, G.W. (1978). A netting approach to automatic radar track initiation, association and tracking in air surveillance systems. *AGARD Conference Proceedings No. 252, Strategies for Automatic Track Initiation* (pp. 7-1–7-10). Monterey, CA.

Farina, A., & Studer, F.A. (1985). *Radar data processing*. New York: Wiley.

Fitzgerald, R.J. (1986). Development of practical PDA logic for multi-target tracking by microprocessor. *Proceedings of the American Control Conference* (pp. 889–898). Seattle, WA.

Nahin, P.J., & Pokoski, J.L. (1980). NCTR plus sensor fusion equals IFFN. *IEEE Transactions on Aerospace and Electronic Systems*, AES-16(3), 320–337.

Popoli, R., & Blackman, S.S. (1987). Expert system allocation for the electronically scanned antenna radar. *Proceedings of the American Control Conference* (pp. 1821–1826). Minneapolis, MN.

Reid, D.B. (1979). An algorithm for tracking multiple targets. *IEEE Transactions on Automatic Control*, AC-24(7), 843–854.

Stallard, D.V. (1987). An angle-only tracking filter in modified spherical coordinates. *Proceedings of the AIAA Guidance, Navigation and Control Conference* (pp. 542–550).

Trunk, G.V., & Wilson, J.D. (1987). Association of DF bearing measurements with radar tracks. *IEEE Transactions on Aerospace and Electronic Systems*, AES-23, 438–447.

25
Joint Probabilistic Data Association in Distributed Sensor Networks*

Kuo-Chu Chang,
Chee-Yee Chong, and
Yaakov Bar-Shalom

A distributed multitarget tracking problem is considered in this chapter. The Joint Probabilistic Data Association (JPDA) algorithm, which has been successfully used for tracking multiple targets in a cluttered environment, assumes a centralized processing architecture. It assumes that measurements are transmitted to a central site and processed. In some applications, however, it may be desirable for the sensor measurements to be processed at or near the sensors instead of transmitting them to the central processor. The local processed results are then sent over a communication network to be used by other processors. This chapter presents a distributed version of the JPDA algorithm which is applicable under such a situation.

1. INTRODUCTION

The tracking of multiple targets using data from multiple sensors occurs in many military and civilian applications. In some applica-

---

* Thanks are due to an anonymous reviewer for his many constructive suggestions.

tions, the data are collected by a network of sensors distributed over a large geographic region. In such distributed sensor networks (DSN), because of considerations such as reliability, survivability, and communication bandwidth, centralized processing is either undesirable or infeasible. Instead, the sensors supply data to a set of local processors/nodes which are connected by a communication network. The nodes process the local sensor data and exchange processing results with other nodes. Examples of possible DSN include the tracking of targets by multiple sensing/battle-management stations in the Strategic Defense Initiative (SDI).

The key problem in multitarget tracking is data association, that is, the association of the measurements from single or multiple sensors to the same targets. Many different approaches have been proposed for data association in a centralized framework (Bar-Shalom & Tse, 1975; Reid, 1979; Fortmann, Bar-Shalom, & Scheffe, 1983; Morefield, 1977; Singer, Sea, & Housewright, 1974), in which all the sensor measurements are transmitted to a centralized site where they are processed. One such approach is the Joint Probabilistic Data Association (JPDA) algorithm (Fortmann et al., 1983). In this algorithm the data association problem is handled by computing the joint posterior probabilities of measurement associations with multiple targets in clutter. These probabilities are then used to update a set of Gaussian distributions representing (suboptimal) Bayesian estimates of the target locations.

Several distributed tracking algorithms for DSN have been proposed. In Tenney and Delaney (1984), a distributed acoustic tracking schemes was discussed; in Mucci, Arnold, and Bar-Shalom (1985), the coordination of multiple sensors to associate track segments was investigated; and in Chong, Mori, and Chang (1985), a multiple hypotheses approach was used where hypotheses were formed and communicated from each local node. This chapter presents a distributed tracking scheme based on the JPDA algorithm where both data association and distributed estimation are considered. In this scheme, each node first performs the tracking functions with the JPDA algorithm using the local sensor measurements and then sends the processed results to other nodes. The receiving node then fuses the information from other nodes with its local information to arrive at a better estimate. By adopting the linear fusion algorithm of Chong (1979) and Speyer (1979), a distributed version of the JPDA algorithm which takes into account the fusion problem is derived in this chapter.

Section 2 describes a simple two-node DSN structure and formulates the problem. Algorithm derivation and discussion are given in Section 3. Numerical simulation results are presented in Section 4.

2. PROBLEM FORMULATION

For simplicity, we consider a two sensor/processor (node) situation with the structure given in Figure 25.1. Each local node processes the local sensor measurements and sends the local estimates periodically to the global processor (fusing node). After processing the results, the global processor sends back the global estimates to each local node.

The target dynamics are modelled as

$$x_{k+1}^t = F_k^t x_k^t + w_k^t \qquad k = 0, 1, \ldots \qquad (1)$$

where x_k^t is the state of target t at time k, F_k^t is a known matrix, and w_k^t is the white Gaussian process noise with zero mean and known variance

$$E(w_k^t w_j^{t'}) = Q_k^t \delta_{kj} \qquad (2)$$

and δ_{kj} is the delta function.

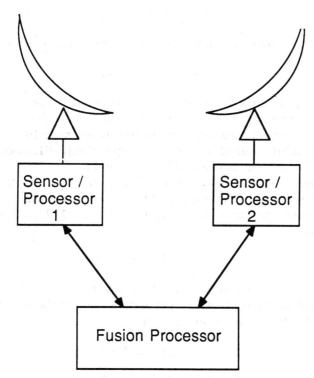

Figure 25.1. A DSN structure.

The measurements of sensor i from target t are modelled as

$$z_k^i = H_k^i x_k^t + v_k^i, \quad k = 1, 2, \ldots; i = 1, 2, \quad (3)$$

where v_k^i is an independent Gaussian measurement noise with zero mean and known variance

$$E(v_k^i v_j^{i'}) = R_k^i \delta_{kj}. \quad (4)$$

We assume the measurements to be validated by selecting an appropriate gate. Denote the set of validated measurements at each time k of sensor i as

$$Z_k^i = \{z_{k,j}^i\}_{j=1}^{m_k^i}, \quad (5)$$

where m_k^i is the total number of validated measurements, and j indexes the set. Let $Z^{i,k}$ be the accumulated validated measurements for sensor i at time k,

$$Z^{i,k} = \{Z_l^i\}_{l=1}^k. \quad (6)$$

The local minimum variance estimate of target t for sensor i is then

$$\hat{x}_{k|k}^{i,t} = \int x_k^t p(x_k^t \mid Z^{i,k}, Y^{i,k}) dx_k^t, \quad (7)$$

where $Y^{i,k} = \{Y_l^i\}_{l=1}^k$ and Y_l^i denotes the information received by node i during the sampling period from time $l - 1$ to l. Note that here Y_l^i is defined to be the information sent by the fusion node to node i. It includes the information of the other node up to time $l - 1$, since this is sent to the fusion node between time $l - 1$ and l.

Assuming perfect communication of the sufficient statistics, the information received $Y^{i,k}$ is equivalent to the actual accumulated measurements from the other sensor up to time $k - 1$. Eq. (7) can be rewritten as

$$\hat{x}_{k|k}^{i,t} = \int x_k^t p(x_k^t \mid Z^{i,k}, Z^{\bar{i},k-1}) dx_k^t, \quad (8)$$

where $\bar{i}$ represents the sensor other than sensor i.

The global minimum variance estimate assuming the sensor data are communicated to the fusion node is

$$\hat{x}_{k|k}^t = \int x_k^t p(x_k^t \mid Z^{1,k}, Z^{2,k}) dx_k^t. \quad (9)$$

The question now is how the global estimate can be constructed by fusing together the local estimates; specifically, how the global estimate is to be calculated, and what necessary and sufficient information is to be passed between the local nodes.

3. ALGORITHM

To account for false measurements from both interfering sources (other targets) and random clutter, validation gates about the predicted measurements are formed in the JPDA algorithm. Then data association is performed by formulating all the feasible joint events which associate the validated measurements to the targets. For details, see Bar-Shalom and Tse (1975), Fortmann et al. (1983), and Appendix A. With this algorithm, the local estimate of each target t is given by

$$\hat{x}_{k|k}^{i,t} = E\{x_k^t \mid Z^{i,k}, Y^{i,k}\}$$
$$= \sum_{j=0}^{m_k^i} E\{x_k^t \mid \chi_{k,j}^{i,t}, Z^{i,k}, Y^{i,k}\} P\{\chi_{k,j}^{i,t} \mid Z^{i,k}, Y^{i,k}\}, \quad (10)$$

where $\chi_{k,j}^{i,t}$ is the event where $z_{k,j}^i$ is the correct return from the target t and $\chi_{k,0}^{i,t}$ is the event where none of the validated returns of sensor i comes from target t.

$$P\{\chi_{k,j}^{i,t} \mid Z^{i,k}, Y^{i,k}\} = \beta_{k,j}^{i,t}$$
$$= \sum_{\chi_k^i} P\{\chi_k^i \mid Z^{i,k}, Y^{i,k}\} \hat{\omega}_{jt}^i(\chi_k^i), \quad j = 1, \ldots, m_k^i, (11)$$

where χ_k^i are the feasible joint events defined as

$$\chi_k^i = \bigcap_{j=1}^{m_k^i} \chi_{k,j}^{i,t} \quad (12)$$

and $\hat{\omega}_{jt}^i(\chi_k^i)$ is the binary measurement-target association indicator (for details, see Fortmann, et al., 1983, and Appendix A).

The local estimates given in Eq. (10) can be rewritten as

$$\hat{x}_{k|k}^{i,t} = \sum_{j=0}^{m_k^i} \beta_{k,j}^{i,t} \hat{x}_{k,k,j}^{i,t}, \quad (13)$$

where, for $j \neq 0$,

$$\hat{x}_{k|k,j}^{i,t} = F_{k-1}^t \hat{x}_{k-1|k-1}^{i,t} + W_k^{i,t}(z_{k,j}^i - H_k^i F_{k-1}^t x_{k-1|k-1}^{i,t})$$
$$= \hat{x}_{k|k-1}^{i,t} + W_k^{i,t}(z_{k,j}^i - H_k^i \hat{x}_{k|k-1}^{i,t}) \quad (14)$$

is the estimate conditioned on measurement j being correct,

$$W_k^{i,t} = P_{k|k-1}^{i,t} H_k^{i\prime} [H_k^i P_{k|k-1}^{i,t} H_k^{i\prime} + R_k^i]^{-1} \tag{15}$$

and

$$P_{k|k,j}^{i,t} = (I - W_k^{i,t} H_k^i) P_{k|k-1}^{i,t} \tag{16}$$

is the error covariance associated with Eq. (14). The error covariance associated with Eq. (13) is (Bar-Shalom & Tse, 1975; Bar-Shalom & Jaffer, 1972):

$$P_{k|k}^{i,t} = \beta_{k,0}^{i,t} P_{k|k-1}^{i,t} + \sum_{j=1}^{m_k^i} \beta_{k,j}^{i,t} P_{k|k,j}^{i,t}$$

$$+ \sum_{j=0}^{m_k^i} \beta_{k,j}^{i,t} [\hat{x}_{k|k,j}^{i,t} \hat{x}_{k|k,j}^{i,t}{}' - \hat{x}_{k|k}^{i,t} \hat{x}_{k|k}^{i,t}{}']. \tag{17}$$

Observe here that $\hat{x}_{k|k,0}^{i,t} = \hat{x}_{k|k-1}^{i,t}$ and $P_{k|k,0}^{i,t} = P_{k|k-1}^{i,t}$.

Now, assume the pdf of the initial state is Gaussian with mean $x_{0|-1}^t$ and covariance $P_{0|-1}^t$, and that they are known to all the local nodes. We will describe the minimum information the local nodes used to communicate with each other, and how the global estimates can be constructed.

From Eq. (9), the global estimate is

$$\hat{x}_{k|k}^t = E\{x_k^t \mid Z^{1,k}, Z^{2,k}\}$$

$$= \sum_{j=0}^{m_k^1} \sum_{t=0}^{m_k^2} E\{x_k^t \mid \chi_{k,j}^{1,t}, \chi_{k,l}^{2,t}, Z^{1,k}, Z^{2,k}\} P\{\chi_{k,j}^{1,t}, \chi_{k,l}^{2,t} \mid Z^{1,k}, Z^{2,k}\}. \tag{18}$$

The first term of the right-hand side of Eq. (18) is the global estimate of x_k^t given that the jth measurement from sensor 1 and the lth measurement from sensor 2 are the correct measurements. This can be constructed, under the condition that the measurement errors from two sensors are independent, by combining the local estimates $\hat{x}_{k|k,j}^{1,t}$ and $\hat{x}_{k|k,l}^{2,t}$ through the estimation method of Chong (1979) (see Appendix B). The result is

$$\hat{x}_{k|k,j,l}^t = E\{x_k^t \mid \chi_{k,j}^{1,t}, \chi_{k,l}^{2,t}, Z^{1,k}, Z^{2,k}\}$$

$$= P_{k|k,j,l}^t [P_{k|k,j}^{1,t}{}^{-1} \hat{x}_{k|k,j}^{1,t} + P_{k|k,l}^{2,t}{}^{-1} \hat{x}_{k|k,l}^{2,t}$$

$$- P_{k|k-1}^{1,t}{}^{-1} \hat{x}_{k|k-1}^{1,t} - P_{k|k-1}^{2,t}{}^{-1} \hat{x}_{k|k-1}^{2,t} + P_{k|k-1}^t{}^{-1} \hat{x}_{k|k-1}^t], \tag{19}$$

where

$$P^t_{k|k,j,l} = [P^{1,t}_{k|k,j}{}^{-1} + P^{2,t}_{k|k,l}{}^{-1} - P^{1,t}_{k|k-1}{}^{-1} + P^t_{k|k-1}{}^{-1}]^{-1} \quad (20)$$

is the associated covariance of $x^t_{k|k,j,l}$. And similar to Eq. (17), $\hat{x}^t_{k|k,0,0} = \hat{x}^t_{k|k-1}$ and $P^t_{k|k,0,0} = P^t_{k|k-1}$. When two nodes communicate every scan, the global and the local prior estimates are the same. In this case Eqs. (19) and (20) can be further simplified as shown in Appendix B. Eqs. (14) and (16) can also be modified as shown later in Figure 25.2.

Assuming that the measurements from the two sensors are independent given the target states and that the events χ^1_k and χ^2_k defined in Eq. (12) are independent given the target states, then the second factor in the right-hand side of Eq. (18) is

$$P\{\chi^{1,t}_{k,j}, \chi^{2,t}_{k,l} \mid Z^{1,k}, Z^{2,k}\}$$

$$= \sum_{\chi^1_k} \sum_{\chi^2_k} P\{\chi^1_k, \chi^2_k \mid Z^{1,k}, Z^{2,k}\} \hat{w}^1_{jt}(\chi^1_k) \hat{w}^2_{lt}(\chi^2_k)$$

$$= \beta^t_{k,j,l}, \quad (21)$$

where

$$P\{\chi^1_k, \chi^2_k \mid Z^{1,k}, Z^{2,k}\}$$

$$= \frac{1}{c} \int \cdots \int p\{\chi^1_k, \chi^2_k, Z^1_k, Z^2_k \mid x^{t_1}_k, \ldots, x^{t_T}_k, Z^{1,k-1}, Z^{2,k-1}\}$$

$$\cdot p(x^{t_1}_k, \ldots, x^{t_T}_k \mid Z^{1,k-1}, Z^{2,k-1}) dx^{t_1}_k \cdots dx^{t_T}_k$$

$$= \frac{1}{c} \int \cdots \int p\{\chi^1_k, Z^1_k \mid x^{t_1}_k, \ldots, x^{t_T}_k, Z^{1,k-1}, Z^{2,k-1}\}$$

$$\cdot p\{\chi^2_k, Z^2_k \mid x^{t_1}_k, \ldots, x^{t_T}_k, Z^{1,k-1}, Z^{2,k-1}\} p(x^{t_1}_k, \ldots, x^{t_T}_k \mid Z^{1,k-1}, Z^{2,k-1}) dx^{t_1}_k \cdots dx^{t_T}_k$$

$$= \frac{1}{c_1} \int \cdots \int \frac{p(\chi^1_k, Z^{1,k}, Z^{2,k-1}, x^{t_1}_k, \ldots, x^{t_T}_k) p(\chi^2_k, Z^{1,k-1}, Z^{2,k}, x^{t_1}_k, \ldots, x^{t_T}_k)}{p(x^{t_1}_k, \ldots, x^{t_T}_k \mid Z^{1,k-1}, Z^{2,k-1})} dx^{t_1}_k \cdots dx^{t_T}_k$$

$$= \frac{1}{c_1} p(\chi^1_k, Z^{1,k}, Z^{2,k-1}) p(\chi^2_k, Z^{1,k-1}, Z^{2,k})$$

$$\cdot \int \cdots \int \frac{p(x^{t_1}_k, \ldots, x^{t_T}_k \mid \chi^1_k, Z^{1,k}, Z^{2,k-1}) p(x^{t_1}_k, \ldots, x^{t_T}_k \mid \chi^2_k, Z^{1,k-1}, Z^{2,k})}{p(x^{t_1}_k, \ldots, x^{t_T}_k \mid Z^{1,k-1}, Z^{2,k-1})} dx^{t_1}_k \cdots dx^{t_T}_k$$

$$= \frac{1}{c_2} P(\chi^1_k \mid Z^{1,k}, Y^{1,k}) P(\chi^2_k \mid Z^{2,k}, Y^{2,k}) \gamma(\chi^1_k, \chi^2_k), \quad (22)$$

where the assumption that two nodes communicate every scan and that the information received from their communication is sufficient to be equivalent to the information from actual measurements has been made (see Eqs. (7) and (8)), c, c_1 and c_2 are normalization constants, and

$$\gamma(\chi_k^1, \chi_k^2) = \prod_{j=1}^{T} \left\{ \frac{(\det P_{k|k-1}^{t_j})^{1/2}(\det S_k^{t_j})^{1/2}}{(\det P_k^{1,t_j}(\chi_k^1))^{1/2}(\det P_k^{2,t_j}(\chi_k^2))^{1/2}} \right.$$

$$\cdot \exp\left(-\frac{1}{2}\right) \left[\hat{x}_k^{1,t_j}(\chi_k^1)' P_k^{1,t_j}(\chi_k^1)^{-1} \hat{x}_k^{1,t_j}(\chi_k^1) \right.$$

$$+ \hat{x}_k^{2,t_j}(\chi_k^2)' P_k^{2,t_j}(\chi_k^2)^{-1} \hat{x}_k^{2,t_j}(\chi_k^2)$$

$$\left. \left. - \hat{x}_{k|k-1}^{t_j}{}' P_{k|k-1}^{t_j}{}^{-1} \hat{x}_{k|k-1}^{t_j} - \hat{x}_k^{t_j} S_k^{t_j-1} \hat{x}_k^{t_j} \right] \right\}, \quad (23)$$

where

$$S_k^{t_j} = [P_k^{1,t_j}(\chi_k^1)^{-1} + P_k^{t_j}(\chi_k^2)^{-1} - P_{k|k-1}^{t_j}{}^{-1}]^{-1} \quad (24)$$

$$\hat{x}_k^{t_j} = S_k^{t_j}[P_k^{1,t_j}(\chi_k^1)^{-1}\hat{x}_k^{1,t_j}(\chi_k^1) + P_k^{2,t_j}(\chi_k^2)^{-1}\hat{x}_k^{2,t_j}(\chi_k^2) - P_{k|k-1}^{t_j}{}^{-1}\hat{x}_{k|k-1}^{t_j}] \quad (25)$$

and

$$\hat{x}_k^{i,t_j}(\chi_k^i) = \begin{cases} \hat{x}_{k|k,l}^{i,t_j} & \text{if } \exists\, l \ni \hat{w}_{lt_j}^i(\chi_k^i) = 1 \\ \hat{x}_{k|k,0}^{i,t_j} & \text{otherwise} \end{cases} \quad (26)$$

$$P_k^{i,t_j}(\chi_k^i) = \begin{cases} P_{k|k,l}^{i,t_j} & \text{if } \exists\, l \ni \hat{w}_{lt_j}^i(\chi_k^i) = 1 \\ P_{k|k,0}^{i,t_j} & \text{otherwise.} \end{cases} \quad (27)$$

For detailed derivation, see Appendix C. From Eq. (22) we can see that χ_k^1 and χ_k^2 are not independent, the correlation term $\gamma(\chi_k^1, \chi_k^2)$ reflects the influence of the actual measurement locations to the probabilities of the combined joint events.

Combining Eqs. (19) and (21) into Eq. (18) yields

$$\hat{x}_{k|k}^t = \sum_{j=0}^{m_k^1} \sum_{l=0}^{m_k^2} \beta_{k,j,l}^t \hat{x}_{k|k,j,l}^t. \quad (28)$$

Similarly to Chang and Bar-Shalom (1984), the associated covariance is obtained as (see Appendix D)

$$P_{k|k}^t = \beta_{k,0,0}^t P_{k|k-1}^t + \sum_{j=0}^{m_k^1} \sum_{l=0\,(j+l\neq 0)}^{m_k^2} \beta_{k,j,l}^t P_{k|k,j,l}^t$$

$$+ \sum_{j=0}^{m_k^1} \sum_{l=0}^{m_k^2} \beta_{k,j,l}^t [\hat{x}_{k|k,j,l}^t \hat{x}_{k|k,j,l}^{t\prime} - \hat{x}_{k|k}^t \hat{x}_{k|k}^{t\prime}]. \qquad (29)$$

From the above, we can see that the information that each local processor has to send out to the fusion node is the local estimates $\hat{x}_{k|k-1}^{i,t}$ and $\hat{x}_{k|k,j}^{i,t}$ of each target t, and the feasible events χ_k^i with their probabilities. The covariances $P_{k|k,j}^{i,t}$ need not be communicated if the local measurement error variances are available to the fusion node. A summary diagram of the algorithm is given in Figure 25.2.

So far, lossless communications have been assumed to take place every scan. In general, to conserve the communication bandwidth, two nodes may communicate less frequently than the frequency of measurements. In that case, the latest local estimates are no longer sufficient to construct the global estimates due to the propagation of the same process noise from target dynamics between communications. However, if the process noise is zero or relatively small, the combining (fusion) of the local estimates can be approximated by using Eqs. (19), (20) and (23)–(25) with the prior estimates $\hat{x}_{k|k-1}^t$ and $P_{k|k-1}^t$ replaced by the extrapolations of the global estimates from the previous communication time, $\hat{x}_{k|k-n}$, and the corresponding error covariance $P_{k|k-n}^t$. When information is lost in communication, the situation is more complicated. This is similar to the case where the communication pattern is arbitrary. A separate information graph-tracing mechanism (Chong, Mori, Fehling, Chang, & Wishner, 1984) is needed to derive the fusion formula. The idea is to identify the common prior information and take it into account in fusion. The details will not be discussed in this chapter.

To determine whether the local estimates correspond to the same target, each track estimate is tagged with an identification tag. Two local track estimates can be fused only when they have the same tag. In general, when nodes have different sensor coverages, then each node has two kinds of track information. One is the local track information, which contains the tracks only detectable by the local sensors, and the other is the common track information which contains the tracks in the common sensor coverage region. In order to establish the common tracks, each node has to know not only its own sensor coverage but also the coverage of the nodes with which it communicates. The track information is communicated with a unique identification tag for each track. Then after receiving the track information, each node is able to tell whether the information contains the tracks it is already tracking. If so, the fusion algorithm described above can be used to obtain the global estimates; otherwise, a new track will be initiated if

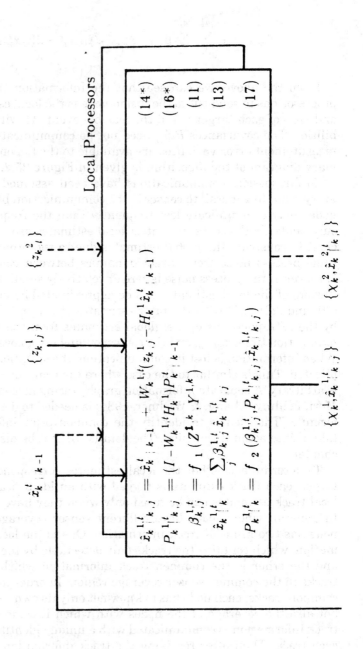

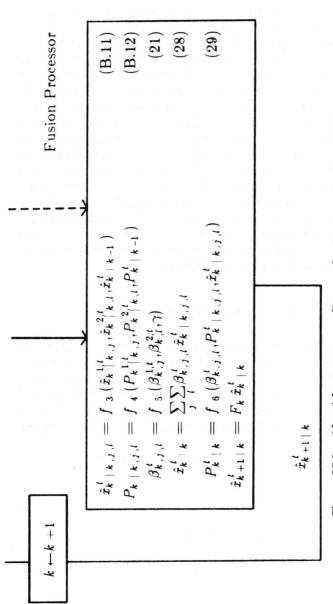

Figure 25.2. Algorithm summary diagram for Communication Period = 1.

the track is about to cross into the local sensor coverage (Tenney & Delaney, 1984).

The algorithm can be extended to the case where there are N nodes, each communicating with the fusion node, but not with each other. The details are derived in Appendix E. In this case, at each scan the local node processes its own measurements from the local sensors and then sends the results to the fusion node. The fusion node then combines all the received information, constructs the global estimates and sends those back to each node. In the other case where each node can talk to all the other nodes, the situation is different. In that case, each node acts as a fusion node. At each scan, after each local node processes its own measurements, it will broadcast the results to all the other nodes. When a node receives the results from all the other nodes, it will then serve as a fusion node and combine the information into the global estimates. The global estimates become the prior information for the next scan and do not have to be sent out, because under a perfect communication assumption all nodes should conclude exactly the same results. The fusion algorithm in these two cases is the same, although the communication architectures are different.

4. SIMULATION RESULTS

The two-node scenario as given in Section 2 is considered. Simulations were carried out for two targets modeled as nearly constant velocity objects in a two-dimensional plane with process noise that can account for slight changes in the velocity. Targets 1 and 2 travel with speed of 0.5 km/s on courses of 82° and 98° respectively. Their trajectories cross at about the middle of the 35-second period, which results in severe interference.

The plant equation for this model, discretized over time intervals of length T, is

$$x_{k+1} = Fx_k + Gw_k \tag{30}$$

where, using Cartesian coordinates the state is

$$x = [x \; \dot{x} \; y \; \dot{y}]' \tag{31}$$

and

$$F = \begin{bmatrix} 1 & T & 0 & 0 \\ 0 & 1 & 0 & 0 \\ 0 & 0 & 1 & T \\ 0 & 0 & 0 & 1 \end{bmatrix} \tag{32}$$

$$w = [w_1 \ w_2]' \tag{33}$$

$$G = \begin{bmatrix} T/2 & 0 \\ 1 & 0 \\ 0 & T/2 \\ 0 & 1 \end{bmatrix} \tag{34}$$

$$E[w_k] = 0; \quad E[w_k \ w_j'] = Q\delta_{kj}. \tag{35}$$

It is assumed that only position measurements are available

$$z_k^i = Hx_k + v_k^i, \tag{36}$$

where

$$H = \begin{bmatrix} 1 & 0 & 0 & 0 \\ 0 & 0 & 1 & 0 \end{bmatrix} \tag{37}$$

$$Ev_k^i = 0; \quad E[v_k^i v_j^{i'}] = R^i \delta_{kj}. \tag{38}$$

The initial 99% confidence ellipse areas were about 10 km², with x and y position confidences of ±1.8 km.

Measurement data were created by true motion (with sampling time $T = 1$ s and process noise $\sqrt{Q_{ii}} = 5 \cdot 10^{-2} \times speed$), adding noise to the computed true measurements, and then adding false measurements. The standard deviations of measurement errors were 0.3 km for the x-coordinate and 0.15 km for the y-coordinate for sensor 1, and 0.15 km for the x-coordinate and 0.3 km for the y-coordinate for sensor 2. True measurements were detected with probability 0.67. The number of clutter points was Poisson-distributed and their locations in the measurement space were uniformly distributed over the field-of-view of each sensor. The clutter density was 0.3/km². This gave about one false detection per gate (99%).

To simplify the simulation, both sensors were assumed to have the same fields-of-view (coverage), and a broadcast-type communication was assumed in the distributed case. Based on the above data, several tracks were created and three communication schemes were examined:

a. decentralized—no communication between nodes
b. centralized—all sensors send measurements to a central node
c. distributed—two nodes interchange information every five scans

The centralized scheme can be regarded as the case in which sensors communicate to each other every scan. In the distributed case, since two nodes do not communicate every scan, the latest local estimates are no longer sufficient to construct the global estimates due to the propagation of the same process noise from target dynamics. However, because of the relatively small standard deviation of the process noise, as mentioned in the previous section, the combining of the local estimates can be approximated by using Eqs. (19), (20) and (22)–(24) with the prior track information $\hat{x}^t_{k|k-1}$ and $P^t_{k|k-1}$ replaced by the extrapolations of the global estimates from the previous communication time, $\hat{x}^t_{k|k-n}$ and the corresponding covariance $P^t_{k|k-n}$.

The simulation results of a sample run given in Figures 25.3 through 25.7 show the differences between the three schemes. As one can expect, the centralized scheme has the best performance and the decentralized scheme performs the worst. Figures 25.3 and 25.4 show the tracking results of node 1 and node 2 using the decentralized scheme. As can be seen, two targets were switched in Figure 25.3 and one target was lost in Figure 25.4. Note that the tracking environment here is much more difficult than in Chang and Bar-Shalom (1984),

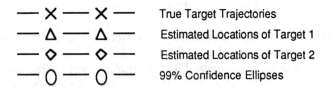

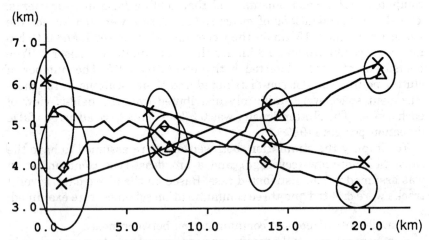

Figure 25.3. Tracking results of sensor 1 with decentralized communication scheme (one sample run).

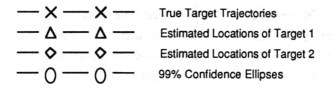
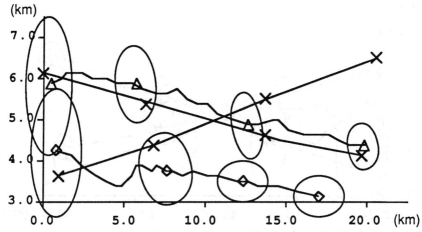

Figure 25.4. Tracking results of sensor 2 with decentralized communication scheme (one sample run).

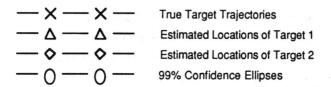
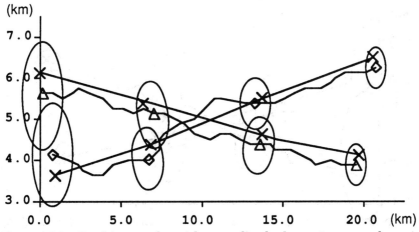

Figure 25.5. Tracking results with centralized scheme (one sample run).

625

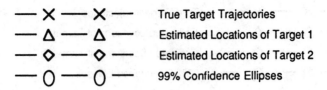
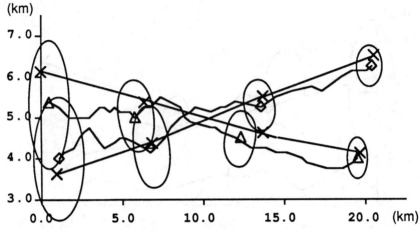

Figure 25.6. Tracking results of sensor 1 with distributed communication scheme (one sample run).

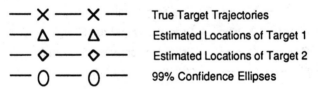
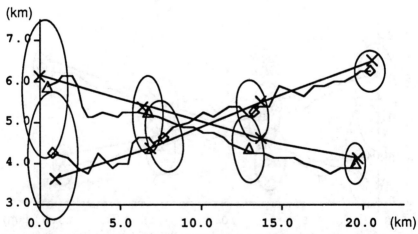

Figure 25.7. Tracking results of sensor 2 with distributed communication scheme (one sample run).

where the probability of detection was higher and the measurement errors were smaller. Figure 25.5 shows results of the centralized case, and as can be seen, the two targets were both tracked. The results of the distributed case are shown in Figures 25.6 and 25.7 for node 1 and node 2. The estimated trajectories were less smooth compared to the results of centralized scheme (see Figure 25.5), nevertheless, none of the tracks were lost. Monte Carlo simulations of 50 runs were obtained for each of the schemes. The rms position and velocity errors of the results are given in Table 25.1. The results of the centralized case represent the best achievable performance given the simulation models and can be used to compare the performance of other schemes. As can be seen in Table 25.1, the distributed scheme performs reasonably well given that the two nodes only communicate every five scans. The rms position errors of distributed case are about 20% higher than that of centralized case. However, in the decentralized case, the rms position errors are about 50% higher than that of the centralized case which reflects the fact that less information was processed in each node.

5. CONCLUSION

A distributed version of the JPDA algorithm has been discussed which takes into account the information fusion in a distributed sensor network. A two-node scenario was examined and the extension of the algorithm to a multiple-node case was also given. A broadcast-type communication has been assumed. In general, when dealing with arbitrary communication, the situation is more complicated and a separate information graph-tracing mechanism is needed (Chong et al., 1984).

Table 25.1. Simulation results

	Centralized Case	Decentralized Case		Distributed Case	
		Node 1	Node 2	Node 1	Node 2
RMS Position Error	0.2463	0.3564	0.3812	0.2919	0.3092
RMS Velocity Error	0.0487	0.0553	0.0611	0.0504	0.0523

The algorithm was derived assuming lossless communication of the sufficient statistics. In addition to the increase in reliability, the algorithm may also require less communication than the transmission of all the measurements. This can happen in the following situations: when the clutter density is high or a large number of sensor measurements are processed at each node, or when the frequency of communication is less than the frequency of measurements. In the latter case, the algorithm will be suboptimal because the local latest estimates are no longer sufficient to construct the global estimates due to the propagation of the same process noise between communication times. When information is lost in communication, the situation is similar to the case where the communication pattern is arbitrary and extra care with information graph tracing mechanism (Chong et al., 1984) needs to be taken to obtain the global estimates. Simulation results have been given which show good performance of the distributed algorithm with reduced communication frequency.

Appendix A. Joint Probabilistic Data Association

The key to JPDA algorithm is the evaluation of the conditional probabilities of the following feasible joint events,

$$\chi_k^i = \bigcap_{j=1}^{m_k^i} \chi_{k,j}^{i,t_j}, \tag{A.1}$$

where for each sensor i, $\chi_{k,j}^{i,t_j}$ is the event in which measurement j originated from target t_j and $0 \leq t_j \leq t_T$ (total number of targets). The feasible events are those for which no more than one measurement originates from each target, and no two targets share the same measurement.

Define the validation matrix (Fortmann et al., 1983) as follows:

$$\Omega^i = [\omega_{jt}^i], \quad j = 1, \ldots, m_k^i; \quad t = 0, 1, \ldots, t_T \tag{A.2}$$

with binary elements to indicate whether measurement j lies in the validation gate for target t. Index $t = 0$ stands for "no target."

Each joint event χ_k^i can be represented by a matrix

$$\hat{\Omega}(\chi_k^i) = [\hat{\omega}_{jt}^i(\chi_k^i)] \tag{A.3}$$

consisting of the units in Ω corresponding to the associations assumed in event χ_k^i. Thus

$$\hat{w}^i_{jt}(\chi^i_k) = \begin{cases} 1 & \text{if } \chi^i_{k,jt} \text{ occurs} \\ 0 & \text{otherwise.} \end{cases} \quad (A.4)$$

In terms of the matrix $\hat{\Omega}(\chi^i_k)$, define the measurement association indicators

$$\tau_j(\chi^i_k) = \sum_{t=1}^{t_T} \hat{w}^i_{jt}(\chi^i_k), \quad j = 1, \ldots, m^i_k \quad (A.5)$$

$$\delta_t(\chi^i_k) = \sum_{j=1}^{m^i_k} \hat{w}^i_{jt}(\chi^i_k), \quad t = 1, \ldots, t_T. \quad (A.6)$$

The probability of a joint event conditioned on all the measurements up to the present time is obtained as (Fortmann et al., 1983),

$$P\{\chi^i_k \mid Z^{i,k}\} = \frac{1}{c} p[Z^i_k \mid \chi^i_k\, Z^{i,k-1}] P\{\chi^i_k \mid Z^{i,k-1}\}$$

$$= \frac{\lambda^\phi}{c'} \prod_{j:\tau_j=1} f_{t_j}[z^i_{k,j}] \prod_{t:\delta_t=1} P^t_D \prod_{t:\delta_t=0} (1 - P^t_D) \quad (A.7)$$

where λ is the density of false measurement, ϕ is the total number of false measurements in event χ^i_k, $f_{t_j}[\cdot]$ is the probability density of the predicted measurements from target t_j for time k, P^t_D is the probability of detection of target t, and c and c' are normalization constants.

The probabiity $\beta^{i,t}_{k,j}$ that measurement j belongs to target t may now be obtained by summing over all feasible events χ^i_k for which this condition is true:

$$\beta^{i,t}_{k,j} = \sum_{\chi^i_k} P\{\chi^i_k \mid Z^{i,k}\} \hat{w}^i_{jt}(\chi^i_k), \quad j = 1, \ldots, m^i_k;\ t = 0,1, \ldots, t_T \quad (A.8)$$

$$\beta^{i,t}_{k,0} = 1 - \sum_{j=1}^{m^i_k} \beta^{i,t}_{k,j}. \quad (A.9)$$

The state estimation for target t from sensor i is then

$$\hat{x}^{i,t}_{k|k} = E\{x^t_k \mid Z^{i,k}\}$$

$$= \hat{x}^{i,t}_{k|k-1} + \sum_{j=1}^{m^i_k} \beta^{i,t}_{k,j} W^i_k (z^i_{k,j} - H^i_k \hat{x}^{i,t}_{k|k-1}) \quad (A.10)$$

Appendix B. Proof of the Fusion Equations

In the following derivation, the superscript t is dropped for simplicity from the notation. The two local a priori and a posteriori estimates $\hat{x}^1_{k|k-1}$, $\hat{x}^2_{k|k-1}$ and $\hat{x}^1_{k|k,j}$, $\hat{x}^2_{k|k,l}$ and their corresponding covariance matrices $P^1_{k|k-1}$, $P^2_{k|k-1}$ and $P^1_{k|k,j}$, $P^2_{k|k,l}$ are used together with the global a priori information $\hat{x}_{k|k-1}$, and $P_{k|k-1}$, to find the global estimates $\hat{x}_{k|k,j,l}$.

Assume $jl \neq 0$; using the concept of the information filter (Anderson & Moore, 1979, p. 139), we have

$$P^i_{k|k,j}{}^{-1} = P^i_{k|k-1}{}^{-1} + H^i_k{}' (R^i_k)^{-1} H^i_k \tag{B.1}$$

$$P^{-1}_{k|k,j,l} = P^{-1}_{k|k,j} + H^{2'}_k (R^2_k)^{-1} H^2_k = P^{-1}_{k|k-1} + H^{1'}_k (R^1_k)^{-1} H^1_k + H^{2'}_k (R^2_k)^{-1} H^2_k \tag{B.2}$$

where $P_{k|k,j}$ is the associated error covariance of the global estimate updated by the jth measurement from sensor 1, which will be given in Eq. (B.5).

Eq. (20) follows from Eqs. (B.1) and (B.2). With the standard Kalman filter equations, we have

$$\begin{aligned}\hat{x}^i_{k|k,j} &= \hat{x}^i_{k|k-1} + P^i_{k|k-1} H^{i'}_k [H^i_k P^i_{k|k-1} H^{i'}_k + R^i_k]^{-1} (z^i_{k,j} - H^i_k \hat{x}^i_{k|k-1}) \\ &= \hat{x}^i_{k|k-1} + P^i_{k|k,j} H^{i'}_k (R^i_k)^{-1} (z^i_{k,j} - H^i_k \hat{x}^i_{k|k-1}). \end{aligned} \tag{B.3}$$

Given the jth measurement from sensor 1, the global estimate is

$$\hat{x}_{k|k,j} = \hat{x}_{k|k-1} + P_{k|k,j} H^{1'}_k (R^1_k)^{-1} (z^1_{k,j} - H^1_k \hat{x}_{k|k-1}) \tag{B.4}$$

where

$$P_{k|k,j}{}^{-1} = P_{k|k-1}{}^{-1} + H^{1'}_k (R^1_k)^{-1} H^1_k \tag{B.5}$$

is the associated error covariance.

Similarly, the global estimate given the jth measurement from sensor 1, and the lth measurement from sensor 2 is:

$$\begin{aligned}\hat{x}_{k|k,j,l} &= \hat{x}_{k|k,j} + P_{k|k,j,l} H^{2'}_k (R^2_k)^{-1} (z^2_{k,l} - H^2_k \hat{x}_{k|k,j}) \\ &= \hat{x}_{k|k-1} + P_{k|k,j} H^{1'}_k (R^1_k)^{-1} (z^1_{k,j} - H^1_k \hat{x}_{k|k-1}) \\ &\quad + P_{k|k,j,l} H^{2'}_k (R^2_k)^{-1} (z^2_{k,l} - H^2_k \hat{x}_{k|k-1}) \\ &\quad - P_{k|k,j,l} H^{2'}_k (R^2_k)^{-1} H^2_k P_{k|k,j} H^{1'}_k (R^1_k)^{-1} (z^1_{k,j} - H^1_k \hat{x}_{k|k-1}) \\ &= \hat{x}_{k|k-1} + P_{k|k,j,l} [H^{2'}_k (R^2_k)^{-1} (z^2_{k,j} - H^2_k \hat{x}_{k|k-1}) \\ &\quad + H^{1'}_k (R^1_k)^{-1} (z^1_{k,l} - H^1_k \hat{x}_{k|k-1})] \end{aligned} \tag{B.6}$$

where the equalities

$$P_{k|k,j,l}H_k^{2'}(R_k^2)^{-1} = P_{k|k,j}H_k^{2'}(H_k^2 P_{k|k,j}H_k^{2'} + R_k^2)^{-1} \quad (B.7)$$

and

$$P_{k|k,j,l} = P_{k|k,j} - P_{k|k,j}H_k^{2'}(H_k^2 P_{k|k,j}H_k^{2'} + R_k^2)^{-1}H_k^2 P_{k|k,j} \quad (B.8)$$

have been used.

By multiplying Eqs. (B.1) and (B.3), we have

$$P_{k|k,j}^{i}{}^{-1}\hat{x}_{k|k,j}^{i} = P_{k|k-1}^{i}{}^{-1}\hat{x}_{k|k-1}^{i} + H_k^{i'}(R_k^i)^{-1}z_{k,j}^{i}. \quad (B.9)$$

Then multiplying Eqs. (B.2) and (B.6) with the substitution of Eq. (B.9), we obtain

$$\begin{aligned}
P_{k|k,j,l}^{-1}\hat{x}_{k|k,j,l} &= P_{k|k-1}^{-1}\hat{x}_{k|k-1} + \sum_{i=1}^{2} H_k^{i'}(R_k^i)^{-1} H_k^i \hat{x}_{k|k-1} \\
&\quad + H_k^{1'}(R_k^1)^{-1}(z_{k,j}^1 - H_k^1 \hat{x}_{k|k-1}) \\
&\quad + H_k^{2'}(R_k^2)^{-1}(z_{k,l}^2 - H_k^2 \hat{x}_{k|k-1}) \\
&= P_{k|k-1}^{-1}\hat{x}_{k|k-1} + H_k^{1'}(R_k^1)^{-1} z_{k,j}^1 + H_k^{2'}(R_k^2)^{-1} z_{k,l}^2 \\
&= P_{k|k-1}^{-1}\hat{x}_{k|k-1} + P_{k|k,j}^{1}{}^{-1}\hat{x}_{k|k,j}^{1} + P_{k|k,l}^{2}{}^{-1}\hat{x}_{k|k,l}^{2} \\
&\quad - \sum_{i=1}^{2} P_{k|k-1}^{i}{}^{-1}\hat{x}_{k|k-1}^{i}
\end{aligned} \quad (B.10)$$

which gives the expression in Eq. (19).

When two nodes interchange information every scan, they will have the same prior estimates as the global node has. In this case, Eqs. (19) and (20) can be further simplified to

$$\hat{x}_{k|k,j,l} = P_{k|k,j,l}[P_{k|k,j}^{1}{}^{-2}\hat{x}_{k|k,j}^{1} + P_{k|k,l}^{2}{}^{-1}\hat{x}_{k|k,l}^{2} - P_{k|k-1}^{-1}\hat{x}_{k|k-1}], \quad (B.11)$$

where

$$P_{k|k,j,l} = [P_{k|k,j}^{1}{}^{-1} + P_{k|k,l}^{2}{}^{-1} - P_{k|k-1}^{-1}]^{-1}. \quad (B.12)$$

Appendix C. Derivation of the Correlation Factor

From Eq. (22),

$$\gamma(\chi_k^1, \chi_k^2)$$
$$= \int..\int \frac{p(x_{k1}^{t_1},..,x_{kT}^{t_T} \mid \chi_k^1, Z^{1,k}, Z^{2,k-1}) p(x_{k1}^{t_1},..,x_{kT}^{t_T} \mid \chi_k^2, Z^{2,k}, Z^{1,k-1})}{p(x_{k1}^{t_1},..,x_{kT}^{t_T} \mid Z^{1,k-1}, Z^{2,k-1})}$$
$$\cdot dx_k^{t_1}..dx_k^{t_T}$$

$$= \prod_{j=1}^{T} \int \frac{p(x_k^{t_j} \mid \chi_k^1, Z^{1,k}, Z^{2,k-1}) p(x_k^{t_j} \mid \chi_k^2, Z^{2,k}, Z^{1,k-1})}{p(x_k^{t_j} \mid Z^{1,k-1}, Z^{2,k-1})} \, dx_k^{t_j}$$

$$= \prod_{j=1}^{T} \int \frac{p(x_k^{t_j} \mid \chi_k^1, Z^{1,k}, Y^{1,k}) p(x_k^{t_j} \mid \chi_k^2, Z^{2,k}, Y^{2,k})}{p(x_k^{t_j} \mid Z^{1,k-1}, Z^{2,k-1})} \, dx_k^{t_j}$$

$$= \prod_{j=1}^{T} \int \frac{N_1(x_k^{t_j} - \hat{x}_k^{1,t_j}(\chi_k^1); P_k^{1,t_j}(\chi_k^1)) N_2(x_k^{t_j} - \hat{x}_k^{2,t_j}(\chi_k^2); P_k^{2,t_j}(\chi_k^2))}{N_3(x_k^{t_j} - \hat{x}_{k|k-1}^{t_j}; P_{k|k-1}^{t_j})} \, dx_k^{t_j} \quad \text{(C.1)}$$

where $\hat{x}_k^{t_j}(\chi_k^i)$ and $P_k^{t_j}(\chi_k^i)$ are given in Eqs. (26) and (27). Define

$$N_4(j) = \frac{\dfrac{N_1(j) N_2(j)}{N_3(j)}}{\int \dfrac{N_1(j) N_2(j)}{N_3(j)} \, dx_k^{t_j}}. \quad \text{(C.2)}$$

Assume $N_4(j)$ is Gaussian with mean $\hat{x}_k^{t_j}$ and covariance $S_k^{t_j}$, since

$$\frac{N_1(j) N_2(j)}{N_3(j)} = \frac{(\det P_{k|k-1}^{t_j})^{1/2}}{\sqrt{2\pi} (\det P_k^{1,t_j})^{1/2} (\det P_k^{2,t_j})^{1/2}}$$
$$\cdot \exp\left(-\frac{1}{2}\right) [(x_k^{t_j} - \hat{x}_k^{1,t_j}(\chi_k^1))' P_k^{1,t_j}(\chi_k^1)^{-1} (x_k^{t_j} - \hat{x}_k^{1,t_j}(\chi_k^1))$$
$$+ (x_k^{t_j} - \hat{x}_k^{2,t_j}(\chi_k^2))' P_k^{2,t_j}(\chi_k^2)^{-1} (x_k^{t_j} - \hat{x}_k^{2,t_j}(\chi_k^2))$$
$$- (x_k^{t_j} - \hat{x}_{k|k-1}^{t_j})' P_{k|k-1}^{t_j}{}^{-1} (x_k^{t_j} - \hat{x}_{k|k-1}^{t_j})] \quad \text{(C.3)}$$

one can easily obtain Eqs. (24) and (25). Then from Eq. (C.2),

$$\gamma(\chi_k^1, \chi_k^2) = \prod_{j=1}^{T} \frac{\dfrac{N_1(j) N_2(j)}{N_3(j)}}{N_4(j)} \quad \text{(C.4)}$$

which results in Eq. (23).

Appendix D. Covariance Derivation

The covariance associated with the global estimate $\hat{x}^t_{k|k}$ is

$$P^t_{k|k} = \int [x^t_k - \hat{x}^t_{k|k}][x^t_k - \hat{x}^t_{k|k}]' \, p(x^t_k \mid Z^{1,k} Z^{2,k}) dx^t_k \quad \text{(D.1)}$$

Using the total probability theorem and Eqs. (18) and (21), the above can be rewritten as

$$P^t_{k|k} = \sum_{j=0}^{m^1_k} \sum_{l=0}^{m^2_k} \beta^t_{k,j,l}$$

$$\cdot \int [x^t_k - \hat{x}^t_{k|k}][x^t_k - \hat{x}^t_{k|k}]' \, p(x^t_k \mid \chi^1_{k,j}, \chi^2_{k,l}, Z^{1,k} Z^{2,k}) dx^t_k$$

$$= \sum_{j=0}^{m^1_k} \sum_{l=0}^{m^2_k} \beta^t_{k,j,l}$$

$$\cdot \int [(x^t_k - \hat{x}^t_{k|k,j,l}) + (\hat{x}^t_{k|k,j,l} - \hat{x}^t_{k|k})][(x^t_k - \hat{x}^t_{k|k,j,l}) + (\hat{x}^t_{k|k,j,t} - \hat{x}^t_{k|k})]'$$

$$\cdot p(x^t_k \mid \chi^1_{k,j}, \chi^2_{k,l}, Z^{1,k} Z^{2,k}) dx^t_k \quad \text{(D.2)}$$

With Eq. (28), after some algebra, one obtains Eq. (29).

Appendix E. Extension to N Node Case

For N node case, similar to Eqs. (18) through (27), the global estimates can be obtained as

$$\hat{x}^t_{k|k} = E\{x^t_k \mid Z^{1,k}, \ldots, Z^{N,k}\}$$

$$= \sum_{j_1=0}^{m^1_k} \cdots \sum_{j_N=0}^{m^N_k} E\{x^t_k \mid \chi^{1,t}_{k,j_1}, \ldots, \chi^{N,t}_{k,j_N}, Z^{1,k}, \ldots, Z^{N,k}\}$$

$$\cdot P\{\chi^{1,t}_{k,j_1}, \ldots, \chi^{N,t}_{k,j_N} \mid Z^{1,k}, \ldots, Z^{N,k}\} \quad \text{(E.1)}$$

where, with the similar proof as in Appendix B,

$$\hat{x}^t_{k|k,j_1,\ldots,j_N} = E\{x^t_k \mid \chi^{1,t}_{k,j_1}, \ldots, \chi^{N,t}_{k,j_N}, Z^{1,k}, \ldots, Z^{N,k}\}$$

$$= P^t_{k|k,j_1,\ldots,j_N} \left[\sum_{i=1}^{N} P^{i,t}_{k|k,j_i}{}^{-1} \hat{x}^{i,t}_{k|k,j_i} - \sum_{i=1}^{N} P^{i,t}_{k|k-1}{}^{-1} \hat{x}^{i,t}_{k|k-1} + P^t_{k|k-1}{}^{-1} \hat{x}^t_{k|k-1} \right]$$

$$\quad \text{(E.2)}$$

and the associated covariance is

$$P^t_{k|k,j_1,\ldots,j_N} = \left[\sum_{i=1}^{N} P^{i,t}_{k|k,j_i}{}^{-1} - \sum_{i=1}^{N} P^{i,t}_{k|k-1}{}^{-1} + P^t_{k|k-1}{}^{-1} \right]^{-1}. \quad (E.3)$$

The second term of Eq. (E.1) is

$$P\{\chi^{1,t}_{k,j_1}, \ldots, \chi^{N,t}_{k,j_N} | Z^{1,k}, \ldots, Z^{N,k}\}$$

$$= \sum_{\chi^1_k} \cdots \sum_{\chi^N_k} P\{\chi^1_k, \ldots, \chi^N_k | Z^{1,k}, \ldots, Z^{N,k}\} \hat{w}^1_{j_1,t}(\chi^1_k) \cdots \hat{w}^N_{j_N,t}(\chi^N_k) \quad (E.4)$$

where, similar to Eq. (22),

$$P\{\chi^1_k, \ldots, \chi^N_k | Z^{1,k}, \ldots, Z^{N,k}\}$$

$$= \frac{1}{c_N} \prod_{i=1}^{N} P(\chi^i_k | Z^{i,k}, Y^{i,k}) \gamma(\chi^1_k, \ldots, \chi^N_k) \quad (E.5)$$

and with a similar derivation as in Appendix C,

$$\gamma(\chi^1_k, \ldots, \chi^N_k) = \prod_{j=1}^{T} \left\{ \frac{(\det P^{t_j}_{k|k-1})^{(N-1)/2}(\det S^{t_j}_k)^{1/2}}{(\det P^{1,t_j}_k(\chi^1_k))^{1/2} \cdots (\det P^{N,t_j}_k(\chi^N_k))^{1/2}} \right.$$

$$\cdot \exp\left(-\frac{1}{2}\right) \left[\sum_{i=1}^{N} \hat{x}^{i,t_j}_k(\chi^i_k)' P^{i,t_j}_k(\chi^i_k)^{-1} \hat{x}^{i,t_j}_k(\chi^i_k) \right.$$

$$\left. \left. - (N-1)\hat{x}^{t_j}_{k|k-1}{}' P^{t_j}_{k|k-1}{}^{-1} \hat{x}^{t_j}_{k|k-1} - \hat{x}^{t_j}_k{}' S^{t_j}_k{}^{-1} \hat{x}^{t_j}_k \right] \right\} \quad (E.6)$$

$$S^{t_j}_k = \left[\sum_{i=1}^{N} P^{i,t_j}_k(\chi^i_k)^{-1} - (N-1)P^{t_j}_{k|k-1}{}^{-1} \right]^{-1} \quad (E.7)$$

$$\hat{x}^{t_j}_k = S^{t_j}_k \left[\sum_{i=1}^{N} P^{i,t_j}_k(\chi^i_k)^{-1} \hat{x}^{i,t_j}_k(\chi^i_k) - (N-1)P^{t_j}_{k|k-1}{}^{-1} \hat{x}^{t_j}_{k|k-1} \right], \quad (E.8)$$

where $\hat{x}^{i,t_j}_k(\chi^i_k)$ and $P^{i,t_j}_k(\chi^i_k)$ are the same as in Eqs. (26) and (27).

By combining Eqs. (E.2) and (E.4), the conditional mean and associated covariance can be obtained similarly to Eqs. (28) and (29). This completes the derivation.

REFERENCES

Anderson, B.D.O., & Moore, J.B. (1979). *Optimal filtering.* Englewood Cliffs, NJ: Prentice-Hall.

Bar-Shalom, Y., & Jaffer, A. (1972). Adaptive nonlinear filtering for tracking with measurements of uncertain origin. *Proceedings of the 11th IEEE Conference on Decision and Control* (p. 246). New Orleans, LA.

Bar-Shalom, Y., & Tse, E. (1975). Tracking in a cluttered environment with probabilistic data association. *Automatica, 11,* 451–460.

Chang, K.C., & Bar-Shalom, Y. (1984). Joint probabilistic data association for multitarget tracking with possibly unresolved measurements and maneuvers. *IEEE Transactions on Automatic Control,* AC-29(7), 585–594.

Chong, C.Y. (1979). Hierarchical estimation. *Proceedings of the MIT/ONR C^3 Workshop.* Monterey, CA.

Chong, C.Y., Mori, S., & Chang, K.C. (1985). Information fusion in distributed sensor networks. *Proceedings of the American Control Conference* (pp. 830–835). Boston, MA.

Chong, C.Y., Mori, S., Fehling, M.R., Chang, K.C., & Wishner, R.P. (1984, July). *Distributed hypothesis testing in distributed sensor networks* (Interim Rep. TR-1048-02). Mountain View, CA: Advanced Information & Decision Systems.

Fortmann, T.E., Bar-Shalom, Y., & Scheffe, M. (1983). Sonar tracking of multiple targets using joint probabilistic data association. *IEEE Journal of Oceanic Engineering,* OE-8(3), 173–184.

Morefield, C.L. (1977). Application of 0-1 integer programming to multitarget tracking problems. *IEEE Transactions on Automatic Control,* AC-22(7), 302–312.

Mucci, R., Arnold, J., & Bar-Shalom, Y. (1985). Track segment association with a distributed field of sensors. *Journal of the Acoustical Society of America, 78*(4), 1317–1324.

Reid, D.B. (1979). An algorithm for tracking multiple targets. *IEEE Transactions on Automatic Control,* AC-24(7), 843–854.

Singer, R.A., Sea, R.G., & Housewright, K. (1974). Derivation and evaluation of improved tracking filters for use in dense multitarget environments. *IEEE Transactions on Information Theory,* IT-20(4), 423–432.

Speyer, J.L. (1979). Computation and transmission requirements for a decentralized Linear-Quadratic-Gaussian control problem. *IEEE Transactions on Automatic Control,* AC-24(2), 266–269.

Tenney, R.R., & Delaney, J.R. (1984). A distributed aeroacoustic tracking algorithm. *Proceedings of the American Control Conference* (pp. 1440–1450). San Diego, CA.

26
Optimal Distributed Decision Fusion

Stelios C.A. Thomopoulos,
Ramanarayanan Viswanathan, and
Dimitrios K. Bougoulias

The problem of decision fusion in distributed sensor systems is considered in this chapter. Distributed sensors pass their decisions about the same hypotheses to a fusion center that combines them into a final decision. Assuming that the sensor decisions are independent from each other conditioned on each hypothesis, we provide a general proof that the optimal decision scheme that maximizes the probability of detection at the fusion for fixed false alarm probability consists of a Neyman-Pearson test (or a randomized N-P test) at the fusion and likelihood-ratio tests at the sensors.

1. INTRODUCTION

Systems of distributed sensors monitoring a common volume and passing their decisions into a centralized fusion center which further combines them into a final decision have been receiving a lot of attention in recent years (Conte, D'Addio, Farina, & Longo, 1983). Such systems are expected to increase the reliability of detection and be fairly immune to noise interference and to failures. In a number of papers the problem of optimally fusing the decisions from a number of sensors has been considered. Tenney and Sandell (1981) have considered the Bayesian detection problem with distributed sensors without considering the design of data fusion algorithms. Sadjadi (1986) has considered the problem of hypothesis testing in a distributed environment and has provided a solution in terms of a number of coupled nonlinear equations. The decentralized sequential detection problem has been investigated in Teneketzis and Varaiya (1984) and Teneketzis (1982). In Tsitsiklis and Athans (1985) it was shown that the solution of distributed detection problems is nonpolynomial complete. Chair and Varshney (1986) have solved the problem of data fusion when the a priori probabilities of the tested hypotheses are known and the likelihood-ratio (L-R) test can be implemented at the receiver. Thomopoulos, Viswanathan, and Bougoulias (1986, 1987) have derived the optimal fusion rule for unknown a priori probabilities in terms of the Neyman-Pearson (N-P) test.

For the "parallel" sensor topology of Figure 26.1, Srinivasan (1986) has shown that the globally optimal solution to the fusion problem that maximizes the probability of detection for fixed probability of false alarm when sensors transmit independent, binary decisions to the fusion center, consists of L-R tests at all sensors and a N-P test at the fusion center. This test will be referred to as N-P/L-R hereafter. The proof of the optimality of the N-P/L-R test in Srinivasan (1986) is based on the (first-order) Lagrange multipliers method which does not

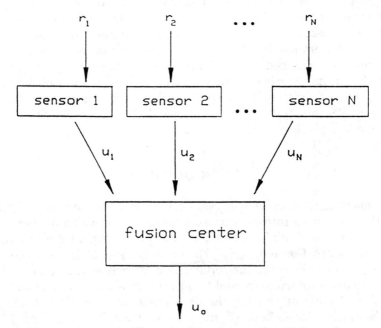

Figure 26.1. Distributed sensor fusion. Parallel topology.

always yield the optimal solution as it is shown by the example in Viswanathan and Thomopoulos (1987). For the paradigm in Viswanathan and Thomopoulos (1987), the Lagrangian approach fails to yield an optimal solution. Instead, it yields a solution which is by far inferior to the optimal solution (see Figure 26.2). A detailed description and analysis of this singular case is given in Viswanathan and Thomopoulos (1987) and Thomopoulos, Viswanathan, and Bougoulias (1988). A theoretical explanation of the failure of the Lagrange multipliers method can be found in Hestenes (1975, chapter 5), Thomopoulos and Viswanathan (1988), and Thomopoulos, Bougoulias, and Zhang (1988).

In general, if the optimal solution lies on the boundary of the domain of x (as in the decision fusion paradigm in Viswanathan and

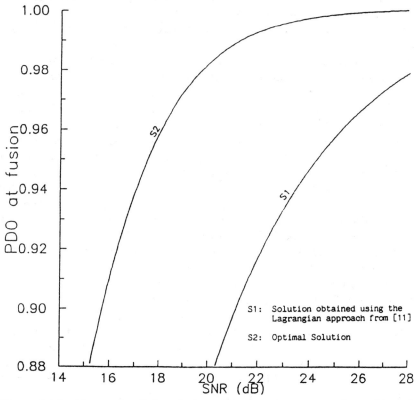

Figure 26.2. Example of singularity of Lagrangian approach used in Srinivasan (1986) for decision fusion. Three identical sensors in slow-fading Rayleigh channel. Paradigm taken from Viswanathan and Thomopoulos (1987).

Thomopoulos (1987), the Lagrangian formulation fails to guarantee the convexity of the objective function, and thus the optimality of the solution obtained using the Lagrange multipliers method. In that sense, the proof of optimality of the N-P/L-R test for the parallel sensor topology in Srinivasan (1986), which is based on a Lagrangian formulation, is incomplete. We give a complete proof of the optimality of the N-P/L-R test for the distributed decision fusion problem that does not depend on the Lagrangian formulation.

2. OPTIMALITY OF N-P/L-R TEST IN DISTRIBUTED DECISION FUSION

A number of sensors N receive data from a common volume. Sensor k receives data r_k and generates the first stage decision u_k, $k = 1, 2, \ldots, N$. The decisions are subsequently transmitted to the fusion center where they are combined into a final decision u_0 about which of the hypotheses is true (Figure 26.1). Assuming binary hypothesis testing for simplicity, we use $u_i = 1$ or 0 to designate that sensor i favors hypothesis H_1 or H_0, respectively. In order to derive the globally optimal fusion rule we assume that the received data r_k at the N sensors are statistically independent, conditioned on each hypothesis. This implies that the received decisions at the fusion center are independent conditioned on each hypothesis. Improvement in the performance of conventional diversity schemes is based on the validity of this assumption (see Chapter 27). Given a desired level of probability of false alarm at the fusion center, $P_{F_0} = \alpha_0$, the test that maximizes the probability of detection P_{D_0} (thus minimizing the probability of miss $P_{M_0} = 1 - P_{D_0}$) is the N-P test (Van Trees, 1968; Difranco & Rubin, 1980). Because of the comparison to a threshold, this test is referred to as a threshold optimal test.

Next we prove that the optimal solution to the fusion problem involves an N-P test at the fusion center and L-R tests at the sensors.

Let $d(u_1, u_2, \ldots, u_N)$ be the (binary) decision function (rule) at the fusion. Since $d(u_1, u_2, \ldots, u_N)$ is either 0 or 1, and all the possible combinations of decisions $\{u_1, u_2, \ldots, u_N\}$ that the fusion center can receive from the N sensors are 2^N, the set of all possible decision functions contain 2^{2^N} d functions. However, not all these functions d can be threshold optimal as the next Lemma states.

Lemma 1. Let the sensors' individual decisions u_k be independent from each other conditioned on each hypothesis. Let $P_{F_i} = P(u_i = 1 \mid H_0)$ be the false alarm probability and $P_{D_i} = P(u_i = 1 \mid H_1)$ be the probability of detection at the ith sensors. Assuming, without loss of generality, that for every sensor $P_{D_i} \geq P_{F_i}$, a necessary condition for a fusion function $d(u_1, u_2, \ldots, u_N)$ to be threshold optimal is

$$d(A_k, U - A_k) = 1 \Rightarrow d(A_n, U - A_n) = 1 \text{ if } A_n > A_k \qquad (1)$$

where $U = \{u_1, u_2, \ldots, u_N\}$ denotes the set of the peripheral sensor decisions, A_k is a set of decisions with k sensors favoring hypothesis H_1 (whereas the complement set of decisions $U - A_k$ favors hypothesis H_0), and A_n is any set that contains the decisions from these k sensors. (The symbol ">" is used to indicate "greater than" in the standard multidimensional coordinate-wise sense, i.e., $A_n > A_k$ if and only if $u_{n_i} \geq u_{k_i} \forall i, i = 1, 2, \ldots, N$, with at least one holding as a strict inequality, where $u_{n_i}(u_{k_i})$ indicates the decision of the same ith sensor in the $A_n(A_k)$ decision set.)

Proof. Let $P_{F_i} = P(u_i = 1 \mid H_0)$ be the false alarm probability and $P_{D_i} = P(u_i = 1 \mid H_1)$ be the probability of detection at the ith sensors. $d(A_k, U - A_k) = 1$ implies that the likelihood ratio

$$\frac{p(A_k, U - A_k \mid H_1)}{p(A_k, U - A_k \mid H_0)} = \frac{p(A_k \mid H_1) p(U - A_k \mid H_1)}{p(A_k \mid H_0) p(U - A_k \mid H_0)} > \lambda_0 \qquad (2)$$

which in turn implies that, for $A_n > A_k$,

$$\begin{aligned}
&\frac{p(A_n, U - A_n \mid H_1)}{p(A_n, U - A_n \mid H_0)} \\
&= \frac{p(A_k \mid H_1) p(A_n - A_k \mid H_1) p(U - A_n \mid H_1)}{p(A_k \mid H_0) p(A_n - A_k \mid H_0) p(U - A_n \mid H_0)} \\
&\geq \frac{p(A_k \mid H_1) p(U - A_k \mid H_1)}{p(A_k \mid H_0) p(U - A_k \mid H_0)} > \lambda_0
\end{aligned} \qquad (3)$$

since, under the assumption that $P_{D_i} \geq P_{F_i}$ for every sensor i,

$$\frac{P(u_i = 1 \mid H_1)}{P(u_i = 1 \mid H_0)} = \frac{P_{D_i}}{P_{F_i}} \geq \frac{P(u_i = 0 \mid H_1)}{P(u_i = 0 \mid H_0)} = \frac{1 - P_{D_i}}{1 - P_{F_i}} \qquad (4)$$

From (3), it follows that $d(A_n, U - A_n) = 1$.

Remark 1. Functions that do not satisfy Eq. (2) cannot lead to the set of optimal thresholds. A function d that satisfies Lemma 1 is called a monotone increasing function in the context of switching and automata theory, as in Table 26.1 (Harrison, 1965).

Table 26.1. Number of monotone increasing functions and percentage of reduction.

Number of Sensors N	Number of Monotone Functions	Number of all Possible 2^N Functions	Percentage Reduction
1	3	4	25
2	6	16	62.5
3	20	256	92.19
4	168	65,536	99.74
5	7,581	4.2949673×10^9	99.99982
6	7,828,354	1.8446744×10^{19}	100

Remark 2. If $P_{D_i} = P_{F_i}$ for all sensors, the L-R at the fusion is degenerated to one, identically for any combination of the peripheral decisions (Thomopoulos et al., 1987). Hence, **for any likelihood test**, the false alarm probability P_{F_0} and the detection probability P_{D_0} at the fusion are either a) **both one**, if the threshold is less or equal to one, or b) **both zero**, if the threshold is greater than one. In the first case, the fusion rule always favors hypothesis one, independent of the combination of sensor decisions, that is, $d(U) = 1$ for all Us, which is a monotone increasing function satisfying Lemma 1. In the second case, the fusion rule always favors hypothesis zero, independent of the combination of sensor decisions, that is, $d(U) = 0$ for all Us, which is a monotone increasing function satisfying Lemma 1.

Remark 3. If $P_{D_i} \leq P_{F_i}$ for all sensors, the inequality in Eq. (3) is reversed, and Lemma 1 still holds with all threshold optimal decisions at the fusion being monotonically increasing functions of the sensor decisions.

Remark 4. If for some sensors $P_{D_i} \geq P_{F_i}$ while for some others $P_{D_j} \leq P_{F_j}$, Lemma 1 does not hold. However, this is an uninteresting case, for if we wish to maximize the detection probability at the fusion, we would either ignore the sensors for which $P_{D_j} \leq P_{F_j}$, or randomize their decisions by flipping coins and deciding with probability $1/2$ for either one of the two hypotheses.

Lemma 2. For any fixed threshold λ_0 and any fixed monotonic function $t(u_1, u_2, \ldots, u_N)$, P_{D_0} is an increasing function of the P_{D_i}s, $i = 1, 2, \ldots, N$.

Proof. The decision function that corresponds to the likelihood test at the fusion is contained in the set of monotone functions of N variables. Consider one such monotone increasing decision function $d(u_1, u_2, \ldots, u_N)$. The function d, when expressed in sum of product form in the Boolean sense (Harrison, 1965), contains only some of the literals $u_1, \ldots, u_N$ in the uncomplemented form and none of the complemented variables $(\bar{u}_1, \bar{u}_2, \ldots, \bar{u}_N)$. Since the random variables $u_1, u_2, \ldots, u_N$ are statistically independent, it is possible to compute P_{D_0} knowing the P_{D_i}s (Thomopolous et al., 1987, Eqs. (20–22)). Taking partial derivatives of the P_{D_0} w.r.t. P_{D_i}s, one obtains that $(\partial P_{D_0}/\partial P_{D_i}) > 0 \; \forall i$, which is the desired result. (As an illustration, consider the function $d(u_1, u_2, u_3) = u_1 + u_2 u_3$. For this function $P_{D_0} = P_{D_1} + P_{D_2} P_{D_3} - P_{D_1}(P_{D_2} P_{D_3})$, from which $(\partial P_{D_0}/\partial P_{D_i}) > 0$, $i = 1,2,3$.)

Theorem 1. Under the assumption of statistical independence of the sensor decisions conditioned on each hypothesis, the optimal decision fusion rule for the parallel sensor topology consists of an N-P test (or a randomized N-P test) at the fusion and L-R tests at all sensors.

Proof. Given the decisions $u_1, u_2, \ldots, u_N$ at the fusion center, the best fusion rule which achieves maximum P_{D_0} for fixed $P_{F_0} = \alpha_0$ is the N-P test (assuming that the false alarm probability α_0 is realizable by an N-P test at the fusion; the randomized case is treated separately afterwards). Call the best test at the fusion center $t(u_1, \ldots, u_N) \gtreqless_{H_0}^{H_1} \lambda_0$. From Lemma 1, it follows that the decision function that corresponds to the above test must be one of the monotone increasing functions $d(u_1, u_2, \ldots, u_N)$. Assume that the individual sensors use some test other than the L-R test and are operating with $\{(P_{F_i}, P_{D_i}) \; \forall i\}$ such that the condition $P_F = \alpha_0$ is met. From Thomopoulos et al. (1986, 1987) it is seen that P_{F_0} is a function of the P_{F_i}s only, and that P_{D_0} is a function of the P_{D_i}s only. Furthermore, from Lemma 2, P_{D_0} is a monotonic increasing function of the P_{D_i}s. Therefore, the L-R tests at the sensors which operate with $(P_{F_i}^* = P_{F_i}, P_{D_i}^*)$ lead to the best performance at the fusion, since in this case, the achieved $P_{D_0}^*$ is greater than or equal to P_{D_0} that can be achieved with any other test at the sensors.

If the false alarm probability α_0 is not achievable by an N-P test, a randomized N-P maximizes the probability of detection at the fusion for the given false alarm probability. Let the best randomized N-P test at the fusion center be $t(u_1, \ldots, u_N) \gtreqless_{H_0}^{H_1} \lambda_0$ w.p. p, resulting in false alarm probability P_{F_0}, and $\bar{t}(u_1, \ldots, u_N) \gtreqless_{H_0}^{H_1} \bar{\lambda}_0$ w.p. $1 - p$, resulting in false alarm probability $\bar{P}_{F_0}$. The thresholds λ_0 and $\tilde{\lambda}_0$ are chosen so that the total false alarm at the fusion is

$$P_{F_0} = pP_{F_0} + (1-p)\tilde{P}_{F_0} = \alpha_0. \qquad (5)$$

Thus, the corresponding detection probability at the fusion is

$$P_{D_0} = pP_{D_0} + (1-p)\tilde{P}_{D_0}. \qquad (6)$$

Since the probability p is fixed from the constraint (5), the detection probability in (6) is maximized if each one of the P_{D_0} and $\tilde{P}_{D_0}$ is maximized. But, according to the part of the proof in the nonrandomized N-P test above, each one of these two detection probabilities is maximized if an L-R test is used at the sensors. Hence, the Theorem is also proven for the randomized N-P/L-R test.

A precise characterization of the set of fusion functions that satisfy Theorem 1, indicated as R_N in Table 26.2, can be found in Thomopoulos et al. (1988).

3. CONCLUSIONS

A general proof that the optimal fusion rule for the distributed detection problem of Figure 26.1 involves an N-P test (or a randomized N-P test) at the fusion and L-R tests at all sensors has been provided. The proof does not suffer from the weaknesses of the Lagrange-multipliers-based proof in Srinivasan (1986).

Table 26.2. Total number of functions searched for the set of optimal thresholds.

Number of Sensors N	L_N (is number of Monotone Functions −2)	Total Number of Functions R_N	Percentage Reduction
1	1	1	0.00
2	4	2	50.00
3	18	9	50.00
4	166	114	31.13
5	7,579	6,894	9.03
6	7,828,352	7,786,338	0.54

REFERENCES

Chair, Z., & Varshney, P.K. (1986). Optimal data fusion in multiple sensor detection systems. *IEEE Transactions on Aerospace and Electronic Systems,* AES-22(1), 98–101.

Conte, E., D'Addio, E., Farina, A., & Longo, M. (1983). Multistatic radar detection: Synthesis and comparison of optimum and suboptimum receivers. *IEE Proceedings Part F, Communications, Radar and Signal Processing, 130*(6), 484–494.

DiFranco, J.V., & Rubin, W.L. (1980). *Radar detection.* Dedham, MA: Artech House.

Harrison, M.A. (1965). *Introduction to switching and automata theory.* New York: McGraw-Hill.

Hestenes, M.R. (1975). *Optimization theory: The finite dimensional case.* New York: Wiley.

Sadjadi, F.A. (1986). Hypothesis testing in a distributed environment. *IEEE Transactions on Aerospace and Electronic Systems,* AES-22(2), 134–137.

Srinivasan, R. (1986). Distributed radar detection theory. *IEE Proceedings Part F, Communications, Radar and Signal Processing, 133*(1), 55–60.

Teneketzis, D. (1982). The decentralized Wald problem. *Proceedings of the IEEE International Large-Scale Systems Symposium* (pp. 423–430). Virginia Beach, VA.

Teneketzis, D., & Varaiya, P. (1984). The decentralized quickest detection problem. *IEEE Transactions on Automatic Control,* AC-29(7), 641–644.

Tenney, R.R., & Sandell, Jr., N.R. (1981). Detection with distributed sensors. *IEEE Transactions on Aerospace and Electronic Systems,* AES-17(4), 501–510.

Thomopoulos, S.C.A., & Viswanathan, R. (1988, January). *Optimal and suboptimal distributed decision fusion* (Tech. Rep. TR-SIU-DEE-87-5). Southern Illinois University, Carbondale: Department of Electrical Engineering.

Thomopoulos, S.C.A., Bougoulias, D.K., & Zhang, L. (1988). Optimal and suboptimal distributed decision fusion. In C.W. Weaver (Ed.), *Proceedings of the SPIE, vol. 931, Sensor Fusion* (pp. 161–167). Orlando, FL.

Thomopoulos, S.C.A., Viswanathan, R., & Bougoulias, D.K. (1986). Optimal decision fusion in multiple sensor systems. *Proceedings of the 24th Allerton Conference* (pp. 984–993). Monticello, IL.

Thomopoulos, S.C.A., Viswanathan, R., & Bougoulias, D.K. (1987). Optimal decision fusion in multiple sensor systems. *IEEE Transactions on Aerospace and Electronic Systems,* AES-23(5), 644–653.

Thomopoulos, S.C.A., Viswanathan, R., & Bougoulias, D.K. (1988). Optimal and suboptimal distributed decision fusion. *Proceedings of the 22nd Annual Conference on Information Sciences and Systems* (pp. 886–890). Princeton, NJ.

Tsitsiklis, J., & Athans, M. (1985). On the complexity of distributed decision problems. *IEEE Transactions on Automatic Control,* AC-30(5), 440–446.

Van Trees, H.L. (1968). *Detection, estimation, and modulation theory* (Vol. 1). New York: Wiley.

Viswanathan, R., & Thomopoulos, S.C.A. (1987, April). *Distributed data fusion* (Tech. Rep. TR-SIU-DEE-87-4). Southern Illinois University, Carbondale: Department of Electrical Engineering.

27
Optimal Serial Distributed Decision Fusion

Stelios C.A. Thomopoulos,
Ramanarayanan Viswanathan, and
Ramakrishna J. Tumuluri

The problem of distributed detection involving N sensors is considered in this chapter. The configuration of sensors is serial in the sense that the $(j - 1)$th sensor passes its decision to the jth sensor and that the jth sensor decides using the decision it receives and its own observation. When each sensor employs the Neyman-Pearson test, the probability of detection is maximized, for a given probability of false alarm, at the Nth stage. With two sensors, the serial scheme has a performance better than or equal to the parallel fusion scheme analyzed in the literature. Numerical examples illustrate the global optimization by the selection of operating thresholds at the sensors.

1. INTRODUCTION

The theory of distributed detection is receiving a lot of attention in the literature (Srinivasan, 1986; Ekchian & Tenney, 1982; Viswanathan, Thomopoulos & Tumuluri, 1987; Thomopoulos, Viswanathan, & Bougoulias, 1987). Typically, a number of sensors process the data they receive and decide in favor of one of the hypotheses about the origin of the data. In a two-class decision problem, the hypotheses would be signal present (H_1) or the signal absent (H_0). These decisions are then sent to a fusion center where a final decision regarding the presence of the signal is made. This scheme, which can be termed parallel decision making, is shown in Figure 27.1. In order to maximize the probability of detection at the fusion center for a fixed probability of false alarm, the tests used at the fusion center and at the sensors must be Neyman-Pearson (N-P) (Srinivasan, 1986; Thomopoulos et al., Chapter 26). The above result is based on the assumption that the data at the sensors conditioned on the hypothesis are statistically independent. If the conditional independence is removed, the threshold of the N-P tests becomes data dependent and does not yield any easy solution for optimization (Tsitsiklis & Athans, 1985).

We consider a serial distributed decision scheme (Figure 27.2). (In Ekchian and Tenney (1982) this is called a tandem network.) Though the serial fusion is very sensitive to link failures, its performance analysis is of interest. In Ekchian and Tenney (1982), the tandem network was analyzed with Bayes's cost as the optimality criterion. Though analytical equations are given, no performance analysis for typical channels or comparison of performance with respect to the parallel fusion was provided. Here we aim to fill this gap.

In Section 2 we derive the relevant equations describing the operation of the serial scheme based on the knowledge that all the sensors employ the N-P test. In Section 3 we show that the global optimality is guaranteed when each stage employs the N-P test. Section 4 examines

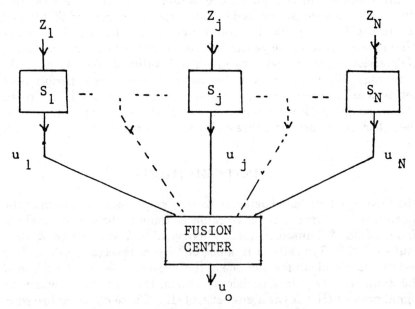

Figure 27.1. Parallel decision fusion.

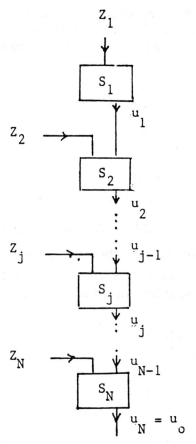

Figure 27.2. Serial decision fusion.

the conditions under which the performance of the serial scheme is definitely not inferior to the parallel scheme. Some numerical examples are also presented to illustrate the performance.

2. DEVELOPMENT OF KEY EQUATIONS

Consider the serial configuration of distributed sensors shown in Figure 27.2. Denote the sensor decisions as $u_1, u_2, \ldots, u_v$. The jth sensor receives the decision u_{j-1} and its own observation Z_j to make its decision u_j. The decision u_N at the Nth sensor is the fused decision about the hypotheses. We assume that the data at the sensors, conditioned on each hypothesis, are statistically independent. This implies that Z_j and u_{j-1} are also conditionally independent. As mentioned earlier, the jth sensor employs an N-P test using the data (Z_j, u_{j-1}). The optimality of this assumption is explored in the next section.

Denoting the distributions of Z_j as $p(Z_j | H_1)$ and $p(Z_j | H_0)$, the likelihood ratio becomes

$$\frac{L(Z_j, u_{j-1} | H_1)}{L(Z_j, u_{j-1} | H_0)} = \frac{p(Z_j | H_1)[P_{D,j-1} \delta(u_{j-1} - 1) + (1 - P_{D,j-1})\delta(u_{j-1})]}{p(Z_j | H_0)[P_{F,j-1} \delta(u_{j-1} - 1) + (1 - P_{F,j-1})\delta(u_{j-1})]} \quad (1)$$

where

$$P_{D,j-1} = \Pr(u_{j-1} = 1 | H_1)$$

$$P_{F,j-1} = \Pr(u_{j-1} = 1 | H_0)$$

$u_{j-1} = k$ implies that the $(j-1)$th sensor decides H_k, $k = 0, 1$, and $\delta(x)$ is the Kronecker delta function defined as $\delta(x) = \begin{cases} 1 & x = 0 \\ 0 & x \neq 0 \end{cases}$ and $L(\ )$ is the likelihood function (Mood, Graybill, & Boes, 1974).

Therefore, the test at the jth sensor is given by

$$\frac{p(Z_j | H_1)}{p(Z_j | H_0)} \frac{P_{D,j-1}}{P_{F,j-1}} \underset{H_0}{\overset{H_1}{\gtrless}} t, \quad \text{if } u_{j-1} = 1$$

$$\frac{p(Z_j | H_1)}{p(Z_j | H_0)} \frac{1 - P_{D,j-1}}{1 - P_{F,j-1}} \underset{H_0}{\overset{H_1}{\gtrless}} t, \quad \text{if } u_{j-1} = 0 \quad (2)$$

where t a threshold to be determined.

Equivalently,

$$\Lambda(Z_j) \underset{H_0}{\overset{H_1}{\gtrless}} \begin{bmatrix} t_{j,1}, & \text{if } u_{j-1} = 1 \\ t_{j,0}, & \text{if } u_{j-1} = 0 \end{bmatrix} \quad (3)$$

where

$$\Lambda(Z_j) = \frac{p(Z_j | H_1)}{p(Z_j | H_0)}$$

and

$$\frac{t_{j,1}}{t_{j,0}} = \frac{P_{F,j-1}}{P_{D,j-1}} \frac{1 - P_{D,j-1}}{1 - P_{F,j-1}}.$$

Many times it is convenient to use the log likelihood ratio, $\ln \Lambda(Z_j) = \Lambda^*(Z_j)$. Hence,

$$\Lambda^*(Z_j) \underset{H_0}{\overset{H_1}{\gtrless}} \begin{bmatrix} t_{j,1}^*, & \text{if } u_{j-1} = 1 \\ t_{j,0}^*, & \text{if } u_{j-1} = 0 \end{bmatrix} \quad (4)$$

and

$$t_{j,1}^* = t_{j,0}^* + \ln\left(\frac{P_{F,j-1}}{1 - P_{F,j-1}} \frac{1 - P_{D,j-1}}{P_{D,j-1}}\right), \quad j = 2, \ldots, N.$$

For the first stage, $t_{1,1}^* = t_{1,0}^*$.

2.1. False Alarm and Detection Probabilities

At the jth stage, the false alarm probability is given by

$$\begin{aligned} P_{F,j} = & \Pr(\Lambda^*(Z_j) > t_{j,0}^* \mid H_0, u_{j-1} = 0) \Pr(u_{j-1} = 0 \mid H_0) \\ & + \Pr(\Lambda^*(Z_j) > t_{j,1}^* \mid H_0, u_{j-1} = 1) \\ & \times \Pr(u_{j-1} = 1 \mid H_0). \end{aligned} \quad (5)$$

Let

$$\begin{aligned} a_j &= \Pr(\Lambda^*(Z_j) > t_{j,0}^* \mid H_0) \\ b_j &= \Pr(\Lambda^*(Z_j) > t_{j,1}^* \mid H_0) \\ c_j &= \Pr(\Lambda^*(Z_j) > t_{j,0}^* \mid H_1) \\ d_j &= \Pr(\Lambda^*(Z_j) > t_{j,1}^* \mid H_1). \end{aligned} \quad (6)$$

Using Eqs. (5), (6), and the conditional independent assumption, we have

$$P_{F,j} = a_j(1 - P_{F,j-1}) + b_j P_{F,j-1}. \quad (7)$$

Similarly,

$$P_{D,j} = c_j(1 - P_{D,j-1}) + d_j P_{D,j-1}. \quad (8)$$

Knowing the distribution of the observations Z_j and using Eqs. (4), (6)–(8), it is possible to compute the $P_{D,j}$s recursively provided the $P_{F,j}$s are specified. If the $P_{F,j}$s are kept the same, the serial configuration exhibits some nice properties (Viswanathan et al., 1987). However, for a given $P_{F,N}$ at the Nth stage, this procedure does not guarantee a maximum $P_{D,N}$. In order to globally optimize the performance, that is, to maximize $P_{D,N}$ for a given $P_{F,N}$, we need a multidimensional search with respect to the variables $P_{F,j}$s, $j = 1, 2, \ldots, (N-1)$. The results obtained using the numerical search procedure are presented in Section 4.

In Figure 27.3 a functionally equivalent form of the serial decision fusion is shown. Each sensor, except the first one, sends two decisions $u_{j,0}$ and $u_{j,1}$ depending on whether the previous sensor decides a 0 or a 1, respectively. These decisions are arrived by using Eq. (3). The fusion center uses the decision from the first sensor and sequentially picks the appropriate decisions from the sensors to arrive at the final decision u_0 which is either $u_{N,0}$ or $u_{N,1}$. Performance-wise, the configuration in Figure 27.3 is equivalent to the serial scheme. The equivalent configuration does not have the time delay problem associated with the serial configuration. However, both are highly sensitive to link failures.

3. GLOBAL OPTIMALITY

The global optimization problem is to find the tests at each stage of the serial configuration such that the probability of detection $P_{D,N}$ is max-

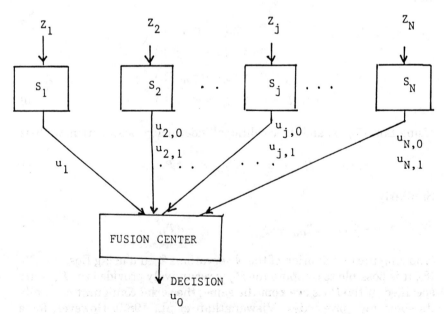

Figure 27.3. Functionally equivalent configuration of serial network.

imized for a given $P_{F,N}$. Here, we show that the global optimality is achieved when each sensor employs the N-P test.

Theorem 1. Given that the observations at each stage in a serial distributed detection environment with N sensors are independent identically distributed (IID), the probability of detection is maximized for a given probability of false alarm at the Nth stage, when each stage employs the N-P test.

Proof. Consider the last two stages. At the Nth stage, the N-P test using the data (Z_N, u_{N-1}) maximizes $P_{D,N}$ for a fixed $P_{F,N}$ (Van Trees, 1968; Srinath & Rajasekaran, 1979). Let

$$L^* = \ln\left(\frac{p(Z_N, u_{n-1} \mid H_1)}{p(Z_N, u_{n-1} \mid H_0)}\right)$$

$$\Lambda^*(Z_N) = \ln\left(\frac{p(Z_N \mid H_1)}{p(Z_N \mid H_0)}\right). \tag{9}$$

Refer to $\Lambda^*(Z_N)$, $P_{F,N-1}$, and $P_{D,N-1}$ as Λ^*, P_F and P_D, respectively, for simplicity. Then,

$$\Pr(L^* < \lambda \mid H_1) = P_D \Pr\left(\Lambda^* + \ln\left(\frac{P_D}{P_F}\right) < \lambda \mid H_1\right)$$
$$+ (1 - P_D) \Pr\left(\Lambda^* + \ln\left(\frac{1 - P_D}{1 - P_F}\right) < \lambda \mid H_1\right). \tag{10}$$

Denote the cumulative distributions and the density functions of Λ^* under H_1 and H_0 as $F_1^*(\ )$, $f_1^*(\ )$ and $F_0^*(\ )$, $f_0^*(\ )$, respectively. Since the left-hand side of Eq. (10) is one minus the probability of detection, we have

$$1 - P_{D,N} = P_D F_1^*\left(\lambda - \ln\left(\frac{P_D}{P_F}\right)\right)$$
$$+ (1 - P_D) F_1^*\left(\lambda - \ln\left(\frac{1 - P_D}{1 - P_F}\right)\right). \tag{11}$$

Similarly,

$$1 - P_{F,N} = P_F F_0^*\left(\lambda - \ln\left(\frac{P_D}{P_F}\right)\right)$$
$$+ (1 - P_F) F_0^*\left(\lambda - \ln\left(\frac{1 - P_D}{1 - P_F}\right)\right). \tag{12}$$

We require, for a fixed $P_{F,N}$ and for any arbitrary but fixed P_F at the $(N-1)$th stage, that the $P_{D,N}$ be a monotonic increasing function of the P_D at the $(N-1)$th stage. Observe that if the P_D of the $(N-1)$th stage is changed, then the threshold λ at the Nth stage changes in order that $P_{F,N}$ remains fixed. Taking the derivative of (12) w.r.t. P_D and equating the result to zero, we obtain

$$\frac{d\lambda}{dP_D} = \frac{\frac{P_F}{P_D}f_0^*(x_1) - \frac{1-P_F}{1-P_D}f_0^*(x_2)}{P_F f_0^*(x_1) + (1-P_F)f_0^*(x_2)}. \tag{13}$$

Similarly,

$$\frac{d(i - P_{D,N})}{dP_D} = F_1^*(x_1) - F_1^*(x_2)$$

$$+ \left[P_D f_1^*(x_1) \left(\frac{d\lambda}{dP_D} - \frac{1}{P_D} \right) \right.$$

$$\left. + (1 - P_D) f_1^*(x_2) \left(\frac{d\lambda}{dP_D} + \frac{1}{1 - P_D} \right) \right]. \tag{14}$$

A reasonable requirement is that $P_D > P_F$. This implies that $F_1^*(x_1) - F_1^*(x_2)$ is less than zero. Hence, a sufficient condition for $\frac{dP_{D,N}}{dP_D} > 0$ is that the term in the brackets in Eq. (14) be less than or equal to zero. After some simplification, using Eq. (13), we obtain the following sufficiency condition:

$$\frac{\frac{f_1^*(x_2)}{f_0^*(x_2)}}{\frac{f_1^*(x_1)}{f_0^*(x_1)}} \leq e^{x_2 - x_1}. \tag{15}$$

However, from the result that the likelihood ratio of the likelihood ratio is the likelihood ratio itself (Van Trees, 1968, p. 46), it follows that Eq. (15) is satisfied with equality.

4. PERFORMANCE ANALYSIS

4.1. Numerical Results

By using the algorithm developed in Section 2, we can obtain the best $P_{D,N}$ for a given $P_{F,N}$ by using a search procedure on the variables,

$P_{F,i}$, $i = 1, \ldots, (N - 1)$. We have recursively used the one-dimensional optimization routine FMIN (Forsythe & Malcom, 1977) for this purpose. The algorithm also requires the zero of a function in order to obtain the thresholds at each stage (7). The ZEROIN routine in Forsythe and Malcom (1977) is used to solve for the zeros. The convergence to the optimum value is obtained in the case of two sensors and three sensors. For performance comparison, we also considered the following parallel fusion schemes: two sensors, identical thresholds at the sensors, AND/OR rules; and three sensors, identical thresholds at the sensors, AND/OR majority logic rules. In the three-sensor case we also consider two other rules, termed $F1$ and $F2$. $F1$ corresponds to the Boolean function $u_0 = u_1 + u_2 u_3$ and $F2$ corresponds to $u_0 = u_1(u_2 + u_3)$. For $F1$ and $F2$, sensors numbered 2 and 3 operate at the same thresholds. In all the cases the observations at the sensors are taken to be IID. Two channel models, namely the constant signal detection in additive white Gaussian noise (AWGN) and the detection of a slowly fluctuating Rayleigh target (Srinivasan, 1986; DiFranco & Rubin, 1968) are considered.

Figures 27.4–27.6 show the performance of two sensors in AWGN channel and Figures 27.7–27.9 show the performance with three sensors. The curve named parallel is the best of the several parallel decision rules mentioned above and the data fusion corresponds to the centralized detection scheme which uses data available at all the sensors. With two sensors, the serial performs better than the parallel, especially at larger signal-to-noise ratios. With three sensors, the performance of the two schemes are nearly the same. Also, either of them is poor compared with the data fusion. This is due to the loss associated with the distributed detection. In Rayleigh target detection with two or three sensors, the OR rule is better than the rest of the parallel fusion rules. Moreover, the numerical computation shows that the serial is equivalent to OR for this channel. Theoretically establishing the equivalence has not been possible. In the sense that the serial is only as good as the OR rule, one can term the Rayleigh channel as conservative (Theorem 2 in the next subsection implies that the serial should be at least as good as the OR rule). Figures 27.10–27.15 show the performances of different schemes for the Rayleigh target detection. In Figures 27.13–27.15, the performances of $F1$ and $F2$ are equivalent and hence the corresponding graphs coincide.

4.2. Comparison with Parallel Scheme

An optimal parallel fusion is the parallel scheme of Figure 27.1 which gives the largest possible probability of detection for a given proba-

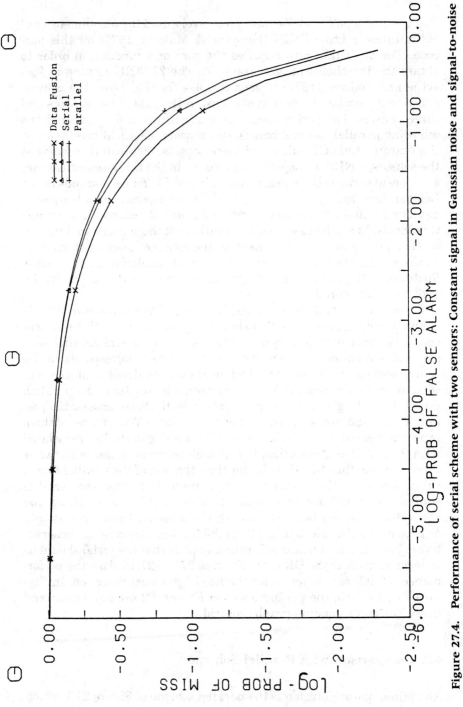

Figure 27.4. Performance of serial scheme with two sensors: Constant signal in Gaussian noise and signal-to-noise ratio of 5 dB.

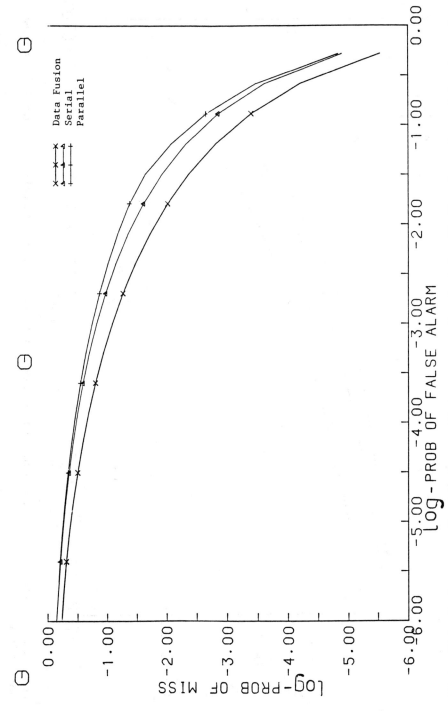

Figure 27.5. Performance of serial scheme with two sensors: Constant signal in Gaussian noise and signal-to-noise ratio of 10 dB.

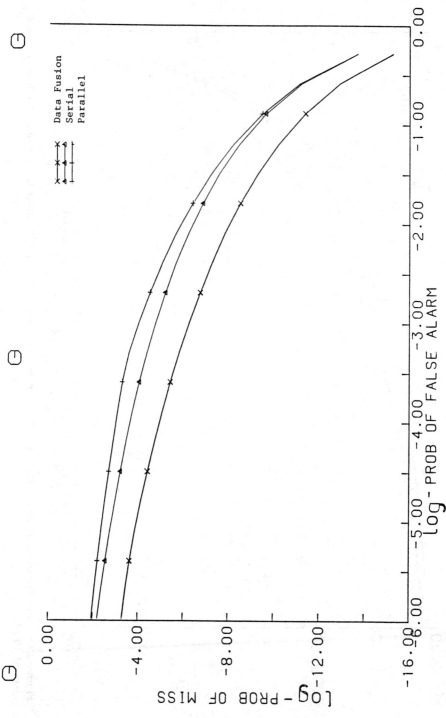

Figure 27.6. Performance of serial scheme with two sensors: Constant signal in Gaussian noise and signal-to-noise ratio of 15 dB.

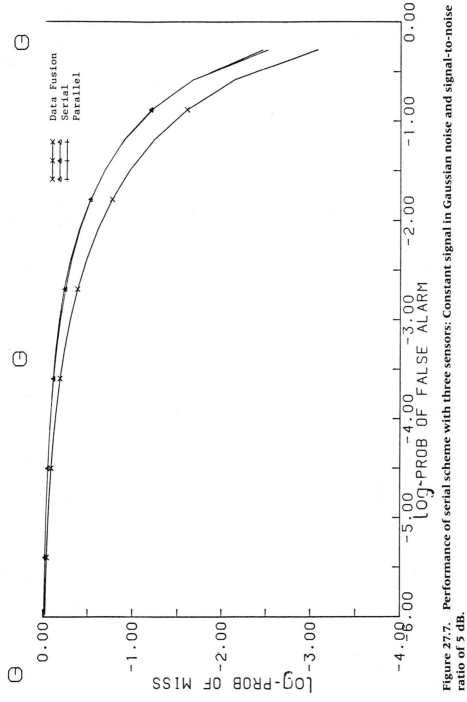

Figure 27.7. Performance of serial scheme with three sensors: Constant signal in Gaussian noise and signal-to-noise ratio of 5 dB.

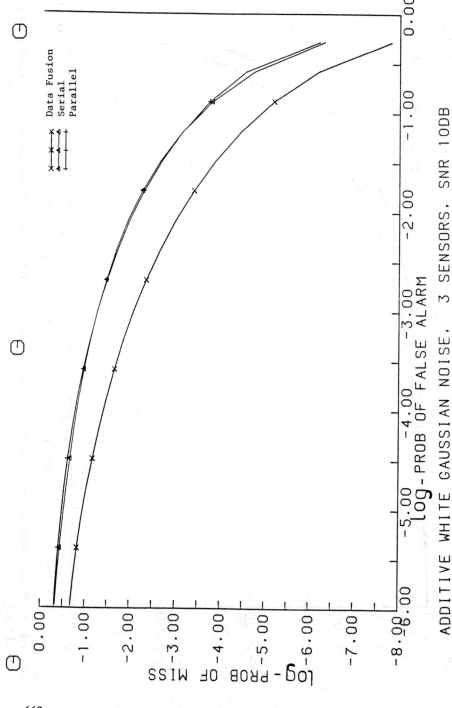

Figure 27.8. Performance of serial scheme with three sensors: Constant signal in Gaussian noise and signal-to-noise ratio of 10 dB.

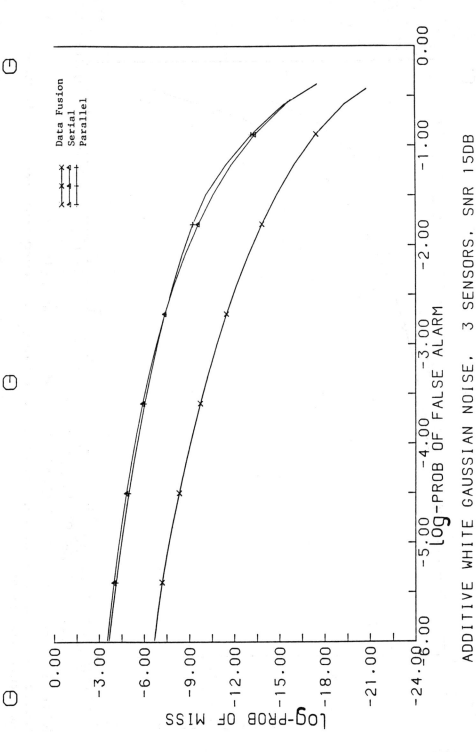

Figure 27.9. Performance of serial scheme with three sensors: Constant signal in Gaussian noise and signal-to-noise ratio of 15 dB.

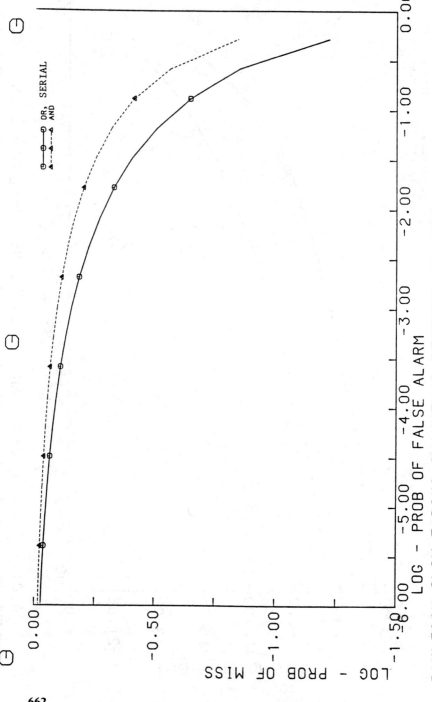

Figure 27.10. Performance of serial and parallel schemes for Rayleigh target detection with two sensors: Energy-to-noise density ratio of 5 dB.

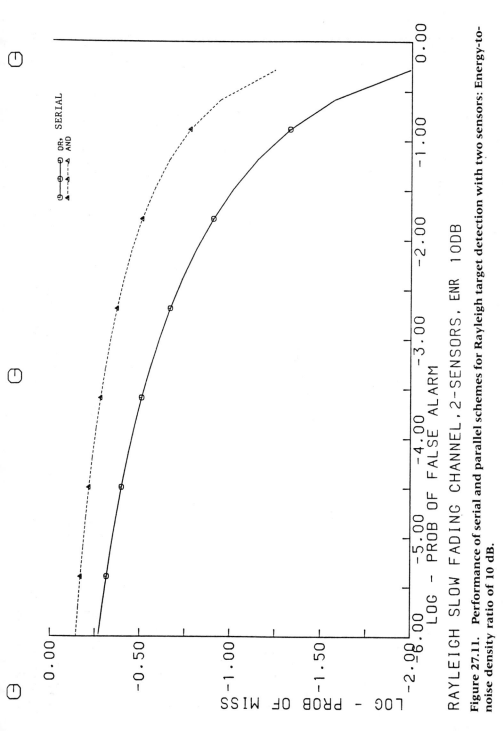

Figure 27.11. Performance of serial and parallel schemes for Rayleigh target detection with two sensors: Energy-to-noise density ratio of 10 dB.

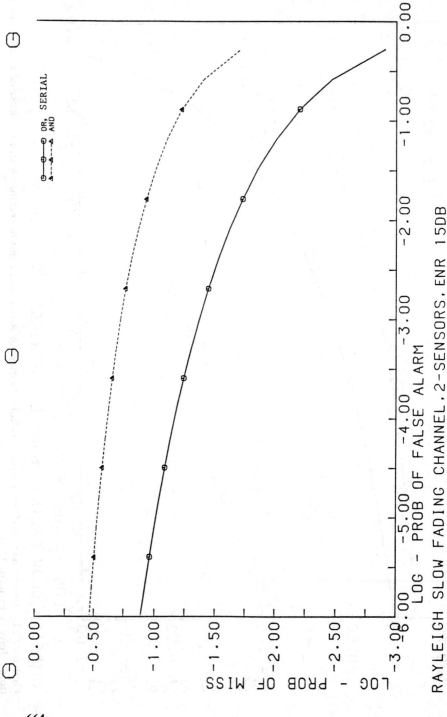

Figure 27.12. Performance of serial and parallel schemes for Rayleigh target detection with two sensors: Energy-to-noise density ratio of 15 dB.

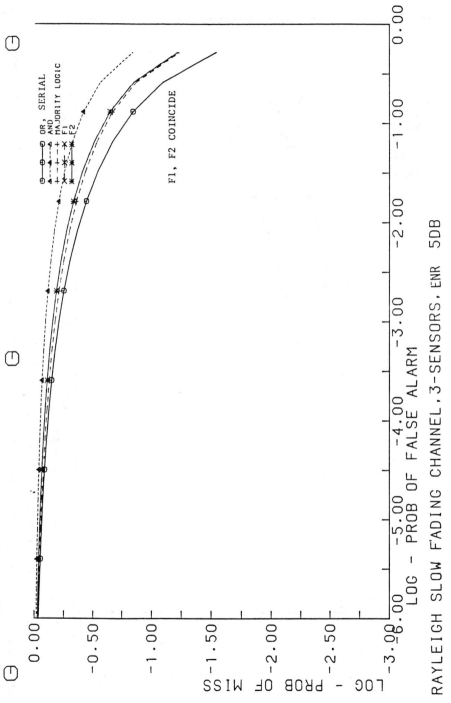

Figure 27.13. Performance of serial and parallel schemes for Rayleigh target detection with three sensors: Energy-to-noise density ratios of 5 dB.

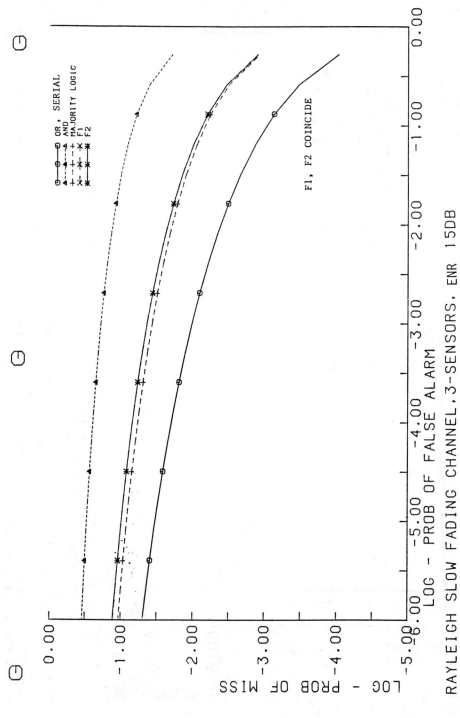

Figure 27.14. Performance of serial and parallel schemes for Rayleigh target detection with three sensors: Energy-to-noise density ratio of 10 dB.

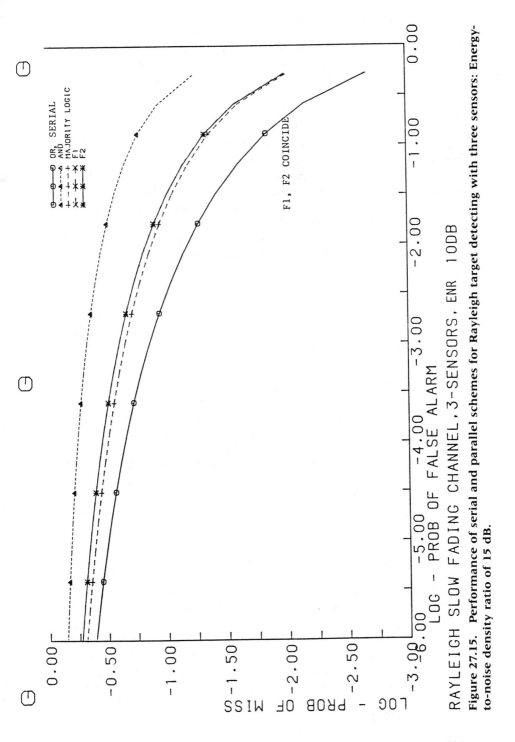

Figure 27.15. Performance of serial and parallel schemes for Rayleigh target detecting with three sensors: Energy-to-noise density ratio of 15 dB.

bility of false alarm at the fusion. Only a monotone increasing switching function, called the positive unate function (Harrison, 1965), qualifies as a candidate for the optimal fusion switching function. This can be easily proved from the requirement that the optimal scheme employs a likelihood ratio test at the fusion. One property of the monotone increasing function is that the function, when expressed as a sum of products, does not contain any complemented variables. A switching function which can be expressed as a sequence of two input and one output functions is a positive unate function and hence qualifies as a candidate for the optimal parallel fusion function. An example of one such switching function of three variables is shown in Figure 27.16, which also shows the serial scheme with three sensors.

Theorem 2 (given below) establishes a sufficient condition for the performance of the optimal serial scheme not to be inferior to the performance of the optimal parallel scheme.

Theorem 2. If the switching function corresponding to the optimal parallel fusion can be realized in terms of a sequence of two variable functions with single output, then the optimal serial scheme is better than or equal to the optimal parallel scheme.

Proof. Consider the conservative situation in which the decision variable u_1 in Figure 27.16(a) and (b) are identical and each stage of the serial scheme operates at the corresponding false alarms of the parallel scheme. (In the Appendix we show that it is possible to achieve such an operation.) The u_2 in Figure 27.16(b) is a function of u_1 and the observation Z_2. Since the mapping of (u_1, u_2) to $\hat{u}_2$ in the parallel is contained in the mapping of (u_1, Z_2) to $\hat{u}_2$ in the serial, the detection power $P_{D,2}^*$ attained at $P_{F,2}$ in the serial is greater than or equal to $P_{D,2}$. Similarly, u_0 in the parallel is a function of u_2 and u_3 only, whereas in the serial it is a function of $\hat{u}_2$ and the observation Z_3. It is observed that the $\hat{u}_2$ of the serial has the same false alarm $P_{F,2}$ of the parallel but has a greater than or equal power. For the serial case, the proof of Theorem 1 shows that the detection probability of any stage operating at a certain false alarm is a monotone nondecreasing function of the detection probability of the previous stage operating at some false alarm. It then follows that $P_{D,0}^*$ is greater than or equal to $P_{D,0}$. By induction the proof is complete for any N. Conservatively it is assumed that the false alarm at each stage of the serial is identical to the one in the parallel scheme. If the serial scheme false alarms are optimized then definitely $P_{D,0}^*$ cannot be less than $P_{D,0}$.

Optimal Serial Distributed Decision Fusion 669

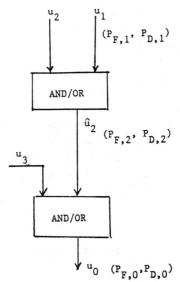

Figure 27.16(a). Example of two input and one output parallel fusion function with three sensors.

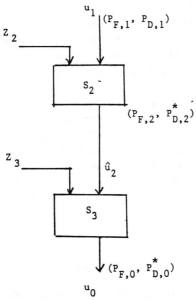

Figure 27.16(b). Serial scheme with three sensors.

From Theorem 2, we observe that for the case of two sensors, the optimal serial is better than or equal to the optimal parallel scheme. With three sensors, it is better or equal unless the optimal parallel is a majority decision logic. In such a case, only an actual performance assessment determines which is better. As mentioned earlier, in the case of Rayleigh channel with two or three sensors, the numerical results show that the optimal serial is just equivalent to OR. In this sense the Rayleigh channel can be termed conservative. Also, in Figures 27.7–27.9, over the range of false alarms where the parallel outperforms the serial, the best of the parallel is the majority decision rule. In the range where serial is better, the best of the parallel belongs to the class of Theorem 2.

5. CONCLUSION

A serial distributed network of N sensors detecting the presence or absence of a signal is analyzed. When the sensor observations conditioned on the hypothesis are statistically independent, the sensors employ the N-P test for maximizing the detection probability for a given false alarm probability at the Nth stage (Theorem 1). For certain noise distributions, the parallel structure requiring its fusion scheme to belong to a certain class of switching functions is not superior to the serial scheme (Theorem 2). As a drawback, any serial network is vulnerable to link failures. Some numerical examples illustrate the performance of the optimal serial decision scheme.

In the case of Rayleigh target detection with two and three sensors, the performances of the serial and the OR fusion rule are equal. For AWGN channel and two sensors, the serial performs better than the parallel. However, with three sensors the performance is essentially the same. It is not known whether there exists any channel, practical or hypothetical, such that the serial is better than the parallel for a distributed network with three or more sensors. Considering the complexity of the serial scheme and the results from this limited study, the choice seems to favor the parallel fusion for the distributed detection problem.

Appendix

It is shown here that any false alarm is realizable at any stage of a serial configuration. Let us denote for simplicity $P_{F,j-1}$, $P_{F,j}$, $P_{D,j-1}$, $t_{j,1}$,

$t_{j,0}$, a_j, and b_j by α, α_0, β, t_1, t_0, a, and b, respectively. Therefore, using Eqs. (2), (3), and (7)

$$\alpha_0 = (1 - \alpha)a + \alpha b$$

$$t_0 = t\frac{1 - \alpha}{1 - \beta}$$

$$t_1 = t\frac{\alpha}{\beta} \tag{A1}$$

The likelihood ratio Λ (from Eq. (3)) and hence a and b are continuous functions of t. Hence, for a fixed α, α_0 is a continuous function of t. Let the support of the distribution of Λ be between t_l and t_h ($t_l \geq 0$ and $t_h \leq \infty$). As t_0 approaches t_l, a, b, and α_0 approach 1 and as t_1 approaches t_h, a, b, and α_0 approach 0. Therefore, any α_0 in (0, 1) can be obtained.

Please note that the method employed here was suggested by a reviewer.

REFERENCES

DiFranco, J.V., & Rubin, W.L. (1968). *Radar detection*. Englewood Cliffs, NJ: Prentice-Hall.

Ekchian, L.K., & Tenney, R.R. (1982). Detection networks. *Proceedings of the 21st IEEE Conference on Decision and Control* (pp. 686–690). Orlando, FL.

Forsythe, G.E., & Malcom, M.A. (1977). *Computer methods for mathematical computations*. Englewood Cliffs, NJ: Prentice-Hall.

Harrison, M.A. (1965). *Introduction to switching and automata theory*. New York: McGraw-Hill.

Mood, A.M., Graybill, F.A., & Boes, D.C. (1974). *Introduction to the theory of statistics*. New York: McGraw-Hill.

Srinath, M.D., & Rajasekaran, P.K. (1979). *An introduction to the statistical theory of signal processing*. New York: Wiley.

Srinivasan, R. (1986). Distributed radar detection theory. *IEE Proceedings Part F, Communications, Radar and Signal Processing, 133*(1), 55–60.

Thomopoulos, S.C.A., Viswanathan, R., & Bougoulias, D.K. (1987). Optimal decision fusion in multiple sensor systems. *IEEE Transactions on Aerospace and Electronic Systems, AES-23*(5), 644–653.

Tsitsiklis, J., & Athans, M. (1985). On the complexity of distributed decision problems. *IEEE Transactions on Automatic Control, AC-30*(5), 440–446.

Van Trees, H.L. (1968). *Detection, estimation, and modulation theory* (Vol. 1). New York: Wiley.

Viswanathan, R., Thomopoulos, S.C.A., & Tumuluri, R. (1987). Serial decision in multiple sensor fusion. *Proceedings of the 21st Annual Conference on Information Sciences and Systems* (p. 124). Baltimore, MD.

Author Index

A

Abidi, M.A., 359, *371*, 548, *557*
Adam, J.A., 21, *24*
Aggarwal, J.K., 23, *26*, 121, 359, 369, *370*, *372*, *373*, *374*, 379, 393, *406*, 481, *493*
Agin, G., 408, *438*
Aguilera, R.A., 379, *405*
Ahuja, N., 468, *492*
Aida, S., 417, *439*
Aiello, N., 74, *79*
Albert, A., 268, *282*
Albus, J.S., 37, 38, 40, *44, 46, 48,* 141, *152,* 218, *238,* 408, *440,* 542, 548, *558, 560*
Ali, M., 32, *47*
Ali, S.M., 223, *238*
Allen, P.K., 23, 24, *24, 25,* 34, *44, 137, 258,* 370, *370,* 408, 426, *438*
Ajjimarangsee, P., 162, *179*
Anderegg, D., 571, *594*
Anderson, B.D.O., 630, *635*
Anderson, J.A., 32, *46*
Anderson, T.L., 446, *460*
Andress, K.M., 449, *460, 463*
Arbib, M.A., 22, *26,* 115, *119,* 122, 124, *137,* 470, *493*
Arkin, R.C., 446, *460*
Arnold, J.F., 551, *558, 561,* 612, *635*
Asada, H., 430, *439*
Asada, M., 450, *460*
Asakawa, K., 446, *464*
Athans, M., 552, *562,* 638, *645,* 648, *671*
Ayache, N., 157, *179,* 263, *282,* 359, *370, 371, 372,* 496, 507, 508, 525, 532, *537, 538*

B

Bachman, C.G., 365, *370*
Ballard, D., 359, *370*
Bajcsy, R., 23, *24, 258,* 426, *438*
Balchen, J.G., 23, *26,* 41, *44*
Bannerot, R.B., 380, *405*
Baran, R.H., 363, *370*
Barbera, A.J., 37, *44,* 218, *238*
Barhen, J., 34, *44*
Barnard, S.T., 77, *77,* 359, *370*
Barnett, J.A., 324, *324,* 329, *353*
Barniv, Y., 18, *25*
Barnes, D.P., 218, *239*
Barrouil, C., 542, 543, 544, *561*
Barrow, H., 143, *151*
Bar-Shalom, Y., 550, 551, *558, 559, 561,* 580, *594,* 598, 601, *608,* 612, 615, 616, 618, 624, *635*
Bastuscheck, C.M., 359, *371*
Bauzil, G., 453, *460*
Beer, C., 294, *306*
Beer, R.D., 446, *460*
Belknap, R., 174, *179*
Bendat, J., 286, *306*
Beni, G., 41, *44,* 98, *108*
Benning, C., 378, *405*
Benser, E.T., 362, *371*
Bentley, J.L., 147, *151*
Berry, R., 451, *460*
Besl, P., 393, *405*
Bestavros, A.A., 446, *460*
Bhanu, B., 43, *45, 46,* 83, 97, 98, 100, 101, *108,* 144, *151,* 362, *371*
Bhattacharyya, A., 223, *238,* 284, *306*
Bianchini, G.L., 40, *45,* 123, *137,* 218, *239, 259*
Biegel, J.D., 385, *406*

673

Biggers, K., 83, *109*
Binford, T.O., 426, *439,* 457, 459n, *463*
Birk, J., 208, *216*
Bixler, J.P., 451, *460*
Black, M.S., *239,* 543, *562*
Blackman, S.S., 42, *44,* 550, *558, 559,* 598, 605, 607, *608, 609*
Blahnik, C., 543, *560*
Boarnet, M., 548, *559*
Boes, D.C., 650, *671*
Bogler, P.L., 168, *179,* 603, 604, 605, *608*
Bohner, M., 378, *406*
Bolle, R.M., 263, *282,* 496, *537*
Bolles, R.C., 151, *151,* 408, *438*
Bonasso, R.P., Jr., 547, *558,* 581, *594*
Boudreau, E.J., 19, *25,* 549, *558*
Bougoulias, D.K., 549, 557, *562,* 638, 639, 643, *645,* 647, 648, *671*
Boyer, K., 218, *239*
Boyter, B.A., 359, *372*
Brady, M., 430, *439*
Brain, A., 543, *560*
Briot, M., 453, *460, 462*
Britting, K.R., 552, *558*
Broida, T.J., 550, *558*
Bromage, R.C., 592, *594*
Brooks, M., 19, *25*
Brooks, R.A., 19, 23, *25,* 243, *259,* 426, *439,* 446, 449, *461,* 469, 474, *492,* 496, *537*
Brown, C.E., 359, 365, *370, 371*
Brown, D.E., 550, *558*
Brown, R.V., 592, *594, 595*
Brown, W.M., 362, *371*
Browse, R.A., 34, *47*
Brumback, B.D., 553, *558*
Bryson, A.E., Jr., 243, *259*
Brzakovic, D., 359, *372*
Buchanan, B.G., 61, *77,* 174, *179*
Buede, D.M., 168, *179,* 552, *558*
Bukowski, M.E., 388, *405*
Bullock, T.E., 19, *25,* 549, *558*
Burge, J.W., 141, *152*
Burks, B.L., 457, *461, 465*
Burton, M., 378, *405*
Buser, R.G., 367, *373*

C

Caillas, C., 444, *463*
Cain, M.P., 363, *371*

Cain, R.A., 151, *151,* 543, *560*
Campo, L., 601, *608*
Capocaccia, G., 39, *44*
Carlson, 284, *306*
Casasent, D., 14, *25,* 378, 379, *405*
Castelaz, P.F., 363, *371*
Cernuschi-Frias, B., 359, *372*
Chair, Z., 552, *558,* 638, *645*
Chandrase karon, B., 14, *25*
Chang, K.C., 550, 551, *558, 560,* 612, 618, 624, 627, 628, *635*
Charniak, E., 59, *77*
Chatila, R.G., 243, *259,* 444, 453, *462, 463,* 496, *538*
Chatterjee, P.S., 168, *179*
Cheeseman, P., 243, *259,* 263, *282,* 496, *538,* 542, 543, 544, *561*
Chen, S., 24, *25,* 121, *137,* 163, *179,* 460, *461,* 468, 470, 475, 481, 482, 483, 484, 492, *493*
Cheng, Y., 165, *179*
Chern, C.H., 218, *239*
Chern, M.Y., 218, *238*
Chiel, H.J., 446, *460*
Chien, C., 359, *372*
Chinnis, J.O., 592, *594*
Chiu, S.L., 124, *137,* 218, *238*
Chong, C.Y., 550, 551, *558, 560,* 612, 616, 619, 627, 628, *635*
Choudry, A., 542, *559*
Clark, J.J., 155, *179,* 446, *460*
Clifford, G.E., 389, *405*
Clifford, S.P., 164, *179*
Clocksin, W.F., 61, *77*
Cohen, M.S., 592, *594*
Cohen, P., 581, *594*
Cohn-Vassen, S., 426, *439*
Coles, L.S., 451, *464*
Comparato, V.G., 547, *559*
Conte, E., 637, *645*
Cooper, D.B., 263, *282,* 359, *372,* 496, *537*
Cowen, J.D., 112, *119*
Cox, J.A., 362, *371*
Crane, R.L., 189, *216*
Cromwell, R.L., 42, *46,* 449, *463*
Crowley, J.L., 262, *282,* 447, 453, *461,* 496, *537*
Culbert, C., 548, *559*
Currie, N.C., 365, *371*

D

D'Addio, E., 637, *645*
Daily, M., 444, 455, *461*
Damasio, A., 39, *44*
Dana, M.P., 550, *559*
Darmon, C.A., 496, *537*
Davidson, J.L., 163, *180*
Davis, L.S., 303, *306,* 455, *465,* 546, *559*
Dean, T., 448, *462*
Deb, S., 550, *559, 561*
DeCurtins, J., 543, *560*
de Figueiredo, R.J.P., 548, *560, 562*
Delaney, J.R., 612, 622, *635*
Delashmit, W.H., 362, *371*
Delcroix, C.J., 359, *371*
Deley, G.W., 605, *608*
Demirbas, K., 551, *559*
Dempsey, E.P., 84, *109*
Dempster, A.P., 328, *354*
Deo, N., 229, *239*
de Saint Vincent, A.R., 453, *462*
de Saussure, G., 457, *461, 465*
Dessen, F., 41, *44*
DeWitt, D.P., 380, 383, 387, 389, *405*
Didday, R.L., 115, *119*
Didocha, R.J., 544, *559*
Di Franco, J.V., 640, *645,* 655, *671*
Donath, M., 446, *460*
Donner, M.D., 85, *108*
Dougherty, E.R., 24, *25,* 162, *180*
Dove, D.L., 455, *463*
Drazovich, R.J., 122, *137*
Dress, W.B., 34, *44, 45*
Drummond, O.E., 550, *559*
Duane, G., 161, *179,* 369, *371*
Duda, R.O., 64, 69, 77, *78,* 231, *239,* 287, *306,* 338, *354*
Duinker, W., 542, *559*
du Lac, S., 33, *46,* 113, 119, *119, 120*
Dunlay, R.T., 455, *462*
Durrant-Whyte, H.F., 24, *25,* 137, 157, 167, *179, 180,* 218, *239, 259,* 263, 266, 280, *282,* 496, *538*

E

Eaves, J.L., 365, *371*
Edelman, G.M., 115, *120*
Eggleston, P.A., 367, *371*
Einstein, J.R., 457, *465*
Ekchian, L.K., 647, 648, *671*

Elfes, A.E., 218, *239,* 448, *462*
El Nahas, M.Y., 365, *373*
Englemore, R., *259*
Erkmen, A.M., 329, *354,* 361, *374*
Erman, L.D., 75, *78*
Esterly, S.D., 33, *46,* 113, *120*
Estrada, R., 551, *558*
Everett, H.R., 451, *462*
Ezquerra, N.F., 365, *371*

F

Fai, W.S., 81, 82, *108*
Falb, P.L., 470, *493*
Farhat, N.H., 33, *45*
Farina, A., 598, *609,* 637, *645*
Faugeras, O.D., 157, *179,* 263, 273, *282,* 359, *370, 371,* 495, 496, 498, 500, 501, 507, 525, 532, *537, 538*
Faverjon, B., 263, *282,* 359, *371,* 496, 508, *537, 538*
Faux, I.D., 413, *439*
Feezell, R.R., 457, *465*
Fehling, M.R., 619, 627, 628, *635*
Feigenbaum, E.A., 61, 75, 77, *78, 79*
Felterly, D., 378, *405*
Ferrer, M., 453, *462*
Ferrier, N.J., 446, *460*
Fickas, S.F., 75, *78*
Fikes, R.E., 61, *78*
Finkel, L.H., 115, *120*
Finkel, R.A., 147, *151*
Fischler, M.A., 14, *25,* 59, 66, 72, *78,* 310, 318, *324, 325, 370,* 547, *559*
Fisher, R.B., 408, *439*
Fitzgerald, M.L., 37, *44,* 218, *238*
Fitzgerald, R.J., 599, *609*
Flachs, G., 284, 285, *306, 307*
Flick, T.E., 226, *239*
Flynn, A.M., 23, *25,* 451, *462*
Foley, J.D., 141, *151*
Forsythe, G.E., 655, *671*
Fortmann, T.E., 550, 556, *558, 559,* 580, *594,* 598, *608,* 612, 615, *635*
Fowler, C.A., 546, *559,* 564, *594*
Fowler, D.W., 388, *405*
Fox, C.S., 367, *373*
French, H.B., 362, *371*
Fostel, N.J., 218, *239*
Foster, J.L., 184, *216*
Franklin, J., 546, *559*

Friedman, J.H., 147, *151*, 303, *306*
Frisby, J.P., 178, *180*, 272, *282*
Fu, K.S., 128, *137*, 303, *306*, 329, *354*
Fukunaga, K., 226, *239*, 284, 295, *306*, *307*

G

Gantmacher, F.R., *533*, *538*
Garvey, T.D., 66n, 68, 72, 75, *78*, 310, 318, *324*, *325*, 329, *354*, 547, *559*, *592*, *594*
Gelatt, C.D., 76, *78*
Gelb, A., 268, *282*
Gelfand, J.J., 40, 43, *45*, *48*
Gelfand, S., 303, *307*
Geman, D., 164, *180*
Geman, S., 164, *180*
Gesing, W.S., 555, *559*
Giannesini, F., 128, *137*
Giardina, C.R., 24, *25*, 162, *180*
Ginsberg, I.W., 392, *406*
Giralt, G., 444, 453, *462*
Glanz, F.H., 542, *561*
Glicksman, J., 450, *463*
Goel, A., 14, *25*
Goldfarb, L., 131, *138*
Goldwasser, S.M., 218, *239*
Gonzalez, R.C., 546, 548, *557*, *562*
Goodman, I.R., 580, *595*
Gossard, W.H., 592, *595*
Goto, Y., 444, 456, *462*
Graf, D.H., 33, *45*
Graham, O., 548, *560*
Grandjean, P., 453, *462*
Graybill, F.A., 650, *671*
Greenwood, D., *595*
Gremban, K.D., 444, 455, *463*, *465*
Grettenberg, T.L., 223, *239*
Grimson, W.E.L., 42, *45*, 361, *371*, 408, *439*
Grinaker, S., 378, *406*
Groen, F.C.A., 541, 545, *559*, *560*
Grossberg, S., 115, *120*
Grupen, R., 34, *45*
Guez, A., 552, *560*
Gustafson, D.E., 303, *307*
Gutfinger, D., 367, *373*
Guyote, M.F., 543, *560*

H

Haar, R., 141, *152*, 408, *440*
Hackett, J.K., 23, *25*, 359, *371*

Hackwood, S., 41, *44*, 98, *108*
Hager, G.D., 41, *45*
Hall, D.K., 184, *216*
Hall, E., 451, *460*
Hamel, W.R., 457, *461*, *464*
Handelman, D.A., 40, *45*
Hannah, M.J., 408, *438*
Hannon, S.M., 367, *371*
Hansen, A.R., 75, *78*
Hansen, C., 43, *45*, *46*, *108*, 359, *372*
Hanson, A.R., 174, *179*, *180*
Hanusa, H., 141, *152*
Haralick, R., 408, *440*
Hardy, N.W., 218, *239*
Harmon, L., 417, *439*
Harmon, S.Y., 39, 40, *45*, 123, *137*, 218, *239*, *259*, 443, 444, 445, 451, 453, 454, *462*, *463*
Harris, J., 444, 455, *461*
Harrison, M.A., 643, *645*, 668, *671*
Harrison, M.C., 165, *180*
Hart, P.E., 61, 64, 69, *77*, *78*, 231, *239*, 287, *306*, 338, *354*
Hartline, P.H., 21, *26*
Hartnett, J.R., 389, *406*
Hartson, C.T., 32, *47*
Hashimoto, M., 243, 246, *259*
Hata, S., 542, *561*
Hayes-Roth, F., 141, *152*
Haynes, L.S., 37, *44*
Hebert, M., 444, *463*, 496, 500, 501, *538*
Heer, E., 457, *465*
Henderson, T.C., 22, 24, *25*, 34, 36, 43, *45*, *46*, *47*, 81, 82, 90, 91, 92, 93, *108*, *109*, 122, *137*, 144, 148, *151*, *152*
Henkind, S.J., 165, *180*
Hertzberger, L.O., 542, *559*
Hestenes, M.R., 639, *645*
Hester, C.F., 379, *405*
Hewes, R.P., 542, *560*, *561*
Hg, W.W., 385, *405*
Hilbert, D., 426, *439*
Hildreth, E., 359, *372*, 416, *439*
Hillis, D., 143, *152*
Hillis, W.D., 21, *25*, 408, 417, *439*
Himayat, N., 40, *46*
Hinderer, J., 378, *405*
Hinton, G.E., 32, 33, *45*, *46*, *48*
Ho, Y.C., 243, *259*
Hodges, D.A., 451, *464*

Holm, W.A., 14, *25*
Hong, L., 359, *372*
Hong, T.H., 39, *46*, 444, *464*
Hoogerwerf, A.C., 23, *26*, 32, *47*
Hopfield, J.J., 33, *46*
Horaud, P., 408, *438*
Horn, B.K.P., 200, 208, *216*, 359, *372*, 392, *405*
Hornak, L.A., 41, *44*, 98, *108*
Hoschette, J.A., 366, *372*
Housewright, K., 612, *635*
Hovanessian, S.A., 41, *46*, 366, *372*
Howard, I.P., 20, *25*
Howarth, M.P., 543, *560*
Howell, J.R., 380, 383, *405, 406*
Hsia, J.J., 392, *406*
Hsiao, M., 18, *25*
Hu, H., 157, *180*
Hu, M.K., 427, *439*
Huber, P.J., 18, *25*
Hudimoto, H., 223, *239*
Hummel, R.A., 76, *78*
Hung, Y.P., 359, *372*
Huntsberber, T.L., 168, *179*
Huntsberger, T.L., 162, 168, 173, *179, 180*
Hutchinson, S.A., 42, *46*
Hvedstrup-Jensen, G., 378, *406*
Hwang, J.N., 32, *47*

I
Ikeuchi, K., 41, *46*, 392, *405*
Ikonomopoulos, A., 542, 545, *560*
Incropera, F.P., 380, 383, 387, 389, *405*
Ishizuka, M., 329, *354*
Isik, C., 450, *463*
Iverson, D.E., 550, *560*

J
Jackel, J.L., 41, *44*, 98, *108*
Jacobson, S., 83, *109*
Jaffer, A., 616, *635*
Jain, R., 123, *138*, 393, *405*
Jakubowicz, O.G., 19, *25*, 33, *46*
Jarem, J.M., 385, *405*
Jayaramamurthy, S.N., 173, *180*
Jaynes, E.T., 65, *78*
Jazwinsky, A.M., 496, 532, *538*
Johnson, C.P., 387, *406*
Johnson, D., 40, *46*
Johnston, E., 421, *440*

Jones, J.P., 457, *461*
Jordan, J., 284, 285, *306, 307*
Jorgensen, C.C., 34, *44*, 449, *463*

K
Kabrisky, M., 368, *373, 374*
Kadota, T.T., 223, *239*
Kahn, G., 90, *109*
Kailath, T., 223, *239*, 284, *307*
Kak, A.C., 24, *25*, 42, *46*, 121, *137*, 218, *239*, 449, *460, 463*
Kalman, R.E., 470, *493*
Kam, M., 552, *560*
Kamat, S.J., 174, *180*
Kanade, T., 41, *46*, 408, *440*, 444, 451, *463, 465*
Kanoui, H., 128, *137*
Kashyap, R.L., 165, *179*
Kassis, S.Y., 362, *372*
Kay, M.G., 23, *26*, 443, *464*
Keirsey, D., 444, 455, *461*
Keller, J.M., 168, *180*
Keller, R.M., 88, 90, *109*
Kelley, R.B., 208, *216*, 545, *560*
Keng, J., 378, *405*
Kent, E.W., 37, 39, *46, 48*
Kessener, R., 141, *152*
Kessenere, R., 84, *109*
Kim, J.H., 378, *406*
Kim, Y.C., 393, *406*
Kingslake, R., 208, *216*
Kinoshita, G., 417, *439*
Kirkpatrick, S., 76, *78*
Kirmani, S., 284, *307*
Kjell, B.P., 21, *25*
Klass, P.J., 546, *560*
Klein, L.A., 362, *372*
Klema, V.C., 249, *259*
Knudson, E.I., 33, *46*, 113, 119, *119, 120*
Knutti, D.F., 83, *109*
Kobayashi, H., *239*
Kohl, C.A., 367, *371*
Kohonen, T., 32, 33, *46*
Komen, E.R., 541, 545, *559*
Konishi, M.J., 113, *120*
Koral, R.L., 387, 388, *406*
Kosaka, M., 580, *595*
Kraft, L.G., III., 542, *561*
Kremers, J.H., 543, *560*
Kriegman, D.J., 457, 459n, *463*
Krihe, T.F., 284, *307*

Author Index

Krishen, K., 548, *560, 562*
Krotkov, E., 444, *463*
Kuhlmann, H., 141,*152*
Kullback, S., 223, *239*
Kumar, M., 388, *406*
Kung, S.Y., 32, *47*
Kuperstein, M., 115, *120*
Kushner, T.R., 455, *465*
Kweon, I.S., 444, *463*
Krzysztofowicz, R., 550, 552, *560*

L

Labonski, P., 552, *560*
Laganiere, R., 36, *47*
La Jeunesse, T.J., 122, *137*, 184, *216*
LaLonde, W.R., 33, *45*
Landa, J., 164, *180*
Lane, S.H., 40, *45*
Laub, A.T., 249, *259*
Lauber, A., 23, *26*
Laumond, J.P., 243, *259*, 453, *461*, 496, *538*
Lawton, D.T., 450, *463*
Lee, D.A., 189, *216*
Lee, I., 218, *239*
Lee, J.S.J., 162, *180*
Lee, M.H., 218, *239*
Lee, R.H., 18, *26*
Le Moigne, J.J., 455, *465*
Levi, P., 443, *463*
Levitt, T.S., 450, *463*
Liang, E., 455, *465*
Limperis, T., 392, *406*
Lin, M., 359, *372*
Lin, Y.J., 378, *406*
Linden, T.A., 455, *463*
Linsenmayer, G.R., 592, *595*
Loebbaka, K., 451, *460*
London, P.E., 75, *78*
Long, D., 550, 552, *560*
Longo, M., 637, *645*
Lowe, D., 504, *538*
Lowerre, B.T., 75, *78*
Lowrance, J.D., 66n, 68, 72, 75, *78*, 320, 321, *325*, 329, *354*
Lowrie, J.M., 455, *463*
Lozano-Pérez, T., 361, *371*, 408, *439*, 469, 474, *492*
Lu, S.Y., 329, *354*
Lumia, R., 39, *48*, 548, *560*

Luo, R.C., 23, *26*, 43, *47*, 359, 360, *372*, 443, *464*, 543, *560*
Lustman, F., 359, *372*, 500, *538*
Lyons, D.M., 22, *26*, 122, 124, *137*
Lyons, D.W., 544, *559*

M

MacQueen, D., 90, *109*
Magee, M.J., 359, *370*, *372*
Mahaffey, F.K., 571, *595*
Malcolm, C., 545, *560*
Malcom, M.A., 655, *671*
Manges, W.W., 457, *465*
Mann, R.C., *26*, 457, *464*
Mansbach, P., 37, 39, *48*
Marce, L., 444, *464*
Marchette, D.J., 34, *47*
Maren, A.J., 32, *47*
Marr, D., 143, *152*, 416, *439*
Marra, M., 444, *465*
Marsh, J.P., 455, *463*
Marsh, K.A., 206, *216*
Martin, J.F., 124, *137*, 206, *216*, 218, 238, *239*, 543, *562*
Martin, W.N., 481, *493*, 550, *558*
Matlock, H., 387, *406*
Matsusita, K., 223, *239*, 284, *307*
Matthies, L., 253, *259*
Maybeck, P.S., 18, 19, *26*, 157, *180*, 552, 554, *561*
Mayersak, J.R., 547, *561*
Mayhew, J.E.W., 178, *180*, 263, 272, *282*
McCain, H.G., 37, *47*
McClelland, J.L., 32, *47*
McConnell, C., 450, *463*
McDermott, D., 59, *77*
McKendall, R., 160, *180*
Meisel, W.S., 303, *307*
Mellish, C.S., 61, *77*
Mendelson, E., 59, *79*
Mesegner, J., 543, *560*
Meystel, A., 448, 450, *463*, *464*, *465*
Michalopoulos, D.A., 303, *307*
Michener, J.C., 84, *109*, 141, *152*
Middelhoek, S., 23, *26*, 32, *47*
Miller, D.P., 451, *460*, *464*
Miller, J., 451, *464*
Miller, W.T., III, 542, *560*, *561*
Mills, J.P., 368, *373*, *374*
Miltonberger, T., 36, *47*

Minsky, M.L., 32, *47*
Minsky, V., 32, *47*
Mintz, M., 160, *180*
Mitiche, A., 23, *25*, *26*, 36, 43, *46*, *47*, 121, *137*
Mitter, S.K., 303, *307*
Mitzel, J.H., 364, *372*
Mochizuki, J., 542, *561*
Moezzi, S., 359, *373*
Mohri, A., 417, *439*
Moiseff, A., 113, *120*
Mood, A.M., 650, *671*
Moore, D.S., 62, *79*
Moore, J.B., 630, *635*
Moore, R.C., 62, *79*
Moran, T.J., 189, *216*
Moravec, H.P., 218, *239*, 451, *464*, *465*
Morawski, P., 546, *559*
Morefield, C.L., 612, *635*
Moregan, A., *259*
Morgan, D., 36, *47*
Morgenthaler, D.G., 444, *465*
Mori, M., 417, *439*
Mori, S., 551, *558*, 612, 619, 627, 628, *635*
Moriarty, J.D., 408, *440*
Morley, D.J., 124, *137*, 218, *238*
Morrison, D.F., 268, *282*
Morse, J.B., 363, *371*
Mucci, R.A., 551, *558*, *561*, 612, *635*
Mulgaonkar, P., 408, *440*
Muller, R.E., Jr., 543, *560*

N

Nagalia, S., 141, *152*, 408, *440*
Nagata, S., 446, *464*
Nahin, P.J., 550, *561*, 581, *595*, 603, *609*
Naim, A., 552, *560*
Nandhakumar, N., 369, *373*, 378, *406*
Nash, C., 468, *492*
Nashman, M., 37, *48*
Nasrabadi, N.M., 164, *179*
Nelson, W.R., 83, *109*
Nesbit, R.F., 546, *559*, 564, *594*
Nettleson, J.E., 367, *373*
Nevatia, R., 426, *439*
Newman, E.A., 21, *26*
Nicodemus, F.E., 392, *406*
Nii, H.P., 74, 75, *79*, *259*
Nii, P.H., 122, *137*

Nilsson, N.J., 60, 61, 71, *78*, 338, *354*, 451, *464*
Nitzan, D., 408, *439*, 542, 543, 544, *561*, *562*
Noreils, F.R., 453, *464*

O

Ohman, C., 385, *406*
Ohta, Y., 132, *137*
Olin, K.E., 378, *406*, 444, 455, *461*
Olsen, D.R., 84, *109*
Orr, G., 36, *47*
Oshima, M., 408, *439*
Oskard, D.N., 444, *464*
Ostevold, E., 378, *406*
Overton, K.J., 408, 417, *439*
Ozaki, H., 417, *439*

P

Paek, E., 33, *45*
Palombo, L., 37, *48*
Panangaden, P., 81, 91, 92, 93, *109*
Pap, R.M., 32, *47*
Papert, S.A., 32, *47*
Papoulis, A., 285, *307*
Pasero, R., 128, *137*
Pattipati, K.R., 550, *559*, *561*
Pau, L.F., 123, 132, 133, *137*, 358, 365, *373*
Paul, R.P., 243, 246, *259*
Pauly, J., 378, *405*
Pavilidis, T., 143, *152*, 164, *180*
Payne, B., 571, *594*
Payton, D.W., 378, *406*, 444, 446, 455, 456, *461*, *464*
Pearce, J.A., 384, *406*
Pearl, J., 36, *47*
Pearson, J.C., 43, *48*, 115, *120*
Pellionisz, A.J., 32, *47*
Penna, M., 475, 481, 482, *493*
Peppers, N., 543, *560*
Peterson, R.M., 43, *48*
Petriu, E.M., 545, *560*
Pfaff, G., 84, *109*, 141, *152*
Pierluissi, J.H., 385, *405*
Piersol, A., 286, *306*
Pietsch, R., 19, *25*
Pin, F.G., 457, *465*
Pinz, B.E., 40, *45*, 123, *137*, 218, *239*, *259*
Pittard, C.L., 550, *558*

Pokoski, J.L., 550, *561*, 581, *595*, 603, *609*
Pollard, S.B., 178, *180*, 263, 276, *282*
Ponce, J., 430, *439*
Popoli, R., 607, *609*
Porrill, J., 178, *180*, 263, 272, *282*
Porter, A.L., 543, *561*
Potmesil, M., 413, 414, *439*
Prade, H., 329, *354*
Prata, A., 33, *45*
Pratt, M.J., 413, *439*
Pridmore, T.P., 178, *180*, 272, *282*
Priebe, C.E., 34, *47*
Psaltis, D., 33, *45*

R
Raczkowsky, J., 544, *561*
Raibert, M., 143, *152*
Rajasekaran, P.K., 653, *671*
Randell, B., 92, 93, *109*
Rao, A.R., 122, *138*
Rao, B.Y.S., 157, *180*
Rauch, H.E., 581, *595*
Ray, R., 208, *216*
Reboh, R., 69, *78*
Reedy, E.K., 366, 365, *371, 373*
Regazzoni, C.S., 39, *44*
Reid, D.B., 555, *559*, 599, *609*, 612, *635*
Reiser, K., 444, 455, *461*
Rembold, U., 544, 545, *561*
Repko, M.C., 545, *560*
Reynolds, S., 40, *46*
Ribes, P., 453, *460*
Richardson, J.M., 206, *216*
Richmond, J.C., 392, *406*
Rigaud, V., 444, *464*
Riseman, E.M., 75, *78*, 174, *179, 180*
Ritter, G.X., 163, *180*
Robb, A.M., 451, *464*
Roberts, B.A., 449, *463*
Rock, I., 412, *439*
Rodger, J.C., 34, *47*
Rodrigues, O., 534, *538*
Rogers, S.K., 368, *373, 374*
Roggemann, M.C., 368, *373*
Rohde, R.S., 367, *373*
Rojder, P., 23, *26*
Rosenblatt, J.K., 444, 446, 455, *461, 464*
Rosenfeld, A., 421, *440*
Rosenthal, D.S., 84, *109*, 141, *152*
Roshenaw, W.M., 389, *406*

Rossini, F.A., 543, *561*
Rubin, W.L., 640, *645*, 655, *671*
Rumelhart, D.E., 32, 33, *47, 48*
Ruokangas, C.C., *239*, 543, 544, *562*
Rurkowski, W., 37, *48*
Ruspini, E.H., 581, *595*
Ryu, Z.M., 384, *406*

S
Sabin, M., 84, *109*, 141, *152*
Sadjadi, F.A., 638, *645*
Safranek, R.J., 218, *239*
Samet, H., 468, *493*
Sandell, N.R., Jr., 552, *562*, 637, *645*
Sanderson, A.C., 218, *239*
Sangsuk-iam, S., 19, *25*
Savely, R.T., 548, *559*
Scheff, K., 164, *180*
Scheffe, M., 556, *559*, 580, *594*, 612, *635*
Schoenwald, J.S., 206, *216, 239*, 543, *562*
Schott, J.R., 385, *406*
Sea, R.G., 612, *635*
Seashore, C.R., 366, *372, 373*
Sekiguchi, M., 446, *464*
Selzer, F., 367, *373*
Serra, J., 132, *138*
Sevigny, L., 378, 379, *406*
Shafer, G., 66, *79*, 167, *180*, 309, 311, 312, *325*, 328, 329, 330, 333, *354*, 581, *595*
Shafer, S.A., 253, 255, *259*, 456, *464*
Shaffer, C.A., 444, *464*
Shah, M., 23, *25*, 359, *371*
Shapiro, J.H., 367, *371*
Shapiro, L., 408, *440*
Sharp, D.H., 112, *119*
Shaw, S.W., 40, *46*, 548, *562*
Shepp, L.A., 223, *239*
Shilcrat, E., 81, 91, 92, 93, *108, 109*
Shirai, Y., 408, *439*
Shneier, M.O., 37, 39, *46, 48*, 141, *152*, 408, *440*
Shortliffe, E.E., 69, *79*
Shortliffe, E.H., 174, *179, 354*
Shumaker, R., 546, *559*
Siddalingaiah, 455, *465*
Siegel, R., 383, *406*
Sikka, D.I., 40, *48*
Silvey, S.D., 223, *238*
Sinclair, P.L., 451, *464*
Singer, R.A., 612, *635*

Sjoberg, R.W., 392, *405*
Slagle, J.R., 592, *595*
Smirnov, V., 284, *307*
Smith, M.H., 451, *464*
Smith, R.C., 243, *259*, 263, *282*, 496, *538*, 542, 543, 544, *561, 562*
Smith, R.G., 142, *152*
Smithers, T., 545, *560*
Snyder, W., 24, *25, 137*
Sobek, R., 451, 453, *462, 464*
Sood, D., 545, *560*
Spence, C.D., 43, *48*
Speyer, J.L., 556, *562*, 612, *635*
Srinath, M.D., 553, *558*, 653, *671*
Srinivasan, B., 455, *465*, 647, 648, 655, *671*
Srinivasan, R., 638, 640, 644, *645*
Stallard, D.V., 602, *609*
Stamper, E., 388, *406*
Stansfield, S.A., 360, 361, *374*
Starkey, R.J., Jr., 570, *595*
Stasz, C., 141, *152*
Stauffer, R.N., 23, *26*
Stentz, A., 255, *259*, 444, 451, 456, *462, 464, 465*
Stephanou, H.E., 329, *354*, 361, *374*
Sterling, L.S., 446, *460*
Stewart, S.A., 363, *371*
Stone, N.L., 570, *595*
Strat, T.M., 68, *78*, 592, *594*
Stroch, C., 387, *406*
Studer, F.A., 598, *608*
Stuelpnagel, J., 501, *538*
Sunshine, C., 141, *152*
Suzuki, Y., 223, *239*
Swerling, P., 63, *79*
Swonger, C.W., 362, *371*
Swyt, D.A., 37, *48*

T

Tahani, H., 168, *180*
Takahashi, M., 542, *561*
Takata, M., 417, *439*
Talou, J.C., 453, *460, 462*
Tanner, R., 143, *152*
Tatman, J.A., 368, *373*
Taylor, G.E., 42, *48*
Taylor, J.W.R., 586, *595*
Taylor, P.M., 42, *48*
Teneketzis, D., 638, *645*
Tennenbaum, J., 143, *151*

Tenney, R.R., 552, *562*, 612, 622, *635*, 637, *645*, 647, 648, *671*
Thepchatri, T., 387, 389, *406*
Therrien, C.W., 24, *26*
Thomas, M., 455, *463*
Thomopoulos, S.C.A., 35, *48*, 557, *562*, 638, 639, 640, 642, 643, *645*, 647, 648, 651, *671*
Thompson, D.H., 457, *465*
Thompson, J.C., 544, *559*
Thorpe, C.E., 255, *259*, 451, 456, *464, 465*
Tikheyeva, A., 284, *307*
Toet, A., 369, *374*
Tomita, F., 408, *440*
Tong, C.W., 368, *373, 374*
Toscani, G., 496, 498, *537, 538*
Tou, J.T., 23, *26*, 41, *48*, 546, *562*
Toussaint, G., 284, *307*
Triendl, E., 148, *152*, 457, 459n, *463*
Trunk, G.V., 600, *609*
Tsai, W., 360, *372*
Tse, E., 612, 615, 616, *635*
Tseng, D., 444, 455, *461*
Tsitsiklis, J.N., 552, *562*, 638, *645*, 648, *671*
Tucker, R.L., 388, *405*
Tuijnman, F., 542, *559*
Tumuluri, R., 651, *671*
Turk, M.A., 444, 455, *463, 465*
Turner, R., 62, *79*

U

Ullman, S., 486, *493*
Ulvila, J.W., 592, *594, 595*

V

Vaisset, M., 444, 453, *462*
Valeton, J.M., 369, *374*
Van Dam, A., 141, *151*
van Ruyven, L.J., 369, *374*
Van Trees, H.L., 287, *307*, 640, *646*, 653, 654, *671*
Van Vleet, W.B., 18, *26*
Varaiya, P., 638, *645*
Varshney, P.K., 40, *48*, 552, *558*, 638, *645*
Vecchi, M.P., 76, *78*
Vernazza, G., 39, *44*
Viswanathan, R., 557, *562*, 638, 639, 643, *645*, 647, 648, 651, *671*
Vreeburg, M.A.C., 541, 545, *559, 560*

W

Waku, S., 419, *439*
Waldron, S., 448, *465*
Wallace, R., 451, *465*
Waltz, E.L., 552, *558*, 576, *595*
Wang, P.Y., 21, *25*
Wang, Y.F., 359, *374*
Wanner, E., 592, *595*
Warmerdam, T.P.H., 541, 545, *559, 560*
Washburn, R.B., 550, *559, 561*
Waxman, 455, *465*
Wechsler, H., 33, *48*
Weisbin, C.R., 457, *461, 464, 465*
Weitz, E., 34, 43, *45, 46*
Wesley, L.P., 75, *79*
Wesson, R., 141, *152*
Westphal, C., 123, *137*
Weymouth, T.E., 359, *373*
Wheatley, T., 37, *48*
Whittaker, W., 451, *465*
Wilkins, D.E., 61, *79*
Williams, R.J., 33, *48*
Williams, T.D., 174, *180*
Wilson, J.D., 600, *609*
Wilson, J.N., 163, *180*
Wirth, N., 83, *109*
Wise, K.D., 23, *26*
Wishner, R.P., 619, 627, 628, *635*

Wohl, J.G., 565, 568, *595*
Wohl, R., 570, *595*
Wolberg, G., 164, *180*
Wong, A.K.C., 131, *138*
Wong, V., 444, 455, *461*
Wood, J.E., 83, *109*
Woodham, R.J., 392, *406*
Wright, J.D., 96, *109*
Wright, W.A., 164, *180*

X

Xiao, S., 123, *137*

Y

Yager, R.R., 329, *354*
Yang, H.S., 218, *239*
Yao, J.P.T., 329, *354*
Yen, J., 168, *180*
York, B., 413, *440*
Yuille, A.L., 155, *179*, 430, *439*

Z

Zadeh, L.A., 167, 173, *180*
Zeytinoglu, M., 160, *180*
Zhang, L., 639, *645*
Zheng, Y.F., 42, *48*
Zimmerman, G.L., 33, *48*
Zucker, S.W., 76, *78*

Subject Index

A

Adaptive learning, 40
AGE knowledge base development system, 74
Alpha-beta search, 71
ANALYST, expert system, 547
Animal behavior paradigm, 445
Artificial intelligence, 22, 49, 363, 379, 450, 546, 598, 608
Assembly, industrial, 545
Associative memory, 33, 449
Automatic guided vehicles, 443
Automatic target recognition (ATR), 12–14, 362–369
Autonomous land vehicle, DARPA, 455, 546

B

Barn owl, 111
Battle management systems (see Command and control)
Bayes's rule, 64, 165, 603
Bayesian estimation
  command and control, 581
  formalism, 165–167
  inference, 241, 243, 253, 309
  multi-Bayesian approach, 167
  networks, 35
  pixel-level fusion, 161
  target detection, 603
  target tracking, 612
Behavioral schemata, 446
Blackboard architecture, 49, 74, 122
  distributed, 4, 39, 123
  object-oriented, 39
  use on mobile robot, 454
Brain organization, 112
Bryson–Frazier smoother, modified, 555

C

Calibration, 19, 262, 269
  camera, 393
  error, 249, 276
  stereo, 498
Cerebellar Model Articulation Controller (CMAC), 40
Certainty factor, 174 (see also Production rules)
CODGER, 123
Command and control, 546, 563–594
  antisubmarine warfare, 569
  architectures, 576–584, 587–594
  decision support, 564–566
  landbattle battlefield warfare, 571
  multisensor fusion, 563, 567, 584–586
  tactical air warfare, 570
  type of sensor information, 572–576
Complementary information (see Information)
Conductivity measure, 361
Confidence distance measure, 227
Connection machine, 21
Consensus, measuring sensor (see Generalized entropy criterion)
Convection heat transfer, 386
Coon's surface patch (see Representations)
Correspondence (see Registration)
Cueing, 6, 50, 73, 298–302, 416, 584
  interaural intensity, 113

D

DARPA's Strategic Computing Program, 546
Data abstraction, benefits of, 83
Data association, 18, 549, 578–580, 598–601

central- vs. sensor-level tracking, 600
Joint Probabilistic Data Association
   algorithm, 611–631
metrics for, 578
nearest-neighbor vs. all-neighbors, 598
sequential vs. deferred, 599
Data fusion (see Multisensor fusion)
Decision
   fusion (see Target detection and tracking)
   networks, 36
   rule, 581
   tree, 360
Decision-level fusion (see Multisensor fusion, symbol-level fusion)
Dempster's rule of combination, 67, 312–316, 327, 333, 583, 605
Dempster–Shafer evidential reasoning, 66, 167–173, 309–325, 327–334, 449, 581–583, 604
Differential geometry, 430
Disparity space, 271
Distance
   Bhattacharyya, 223, 284
   J-divergence, 223, 284
   Kolmogorov's variational, 284, 290
   Kolmogorov–Smirnov, 283, 290
   Mahalanobis, 295
   Matsusita, 223, 284
Distributed blackboard (see Blackboard architecture)
Distributed sensor systems, 550, 557, 605
   data association, 611–634
   optimal fusion for parallel topology, 637–644
   optimal fusion for serial topology, 647–670
   parallel vs. serial topology, 557, 655–670

E

ϵ-contamination, 160, 167, 266
Electro-optical sensors, 365, 368
EMYCIN expert system, 174
Entropy (see Generalized entropy criterion)
ESPRIT program, 542, 544
Evidential propositional calculus, 309–325
Evidential reasoning (see Dempster–Shafer evidential reasoning)

Expert systems, 174, 328, 363, 547, 580, 589, 598, 607
Extended Kalman filter (see Kalman filter)

F

Fault tolerance, 92–96, 112
Feature selection, 146
Feature space mapping, 283–306
Feature-level fusion (see Multisensor fusion)
Fiducial points, 395
Forward-looking infrared (FLIR), 365, 367
Fourier descriptors, 475
Frames, 61
Function equation language, 91
Fusion (see Multisensor fusion)
Fuzzy set, 608

G

Gauss–Markov estimation, 262, 267–269
Gaussian curvature, 424, 426, 430, 434
Generalized entropy criterion, 327–353
Generalized evidence processing, 35
GEOMSTAT, 261, 273
Gibbs distribution, 164
GISTER, 68
Graph representations (see Representations)
Graphics Kernel System, 84
Grid representations (see Representations)
Guiding (see Cueing)

H

Heat flux, 379, 385–391
HERMIES, mobile robot, 457
Hierarchical Phase-Template paradigm (see Multisensor integration)
Highly redundant sensing, 23
HILARE, mobile robot, 156, 453

I

IDEF diagram, 587–591
Image algebra, 163
Industrial trucks, 542
Inertial navigation, 552
Inference, 49, 598
   backward-chaining, 70, 174, 583, 587, 589
   Bayesian (see Bayesian estimation)
   forward-chaining, 70, 174, 583

Subject Index 685

logical, 59–62
probabilistic, 64 (*see also* Bayesian estimation)
Inferential information-integration module, 54
Inferior colliculus, 111
Information
  complementary, 14, 408
  entropy 9 (*see* Generalized entropy criterion)
  less costly, 15
  more timely, 15
  redundant, 14, 159
Infrared
  images, 376
  sensors, 365
Inspection, industrial, 544
  integrated circuit, 132

J

Joint Probabilistic Data Association algorithm (*see* Data association)

K

Kalman filter, 157–160, 243, 253, 262, 457, 553, 601, 607
  adaptive, 157
  extended, 157, 359, 495, 506–508, 532
  fixed-coefficient filters, 601
  measurement model, 158, 497, 532
  state–space model, 157, 506
kd-tree, 147
Kirchhoff approximation, 203

L

Lagrange multipliers, 638
Lambert's law, 203, 474
Lambertian surface, 392, 400
Laser radar (LADAR), 298–302, 365, 367
Likelihood-ratio test, 637–644
Location data, 160
Logic
  Boolean, 309, 311
  fuzzy, 173, 450
  modal, 62
  nonmonotonic, 62
  propositional, 59
  temporal, 62
Logical behaviors, 34
Logical filters, 161
Logical sensor, 4, 85–92, 139, 141, 242
  automatic generation, 98–101
  definition, 85
  fault tolerance, 92–96
  formal aspects, 87
  network, 94
  specification language, 88–92, 101
  specification system, 81, 92, 102–108

M

Maps (*see also* World model)
  acoustic map, 112
  Cartesian elevation, 456
  computational, 113
  neuronal, 111
  self-organizing, 33
  visual, 112, 495
Markov random field, 9, 161, 164
Marr–Hildreth edge operator, 416
Matching (*see* Registration, stereo)
Material handling, industrial, 542
Mathematical morphology, 162
Maximum entropy principal, 65
Microwave radar, 548
Millimeter-wave (MMW) radar, 365
Mobile robots, multisensor-based, 443–460
  control strategies, 444–446
  high-level representations, 447–450
  role of perception, 444
  selected examples, 451–459
  "walk-around" algorithm, 488–492
Modus ponens, 51, 59
Moment invariants, 360, 427
Moore–Penrose pseudoinverse, 268
Multilayer Perception, 32
Multisensor fusion, 3, 121, 155, 184, 242, 479–487, 563, 597
  acoustical and optical data, 200–216
  advantages, 189–191, 379, 550, 567, 572–576
  attribute fusion, 129–132
  Bayesian estimation, symbol-level fusion using (*see* Bayesian estimation)
  binocular fusion, 10
  consensus, measuring (*see* Generalized entropy criterion)
  Dempster–Shafer evidential reasoning, symbol-level fusion using (*see* Dempster–Shafer evidential reasoning)

686 Subject Index

dynamic, 468, 484–487
feature-level fusion, 7, 10, 357, 283–306, 506–525, 551, 572, 578–580
geometrical methods, 250–255, 261–281
Kalman filter, signal-level fusion using (*see* Kalman filter)
neuronal mechanism, 115–117
pixel-level fusion, 7, 9, 160–164, 357, 362, 368
problems, 481
production rules, symbol-level fusion using (*see* Production rules)
reduction in uncertainty, 457
registration (*see* Registration)
signal-level fusion, 7, 9, 156–160, 222–234, 357, 362, 550, 553
signals-to-symbols phenomenon, 14, 56
static, 468, 482–484
stereo vision, 245, 271–273
symbol-level fusion, 7, 11, 164–177, 309–325, 358, 362, 551
thermal and vision, 375–405, 483
vision and acoustic, 113
vision and tactile, 234–238
weighted average, signal-level fusion using, 156
weighted least squares, 243
Multisensor integration, 3, 29–48
adaptability, 4, 29
blackboard architecture, control using (*see* Blackboard architecture)
control structures, 35–40, 69–77
cueing (*see* Cueing)
Hierarchical Phase-Template paradigm, 30, 218–220
hierarchical structures, 4, 29, 113, 124–129
guiding (*see* Cueing)
logical sensors (*see* Logical sensors)
modularity, 4, 29, 113, 174, 192–199
NBS sensory and control hierarchy, 4, 37–39, 545, 548
paradigms and frameworks, 30–35, 408
problems, 193
sensor management, 584
sensor selection strategies, 40–42
vision and touch, 407–438
Multisensor integration and fusion
advantages, 14–17, 550, 567, 572–576

biological examples, 19–21, 111–119, 162
future research directions, 21–23
generic models, 4–7, 54–58
is more always better?, 550
industrial applications, 541–545
information provided by (*see* Information)
military applications, 545–548, 563–594
mobile robots, multisensor-based (*see* Mobile robots)
problems, 17–19, 408
space applications, 548
surveys and reviews, 23
Multisensor Kernel System (MKS), 82, 139–151, 242
MYCIN expert system, 69, 329

N

National Bureau of Standards (*see* NBS sensory and control hierarchy
National Institute of Standards and Technology (*see* NBS sensory and control hierarchy)
NAVLAB, mobile robot, 456
NBS sensory and control hierarchy (*see* Multisensor integration)
Neural networks, 22, 32–34, 111, 363–365, 449
Neurobotics, 32
Neyman–Pearson test, 637–644, 647–670
Nucleus laminaris, 113
Nusselt number, 387

O

Object apprehension, 360
Object recognition, 357–370, 407–438
military applications, 546
Object surface radiosity, 381
Object-oriented programming paradigm, 4, 34
Octree (*see* Representations)
Optic tectum, 112, 162
Optical flow, 359
OWL language, 85

P

Part fabrication, industrial, 543
Pattern recognition, 130, 602
Perceptual reasoning, 71–74, 309
Pit vipers, 21

Subject Index

Pixel-level fusion (see Multisensor fusion)
Planck's equation, 380
Planning methods, 75
Predicate calculus, 59
Printed circuit boards, 542
Production rules, 35, 61, 173–177, 404, 450, 547, 580, 607
Prolog, 61, 430
Prospector, 69, 71

R

Radar cross section, 484, 549
Radiation, blackbody, 380
Rattlesnakes, 21, 162
REDIFLOW simulator, 92
Redundant information (see Information)
Registration, 6, 18, 19, 392, 395, 481 (see also Data association)
　stereo, 495, 500–506, 534–537
Relaxation, 76, 164, 392
Remote sensing, 553–555
Representations, 124–129 (see also Mobile robots, high-level representations)
　Coon's surface patch, 413
　graph, 449
　grid, 447–449
　labeled regions, 450
　maps (see Maps)
　occupancy grids, 448
　semantic nets, 61, 122
　spatial proximity graph, 140, 143–146
　spherical octree, 476–479
　Voronoi diagram, 450
Retinotopic coordinates, 114
Reynolds number, 387
Robot
　industrial, 541
　mobile (see Mobile robots)
　schemas, 22
Robust statistics, 18, 160
Rockwell's Automation Sciences Testbed, 543
Rodirigues formula, 534
Rotation matrices, exponential representation, 533
Rule-based systems (see Production rules)

S

Scene understanding, 121, 357, 393–405
Self-organization, 112

Semantic nets (see Representations)
Sensor
　allocation (see Target detection and tracking)
　calibration (see Calibration)
　combinations, 122
　　automatic target recognition, 365–369
　　mobile robots, 451
　effect cube, 31
　error, 547
　failure, 7, 19
　fusion (see Multisensor fusion)
　integration (see Multisensor integration)
　model, spherical, 470–476
　physical features of, 96
　registration (see Registration)
　selection, 6
　smart, 23, 83, 147
Shafer's theory of evidence (see Dempster–Shafer evidential reasoning)
Signal-level fusion (see Multisensor fusion)
Simulated annealing, 33, 76, 164, 449
Situation assessment, sensing system for, 141
Smart sensor (see Sensor)
Space shuttle, 548
Space station, NASA, 548
Spatial proximity graph (see Representations)
Specular reflection, 400, 548
Spherical harmonics, 475
Stanford Mobile Robot, 457
State-transition networks, 62
Statistical
　decision theory, 160
　reasoning, 63
Stereo
　reconstruction, 498–500, 514, 532
　vision, 407–438
Stochastic image algebra, 163
Strategic Defense Initiative, 21, 612
Subsumption architecture, 446
Symbol-level fusion (see Multisensor fusion)
SYNGRAPH, 84

T

Tactile sensing, 417–421
Target detection and tracking, 363,

549–552, 568, 572–576, 597–608, 611–634
  active and passive data, 602
  architectures, 576–584
  characteristics of fused information, 584–506
  data association (see Data association)
  decision fusion, 552, 557, 637–644, 647–670
  distributed sensor systems (see Distributed sensor systems)
  measurement fusion, 551
  multiple hypothesis tracking, 599
  probabilistic fusion, 552
  sensor allocation, 549, 598, 606–608
Target tracking (see Target decision and tracking)
Terregator, mobile robot, 456
Texture recognition, 302–305
Thermal images, 376
Tie space mapping, 295–297
Tie statistic, 283, 287–305
Topographic projection, 114
Tracking (see Target detection and tracking)
Tri Service Laser Radar, 367

U

U-D covariance factorization filter, 157, 555
Uncertainty
  reasoning, 62–69
  ellipsoid, 248–250
  manifold, 449
Utah/MIT dexterous hand, 83
Utility theory, 607

V

Ventriloquism, 19
Virtual input devices, 84

W

Weighted average (see Multisensor fusion)
Weighted least squares (see Multisensor fusion)
World model, 6